BOOKS BY HOWARD I. CHAPELLE

*The Baltimore Clipper*
*History of American Sailing Ships*
*Yacht Designing and Planning*
*American Sailing Craft*
*Boatbuilding*
*History of the American Sailing Navy*
*American Small Sailing Craft*
*The Search for Speed Under Sail*
*The American Fishing Schooners*

*HOWARD I. CHAPELLE*

# Boatbuilding

*A Complete Handbook of*
*Wooden Boat Construction*

*Foreword by Jon Wilson*

W · W · NORTON & COMPANY

NEW YORK · LONDON

The text of this book is composed in Janson with the display set in Typositor Latin Elongated and Caslon 471. Manufacturing by The Courier Companies, Inc. Frontmatter design by Marjorie J. Flock.

Library of Congress Cataloging-in-Publication Data

Chapelle, Howard Irving.
    Boatbuilding: a complete handbook of wooden boat construction /
    Howard I. Chapelle ; with a new foreword by Jonathan Wilson
        p.    cm.
    Originally published: New York: Norton, © 1941. With new introd.
    Includes index.
    1. Ships, Wooden—Design and construction.    2. Boatbuilding.
    I. Title.
    VM144.C27    1994
    623.8′207—dc20                                                      94-14556

                    ISBN 0-393-03554-9

W. W. Norton & Company, Inc., 500 Fifth Avenue, New York, N.Y. 10110
W. W. Norton & Company Ltd., 10 Coptic Street, London WC1A 1PU

                    3 4 5 6 7 8 9 0

# CONTENTS

# LIST OF ILLUSTRATIONS

## TEXT ILLUSTRATIONS

# List of Illustrations

# List of Illustrations

# List of Illustrations

# List of Illustrations

## List of Illustrations

# List of Illustrations

# FOREWORD

*I*T WAS my good fortune to grow up in a house in which the first edition of Howard I. Chapelle's *Boatbuilding* stood easily at hand on a bookshelf. It belonged to my grandfather, who turned seventy the year that first edition appeared, and I can well imagine how he thrilled to its every page. He had been around boats since boyhood; among his forebears were shipwrights and sea captains, and he was very familiar with the construction of yachts and boats. Yet, although he and other determined students or enthusiasts could find an occasional small book on the subject of building specific types of craft, there was nothing of substance which explored and revealed so many of the intricacies of this mysterious art and science. Thus, *Boatbuilding* became the first broad examination of traditional methods, and in this alone it probably would have found good success. But it had greater strengths and virtues, and they lay in the breadth of the author's scholarship, and in his ability to convey, through his numerous sketches and plans, a sense of the romance which is so much a part of designing, building, and sailing wooden boats. And *Boatbuilding*, like his *Yacht Designing and Planning*, *American Small Sailing Craft*, and others, finds much of its enduring value in its ability to inspire on both a visual and cerebral level in every chapter.

Although Howard Irving Chapelle (1901–1975) was completely at home at his typewriter, his drafting table, and in museum curatorial offices, his career and reputation sprang from the years he spent working in the field—around, on, and under the many vessels and small craft which were fast disappearing from the waterfront. He grew up around the harbor of New Haven, Connecticut, and sailed a traditional New Haven Sharpie, a local boat for oyster fishing. Although as a young man in 1918 he had been admitted to the prestigious Webb Institute of Naval Architecture, he decided instead to go to work for an upstate New York boat-builder, where he gained a firsthand sense of how different boats were constructed. From there he moved to New York City, where he worked in the offices of two eminent yacht designers, Charles Mower and William Gardner, and from there to New Bedford, Massachusetts, where he worked with yacht and working-vessel designer William Hand, who had himself worked under the direction of Thomas McManus, one of the great designers of the Gloucester fishing schooners. In addition, Chapelle worked with well-known Massachusetts designers Walter McInnis and John Alden.

During all these years his interest in the art and history of yacht, boat, and vessel design remained deep. By 1930, he had set up a design office of his own, and written a book called *The Baltimore Clipper*, published under the aegis of the prestigious Marine Research Society of Salem, Massachusetts. Five years later, W. W. Norton was to publish his ambitious *History of American Sailing Ships*, a scholarly yet popular study which has also endured through the decades; and in 1936, *Yacht Designing and Planning*. The latter invited readers—for the first time on any broad scale—to become more deeply involved in the creation of their dream boats by providing easy and illustrated access to the scientific and artistic principles which inform such creations. No other work before or since had done quite so much to provide this access. He had been inspired, no doubt, by his success as the author of a series of popular articles in *Yachting* magazine during this period, which were subsequently published in the book *American Sailing Craft* in 1936. But his true passion at the time was field research. During 1936 and 1937, he was a regional director for the Historic American Merchant Marine Survey (HAMMS), a WPA project; it was a charge which suited his passion perfectly. From a program designed to record, through measurements and drawings, the hull shapes and construction details of a wide variety of (primarily wooden) merchant vessels in this country, the information gathered by HAMMS teams remains one of the richest and most intriguing collections in the National Museum of History and Technology. During this period Chapelle also designed and had built for himself a yacht based upon the lines of the New England Pinky schooner, predecessor to the Banks schooner; and, more importantly to history, he organized and prepared the material for his great classic, *Boatbuilding*, which appeared in 1941. A further example of Chapelle's increasingly successful blend of popular scholarship, this book, like several of his others, has remained continually in print ever since.

Following his wartime stint in the U.S. Army Transportation Corps, and another year or so of studying, measuring, and drawing watercraft from the Great Lakes to Nova Scotia, Chapelle's *History of the American Sailing Navy* appeared in 1949, followed in 1951 by the wonderful *American Small Sailing Craft*, perhaps one of the most influential studies of traditional small boats ever published, and the undisputed chief inspiration for much of the continuing work and play in the field of traditional wooden small craft today. But Chapelle's commitment was not only to North American craft; during two different years, including one under a Guggenheim Fellowship, he studied the collections of Admiralty drawings at England's National Maritime Museum. In 1956 and 1957, he studied Turkish fisheries and vessels, and reported his findings to the Food and Agriculture Organization of the United Nations; years later he served as a consultant to a new maritime museum in Singapore. In 1957 he was also appointed curator of the Museum of Transportation at the Smithsonian Institution, and in 1964, under his direction, the Hall of the American Merchant Marine was opened there. In 1967 his book *The Search for Speed Under Sail* was published and that same year he was appointed senior historian at the Smithsonian. It was during these two decades that Chapelle's name grew to be so widely synonymous with traditional vessels and small craft, and he became a hero and mentor to historians, scholars, and boatbuilders alike. His last book published was *The American Fishing Schooners 1825–1935*, which appeared in 1973. He had been working on material for a similar volume about American pilot schooners when he passed away in the summer of 1975, and it surely would have found an equally enthusiastic response. In all, he left a tremendous body of work. It was not without flaw, for it would be nearly impossible to accomplish so great an amount without occasional error; but it was incomparable not only in volume, but in its power to inspire new and further research among present and future scholars and enthusiasts, which it continues to do today.

It is quite extraordinary that such works as *Boatbuilding* and *Yacht Designing and Planning* and *American Small Sailing Craft* have remained so enduringly valuable in the field of yachting and boating. Despite the evolutions and changes in the way the world thinks about yachts, boats, and vessels, the depth, breadth, and durability of Howard Chapelle's work is timeless. One might be inclined to think that the methods described, for example, in *Boatbuilding* must surely be out of date a half-century later, but it is not so. On the contrary, there remains a widespread and deep commitment to traditional wood construction techniques for their simplicity and strength, and for their accessibility to all—whether amateur or professional—who respond to the fragrance of wood shavings and the lure of fresh and salt water. And though the tools and materials for traditional boatbuilding might not seem easily accessible, they are, indeed, and even the seemingly very hard to find, if you know where to look. And as for the designs themselves, which for decades have inspired both amateur and professional boatbuilders, they are still available—from the Smithsonian Institution, and from the Chesapeake Bay Maritime Museum, both of which house collections of Chapelle's notes, sketches, and plans. But there are many other sources as well, of plans created by designers deeply influenced by the craft which Chapelle worked so hard to share with the world. For virtually no designer of consequence in this country is unaware of Chapelle's enormous legacy. Many museums exhibit the very kind of craft which are herein described, and many individuals and groups work hard to excite and inspire broader interest. The Traditional Small Craft Association is a national organization devoted to the construction, use, and enjoyment of such craft, not as historical objects, but as wonderful, sophisticated, and timeless examples of maritime art and industry. And if the enthusiasm of the last two and a half decades is any indicator, the future of traditional wooden yachts and boats is very bright, indeed.

JON WILSON

Editor, *WoodenBoat* magazine

# *PREFACE*

*A*NY man having a fair amount of skill with carpenter's tools can build a boat of some kind. Each passing year offers proof of this by the steadily increasing number of home-built craft, many of which would not shame a professional boatbuilder. The yachtsman builds a dinghy, small racer, or moderate-sized cruiser. The fisherman turns out an automobile-engine-powered fishing launch. The farmer, during the winter, may build a powerboat with which to carry produce. The sportsman may try a hand at a canoe or hunting craft of some sort. Even the seaside cottager is often tempted to knock together a flat-bottom rowing skiff.

However, many would-be boatbuilders become discouraged long before their self-imposed task is completed. This is caused by an improper choice of design for the boat to be built—considering the skill and equipment of the builder—or by a lack of definite information on how to accomplish certain portions of the work. There are, of course, a great many magazine articles and books describing in more or less detail, and with accuracy, the methods of building certain individual designs. Too often, however, these are neither the type wanted nor the size necessary, in the eyes of the amateur builder. Very often he knows of a design he wishes to follow, or has plans at hand; what he requires is information and instruction.

This book is designed to answer that need and to indicate whether the design chosen is proper in relation to the amount of skill and experience possessed by the builder; or whether it is proper in relation to tools and facilities available. It will serve as a workshop handbook, giving detailed instructions on how to go about each part of a job and its proper sequence, as well as what must be looked forward to, while performing a given operation.

The advantages and disadvantages of each type of construction suitable for amateurs will be described.

It is impossible to describe all the variations of construction, but those most suited to amateur work are explained. The sketches, taken from memorandums of actual construction details, are intended to serve as guides when details are missing in plans being used. It is assumed that cost is of prime importance and that the builder-to-be has relatively few tools and no expensive shop equipment. It is on this assumption that much of the advice in this book is based. Time may also be an important factor, and this is referred to in the text, with special regard to selection of a quickly built design. It is also assumed that the builder-to-be has some skill in carpentry, is able to read blueprints, and knows the names of the various parts of the structure of a boat.

The author wishes to acknowledge his obligations to Worthington Mansfield, George Stadel, George Buckhout, Larry Huntington, Eric Steinlein, "Bud" MacIntosh, and "Herb" Johnson for the information and suggestions they have so freely given.

Among the books consulted are *Small Boat Building* by Patterson; *Amateur Boat Building* by Crosby; *Boatowner's Sheet Anchor* by Lane; *Boat Building Materials and Methods* by Lindley-Jones: *Small Yacht Construction and Rigging* by Hope; *Boat Building Simplified* by Ashcroft; *Canoe and Boat Building for Amateurs* by Stephens; and *The Sea Boat* by Leslie. In addition, the works of Dixon Kemp, Kunhardt, and Arthur Tiller, and a great number of articles in yachting magazines, have been used as references.

Marine hardware catalogues have been of great assistance, particularly those of Merriman Bros., Inc., of Boston, Mass.; E. J. Willis Company, 91–93 Chambers Street, New York City; Wilcox, Crittenden & Company, Inc., Middletown, Conn.; Edson Manufacturing Corporation, South Boston, Mass.; Kelvin & Wilfred O. White Company, Boston, Mass.; the James Walker Company, Baltimore, Md.; and Elisha Webb & Son Company of Philadelphia, Penn.; also of the well-known British house, Simpson Lawrence & Company, Glasgow (C 1), Scotland.

HOWARD I. CHAPELLE

*Cambridge, Maryland*

# INTRODUCTION

*T*HE beginner will be helped a great deal in building his first boat if he has in mind an outline of the various operations necessary. First, then, is the choice of model, size, and design of the boat to be built. Next, plans must be secured; the less the knowledge and experience of the builder, the greater the importance of complete and carefully made plans. From these drawings a list of materials, fastenings, fittings, hardware, tanks, sails, rigging, and other things necessary to build the boat must be made and ordered. It is usually possible to judge from the plans what tools will be required.

When the plans, and specifications either on the plans or attached to the design, have been studied, the builder must find a proper place to make a full-sized drawing of the plan marked "lines." It is this stage of building that is so often neglected, and this is the most common cause of trouble later on. Not only must the cross sections of the hull, called "molds" or "forms," be drawn; the whole projection of the form of the boat as shown in the "lines" must be reproduced full size. On this, after certain projections are made which will be described in the proper place, the construction shown in the design plans must be superimposed in more or less detail. From this drawing or "mold loft work" patterns will be made of each timber to be sawn and shaped, by which the rough stock can be cut to proper form. When patterns and the hull molds, or section forms, are complete and have been checked, the builder is ready to start actual construction.

When a place in which to build has been chosen, and material and tools collected, the builder proceeds to shape the timbers of the backbone or keel by means of the patterns made from the mold loft work. This will include all pieces of timber making up the keel, centerboard case if one is used, stem and stern members.

As each piece is shaped and fastened together, the structure is marked with the lines transferred to the patterns from the mold loft work for reference and the whole is carefully checked. When the backbone is complete and all stations necessary marked off from the mold loft patterns, the builder proceeds to the construction of the "stocks." If the boat is small and is to be built upside down, this structure may be in the form of a low table; or, if right side up, then a single timber supported by posts may serve as the stocks. If the boat is large, then the keel is set and plumbed on blocks, or posts, to get it at a proper working height above the ground or floor. It is very important that the stocks be so arranged that the keel has the same relation to a level line on the stocks that it had in the "lines" and mold loft work.

Next the builder gets out his molds, which are the cross sections of the hull shown in the "lines," from his mold loft patterns; the latter are of thin wood, or of cardboard if the boat is small. These molds are made up of rough timber of sufficient thickness to have the required strength. These, when shaped and squared up so as to coincide with the patterns, are placed in the proper position on the backbone, squared and plumbed, then secured with stays and shores. Great care should be taken to see that the molds are square to the center line of the keel (which is, of course, the center line of the boat) and that the marks representing sheer on each side are level; also that the mold, viewed from the boat's broadside, is plumb, so that its angle with the keel coincides with that shown in the "lines." The stem and stern are checked to see that they are plumb and properly shored. The transom, if not already in place, is made up and set, plumbed, checked, and secured. Then the builder battens off the hull with narrow strips of wood called "ribbands." These serve to fair up the molds and to help hold them in place; also the ribbands will give something to secure clamps to, when framing, if the hull has bent frames. The ribbands are nailed to each mold and to the stem and transom. They are spaced at some convenient distance apart to permit timber and clamps to be passed into the hull. This stage of construction enables the builder to see the form of the boat. Now, if there are heavy longitudinal timbers (such as shelves and stringers) to be placed, they are made up and fitted into notches cut in the molds to receive them. Sometimes this is left until the boat is planked, but this should depend upon the method of construction employed rather than upon the whim of the builder, as will be explained later.

If the boat is to have steam-bent frames, the stock is now prepared as to size and then a steam box or boiler is made. The keel is notched or "boxed" at each place where the heel of a frame will rest if the plans so require. It is usual to mark the position of each frame on the uppermost ribband, or sheer clamp, if one is in. The frames are then placed in the steam box and left until they are sufficiently pliable to bend to the sharpest curve required without breaking. While hot, they are placed in the boat; the heel is nailed and then the frame bent against the ribbands, C-clamps being used to hold them into the proper curve. Care is taken that they lie parallel with heads to the marks on the top ribband or sheer clamp. When they are cool and have set to shape, a few nails will hold them to the ribbands. It usually takes two men to frame a boat in this fashion. When the frames are cold and set, the floor timbers are made up from mold loft patterns, fitted and fastened to each pair of frames and to keel. If sawn frames are required, they are made up as molds.

The planking is the next step. After carefully selecting his stock, the builder lays off the number of belts or "strakes" of planking the boat is to have, with regard to the width of planking available, on the frames or molds and on stem and stern. When this is done he planks up, removing ribbands as the strakes reach them. Usually he will put on the lowest, then the highest strakes, then those in between. As a strake is shaped and fitted on one side it is used as a pattern for the other side; both are secured in place before another strake is made up. When the hull is planked it is usually planed off fairly smooth, final sanding being left until the interior of the hull is complete.

The next step depends upon the size of the boat and how she is set up on the stocks. If large and right side up, and if the shelves, clamps, and stringers are in place, the deck beams are made up from mold loft patterns and some of them bolted into place, and knees put in, before the rough molds are knocked apart and removed. If the boat is without longitudinal members, the hull is stayed across at sheer and bilge with pieces of plank nailed to pairs of frames, the molds removed, and the longitudinal members fitted. If the boat is upside down, she is tied together with stay timbers and turned over before the molds are removed.

The deck beams, carlins, knees, and blocking made up from the mold loft patterns are located, fitted, and secured. At this point the builder usually puts in the engine and tanks, the large bulkheads, and the fittings that require room to install easily. When he is satisfied that enough of such work is done, he lays the deck, fits the bitts, and makes up the hatch frames and cabin trunk. Then he puts in the cabin roof beams and lays the roof. If both or either the deck and cabin roof are canvas covered, he does this before securing any of the hatch frames in place. Then, when the deck is completed, he builds the rails; after this he may complete the deck fittings and install the hardware outboard. The interior is next completed, the plumbing installed, and all cabin fittings placed. When the engine piping and wiring are finished, the cockpit is completed.

Now the hull may be finished; any deck fittings or hardware not installed are secured and all outside smoothing is done. When the planing and sanding are completed, the boat is painted inside and out. While this is drying the builder can get out the spars, fit the rigging hardware and prepare to step the masts, put over the rigging, and get the sails ready to bend. When all is ready, the launching takes place, the spars are stepped, and the rigging set up. Then sails are bent, the motor tested, and a trial takes place. After this adjustments or small changes are necessary, as a rule, so these are done by the builder before he considers the job complete.

This, of course, is nothing more than a bare outline of the operations necessary to build a boat, and the sequence may vary a little in certain types of construction.

The most important requirements in a builder are accuracy and patience. The beginner should have no feeling of haste. He must plan each operation well in advance and try to see not only that particular job but the one following it; by this means he will avoid having to undo some work already completed in order to get at a fastening, or to fit some member later on.

In every amateur boatbuilder's shop there should be a "moaning chair"; this should be a comfortable seat from which the boat can be easily seen and in which the builder can sit, smoke, chew, drink, or swear as the moment demands. Here he should rest often and think about his next job. The plans should be at hand and here he can lay out his work. By so doing he will often be able to see mistakes before they are serious and avoid the curse of all amateur boatbuilders: starting a job before figuring out what has to be done to get it right.

# Boatbuilding

# CHAPTER ONE

# *PLANS*

*T*HE obvious first step in building a boat is, of course, to obtain plans. When these are once chosen, the size, type, rig, and accommodation of the finished boat are established. The cost and the amount of labor necessary to build the boat are also decided. Even the number and kind of tools and the equipment required will depend upon the plans chosen. It is hardly necessary to stress the fact that, aside from these matters, the behavior of the boat under sail and motor, her appearance, and, last but not least, the comfort to be had in her, are all decided upon when the plans are selected. Obviously, then, the plans are of the utmost importance and a great deal of thought must be given to the selection of them. The builder must decide for himself which model of boat and design he wishes to build; what pleases his eye, what fits his particular requirements as to wind and water, use and cost. Nevertheless, the following information will serve as a guide to the beginner.

## *Time*

Most amateur builders do not care to spend more than a year in constructing a boat. The exact number of hours required to build a boat is an important consideration, particularly as the amateur builder usually works after business hours and on holidays and week ends. If a man is building a boat alone, he would not work over 936 hours a year if he spent two hours every weekday and eight hours every week end on the job. Of course, very few men with this amount of time to spend in building would actually be able to do so; in practice they would probably have trouble in reaching a total of much over 700 hours. Even with the uncertain help of friends it is doubtful if a total of 900 hours would be reached. Furthermore, the effectiveness of the hours spent on the job depends upon the skill of the builder in handling tools. Most amateur builders are unable, for this reason, to make the most of the time they allot to the work. Often mistakes are made and a task must be done over, with a resulting loss in time. In the case of the outright beginner this becomes particularly important as a cause of discouragement, since progress may become very slow. It seems apparent, on this assumption, that there are certain limitations on boats suitable for amateur construction.

## Size

The chief of these limitations is size. This does not mean length alone; rather it is best represented by weight, or "displacement." The three dimensions—length, breadth, and draft of water—give a working idea of the actual size of a boat. It must be remembered that the greater the cabin space required, the greater the space inside the hull must be and therefore the greater the displacement; or, in other words, the greater the size actually becomes.

To make the matter clearer, a boat 40 feet long on deck, 11 feet beam, and 6 feet draft is usually a good deal heavier than one 40 feet by 9 feet by 4 feet. The first boat, weighing more, has greater cabin space and therefore takes more material to build, which in turn represents more hours of labor and more cost than would be required to build the second and lighter boat.

Suppose these boats are both of the common round-bottom class and that they have very meager cabin furniture, simply arranged; the number of effective working hours required to build the hull, cabin, deck furniture, and spars, and to paint and finish, would be about 980; add to this the hours necessary to install engine, tanks, wiring, plumbing, rigging, and ironwork, and the total is well over 1,400 working hours for the heavier boat. The total for the second and lighter boat, on this basis, would be about 1,100 hours. Of course, this comparison is based on specific examples that are reasonably alike in all but displacement. Differences in model, finish, and detail would have qualifying effects on such a comparison. Lest it be assumed that the differences in weight, or displacement, could be accounted for in ballast and not in work and material, it must be made plain that the heavier a boat is in displacement, the stronger and heavier must be her construction, if she is to be a soundly built job.

The question of how large a boat an amateur builder should undertake depends wholly upon the following factors: his skill, time allotted for building, help available, and the model and finish of the boat shown in the design to be followed. As a general guide, however, it is possible to set up certain standards of maximum size that should not be exceeded. For a man who has never built a boat before, and whose skill in the use of tools is not great, a boat weighing between 2 and 3 tons is about as large a craft as he should attempt to build alone. In length, such a boat might fall between 24 and 30 feet, perhaps, depending upon model and type. If he has no allotted time for building then the size might be increased slightly, but this is not recommended; slow progress, which would naturally result, would be very likely to discourage him. Two such amateurs could build a boat up to 4 or 5 tons displacement, say, of lengths between 28 and 35 feet. Even the most skilled amateur would do well to take 14 tons displacement and 40 to 45 feet length on deck as the largest boat he can build at home, with occasional help. Such a boat would require about a year and a half to build under the best conditions that a beginner can expect; probably two years would be required. Since it is extremely important that the beginner not hurry his work, it is really a mistake to attempt to set an exact building period; on the other hand, few men wish to spend as long as two years building one boat. For that reason, regardless of model, a boat exceeding 45 feet in length on deck and 14 tons displacement is too large for home construction. As a general rule, the larger the boat chosen by an amateur builder, the simpler she must be in construction, model, and arrangement. Fancy finish is usually out of the question in a large, "home-built" boat.

### Model

The model of the boat chosen for amateur construction must be subject to certain qualifications as to suitability. For this reason it may well be classed as another important limitation—as important as size and closely related to that consideration.

Model is taken to mean basic design. For practical purposes there are assumed to be three basic hull forms, graded according to the shape of their midsection, or largest transverse section: flat-bottom, V-bottom, and round-bottom. Each basic model is sub-divided into a number of "types" which represent variations in the basic model, the result of the application of a model to some given condition or requirement.

### Flat-Bottom Model

The first to be considered is the flat-bottom model of boat. Of all models this form of boat is the easiest to build; it requires the fewest tools and the least hours of work to complete in any given length. In type it is usually classed as follows: scow, punt, skiff, or sharpie. The scow is nothing more than a rectangular box with the two narrow ends sloping outward from the bottom, usually with shoal upright transoms or end timbers finishing off these sloping ends on top. The punt is an improved and developed scow, having the bottom well rockered fore and aft, flaring sides and raking transoms at bow and stern. The skiff is marked by a sharp bow and has less rocker to the bottom in profile forward; aft she is like a punt. These three types are usually built for rowing in lakes and rivers, but occasionally they are used as sailing craft. In the latter case they commonly have centerboards. In some localities the punt and skiff types are fitted with power and are used for fishing. The sharpie is really an enlarged skiff; sometimes, however, it has either a sharp stern like a canoe or a rounded stern something like that seen on the towboats used along the coast.

EXAMPLES. The flat-bottom model is suited for protected waters, but is occasionally used along the coast when built to sufficient size. Large-powered scows are seen in harbors and rivers; formerly such boats were commonly fitted with sail, either sloop or schooner rigged. Others of this class were punt shaped. The New Jersey oyster garvey, the Maine scow sloop, and the San Francisco scow schooner represent examples of the practical use of such hull forms. The skiff is also used under power and sail by fishermen or watermen along the coast. The sharpie, ranging from 18 to 60 feet in length, is usually a sailboat, but sometimes it is fitted with a motor. Boats of this class are in favor for shoal water work of all types; formerly they were very popular with oystermen on Long Island Sound, the Carolinas, and Florida

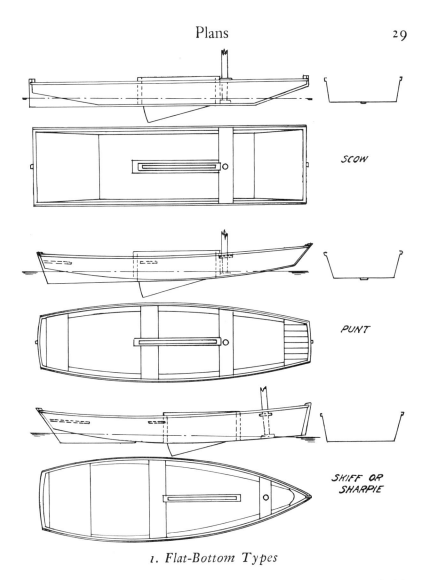

SCOW

PUNT

SKIFF OR
SHARPIE

*1. Flat-Bottom Types*

waters. Many of the Chesapeake Bay crabbing boats are of this same general type. The use of flat-bottom hulls for pleasure craft was largely a development of the designs evolved in commercial boats, where shoal draft and cheapness were important.

The flat-bottom hull is commonly seen in the very small sailing classes, as dinghies and prams, and occasionally as small cruisers. Whether rowing, sailing, or power hulls, the designs are marked by light displacement, slight or moderate rocker to the bottom fore and aft, and simple construction.

DESIGN. Observation indicates that for sailing, or power, the flat-bottom hull should be relatively narrow in proportion to length and that the rocker of the bottom fore and aft should be moderate. In sharp-bowed craft, the line of the bottom, viewed in profile, should conform to a general rule. The heel of the stem should either touch the water or be just clear of it. From this point the line of bottom, or chine, should run straight and sloping downward for about one third the water-line length of the boat; from there it should go into a reasonably gentle curve through the middle third, and then should again become straight, or very

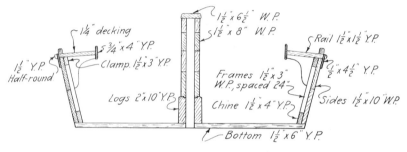

*2. Typical Flat-Bottom Hull Construction*

nearly so, and run upward to the stern. Even in rowing skiffs this general form is quite important. Much of the prejudice against flat-bottom dinghies can be traced to the neglect of this matter on the part of their designers and builders; if there is curvature in the forward third of the chine, in profile, the boat will row heavily. Flare is also important, for it not only aids in seaworthiness and stability under sail but also gives increased power to carry loads. The Gloucester Fishing Dory is a good example of a flat-bottom hull designed for rough water work and load carrying; it is also a good example of the effect of flare on sea-keeping ability in flat-bottom hulls.

CONSTRUCTION. The usual construction of a flat-bottom hull is to make up the sides of one or more strakes; the bottom is cross planked. Longitudinal stringers are placed at chine and sheer and secured to stem and transom or post. The planking of the sides is fastened to these and the bottom is fastened to the chine stringers. Along the sides cleats are worked in, vertically between chine and sheer, to serve as frames. Except in the large sharpies there is rarely any keel structure. A plank worked in along the center line, either inside or outside of hull, serves the purpose. A skeg or outside keel is sometimes used; this is merely spiked to the fore-and-aft plank on the center line and to the bottom planking. In a small boat only one or two molds are used, in addition to the transom.

Bottom Laid Fore and Aft. A few flat-bottom boats are planked fore and aft on the bottom. There are no advantages to this, and some disadvantages; a boat planked this way needs regular sawn frames and so is usually heavier than a cross-planked hull. Also there is often weakness in a sailing boat so built, unless she

*3. "Curved Sides and Flat-Bottom" Sailing Dory*

is well braced. The dory is the only well-known example of a working flat-bottom boat being planked fore and aft on the bottom. Due to their narrow bottom this can be done with two or three wide plank, so there is some saving of time in building. The necessity for making it possible for these boats to nest inside one another makes fixed thwarts or cross bracing out of the question and sawn frames are therefore required to keep the sides in shape. Since these frames must be used anyway, the fore-and-aft bottom plank naturally follows.

Curved Side. In an attempt to improve on the appearance of flat-bottom craft, designers sometimes employ curved sides in cross section; a common example is the stock sailing dory. There is no real advantage, other than appearance, in this idea and it makes the flat-bottom boat quite a bit more difficult to build. The chief advantage of a flat-bottom hull being her ease of construction, there can be no common-sense excuse for adding anything to complicate the building. A well-designed flat-bottom hull can be made very attractive in appearance by proper sheer and flare,

combined with simple, straight-line stem and stern, if her freeboard and beam are both small in proportion to length. High
freeboard or very high deck structures, such as cabin trunks, are
not possible in a well-proportioned flat-bottom boat in lengths
up to 45 feet overall. It is evident, then, that full headroom (6
feet 1 inch by rule of practice) is not practical in this class of boat.

SEAWORTHINESS. While it is true that flat-bottom craft are used
in rough water (the Gloucester Dory, or "Bank Dory," for example), the model is not suited for this purpose, generally speaking. The sharpie type, in lengths between 28 and 60 feet, has gone
to sea and, in proper hands, will stand a good deal of punishment;
but her crew will receive as much as the boat. The large sharpies
pound heavily under bad weather conditions; so severe is this
pounding that there is danger that the calking may be knocked
out of the seams in the bottom. Large flat-bottom craft are inclined to be unmanageable in a heavy-breaking sea. The model is
suited to small craft or those used alongshore and in protected
waters, not for deep-water cruising.

There is one further modification in the flat-bottom model.
In this the bottom has some curve athwartships, but the sides are
flat. This is seen in small racing classes, such as the well-known
"Star Class" boat. This has the advantage in that it gives greater
speed in light weather than is usually possible with a boat having
the conventional flat bottom. Frames are usually required and
the bottom is planked fore and aft.

SAILING QUALITIES. A general idea of the sailing qualities of
flat-bottom models of good design can be given as an aid in forming an opinion on the suitability of the class for a given condition. The boats will run very fast in strong winds and smooth
water. The long, narrow boats are fast reaching and running under such conditions. Most flat-bottom boats are a little slow in
drifting weather. They will go to windward but will not point
as high as a good round-bottom boat should do. Their worst sailing is done to windward, in light airs and in a choppy sea. Under
such conditions they pound and lose headway. In strong winds
they usually carry a strong weather helm. They sail best when
the weather chine is just clear of the water and in rough water
work when given some heel. They require much larger centerboards than do most round-bottom boats; this, incidentally, is
one of their objectionable features when planning a cabin layout

for cruising, as the case invariably divides the cabin in two parts. Windage is a very important matter in the sailing of most flat-bottom types and should be kept to a minimum. High freeboard, large or high cabin trunks, and excess rigging should be avoided.

FOR POWER. As a motorboat, the flat-bottom model is suited only for protected waters. It will carry heavy weights on a small

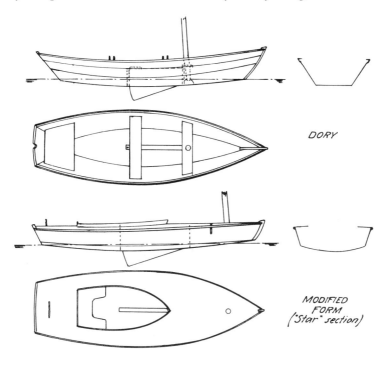

DORY

MODIFIED
FORM
("Star" section)

*4. Flat-Bottom Types*

draft of water and is fairly efficient with engines of low power. It is a mistake to attempt to drive a hull of this model at high speed. The punt type of hull is widely used as a commercial powerboat; it is a very efficient carrier and cheap to build. Sharpie-type power cruisers are sometimes seen; usually they are very small and are powered with outboard engines. It is a mistake to attempt to build a wide boat for this purpose, if power is to be used efficiently.

JUDGING FOR BUILDING. There is one way of telling whether

a design of a flat-bottom model is going to be difficult to build; in the part of the "lines" showing the cross sections look at the sides. If the lines of these as shown in the various sections are parallel, or nearly so, the side will bend into place without having to be twisted. If not parallel to a marked degree, the sides will have to be rolled in or out—and this is not easy if the plank is not very thin. To bring a flat side into a curved rabbet line at the stem

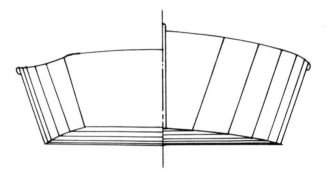

*5. Body plan of straight-sided skiff with parallel sections indicating an easily planked hull. Transom side is not parallel to sections as it is raking in profile. This does not affect planking, however.*

is likely to cause trouble too. If the stem is to be curved, this should be only in the profile of the stempiece, not in the rabbet.

CONCLUSION. A properly designed flat-bottom boat is undoubtedly the best subject for an amateur's first attempt. It offers a wide range of choice of types which fulfill the needs of at least the majority of beginners. Even if the amateur intends to build a different model, the flat-bottom dinghy will serve to practice on and to experiment with; the labor is not lost, since a useful boat will result.

## V-Bottom Model

The V-bottom model has become very popular with amateur builders during the last thirty years. It is a more seaworthy model than the flat-bottom and is usually somewhat roomier since it is possible to employ greater displacement and beam. The V-bottom

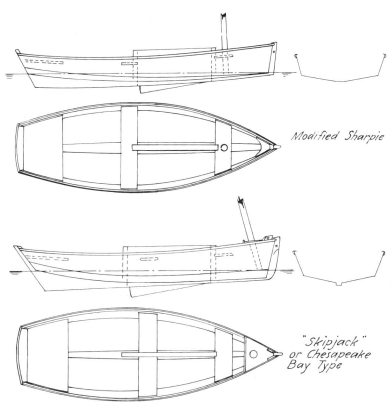

*Modified Sharpie*

*"Skipjack"
or Chesapeake
Bay Type*

*6. V-Bottom Types*

is the outgrowth of the flat-bottom and was developed through the necessity of getting greater displacement in a given length than was desirable in the latter model. Because of the straight-line sections usually employed, the V-bottom is looked upon as a very suitable type for beginners. As will be explained, this may or may not be true, depending upon the exact shape and construction methods shown in a design.

TYPES. As in the case of the flat-bottom model, the V-bottom may be divided into types or classifications. The first is the "modified" sharpie, having either dead rise at the stern, or stern and bow, or a slight amount all along the bottom. A great many small racers and some cruisers might be said to fall in this classification.

The well-known Chesapeake Bay Skipjacks may be taken to represent the next type, having a good deal of beam and more dead rise than the modified sharpies. The third type is that seen so often in yachts, characterized by much lift to the chine fore and aft, a great deal of dead rise, and a rockered keel with centerboard or fin. The fourth type is usually employed in motorboat hulls designed for high speed. In this both the sides and bottom are curved in section; sometimes only the sides are curved. This form

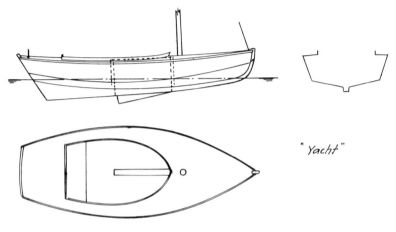

"Yacht"

7. *V-Bottom Types*

is best represented by the stock high-speed runabout. There have been a large number of variations in the V-bottom model, employing two chines on each side, variously curved sections, or scow- and punt-type hull plan and profile. The outboard racing boats, hydroplanes, and certain classes of highly specialized and restricted racing craft, both sail and power, may be said to illustrate these variations in the V-bottom model.

SEAWORTHINESS. The V-bottom model's seaworthiness is less easy to rule upon than that of flat-bottom types. Much depends upon the exact design rather than type classification, except, of course, where racing craft (either power or sail) are concerned. The modified sharpie and the yacht-type dead-rise model (dead rise is another name for a V-shaped bottom, though the term is also used in reference to the rising bottom or "floors" of round-bottom boats) have often been used in deep-water cruising. These two types and the Chesapeake Bay type are used for commercial craft, both power and sail. The Bay Skipjack is not as seaworthy as the other two models because of her proportionately greater beam. Power dead-rise boats are used all along the Atlantic coast of the United States for both work and pleasure. Dead-rise working craft have been built as long as 90 feet and the common dead-rise power yacht is often over 50 feet in length. Stock-boat builders have developed many V-bottom power and sailing cruisers.

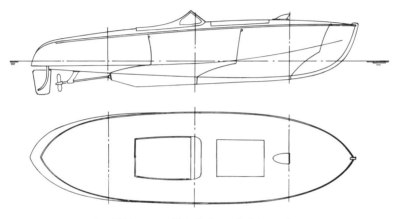

*8. V-Bottom High-Speed Motorboat*

The majority of types having a V-bottom are designed for use in protected waters. In almost all hulls having this form there is some pounding in rough water. In power craft this takes place when driven fast, even in a moderate sea. In sailing hulls it takes place when the hull is heeled at certain angles, which vary with the individual design. In sailing V-bottom craft the pounding is rarely as severe as it would be in an upright, flat-bottom boat. A dead-rise hull does not have the power to carry sail, that a flat-bottom boat of the same length and breadth would have, without the addition of ballast. This is not necessarily an objectionable feature.

SAILING QUALITIES AND DESIGN. The sailing qualities of the V-bottom hull are somewhat like those of the flat-bottom types, but with improved windward qualities if well designed. They will rarely point as high as a well-designed round-bottom boat, though this is not the case with exceptional designs. It seems probable, from observation, that some designs are adversely affected by excess beam and windage. The effect of the chine may also be the cause of poor sailing. Too much rocker in the chine (in profile) is damaging to speed, as tank tests have indicated. In many designs the chine is carried very high, forward and aft, in an effort to overcome pounding. Apparently this is very harmful to speed. The chine ought not to be too deeply immersed amidships but, on the other hand, should not be out of water when at rest or a very uneasy boat is likely to result. All chine hulls having the sharp, conventional bow seem to benefit by greater sharpness than would be common in round-bottom boats. The exception to this is in long, low, narrow, very light sailing hulls of the racing type, where a full bow is often effective. Designers sometimes attempt to produce a deep keel hull, having a good deal of headroom, by employing great dead rise. Such designs are usually complete failures in speed and sail-carrying power. While it is possible to use a keel in place of a centerboard in the V-bottom, this ought to be in the form of a fin, rather than a part of the hull form, to avoid the undesirable effects of excessive rise of bottom. The angle of the bottom at amidships ought not exceed 18 degrees from the horizontal in V-bottom craft. The most common faults found in V-bottom yacht designs are too much rocker to chine, or to both chine and rabbet, too much dead rise, or too much beam or freeboard.

POWER DESIGN. Power hulls differ in characteristics of design according to the type and required speed. Low-speed hulls are usually long, sharp, and narrow; in profile their chines have little curve. The chine is usually at, or a few inches above, the water line at the bow, runs straight and sloping downward to a few inches below the water line at about one third the water-line length from the bow, then curves gently and comes out of the water at the stern in a long, flat curve or straight line. The chines are not deeply immersed and there is usually a rather deep forefoot. The transom is either clear of the water or immersed very little. In high-speed hulls the chine is usually rather high at the bow and has a good deal of curve in profile forward. The chine enters the water well amidships and then runs downward in an almost straight line so that the greatest depth the chine is immersed is abaft amidships or at the transom. In very fast hulls, having sufficient power, there are one or more steps in the bottom running from chine to chine; these are hydroplanes. In all high-powered craft the transom is well immersed when boat is at rest. The forefoot is very shallow in these boats; the stem is well curved, in profile, and the bow is full on deck.

CONSTRUCTION. The methods of constructing V-bottom types are many. Some are easily followed by the amateur builder but

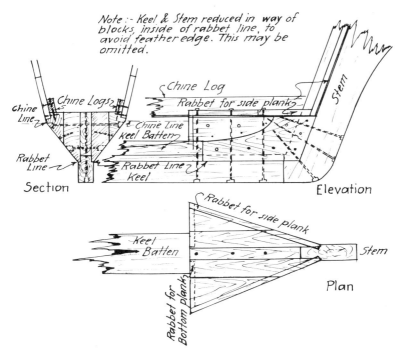

*9. Block Forefoot of Five Pieces, Chesapeake Bay Fashion*

others drive even the skilled professional to the moaning chair in despair. The easiest type of V-bottom hull to build is the modified sharpie. This type has no forefoot as a rule; the chine and rabbet line of the keel meet at the heel of the stem. The sections are usually straight sided; the rabbet of the stem is straight, or nearly so. The stern may be sharp or have a transom, set raking or upright. Usually the keel has no rabbet cut into it; there is an inner member, the "keel batten," which backs up the bottom planking along the keel. The chine timbers are like those of most flat-bottom types; so is the side framing. The bottom is cross planked, but at an angle to the center line of the hull with the outboard ends of each plank further aft than at the keel. This is usually done so that the planks at the transom will be nearly parallel sided; the boats having plumb transoms or sharp sterns do not require this method of planking the bottom, though it is sometimes done. The forefoot is made most easily of a block secured to heel of stem and to keel and hewn to fair off with the bottom, when planked. In such construction the keel need not

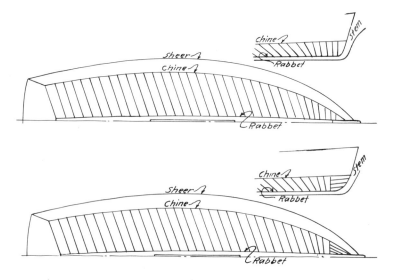

*10. Cross-Planked V-Bottom with Staving at Forefoot*

be carried to the stem unless there is an outside shoe or "gripe." If the rabbet line of the keel is lower than the chine at the stem, the bottom planking becomes a little more difficult. Usually the easiest way is to plank the bow, between keel and chine, with narrow, thick staving for a few feet abaft the stem; this is then planed off to the thickness of the rest of the bottom planking, when that is laid. Sometimes it is better to lay the plank fore and aft, using thick staving, for a few feet, then cross plank the bottom. If the height between chine and keel rabbet at the stem is not great, then it is possible to form the fore part of the bottom by securing blocks on either side of the keel batten with dowels;

the blocks are deep enough to fill the height between rabbet of keel and chine, of course; then hew off the blocks fair to outside of bottom plank when laid. This is perhaps the best method when the forefoot is angular and the bow fairly full. Vertical staving, however, is often used in place of blocking.

In this class of work no sawn frames are required in the bottom, but if the boat is wide there are often two fore-and-aft battens inside, one on each side of the keel, parallel to it, and about half-way between chine and keel amidships. It is easiest to fit the outside keel or shoe before the bottom is laid. Boats having these features of construction ought to have strong deck framing, with a number of hanging knees, braces, or solid bulkheads to give them strength enough to stand strains set up by waves or, if a sailing boat, by the spars.

BOTTOM LAID FORE AND AFT. In yacht designs it is common to require the bottom to be planked fore and aft. This occasionally causes a good deal of trouble to the inexperienced builder. With this method of planking the bottom, sawn frames are required. It is also necessary to fit the garboard in the same manner as in round-bottom hulls. Usually all bottom plank run to the rabbet of the stem, which requires spacing and fitting like the garboard. Should there be much twist in these planks they may have to be steamed, particularly if the bow is full. Steamed planking is one of the reasons why professional builders often claim the V-bottom is as hard to build as a round-bottom hull; fitting the bottom plank to some designs will cause the amateur to wear the moaning chair to footstool height.

When the bottom plank, laid fore and aft, does not run to the stem but ends on the chine, the long, narrow points formed by the acute angle at which the chine crosses each plank will usually cause trouble when the calking is being done.

BATTEN SEAM CONSTRUCTION. Some plans call for the seams of the topsides, and of the fore-and-aft bottom plank, to be backed up inside by a batten, to which each plank is to be fastened as well as to the frames. This is known as "batten seam construction." Excellent for hulls subject to vibration, such as lightly built, high-speed power hulls, it is not wholly suited for amateur construction, unless the hull form is one that is easily planked. The battens cannot be placed until the planking has been laid off on the hull in accordance with the *width of plank available*,

*after it has been shaped and fitted.* If this is not done, the builder
is likely to find he cannot get out a plank the width required by
an arbitrary spacing of the battens. Since the battens must be let
into the sawn frames, or molds, before the plank is fastened, the

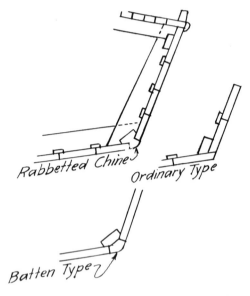

*11. Batten Seam Construction and Chines*

construction makes slow progress. With this type of construction, it is common in fast powerboats to use closely spaced steam-
bent frames between the wide-spaced sawn frames, to give greater
strength to the hull.

RABBETED KEEL AND CHINE. Sometimes a design will require
a rabbeted keel; this will add to the labor required of the builder,
but is not beyond the skill of a reasonably good carpenter. On the
other hand, rabbeted chines are to be avoided as they require a
great deal of mold loft and carpenter skill to make and fit. Such
chines are sometimes employed in high-speed motorboat designs
intended to be built by highly skilled professional builders. It
must be remembered that the V-bottom is particularly suited to
high-speed motorboat design and is used for this reason alone,
not because it is necessarily easy to build. Because of this, complicated construction methods are often shown in a design of a

fast-power V-bottom in order to give strength with a minimum of weight. As a general rule, light, strong construction requires great skill on the part of the builder since every member must fit exactly and be well fastened.

PLYWOOD CONSTRUCTION. In recent years plywood has been used for planking both flat- and V-bottom small craft. The material used for this is made with a waterproof binder between the veneers; no other will serve. While plywood is not affected by water in contact with its faces, it may be harmed by water in contact with its edges. To prevent this, seams and raw edges

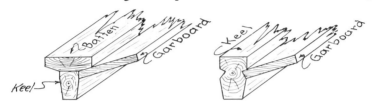

*12. Batten Keel and Rabbeted Keel*

are protected with a waterproof tape or cement. The lasting qualities of plywood hulls seem good if properly built and the construction is suited to small dinghies and similar craft. It is expensive in large boats. As it is very flexible, a number of closely spaced battens are employed between the frames to stiffen the skin of the hull; this increases the labor, so there is little saving, except in weight, over a planked hull. The source of most trouble in plywood, particularly the thinner sheets, is due to faulty manufacture; the inner plys (or core) are not closely butted and the sheet will fracture if bent in the vicinity of the open butt. In most sheets of plywood the inner ply (or core) is of fir, which is subject to quick rot. Therefore, the plywood should be well protected with paint, or canvas covered, to get the greatest life. In small cruisers that must be light, canvas-covered plywood makes an excellent deck or cabin roof if the required curvature is not too great. Plywood cannot be bent in more than one direction; the bending qualities of a sheet are best represented by a square of paper. Pressed fiberboards of certain classes may be used in the same manner and for the same purposes as plywood. These materials, plywood and fiberboards, are much used for cabin bulkheads if their binder is waterproof.

Multi-Chine Types. Hulls having more than one chine on each side are sometimes designed for amateur construction. These boats most commonly have two chine lines on each side and are planked fore and aft. It is doubtful if there is any particular ad-

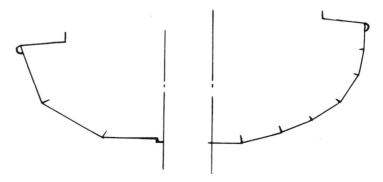

*13. Sections Showing Multi-Chine Hull Forms*

vantage to such hull shape, but some designers and builders prefer it to the orthodox single chine. The planking has to be spaced and fitted as in a round-bottom boat, though it is a little easier to get the plank in place. The chines are generally backed with a batten, beveled to fit the angles of the frames and plank. A better construction, though harder to do, is to lap the edges of the planks at these chines and omit the chine battens. This is the sailing dory construction; by multiplying the number of chines, a round-bottom hull results.

## Round-Bottom Model

The round-bottom model is considered by most amateur builders too difficult to construct. This is not wholly correct; while it is true that some designs are beyond amateur means, both in skill and equipment, there are designs that are really no more difficult to build than a V-bottom model having the bottom fore and aft planked. The means of classification of the round-bottom model must vary from the rather simple method used in the other models. The clearest way, most suited to establishing the relation of a design to suitability for amateur construction, is to divide the

model's types according to midsection and then subdivide according to use and methods of construction.

U-Section. The first midsection form is that which might best
be called the "dinghy section"—almost U-shaped. This midsection is used not only for dinghies, but also for powerboats and
even larger sailing yachts than dinghies. It is probably the easiest
form to frame as there are commonly no reverse curves in the sections. There are a number of ways of planking this hull form,

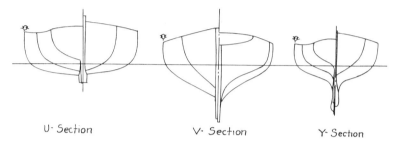

*14. Classification of Round-Bottom Types by Midsection, Showing
Effect of Midsection on Other Sections in the Hull*

clench or lap-strake, carvel, strip and diagonal. With the latter
two methods of planking, the usual bent framing may be largely
or entirely omitted. The clench or lap-strake and the diagonal
methods are the lightest and strongest; they are excellent for
dinghies. Clench planking is sometimes used in the bottoms of
high-speed powerboats. It requires a good deal of skill to build a
lap-strake hull, but it is not beyond the capabilities of a good amateur carpenter. The diagonal method, highly developed in England under the name "Ashcroft System," is particularly designed
for amateur building. It is not to be confused with the regular,
double-skin type of planking which is very difficult for the ordinary amateur. Carvel or smooth-skin planking is the orthodox
method; it is suitable for boats having planking not less than $\frac{3}{8}$ of
an inch thick. It is not quite as difficult to do as lap-strake, but
more difficult than the Ashcroft method.

In some designs having carvel planking the seams are backed
up with battens; this is known as "ribband carvel" or batten seam
construction. It is subject to the same objections as the batten

seam construction described for V-bottom craft (batten seam construction, page 41), with the additional drawback of having to pad the steam-bent frames between the battens. These make it unsuitable for amateur construction in most cases. Its advantages and uses are those of the same method applied to V-bottoms, already mentioned. Strip planking is made up of narrow strips,

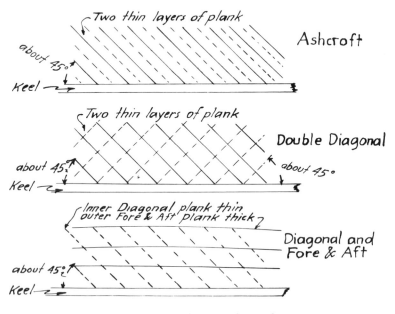

*15. Types of Diagonal Planking*

edge nailed. It is relatively easy to do, as far as fitting is concerned, but is somewhat laborious in fastening. A strong but heavy method of planking, it is well suited to amateur building. Small craft having the dinghy section are sometimes carvel planked and then canvas covered; this method is also suited to amateur building, but is limited to canoes and the smaller class of dinghies. All of these planking methods will be explained in a later chapter. The dinghy-section round-bottom hull is easiest to build when it is not wide in proportion to its length. It is a pretty general rule that all wide hulls are much more difficult to build than narrow ones.

Sailing Qualities of U-Section. The sailing qualities of this section are usually excellent and so it is commonly used for small racing craft, either centerboard or fin keel. In Europe it has been used successfully in small auxiliary cruisers. With proper design, it has been used in large sailing craft having centerboards.

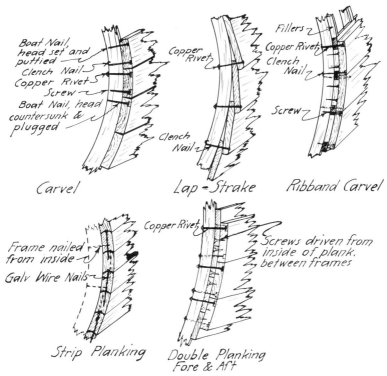

Boat Nail, head set and puttied
Clench Nail
Copper Rivet
Screw
Boat Nail, head countersunk & plugged
Clench Nail

Carvel

Copper Rivet
Clench Nail

Lap-Strake

Fillers
Copper Rivet
Clench Nail
Screw

Ribband Carvel

Frame nailed from inside
Galv Wire Nails

Strip Planking

Copper Rivet
Screws driven from inside of plank, between frames

Double Planking
Fore & Aft

*16. Common Types of Planking and Methods of Fastening Used for Each*

U-Section for Powerboats. For power craft, the section is also a very good one. It is used in most round-bottom powerboats, either launches or cruisers. Generally the hull has a skeg or fin keel aft to protect the propeller and rudder, and to help in steering. It is suited to low- and medium-speed motorboats. When long and rather narrow, this hull form will drive easily with low power. In recent years boats have been built with the dinghy form forward and chines aft for high-speed work in rough water. This form is not easy to build and, like most high-speed hull forms, is unsuited to amateur building.

V-SECTION. The next form of hull, the V-section, partakes of the V-bottom; it is really a V-bottom with round bilges. It usually has reverse curves in the aftersections. Primarily it is a sailing hull, but it is so used in a modified form in seagoing powerboats and in tugs. In the small sizes it is usually seen in sailing cruisers, keel or centerboard, having all or most of their ballast inside. For this reason, it is generally more heavily built than the dinghy-section hull. In sailing craft this form of hull requires ballast, the amount usually depending upon the relation of depth to beam. It is usually easy to frame, only a little more difficult than the dinghy form. It is also rather easily planked, though if full ended or wide this is not true. The greatest trouble is usually aft, in the run, where there is often a good deal of twist in the bottom planking. It may be planked lap-strake, carvel, or strip. Neither batten seam construction nor diagonal planking is suited to the usual design for this form of hull. Diagonal planking can be used, however, if there are no reverse curves in the aftersections. It makes an excellent sailing hull for rough water and was much used, therefore, in small fishing craft having sail, with or without centerboard. It is suited to low-speed power craft only.

Y-SECTION. The third form of hull belonging to the round-bottom model may be described as having a Y-section, shaped something like a wineglass. This is the popular form for the more expensive sailing cruisers and racers having all, or practically all, of their ballast outside. The keel is usually very wide and heavy. It may be safely said that most designs having this midsection are unsuited to amateur construction, not necessarily because the hull form is difficult to frame or plank but because of the massive keel and ballast casting. Some designs are easily framed and planked, but as a rule boats having this section are harder to frame and plank than those having the dinghy or V-section. Hulls having the Y-section are usually carvel planked, though in some cases strip planking could be used. Expensive racers are often double planked, but this requires greater accuracy in planking than most amateurs are likely to possess. The hulls having the Y-section are not suited to much speed under power, so this hull form is not used in motorboats.

HARD TO BUILD FEATURES. The foregoing classification of the round-bottom model is somewhat arbitrary, for there are designs that do not fall into such clear-cut divisions of hull form. In order to help the amateur choose a design for a round-bottom model, the portions of a design that are hard to build, and which therefore decide its suitability for home building, will be outlined. As has been mentioned, the dinghy section, when given great beam, is difficult to plank. This is generally true of the V- and Y-sections also. If the boat is full on deck forward and fine on the water line, having great flare outward to the sides forward, she will be difficult to plank. If there is a sharp reverse curve aft, she will require careful spacing of the strakes. Fullness in the forefoot or in the stern near the lower part of the sternpost will make a trying job of planking. Very sharp curves in the sections, such as those at the bilge, often give trouble too. The oval stern, or elliptical transom, is much more difficult to shape and finish than the transom having angular corners at the deck or sheer line, in plan view. The transom having curves across its face is more difficult to frame and plank than one that is flat. When the rabbets of the stem and sternposts are well curved, the ends of the planking resting in them (called "hood ends" by builders) are long and sharply pointed; they are usually very difficult to fit.

FRAMING. Framing the round-bottom model is an important factor in ease of building. Some types that are planked diagonally or with strips require no frames, or at least very few. Framing is done, with other types of planking, in two ways: steam-bent or sawn to shape. The former is used in nearly all small craft of the round-bottom model. In light boats the steam-bent frames are small and closely spaced. In larger craft the frames become wide and thick, the spacing greater. Sawn frames are usually made up of two layers, with the butts staggered to obtain strength. They are heavier, but stiffer, than steam-bent frames. If made of natural crooks or knees, the sawn frame is very strong; in such cases it is not necessary to double the frames except where the joints, or butts, come.

BENT FRAMES. Steam-bent framing requires molds to be set up and ribbanded off before framing. Boats having sharp curves in the sections, reverse curves, curves near to the keel rabbet, or rounded-in sheers (streamlining), are difficult to frame. If the frames are of large section or are bent on edge they will be

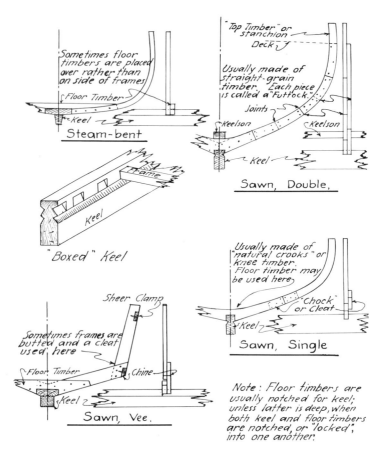

Sometimes floor timbers are placed over rather than on side of frames

Floor Timber

Keel

Steam-bent

Frame

Keel

"Boxed" Keel

Sheer Clamp

Sometimes frames are butted and a cleat used here

Floor Timber

Chine

Keel

Sawn, Vee.

"Top Timber" or stanchion

Deck

Usually made of straight-grain timber. Each piece is called a "Futtock."

Joints

Keelson                    Keelson

Keel

Sawn, Double,

Usually made of "natural crooks" or knee timber. Floor timber may be used here

"Chock" or Cleat

Keel

Sawn, Single

Note: Floor timbers are usually notched for keel; unless latter is deep, when both keel and floor timbers are notched, or "locked", into one another.

*17. Types of Framing*

difficult to bend. If the frames must be of large section, then they ought to be wide and rather thin, instead of square, and bent on the flat (wide face to the planking and ribbands), to be suitable for amateur builders. In some localities it is either very difficult or impossible to get timber that can be steam bent.

SAWN FRAMES. Sawn frames must be all laid down in the mold loft and patterns made; the bevels must be taken from the mold loft drawing. It takes much longer to frame with sawn timbers than with bent ones. However, it is not necessary to set up molds when building with sawn frames and it is much easier for the builder to check his work against the "lines" plan. The builder is more likely to have a boat exactly like the "lines" with sawn frames than with steam-bent frames. Hard curves in the sections are less troublesome to the builder with this mode of framing. If the frames are of thick timber, a power band saw with tilting frame or table is almost a necessity. In fact, to saw frames out by hand, even for a small boat, is a laborious task, added to which the bevels have to be cut on the face of the frames. Therefore, unless the frames required are few in number, sawn frames are not suited for most amateur-built round-bottom boats.

## Heavy Keels and Outside Ballast

Heavy timbers cannot be easily worked by hand. Much of the shaping of the wide, deep keels, required in most outside ballasted hulls, must be done with power tools or with the adz, a highly dangerous instrument in unskilled hands. Then, too, the ballast casting is a difficult problem. If the ballast is of iron, and if the casting has curved sections (as is so often the case in modern yachts), an accurate pattern must be made, allowing for shrinkage. Arrangements for fastening the ballast casting to the keel must also be properly made on the pattern. This is beyond the skill and knowledge of most amateur builders. If the work is hired out, it is quite expensive. If the ballast casting is of lead and not too massive, the amateur builder may be able to cast it in his shop. Shrinkage is a matter of small importance in lead castings of the size an amateur is likely to undertake, so no allowance need be made on that score. It is also possible to make the pattern and mold without having great skill. Lead can be drilled and planed with hand tools, so the fastenings can be bored when the casting is completed. This is a decided advantage in building. Two men can cast a lead keel of 1,500 pounds without great difficulty if they make proper preparations. Smaller lead keels can be cast more easily, of course. The design having the ballast keel angular in section (straight sided and flat on top and bottom) is most suited to amateur construction. In spite of the greater cost of lead, compared to iron, the builder will usually find that the saving in pattern cost, foundry work, and transportation made possible by casting the lead ballast keel himself will more than make up the difference. If the keel casting is too heavy to be handled by two men, it should be cast alongside the stocks and secured to the keel before the latter is placed on the stocks. Inside ballast is no problem, of course, but cannot be used in all designs of round-bottom hulls.

## Expensive Materials

In selecting a design from which to build, the beginner should avoid those requiring expensive materials. Mistakes in workmanship are hard to avoid and the loss in spoiled material may run to a large amount of money. Racing craft, except the few classes that were designed primarily for amateur building, should never be attempted by the beginner. He would be wise to try a simple design, flat- or V-bottom, for his first attempt.

## Source of Plans and Cost

The model having been chosen and the size, rig, type, and accommodation decided, plans must be obtained. It will be very helpful to have the advice of some other builder in this matter. Plans may be obtained by ordering them from the professional designers whose advertisements may be found in yachting magazines. Or, if the proper plan can be found, it may be possible to use the "how-to-build" articles in yachting and mechanics' magazines, hobby magazines, or books. Those in the yachting papers and books are usually the better designed since the editors know they will be criticized by experienced yachtsmen as well as by professional designers. Unfortunately, many plans used in mechanical and hobby magazine articles are not the work of experienced or professional boat designers. For this reason, advice is very helpful when choosing from such sources. If plans are chosen from a published source, magazine or book, the cost is very low. If a designer is required, the cost will be a good deal greater. There is no fixed scale of fees for boat designing. This is particularly true where very cheap or small boats are concerned. Large yachts are designed on a percentage basis, just as houses are. This percentage is usually from 6 per cent to 10 per cent of the estimated building cost taken for an average building yard. In most offices having a staff of draftsmen a minimum fee is established, usually between fifty and one hundred dollars. This is applied to all designs in which the percentage would run under the established minimum. When the design is of a boat estimated to cost over the minimum, the exact percentage will vary with the type, size, and accommodation. In other words, if a small boat is designed, having a complicated arrangement, the design fee may be higher than for a larger boat having a simple arrangement. If inspection, or inspection and supervision, is desired, the fee usually reaches 10 per cent, or even more.

### Stock Plans

Some designers have "stock" plans; these are plans on hand that they will sell for a low price. These have usually been made to fill a demand for a special type and size, or are old designs that have become more or less obsolete. Very often these plans are excellent and tested designs. However, there is one disadvantage in their use: they cannot be altered in any respect except at an additional cost. If changes are wanted it is wise to have a special design made rather than to ask a designer to make changes in a stock plan. Since the prices of stock plans are usually low, the designer cannot give much time to advice and assistance. If an amateur wishes to build a boat which will require professional advice from the designer, he would do well to have a special design drawn for his particular needs. Some designers do not have stock plans —very few, indeed, have catalogues of available designs—so it is very necessary that inquiries from amateur builders be very complete as to requirements.

### Choice of Designer

Choosing the designer is an important matter. It is not difficult for the amateur builder to find examples of the work of the designers listed in the advertising sections of yachting magazines. He may be able to see finished boats in his vicinity, or at least can find examples of designs in the "Design" section of the magazine or in articles. Then, too, there are a number of books showing plans of various types of boats and yachts by specialists in each type. Some designers specialize in small craft, some in large, or in racing boats, or cruisers, or powerboats—wherever their personal interest is greatest. Not all designers are interested in the types of craft suitable for amateur construction. The choice of designer is best made by finding one who specializes in the desired type and who has some interest in amateur problems. An experienced designer may refuse to design a boat of a given type or appearance because he is not interested in it or has objections to it; in that case he will state his reasons or refer the inquirer to a specialist in the type desired.

## Ordering Plans

When the designers specializing in a given type are discovered, the amateur builder can write them for quotations on the design of the boat to be built. It is highly important that the designers be given all the pertinent information possible: general dimensions, type, rig, engine, accommodations, and the fact that the boat is to be amateur built. Also a sketch should be given of the cabin arrangement or of the general appearance desired. It is a good idea to give some information on the timber available in the district in which she will be built. Do not ask for just "plans of a 30-foot yawl"; tell exactly what you require. It is sometimes helpful to send the designers photos, or clippings of a plan published in some magazine, showing a boat approximately like the one wanted. Sometimes it may be desirable to have the designers submit sketches of their ideas; for sketches there is usually a small charge, but they are only necessary when large boats are being discussed or when there is doubt as to the proper arrangement of accommodations. Ordinarily sketches are not required if the inquirer is specific in his request for a quotation. Some of the designers approached may refuse to design the boat according to the exact requests of the amateur and will state reasons. These should be carefully considered as designers can make a more accurate study of a proposed boat than is possible by an amateur builder. While it is possible that there is a misunderstanding of requirements or prejudice on the part of the designer, it is likely that any objections he may raise are founded on practical considerations. When the quotations are received and the correspondence compared, a choice of designer can be made and the plans ordered. If the design is to be a new one, remember that the designer will require time to make the drawings; also it may be necessary to have some correspondence in regard to possible

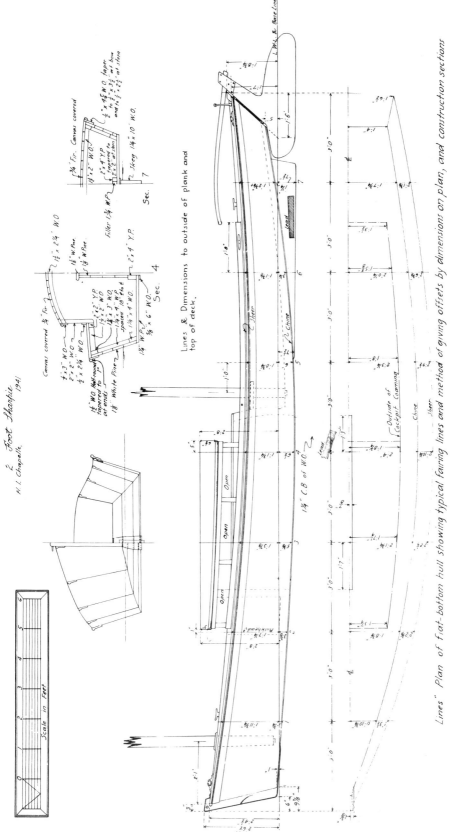

PLATE 1. Lines of a 24-foot sharpie. Sail plan shown on Plate 7.

"Lines" Plan of flat-bottom hull showing typical fairing lines and method of giving offsets by dimensions on plan, and construction sections

changes as the plans progress. It is very important that the plans
be final, that no changes in shape, dimensions, rig, or accommodations be considered after the plans are once finished.

## The Lines

When the blueprints of the design arrive, it will be found that
they are made up of a number of sheets or plans, unless the boat
is a very small and simple one. One of the plans will be the "lines."
This shows the shape of the boat. In it are three elevations or
views: the profile or sheer plan (or view), showing the appearance of the hull seen broadside on; the half-breadth plan, showing
one half the hull seen from above; and the body plan, showing the
transverse or cross sections of one half the hull. Only half of the
hull is shown because both sides are alike in shape and dimensions.

FLAT-BOTTOM LINES. If the boat is a flat-bottom model, the
lines show the profile of the top of the hull or "sheer" line, the
profile of the bottom or "chine" line, and the profile shape of
both bow and stern in the sheer plan. The half-breadth plan shows
the same, viewed from above, giving the outline of the deck or
sheer line and of the bottom or chine line as seen from this point
of vantage. The half-breadth plan will also show the half-thickness
of the stem (and sternpost if sharp sterned) and the half-width
of the transom at top and bottom. If there is a keel or skeg, its
outline is shown in the sheer plan and its half-breadth in the half-
breadth plan. The body plan shows sections taken at selected
points indicated in the other two views, and the end-on shape of
bow and stern; usually the half-breadth of the skeg or fin is again
shown. The positions of the masts and deck structures are usually
drawn in the lines and there are dimensions given for placing sections, and for profile of stem and stern, that will be required to
make the full-sized drawings necessary for building. (Plate 1.)

V-BOTTOM LINES. If the hull is V-bottom, the lines will show
the same things as in the case of the flat-bottom boat, with the
addition of the profile and half-breadths of the keel, at its bottom and where it meets the bottom plank (rabbet line). The sections in the body plan will show the amount of vee or dead rise in
the bottom, of course. (Plate 2.)

ROUND-BOTTOM LINES. If the hull is round-bottom, there are a
number of additional lines, or longitudinal sections, required. In

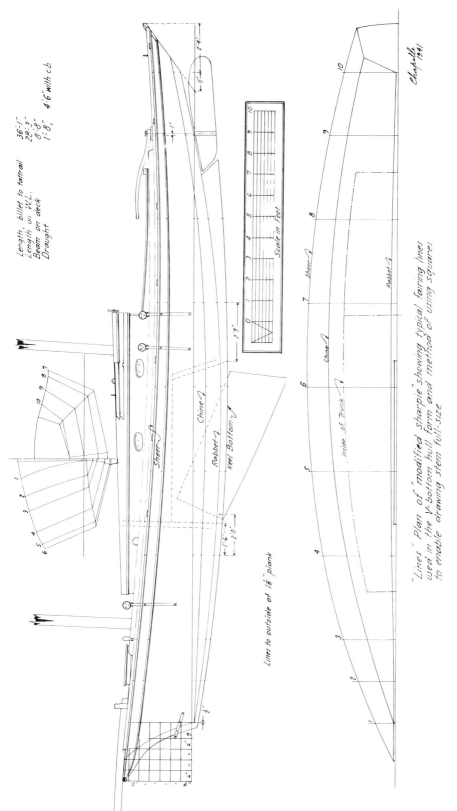

Length, billet to taffrail 36'-1"
Length on W.L. 28'-3"
Beam on deck 8'-8"
Draught 1'-8", 4'-6" with c.b.

Lines to outside of ⅛" plank

Sheer
Chine
Rabbet
Keel Bottom

Scale in Feet

Sheer
Chine
Inside of Trunk
Rabbet

Chapelle 1941

"Lines" Plan of "modified sharpie" showing typical fairing lines
used in the v-bottom hull form and method of using squares
to enable drawing stem full-size.

PLATE 2. Lines of a 36-Foot Modified Sharpie

the sheer plan the profile not only shows the sheer line, rabbet line, and profile of bow and stern, but also a number of straight lines parallel to the load water line, or to an arbitrary base line; these are the location or heights at which the longitudinal sections, called "water lines," will be taken. On the profile will be seen long curves marked "buttocks"; these are the outlines of a number of equally spaced longitudinal sections, taken through the hull vertically and parallel to the center line of the hull. The half-breadth plan shows the outline of the water lines, shown as straight lines in the sheer plan; while the buttocks are shown as straight lines in the half-breadth plan, parallel to the center line, they are shown as curved lines in the sheer plan. The half-breadth plan will show the half-width of the rabbet along the keel and stem and sternpost; sometimes the half-width of the bottom of the keel and the face of the stem and sternposts are also shown. The body plan shows the cross sections located by vertical straight lines on the other two views. These are crossed by horizontal straight lines, representing the straight lines called water lines in the sheer plan and the curved water lines in the half-breadth plan. There are also vertical straight lines crossing the body plan sections; these are the buttocks, shown as curves in the sheer plan and as straight lines in the half-breadth plan. The end-on elevation of the rabbet line, along the keel and up both stem and sternpost, will also be shown, and the same view of the bottom of the keel and the face of the stem and sternpost may be shown. Across the sections in the body plan are some sloping straight lines, meeting and crossing in the center line of the plan. It will be noted that each pair has its outer ends at the same height from the nearest water line or from the base line and out the same distance from the center line. These are the "diagonals"; their projection through the hull longitudinally is represented by a number of long sweeps or curves superimposed on the half-breadth plan, or opposite to its center line. The projection of all of these sections is required to fair the shape of the boat; fairing means to develop curves around which a batten, plank, or steam-bent frame can be bent without breaking or having humps and waves. The whole of the lines for a round-bottom hull should be drawn full size and checked before building, as will be described later. (Plate 3.)

WHAT LINES REPRESENT. It is important that the builder be able to visualize the lines in the plan as the completed boat. To do

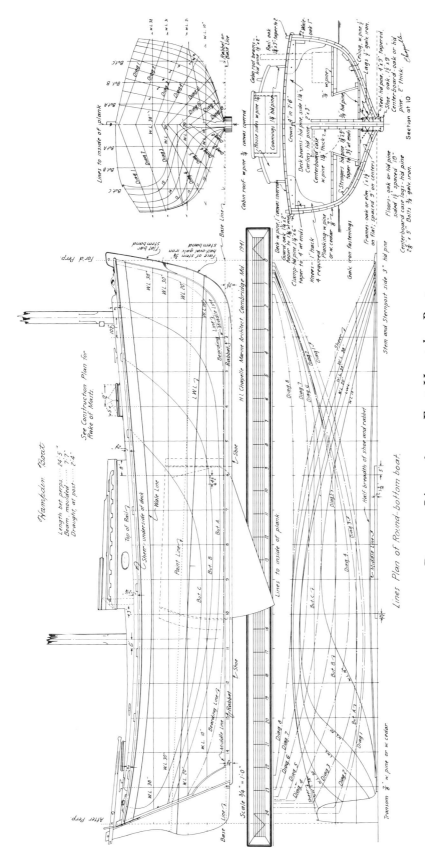

PLATE 3. *Lines of a 24-Foot Hampden Boat*

this, it is necessary to know what water lines, buttocks, diagonals, and sections really indicate as to the shape of the boat. Suppose a solid wax model of the boat is at hand, made to the same scale as the drawing of the lines. If this model is split lengthwise, two half-models result. Take one of these, whose bow and stern will coincide with those drawn when laid on the lines. This is the half-model that the lines must show in such a manner that any section can be projected and enlarged to full size. When the half-model is laid on the lines so that its flat back coincides with the sheer plan, it will be obvious that the sheer line and the rest of the profile of the model will coincide with the drawing. Now cut the model in parallel slices coinciding with the straight water lines in the sheer plan and perpendicular to the flat back. The outlines of these slices will coincide with their respective water lines when laid on the half-breadth plan. If cut transversely in the same manner, coinciding with the vertical section lines in the sheer plan, each section in the body plan will be duplicated. If cut longitudinally to coincide with the buttock lines shown on body and half-breadth plans, the sections obtained are those shown in the sheer plan. In the same manner the shape of the diagonals can be verified. It can be seen that there is a definite relation between each section cut and the shape of the hull. The use of the various sections obtained in the lines will be explained when the making of full-sized drawings is discussed.

### *Offsets*

Attached to the lines, or on a separate sheet, will be found a Table of Offsets. (Plate 4.) These are the necessary dimensions to make the full-sized drawing and to reproduce each section or line shown in the "lines" plan. It will be noticed that the height and breadth of each water line and buttock, the sheer line, rabbet, and every other curved line are given with the dimension taken from base and center line opposite the proper line name and under the number of each station, or section, number. The dimensions are given in feet, inches, and eighths; thus: 7–6–3, meaning 7 feet 6⅜ inches. Sometimes the signs + and — are placed after the dimensions; this merely means the dimension is either full or scant by 1/16 or 1/32 of an inch. Some designers show all the dimensions required to lay the boat down full size on the offset table;

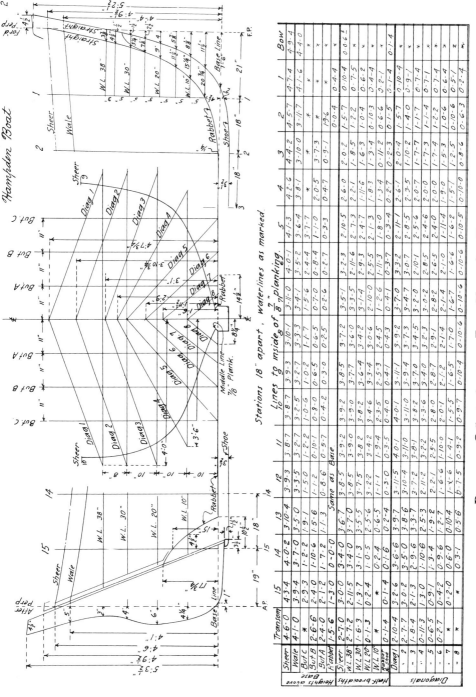

PLATE 4. *Offsets for a 24-Foot Hampden Boat*

others put dimensions on both the lines and offsets, so that both
are required in making the full-sized drawings. There are many
methods of showing the dimensions of the bow and stern. If simple in detail, dimensions are commonly used, but if there is decora-
tion or other complications the stem and stern may be shown in
the offset plan, superimposed over a series of squares for which
dimensions are given. By this means enlarging to full size can be
easily and accurately done (see Plate 2).

## Construction Plan

There will be a "construction plan" in the set of blueprints
(Plates 5 and 6); this usually shows an inboard profile made
as though the hull were split lengthwise. By this means a true projection can be made of the appearance of the hull frame. Here you
will see the shape of the pieces of timber making up the keel, deadwood, and stem and sternpost. The location of the bilge stringers
and other longitudinal members is shown. The position of the deck
framing can be seen. It is usual to show the mast positions, shape
of the steps, height of cabin trunk, cabin and cockpit floor, propeller shaft position and dimensions, engine beds, and the other
structural members required by the designer. On the same plan
will be a midsection, showing a cross section or "typical construction section." Here will usually be given the timber sizes and other
building specifications not given elsewhere. The third elevation is
a plan view of half the deck framing where dimensions and timber sizes required are given so that an accurate deck arrangement
can be laid out. It is general practice to omit some dimensions on
the construction plan; therefore the builder will have to scale the
size of many members (particularly in the deadwood and ends of
the hull) from the blueprint. On this plan the keel, stem and stern,
and all deadwood members, the profile of cabin trunk and the
roof framing, and the whole of the deck framing shown in the
plan view, must later be drawn full size.

## Joiner, or Cabin, Plans

If the boat has a cabin there will be a plan similar to the construction plan which shows two or three views of the cabin arrangement. This plan has an inboard elevation showing one side

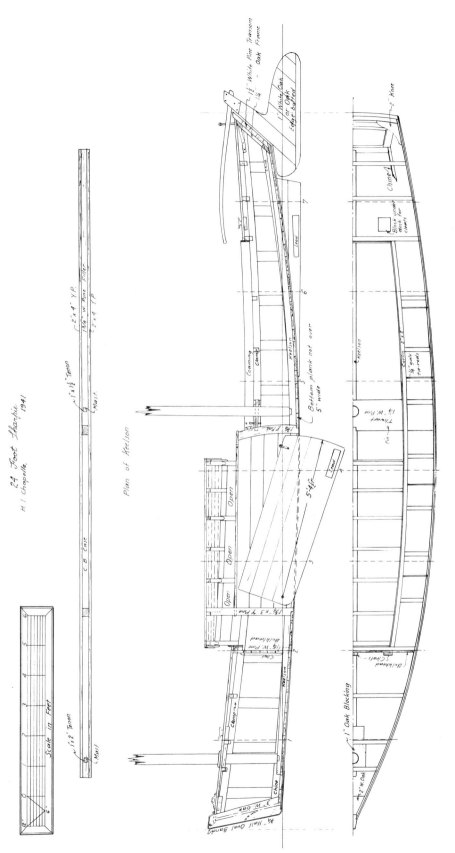

PLATE 5. *Construction plan for a 24-foot Sharpie. Lines shown in Plate 1.*

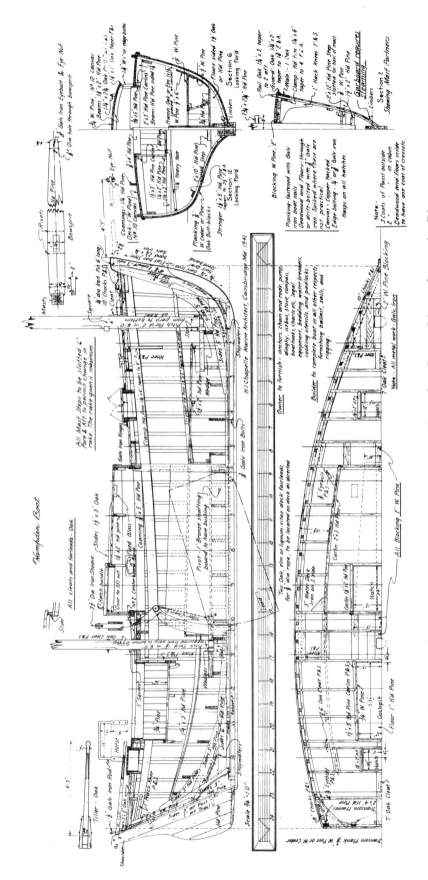

PLATE 6. Construction plan for a 24-foot Hampden Boat. Lines shown in Plate 3.

of the cabin furniture, with some important dimensions. The plan view shows the whole cabin arrangement when viewed from above; it is usual to show both sides of the boat in this since the two sides of a boat's cabin may not be alike. Additional dimensions are usually shown here. There may also be a section or two showing the important details in the cross sections of the cabin. If the boat is large, or has a good deal of cabin furniture, there may be a separate plan showing a number of sections. These one or two drawings are usually referred to as "joiner plans." Both the construction and joiner plans are, to some extent, merely pictures with only the important dimensions given; the less important must be scaled from the blueprints.

### Sail Plan or Outboard Profile

If the boat has spars and sails, there will be a "sail plan" (Plates 7 and 8), showing shape and dimensions of the sails, spar dimensions, and details of the rigging. This plan also gives a picture of the outboard appearance of the hull. If the design is for a motorboat, there is an outboard profile instead of a sail plan, serving the same purpose. Occasionally there may be separate detail drawings, or some may be included in the construction, joiner, and sail plans. Equipment (such as deck and cabin fittings) and all important hardware are listed on the construction and joiner plans. Common practice is to give some maker's or dealer's name and his catalogue number; it should be understood that this is generally for guidance to type and size in purchasing and that similar equipment and hardware from other catalogues will serve.

### Specifications

In small craft there are usually no specifications, as these are made a part of the plans. In large boats and most cabin craft additional information to the plans may be needed. The designer may therefore furnish a number of typewritten or blueprinted pages, usually in pamphlet form. These contain all the necessary information to supplement the plans. The kind and size of timber to be used in each part of the boat, fastenings, method of building, hardware, fittings, plumbing, engine installation, painting, and other information are found in the specifications.

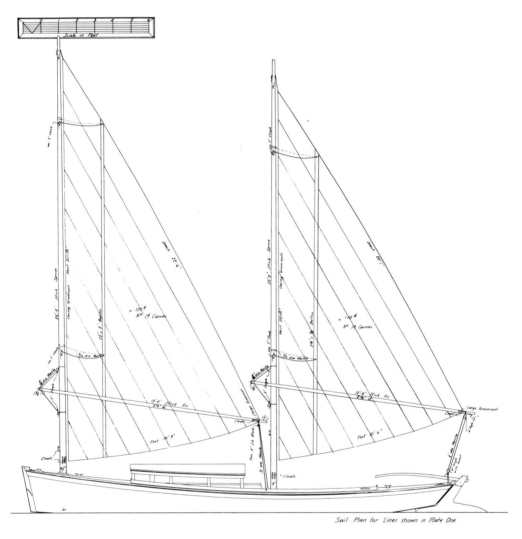

Sail Plan for Lines shown in Plate One.

PLATE 7. *Sail Plan for a 24-Foot Sharpie*

## *Details*

When the plans are studied, some details may appear to be missing. In this case read all the notes on the plans carefully and then turn to the specifications. The missing details may be referred to there. If not found, the builder can write to the designer for instructions. The amount of detail shown on plans varies with the designers. Very often the detail of construction not shown on a plan is a matter of common building practice and the designer feels he need not bother to show it. If he is asked to furnish detail drawings there will be a charge for them. In most boats a completely detailed set of plans would be unnecessarily expensive. Perhaps the best attitude the builder can take in regard to the plans is that what is shown is important and should be followed; what is not shown is not important and the builder can therefore do it as he thinks best. Timber sizes noted on the plans are usually dimensions of the lumber before being finished, unless marked "f" (finished size).

## *Lumber List*

Few designers will attempt to furnish a list of lumber required; this must be taken from the blueprints by the builder. The way to do this is to pick out each piece in the deadwood, for example, and scale its dimensions. Then note its greatest thickness. Allow a little margin for shaping all around. When all the pieces are listed, go over them and rearrange them so that all pieces of the same width and thickness are together. Do this for all timber required. For planking and framing it is usual to add from 10 per cent to 20 per cent for loss through breakage or waste. Now the list should be converted to commercial sizes of timber. All timber is sold by the board foot, 1″ x 12″ x 12″; in most sections of the country there are standard sizes of commercial stock. The common lengths are 10–12–14–16–18–20–22–24 feet. The standard widths and thicknesses are 1″ x 2″, 1″ x 4″, 1″ x 6″, 1″ x 8″, 1″ x 10″, 1″ x 12″, 2″ x 4″, 2″ x 6″, 2″ x 8″, 2″ x 10″, 2″ x 12″, 2″ x 14″, 2″ x 16″, 3″ x 6″, 3″ x 8″, 3″ x 10″, 3″ x 12″, 3″ x 14″, 3″ x 16″, 4″ x 4″, 4″ x 6″, 4″ x 8″, 6″ x 6″, 6″ x 8″, 6″ x 10″, 6″ x 12″, 8″ x 8″, 10″ x 10″, 10″ x 12″, 12″ x 12″, 12″ x 14″. Some lumber dealers will furnish out-sizes, such as 2″ x 2″, 3″ x 3″, 2″ x 3″, and others, at no additional cost; but in most cases an order for a lot of 2″ x 2″ 's will require sawing from 2″ x 6″ 's. The reason 2″ x 2″ 's cannot be made by ripping 2″ x 4″ 's is that the actual dimensions of commercial standard stock is under the sizes given; take a 2″ x 8″, 14 feet long, as an example; it would actually be about 1⅞″ x 7⅞″ and about 13′–11″ long. Due to checks in the ends of timber it is well to consider a 14′–0″ piece as actually being 13′–6″. If greater lengths are required than 24′ a premium will usually be paid.

The cost of sawing and the waste will be figured in when the dealer makes up timber not of standard sizes. Occasionally the "standard" sizes vary somewhat from those given, but this is unusual. Now, by going over the list of timber sizes required for the boat and adding those of the same width and thickness, it is possible to find out how many lengths of commercial stock will be required. By comparing thickness and widths of the required lumber with the stock sizes it is possible to select the properly dimensioned commercial stock. The cost of lumber is usually given "per thousand board feet." When the unit price is known, it is possible to estimate the cost of the lumber to be ordered from the completed list. If it is desired to have any of the stock reduced to some odd thickness or width, the cost of such work will have to be added to the cost of the lumber. Most dealers have mills for this purpose and will give an estimate. Order timber by commercial standard size, whenever possible, and be sure to state the kind of timber required. Excepting pine, spruce, and cypress, it is usually cheaper to order random widths, whenever possible, than specified widths.

Grading of lumber varies a good deal with the timber and location; the highest grade ("clear of knots on one side and free of rot, shakes, or checks, and other faults on the other side") should be ordered for all hardwood material such as oak, maple, and mahogany. This grade is called "Firsts" in the lumber trade, and the next grade "Seconds." Stock for steam-bent frames should be specially listed and the dealers informed of the purpose for which it is to be used. It should be "Firsts" and should be of young timber, not dried. Old, large oak trees will not do for bent timbers. All softwood timber should be "Select." This is subdivided into A, B, C, and D. Select A and B are suited for "bright" or natural

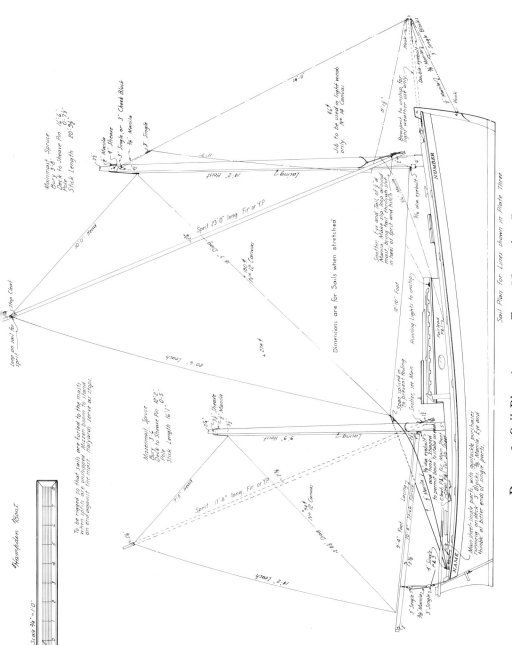

PLATE 8. *Sail Plan for a 24-Foot Hampden Boat*

finish while C and D are suited for paint finish. The Select grade, when bought in plank, is called "Number One" grade.

Planking for hulls may be bought in some varieties of lumber "flitch sawn," which means that each plank has bark on its edges so that the builder may get the greatest benefit from the shape of the tree. Cedar is commonly sold this way. If possible, the builder should see the lumber stock of the dealer before ordering. Decking, when painted or finished bright, should be ordered "quarter-sawn." If the dealer specializes in boatbuilding timber the decking should be ordered to finish size. Steam-bent frames should likewise be ordered to finish size and at least 2 feet longer than the maximum length required in the hull. Air-dried stock is the best for boatbuilding timber, but is almost impossible to obtain in most sections of the country. For this reason kiln-dried stock must be accepted. Some woods, such as teak, should not be too dry when used for planking. White cedar, white pine, and longleaf yellow pine are considered the best planking from among our native timbers; loblolly (Virginia or North Carolina) pine is also used to some extent. Cedar and white pine are the easiest to work. Longleaf yellow pine may be used for keels, deadwood, stem and sternposts, stringers, and clamps, in place of white oak. Steam-bent frames can be made of rock elm instead of white oak. Fir and spruce are sometimes used in hull construction, for plank and framing (not steam bent), but are short lived compared to the others mentioned; they are suited, however, to spar building.

### Hardware List

When the lumber has been ordered, the hardware and fittings must be listed, checked against marine hardware dealers' catalogues, and ordered. The fastenings should be roughly estimated and ordered. There is no ready rule for estimating quantities of fastenings, but an estimate can usually be made from the blueprints, allowing at least three fastenings per plank per frame. Keel fastenings average about two per frame, frame fastenings (to keel, floors, and to longitudinal members) about twelve per frame. Materials and fastenings will be dealt with in later chapters. When ordering deck and cabin fittings be sure to order the required number, size, and type of fastening for each item. Sails, rigging, and motor can also be ordered prior to building if desired.

Before starting to work on the boat, the builder should take time to study the plans carefully. It would be well to try to find out what steps will be required to build the boat in the easiest way, to decide what the best sequence of jobs seems to be, and to see that the plans are fully understood.

## Selecting Place in Which to Build

While this study is being made, a place in which to build must be found. To the average city man this is a great problem. Garages are often used, or sometimes space may be rented in an old warehouse or loft. If a building is to be used, it is very important that definite plans and measurements be made so that it is certain that the finished boat can be removed without tearing apart the building. This has been a standing joke among amateur builders for years, but is often overlooked in spite of that. If the boat is to be built in the winter, then heating must be considered. No man can work well, or be accurate, when he is physically uncomfortable. If no building is available and the boat is to be constructed in the open, then she must be built in warm weather. Obviously, the space in which the boat is to be built must be suitable for the size of hull chosen. No guide can be given that covers all eventualities, but if possible the building space should be 1½ times the over-all length of the hull, 4 times the beam, and 1½ the height, keel bottom to cabin roof top. The boat should not be built close to any wall or obstruction that will prevent the builder from handling timber easily or from being able to stand back and look at his work. There must be space for tool and material storage, room for a workbench and for the usual visitors. A floor or bench suitable for the full-sized drawings must be provided for. *In any case, the full-sized plan should be in existence the whole time the boat is building* so that the drawing can be referred to.

Making the full-sized plans is the next step.

# CHAPTER TWO

# LOFTING

## Reason for Lofting

LOFTING the plans, that is, drawing them full size, is the foundation of good workmanship in building a boat. Because this is usually a tedious task and because the builder is impatient to see the hull take shape, lofting is often scamped, even by professional builders who know better. Making the full-sized drawings avoids much "trying and fitting," which represents a great saving in time and labor. In the lofting of the plans the builder has an opportunity to preview the details of building before setting up the hull and this aids greatly in planning the required sequence of operations. Too often only the lines of the boat are "laid down" full size; this enables the molds and backbone to be shaped according to the design, it is true, but leaves much timber to be shaped by trial and error when actual construction starts. By lofting part of the construction and joiner plans as well as the lines, this can be avoided. Mistakes made in the full-sized plan can be easily corrected, which is not true of the full-sized hull; very often what appeared to be a serious problem when studying the plans becomes self-explanatory when drawn full size. Sometimes errors are found in the plans, designers being human, and lofting will expose and correct them. While making the full-sized plans, the builder should build the boat mentally, to get the full advantage of the operation. Plenty of time must be allowed for the task and it should be borne in mind that there was never a boat built in which too much lofting had been done.

## Lofting Space

In order to make the full-sized plans, a mold loft must be provided. For a small boat, a large piece of paper or cheap plywood will serve. If there is no room for the loft drawing in the work-shop, it is possible to lay down the plans of a boat up to 45 feet long on paper and so preserve the plan for reference. Under such conditions, paper may be joined in order to get sufficient size. Usually it is possible to make such a plan in some attic or other place where it is possible to lay down the whole roll or sheet. Sometimes, when space is lacking, the plan must be made in two or even three sections; but this is not recommended for a begin-ner. In a well-equipped boatyard there is a "mold loft," a shed or floor giving enough space for making full-sized plans. Here it is customary to make the drawing on the floor, in pencil and colored crayons; the floor is sanded smooth, or sanded and painted flat gray, or white. This is the most satisfactory method. Therefore, if there is space, the amateur builder should build a temporary loft, even if it must be outside the shop. Such a floor may be constructed by joining sheets of plywood or by laying a cheap but smooth floor on bearers or sawhorses. The floor should not only be smooth, but should also be flat, without humps or ridges. In picking up patterns it is desirable to be able to drive nails into the drawing on the floor. If paper must be used, heavy, rosin-sized building paper will serve, though it will be difficult to avoid tearing it. Do not use cheap wrapping paper, since it stretches with dampness, is easily torn, and is not a good working surface. The thick paper will give enough strength to permit drawing of lines while the paper lies on a rather irregular surface, such as most attic floors. It is possible to make the loft drawing on paper using an apartment floor, but this makes picking up patterns somewhat troublesome (unless you wish to break a lease).

The amount of space to lay down a boat properly, in one section, is easily decided. There should be sufficient length to permit the battens, used to fair in the profile and half-breadth plans, to extend from 3 to 6 feet beyond the bow and stern. In other words, a boat 24 feet long would require a lofting space about 30 feet long. As to width, the space required is about one and a half times the depth from base to highest point on the cabin roof or sheer, or one and a half times the beam, whichever is the greatest. To lay down a boat in two sections requires a loft length equal to half the length of the hull plus the spacing of two sec-tions shown on the lines drawing plus 4 to 6 feet. Thus, a 24-foot

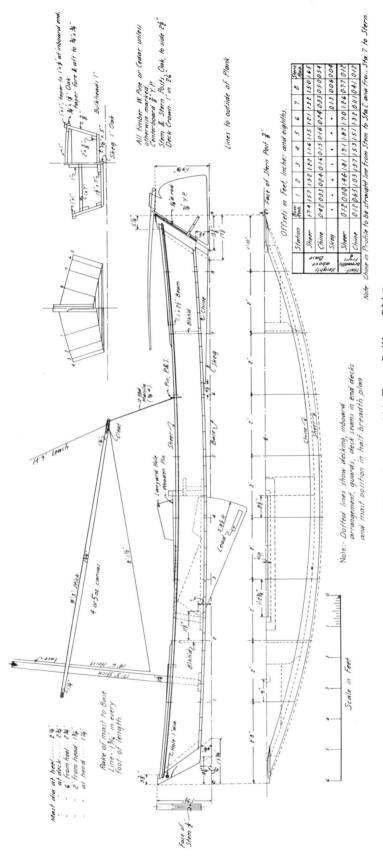

PLATE 9. Plans for an 18½-Foot Sailing Skiff

hull having stations or sections spaced 2 feet would require a loft length of 12 plus 4 plus 4, or 20 feet. The extra length, in each case, is desirable so that the curves formed by the battens can be continued beyond the ends of the hull in order that they may be fair and without flat or straight "spots." The width of the loft space is fixed by the room required for profile or half-breadth, whichever is largest, because these views are superimposed. Enough additional space for the battens, used in the body plan (also superimposed on the profile), to lay fair is required. Of course there must also be enough room to work around the plan on the floor. If paper is used for lofting it need only be large enough to contain the actual drawing, but the same amount of working space is required as for lofting on a floor.

## Battens

Battens must now be prepared. These are long, narrow strips of wood used to guide the drawing of curved lines on the floor or paper. They should be made of clear white pine if possible, though any flexible wood will do. The edges of the batten must be straight and smooth. A number of battens are required—say, three long and three short ones. One, to be used for the sheer line and other long, gentle curves, should be quite stiff, about ½ inch or ¾ inch by 1½ inches or 2 inches, to be bent with the wide side on the floor, and 3 or 4 feet longer than the boat. Another batten of the same length, about ½ inch by 1 or 1½ inches at the middle, tapered to ½ inch by ¾ or 1 inch at the ends (with all the taper taken on one edge), can be used for water lines, buttocks, and diagonals. A third long batten is useful; this should be about ¾ inch square, ⅜ inch for a small boat (under 16 feet in length). These battens may have to be spliced and this should be done near the middle of the length. A scarf must be used, fastened with glue, rivets, or screws; it should be between 14 and 24 inches long, well secured.

Short battens will be required for drawing the body plan of a round-bottom hull; these should be a couple of feet longer than the girth of any half-section shown in the body plans. They should be between ¼ and ½ inch square. One should be tapered at each end, by ⅛ inch, and another should be reduced toward its middle. The third should be parallel sided. For dinghies and canoes, drafting battens can be used for the body plan; these are of hard rubber, or of Celluloid, obtainable from stores selling drafting supplies. To hold battens in place, nails can be used. For the larger battens use 1½- or 2-inch wire nails (sixpenny common or finishing brads); for the small battens 1 inch (two-penny finishing brads). If more than one boat is going to be built, then get two-dozen common scratch awls; these have tempered steel points held in a wooden handle and may be forced into the floor without hammering. If paper is being used, on a floor that must not be marred, battens may be held in place fairly well by using a number of old-fashioned flatirons, obtainable from any mail-order house. The battens may be painted if desired; black is the best color as a rule.

## Tools

For marking the floor or paper, the ordinary carpenter's pencil, hard lead, sharpened to a chisel point, is best. Colored pencils or crayons (hard) can be used to advantage, as the colors will serve to identify certain lines on the loft plan. The only other tools required are a steel square 16 by 24 inches (or a large

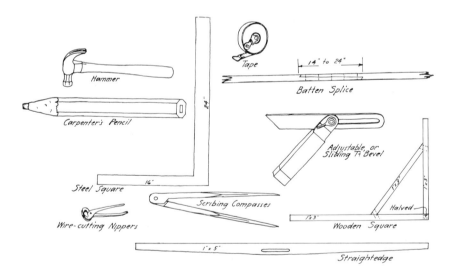

*18. Lofting Tools*

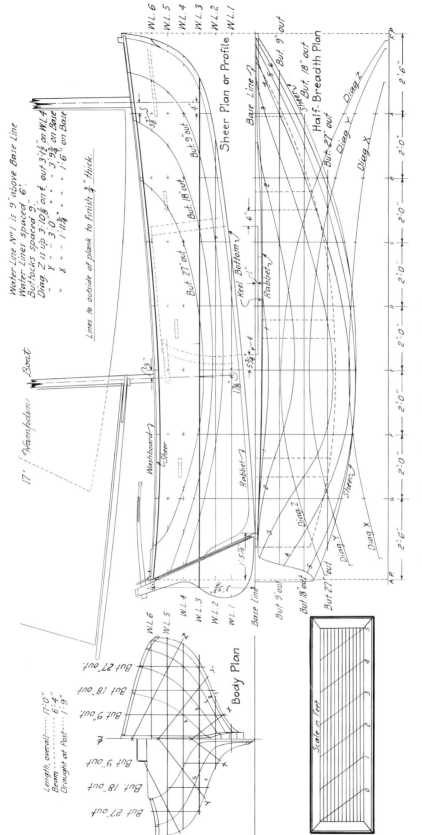

PLATE 10. *Lines of a 17-Foot Hampden Boat*

Water Line Nº 1 is 9" above Base Line
Water Lines spaced 6".
Buttocks spaced 9".
Diag. Z is up 3'-10⅛ on ℄, out 3'-1½ on WL.4
" Y " 3'-0 " " 3'-9¾ on Base
" X " 1'-11¾ " " 1'-6", on Base

Lines to outside of plank to finish ⅞" thick.

17' Hampden Boat

Sheer Plan or Profile

Half-Breadth Plan

Body Plan

Length, overall ----- 17'-0"
Beam ------------- 6'-4"
Draught at Post --- 1'-9"

Scale in Feet

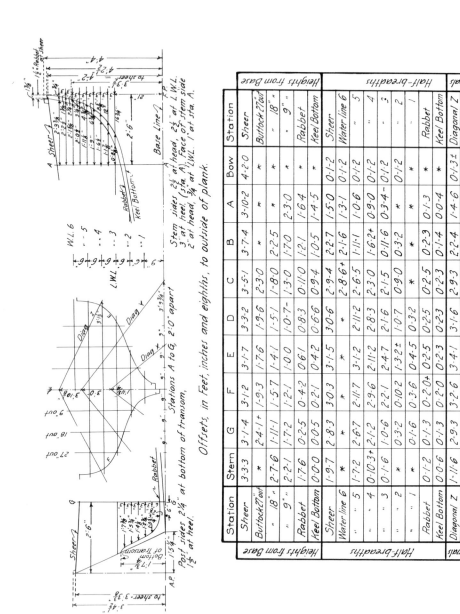

Offsets, in Feet, inches and eighths, to outside of plank.

Stem sides 2½ at head, 2½ at L.W.L. 3" at heel (sta. A). Face of stem side 2" at L.W.L., ¾" at sta. A.

Stations A to G, 2'-0" apart.

Post sides 2¼ at bottom of transom, 1½ at heel.

| Station | Bow | A | B | C | D | E | F | G | Stern |
|---|---|---|---|---|---|---|---|---|---|
| **Heights from Base** | | | | | | | | | |
| Sheer | 4-2-0 | 3-10-2 | 3-7-4 | 3-5-1 | 3-3-2 | 3-1-7 | 3-1-2 | 3-1-4 | 3-3-3 |
| Buttock 27 out | * | * | * | 2-3-0 | 1-9-6 | 1-7-6 | 1-9-3 | 2-4-1+ | * |
| " 18" | * | 2-3-0 | 2-2-5 | 1-8-0 | 1-5-1 | 1-4-1 | 1-5-7 | 1-11-1 | 2-7-6 |
| " 9" | * | 2-3-0 | 1-7-0 | 1-3-0 | 1-0-7- | 1-0-0 | 1-2-1 | 1-7-2 | 2-2-1 |
| Rabbet | * | 1-6-4 | 1-2-1 | 0-11-0 | 0-8-3 | 0-6-1 | 0-4-2 | 0-2-5 | 1-7-6 |
| Keel Bottom | * | 1-4-5 | 1-0-5 | 0-9-4 | 0-6-6 | 0-4-2 | 0-2-1 | 0-0-5 | 0-0-0 |
| **Half-breadths** | | | | | | | | | |
| Sheer | 0-1-2 | 1-5-0 | 2-2-7 | 2-9-4 | 3-0-6 | 3-1-5 | 3-0-3 | 2-8-3 | 1-9-7 |
| Water line 6 | 0-1-2 | 1-3-1 | 2-1-6+ | 2-8-6+ | 2-11-2 | 3-1-2 | 2-11-7 | 2-6-7 | 1-7-2 |
| " 5 | 0-1-2 | 0-9-0 | 1-6-2+ | 2-6-5 | 2-8-3 | 2-11-2 | 2-9-6 | 2-1-2 | 0-10-3+ |
| " 4 | 0-1-2 | 0-3-4 | 0-11-6 | 2-3-0 | 2-1-6 | 2-4-7 | 2-2-1 | 1-0-6 | 0-1-6 |
| " 3 | 0-1-2 | 0-1-2 | 0-1-6 | 2-1-5 | 1-0-7 | 1-3-2± | 0-10-2 | 0-3-2 | * |
| " 2 | * | * | 0-3-2 | 0-9-0 | 0-3-2 | 0-4-5 | 0-3-6 | 0-1-6 | 0-1-6 |
| " 1 | * | * | * | * | 0-3-2 | 0-2-5 | 0-2-0+ | 0-1-3 | 0-0-6 |
| Rabbet | * | 0-1-3 | 0-2-3 | 0-2-5 | 0-2-5 | 0-2-5 | 0-2-0+ | 0-1-3 | 0-1-2 |
| Keel Bottom | * | 0-0-4 | 0-1-4 | 0-2-3 | 0-2-3 | 0-2-3 | 0-2-0 | 0-1-3 | 0-0-6 |
| **Diagonals** | | | | | | | | | |
| Diagonal Z | 0-1-3± | 1-4-6 | 2-2-4 | 2-9-3 | 3-1-6 | 3-4-1 | 3-2-6 | 2-9-6 | 1-11-6 |
| " Y | 0-1-3+ | 1-0-6 | 1-7-5- | 2-0-5+ | 2-3-6+ | 2-5-3 | 2-3-4 | 1-9-6 | 1-2-3 |
| " X | 0-1-6÷ | 0-4-5 | 0-9-2 | 1-0-2 | 1-1-7 | 1-2-7± | 1-1-0 | 0-8-5 | 0-3-2 |

PLATE 11. *Offsets for a 17-Foot Hampden Boat*

wooden square may be made), a 6-foot rule, a compass or scribe, chalk line and chalk, hammer, steel tape, wooden straightedge (3 to 6 feet long), wire-cutting nippers or pliers, erasers, jackknife, and a sliding T bevel. A wooden mallet is useful in picking up patterns. Have plenty of pencils and crayons at hand. If laying down the loft plan on paper, adhesive is necessary to join the sheets together and to repair tears.

## *Plans*

The plan to be laid down first is the lines. To do this, the offsets must be at hand, of course. As mentioned on page 60, the offsets give the measurements of the lines in feet, inches, and eighths; thus: 6–8–4, or 6 feet, 8 inches and ⅛ inch.

## *Base Line and Stations*

To start, strike a base line near one side of the floor or paper. This is to be the base line shown in the profile (in the lines) or may be the load water line, from whichever the heights in the offsets are measured. It will also be used as the center line of the half-breadth plan; so allow the necessary room. The line should be struck with a chalk line if the boat is longer than any straightedge at hand. If there is any doubt about the use of the chalk line, try this. Stretch a thin fish line between nails just clear of the floor or paper. Draw taut; make pencil marks *directly under* the line, about 30 inches apart. Then draw a line with pencil and straightedge from mark to mark. All lines should be sighted on the floor as the eye will seek any irregularity in a line. Always sight lines from both ends. The base line should be a couple of feet longer than the hull to be laid down. A base line batten can be used to advantage in setting off the offsets. This is a straight strip of wood, about ½ inch by 2 inches, nailed to the floor below the base line with the top edge coinciding with the base line. This batten serves as a stop against which the end of the rule may be jambed, with no danger of overrunning the base line with the rule and so getting a short dimension. On the base line measure and set off the stations given in the lines and offsets; number them according to the lines. With the square erect perpendiculars at each station, taking care to be accurate. With the straightedge extend the perpendiculars far enough to exceed the greatest measurement on the stations, either in the profile or half-breadth.

## Water Lines in Profile

The water lines shown in the profile view of the lines must now be drawn. Measure up the distance each is above the base line (or above and below the load water line if that is used as the base) on the end stations. These end stations are usually referred to as the fore and after perpendiculars. When the heights of the water lines are set off accurately, the lines are drawn in the same manner as the base line.

## Profile, Outline of Sheer

The next step is to lay down the profile view. Begin by setting off the sheer line, bow to the same hand as in the lines plan; measure up the height on each station, as given in the offsets, from the base line. At the proper dimension make a pencil mark and if possible drive in a nail. Take the long sheer batten and lay it on the floor against the nail, or mark, on the fore perpendicular, with the ends of the batten extending beyond the fore perpendicular a little less than at the after perpendicular. When the batten is tight against the nail, or mark, on the fore perpendicular, drive a nail through the batten or against the back of it opposite the nail in the fore perpendicular. This new nail is to hold the batten in place. If nails cannot be used, put one of the holding weights in its place. Now bend the batten along the line of nails, or marks, representing the sheer heights, securing it with nails or weights as it touches each station mark in turn. When the stern is reached, it is probable that the batten will bend so stiffly that it will not meet the station marks in one or two stations ahead of the stern. Spring up the extending and free end of the batten until it does meet the marks, and secure. Do the same at the bow. It is very important that the free ends of the batten always be sprung and secured so that it is possible to remove the holding weight or nail at any one of the forward or after stations without the batten's moving. With the batten secured, look along its length from each end; if there are waves, humps, or dips, remove the nail or weight at the place they occur and correct by allowing the batten to spring a little.

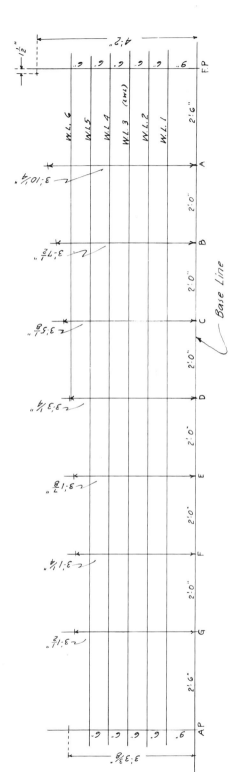

PLATE 12. *Lofting a 17-foot Hampden Boat. First stage—setting off sheer in profile.*

Sometimes a mistake in the offsets will be found and it will then be necessary to make a correction. If it is apparent that one offset is wrong, let the batten pass through the points on all the other stations fairly; the spot where it crosses the station, whose offset is out, is the corrected height. If it is found that the batten is too stiff to stay in place while being bent, remove it and try another, or cut down the size of the one used. The batten can be too limber, however, so care must be taken in choosing the right one. If the batten is too limber, it will not lay fair between the stations; if too stiff, it will jump out of position, or break, when being forced to the required curve. When the batten is fair, all offsets corrected, and you are certain that it is in accordance with the lines plan, draw in the line and remove the batten. Mark the line by its name and note whether it is the top or underside of rail or deck.

### Profile of Keel, Stem, and Stern

Now the profile of the keel can be laid off. Measure up on each station from the base line the given offset and make a mark or drive a nail. If the keel bottom is curved, lay off in the same manner as the sheer, but do not attempt to force the batten around the sharp curves at the stem. Then, from the lines or offsets, set off the dimensions for the profile of the stem; fair in with a light batten (one of those prepared for the body plan sections). In the same manner lay off the dimensions for the profile of the stern and draw in with straightedge or batten and pencil.

### Fairing with Light Batten, Forefoot

In using the light battens, remember that the retaining nails or weights must be close together, as obviously so must the stations or dimension marks. Always be certain that the batten is a couple of feet longer than the line to be faired. If it is necessary to join two curves of different degree—as, for example, the forefoot and a curved keel—draw in the gentle curve with as stiff a batten as possible, handling it like the sheer curve, and then put in the sharper curve with a thin batten, part of which must follow exactly the line of the gentle curve for at least a couple of feet. Thus a portion of the sharp curve is superimposed on the gentle

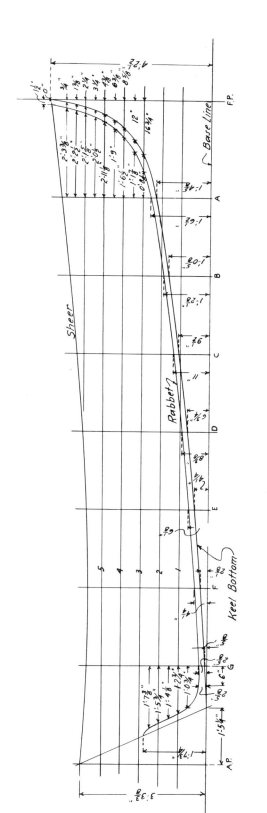

PLATE 13. *Lofting a 17-foot Hampden Boat. Second stage—setting off rabbet and keel bottom in profile.*

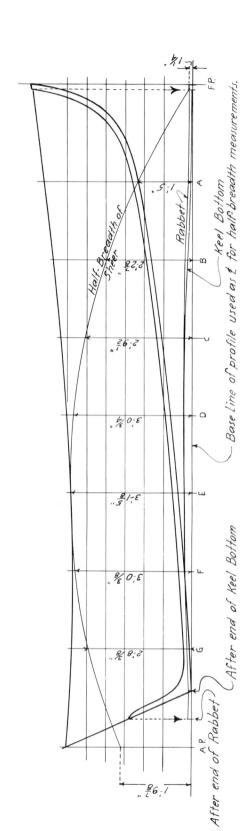

PLATE 14. *Lofting a 17-foot Hampden Boat. Third stage—setting off half-breadths of sheer, rabbet, and keel bottom.*

curve and their joining is fair. The same treatment must be applied to a sharp or gentle curve fairing into a straight line.

## Profile of Keel, Rabbet

If the keel is straight, it is usual to give only the offset heights at the two stations marking the limits of the straight portion of the line. When the keel bottom, stem and stern profile, and sheer are drawn in, the rabbet line should be set off and faired in. This is done in the same manner as the keel bottom and stem and stern profiles. However, it is time to take notice of whether the lines were drawn to the outside of the plank, as is commonly the case, or to the inside of the planking. If the lines are to the outside of the planking, then the rabbet drawn on the mold loft drawing is the line of intersection of the outside face of the keel and plank. The rabbet eventually will have to be represented by three lines: the rabbet, inner or margin line, and upper or bearding line. For the moment, however, the other rabbet lines must wait. If the lines should be to the inside of the plank, as in Plate 3, then the line laid off on the loft plan is the innermost corner of the rabbet, the middle or margin line. If this is a straight line, the rabbet line will have a slight curve, as will be found when projected.

## Marking Staffs

To save time, in most boats it is well to have marking staffs at hand. These are thin, narrow battens, straight and smooth, long enough to equal the greatest half-breadth and height given in the offsets. The staff used to record the heights should be separate from the one used for the half-breadths. Take the staff chosen for the heights and measure off each height to keel bottom, rabbet, and sheer, station by station, and mark each by its name and station number. To do this, lay the staff along each station with heel snug against the base line batten and tick off the proper heights. This will enable the corrections in fairing to be transferred later to the body plan without error or extra measuring.

## Half-Breadth Plan, Sheer, Rabbet, Keel

Next set off the half-breadth of the sheer line. The base line for the profile will be used as the center line now. On each station set off the half-breadth offset given in the tables. Measure on the profile at the stem the point where the rabbet of the stem intersects the sheer, using the forward perpendicular for the base line. Transfer this distance to the center line. From the offset table take the half-breadth of the sheer at stem and set it off perpendicular to the center line at the point just obtained. This is the fore end of the sheer line. Obtain the end at the stern in the same manner. Sweep in the line with batten and pencil. Now lay off the half-breadths of the rabbet and keel bottom in the same manner. The end of the rabbet at the stern will be decided by the type of stern in the design; its fore-and-aft position is obtained in the same way as the fore end of the sheer. Mark the measuring staff for the lines faired in so far in the half-breadth plan.

### Body Plan Position

Some builders proceed to fair in all the water lines next, but it is safest to fair in the body plan at this stage. Errors can be more readily checked if the loft plan is drawn in the same sequence as the design plan, in which the body plan is drawn when the lines described previously have been faired in. For the center line of the body plan it is customary to take the station at amidships (or the one giving the largest section area) and to draw the sections or mold forms on both sides of this. There is no particular importance to this location except that it puts the body plan in the center of the work and so is handy from all parts of the loft plan. Some builders draw the body plan on a separate drawing board, if the boat is small, in which case a base line, center line, and water lines have to be drawn with *exactly* the same spacing as on the large plan. We will assume that the body plan is on the floor, however, as the procedure is the same as far as fairing is concerned.

### Body Plan Drawing Sections

Taking the midsection station on the profile as the center line of the body plan, space off the buttock lines shown in the design according to the measurements given in either the lines or offsets. The buttocks must be exactly parallel to the center line and spaced equally on each side. Next draw in the diagonals, dimen-

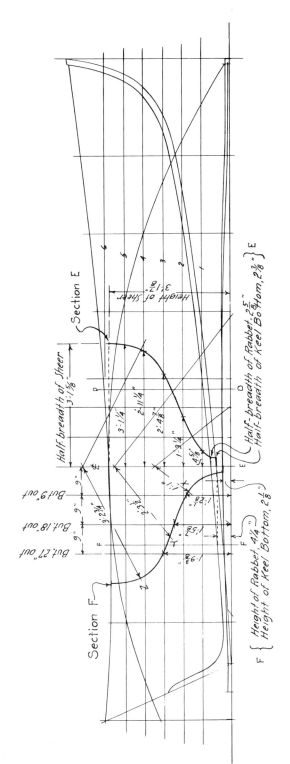

PLATE 15. Lofting a 17-foot Hampden Boat. Fourth stage—drawing sections in the body plan.

sions for the location of which may be obtained from the same plan and table. Note particularly the place each diagonal crosses the water lines and compare these with the lines plan; this will indicate any error, either in the loft plan or offsets. Now a base line batten may be tacked on either side of the center line, the side chosen depending upon which portion of the body plan is to be laid off first. Usually it is easiest to lay out the forward sections first. It is supposed that the profile of the hull on the loft plan heads the same way as in the lines. In this case the body plan may as well be made to follow the same arrangement as in the lines, for ease in comparison.

Suppose the bow sections are to be laid off first. Take the measuring staff made for the profile, or heights, and begin to lay off the sheer heights for the fore sections. Take two spots for each so that horizontal lines can be drawn from the center line outward, parallel to the base line. Do this for the rabbet and keel bottom, marking the station and identification for each. Then take the measuring staff for the half-breadths, lay it along each horizontal line, and tick off the half-breadths of sheer, rabbet, and keel bottom for the corresponding station. Turn to the offset table and select the foremost station. Begin by setting off each water-line half-breadth for this station on the loft body plan, taking care to be exact in reading and laying off dimensions. Be sure to get the water lines correctly numbered or identified on the loft plan so that mistakes in plotting can be avoided. Each offset must be measured from the center line out, with the rule laying along the horizontal line representing the water line or half-breadth. When the water-line offsets are marked, either by pencil or nails, pick out the heights of the buttocks in the offset table. These must be set off vertically from the base line on the buttock lines, on the loft body plan, corresponding with those in the lines plan, of course. This is emphasized as it is very easy to misread offsets, and thereby set them off on the wrong line, or to take the wrong station. Set off the buttock heights, then, in the same manner as was done with the water-line offsets, but measuring vertically from the base line.

Next find the diagonal offsets on the offset table. These must be set off on the corresponding diagonals on the loft body plan. Measure from the center line of the body plan, that is, from the point where this line intersects each diagonal. Again the rule must lay along the line in setting off measurements, sloping downward from the horizontal according to the slope of the diagonal. When these are completed, the section may be faired in with a batten. In the sections at bow and stern some offsets for water lines, buttocks, and diagonals may be found missing on the offset table. This is because the fairing lines omitted may fall outside the limits of the section or because they may coincide too closely in position with the sheer or rabbet lines. In fairing in the sections it is probable that the batten will show that humps will result if it is forced to meet every offset mark. Therefore, some corrections must be made, but never at sheer or rabbet, in order that the batten lay fair; it should pass through the majority of the offsets set off as explained in regard to the sheer line. Every station, or section, shown in the lines, including the stern elevation of the transom, must be drawn in the loft plan in the manner explained for the foremost station, the base line batten at center line being shifted when necessary.

## Fairing Body Plan Sections

In fairing in the sections, certain general principles must be observed. If the hull form is of the dinghy or U-section model, the bottom will be straight in section for a short distance out from the keel. This is the "dead rise of the floors" and must be correctly drawn on the loft plan. If one does not take care, the batten will tend to make the dead rise of the floors curved instead of straight. When fairing such a section, the batten must be forced where it fairs into the bottom. The need for this can be judged very easily by studying the section as shown in the lines plan while fairing it in on the loft plan. This applies, of course, to round-bottom hulls of all types in which such section forms exist. In fairing reverse curves, in the sections or elsewhere, there must be a short portion that is dead straight between the reverses. If this is not done, a hump will form in the section at the point where the curve reverses. Again note the section form shown in the lines, in order to find out what is required. The whole idea of drawing the loft plan is to reproduce the designed lines as closely as possible. It must be emphasized, however, that fairing in the sections must under no circumstances require changes in the sheer and rabbet positions as transferred from the profile and half-breadth on the loft plan. If the design is well drawn, there ought to be no marked alterations required in the offsets to fair the lines. It is necessary that the batten be shifted about a bit if the offsets do not seem to fair, adding a little to one offset and subtracting a little from another. It pays to be careful in all loft work, to check and compare at every step.

## Fairing Lines

Now the body plan is complete and the rest of the fairing may begin. The choice of which to fair in first—water lines, diagonals, or buttocks—depends wholly upon the form of the boat. Lines which cross the sections in the body plan at, or nearly at, right angles are the most useful fairing lines since it is possible to find their exact intersection. So in the afterbody (sections toward the stern) the bottom is best faired by the buttocks, the topsides by the water lines; in the forebody (sections toward the bow) the water lines will serve. The diagonals usually serve to fair in the middle third of the boat's length and the topsides to the best advantage.

## Fairing Buttocks

Let us suppose it has been decided to fair in a buttock first. Take one about one quarter the beam of the boat, out from the center line, whichever buttock is nearest to this position in the body plan. The measuring staff for heights should be marked for the buttock, taking off the heights from base line to where the buttock intersects each section in the body plan, by laying it along the chosen buttock line and ticking the batten as previously explained. Lay the measuring staff on each station in turn, on the profile, and mark the height at which the buttocks crossed it in the body plan. Fair these points in with a batten, but do not attempt to run the whole line in. Only fair the sections from just forward of amidship to the stern. This should require no alteration in the heights marked on the stations; but, if it does, then the body plan must be changed so that the section there coincides with the changed offset height in the profile. The remaining buttocks in the afterbody may be faired in, in the same way; but if any of these run up the side of the hull aft, omit them for the

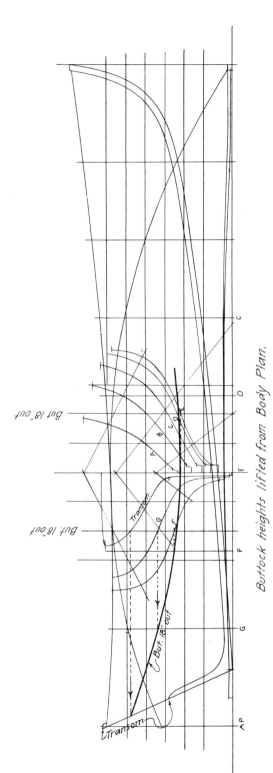

Buttock heights lifted from Body Plan.

PLATE 16. Lofting a 17-foot Hampden Boat. Fifth stage—fairing first buttock.

time being. Now the buttocks may be drawn on the half-breadth
plan—in which they are straight lines parallel to the center line.
Measure these off in the same manner that the water lines were
in the profile. If, in the loft plan, they should coincide, so much
the better. Perhaps the superimposed lines are becoming confus-
ing; if so, they may be traced over with colored crayons—say,
the water lines in blue, buttocks in green or yellow, and diagonals
in black. Save red for the construction drawing which comes
later.

## Fairing Water Lines, Ends

Leaving the buttocks, turn to the water lines. Make a measuring staff for the half-breadths of the load water line in the body
plan. Transfer these to the corresponding stations on the half-
breadth plan. Now the ends of the load water line must be found.
On the profile, measure in along this water line to the rabbet and
face of the stem, using the forward perpendicular as a base.
Transfer these measurements to the center line of the half-
breadth plan and square up the half-breadths of the rabbet and
face of stem; these points are the forward end of the load water
line. If the stem sides are not faired to the side of the planking,
but form an angle to it in the half-breadth plan, only the rabbet
need be found as the end of the water line. The same operation
may be performed at the stern. If a large enough wooden square
can be made, these points may be obtained by placing the square
on the center line (or base line batten of the profile) and squaring
the intersection of water line and rabbet down to the proper
place. On the profile, measure the points of intersection of the
load water line with the buttocks already faired in. Square these
down to the respective buttocks on the half-breadth plan. This
gives additional fairing points. Through this sweep a curve with
batten, pencil, or crayon. Again, if there is any variation from the
offsets in the sections, the latter must be corrected. Where the
water line crosses the buttocks on the half-breadth plan will be
the hardest to check for position as the angles are so acute on the
profile that they will be difficult to establish accurately. Even so,
the projection of these to the half-breadth plan is highly desirable. All the water lines can now be faired in, following the
method employed in the load water line.

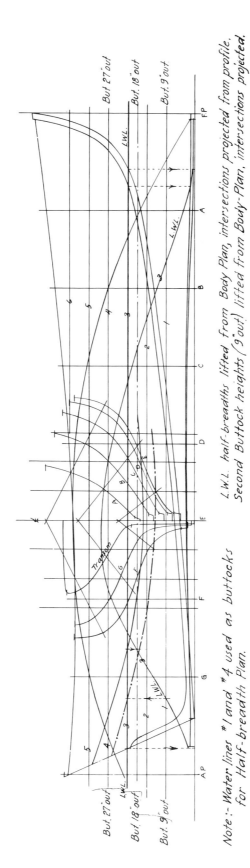

Note:- Water-lines #1 and #4 used as buttocks
for Half-breadth Plan.

L.W.L. half-breadths lifted from Body Plan, intersections projected from profile.
Second Buttock heights (9″out) lifted from Body-Plan, intersections projected.

PLATE 17. Lofting a 17-foot Hampden Boat. Sixth stage—fairing first water line and second buttock.

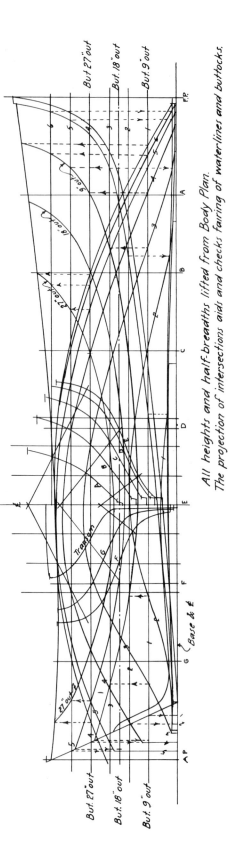

All heights and half-breadths lifted from Body Plan.
The projection of intersections aids and checks fairing of water-lines and buttocks.

PLATE 18. Lofting a 17-foot Hampden Boat. Seventh stage—fairing water lines and buttocks and projecting their ends and intersections.

## Finishing Buttocks, Bow and Stern Ending

The buttocks can now be finished on the profile. Square up the intersections of the straight-line buttocks with the water lines on the half-breadth plan to the profile, spotting each intersection on its respective water line. Do the same with the intersection of the buttocks with the sheer line. This gives additional points which enable the buttocks to be completed on the profile. If not fair, the water lines or sections, or both, may have to be altered. Due to the rake or curvature of the stern, it may not be possible to complete the buttocks and water lines close to the transom until its true shape has been projected in the profile. It has been assumed that the transom is flat in the design being lofted, but if this is not the case the transom outline must be drawn in the profile and half-breadth plans before the water lines and buttocks can be properly faired.

## Sharp Stern

In a sharp stern, with either the usual straight sternpost or the overhanging "canoe stern," the fairing is the same as at the bow, and no further directions are required. Water line and buttock ends are projected as at bow.

## Plumb Flat Transom

If the transom has no rake, that is, stands parallel to the section or station lines in the profile, and is flat across its face, its true shape is shown in the body plan and its outboard edge is represented by a straight line (coinciding with the transom center line) in the profile plan. Water line and buttock ends are taken from offset table.

## Raking and Flat Transom

If the transom is raking in the profile but is flat across its face, the outboard edge in the profile coincides with the center line but the elevation in the body plan is not its true shape. To lay off the shape of this transom in the half-breadth plan, set off the distance its face is from the after perpendicular in each water line

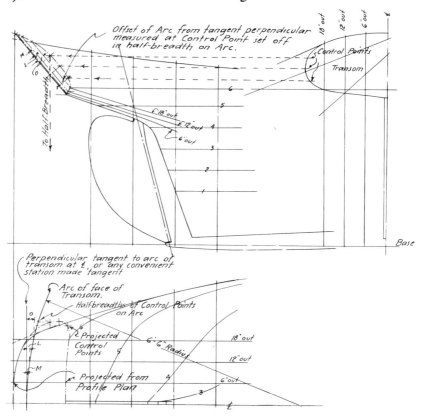

*19. Projection of outboard edge of transom in profile and half-breadth plans to end water lines and buttocks. See text.*

in the profile, transfer these distances to the half-breadth center line, and erect perpendiculars. Now measure each water-line half-breadth in the transom on the body plan and set off on the corresponding water line in the half-breadth transom. Then measure the intersections of the buttocks with the transom, square to the after perpendicular in the profile, and set the distances off on the corresponding buttocks in the half-breadth plan. Set off the top of transom in the body plan if it can be done by offsets, transfer the heights this intersects the buttocks there to the profile, and square these points down to the buttock lines in the half-breadth plan. The position of the bottom of the transom is found by squaring it down from the profile (where it has been established) to the half-breadth center line, where its half-breadth is set off perpendicularly, as measured from the body plan. By drawing a curve, or curves, through the points obtained, the shape of the transom as viewed from directly below is outlined on the half-breadth plan, and the end of each water line and buttock is marked for completing the fairing. Before leaving the transom, set off the thickness of the transom planking and of the stern frame in the profile plan, the lines of which are straight and parallel to the original transom line there.

## Remarks

In the type of transom described so far the projection of the outboard edge in the profile and half-breadth loft plans are really of small importance, since the points on the transom may be readily obtained directly from the offsets as previously explained. Nonetheless, the projection of the transom of the sloping or raking type is good practice, since it will aid in understanding the principles of projection that are employed in the more difficult shapes.

## Plumb and Curved Transom

If the transom is perpendicular in profile but is curved across its face, the center line of the transom in the profile is a vertical straight line, probably the after perpendicular. The apparent shape of the transom, as seen from dead aft, is shown in the body plan. The amount of curvature is shown in the half-breadth plan. Due to the fact that the outboard edge of the transom does not coincide with the center line in the profile, it is impossible to end the water lines and buttocks (or chine line) until it is projected in the profile and established on the half-breadth plan. The radius of the face of transom is given on the half-breadth plan in the designer's lines drawing. Make a trammel by boring a hole for a pencil in a batten somewhat longer than the required radius. Measure off this radius dimension along the batten from the pencil point, and at the required distance drive a nail through the batten as a pivot point. Lay the trammel on the half-breadth plan with the pivot on the center line and the pencil point on the same line where the transom center line is established by squaring it down from the profile. Sweep in an arc a little longer than from center line to sheer-line half-breadth. On a measuring staff, tick off the half-breadths of each water line at the transom on the body plan. Set these off square to the center line on the arc in the half-breadth plan; this will require shifting the batten for each half-breadth in order to keep it square and yet have the tick-mark for half-breadth fall on the arc. Identify each mark as the end of a water line; these may now be completely faired in on the half-breadth plan. To obtain the ends of the buttocks in the profile, square up their intersections with the arc in the half-breadth plan to the profile; then carry over the heights from the body plan, square to the base line, of course. This will establish the ends of the buttocks in the profile so that they may be faired completely.

The chine and sheer lines are projected in the same manner as water lines. It will be wise, for the sake of clarity, to project the ends of the water lines on the half-breadth to the corresponding water lines on the profile, doing the same with sheer and chine, if one exists, so as to draw in the side elevation of the outboard edge of the transom. This line passes through the buttock ends, of course, and the buttocks on the face of the transom are vertical lines parallel to the center line, squared up from these ends. If the top of the transom can be established from the plans, it is drawn on the body plan and the heights of the buttocks, intersections (and center line) are carried over to the profile transom buttocks and center line, where the top may be drawn in profile. If the top of the transom is at deck level, however, the deck crown will have to be drawn before the top can be shown in the body plan. The transom just described is most common in motorboats. The inside of the transom plank and frame should be set off on the profile as parallel lines to the transom center lines. These should be drawn on the half-breadth plan by reducing the radius by the required amount so that the arcs are all parallel. This stern is now completely drawn, for the time being; but later it will be necessary to project its shape when laid out flat.

## Raking and Curved Transom

The third type of transom is the most difficult to build and is rather tedious to project, though it is one of the handsomest sterns used today. This transom rakes in profile and is curved across its face. Not only must its shape be projected on the profile and half-breadth plans, but later it is necessary to expand its shape when laid flat. The first step is to establish the shape of its outboard edge in the profile and half-breadth so that the ends of the water lines and buttocks may be established, as well as the ends of such diagonals as cross it in the body plan. Inspection of the lines plan will show that the designer has given the radius of the face of the transom by a dimension line and measurement; the former is drawn perpendicular to the center line of the transom in the profile. This dimension line is usually drawn so that it passes through the outboard edge of the transom, where it is farthest from the center line in the profile; this represents the widest part of the transom. It will also be found that the apparent shape of the transom is established in the body plan by offsets on sheer, water lines, rabbet, buttocks, and diagonals, so that it can be drawn in the loft body plan. It is usual to establish the top of the transom in the body plan also. The rake of the center line of the transom is given by dimensions on the lines plan. It is also usual to give dimensions that will enable the sheer half-breadth to be carried to the transom edge in cases where it does not intersect the edge of the transom, but curves in and up to pass over the top. When this is done, the resulting transom is elliptically shaped in the body plan, well and unfavorably known as "the loftsman's curse" for reasons that will become plain when it is lofted.

The first step in projecting this class of transom is to draw it in the body plan and to set off the rake of the center line in the profile, to find the outline of the stern overhang. Then a trammel is made to the required radius (as described on page 97). Place the trammel on the half-breadth plan so that the pivot is on the center line and the pencil is on the intersection of the after perpendicular (or aftermost station) and the center line. Sweep in an arc from center line to a little outside of the sheer line. Then erect two short perpendiculars inboard on the transom center line in the profile, say, one at or close to the bottom and the other close to the top (or sheer line) of the transom. Next, with a measuring staff, tick off the distances on each buttock from the after perpendicular to the intersection of the arc, on the half-breadth plan. Transfer these distances to the profile and set them off on the two perpendiculars to the transom center line, measuring from the latter. Draw lines through the points thus set off. These lines are inboard of the transom center line and parallel to it. They are the buttocks, as viewed from the side, on the face of the transom. Then transfer the heights of the buttocks at the bottom and top of the transom, in the body plan, to the profile and set them off on the sloping buttocks previously drawn, measuring square to the base line. This step enables the buttocks to be completed on the profile since the after ends are now established.

Next make a mark or series of marks on the outboard edge of the transom in the body plan. One of these should be at the point of greatest beam in the apparent transom shape. Measure the height of these on the body plan and transfer them to the profile, measuring square to the base line. Set off the heights of the points on the profile of the transom, making short, horizontal lines a few inches ahead of the center line of the transom. With the measuring staff, pick off the half-breadths of the marks on the transom in the body plan, taking care that the offset is taken square to the center line. Transfer these offsets to the arc in the half-breadth plan, keeping the measuring staff square to the center line as the distances are ticked off for each half-breadth on the arc; this will necessitate shifting the staff to keep it square and to bring the half-breadth tick-mark to the arc. Identify these marks plainly in the body plan, half-breadth, and profile. With a measuring staff, set off the distances between the after perpendicular and these half-breadth offsets on the arc in the half-breadth plan, keeping the staff square to the after perpendicular. Next transfer these to the profile, setting off with the staff square with the center line of the transom in profile and shifting it so as to have each tick-mark intersect its corresponding horizontal line. This will give enough points on the profile to enable the loftsman to sweep in the outboard edge of the profile when the sheer line, or point approximating it, has also been projected in the manner just described. It is impossible to utilize the water lines in this projection because they do not intersect the transom face at right angles and are not true radii for the plane to be projected.

It may be desirable to add more buttocks or marks on the body plan in order to obtain enough points on the profile to fair in the correct shape of the outboard edge in that elevation. When the outboard edge of the transom has been drawn in the profile, it can be drawn in the half-breadth plan to obtain the ends of the water lines and, later, to check the ends of the diagonals aft. Square down the ends of all water lines intersecting the outboard edge of the transom in profile to the half-breadth plan, as lines square to the center line of the latter. Take the half-breadths of these from the body plan and set them off on the corresponding lines in the half-breadth plan. Square down the ends of the buttocks and the transom bottom at rabbet. It is an excellent plan to set off all the other points used to find the outboard edge of the transom in profile to the half-breadth, taking them as water lines have been. This will give a large number of points on the half-breadth plan through which the outline of the transom can be drawn, as seen from directly below. Do not hesitate to add a number of control points in laying off the three views of this type of transom. It is due to shirking this that builders find the transom pattern wrong when they come to set it up.

## *Accuracy*

It is worth while to take pains to be extremely accurate in making the projections necessary in the lofting of the lines. This becomes of tremendous importance when such transoms as the last described are to be developed. Due to the number and tediousness of the projections required, even professional builders are inclined to try "short cuts," with the result that both builder and designer wonder why the stern does not look right on the finished hull.

## *Fairing and Ending Diagonals*

The diagonals should now be faired in. They will be superimposed over the half-breadth plan in the loft. To avoid confusion, it is best to use the uppermost buttock in this plan as the center line for setting off the diagonal offsets, with the curves downward, or opposite to those of the water lines. Having chosen the center line for the diagonals, the first step is to establish the ends of the diagonals on this line. On the body plan measure the height at which the uppermost diagonal crosses the outboard edge of the transom and transfer this to the outboard edge of

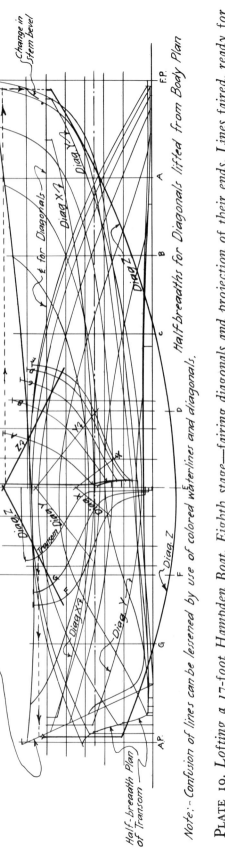

Centerline and outboard edge
of transom coincide in profile

Change in
Stem bevel

Half-breadth Plan
of Transom

Note:– Confusion of lines can be lessened by use of colored waterlines and diagonals.

Half-breadths for Diagonals lifted from Body Plan

PLATE 19. Lofting a 17-foot Hampden Boat. Eighth stage—fairing diagonals and projection of their ends. Lines faired, ready for expansion of transom and other detailing.

the transom in the profile. Measure the distance this new-found point is before the after perpendicular and square this down to the center line for the diagonals. Measure the width of the transom in the body plan, along the diagonal, transfer this to the center line of the diagonal at the point previously found, and set it off perpendicular to the center line. This is the end of the upper diagonal at the stern. To find the forward end, draw the half-breadth of the stem rabbet, on the body plan, as shown in the lines plan. This may be taken from the profile and half-breadth plan instead of from offsets, if desired. Measure the height the uppermost diagonal crosses the rabbet in the body plan, square this to the rabbet on the stem profile, measure this point from the forward perpendicular, and square this distance down to the diagonal center line.

Next measure the distance from center line to rabbet, along the diagonal, on the body plan and set this dimension off square to the diagonal center line at the point just projected. This is the forward end of the uppermost diagonal. The half-breadths of the uppermost diagonal will now be measured in the body plan. The measuring staff is laid along the diagonal and the distances at which the diagonal crosses each station, measured from the center line, are ticked off. The staff is then transferred to the diagonal center line and from this the half-breadth of the diagonal at each station is set off. When all the stations are marked, a line is faired through the points obtained, running from end to end. If it is found that this curve, when fair, misses some of the station marks, it is well to check the measuring staff before changing the station on the body plan as it is very easy to make an error in setting off the diagonals. This is particularly true in the sections in the stern, where a diagonal passes through the portion below the bottom of the transom. Fair in all other diagonals in the same way that the uppermost has been worked out. The ends of diagonals under the transom or on the sternpost are obtained as at the bow.

### Correcting Body Plan

It may be found that, in making changes in the body plan to agree with the faired diagonals, it will be necessary to refair some of the water lines or buttocks. This may seem a tedious job, but it must be done if trouble is to be avoided later. When the lines are faired to the builder's satisfaction, he can draw in the location of the masts on the profile and lay off the cabin trunk or cockpit outlines on both profile and half-breadth plan. These are sometimes given on the lines drawing but, if not, will be found on the construction drawing.

## Deducting Plank Thickness in Body Plan Sections

If the original lines plan was drawn to the outside of the planking, as is the usual custom, the thickness of the plank must be deducted from each section in the loft body plan. Turn to the construction or lines plan, whichever shows the "construction midsection," or consult the specifications, to find the thickness of the planking. As has been mentioned, the thickness given for the planking is usually the rough size, when finished on the boat; the thickness will be a little less than this. This matter is not important on a cruising boat, but on a racer the deduction for planking must be very accurate or the boat may be narrower than the plans call for. In thin planking, under ¾ inch thick, use a thickness ¹⁄₁₆ inch less than given in the plans; in planking under 1¼ inches deduct ⅛ inch from the given size. Set the compass to the thickness decided upon and, beginning with the foremost section on the loft body plan, sweep a series of small arcs along the curve of its outline. The compass pivot point must be on the curve and the arcs should be inboard, of course.

These arcs should be close together where the curve of the section is sharp, and further apart where the curve is gentle. They may be taken 2 or 3 inches apart on sharp curves and 4 to 6 inches apart on gentle curves. Through the arcs sweep in a curve with a batten in order to set off the inside of the planking. Care must be taken that the batten is tangent to each arc, so that it is parallel to the original section curve. This new line may be drawn in red. At the point where the rabbet is set off on the section curve, the new line must be ended. Set a square on the original section, one blade along the original section curve as far as it will go outboard from the rabbet with apex at the rabbet. Mark the place where the other arm crosses the new curve; this is the lower end of the new curve and is the position of the inner line of the rabbet on this section. The top of the new curve must be found. Find out from the lines if the sheer was drawn as the top or underside of the deck. If the latter, the upper end of the new curve is on the same horizontal line as the original section curve's sheer mark. If the sheer line is the top of the deck, subtract the finished thickness of the deck from the horizontal sheer mark, for the original section curve, and make another short horizontal line on the new curve. This is the sheer to the inside of plank. Perform the same operation on all the sections in the body plan, including the transom. We now have the correct shape for each mold form which will control the shape of the boat when set up and framed.

## Keel Structure in Profile and Scaling Blueprints

The next step is to lay off the keel construction in profile. It will be necessary to scale the blueprint of the construction plan to do this. Always scale from the nearest station for fore-and-aft position, and from the nearest water line for height (if the base is not closer than a water line). This is done to avoid accumulating the error in scaling which would result in taking long measurements on a blueprint. All blueprints stretch and shrink, stretching in the direction the paper runs through the blueprint machine and shrinking at right angles to this direction. It is quite important that the loft work on the keel profile be carefully worked out. Every piece of timber making up the keel, deadwood, stem and sternposts, centerboard case, skeg and rudder should be accurately shown in profile. The center line of the propeller shaft should be laid off and the location of bearings or stuffing boxes shown. All jogs in timbers, to lock them together, must be correctly drawn. It is necessary that the heels of the frames be drawn in, accurately spaced, so that the floor timbers may be located and later drawn in. If the keel is jogged for the floor timbers, it is well to show the floors in section (as though cut in two along the center line of the boat) in the profile so as to be able to fix the depth of the jogs. If there is a ballast keel, the bolt positions must be worked out. Sometimes the construction plans show the position of the important bolts in the keel structure; transfer these to the loft profile. It will save time and trouble to show the mast steps, engine beds, and bearers in the loft profile.

## Changes in Deadwood and Keel from Plans

It is often said that it is very important that the builder make no changes from the plans when drawing the loft plan. This is certainly true; yet in working out the keel structure it may be possible to save a great deal of time and money by altering the arrangement of timber in the keel structure. In all fairness, it must be admitted that some designers are pretty careless when laying off the sizes of timber for the keel structure of a design. It is not wholly uncommon to find excessively wide timber called for, or knees that are practically impossible to obtain, due to size or shape. Sometimes this apparent thoughtlessness is due to the conditions existing in the location the design was made. Thus, in New England large knees of hackmatack are available; in some other parts of the country it is almost impossible to get large knees of any timber. In some parts of the West it is not particularly difficult to obtain very wide timber of certain species, but in other sections such timber is simply unavailable. As a result, it may be highly important to make some alteration in the keel structure design in order to use local timber or available stock.

## Rules for Changes

It is quite impossible to give complete and accurate instructions that would meet all conditions that might exist in making alterations from the plans. However, there are some general rules that should be followed. Study the construction plan before making any change whatever in the keel. The fewer the number of seams crossing the rabbet, the less the liability of leakage. All fastenings into the end grain of a timber are weak. All butts in the external keel must be backed by an inside timber in the ends of the hull. If two timbers, say, the keel and stempost, are joined by a knee (in the original construction drawing) which is not available, straight-grained timber may be used in its place; but the ends must extend beyond the arms of the original knee for at least enough space for an additional fastening in each end. Such a change will increase the weight, so great care must be taken in planning any alteration in the keel structure. If the plans call for a keel in a single length and this cannot be obtained, it is permissible to scarf the keel. The location of this should be chosen with care so that the scarf bolts will not interfere with the bolts in the floor timbers or those for the ballast keel.

The length of the scarf should be five to eight times the depth of the timber, or not less than three frame spaces in any case. Before making any marked changes in the keel structure it is wise to submit the proposed alterations to the designer. The builder should remember that too many small pieces worked into the deadwood or keel structure increase the opportunity for rot to start in one of the numerous seams that result. Also it is well to avoid laying out the keel structure so that end grain is exposed in any piece, either inside or out of the hull. Such exposure can be avoided by notching pieces into one another; in the ends of the hull, pieces can be worked in at angles that will further reduce exposure. Of course, it will not be possible to avoid entirely the exposure of some end grain, but the danger can be reduced by rounding off the ends of the members approaching the vertical— arms of knees, for example. No pockets that will hold moisture should be permitted in the top of the keel structure profile.

## *Projection for Rabbet Lines*

When the keel structure is laid out on the loft profile, the inner line of the rabbet and the bearding line will have to be drawn so that it will be possible to rough out the whole rabbet before setting up the keel on the stocks. If this is allowed to wait until the boat is set up, the work is measurably increased. The first step is to draw the half-breadth of the keel on the loft body plan. It has already been drawn outside the rabbet line. Take the heights of the top of the keel structure from the profile at each station and transfer to the body plan; there outline the half-section of the keel structure at each mold section. By so doing, the position of the bearding line at each mold station is found. The bearding line is formed by the intersection of the *inside* of the planking with the face or side of the keel, just as the rabbet was formed by the intersection of the *outside* of the planking with the side of the keel. The inner line of the rabbet was established on each section by finding the keel end of the line representing the inside of the planking of each section. The heights of the inner line of the rabbet should be transferred to the profile for each station. Do the same for the bearding line. Enough points will be obtained from

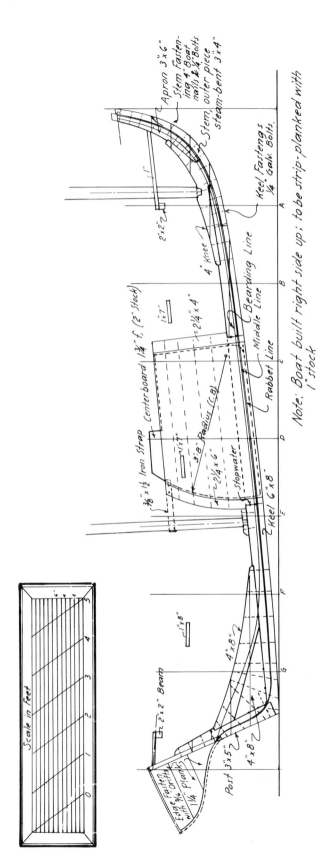

Scale in Feet

Note: Boat built right side up; to be strip-planked with 1" stock

PLATE 20. Lofting a 17-foot Hampden Boat. Ninth stage—deadwood and keel lay-down, rabbet lines, and transom. (Rough timber sizes marked.)

the body plan to establish the curve of these lines on the profile through the mid-body of the hull, but more will be required before the two lines can be drawn on stem and sternposts.

To get these, we go to the half-breadth plan. With the compass, set off the *inside* of the planking on each water line at the stem and sternposts, running from the rabbet of each a couple of feet inboard, and sweep in the curve of the inside of plank of each water line, establishing the inner line of the rabbet as done in the body plan sections. Next draw in the half-breadth line of the keel in the half-breadth plan. Where this crosses the line of the

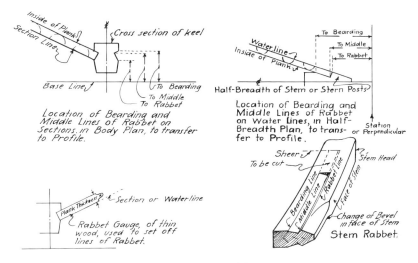

20. *The Rabbet*

inside of plank for each water line is the position of the bearding line for each water line. Square these points (for inner line of rabbet and for bearding line) up to the profile to the corresponding water lines there. Perform the same operation on the sheer line. By doing this at bow and stern enough points should be obtained to complete the fairing in of the inner rabbet and bearding lines on the profile. If not enough are found, then it is necessary to run in a few more water lines or sections, drawing them in only close to the keel or to stem and sternposts, to fill in the gaps caused by too wide a spacing of sections and water lines in the original design plans.

If the lines were designed to the inside of the planking (as in Plate 3), and as in most designs for lap-strake (clench, clinch or clincher-built) hulls, the operation of finding the inside of the planking is reversed so as to establish the outside of the planking at the keel, in order to project the rabbet line. In this class of design the rabbet is replaced on the lines by the inner line, or·margin line, of the rabbet and both the rabbet line itself and the bearding line have to be developed by projection in lofting the lines. The process of obtaining the position of these lines on the profile is the same as described previously.

## Additional Fairing Lines

No special explanation should be required in regard to adding water lines and buttocks to the loft plan. Such lines are set off on the profile body plan and half-breadth, regardless of position, in the same manner as laid off for the lines shown in the designer's plans. Diagonals may be added also, if desired. They are first drawn on the body plan. In laying off diagonals the joining of each pair must be at the same place on the center line and must also be at exactly the same angle; their outer ends must pass through a given water line equidistant from the center line of the body plan.

## Adding Sections

Additional sections may be added at will, in order to project the shape of a bulkhead or to locate properly some particular point on the hull. To draw a new section, erect a perpendicular to the base line on the profile and then project this down, square to the center line of the half-breadth. The location of this line can be established anywhere in the length of the hull without regard to its position in reference to any other section line. Using a measuring staff, mark on it the half-breadths of the water lines on the new section and transfer to the corresponding water lines on the body plan. Do the same with the diagonals. Then measure the height of the buttock lines, sheer, rabbet, and keel bottom on the new section line in the profile and transpose these to the proper place in the body plan. Then project the half-breadth of sheer, rabbet, and keel bottom to the body plan as previously explained in the setting off of the design sections. A curve through the points thus obtained on the body plan gives the shape of section at the chosen location. The thickness of the planking and the half-section of the keel, position of inner rabbet, and bearding line are found as described for laying down the sections shown in the lines plan.

## Lofting Sawn Frame Hull

The lofting of a sawn frame hull is no different from the method outlined, which is intended for a steam-bent frame hull. In the sawn frame design there are more sections in the body plan. Since most designers give offsets for every other sawn frame, the intermediate frames must be projected on the loft plan. It is common practice to fair up the sections given in the offsets first; when these are complete the intermediates are projected as though they were new sections. Loftsmen do not bother to correct water lines, buttocks, and diagonals for the intermediates unless the shape of the section indicates great errors, or some irregularity in offsets causes doubt as to which should be followed.

## Deck Crown and Pattern

The crown of the deck is laid out as a pattern, as a rule. To make this the crown must be known. This is given in the plans, either in the lines or construction plan. Usually it appears as Crown of Deck 6″ in 10′, the actual figures varying with the beam of the boat and the amount of crown in the deck the designer requires. It will be noticed that the length specified for a given crown is equal to or very slightly greater than the greatest width of the hull on deck. The amount of crown or bow-up of the deck is measured at the middle of this width; if the length for crown is 10 feet and the height of crown 6 inches, the latter is at the middle of a straight line 10 feet long, represented by a perpendicular 6 inches high. A curve passing through the ends of the 10-foot line and the top of the 6-inch perpendicular is the crown of the deck. This is commonly laid off as a parabolic curve.

First, to prepare to set off the crown, take a piece of thin board (plywood or cardboard will do in small boats) longer than the length given for crown and a few inches wider than height for crown. Near one edge of this strike a straight line and set off the length for crown. Find the middle of this length and erect a perpendicular on which set off height for crown, measuring from the length line. Set the compass to the height of crown and, with the pivot at the intersection of the length and height line, sweep an arc from the length to the height line. Divide the length of the arc within these limits into four equal parts. Divide the portion of the length line between the arc and the height line into

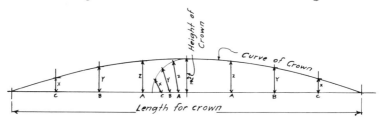

*21. Making Deck Crown Pattern*

four equal parts. Connect each mark on the arc with each mark on the length line by a straight line, beginning with the marks closest to the perpendicular height line.

Next divide the length line, on each side of the perpendicular height line, into quarters—eight parts in all. Erect perpendiculars at each mark, except at the extreme ends. Measure the heights of the sloping lines inside the arc, from length line to arc, and transfer these to each pair of perpendiculars (one on either side of the height line), beginning with the two nearest to the height line. The two ends of the length line will have no height measurement. Run a line through the tops of the heights set off on the quarter perpendiculars, beginning at the extreme ends of the length line and curving up and over the height of crown as set off at the middle of the length line. This is the shape of the deck crown. Cut the board to serve as a pattern, the top of which will be the curve of the crown. The lower edge should be a few inches away from the length line, parallel to it, and perfectly straight.

To use, lay the pattern on the body plan with the height line on the pattern coinciding with the center line of the body plan, and the curved edge of the pattern against the sheer or deck mark of the section. The bottom of the pattern must be at right angles with the center line of the body plan. Sweep in the curve of the top of the pattern from sheer or deck height to center line and the deck crown at the station is found. The pattern can be used to lay off the top of the deck, the underside of the deck, or the underside of any deck beam. It will be noticed that the amount of crown in any section is controlled by the amount of beam of the section. The top of the transom may be drawn on the body plan with this pattern, if not already established (if the top is fixed by the deck crown).

## Transom Expansion

The expansion of the transom, when it rakes or has a curved face, has been mentioned. The usual procedure is to expand the transom to the outside of the planking and deduct the plank thickness. If the transom is very curved, or if the sides of the boat come into it with a very full curve, there is actually a slight error resulting from this; but it is so small that it may be overlooked. The outside face of the transom, when expanded in the usual way, is used to set off the bevels—or angles at which the sides join it—to obtain the sawing shape, or "molded face," of the frame. This is not difficult to do if care is taken. First the various methods used to expand transom forms must be understood.

## Suggestion for Expansion

In small craft, where there is no transom frame and the sides and bottom are therefore fastened to the ends and bottom of the transom plank, the most satisfactory way is to expand the transom at its forward face, or inside of the transom plank line in the profile. This is particularly true when no tilting band saw is available. The usual procedure of getting out the finished transom, in this case, is to saw to the pattern obtained with a handsaw and then to work in the bevels with drawknife and plane after the transom is set up. As will be explained, it is possible to get out the correct bevels of the transom beforehand with a little more work on the loft drawing. Projecting the transom to the inside of its plank is a little more laborious when lofting the lines, but is less productive of error in setting off the bevels. In boats having a transom frame, it is possible to project the transom to the inside of the frame line, if desired, by the method suggested. This should be clear, however; the methods of projection used to expand the transom can be used to obtain the shape of the transom at its after face, forward face, or the forward face of its frame, by changing the position from which to start the projection. In the descriptions that follow the projection is taken at the inside of the transom plank, with one exception.

### Plumb and Flat Transom

In a flat transom, standing plumb, the body plan transom gives the true shape to its outboard face. To obtain the inboard face, draw in an extra section line on the profile and half-breadth plans at the distance forward of the transom face required by the thickness of the transom plank, or plank and frame. Project this to the body plan as explained in the development of extra sections on page 110 and set off the line of the inside of the side planking on the resulting body plan section; this is the required molding face.

### Expansion of Raking Flat Transom

If the transom is flat athwartships and raking in profile, the body plan shows the apparent shape of the after face of the transom. The inner face of the transom plank has been marked on the profile. A section representing this must be projected to the body plan first. Square down the intersections of the line on inside of transom plank with sheer, water lines, buttocks, and rabbet in the profile to the corresponding lines in the half-breadth plan. Draw in the outline of the section there as was done with the outboard face of the transom. Take the half-breadths of water lines, sheer, and rabbet of the new section on the half-breadth plan and transfer them to the body plan in the usual way. Take the heights of buttocks, sheer, and rabbet at inside of transom plank from the profile and set them off on the body plan. Draw in the section on the body plan. The diagonals may be checked as though the new section were the after face of the transom. Now a section is projected that is the forward face of the transom. To make the expansion, the raking line of the inside of the transom plank in the profile is taken as the center line for the expansion drawing, which will stand off from it abaft the

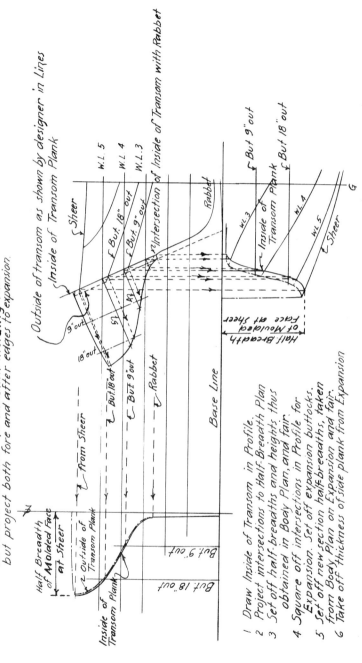

If top of Transom is beveled, use after edge at centerline and sheer to establish molding face but project both fore and after edges to expansion.

(Outside of transom as shown by designer in Lines

Inside of Transom Plank

W.L. 5
W.L. 4
W.L. 3

Sheer

℄ But. 18" out
℄ But. 9" out

Intersection of Inside of Transom with Rabbet

Rabbet

9" out
18" out

℄ From Sheer
℄ But. 18" out
℄ But. 9" out
℄ Rabbet

Base Line

Half Breadth of Molded Face at Sheer

Outside of Transom Plank

Inside of Transom Plank

But 9" out
But 18" out

℄ But. 9" out
℄ But. 18" out

wl 3
wl 4
wl 5

Inside of Transom Plank

℄ Sheer

G

Half Breadth of Molded Face at Sheer

1 Draw Inside of Transom in Profile.
2 Project intersections to Half-Breadth Plan
3 Set off half-breadths and heights thus obtained in Body Plan, and fair.
4 Square off intersections in Profile for Expansion. Set off expansion buttocks.
5 Set off new section half-breadths, taken from Body Plan on Expansion and fair.
6 Take off thickness of side plank from Expansion

22. Expansion of Flat and Raked Transom, 17-Foot Hampden Boat

stern. The height of the rabbet has been established on the raking
line of the inside of the transom plank in the transom profile by
its intersection with the profile rabbet line. At the rabbet height,
square out its half-breadth, taken from half-breadth plan to the
expansion-drawing center line.

The sheer is squared out on the expansion center line and its
half-breadth set off in the same way. At the points where the
water lines intersect the line of inside of transom plank on the
profile, square out water lines (from the expansion center line).
Take their half-breadths from the projected section of the inside
of transom plank in the body plan. Draw buttocks on the expansion plan; these are parallel to the center line of the expansion
drawing. Their spacing from it is the same as in the body and
half-breadth plans. The heights of the buttocks at top and bottom
on the expansion are found by squaring out from the expansion
center line the intersections of the buttock lines with the line of
the inside of transom plank in the profile as projected from the
body plan. Draw in the outline of the expanded transom, through
the points obtained. This is the true shape of the section of the hull
at the position of the forward face of the transom plank. The shape
to inside of plank is obtained by setting it off in the expansion
drawing in the same way as in the sections in the body plan. If the
top of the transom is beveled, project both fore and after edges
at sheer and center line to expansion drawing.

### Expansion of Plumb and Curved Transom

If the transom is perpendicular in profile but curved athwartships, the center line of the inside face of the transom has been
drawn in the profile and the arc of this face in the half-breadth
(page 98). The section at the inside of transom plank, or frame
if desired, is to be projected on the body plan. The heights of the
sheer, rabbet, buttocks, and chine, if one exists, are established
for this section by obtaining the outline of the outboard edge of
the inside of transom plank line, in the profile. This is done in
the same manner as in the outboard face of the transom. The
points of intersection of each water line, sheer, rabbet, chine, if
one exists, and of each buttock line, with the arc of the inside
of transom plank is squared up to the corresponding lines in the
profile from the half-breadth plan. When the outboard edge is

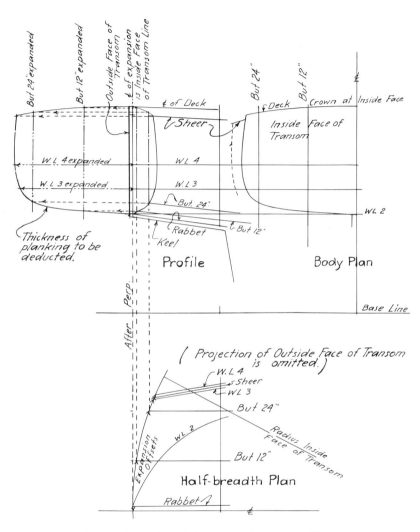

*23. Expansion of upright, curved transom. See text.*

drawn, the heights of sheer, rabbet, buttocks, and chine are transferred to the body plan at their proper places. The half-breadths
of the water lines, sheer, rabbet, and chine are then lifted from
the half-breadth plan, square to its center line, and carried to their
respective lines in the body plan. The outline of the section in

the body plan can then be drawn and the diagonals checked by projecting them as if the new-found station were the transom.

It is now possible to make the expansion drawing. The inside face of the transom plank at center line in the profile is taken as the center line for the expansion. The heights of sheer, rabbet, buttocks, chine, and water lines are squared out from this center line at the heights they were established in the profile at the outboard edge of the inside of transom plank. A batten is now bent around the arc of the line of the inside of the transom plank on the half-breadth plan and the spacing of the buttocks, from the center line, is ticked on the edge of the batten. Also the half-breadths of the water lines, sheer, rabbet, and chine, if one exists, are set off on the batten. When the batten is straight these dimensions are expanded. The expanded offsets are set off on the expansion drawing for water lines, sheer, rabbet, and chine. The expanded spacing of the buttocks is also laid off and these lines are drawn in parallel to the expansion center line. The heights of the buttocks are taken from the profile or body plan section, at the inside of transom plank, and squared off to the expansion buttocks. The top of the transom may be set off from the body plan in the same way. The outline of the expansion is then drawn in, the thickness of the side planking set off, and the true shape of the molded face of the transom plank is the result.

## Expansion of Raking and Curved Transom

The transom set raking, with its face curved athwartships, cannot be easily expanded in the manner applied to other forms of transom. To attempt to set off the molded shape of such a transom is a very involved procedure and it is easier to work from the expanded shape of the transom plank at its outboard face, unless the original lines have been drawn to the inside of the plank. Should it be desired to attempt the projection to the inside of the transom plank or frame, it is necessary to add a large number of water lines and buttocks that will pass through the transom, and these must be faired through the after stations on the profile, half-breadth, and body plans. With these, the projection can be made by following the methods outlined, with a little ingenuity in adaptation. However, this is one of the reasons that the raking and curved transom is not suited for the nonprofessional builder and that even the better professionals have trouble obtaining the proper shape.

The method to be explained will give a reasonably simple method of preparing the transom pattern. The expansion will be made with the line of the outside of transom plank at center line

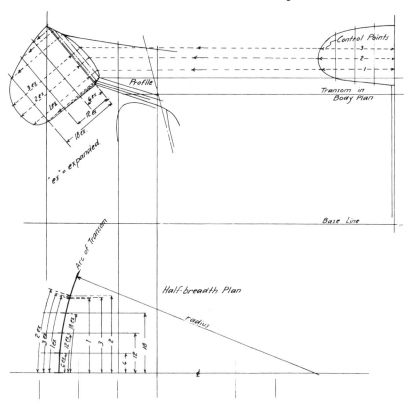

*24. Expansion of raking, curved transom. See text.*

in the profile as the center line for the expansion. Bend a batten around the arc of the face of the transom in the half-breadth plan to get the expanded spacing of the buttocks from the center line. Having marked these on the batten, transfer to the profile and set off at right angles to the expansion center line. Draw in the expansion buttocks parallel to the expansion center line. Square out the intersections of the buttocks, at top and bottom of transom, with the outboard edge in the profile to the corresponding buttocks in the expansion, using the expansion center line as a base. Square out in the same manner, from their position in the profile, all the control points marked for establishing the outboard edge of transom originally. Do the same with sheer, rabbet, and top of transom at center line, identifying each. The expanded half-breadth of each control point, and of the sheer and the rabbet, are obtained by setting off the half-breadth of these in the body plan on a measuring batten, transferring these to the arc of the face of the transom square to the center line in the half-breadth plan and marking there. Then a batten is bent around the arc and the expanded half-breadths set off on it. These are transferred to the expansion and set off on the corresponding heights or lines there. The outline of the transom can now be drawn in the expansion and the thickness of the planking set off. The expanded shape of the transom to the inside of the side planking and to the outside of the transom plank is now formed. To obtain the molded face of the plank or frame, the bevels must be lifted and applied to the expanded shape.

### To Find Bevels

The method of finding the bevels for the transom is the same as for finding the bevels of sawn frames, or for the floor timbers when bent frames are used. Among professional builders methods vary, but that to be explained is perhaps the most common. First, however, it is important that the builder know the reasons for using the method suggested. It might be supposed that the bevels of the frames, transom, and floors might be obtained by the apparently simple method of setting them off from the half-breadth plan with an adjustable bevel, using the intersections of a section line with water lines, buttocks, and diagonals. This would only work at the places where these fairing lines pass through the section, as outlined in the body plan, at right angles. As this is the case in only a few instances, a method giving more control points is necessary. The reason that the bevel must be taken at right angles to the section line, as shown in the body plan, is that it is in this position that the bevel must be used in sawing. First, the method of lifting a bevel for a frame will be explained.

Take a piece of plank or plywood (or heavy cardboard) two

frame spaces long and about 12 inches wide. Down the center of this strike a base line, the length of the board. Then erect perpendiculars to this at three points, measured off to equal the spacing of three frames, edge to edge or center line to center line of the frames—it makes no difference. Extend these perpendiculars across the board. Mark the middle perpendicular with the frame

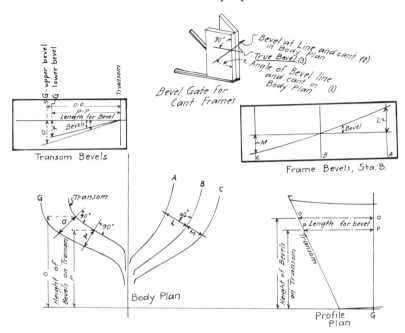

25. Bevel Boards—Measuring Bevels

number (or floor number) whose bevels are required. This will be a "bevel board." Turn to this particular section on the loft body plan and make marks, on its outline, which are spaced to give the desired number of bevel points on the frame or floor outline. Lay a 2-foot rule on one of these marks, laying the rule as nearly at right angles as possible to the section outline at the marked point and noting the exact measurements to the intersection of the rule with the stations on each side of the one chosen. Now take notice of the relative position of the chosen station to the side of the boat, that is, which way the bevel must slope. If the bevel formed is an acute angle it is an "under bevel"; if an obtuse

angle it is a "standing bevel." Bevels are always taken from the side
of the frame or floor that has been represented in the body plan.
Now take the board and set off the distances measured on the
body plan from the chosen station to the adjoining ones on either
side of the middle perpendicular (which represents the chosen
station); one dimension will be above the base line and the other
below, according to which way the bevel stands. A line is now
drawn with a batten from the measurement on one perpendicular
to the measurement on the other, passing through the point of
intersection of the base line with the perpendicular representing
the chosen frame. This line is usually straight, but may be curved
if necessary to pass through the three points required.

   To illustrate the process, let us suppose that three frames or
floor timbers are taken as examples—A, B, and C. These are in
the forebody and C is the farthest forward; B is the frame on
which the bevels are required. The bevel board has been laid
out and the perpendiculars representing the frames drawn. The
bevel points on B are marked in the body plan and the measurements to the stations adjoining (A and C) have been made there,
for one bevel mark. It is found that B in the body plan is the after
face of a frame (or floor) which will make the bevels "under,"
since the forward face must be smaller due to the run of the sides
of the hull toward the bow. Therefore, the measurement on C
on the bevel board will be taken above the base line and that on
A will be below. Since B is the face from which the bevels are
set off, strike in the forward line of the frame on the bevel board
to represent the forward face. Now the bevel line may be drawn
from the measurement on C through the intersection of base and
perpendicular at B and then to the measurement on A. This line
cuts the forward and after lines of the frame B on the bevel board
at the bevels required for the mark on the body plan that was
chosen. From this board the amount of wood to be cut off frame
B on its forward edge, to get the proper bevel, is measured. When
all the bevels for a frame have been marked from the body plan
to the bevel board it is a simple matter to set off the other side of
the frame when one side is already drawn. Had the line B been
the forward side, the bevels would obviously be the opposite and
would be "standing" in order that the after face be the larger,
by the amounts of bevel required at the different marks on the
body plan section. The spacing of the marks on the body plan

station may be any desired amount to give enough points to control the bevel in the band saw or to draw the opposite side of a frame to guide beveling with hand tools.

### Transom Bevels

The bevels of the transom may be taken in the same way, but the spacing of the perpendiculars on the bevel board must vary with each mark plotted when the transom rakes or curves. The reason for this is the variation in distance between the after frame and the outside edge of the transom. To lay out a bevel board for a transom, draw the base and erect a perpendicular near one end and extend across board. Make the marks on the transom for bevel points. Pick off the distance between the transom and the section adjoining, as was done with frames and floors in the body plan. Carry the mark on the transom edge in the body plan to the transom edge in the profile plan and measure the distance to the adjoining station, parallel to the base line of this view or square to the adjoining station. We now have the amount of bevel and the distance between transom edge and next frame or station.

Set off the frame distance on the base line on the bevel board, measuring from the transom perpendicular. Erect a perpendicular and extend across the bevel board. Now set off the bevel measurement below the base on the perpendicular representing the adjoining frame. Draw a line from this to the intersection of base and transom perpendicular. If the transom perpendicular represents the after face of the transom, then the line representing its forward face must be between it and the frame on the bevel board. If the transom perpendicular represents the forward face, then the after face line must be drawn outside of the transom perpendicular on the bevel board and the bevel line projected across it. By so measuring the bevel and distance to adjoining frame for each bevel mark, a tolerably accurate transom will result. If the transom is plumb and flat, it is treated as a body plan section in lifting bevels, of course. Transom bevels are sometimes taken from the half-breadth loft plan, taking the bevels on the sides at the water lines and on the bottom at the buttock line in the loft profile.

## Bevels Required for Cant Frames

In a steam-bent frame hull, the bevels are required at the transom and on the ends of the floor timbers that bind the frames together at the keel. All other bevels may usually be lifted from the loft plan without a bevel board. In sawn frames it is customary to lift three bevels for every buttock or timber that makes up a frame, on each side of the hull. If a sawn frame is canted, the bevels are hard to pick up as the spacing between frames varies with the height above the base line. One method is to make a "gate." This is a pair of short boards hinged along one edge. To these are nailed strips along an edge square to the hinged one, to act as handles and bases on which to stand the gate. The device is used to transfer the apparent bevels to the real bevels; the angle at which a water line or diagonal crosses the line of a section in the body plan is picked off with an adjustable bevel. This is transferred to the gate and marked on the blades, using the hinged edge to represent the line of section. Then the bevel of the chosen line with the section is picked up from the half-breadth plan and, with the bevel set to this and tipped to the angle marked on the gate, the latter is then opened until the sides of the gate are snug to the bevel's arms. The gate blades are now held in place by a weight and the bevel removed. The true bevel may now be found by placing the adjustable bevel against the gate square to the hinged edge. This method is somewhat tedious but easily understood. Cants are rarely used in framing today. The methods of beveling to be used, when such frames are numerous, are best found in old shipbuilding books. The cant frame is one that is not set square to the center line of the hull. It was once used to frame the ends of the hull when very full, to avoid the excessive bevels that would be required if the frames were square to center line.

## Lofting of Flat- and V-Bottom Hulls

The lofting of a flat- or V-bottom hull having straight dead rise and side in section is, of course, very simple compared to the lofting of a round-bottom hull. All fairing is usually done with sheer and chine in a flat-bottom hull; sheer, chine, and rabbet in

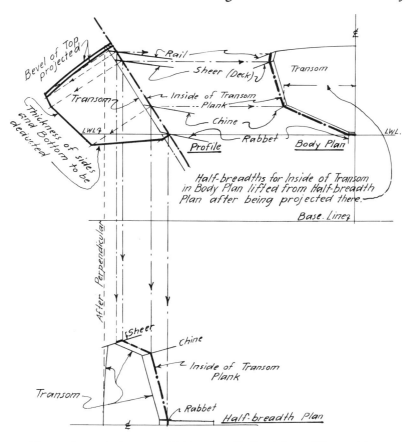

Bevel of Top projected

Thickness of sides and Bottom to be deducted

Transom

LWL?

Profile

Rail

Sheer (Deck)

Inside of Transom Plank

Chine

Rabbet

Body Plan

Transom

LWL.

Half-breadths for Inside of Transom in Body Plan lifted from Half-breadth Plan after being projected there.

Base Line?

After Perpendicular

Sheer

Transom

Chine

Inside of Transom Plank

Rabbet

Half-breadth Plan

*26. Expansion of Transom V-Bottom Hull without Water Lines or Buttocks*

a V-bottom. In a V-bottom only four bevels, two on the side and two on the bottom, need be measured for sawn frames. The bevels of the chine can be lifted from the sections. Four transom bevels, located as on sawn frames, are required for the transom of both V- and flat-bottom hulls. The method of drawing the keel structure, getting the mold shapes, and drawing the rabbet, middle line, and bearing line in a chine hull is the same as that described for round-bottom hulls.

## Rabbet Projection for Faired Posts

Sometimes the lines are faired to the face of the stem and the offsets for the rabbet on stern and stemposts are not given. The rabbet is established in the half-breadth plan, however. This is usually a curved line with the rabbet widest amidships. The profile of the rabbet is also established on the profile for the sections. Transfer the heights of the rabbet to the body plan after it has been faired and set off the half-breadths. These should come on the section outline. The width of stem and sternposts is now set off on the body plan and faired into the rabbet as marked on the sections. Pick up on a measuring batten the half-breadths of the rabbet as indicated by the stem and sternpost half-breadths in the body plan for each water line. Set these half-breadths off on the water lines faired in, in the half-breadth plan, keeping the batten square with the center line and sliding it fore or aft until the offset mark intersects the water-line curve. Mark this and then square the point up to the corresponding water line on the sheer at stem or stern, as the case may be. When all the water lines and the sheer are so treated, it is possible to establish the rabbet on the profile and to be sure that the outside of the planking is fair with the side of the stem, to the forward face of the cutwater.

## Stem Bevels and Finish

Some designers and builders do not fair the lines to the face of stem all the way up to the sheer, but allow the stem to widen out on its face, very suddenly, near the sheer. This should always be done, as it gives strength to the stem and enables it to withstand blows. If there is a bowsprit, the squaring of the stemhead in this manner makes the fitting of the gammon iron much easier and neater. The change in section of the stem, from square to taper, should be located on the profile just below and clear of the gammoning, if not shown in the plans. Another matter having to do with the finish of the stem is the head. In many boats having no bowsprit or stemhead fair-lead (such as is often seen in motorboats) the stem is sawn off flush with the deck. This practice usually spoils the appearance of the whole bow. Whenever possible, the stemhead should come above the deck and finish in a form having its greatest height above the deck at its forward end in profile. The very recent practice of streamlining the bow is an exception to this rule, however.

## Lofting Barrel Bow

The so-called "barrel bow" has been developed by streamlining. It really serves no useful purpose in a small boat designed for sailing, or for ordinary speed under power. Nevertheless, it is often attractive and so may be called for in a design. The methods of building vary; the most common practice is to form the stem of wide plank, doweled and glued together in the fashion used for building model boats called "bread and butter" construction. When the structure is formed, it is shaped with templates in the same manner as a model boat is shaped; then it is hollowed and the after edges of the stem are rabbeted to take the plank of the sides and bottom. The laminations may be vertical or horizontal. The shape of each lamination must be drawn in the loft plan. If the laminations are vertical, then buttocks are drawn in, of the spacing required by the thickness of the laminations or "lifts." If the laminations are horizontal, they are drawn as water lines, of course. These must be faired back from the bow far enough to make certain that the stem structure will fair into the hull when complete. The keel and other longitudinal members notch into the inside of the barrel-bow structure. With certain forms of diagonal planking the barrel bow can be planked up, but this is not true of the conventional methods of planking. Care should be taken, in lofting a barrel bow, to set off both inside and outside of each lift or lamination so that, in making up the stem, fastenings can be worked in that are clear of the outside and inside lines and that will not be disturbed in shaping. By this means, it is possible to use nails or screws to back up the glue used in forming the stem as well as to preserve wooden dowels when shaping.

## Lofting Deck Frame

Let us return to the lofting that was being described. The fairing of the lines had been completed, the projections for mold forms had been made, and the profile of the keel structure had been drawn. Before beginning to lift the templates or patterns, it is a good plan to draw the deck framing on the loft half-breadth plan. This can be done in red crayon. The location of all hatches, their inside dimensions, the shape and position of all deck knees and blocking, and the exact position of every deck beam can be copied from the designer's construction plan. The top of the cabin trunk can be worked out. Sometimes it is possible to use a beam mold, such as was made for the deck crown, that can be used to shape every cabin roof beam. However, it will be found that in many designs the position of the top of the sides and center line of the cabin trunk roof are given by offsets; in this case a mold must be made for every individual beam. This can be done by designing individual beam molds for every width and height of cabin roof beam required. In rare cases it is necessary to fair in the deck with buttocks as though it were the bottom, upside down. This is sometimes necessary in streamlined hulls. It is also possible to lay out and project the cabin trunk sides. To do this, it is necessary to draw the deck and construction section at each station that passes through the trunk. Such projections should also be made at the ends of the trunk. The half-breadth plan will give the length of the trunk sides, which may be expanded with a batten. The height of the trunk sides and cockpit coamings can often be roughed out after such a drawing has been completed.

## Lofting Joinerwork

Usually it is well to wait until the boat is under construction before lofting any of the cabin plan, but for the sake of brevity it will be discussed here. The important bulkheads can be easily lofted and patterns made by which the bulkhead can be completed before the hull is ready to receive it. Anyone who has any knowledge of drafting can work out the shape of any piece of cabin furniture in the loft plan. The importance of this is, perhaps, not so great in amateur building as in professional work, since the amateur rarely has any problem in doing the work inside the hull. The professional builder, however, may have a number of men at work in the hull at one time, and so all the structure completed outside reduces the chances of hindrance through men being in one another's way.

## Cross-Sectioning Timber

It is usually very helpful, in shaping timbers, to have the cross sections at each station drawn out. Cross sections through the keel, showing the exact bevels and cross-sectional shape, are particularly useful in checking the work. Such members as chine logs, keelsons, keel battens, and the sheer clamp, or clamp and shelf, may be cross-sectioned in each body plan section to advantage. This detailing will often show where study must be given the construction prior to the actual building, in order to carry out the designer's intentions correctly.

## Short Cuts in Lofting

The methods of lofting that have been described are not exactly those that are generally followed by professional builders; rather they are those most easily understood. As a builder gains experience, he will work out short cuts and variations desirable in the type of boat he commonly builds. It will be found that the work of some designers requires less lofting than that of others. Some hull forms need relatively little fairing; others a great deal. It is well to remember, however, that work in lofting is work saved in construction.

## Templates and Material

The next step is to make the templates or patterns. These may be made of cardboard if the boat is very small, or of plywood or any thin plank ¼ to ⅜ inch thick if the boat is large. The extent to which the templates are made should depend upon the number of boats to be built on one design. If only one is to be built, no patterns are required for the molds, as their shapes may be transferred directly from the floor or loft drawing to the wood to be used in making the molds used to form the hull.

## Molds and Picking Up

Suppose it is desired to make the molds first. Rough lumber will do for these. The plank used should be wide enough so that not more than four or six pieces will be required to get out the shape of the mold, not including the tiepiece across the top, called the "cross-spall." The thickness of the plank used for the molds should be ample to give strength. In small craft, up to 20 feet in length, ¾- to 1-inch stock will do. For hulls 20 to 30 feet, use 1¼-inch stock; larger boats require molds from 1½ to 27 inches thick. The plank for the molds can be in short lengths and waste timber can be used. The first step is to prepare the loft drawing for picking up. There are many methods of picking up, but for the moment it will be assumed that it is possible to drive nails into the lofting floor. Small wire brads, about ⅜ inch long, will do. The heads should be cut off snug. Drive these along the line of the inside of planking of the foremost section in the loft body plan. The nails should be spaced about 1½ inches apart, 2 inches in large boats. Drive nails along the curve of the section at the inside of planking line, taking care that each nail is directly on the line, with top of nail about ¼ inch above floor. Outline the cross section of the keel, inside the rabbet bearding line, and the center line there, with nails. Lay a plank on the nails in such a way that it covers the maximum part of the section outlined in nails. When this has been found, hit the plank a few raps with a mallet so as to make an impression in the underside of the plank of each nail driven in the body plan section. Turn over the plank and run a line through the nail impressions with a batten and a straightedge so that the exact section, to inside of planking, is outlined on the plank, and so that the outline of half the keel cross section, inside of the bearding line, is drawn.

In the foremost section it should be possible to make a half-mold out of one plank. The plank should be long enough to extend 3 inches or more above the sheer or deck. At the center-line marks in the plank draw the center line to form the lower limits of the mold. Saw out the mold plank along the lines just drawn and plane fair and smooth to the exact line of the section. The notch for the top of keel is sawn out as marked and then the center line is used as a guide to saw for the butt to be formed there. Here there ought to be about 3 inches of width to the plank along the butt—more, if possible—so as to give room for fastening the cleat at the butt. Repeat this operation with another plank to form the duplicate for the other side. Now pull out the nails (with pliers) that were driven into the loft body plan. Lay the first mold plank back on the section, making sure that it coincides exactly with the inside of planking line and with the center line and top of keel. Mark plainly on the plank the lines crossing the section in the body plan (water lines, buttocks, and diagonals), drawing them across the width and edges at the angles formed by the drawing. Also mark plainly the sheer. In some cases it may be desirable to pick up the cross section of such members as the chine log and stringers, or clamps, on the mold plank. When the plank has been marked, turn it over and place the duplicate on top of it. Then mark this plank with the same lines, so that the markings will be on the same face in both halves of the mold when assembled.

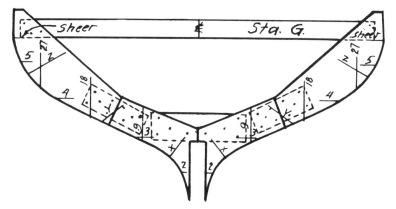

*27. Four-Piece Mold, 17-Foot Hampden Boat, Station G*

Get out the plank used for the cross-spall. Lay it across the section in the body plan so that its underside is at the sheer or deck line and square to the body plan center line; mark both center line and sheer half-breadth on it. Reverse and mark off the other side for sheer half-breadth. Cut spall to proper length. Now lay the two halves of the mold together in the proper position, one half on the body plan section but with markings on plank down, and secure the cross-spall in place to both halves. The cross-spall must be square to the center line and its underside exactly on the sheer or deck marks so that it will be level when the mold is set in place. The cleat holding the two halves together over the keel is next made and fastened. If necessary, this will be notched to fit the top of keel. The width of plank used for cross-spall and cleat should be 3 to 6 inches, depending on the size of boat. The thickness should be the same as the mold stock. Perhaps this is obvious, but it is mentioned in order to emphasize the importance of strength in the molds. These members may be fastened with large screws or with common nails. After ᵗhe mold is fastened together, it should be turned over with markings up and checked with try square and straightedge to make sure that it is properly lined up and put together. The other molds are made in the same manner, but each side of the mold will have to be made of two or three pieces and then cleated together. The corrugated fasteners used for fastening crates, packing boxes, and window screens are very useful in fastening the parts of the mold together before

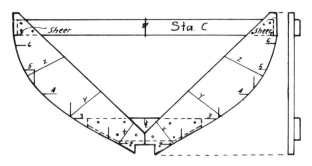

28. *Mold Station C, 17-Foot Hampden Boat*

fitting cleats. The butts formed on the pieces of the mold need come in no special position; their location can be decided by the stock on hand. No mold need be made for the transom. Molds in way of centerboard case can be made in two sections, deducting case thickness if it is intended to set up case with keel. Molds are cleated to case side in setting up, if this is done.

## Other Methods of Picking Up Molds and Patterns

If the loft drawing cannot have nails driven into it, tacks may be set on the drawing with points up and heads on the line. If the drawing is on paper, the wood for the molds may be slid under and the lines transferred by punching through the drawing with a common scratch awl. Various types of toothed wheels are made for this purpose. These are called "tracing wheels" and are used by dressmakers to transfer paper patterns; they may be obtained from mail-order houses. Special battens can be made for picking up. The most common consists of a limber batten, square in section; to this are attached short wooden strips at right angles. The method of attachment is a brass sleeve, shaped like the letter "U," over the end of each short strip. The long batten is then passed through the U. This enables it to be shifted in the attachment. In the ends of the short strips are small holes. The long batten is

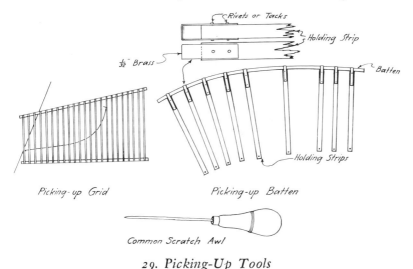

Picking-up Grid                    Picking-up Batten

Common Scratch Awl

*29. Picking-Up Tools*

bent around the section on the loft body plan and held to the curve by awls driven through the holes in the short strips. These, by their attachment to the large batten, hold the section curve and the batten can then be lifted far enough from the floor to slide under a plank, on which the shape of the curve is then traced. The fairing of the batten on the section curve can be controlled by shifting the holding strips as required. Another idea, sometimes employed, is to build a grid of thin battens, consisting of $\frac{1}{4}$- by $\frac{1}{2}$-inch pine strips, about 3 feet long, spaced about 1 inch apart on two 1-inch by $\frac{3}{8}$-inch battens. This grid is laid over the body plan and where the chosen section crosses each batten a tick-mark is made on the grid. This is then transferred to the mold plank and the process reversed. Such a device as this is suitable for lofting small craft such as dinghies and canoes.

*Patterns*

Patterns are picked up from the loft plan in the same manner as molds. The patterns for the wide timbers in the keel may be outlined in skeleton form with narrow battens held together by corrugated fasteners and braces or cleats. The pattern, or template, outline should be the exact shape of the timber for which it is made. The lines on the timber, such as bearding, middle, and rabbet lines, are picked up from the loft plan on the pattern as

*Stem, Knee*
Template in one piece

Cleats

Corrugated Fastener

*Stern, Upper Deadwood*
Template built up, to save stock.

*30. Keel patterns, 17-Foot Hampden Boat. Note station and water-line marks. Mark for bolts also.*

was done in picking up the shape of the molds. These lines are drawn on the pattern in their correct place and shape. When it is necessary to transfer them, nails are driven through the pattern, along the lines, into the timber to be shaped; the outline is traced around the edge of the pattern and all control points are then transferred to the timber. As in the molds, it is very important that all section lines, water lines, and the sheer, when possible, be transferred to the pattern and from there to the timber. The reason for this is that these marks will be necessary to properly fit the timbers together and to set the molds. Patterns should be picked up for every timber in the keel structure, for stem and sternposts and their knees, and for all deck framing. If there is a centerboard, or fin keel, the timbers for this must have patterns. The rudder should be drawn in the loft plan and a pattern made for each individual plank in its structure, if large. When the patterns or templates for the keel are completed, put them together on the mold loft plan to check them against the drawing and to be sure that the lines marked on the various templates coincide as they should. This is a very important check. It will show any errors in outlining the scarfs or laps in the timber patterns. As each pattern is made, make some identifying marks on it and upon the timber in the loft plan, so that its place is known. Patterns should be made for deck knees and blocking if there are many pieces to be cut. With the deck crown pattern and the loft plan it should be possible to get out the deck beams without individual templates.

## Transom Pattern

A light wooden pattern should be made of the expanded transom and the bevel spots marked. The transom template should be complete, like the molds. The amount of bevel to the transom edge is on the bevel board, and if it is desired to make the inside and outside lines of the transom plank or frame this can be done on one pattern. The transom pattern must have the center line, all the water lines, and the buttocks that cross it plainly drawn. It is usually well to mark on the diagonals also; very often these lines are useful in taking measurements necessary to properly set the transom.

## Floor Timbers, Patterns, and Bevels

When the molds and the patterns, or templates, for the keel structure, stem and sternposts, deadwood timber and deck framing are completed, the floor timbers should be projected on the mold loft drawing and patterns made. From the designer's plans the position of the floor timbers can be transferred to the loft profile. From here their shape can be projected to the body plan by the methods used for additional sections (page 110). There is one point that should be made here: it will save time if the *molded face* of the floors be chosen for the body plan section to give under bevels. This means that the after sides of the floor timbers, in the profile, are taken as section lines in the forebody; the forward sides in the afterbody. The bevels for the floor timbers can be measured as for frames (page 120).

## Sawn Frames, Templates For

If the boat has sawn frames, templates are made for every timber, or futtock, that makes up each. The bevel spots, as well as all other identifying lines, must be marked on the pattern. The templates for each frame are put together in a pile, with the bevel board, so that they will not become mixed and hard to pick out when getting out stock. After the individual timbers of a frame are shaped, the whole frame template should be assembled and cleated together to aid in putting the frame together prior to setting up. This will give a handy check for frame shape. No mold forms are necessary, of course. Otherwise the patterns are the same as required for a bent-frame boat.

## Joinerwork Patterns

Now the molds and patterns are complete for the hull frame. If desired, patterns may be made for the cabin joinerwork or for bulkheads. Then the patterns should be stored in the order in which the timber is to be worked.

## Planning Setup

At this stage it is well to begin planning how the hull is to be set up for building. If the boat is small and rather light, it is usually built upside down. On the other hand, a heavy boat, or a large one, is built standing on her keel. If the boat laid down is to be built upside down, it is well to strike a base line on the loft plan representing the floor or building base line. Then the setting-up heights for each mold from this to base line and to the sheer (which is the underside of the cross-spall, remember) can be measured full size and marked on each mold spall. Some builders plan the molds so that the ends above the sheer will reach the floor, when upside down, at the required height. The base line position in relation to the sheer should be carefully chosen to keep clear of the spalls, the stem and sternposts, and the transom top. If the base line is to be the floor, the height of the boat when set up should be considered. There must be plenty of room for the builder to crawl under the hull and there ought to be comfortable sitting headroom between the floor and underside of keel. If the boat is to be built right side up, it is often a trouble saver to establish the building base line in a different position from that in the designer's lines. In this case the corrected heights should be measured from base to rabbet line on each station (or from base to sheer, if desired) and marked on the corresponding molds. The height at which the boat is set up will probably be governed by the headroom in the shop. It is well to set the boat as high as possible, as a rule, to give ample room to work on the bottom, under the bilges. It will be found useful to establish two base lines, one below the keel and one above the sheer, in boats over 30 feet long overall, in some designs.

## Special Cases

If the boat is strip or diagonal planked, the position in which she is set up is particularly important. Usually it is best to set the strip-planked boat right side up. The diagonal-planked hull is easiest built upside down. If such a boat is fairly large, it would be well to start planning the method to be used to turn her over when the planking is done. The gear can be easily rigged, but room is required. Flat-bottom hulls are usually built upside down; so are V-bottom hulls, unless they are large. When boats of these models are large and built right side up, there should be more room between the floor and chines than would be required between floor and keel in a round-bottom model. If the boat has a motor and it is desired to put it in before the hull is moved out of the shop, it is wise to check the headroom to see if it can be hoisted clear of the gunwale or sheer when the boat is complete. If not, it may be necessary to put in the motor before ribbands are fastened to the molds; this will require putting in some floor timbers before setting up the molds. These are possible details that should be considered now and planned ahead.

## Suggestions: Batten Chines and Batten Keel

There remain a few suggestions and remarks concerning lofting. The best method of finding the shape of the notch to be cut in the molds for a chine timber that is carried through the planking (in the same manner as a keel and keel batten) is as follows. Bisect the angle formed by bottom and side in a section in the body plan and draw a line to represent the division. This line should pass through the point of the chine and inboard a few inches. The thickness of the plank on sides and bottom is drawn. From the specifications get the size of the outer chine member. Set off its width square to the bisecting line, with half

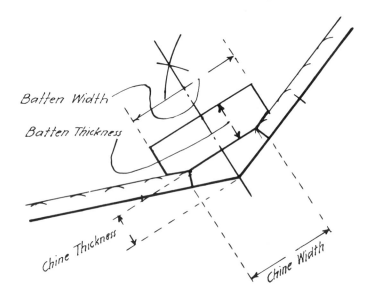

Batten Width

Batten Thickness

Chine Thickness

Chine Width

*31. Layout for Batten Chine*

of the width on each side. Project this until it intersects the outside of plank on both side and bottom; this marks the position of the seams along the outside of the plank at chine. Square in, to the face of the plank of bottom and sides, their thicknesses. Connect these two points and the cross section of the outer member of the chine is drawn. The inner member is laid off with its thickness along the bisecting line, measured from the inside of the outer member. The width is laid off square to the bisecting line with half on either side. Square the edges from the back or inboard face of this member to the inside of plank and the cross section is completed. This not only shows the shape of the notch to be cut in the molds, but also the bevels of each member at the given station. By this means it is possible to lay out the chine members with their proper bevel before fastening into the hull; but it is advised that the bevels be only roughed out so as to leave a little wood for fitting, since the sections may be rather widely spaced. In getting out the batten keel the same methods can be followed. Sawn frames for either flat-sided hulls or the round-bottom model are usually beveled on the inside with the same bevels established for the outside.

## Curved Transom

If the transom is raking in profile and curved very slightly athwartships, it may save time to treat it as a flat-raking transom, picking up the transom expansion pattern to the inside of a thick transom plank, or to the inside of both it and the frame, and then cutting the amount of curvature (to the after face of the transom) out of the thick transom plank. This will work when the amount of curvature across the face of the transom does not exceed ¾ inch, measured in the hull profile at the widest place. If light weight is important, however, this practice is frowned upon.

## Stopwaters

It is a good plan to mark the stopwaters in the keel structure in the loft plan and to indicate them on the templates so that they won't be overlooked. These should be placed so that one goes through a keel scarf at the middle line of the rabbet and another just inside of the bearding line, that is, between middle and bearding line. The rake of the scarf and the distance between middle and bearding line will fix the spacing of the stopwaters. These should be of white pine or cedar and should range from ¼-inch diameter in a small boat to ½ inch in a large one. Common sense is the best guide for exact size; too large a stopwater will cut away the space inside the rabbet lines excessively. There should be two stopwaters in every seam passing through the rabbet in the keel, stem and sternposts, or deadwood structure, whenever space permits. If the space between middle and bearding lines is scant, the outermost stopwater may be located between rabbet and middle lines. If the seam is vertical to the rabbet, one stopwater will have to serve.

## Ballast Pattern

If there is an outside ballast keel of lead that is rounded or shaped in cross section, a full-sized replica will have to be made of softwood, for a pattern. This can be built by gluing together plank and shaping, as was done in directions for the barrel bow, following a plan used for building model boat hulls. If the ballast keel is rectangular in cross section, no pattern will be required; it can be cast in a wooden mold as will be described later. When there is a ballast keel, be careful to draw in the ballast bolts in the loft profile to make certain that they do not foul the bolts required for floor timbers or scarfs; the patterns should show all bolt locations so that these can be laid off on the timbers when shaping them.

## Shaft Log

Take particular care in laying off the shaft log. It is well to draw a number of sections to see how the through-fastenings are going to work out. This will save untold trouble later. Too often it is found that the shaft (or shaft and its tube) is so large that it is difficult, if not impossible, to bore for the through-fastenings or drift bolts without danger of running into the shaft line or

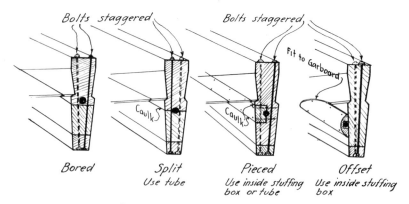

32. Common Shaft Log Construction

running too close to the rabbet when the latter is cut. The greatest danger usually exists when the deadwood is thin. If boring
looks too difficult, or tools are not available, the use of split or
pieced shaft logs may solve the problem. If the deadwood is very
thin, it is usually better to offset the shaft and put a faired strip
over the shaft. In this case the shaft runs along one face of the
deadwood and may or may not be covered by a slotted plank,
rounded on its outer face. Sometimes the designer has shown a
"feather" or strip run in along the seam on both sides of the split
shaft log. If it appears that this is going to be cut by bolts it
might as well be omitted and the hole for the shaft protected
against leakage, through these seams on the sides, by a lead or
brass tube running the full length of the shaft hole, even though
not called for in the plans or specifications. Perhaps the greatest
difficulty in making a shaft log by boring is to avoid fouling keel
drifts or bolts. The longer the shaft hole, the greater the difficulty
in boring. For most amateurs the split, pieced, or offset shaft
holes are the most satisfactory. This subject will be discussed in
greater detail in the next chapter.

This completes the mold loft work. Remember, an eraser will
correct an error in the loft drawing but more than that is required
to correct the same error when actual building begins.

The next step is to shape the backbone and set up.

# CHAPTER THREE

# THE BACKBONE– SETTING UP

## Importance of Lumber Storage

*W*HILE the lofting has been going on, the timber necessary for building should have been delivered. If it is
possible to use the lumber at once, it will suffice to put
it under cover and pile in such a way that the sticks desired first
will be on top. Few home builders can plan on full-time construction, however, and a good deal of time may intervene between the
starting and finish of the boat. During this time it is possible for
some of the timber to be harmed by heat and moisture unless it
is properly stored. This is particularly true of oak, spruce, elm,
and pine. Of course, the space available will govern the storage
of lumber but, if possible, certain precautions should be taken.

## Methods of Storage and Protection

The best way is to pile plank on a level, dry floor, one plank
on top of another. The pile should not be so high as to be easily
knocked over; if there are too many planks for one pile, make
another against the first. On top of these planks put the heavy
timbers, spreading them out so that their weight is evenly dis-
tributed over the length and breadth of the pile of plank. The
weight of the large timbers will keep the plank from warping,
springing, or twisting. Do not put stones or other heavy, but small,
objects on the lumber pile in place of heavy timbers. Concentrated
weights will do more harm than good. If there is no floor available, put a couple of thick, rough plank on sleepers, level, and
then stack the lumber on the platform so formed. If the lumber

is very green and it is hoped to dry it out while building, insert battens under each plank as it is added to the pile. These battens should be about 1 by 2 inches, laid on the flat, spaced about 4 feet apart. Take care that the battens, as they are placed, line up with those below. The bottom plank of the stack should be well off the ground. If the stack is in the open, one end should be lower than the other so that rain water will run off. It may be well to remind the reader that it takes from two to three years to air season timber. If there is a quantity of heavy timber to be seasoned, it may be stacked on end, against a building or fence, leaving air spaces between the timbers. If timbers are to be stored under cover for any great length of time, pack them in a pile as was done with plank, on a level floor, and over them lay some wide planks; erect posts along the sides of the stack and then cleat across the stack. The posts may be toenailed to the floor and the cross cleats nailed to the posts; these will prevent the sticks from twisting. This is a good way to store oak and elm. When oak or elm timber, or plank, is on hand, it is a good plan to paint the butts with orange shellac, red lead, or old paint that is rather thick. This will usually prevent the ends from checking. Piles of lumber should be covered with paper or old sacks to keep dirt and grit from accumulating on the surfaces of the plank; oak may be protected from checking by covering with damp sawdust and salt. If the pile must be in the open, it may be covered with tar paper or tarpaulin. It is not desirable to store lumber overhead in a shop as the heat is usually too great. Also, dust and dirt will accumulate on the upper surface of any timber so stored.

## Tools

The tools required for getting out the backbone depend upon the size and design of the boat to be built. In any case there must be a workbench. This should be fitted with a woodworker's vise, not the iron- or steel-jawed machinist's or metalworking vise. A metal bench stop should also be fitted. For smoothing thin battens, a wooden stop topped with sole leather may be used. This is shown in the accompanying cut. A bench hook can be made of a hardwood plank, as also shown. This is useful in sawing short pieces of wood on the bench, or in working with chisels; it will steady the work and save the top of the bench from becoming

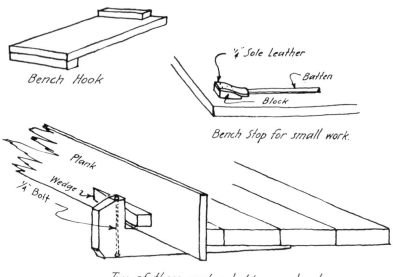

Bench Hook

"¼" Sole Leather
Batten
Block

Bench Stop for small work.

Plank
Wedge
¼" Bolt

Two of these wedge holders on bench
are handy when shaping timber or plank

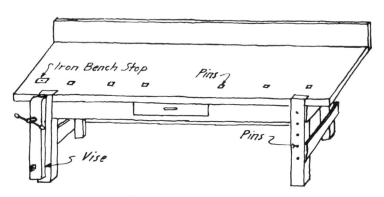

Iron Bench Stop
Pins

Vise

Pins

*33. Workbench for Planking*

cut up. A separate planking bench is useful if there is room. This
may be made against a convenient wall. It does not need to be
wide; 20 inches is ample. On this can be fitted the plank holders
shown in the cut; these and wedges will hold a plank better

than a vise when smoothing up the edges or working with a draw-knife. Tools for getting out the timbers are a cross-cut handsaw, a hand ripsaw, compass saw, broad hatchet, brace and bits, ball peen, hammer, a light sledge hammer, mallet, drawknife, chisels, jack plane, rabbet plane, smooth plane, bullnose plane, and try square. For a small boat, iron C-clamps capable of opening to 8 inches can be obtained at low cost; large C-clamps are very expensive, however.

There are various types of adjustable bar clamps, but on the whole they are not strong enough for holding deadwood timbers.

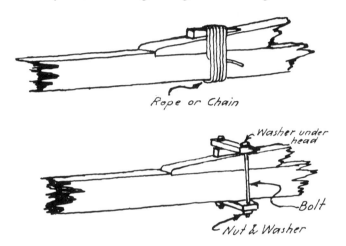

*34. Makeshift Deadwood Clamps*

Makeshift clamps can be fashioned that are better suited to the job. One way of clamping is to take a few turns of rope around the timbers, draw up snug, and tuck under the ends. Then drive a large wedge between rope and timbers. If the rope is well stretched before using, the results are satisfactory. In handling knees by this method, a cleat nailed to each side of the timber will keep the rope from slipping down the slope of the top of the knee. If rope is too light for the work, small chain can be used. Similar results can be had by using a wedge clamp, made of two pieces of oak and two carriage bolts, shown in the cut. This can be taken apart to get it over the ends of timbers, if necessary. Large keels require a broad ax and an adz to shape by hand. If there is a mill handy, it is best to mark the timbers and carry them to the mill to be rough-shaped rather than attempt to work them down with hand tools. Where power tools are available, a band saw will serve for shaping deadwood and keel timbers.

In shaping the rabbet, a carpenter's slick (a large chisel with a blade over 2 inches wide) is very useful. All chisels should be heavy-duty tools. The "framing chisel" is most commonly used, as the "firmer" is too light for work on the keel. The brace should be of the ratchet type. The auger bits should vary according to the work: for hardwood use bits having a single cutter; for planking and joinerwork use the double cutter. Also a selection of ship augers is required. For long holes use the barefoot ship auger (which is started by first boring a shallow hole with an ordinary bit). The ship auger with screw is used in counterboring for plugs in planking and for heavy work, but is not used for long, straight holes, such as the shaft logs require. The ship auger bit is between 13 and 20 inches long; it can be used in an ordinary brace, but when used for long holes an iron stock is welded on to serve as a brace. The stock can be made and welding can be done by any blacksmith. The diameter of the stock should be about the same as the shank of the auger, above the twist.

The saws should be chosen with care; for hardwood and smooth cuts, use saws having 10 or 11 points to the inch; for softwood and rough, quick cuts, use saws having 8 or 9 points to the inch for cross-cut, 5½ points to the inch for rip. The large, one- or two-man cross-cut saws, used in cutting cordwood, are suitable for cutting ends off keel timber. If some fastenings are countersunk, the Foerstner auger bit should be used to counterbore. It is much better than the common bit on sloping surfaces; the expansion bit is useless in this situation. The adz should have a lipped blade, since most cutting will be done across the grain of the wood. A good grindstone is a necessity; high-speed abrasive wheels or grinders are not satisfactory for heavy tools. Hacksaw, or boltcutter, sledge, and spikeset (heavy punch with point cut off) are required for fastening.

### Marking and Cutting Timber

Now the marking of the timbers may be started. Select the pieces for the keel from the lumber pile. Consult your lumber list to be certain you choose the right pieces. With the templates mark the outline of the first piece and cut to the line. After the outline has been cut, lay off the center line and the taper, if the keel is not parallel sided; with adz and broad ax, or with band saw, cut the taper in the sides of timber, to the marks. Finish with a plane. Now lay template or pattern back on the timber and mark the position of stations and water lines, as shown on the template, on the face of the timber. Square these across the top and bottom and mark the opposite side. Drive nails through the template to hold it in position on the timber while marking. The location of the rabbet can be transferred to the timber by driving nails through the template along the rabbet, middle, and bearding lines shown there. If the template is transferred to the opposite side of the timber, the nail holes will guide to spotting and fairing the rabbet lines on that side. When the lines of the rabbet are marked, fair in the lines with a batten, tacked to the timber. Mark the location of bolts, or fastenings, shown on the template. It may appear unnecessary to mark all these lines on the timber, but they will become very important when the keel is being put together and when the molds are being set. If joinerwork is required in the boat being built, these lines and marks on the dead-wood will be of great assistance in getting all measurements correct. One of the greatest causes of trouble and error in setting up the deadwood and molds can be traced to neglect in properly marking the timbers.

After the timber is shaped and marked, the rabbet may be roughly cut, if desired. Mark and cut each timber for keel, dead-wood, stem and sternposts, and knees in the same manner. If there is much change of width in any timber, due to taper, the stations should be marked on with the outline and squared across top and bottom after shaping these surfaces, renewed on the sides from these lines after the sides are cut off to make the taper, and then the rabbet set off by measurements on these stations.

The scarfs should be planed smooth, exactly to the line. Notched timbers may be worked smooth with a bullnosed plane. When cutting the rabbet use a plank gauge and check the bevel at each station on the timber with each station on the loft body plan. Cut the stem and sternposts long at the top, for nailing stays when setting up; the stemhead can be marked, but the shaping may. be done after the deck is laid. Take care to bevel the

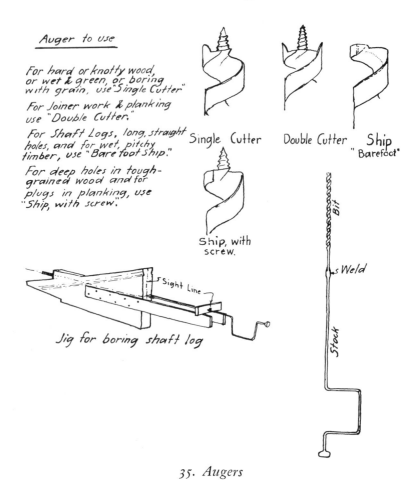

Auger to use

For hard or knotty wood,
or wet & green, or boring
with grain, use "Single Cutter"

For Joiner work & planking
use "Double Cutter."

For Shaft Logs, long, straight
holes, and for wet, pitchy
timber, use "Bare foot Ship."

For deep holes in tough-
grained wood and for
plugs in planking, use
"Ship, with screw."

Single Cutter      Double Cutter      Ship
"Barefoot"

Ship, with
screw.

Bit

Weld

Stock

Sight Line

Jig for boring shaft log

*35. Augers*

stem properly so that the width of its face, or forward edge, will run fairly into the width of the keel bottom. If there is a centerboard, cut the slot in the keel allowing for the tenon of the "ledges," or endpieces as shown in the proper keelpiece template. It is very important that the slot be straight and in line with the center line of the keelpiece. The slot is cut by first boring holes along the slot and then opening up with saw, chisel, and slick.

## Constructing the Transom

The transom is next to be built. If the transom is of a single plank, it is made up from the pattern and the cleats or side frames attached. If the template was made to the molding face of the transom frame, the frame is first marked and shaped, then planked; the whole is then beveled, or left square to be beveled when set up. If the transom is curved, the frame is sawn to the arc of inside of transom plank shown in the half-breadth plan in the loft, then shaped by bending the transom template to the face of the frame. The transom planking is then steamed and bent over a form having a little less radius than the arc of the frame. The steaming of timber will be described when framing is discussed.

The sharper bend in the transom planking is to allow for straightening out, which will take place when the planking is removed from the form. Usually the radius of the form for bending the planking is around one twenty-fourth less than the radius of the transom frame. Little need be said about framing the transom. Flat-bottom craft usually have transoms of either a single plank, or two or three cleated together. Sometimes two-plank transoms are doweled or drifted together instead of cleated. In large flat-bottom boats a transom frame is required; it may be notched for keel, clamps, and chines. If the frame is not notched, the ends of the clamps butt against the frame and are secured by knees, called "quarter knees." Sometimes a center batten is also used, on which the stern knee at center line of hull will bear. The chines do not require knees at transom as the bottom planking, when nailed on, acts as a bracket or knee. V-bottom transoms are framed in a similar manner to flat-bottom transoms.

In large boats the transom frame is halved at chine and sheer; in small craft this is not necessary. Flat-raking transoms for round-bottom hulls have frames differing little from V-bottom transoms. Vertical-curved transoms usually have two or more stiffeners on each side of the center batten; all are halved or notched into the transom frame at bottom and at deck. The clamps are butted against the frame and secured with quarter knees. The keel is notched into the frame. Raking-curved transoms are framed about like raking-flat transoms. The keel is notched into the frame and there may be one or two center battens for the transom knee,

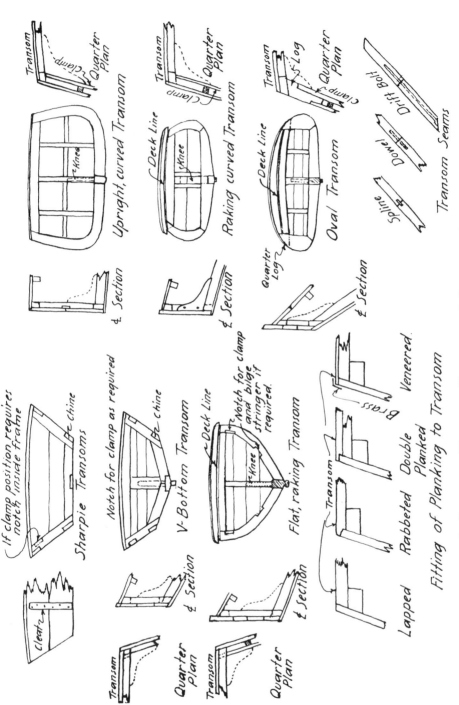

Transom

Quarter Plan

Clamp

Upright, curved Transom

Deck Line

knee

¢ Section

Transom

Quarter Plan

Clamp

Raking curved Transom

Deck Line

knee

¢ Section

Transom

Log

Quarter Plan

Clamp

Oval Transom

Deck Line

Quarter Log

¢ Section

Spline

Dowel

Drift Bolt

Transom Seams

If clamp position requires notch inside frame

chine

Sharpie Transoms

Cleat

¢ Section

Transom

Quarter Plan

Notch for clamp as required

chine

V-Bottom Transom

¢ Section

Transom

Quarter Plan

Deck Line

Notch for clamp and bilge stringer if required.

knee

Flat, raking Transom

¢ Section

Lapped

Rabbeted

Brass

Double Planked

Transom

Veneered

Fitting of Planking to Transom

36. Common Transom Frames and Construction

or a heavy center batten and knee with stiffeners outboard on either side. If the transom is large, the frame is halved at the butts; cleats are used occasionally instead of halving. If the transom planking is reasonably heavy, the transom frame need have no great strength at the butts and joints, since the planking will serve as cleats when secured to the frame.

In the oval transom it will be necessary to fit logs at the sheer, running fore and aft, in order to have means of shaping the tumble-home of the quarters. This log is sometimes secured to the transom by quarter knees let into the top of the log and resting on the transom frame under the deck. In other cases the knee is secured to the inside of the log; the position depends upon where the deck actually is in relation to the sheer. When a few wide planks are used to make up the transom, the seams should be backed with a seam batten or a spline. The frame of curved transoms must be sawn to the proper curve at top and bottom. The sidepieces can usually be shaped out of plank.

The method of fastening the side and bottom planking to the transom is usually specified in the plans; if not, common sense is the best guide. It is common practice to bring the planking past the transom and saw it off flush with the transom face; this is the "lapped" method of fitting. The sides and bottom are nailed, riveted, or screwed to the transom frame, with two fastenings into the ends of the transom planking, in each strake. The "rabbeted" method of fitting is used on highly finished hulls; the planking rabbet in the transom is cut as the side and bottom planking is laid on. Usually there are two small fastenings, driven through the transom planking and into the ends of each side and bottom strake to keep the rabbet closed; the main plank fastenings are driven into the transom frame. Double-planked transoms are usually rabbeted; only the inside transom planking is put up with the frame. The outside transom plank is not put on until the side and bottom planking is in place and trimmed off, projecting a little, along the transom edge. The outer planking of the transom may be easily marked when clamped or shored into place, then removed and accurately rabbeted.

When finally fitted and placed, the two layers of transom planking are secured together by marine glue and screws. The same result is obtained by means of a veneered transom. In this construction the inside planking is put onto the frame and the beveling completed; then the veneer is glued in place with a liberal margin beyond the transom edge all around. This is not cut off until the hull is planked. Sometimes the veneer is put on after the side and bottom planking is completed. The final step is to put a brass binding all around the transom to cover the edge of the veneer. This binding is made of brass or bronze angles, usually formed to shape by brazing. The veneer used is marine plywood, 3-ply, about ³⁄₁₆-inch total thickness. This method gives a seamless transom suitable for varnish finish. The veneered transom is used in powerboat construction and is rarely seen in sailing craft. Rabbeted and veneered transom construction requires a good deal of skill and great care in fitting; it is probable that few amateur builders would attempt to build these types of transoms unaided. As far as practical considerations are concerned, the lapped method is as good as any, since it is strong and lasting. In very large vessels, over 60 feet long, with planking 2 or more inches thick, it is customary to miter the ends of the transom planking into the side and bottom planking; but this never should be done on a small boat. Occasionally the side planking is rabbeted into the transom plank—in small boats, when there is no transom frame; but the practice is not good unless the transom is unusually thick. Screws, nails, or spikes are used for fastening the transom frame together, bolts being required only in the knees. Large vessels have their transom frame bolted and drifted.

## Centerboard Construction

The centerboard construction is usually well detailed in the plans furnished by the designer. The following remarks are intended to give the builder an idea of common construction details that will serve if the designed method cannot be followed for some valid reason. There is no good reason for complicated centerboard trunk construction. Except in large craft, the strains set up on the case, when sailing, are not very great. The centerboard is usually rectangular in shape and is pivoted at its lower forward corner. The lanyard is attached to the after part of the top of the board. This type of board is undoubtedly the best when strength and durability are important. It is sometimes built of a single plank when the boat is small. If this is called for in the plans, put a drift bolt through from top to bottom, edgewise, at the fore and after ends. This will prevent the board from warping. If the board is large, it is best constructed when the planks that form it are narrow. These may be edge-bolted as each piece is set in place, then through-edge bolts driven at each end of the board, top to bottom. The drift bolts can be quite small in diameter; a board 1½ inches thick should be fastened with ⅜-inch diameter, wrought-iron rod, galvanized. The hole for leading these drifts should be about $\frac{5}{16}$ or $\frac{11}{32}$ inch in diameter. The diameter of any edge bolt should not be greater than one third the siding of the smallest timber fastened. This is a rule that applies in all deadwood and keel fastenings. Other proportions will be given later.

The lead ballast for the board should be near the lower after corner; a square or rectangular hole is cut through the board to receive it. The lead can be held in place by nails or spikes driven around the inside of the hole before the lead is poured. A better finish is to chamfer the sides of the hole on both sides of the board, to form a V-section all around the edges of the hole. The lead is poured into the hole with the board laid on its side and level, after the bottom or underside of the hole has had a plank tacked over it. If the ballast casting is large, paint the board and edges of the hole with water glass (such as used for preserving eggs, etc.) to prevent burning. Pour the ballast in one operation; this requires the whole amount of lead to be melted at one time.

The pivot bolt must be bored so that the board will swing in its case properly. The plans should show where the bolt is placed. A heavy board should have a bushing for the pivot bolt, secured to the board. A very fair iron bushing can be made of two pipe flanges, having the flanges let into the board on each side. Bronze bolt and bushing are the highest specification. Wrought-iron bolt and pipe flanges, galvanized, are the next best. The bolt should be fitted with washers, one on each side of the board and one on each side of the case. A lock washer may be used under the nut as the bolt may have a tendency to turn. This is sometimes overcome by using a carriage bolt; the head is covered by a wooden cleat set in white lead or wicking and secured to the case with screws. The nut may be covered in the same manner.

The lanyard is secured to the board by an eyebolt, or screweye, when the board is small and light. When the board is heavy, two straps, one on either side of the board, and through-fastened, are required. The straps may be made of flat-bar, galvanized wrought iron or bronze. If no drill press is available, a breast drill and high-speed, round-stock twist drills will serve to bore holes in metal. The straps should be let into the sides of the board so that they are nearly flush. The length of the straps should be sufficient to permit the lower through-fastening to pass through the plank next below the top one of the board, at least. The top of the straps should stand high enough above the board to give room for a bolt and shackle, or bolt and splice.

If the board is very heavy, the lanyard should be of chain. If extremely heavy, the board should be fitted with an iron rod in place of a lanyard; this is split and welded to form an eye for the bolt in the straps at the top of the board. The rod may be jointed by use of an eye-in-an-eye, if necessary. In some small craft the board is not ballasted, so the rod is not only used to raise the board but is also used to force the board down. Some arrangement is made to hook or lock the handle of the rod when the board is down. One very common way of doing this is to form the handle of the rod in a narrow V shape that will jamb in the case but which will be knocked loose and out if the board touches bottom. When a heavy board is built, it is a good idea to put in a lifting eye on top, at the forward end; this will give something to secure a tackle to, in hoisting out for inspection or repairs. Sometimes the ends of the board are cleated to cover the end grain. The lower and after edges of the board are tapered and faired to ease the flow of water. The lower edge is made full and round, the after edge fined off to about half the thickness of the board. In a large, heavy board the fairing of the after edge is said to increase its life and durability.

## Dagger Boards and Other Types

Small craft are sometimes fitted with "dagger boards." These are blade-shaped boards without pivots, to be lifted out of the case when not in use. They are usually made of one or two planks; in either case edge bolts are driven fore and aft. The top of the board is fitted with stops which rest on top of the case when the board is in position, and so support it. A handle is usually cut in the top of the board for convenience in lifting it out. This type of board should be heavily ballasted. The board should have a marked slope or "drag" to its bottom profile, deep aft and shallow forward, so it will rise if it touches bottom. If the bottom of the board is not rounded, it is common practice to finish it off with a fore-and-aft cleat. The forward, or "leading," edge below the keel should be slightly tapered and rounded; the after, or "trailing," edge should be fined down and faired thin in the well-known streamline form.

In recent years designs have appeared with centerboards shaped somewhat like the letter L, or inverted T. The upright arm of these boards is used to form a lever by which the board is raised and lowered; the lanyard is attached to it. In L-shaped boards, the arm may be fore or aft in the case. The blade of the board in these types is under the cabin floor. The obvious advantage of such designs is that only a short case is required for the arm of an L or inverted T board and so cabin floor space can be utilized to the best advantage as far as joiner arrangement is concerned.

There is one serious disadvantage to these boards, however; their cases are hard to keep tight and form excellent nests for worms and a breeding place for marine growth. Since the greater part of the case must be closed, inspection is practically impossible except by hauling out the boat and dropping the board. These boards seem more likely to wring and twist than the rectangular shape. Metal boards are sometimes employed; they are satisfactory in small craft but much less so in large boats. This is because the metal board is easily bent when touching bottom, particularly when the boat is large enough so that the jammed board will not lift the hull.

## Size of Fastenings

The fastenings used in the board may be worked out by rule if no specification is given in the plans. The through-edge bolts used in the ends of the board, and the drifts, should not be less than one eighth or more than one third the thickness of the board; the diameter of the pivot bolt is one half the thickness of the board.

## Pivot Bolt

The location of the pivot bolt should be governed by the plans, of course. However, one observation must be made. The pivot should be high enough in the board and case so that the board will not be able to swing out of the case, and slot, if the lanyard should break. If the pivot is low—say, in the keel outside of the rabbet—the board will not only swing down and forward so far

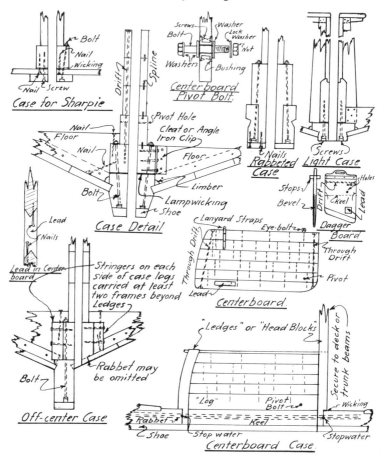

37. *Centerboards and Cases*

that it will be entirely out of the slot, except for a small triangle at the forward end, but will also swing slightly across the slot and jam. In this condition the boat will neither steer nor handle and the captain-owner has an exciting but unpleasant time. The old rule of thumb for placing the pivot was one sixth the length of the board from the fore end and from the bottom of the center-board.

## Centerboard Case Construction

The case is undoubtedly well detailed in the plans, but the cut (page 156) shows the most common methods of fitting. Light cases, such as used in sailing canoes and dinghies, are made of two thick planks fitted to the top of the keel; these are the "case logs." They are secured to the keel by long screws, lampwicking or flannel, well soaked in paint, having been put between the keel and the logs. The endpieces, or "ledges," or "head blocks," are run through the slot to the bottom of the keel; usually the tenon so formed is about half the fore-and-aft width of each ledge timber. This stiffens the case and protects the open grain of the keel at each end of the slot. The tenon may be carried flush to the bottom face of the keel, but if there is a shoe or rubbing strip the bottom of the tenon should be covered by this member. The case sides can be made of thin plank or waterproof plywood, rabbeted into the top of the logs. At the ledges the sides of the case run by, or lap, and are generally through-fastened. The sides may be stiffened by vertical cleats or braces; these are screwed to the outside of logs and case sides. The floor timbers lap over the top of the keel and butt against the case logs. They should be secured to the case cleats; the latter's location can be decided by this. The top of the case can be stiffened by a fore-and-aft seat which can be nailed to the top of the case sides and supported by the top of the case-side cleats. If there is no seat the top can be stiffened with fore-and-aft battens, if necessary.

## Rabbeted Case

If the board is large and the keel is wide enough, the "rabbeted case" is very sound construction. In this the logs are rabbeted deeply enough so that the inside half of each extends through the keel to the shoe. This requires a very wide slot, of course, and should never be used if the keel is going to be severely weakened by it. When the logs are rabbeted in this manner, the shoe is spiked to both keel and logs, where possible, and the logs are through-fastened to the keel with carriage bolts. Wicking is placed in the rabbet, at the top of the keel, where the fastenings pass through the log and keel.

## Common Construction of Case

In flat-bottom craft the rabbeted logs can be used to advantage. It is common, however, to use fairly thick logs resting on top of the cross planks of the bottom, with wicking or flannel soaked in paint between. The bottom planks are nailed to the log, and the shoe through-bolted through bottom planks and log, or screw-fastened in the same manner. The head blocks or ledges usually tenon into the slot the depth of the bottom plank. The same general plan is used for building a case on a batten keel, substituting the batten for the bottom plank in the description. This is the construction generally used in all cheap boats, flat-, V-, or round-bottom. The bolts in the logs are carried through the logs, so that the nuts are exposed on top. When the case springs a leak under the log, a few heaves on the nuts with a wrench will tighten the seam. The through-bolts should have heavy washers under head and nut and should be spaced reasonably close together—say, not over a foot in a 30-to-40-foot hull. In a small boat they may be spaced as closely as 6 inches.

## Securing Floor Timbers to Case or Keel

In the usual centerboard hull, the case logs not only are secured to the keel but also are used to secure the floor timbers to the keel. This is done by notching the floors over the top of the log and spiking, or cleating (or clipping), the end of each floor to the outside face of the logs. It is apparently not necessary to make such fastenings extremely strong, probably because the planking, when in place, tends to force the floors inward against the logs. Screws, spikes, or nails are therefore considered adequate for securing the floor timbers to the case logs.

## Head Blocks, Luting

The head blocks need not be rabbeted or splined for the sides of the case. There is sufficient surface to ensure a tight joint by putting the case together with wet paint or other material in all joints and seams. This is called "luting" and many things may be substituted for wet paint: hot tar, marine glue, or the standard luting mixture. This last is made by using the following formula (the quantities are by volume): to one part of putty add one-half part white lead. Mix until streaks disappear. Add a few drops of linseed oil and work, adding more oil if necessary, until the mixture has the consistency of heavy cream. Then add a very small amount of "turps"; better, merely sprinkle with enough red lead to turn the mixture a very faint pink when well mixed. This will not harden entirely when applied to the surfaces of a joint. Luting is applied to the inside of all joints in a boat; these surfaces are known as "faying surfaces" and, as a result, the act of luting is called "faying." Hot tar, or pitch, is sometimes used for the same purpose, but is annoying to handle.

## Bracing the Case

The forward head block or ledge should be well secured at the top; if possible, it should be carried up to the deck or cabin roof beams. Should it happen to fall between two beams a locking block, formed with a socket to take the ledge end, is required. The after ledge does not need to be extended above the top of the case.

## Cases for Large Boats

Large and heavy centerboard cases should have the sides made up of rather narrow stuff, which should be edge-bolted as set in place on the logs. The tenons at the bottom of the ledges are cross-bolted through the keel athwartships. If possible, stopwaters should be worked in. The ledges should be of white oak if possible. It is common to find the first strake of the case sides, above the logs, somewhat thicker than the next above. This need be done only when the logs are on the light side, due to the narrowness of the keel.

## Off-Center Case Construction

If it is necessary to place the centerboard and case off center, along the side of the keel, the log is usually doubled on the side away from the keel; the doubling piece is carried well fore and aft of the case and is notched over each intervening frame; these are fastened to the doubling from below, prior to planking. The doubling is spiked or screwed to the case log, athwartships. The floors usually lap over the top of the doubling and log and are fastened through the lap. The inner log may be doubled to give a better fastening for the floor timbers along that side of the case. In any case the inner log is through-bolted to the keel. When the centerboard drops alongside the keel there is no rabbet cut along the slot, in the side of the keel toward the board. Sometimes a rabbet is cut in the bottom of the outer log (outboard of the keel) to take the planking instead of merely lapping with the plank. The head blocks are carried to the outside of the planking and their outboard ends are metaled to protect the open grain of the tenon formed. It is usual to back up the head blocks fore and aft of the case, with filler blocks fitted between the extensions of the log-doubling timbers, for the length of one frame; these should be well luted. Sometimes these blocks are really a padding between the notch of the heel tenon of the head blocks and the planking; they are then notched into the ends of the case logs inside of the doubling pieces.

## Rudder Construction

The rudder should be made up of narrow stock if too large to be made of a single plank. The pieces making up the rudder are first shaped to the profile struck off in the loft plans and then edge-bolted together with drifts. The stock is first made, then the first plank drifted to it, then the next is added. If there is only one plank in the rudder, it is still desirable to drive a couple of edge bolts to prevent splitting and warping. Sometimes the planks making up a rudder are notched close to the edge of the blade to avoid feather edges. Many rudders having a more or less straight bottom are cleated there to cover the end grain. Outboard rudders usually have tillers; these either pass through the rudderhead by means of a hole formed by cheeks through-fastened on each side of the head, or the head passes through a slot in the tiller, which is riveted at each end of the slot to prevent splitting. Sometimes a metal sleeve is formed over the rudderhead to form a socket for the tiller. Outboard rudders are usually hung to an outside sternpost, or to the sternpost and transom, with pintles and gudgeons. A screw, or through-eyebolt, is used in place of a gudgeon in the transom of some boats. The bolt on which the rudder pivots, if there is no pin on the pintles, is made in a number of ways. Individual bolts are sometimes used, but the best practice is to use a long pin going through all the pintles and gudgeons; this will allow the rudder to rise without destroying the blade or the pivoting arrangement. The top of this long pin, or rod, may be finished in an eye or bent and stapled into the top of the post or transom, after being bent in a hook. If there is a propeller close to the rudder a stop must be fitted to prevent the blade from fouling the wheel. This can be made of two oak blocks, beveled so that their after face is approximately 35–45 degrees to their base. One of these is placed on each side of the sternpost, with the blade of the rudder confined by their beveled faces. They should be located close to the water line, parallel to it, and well fastened. It is usually necessary to locate them below the water line.

## Rudder Braces

The pintles and gudgeons, sometimes called "rudder braces," are made of bronze, or wrought iron galvanized. The pintle, properly speaking, has a pin which enters the female gudgeon and forms the pivot. However, it is common to call a brace on the rudder the "pintle" and one on the sternpost the "gudgeon," even though they are actually made from the same pattern. Pintles and gudgeons are let in flush in rudder and post. They are throughbolted except when the end fastening of a gudgeon is in the planking; there a large screw is driven.

## Rudderstock Types

Rudders are built with wooden or metal stocks when in the inboard position. In this case the stock passes through the counter or stern overhang by means of a built-up trunk of wood or a metal tube. Wooden-stocked rudders are usually built when the vessel is large. Metal-stocked rudders are used for sailing yachts and powerboats as a rule.

## Wooden Stocks

The wooden-stocked rudder is made with the stock running the full length, in one piece, from rudderhead to the heel of the blade. Where the stock passes through the counter it is round; below the counter it tapers quickly to the upper pintle. Below the upper pintle the stock is shaped so as to be part of the blade. The center line of the stock in the counter is in line with a center line passing through the pins of the rudder pintles. This makes the round portion of the stock offset ahead slightly, in relation to the forward edge of the blade. The pintles are so placed that the

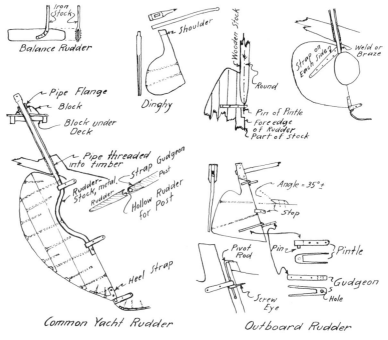

38. Rudder Details

center line of the pins of the pintles is either in line with the forward edge of the rudder blade or very close abaft it. As a result, it is necessary to notch the forward edge of the blade to receive the pintles and to permit them to be engaged with the gudgeons. This notch is made long enough, vertically, so that the rudder can be lifted the height required by the pins in the pintles to pass over the top of the gudgeons before the pintle pins drop into the holes in the latter.

To keep the rudder from being lifted out accidentally, after being shipped, it is "locked" by means of a block inserted in one of the notches so as to fill the space between the bottom of the notch and the underside of the gudgeon. This block is held in place by a screw driven slantwise into either side of the blade, through the block. The lock is usually in the top notch if there are two sets of braces, in the middle notch if there are three and the boat is deep. It should be easily reached from the ground when the boat is on the railway. The forward edge of the rudder blade is beveled on each side to allow the rudder to swing without binding its edge against the sternpost. The latter is sometimes beveled slightly to match the rudder. The forward edge of the rudder blade at its center line (inside the bevels) should be close to the sternpost, not over $\frac{5}{8}$ inch in a large vessel.

The building of this class of rudder proceeds as follows: the stock is made up as to shape, then the first plank of the blade is shaped and drifted to the stock, then the next. When the blade is completed, the rudder is fitted with the pintles and the necessary notches cut. Then the fairing of the trailing edge and the beveling of the forward edge are finished and the pintles fastened in place. It is important to regard the following points in building this type of rudder: the weakest place is just above the upper pintle where the rudderstock tapers from the round to the blade very quickly. There should be room for two drifts without cutting away the wood to a dangerous degree. In other words, the blade should run up on the after side of the stock so that its top is as close as possible to the bottom of the counter and yet permits the blade to be lifted out. Care must be taken in selection of the proper width for the stockpiece and in cutting the notches for the pintles. The latter must not cut through the stockpiece; in fact, it should not be deeper than half the fore-and-aft width of the stock in the blade section. The top of the sternpost must be hollowed to take the offset of the round portion of the rudderstock.

## Metal Stocks

Power craft usually have a wooden or metal rudder blade fitted to a metal stock. In high-speed motor craft the blade and stock are usually in a unit, cast of bronze. In cheaper and slower boats the blade is made of a metal plate inserted in a slot cut in the bottom of the stock and secured with rivets or by welding. The stock may be of galvanized wrought iron or of steel, but the best is bronze, of course. Both types of plate rudders usually have a small amount of area forward of the center line of the stock; they are called balance rudders for this reason. In workboats and sailing craft the balance rudder is usually made with a plank blade and metal stock. The stock is bent aft on each side of the blade to form a lever. In sailing craft the blade for this type of rudder can usually be made of a single plank. The stock runs through a tube in the counter. The balance rudder can be fitted outboard; its construction and hanging follow the usual practice for outboard rudders.

## Metal Stock Construction

The metal-stocked rudder is generally made with a Tobin bronze stock, though iron is used on rare occasions. This is bent to shape, if required to pass around a propeller aperture, and the head is squared to take a tiller or quadrant. It is then bored for rudder-blade bolts. The sternpost is hollowed on its after edge. The forward edge of the rudder blade is also hollowed for the length of the stock; if the latter does not run to the heel of the blade, the forward edge is rounded to fit the hollow of the sternpost below the stock. The planks forming the blade are then fashioned and edge-bolted, the piece nearest the stock being prepared first and the others fastened to it in the usual manner. The whole assembly is then bored to match the stock and through-riveted or through-bolted. The heel of this form of rudder may be fitted with some form of pintle casting, with a gudgeon to match on the post. The gudgeons are mere straps passed around the stock through small slots cut in the fore edge of the wooden blade, aft of the stock. These straps are passed and secured after the rudder is shipped. They are through-fastened in the sternpost. If castings are required, the designer may be able to furnish them or refer the builder to some foundry having patterns. If this is not possible, a pattern must be made; this is a job for a professional patternmaker. In shallow hulls the metal stock is sometimes short and the blade is steadied by a heavy strap passed around the stock, riveted, and brazed, or made as a casting and fitted to the bottom of the stock. If iron or steel stocks are used, the strap is usually welded and no casting made.

## Fairing Rudder Blade

Deep rudders should be well faired along the trailing edge, as a rule, but apparently this is neither necessary nor desirable in shoal rudders, if the area is properly designed with this in view. The hollow sternpost should be carefully faired and shaped so that the rudder will not bind when turned. In fitting any rudder, great care must be taken that the pintles or straps are correctly lined up and the stock is straight so that it will revolve truly on its axis. The size of fastenings in the rudder blade follows the same rule that was given for centerboards.

## Rudder Trunk

If the rudder is inboard, the tube or trunk for the stock must be prepared. The trunk used on large craft is made up somewhat like a centerboard case, in some boats. The forward head block is the sternpost hollowed for the stock, inside the counter, and an after head block is tenoned into the counter's keel (called the "horn-timber"). A hole is drilled for the rudderstock in the latter. This is carefully lined up with the post outside and is lined with a copper tube the depth of the horn-timber. The sides of the trunk are then planked fore and aft with splines or worked in with feathers. Another construction is made by fastening vertical planks on each side of the sternpost, extending a short distance aft of the after face of the latter. The sternpost is first hollowed for the rudderstock, of course. The after head block is rabbeted into the two sidepieces and all three are rabbeted into the horn-timber, at their heel. The after head block should be driven down the rabbets from above. Splines may be used instead of rabbets in the sides and after head block. There is no great difference in either form of construction, as far as any real advantage is concerned. Both may be made tight when properly fitted. The disadvantage of this form of construction is that worms and rot may destroy the trunk in time. To prevent this, some builders run a sheet-copper tube liner through the trunk; this is only necessary when the counter is so low that water is always in the trunk.

## Rudder Tube

Metal-stocked rudders require tubes, as a rule, and the construction is very simple. The tube is cut to length, to extend from a little below the tiller or quadrant to the bottom of the keel or horn-timber. The lower portion is threaded the depth of the horn-timber. A hole a little smaller in diameter than the tube is then bored, taking care to line it through the horn-timber so that the rudderstock will hang correctly when in place. When the hole is bored, the pipe or tube is then screwed into the hole. It is an excellent plan first to paint the hole or to daub it with white lead before starting the pipe. The size of the pipe is usually specified; it should be from $\frac{1}{8}$ to $\frac{1}{4}$ inch greater in inside diameter than the diameter of the rudderstock. It must be of the same metal as the stock. The head of the tube is held by deck blocks worked in between the deck beams and by a finish block shaped to the proper rake of stock and to the deck, above deck. In power craft, and those with tiller below deck, the head of the tube is held by a thwart, or plank run athwartships, at the required height. This should be notched into the frames on either side and supported by two fore-and-aft battens secured to the frames. This thwart must be well fitted and strongly secured. Sometimes a bearing or flange is placed at the head of the tube; if required, this is shown in the plans. Of course, much of this description of the fitting of the rudder and trunk or tube cannot be carried out until the boat is well under construction, but it is necessary to know how the rudder is hung and fitted now so that the work may be planned ahead.

## Mast Steps

If there are masts, and steps are required, they should be shaped, patterns made from the loft drawing being used to shape and notch them correctly. The tenon socket for the heel of the mast can be cut and drain holes bored. These should be so arranged that the socket will drain completely, when in position.

## Shaft Log

The shaft log should be shaped and bored before the keel is assembled. The following is usually the easiest method. The manner of constructing the log without boring a shaft hole has already been discussed in the lofting of this member (page 140) and requires no further reference here. If the shaft hole is to be bored, the log is first shaped and the center line of the shaft hole is carefully struck off on the timber from the template. The center line is then duplicated on the opposite side of the timber and squared across the inside and outside edges, where the shaft will enter and leave the log. Then a fore-and-aft center line is drawn on top of the log and brought to intersect the shaft line at either end, so that the exact points at which the shaft hole will enter and leave the timber are marked. A jig can then be made of two heavy battens; one of these is nailed on each side of the log, parallel to the shaft center line as drawn on the timber and a few inches below it. The hole for the shaft should be started with a single cutter auger bit in the after end of the log. Then a crosspiece is made with a notch which will support the long stock of the ship auger in correct line when boring. This should be secured to the battens as shown in the cut on page 148. If a hole is used in place of a notch, a sight line should be struck on the crosspiece. The hole for starting the boring should be a couple of inches deep. The barefoot ship auger bit, welded to a long stock or brace, can then be used to complete the boring. When boring a long hole the bit should be pulled out and the chips removed from the hole a number of times while the boring is being done. If the bit and its stock are correctly lined up there should be little trouble in getting a true hole. After boring, the hole can be reamed by using a piece of iron pipe of the right diameter and roughing its surface with saw cuts opened with a cold chisel. Another way is to heat the end of the pipe and to burn the hole out smooth. The longer the battens are extended abaft the shaft log, where boring starts, the more accurate the boring is likely to be but the longer the stock on the auger will have to be; and this, in practice, fixes the position of the crosspiece or guide.

The size of the shaft hole is governed by the shaft diameter, of course; the hole diameter should be from one fourth to one third greater than the shaft diameter, the larger hole being required if a tube is used. The tube is usually standard lead tubing, with an inside diameter about 20 per cent greater than the shaft diameter. The hole must be slightly larger than the outside diameter of the tube so that it will enter without driving, which, of course, it will not stand. The tube may be cut to length when the hole is bored;

it should be from 6 to 8 inches longer than the shaft hole so as to leave material to make the flanges. The tube is marked and then removed. The sides are split at each end, almost to the marks; usually four to six splits are made in each end. The tube is coated with white or red lead and inserted; then the flanges are formed inboard and out by carefully bending down the flaps formed by the split ends. These are secured to the timber by brass or copper tacks. Use plenty of lead under the flaps and, after bending, tap flat with a hammer so that the flange is tight and smooth. If any irregularities appear inside the tube, as a result of flanging, be sure to ream them out; they usually can be reached with a file, round or triangular, or can be pounded out with a round piece of wood and a hammer.

## Ballast Keel Casting

If there is a ballast keel to be cast, this should be done before setting up the keel. If it is necessary to have the work done in a foundry, the casting should be ordered while the loft work is being finished. The construction of a mold for a ballast keel that is rectangular in section is simple. The sides are made of two plank on edge, sprung to the taper of the keel. The bottom of the keel can be formed by a plank shaped and sprung between them, at the proper depth. The ends are completed with plank to form the end of the ballast casting. If the sides have flare, the top of the side planks will have to be trimmed straight when bent and flared to the correct shape. If the casting is large, the bottom should be supported by bearers inserted under the bottom and between the sides, of sufficient depth to reach the bottom of the sides. The top of the form can be stayed by crosspieces nailed to the top of the sides, their ends extending out 6 or 8 inches from the side planks. Sections taken from the loft floor can be used as temporary molds to check the shape. This mold should be made of green wood. If holding bolts are to be cast in place, they can be placed in the mold with heads wired to the bottom board and the shanks secured to crosspieces. The centerboard slot can be cast by putting a thick plank on edge in the mold. When ready to pour the casting, the mold is set on solid ground with top level, lengthwise and athwartships. Earth should be packed under the bottom plank, if possible.

Stakes are then driven along the sides to give additional support. A pair should be driven at each crosspiece; the latter can then be nailed to the stakes. After earth has been piled against the sides and tamped, the mold is ready for use. If the keel to be cast is under 1,000 pounds weight, the mold can be made of inch plank; if heavier, the plank should be from 1¼ to 2 inches thick. The mold can be protected against burning by painting with water glass or some of the so-called fire-resistant materials, such as whitewash or so-

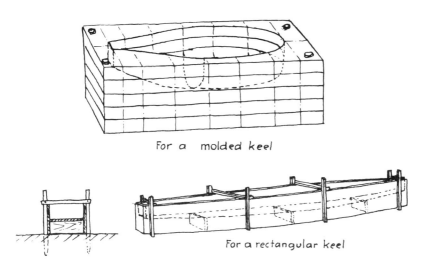

For a molded keel

For a rectangular keel

*39. Ballast Keel Molds*

dium silicate. Before pouring the metal be certain the inside of the mold is dry; no puddles or drops of water must be allowed to be in the mold. When the metal is poured the mold should be allowed to stand for a day or two, so as to cool; then the mold can be knocked apart. Care in handling the casting is necessary as it will bend easily if long and narrow.

## Casting a Molded Keel

If the keel is shaped and is small, it is possible to make a wooden mold and avoid the expense of a pattern, though the building of the mold is somewhat laborious. The mold to be described should not be attempted when the ballast casting has a length greater than 40 inches, a width of over 12 inches, and a depth of over 16 inches. To build a mold for a shaped ballast keel, the ballast casting is faired on the loft plan by water lines spaced 2 inches apart or a little less. The shapes of these water lines are then laid off on each side of a center line on a plank having sufficient width and length to give a few inches margin to the largest water line, and of the thickness required by the water-line spacing in the loft plan. The water-line shape is then sawn out, leaving a little clearance outside of the saw cut and inside the water-line shape. The planks are bolted together when all are prepared and the inside hollowed out carefully to give the proper shape to the casting. This is the reverse of the bread-and-butter method of building a model boat hull or a keel pattern. The mold should be treated as the one first described, when preparing to pour. It should be made of softwood for ease of working, white pine being the most generally used. This is one reason why the construction is unsuited to a large ballast casting. The mold must be staked and banked before pouring unless very small.

## *Foundry Work*

The melting of the lead requires some preparation. First, the lead used is not pure, but is usually impure scrap. Some of this may come from telephone or electric cables, or pipe. This is much cheaper and very nearly as heavy per cubic foot as pure lead. It is important that a small margin in excess of the proposed weight of the ballast keel be allowed when ordering the pig lead. Lead keels usually run a little heavier than estimated; allow about 3 to 5 per cent excess. If a melting pot with a spigot can be borrowed, rented, or purchased, this should be set up on a temporary brick hearth high enough for the spigot to be fed into the mold. A trough can be made of iron or brick, mortared, to carry the hot lead from spigot to mold. If the mold is long, a metal trough is necessary as it will have to be moved from time to time. Fill the pot with pigs and get a hot fire going. When the metal is completely melted, start pouring and at the same time add the additional pigs that are required to keep the pot full and to fill the mold. The new pigs will melt rapidly in the molten metal. In this way it is possible to cast a keel of large size with a rather small pot. The fire can be fed with shavings, waste lumber, or charcoal; it should be kept hot throughout the whole operation. The pouring should not stop for a period long enough for the surface of the metal in the mold to cool. As the metal runs into the mold one man can skim and puddle; most builders use a piece of green oak for puddling or stirring the metal. A skimming ladle should be used to prevent a scum from forming. The trough should be moved occasionally to be sure that the metal is going into the mold evenly and that no air pockets are being formed. If the keel is large, pouring is a four-man job.

## Foundry Work, Small Craft

If the ballast keel is small and the spigot pot is not available, the melting can be done in a small pot such as is used in brass foundries; the pouring can be done by using the tongs with which these pots are handled; a temporary crane and a chainfall are required to lift the pot from the fire and to swing it over the mold in pouring position. It is advisable to plan and try this out before filling the pot.

## Molding Sand

The use of a pattern and molding sand is usually beyond the facilities of the amateur builder. It can be done, however. The assistance of an experienced molder is the best way to learn how to handle the sand. The pattern is placed in a trough of sufficient size, with its top level with the top of the trough. Molding sand is rammed under and around it as the trough is gradually filled. When the trough is filled and the top of the sand leveled off, the pattern is lifted out and the mold formed is cleaned and patched. This requires a bit of patience and care. The ramming of the sand is perhaps the most important part of the operation. The manner of placing the pattern is the part that requires the most knowledge; a two-part mold is a foundry job. If the pattern is such a shape that it cannot be lifted out without breaking the mold, take it to the foundry. Very small ballast keels may be molded by using plaster of Paris instead of molding sand. These may be poured with a ladle.

## Ballast Bolts

In most cases it is hardly desirable to cast the bolts in place, or to try to core for the bolt holes, in a lead keel. It is easier to place the ballast keel in position and to bore from above through holes established in the keel. The boring can be done with twist drills sold as "Electricians' Drills"; these fit a two-chuck brace of the type used by carpenters. The lead can be smoothed up with a hand plane set for a fine cut. The ballast keel bolts should be of bronze if the keel is of lead, of galvanized steel if the ballast keel is of iron. The bolts should be staggered if possible, not all placed on the fore-and-aft center line of the keel. If the keel is heavy a ballast keel bolt should pass through every other floor timber, but this is admittedly open to objections. In most cruiser designs the ballast bolts are set up on the inside of the keel. If the ballast casting is of lead and the bolts of bronze, then there should be lead grommets, or washers, under the head and nut of each ballast bolt. If the ballast casting is of iron and the bolts of steel, grommets of calking cotton well soaked in paint should be used in place of lead. When the ballast casting is ready to be fastened to the keel, the top of the casting can be coated with hot pitch or a sheet of tarred felt, or canvas laid in wet paint can be worked in instead. This will prevent rot in the keel, in the way of the ballast casting. It is a safe rule that all large areas of metal in contact with wood should be insulated in order to prevent the rot that is likely to take place. The "sweating" of metals is the cause of a great deal of rot in keels.

## Ballast Bolts through Floor Timbers

If the design calls for bolts passed through ballast, keel, and floor timbers, there is likelihood of leakage between floor timbers and keel. This can be prevented, in most cases, by putting wicking, laid in wet paint, between keel and floor before fastening the latter in place. The keel should be well calked outside the rabbet. When the bolts pass through the floors great care is required in boring for them and they must be staggered so that they will clear the bolts that secure the floors to the keel. It is best to bore from the top of the floors downward.

When all the keel, deadwood, and backbone timbers are shaped, it is a good plan to place them on the loft profile drawing, if size and weight permit, so as to get one last check. This will show any tendency of the assembled timbers to gain or lose length, due to faulty marking or shaping.

## Assembling Keel

Assembling the backbone can usually be started before setting up the building stocks, unless the keel is very heavy or the boat large. Since most home-built craft are small, it will be assumed that the stocks will not be built until after the keel is wholly assembled. Obviously no directions are necessary as to how the timbers should go together, the loft plan and the patterns or templates having made the builder familiar with the proper setup. All scarfs and laps in the keel and deadwood must be payed with paint, white or red lead, or other luting material before being fastened. As each piece is set in place, its marks are brought to coincide with those on the adjoining timber and then securely clamped before boring for fastenings. If the fastenings are marked on the timbers from the loft plan, care must be taken to bore at the required position and angle.

## Fastenings, Drift Bolts

The fastening most commonly used in the keel is the drift bolt. This is made of galvanized wrought iron or steel rod. It is cut to the required length with a hacksaw or boltcutter. The point is then tapered on an anvil (or block of steel), cold, by blows with a light hammer. It is not necessary to make a long taper, usually less than $\frac{1}{2}$ inch being sufficient. This gives a rounded, blunt point. The boring for drifts must be done with care. The hole should be a little less in diameter than the rod. If the drift is less than 14 inches long, the hole should be bored about $\frac{1}{8}$ or $\frac{1}{16}$ inch less in diameter than the rod, depending on the hardness of the wood; if the hole is long, its diameter should be about $\frac{1}{32}$ inch less than the rod. In very hard wood, or where there is danger of splitting, it is best to bore the hole $\frac{1}{32}$ inch, or even $\frac{1}{64}$ inch, less in diameter than the rod. When the hole has been bored, a clench ring is set over it and the rod driven. Clench rings should be of wrought iron, galvanized. The cast-iron clench rings are useless, since they break when the bolt is driven home. Test the clench rings by

pounding them with a sledge hammer. Inspect a clench ring and
you will see that it has a top and bottom. The latter is flat, like a
washer. The top is crowned and countersunk for the drift-bolt
head. Be sure to set the ring right side up. Drive the drift with a
heavy hammer, using a few heavy blows in preference to many

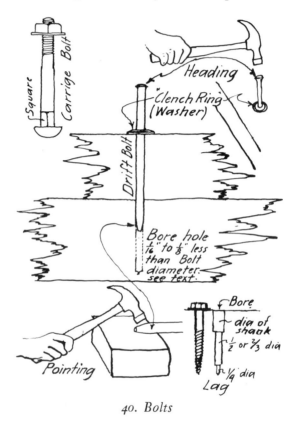

*40. Bolts*

light ones. If the first bolt drives very hard, the next can be lubricated with soft soap. If the hole for the drift is not of sufficient
diameter or not the length of the bolt, a split timber will result.
When the drift is nearly home, shape a head with a light hammer,
by tapping the edges of the top of the rod. The impact of the
sledge used in driving will usually upset the top of the rod to such
an extent that it will only require shaping. If the head mushrooms,
or breaks up, either the bolt is driving too hard or the hammer

used to drive it is too light. When the head has been shaped, the bolt is driven home with its head in the countersink of the clench ring. In order to get a neat, strong job, the clench ring must be the proper size for the rod used.

## Through-Fastening Drifts

The same method may be used in a through-fastening. This class of fastening should be used wherever possible. The drift is usually driven from the outside to the inside of the hull whenever practical. The bolt must be cut about two diameters longer than the hole, plus the two clench rings' thicknesses. This will allow for heading and riveting. The bolt is driven as previously described, headed, and driven home. Then a helper holds a heavy sledge against the head, if the fastening is short, while the point is riveted or headed over a clench ring with a light hammer or small sledge. The outboard end of a through-fastening should be countersunk and plugged.

## Copper and Bronze Fastenings, Drifts

Copper and bronze drift bolts and bronze clench rings are sometimes used. These metals do not have great holding power and are, therefore, generally used for drifts as through-fastenings. The hole for bolts of these metals should be bored to the full diameter of the rod. The impact of driving will swell the bolt and it would hang if the hole were not bored to the same diameter as the rod. Otherwise the driving of bolts of these metals is in no way different from that used for iron or steel drifts. In selecting copper or bronze rod for drifts be sure that the metal is neither too soft nor too brittle; drive a test rod into some waste timber. Annealing the rod may reduce its tendency to break up at the head and in riveting the point.

If clench rings cannot be procured, use as thick a washer as can be obtained for the required diameter of bolt.

## Carriage Bolts

Carriage bolts are also used in fastening keel timbers, particularly when the timbers are too small to drift or where there is great danger of splitting. They also are used to pull timbers together where clamps cannot be used. These bolts have crowned heads and a short portion of their shanks, under the head, is square to prevent turning when the nut is set up. They should be purchased in the proper diameter and length. The latter should be taken as the length of the hole plus about 1½ diameters, to allow for nut and washer. The hole is bored the same diameter as the shank of the bolt. It is a good plan to smear the shank of the bolt with red lead before driving it into its hole. Carriage bolts are made of galvanized steel and bronze.

## Lag Bolts

Lag bolts are really screws with a square head. Made of galvanized steel, bronze, and alloys, they require proper boring to be strong enough for a hull fastening and are not highly regarded by experienced builders. The lag should be measured before boring—the hole for the depth of the shank should be the same diameter as the shank. Three quarters of the length of the screw or thread should then be bored for, using one half or two thirds the shank diameter. The remaining length of the thread should be bored for, using one fourth the shank diameter. This is a troublesome fastening to use because of its changes in boring diameters.

## Spikes

Spikes are sometimes used in keel construction. The square-shanked boat spike is generally preferred. A measurement of a flat side of its shank is used to represent the diameter. Bore a hole for a spike about three quarters the diameter. If the wood is very hard or has a tendency to rend or split, bore a hole seven eighths the diameter of the spike. Round spikes are sometimes used and are often employed for through-fastenings. They are treated as drift bolts both in boring and riveting.

## Hanger Bolts

A hanger bolt is a form of lag bolt which has a threaded shank and nut instead of a head. Used for securing machinery and engines to their beds, it is driven by temporarily adding another nut to the one already on the bolt; this prevents the first nut from jamming, which would happen if it were used alone for a driving head. The hanger bolt must be bored for in the same manner as a lag. It is useful where it is necessary to remove a fitting without disturbing the bolt.

## Screw Bolts

Machine bolts, called "screw bolts" in some sections of the country, are sometimes used in hull construction, but more generally in securing ironwork to the hull or for machinery foundation bolts. The head and nut can be obtained either square or hexagonal; the latter is the traditional form, in some shipbuilding towns, for fastening the gammon iron and bobstay plates to the hull. They are driven in the same manner as carriage bolts.

## Rod Bolts

Another form of bolt sometimes used is made of rod, threaded at both ends. It is driven by screwing a nut on the end to be used as a head. The point is secured with a nut and washer after being driven. A variation of this is a rod threaded at one end with the head formed by upsetting the opposite end. The purpose of rod bolts is to fill a need for bolts whose required lengths cannot be obtained from standard sizes. These bolts are very good through-fastenings and are much cheaper than having carriage or machine bolts made to special lengths.

## Boat Rivets

For small craft, boat rivets can be obtained in sizes ranging from $\frac{3}{16}$ inch in diameter and 2½ inches long, to ⅜ inch in diameter and 12 inches long. These may be used as drifts or as through-fastenings, riveted. Boat rivets can be bought only of galvanized iron; their heads are crowned like a carriage bolt.

## Stove Bolts

Stove bolts are rarely used in keel construction, but are sometimes required in securing deck hardware. They can be obtained in galvanized iron or in bronze, have a head like a screw, and are designed to countersink. The nuts are square.

## Treenails

Hardwood dowels or treenails ("trunnels") are also used occasionally in keel construction, either as through-fastenings or as drifts. Locust or white oak, well air-seasoned, should be used for the treenail. The use of wooden fastenings of this type should be limited to keels in which the timber is reasonably well seasoned. The boring should be done with great care to ensure a drive fit, but not a loose one. After driving the head is cut off and then the exposed end is split with a chisel and a thin oak wedge is driven into the treenail end. As this leaves a flush head, no countersinking is necessary, of course. The point of a through-fastening is treated in the same manner. Treenail, or peg, fastening is very strong if properly done, but a careless piece of work is utterly useless. Treenails can be used in small sizes, ranging from about ⅜ inch in diameter up to 1½ inches; the smaller the diameter, the shorter the length should be, of course.

## Boring, Drawing Bolts, Driving

In boring for a long fastening in hardwood, such as oak, the auger should be greased. It must be withdrawn from time to time, to clear the hole and bit of chips. If a drift bends, or if it is found that it must be withdrawn, use two jacks and an iron clamp. The clamp is set up at right angles to the drift just under the head and the two jacks placed between clamp and timber as close to the drift as possible. If there is no room for jacks it may be possible to withdraw the drift with a claw-end crowbar or "wrecking bar" worked over a block to raise the fulcrum. If the drift is of galvanized iron and the timbers are of oak, do not let a poor fastening stand for any length of time; withdraw it at once. Otherwise it will "set" and be very hard to withdraw. Curiously enough, this is not true of copper drifts; if allowed to stand a few days they will drive or withdraw more easily if they bind. When driving a drift into a countersink it may be driven flush with a sledge and then set into the countersink with a heavy punch or spike set. A spike set should be fitted with a handle so that the holder will not be injured if the driver should miss with the sledge. As was suggested previously, it is well to lubricate all drift bolts with soft soap. Grease may be used instead, but is said to have an ill effect upon the holding power of the fastening, in some timber. Remember to stagger all fastenings; if this is not done, splitting will often occur.

## Building Stocks

When the keel has been assembled, or as much of it as can be conveniently handled, the stocks can be built. On these the hull will rest while being built. Many amateurs make unnecessary trouble for themselves in planning the stocks because of their worry about a base line. If the deadwood is properly marked with water lines and stations there is no reason for extraordinary alarm about a base line. An outside base line, that is, outside the hull, must be used, of course, to set the stocks and keel in the proper position, as shown in the lines and loft plan. Here its usefulness usually ends and an inside base line becomes important. By stretching a line inside the deadwood, at any water-line level, an inside base line is easily obtained. As there are a number of water lines it is possible to run a number of base lines, if it is found that some structure interferes with one. The advantages of this are too obvious to require explanation. There is nothing more useless than an outside base line, once the hull is planked; it cannot be used for height measurements in any practical way. Furthermore, the outside base must usually be stretched offside from the actual center line, if the hull is built right side up, and therefore it is usually out of reach for athwartship measurements. If the hull is built upside down the base line is usually on center and can be utilized to somewhat greater advantage, but once the hull is planked and righted a new base line will be required to finish the deck and cabin. It is plain that the marking of the deadwood is the only practical way that this can be accomplished with any degree of accuracy.

## Setup

The question of how a boat is to be set up—right side up or upside down—has already been discussed in the last chapter. No hard and fast rules can be laid down, but it is general practice to build a small boat upside down except when she is strip-planked. Most clench-built (lap-strake) hulls are also built right side up. The builder must follow the plan that seems best suited to the design and to the working space available. A carpenter's level is required to set up most stocks; a string level is also necessary.

## Building Horse Right Side Up

If the boat is to be built right side up and she is small and light, it is possible to build her on a horse. This is made of timber a little longer and about as wide as the keel, of sufficient depth to be stiff; it is supported by legs, sawhorse fashion. The legs should be nailed to the shop floor or to stakes driven into the ground. The spacing

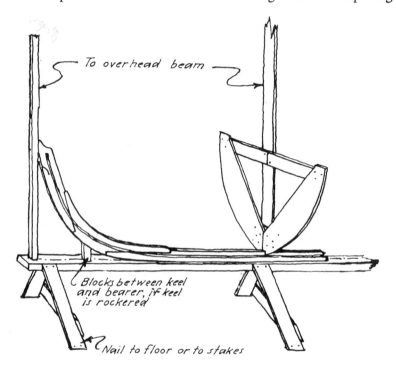

41. *Setup of Small Boat, Built Right Side Up on Building Horse*

of the legs should vary with the weight of the hull; it is usually sufficient to locate a pair of legs at each mold position. A center line is struck off on the top of the bearer and the keel set up. If the rocker of the keel is slight, blocks are set on the bearer to chock up the keel. If the keel is sprung to a long sweep, the blocks must be cut to the proper height and bevel and set at each mold station; in this case the top of the bearer must be level and straight as it will serve as a base line. If the keel is straight the bearer may be leveled, if desired, but in any case should be straight. If the bearer is not leveled, the molds can be set with a steel square from the keel or bearer instead of being plumbed. If the keel is to have drag and so is set at an angle to the base, it is best to set the bearer level and to block up the keel with blocks set at each mold station. When the keel is set in place, it is nailed or cleated to the bearer. The center line of the stem and of the sternpost or transom is then plumbed and each is stayed. These stays are of plank or scantling lumber; they are best secured to a ridgepole supported by posts driven or set in the ground to give 8 or 10 feet headroom, or secured to the roof truss of the shop. Take care to get the top of the keel level athwartships and set at the proper angle to the bearer, or to the proper curve. After all the stays are in place it is a good plan to check the bearer for level and the stem and stern for plumb. The molds will be set on the keel, cleated to the top of the keel by a block nailed or screwed to one face of the mold, and stayed at the center line to the ridgepole. The setting of the molds will be discussed later.

## Timber-bearer Stocks

If the boat has a great deal of rocker or drag, the bearer may be set to the required drag, or the top curved to fit the rocker for a portion of the length of the boat. In this case the bearer is shorter than the hull and is supported by legs, or well-braced posts, nailed to the shop floor or set into the ground. The bearer is commonly made of a piece of heavy scantling on edge, and the keel is secured to it at the ends with side cleats. The base line may be struck across the legs or posts with a chalk line, or a piece of fine wire set up with a turnbuckle may be used. The thickness of the bearer and posts is fixed by the thickness of the keel at each end of the bearer. If the boat is very heavy, posts or legs should be located at each station. The plumbing and staying of the keel are the same as described for the setup on the horse. Care must be taken to be certain that the base line is set level before measuring for cutting off the posts or legs to set the bearer at the proper angle. It is sometimes easiest to lay off the bearer and supports, as well as the base line to be used, on the profile in the loft drawing and to pick up the bearer shape from there, as well as the bevel and height of each

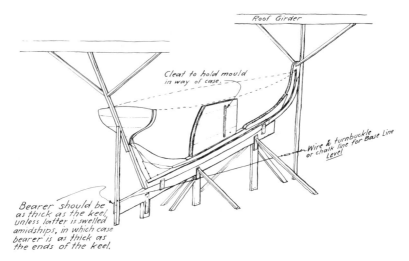

Roof Girder

Cleat to hold mould
in way of case.

Wire & turnbuckle
or chalk line for Base Line
Level

Bearer should be
as thick as the keel,
unless latter is swelled
amidships, in which case
bearer is as thick as
the ends of the keel.

*42. Setup for keel of a heavy boat built right side up in a shop.
Top of bearer under keel usually shaped to profile of keel, but blocks
on bearer will serve the same purpose.*

leg or post. If the ballast keel is not ready, or if it is to be put in
place after the boat is nearly completed, the bearer may be made
to fit the part of the keel left for the ballast casting.

## Post Stocks

Another variation of this setup is to set the keel on a series of
heavy posts. This method is often used when there is no floor in
a shop, or when the boat is built in the open. The posts are set in
the ground in a very secure manner, with the earth well tamped
around each. Care is taken to line them up carefully so that they
stand in a straight line. A level base line is struck across them and
then each may be cut off at the proper height and bevel. The spacing is usually at each mold station and at the extreme ends of the
hull. When the tops are cut off, they may be notched to take the
keel. The usual way of doing this is to use wide posts and notch
the tops alternately right and left; the keel is then wedged against
the standing side of the notch, or temporarily nailed to it. Since
most boats have some swell to the keel, however, it is usually easi-

est to saw the posts to the height of the bottom of the keel and then to cleat the latter to each post with side cleats; these are padded out from the posts, where necessary, to give sufficient breadth for the swelling of the keel. Of course, the posts may be selected to give

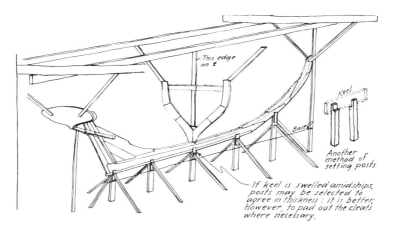

43. *Setup for a heavy boat built right side up, using posts. Common methods of bracing shown. Posts at every station used for a mold.*

the proper width at each station, if desired. The treatment chosen for these setups would ordinarily be governed by the number of boats to be built on the individual stocks. For one boat there is little value in notching, or in using posts of varying widths.

### Stocks for Large Craft

These methods of building stocks would not do for a very large and heavy vessel. In building a large wooden hull the stocks are built first and the keel is assembled on them. First, heavy oak sleepers, somewhat longer than the beam of the boat if possible, are laid on the ground. They are spaced about 6 feet apart and are laid at right angles to a center line representing the keel of the boat. Usually the ground is prepared for the sleepers by leveling and sloping at the angle required for launching. This slope is governed by the weight and size of the boat and the amount of "run" she can be allowed in launching. If there is little space or insufficient depth to permit her to run very far after launching, the slope is slight—about ⅝ inch per foot of length. Normally the declivity is about ¾ inch per foot or a little more, unless the boat is very small or light. One inch to the foot is about the maximum required under any ordinary condition. As the weight and size of a vessel increase, the declivity decreases; a 100-footer would normally be launched at a ¾-inch declivity, while a 400-footer requires only ½ inch. The sleepers are well tamped in place and occasionally staked to prevent their moving. If the ground is soft, piles may be driven to bear their weight. On these sleepers short blocks are laid in order to raise the keel a few feet above the top of the sleepers. The blocks may be cleated together, or iron staples made of ⅜-inch diameter rod, in a shallow U, about 12 inches between points and 5 inches from points to crown, are used. These are driven into the blocks with one point in each. When the blocks are all set and their tops checked to see that the keel will bear on each, the keel is placed on them and assembled. Sometimes the keel is given a little sag in the middle, if it is over 85 feet long, in order to allow for the drooping of the ends which may take place. The amount of sag is about 1 inch in a hundred feet of length. The keel is held in place by short shores nailed to its top and reaching to the sleepers. These keep the keel from capsizing while being fastened together.

The sternpost is then set up, fastened along with the after deadwood, and shored. Then the frames are usually raised as they are assembled on a temporary platform built over the keel and moved as the raised frames make necessary. The first frame to be raised is commonly the aftermost "square frame." This frame is the one farthest aft having a floor athwart the keel. Though they do not actually set at an angle to the keel, the frames which have no floors but have their heels spiked or bolted to the deadwood (even if they have a "strongback" to tie the two parts together in place of a floor timber) are still known as "cants" (see Plate 21). After the aftermost square frame is raised the others are assembled and raised one by one until all the frames are raised. Then the after cants are raised, when the square frames have been plumbed and ribbanded, and shored. The forward cants and the stem are raised last. The stem and stern are well shored after being plumbed. If there is a transom or stern frame this is generally raised with the after cants. When all the frames and cants are secured and faired

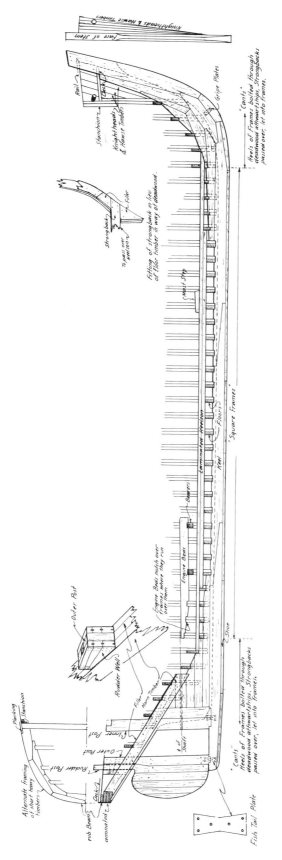

PLATE 21. *Deadwood Plan for a 75-Foot Dragger (Sawn Frames)*

with ribbands, the keelson is secured in place. This general description will be enlarged upon later. The accompanying cut is designed to show the method of setting up a large vessel and of shoring; it does not show all the frames in place nor the usual sequence of operations. As most large vessels nowadays have straight

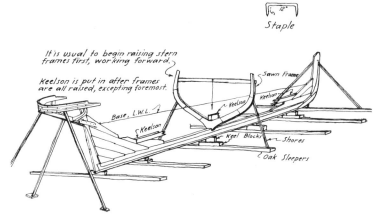

44. Setup for a large vessel built in the open, showing method of shoring, setting of keel blocks, etc. In practice, sleepers are about 4 feet apart. Keel is steadied by short shores to its sides (not shown).

keels, it is easiest to raise frames square to the top of the keel or rabbet if the design permits. Otherwise great care must be taken that the keel is set on the blocks at the angle that will allow the frames to be plumbed in position with a plumb bob or level. This sometimes causes difficulty in setting the launching ways. The appearance of the keel structure of a heavy vessel is shown in Plate 21.

## Building Horse Upside Down

If the hull is to be built upside down and it is small and light, it may be built on a horse. The stem and stern are assembled on the keel and the whole structure is mounted on the horse with the stern blocked up so that the keel is set at the proper angle to the base line; usually the latter is the top of the horse. The molds are set on the horse, between it and the keel, as shown in the accompanying sketch. Usually the molds are made long enough at the tops, above the sheer, to reach the floor when turned upside down and set on the horse. These ends serve as shores and may be toe-nailed or cleated to the shop floor, or nailed to stakes. It will be found convenient to set the cross-spalls at the base line instead of the sheer; this must be laid off on the mold loft drawing, of course,

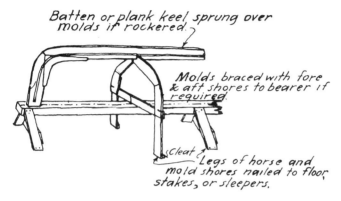

45. *Setup for Small Boat, Built Upside Down on Building Horse*

and the molds marked for sheer and base. When the molds are set in place they should be cleated to the keel and to the horse. If the keel is to be sprung to a curve the molds must be set in place, cleated to the horse, squared and plumbed, and then securely shored, after which the keel may be bent over them, shored to the ridgepole or roof—and the stem and stern secured. The horse should be built in the same manner as described for building right side up: the center line of the boat is struck off on the top of the bearer and the stations marked off.

## Building Table

If the boat is very light, and particularly if frames are used for molds, a building table makes excellent stocks. The table is made of two or more planks shaped roughly to the form of the sheer of the two halves of the boat, one of which is shown in the half-breadth plan in the loft drawing. The center line of the boat is marked and the stations located and squared off to it. Cleats are then nailed or screwed to the table top at each station to which the frames or molds will be secured. The whole structure is placed on legs or posts and securely braced. The frames or molds are made so that their tops are at the base line, which is the table top, of course. The stem and stern are set in place on the table and fastened by shores or uprights to the shop roof or ridgepole. The molds or frames are then fastened to the table and temporarily screwed to the cleats; then they are plumbed, or squared, and

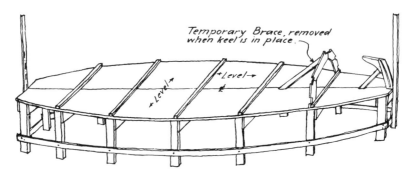

46. *Building table, suitable for very light construction. Boat built upside down. Table-top level, used for base.*

shored. Care should be taken to get the table top as straight as possible, and level in all directions along its surface, before cleating. Experience shows that it is very desirable to locate the table legs or supports at each mold station. This form of stock is very convenient when a number of boats are to be built off one design. The cut shows the appearance of a building-table setup. The molds must be prepared from the mold loft plan by setting off the base line in the building position there and building the molds accordingly.

## Building Upside Down on a Floor

If the shop has a straight, level floor, the setup may be based on it. This is shown in the sketch; the tops of the molds are made to the building base line which is established in the loft drawing. A center line is struck off on the floor and the stations marked and squared to it. The molds are then set up on each station, squared, plumbed, and shored. The tops of the molds are cleated to the floor. Some pains are necessary to get the center line of the molds plumb over the center line on the floor. This can be done by use of a plumb bob if the cross-spalls and molds are properly marked. By a little extra work in the loft drawings it is also possible to pick

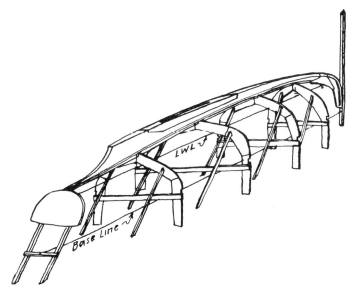

*47. Usual setup when building upside down. Molds carried to floor line; braces off center. Centerboard case not set up with keel.*

off the half-breadths of the tops of the molds at floor level (base line) and to set those off on the floor, by which the molds should automatically center correctly. Once the molds are in place, the keel is set on them and stem and stern plumbed and shored. The keel can be cleated or temporarily screwed to the molds.

## Remarks

It is very important that any setup be firmly built. Not only is the weight of the keel and molds to be considered, but also the strains caused by bending frames, ribbands, clamps, stringers, and planks. These strains are relatively great and the molds and backbone must therefore be well shored and braced. Screws and lags are often used as fastenings in building stocks and setting molds, since they can be removed without destroying timber and can be driven without impact which might disturb the setup before it is wholly fastened in place. It is very important that the molds be set square to the center line and plumb to the base line; no amount of care is too great. It is also very important that the base line, if on the supporting timbers of the stocks, be marked and referenced, as it may be necessary to remove a stretched line or wire from time to time as construction progresses. Emphatically, the keel must be laid at exactly the right curve, or slope to the base line, and the stocks must be adjusted by accurate cutting, blocking, or shimming to permit this. It is utterly useless to be accurate in the mold loft drawing and then careless in setting up. Any mistake in lining up the molds and backbone not only makes the completed boat different from the lines drawing, but also makes trouble in building; nothing fairs properly and all fitting must be done by "try and fit." This always results in a botched job.

## Setting the Molds

Setting the molds on the keel, when it is in place on the stocks, requires careful attention. Since the edges of the molds are not beveled, the molds must be set, in relation to the station lines shown in the loft plan and marked on keel and stocks, to compensate for this when the ribbands are bent into place. The sketches show how this should be done. The molds forward of the point of greatest beam in the hull should be set so that their forward face is on the station line. Those abaft the point of greatest beam should be set with their after face on the station line. These faces of the molds are now the planes used for the sections in the loft body plan. When the ribbands are bent into place around the molds they will touch only on the faces or edges representing the body plan sections in the loft drawing, as will be seen by inspection of the sketches. This is a very important matter and neglect of this precaution will cause unfairness in the hull, or a lot of trimming or "dubbing" of the molds; either will result in a hull whose lines are different from the design, not only in appearance but also in behavior when under power or sail, compared to a boat built correctly.

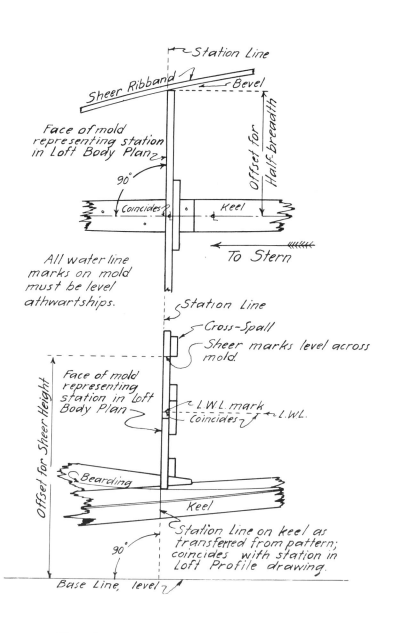

Station Line

Sheer Ribband

Bevel

Face of mold
representing station
in Loft Body Plan

90°

Offset for Half-breadth

Coincides?

Keel

To Stern

All water line
marks on mold
must be level
athwartships.

Station Line

Cross-Spall

Sheer marks level across
mold.

Face of mold
representing
station in Loft
Body Plan

L.W.L. mark

Coincides

L.W.L.

Offset for Sheer Height

Bearding

Keel

Station Line on keel as
transferred from pattern;
coincides with station in
Loft Profile drawing.

90°

Base Line, level

48. How Molds Must Be Set, Aft of Station Having
Greatest Beam

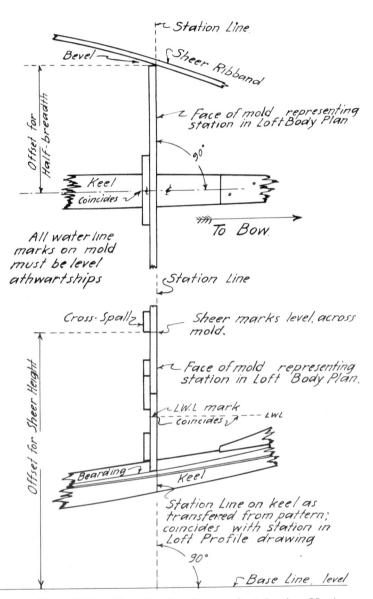

All water line
marks on mold
must be level
athwartships

49. How Molds Must Be Set, Forward of Station Having
Greatest Beam

It is also very important, in setting the molds, to check heights of the sheer against those in the loft drawing. If there is variation it may be necessary to trim the notch for the keel in a mold, or to shim one up. Theoretically, the bottom of a mold should coincide with the bearding line on the keel; but as the bottom of a mold on each side of the keel may end in a long, thin point, which is easily broken or splintered in making or handling, it is not safe to use the bearding line of the rabbet as a reference line. The mold at the greatest beam in a hull is usually set with regard to the bevels formed at the lower water lines. In most cases either the forward or after face may be set to the station line at will, as there is practically no bevel required by the ribbands at this station. Occasionally, however, this is not the case because of what is known as a "raking midsection" in the design. This can be observed by noticing the relation between the points of greatest beam on each water line in the half-breadth plan in the loft drawing. It may be seen that there is no bevel required at the midship mold in the topsides, but below the load water line some bevel is required. Hence the mold should be set so that the face on the station will not require dubbing, when ribbanding. In most hulls having a raking midsection the mold at the point of greatest beam on deck is set with its forward face on the station line.

## Stopwaters

Now that the molds are set in place, the next step is to drill and drive the stopwaters in the keel, if this has not already been done. Stopwaters should be made of white pine or cedar, from ¼ to ½ inch in diameter, and may be purchased as dowel stock from a woodworking mill. The dowels must be cut to length and should be long enough to pass through the keel or deadwood, with a little to spare. Holes are then drilled in the joints and scarfs in the deadwood and keel as described in the chapter on lofting. The stopwaters should be a drive fit in these holes, the ends cut off after driving. It may be well to repeat that a stopwater should be driven in every scarf and butt in keel, stem, and stern, the seam of which passes through the rabbet line. The stopwaters are all located in the rabbet, between the outer rabbet line and the bearding line. If possible, two stopwaters should be driven in every such butt and scarf.

## Ribbands

Ribbanding may now be done. The first step is to cut some battens for these. Yellow pine, green spruce, or fir are generally used for ribbands. For small craft, with light frames and with molds spaced not over 36 inches apart, the ribbands should be from 1¼″ x 1½″ to 1½″ x 2″. In larger hulls, where the molds are spaced 4 feet or more apart, the ribbands should be from 1½ by 2 inches to 2 by 2½ inches. In boats over 40 feet long the ribbands are from 2 by 3 inches to 2 by 4 inches. It is a good plan to make many of the ribbands tapered toward one end and a few tapered toward both ends. There is no rule for spacing the ribbands on the molds. In a small boat the ribbands are usually spaced from 6 to 10

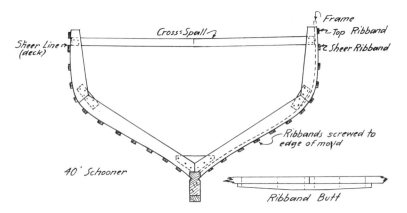

50. *Common method of ribbanding molds. Frame bent to inside of ribbands.*

inches apart; on a 40-foot hull the spacing ranges from 10 to 12 inches. However, much depends upon the shape of the hull. For the moment, the foregoing will serve to estimate the number of ribbands that will be required. If it is not possible to get ribbands in one length they may be scarfed, or butted and spliced. The scarf should be vertical when the ribband is on the hull. The splice is easier to make. The splicing strip is made of a ribband of the same size as the two being joined and is on the top or bottom of the ribband when it is in place. It is usual to begin ribbanding the hull at, or close to, the sheer. If possible, one ribband should be so placed that its top is the sheer line if the hull is right side up, its bottom if the hull is upside down. In a small boat the ribband should be the same size as the rest, but in large hulls, 40 feet long and over, it will be found helpful to make the sheer ribband a little wider than the rest.

When a ribband is in place on one side, put up the one on the other side of the hull, as ribbanding one side of a hull will pull the molds out of line and plumb. When the two sheer ribbands are in place, put up the next two, which should be above the sheer, then the next below the sheer, and then on down. The spacing already suggested can be used as a guide, with these qualifications. Ribbands can be more widely spaced where the molds show that the hull sections have little curve. At the turn of the bilge, however, or wherever else a quick curve appears, the ribbands should be more closely spaced. If the ribbands run too close together at the ends of the hull they may be stopped on a mold short of the stem or stern, in places where there is little fore-and-aft curve. Splices or scarfs in the ribbands should be brought to sections where there is little fore-and-aft curvature also. At the top of the transom let the ribbands run a few feet abaft the transom and tie each pair together athwartships with a short length of rope outside the stern. This will require a little judgment, but it is desirable in order to produce fair curves in the ribbands, between the aftermost mold and the transom. It is necessary to spring the ends together a little before tying them; the amount of spring required can be found by not fastening the ribbands at the aftermost mold and transom. When sprung enough the ribbands will not only bear on the transom, but also on the aftermost mold, without being drawn up to it with fastenings. At the stem and sternposts the ribbands will serve to check the rabbet; if not completed the rabbets may be cut a little to permit the forward ends of the ribbands to end fair in the rabbet against the bearding. If there are quick curves in the hull, the tapered ribbands will permit bending to the required curve without breaking.

In rare cases it will be found necessary to use laminated ribbands to avoid breakage. The best way to fasten ribbands to the molds and to stem and stern is to use oval-headed screws, or lag screws if size permits, with washers under their heads—one fastening at each station. Usually it is best to fasten a ribband amidships and then to work toward the ends, fastening as the ribband bears on the mold (except near the top of the transom, where the ribband ends may be tied in pairs). It is usual to spring the ribbands a little up or down as they are bent into place to hold to a more or less regular spacing at the ends of the hull, but the ribbands should not be forced so much as to bring heavy strains on the molds, tending to lift them from the keel or stocks. The most common error in ribbanding is to space the ribbands too far apart in the hollows of the hull, near the counter and along the rabbet of the keel near the sternpost. This mistake will break frames that must bear on these ribbands, when forced to the sharp bend usually required there. A ribband should be located so that it runs through the sharp hollow that is formed at the junction of the bottom of the counter or stern with the sternpost. Ribbands against which frames will bear when being bent, such as in the "tuck" just mentioned, and along the keel when there is hollow in the sections, should be rounded on the inside to prevent their sharp corners from cramping the frame and breaking it by a cutting action. This is often neglected and is one of the causes of excessive frame breakage. The ribband above the sheer on each side is a desirable feature, when bending frames, as it gives support that will prevent the frame heads from flaring out while they are cooling after being bent in place. In some boats having rather straight sides they may sometimes be omitted. If the molds are of softwood—white pine, for instance—it may be noted that the ribbands are crushing the edge of the molds on which they bear. To prevent this, make some hardwood wedges and force them between ribbands and mold from the face of the mold that does not touch the ribband. This will give the ribband a better support and prevent the crushing of the sharp edge representing the section, by transferring some of the load to the whole edge of the mold. Be careful not to drive the wedges enough to force the ribband away from the mold, however.

If a ribband or other timber requiring great bend has a tendency to break, it is sometimes better to bend it from amidships to the ends at once, and clamp into place, before driving any fastenings, rather than to bend and fasten simultaneously. Lags can be driven with a socket wrench fitted to a brace. The ends of ribbands in the rabbet of stem and sternposts should be secured with screws. If the bow is full on deck, the ends of the ribbands in the rabbet of the stem may be held by cleats nailed or screwed to the sides of

the stem outside of the rabbet, to permit some movement in the ribbands when filling out the deck line, by inserting a staff between
the upper ribbands. If it is not possible to fair out the bow between
the stem and foremost mold in this way, an additional mold will
have to be laid off in the loft plan and made to fill the hull form
out at this place. It may be necessary to make an additional mold
between the transom and the aftermost mold, given in the offsets,
for the same reason. The curves formed by the ribbands must be
fair and they must rest on every mold that they cross. If they do
not, a mistake has been made in either the loft plan or in the setup.
If the spacing of the ribbands at one end of the hull becomes too
great at any one place, and if it is undesirable to spring the ribbands
toward one another, then put in a short ribband at least three
mold spaces long. Ribbands made too small will produce an unfair hull when the framing is in; ribbands too large will force molds
out of line.

## Ribbands Inside of Frames

The most common method of applying ribbands is to place
them on the edges of the molds as just described. In building upside down, however, it is sometimes easier to use a different plan.
With the ribbands put on as previously described, the frames will
be bent on the inside of the ribbands and this requires working
from inside the hull. The other plan is to bend the frames outside
the ribbands and thus be able to work from outside the hull. To
do this, the molds are notched to the depth of the ribband plus
the thickness of the frame, as shown in the cut. The molds are also
notched for sheer and bilge clamps or stringers in the same manner. The sheer clamp is located from the loft drawing and its
notch cut, but the bilge stringer and ribband notches are cut by
bending these members in place and holding them with nails or
clamps, marking where they cross each mold, removing stringer
or ribband, and cutting notches. It is possible to clamp a ribband
to a mold when the clamp will not reach to the inside of the mold
timber by screwing blocks to either the fore or after faces of the
molds. Care must be taken in notching molds to allow the depth
of the ribband plus frame thickness, so that the outside of the
frames (when bent) will be in the correct position in relation to
the edges of the molds. The notches are not beveled and the molds

are set on station lines as previously described, to allow for the omission of the bevels. The advantages of notching the molds are greatest when the hull is built upside down, but occasionally it is desirable to apply this system to a hull built right side up. The only serious disadvantage is that the molds must be completely pulled

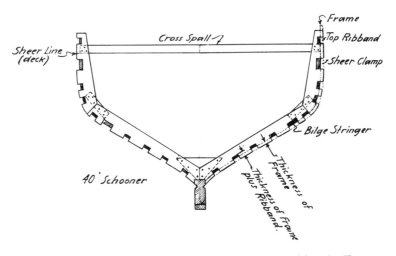

*51. Mold Notched for Clamps, Stringers, and Ribbands; Frames Bent from Outside of All*

apart and the ribbands sawn in two in order to remove them. If a heavy sheer clamp or bilge stringer is required, however, this system works very well and the setup is very strong when the ribbands are in place. It is claimed that building in this way is excellent when the frames must be given very hard bends at garboard or bilge.

## Keel Types, Flat-Bottom Hulls

The general methods for setting up and ribbanding a hull have been discussed. The various classes of keel construction now require attention, as there are certain problems inherent in each type which have some bearing on the methods of assembling or of setting up. The keel structure of most large flat-bottom hulls is made of plank on edge. If there is a centerboard the keel is made of two members running the full length of the structure, with a filler between that is cut in the way of the centerboard slot. The two side members thus form the centerboard case logs. Very often these timbers do not run all the way to the bow, or to both bow and stern, but stop short. This is done to save weight. The side members of the keel and the timber between—the filler—may be butted if necessary. It is important that the butts be well staggered, however. This form of keel is very easy to build and is very strong. In the way of the case some care is required in fitting. This

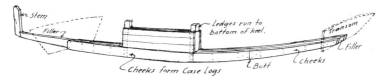

*52. Common Flat-Bottom Hull Keel; See Plate 5*

is particularly true of the case ledges. These run through the keel and to the outside of the bottom planking where their ends are covered by a rub-shoe, or plank, run fore and aft along the bottom. In a few cases the ledges are cut off at the inside of the bottom planking. Some builders drive a stopwater through the keel at the seams formed by the ledges and the filler timber, but perhaps the best way to prevent leaks is to pay the timbers of the keel and the parts of the centerboard case with luting as it is assembled. If the hull is planked fore and aft on the bottom, or is built of plywood, the keel is notched to receive the frames. Plywood hulls are sometimes designed with a temporary plank keel, built somewhat like the one just described, to serve as a template on the building stocks to hold the molds, or frames, in the correct position. This keel is really a bearer and is removed before the hull is decked.

## Keel Types, V-Bottom Hulls

Keels for V-bottom hulls vary in design. Heavy craft may have as complicated a structure as round-bottom types usually have. Plate 22 shows a batten keel for a heavy hull, cross-planked on the bottom. The skeg is merely an appendage built up of narrow stock, bolted, spiked, or drifted to the keel batten. Mast steps are made of blocks screwed or bolted to the top of the keel batten.

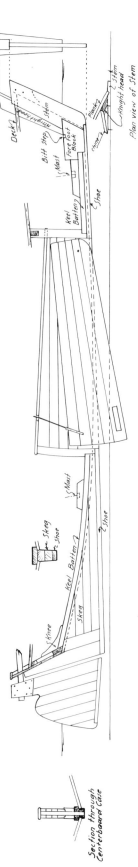

PLATE 22. *Deadwood plan for a heavy V-bottom hull, Batten keel and Skeg*

The construction is simple and cheap. Stopwaters are sometimes placed at the seams of the headledges of the centerboard case.

The methods of forming the forefoot have been discussed in the first chapter, page 40. The block method shown in Plate 22 is one of the many possible variations in construction. Since the forefoot block should be set up with the keel, the variations will be described now. The construction of the forefoot block is decided by the design of the bow and the size of the timber available. The keel batten may be notched into a single block, on which the stem is stepped in a notch or tenon in a very small boat. In a larger boat, where it is not practical to make the block of a single piece, two or more blocks may be doweled together to form the unit. In some craft having a heavy-shaped timber in lieu of a keel batten, this timber is carried to the rabbet of the stem by notching its end to receive the stem timber or by notching the latter to receive the keel. The two side blocks are doweled to the sides of the keel with oak pins and the whole is hewn to shape. The side blocks are then given additional fastenings, usually nails. This is the most common forefoot-block construction, seen in Chesapeake Bay V-bottom craft. The height of the block in these craft is fixed by the height of the bottom of the chine log. The latter is edge-fastened to the blocks. In some craft, however, the block is carried to the top of the chine logs and is notched along the sides to receive them. The disadvantage of the block forefoot is the exposure of end grain in the blocks, which eventually leads to rot.

## Knightheads and Hawse Timbers

Plate 22 shows the "knightheads." These timbers are rarely seen in small craft. They are used in large craft for two purposes: to give additional backing to the planking just abaft the stem and to add strength to the bowsprit. In most craft they may be made of thick plank, shaped in more or less of a triangle and edge-fastened to each side of the stem with spikes or drifts. Their length is decided by the shape of the bow and by the sections of the hull immediately abaft it; knightheads should be carried as low into the hull as the timber and these limitations permit. The top of the knightheads is the underside of the rail cap or the top of the bowsprit in most craft, but occasionally the knightheads are carried higher and their tops exposed. This is the old-fashioned way and has no particular advantage except tradition and perhaps appearance. Knightheads of this description are still to be seen in some Bugeyes and Skipjacks on the Chesapeake. They are inclined to rot at the top, due to the exposed end grain, unless capped with wooden blocks or sheet metal. In small craft the knightheads are usually wide enough fore and aft to take the hawseholes, or the hawsechocks. In large craft, however, additional knightheads are necessary; these are called "hawse timbers" because they back up and support the hawsehole castings or chocks. They are made of timber the same thickness as the knightheads and, like them, step against the side of the stem just above the bearding of the forefoot, or against the foremost frame. They are edge-fastened to the knightheads and to each other. Care must be taken to locate the hawseholes before fastening, so as to avoid driving a drift or spike where it will be necessary to cut the hawseholes later.

The thickness of these timbers is fixed by the thickness of the frames in the hull; the sheer clamp must run inside the knightheads and the hawse timbers to the stem, and is fastened to each. These timbers are rather troublesome to fit due to the excessive bevels required at their bottoms and where the knightheads' sides bear on the sides of the stem. They should be well luted before being fastened. In V-bottom hulls these timbers are more easily fitted than in round-bottom hulls, as they step on the top of the chine logs. There is no practical reason for fitting knightheads in a light hull, of course. They are required in power hulls that will receive hard blows around the stem, as in tugboats and fishermen. In hulls that are very full in the bow, so that there is little space between the middle line and the bearding line of the rabbet on the bow, the knightheads give a better chance to fasten the planking to the bow. However, a stem apron fitted to the after face of the stem in about the same manner as the keel batten is fitted will serve the same purpose if made wide enough. Hence the use of these timbers has been reduced to those vessels having long or heavy bowsprits, or large enough to require support to the hawse.

## Keel Types, Light Keels

Plate 23 shows the types of keels most common in small light craft, such as are usually built by home builders. The dinghy keel is made of a single timber on edge backed with a batten, or is made

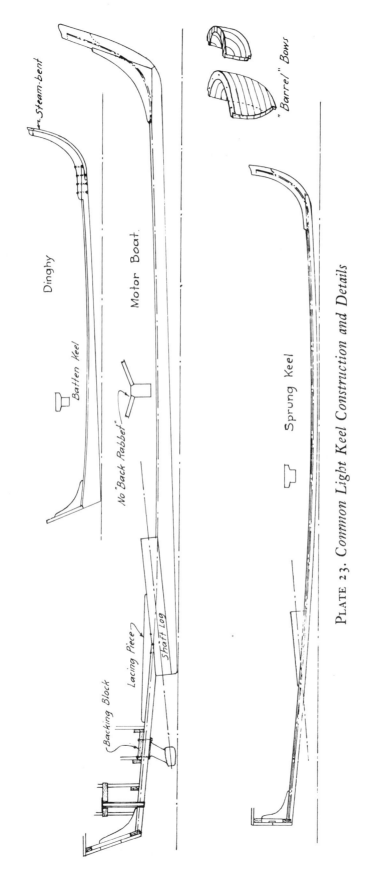

PLATE 23. *Common Light Keel Construction and Details*

"Barrel" Bows

Steam-bent

Dinghy

Batten Keel

Motor Boat

No "Back Rabbet"

Sprung Keel

Backing Block

Lacing Piece

Shaft Log

of a timber of sufficient thickness to be rabbeted. The stem is made of a hackmatack or oak knee, usually in one piece if possible. The transom or stern is secured with a knee to the top of the keel structure. Power launches and cruisers usually have similar keels, but of greater width. Because of the greater length, keels of many powerboats are scarfed; the design should show how and where. In Chapter Two the lengths for scarfing are given. However, the rule is not strictly followed as conditions in a boat keel are not those of a simple beam. The line of a scarf is usually less than 13 degrees to the top or bottom of a timber. In the deadwood, laps or scarfs are often shorter since the necessary strength is obtained by the laminations of the structure. In this part of the hull the laps or scarfs are usually made long enough to permit two or three fastenings to be driven. Laps are usually longer than scarfs in the keel as there is generally less depth of timber involved.

Lacing pieces, which are merely long butt blocks, are used where there is not enough length to form a proper scarf or lap; a lacing piece is shown at the shaft log in the motorboat keel in the plate. Struts for the shaft are usually backed by blocks if the keel is lacking in thickness or depth. In boats having garboards over 1 inch in thickness the rabbet of the keel is sometimes omitted; the top edges of the keel are merely beveled to form the bearing for the edges of the garboard and there is no backing along the keel, and no bearding, of course. This is not very strong construction theoretically, but in practice it seems to work satisfactorily in hulls that have no outside ballast casting or excessive depth of keel outside of the rabbet line. It is not advised for centerboard hulls. The sprung keel is very popular in small or light boats. It may be in one piece, rabbeted, or may be laminated with the top piece forming a keel batten. If the keel must be scarfed due to the lack of timber of sufficient length, it is better to laminate than to attempt to make a proper scarf. If it is thought that the setup will not stand the strain of bending the sprung keel shown in one piece in the plans, lamination is the obvious alternative. Put on the laminations one at a time and fasten together with screws or nails between the molds. The usual method of fitting the shaft log in this type of keel is shown in the plate. A shaft tube is desirable. Lute all joints as the keel is assembled.

## Keel Types, Heavy Keels

The keel structure of a heavy sailing cruiser is shown in Plate 24. The drawing is sufficiently complete to require little explanation. The heel of the sternpost is tenoned into the top of the keel. This is done to prevent the swelling and shrinking of the wood from opening the joint. The tenon is locked with a dowel driven athwart the keel. Usually this is of wood, but metal pins are also often used. The drawing shows the strongest method of building the horn-timber, or keel of a counter. Some designs show the horn-timber set on top of the after deadwood and drifted to it. This is a very poor method of construction as the drifts into the end grain of the deadwood do not hold well. If the design is for a sailing boat, the strains on the counter are great enough to make this method wholly unsuitable. The cheeks of the horn-timber in the plate were to be through-bolted with carriage bolts, through the deadwood. The drawing is supposed to show the whole structure, except the horn-timber, split lengthwise along the center line. The filler of the horn-timber often forms the outside keel of the counter, with the cheeks acting as the back rabbet or keel batten.

## Keel Types, Fin Keels

There are countless variations of the basic types of keel construction, but the design being built from will show the required details. There are two special types, however, that are often used in sailing craft and which differ from the types already described. One of these is the fin keel. The hull of a boat having this type of keel may have a sprung or shaped keel, in a single timber, or laminated. The fin is made up of small pieces of timber edge-bolted and there is usually a ballast casting attached. The fin is attached to the hull with long through-bolts, usually passing through keel and floor timbers. The bolts are staggered athwartships or are raked, and each floor timber takes a ballast bolt and a floor bolt opposite it. This construction is necessary because of the strains set up by the deep fin. It should be added, perhaps, that these strains are not very great when the boat is under sail, unless the vessel is large; the greatest strains are set up when the boat goes aground or is hauled out for the winter. The serious disadvantages

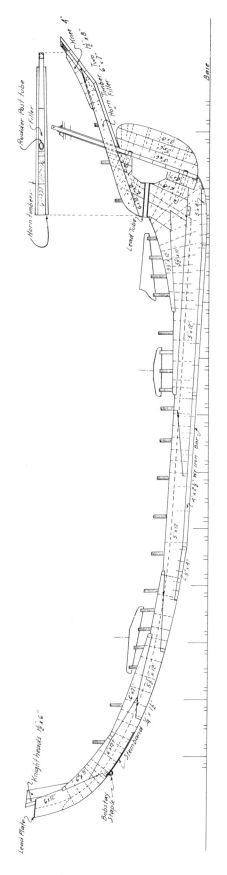

PLATE 24. *Deadwood Plan for a 41-Foot Schooner (Bent Frames)*

in bolting through the floor timbers are the difficulties in boring
the holes for the ballast bolts in correct line and angle, and in stopping the leaks that usually appear under the floor timbers. These
leaks are caused by water getting into the boltholes through the
sides of the fin and leaking into the boat through the seam between
the floor and the keel. This can only be overcome by careful fitting and proper calking.

It is very important that the keel bolts be tight fits in their holes,

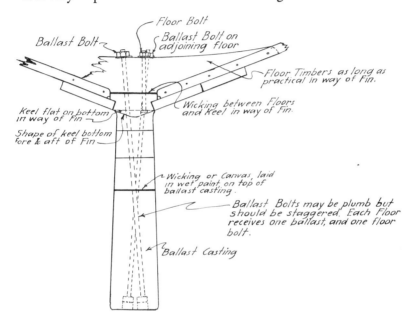

*53. Fin Keel Construction; See Text*

but due to practical difficulties in boring this is not easy to accomplish, except on paper. For that reason it is wise to place wicking
or flannel saturated with paint under each floor timber before
fastening it to the keel. The ballast bolts should have lead or cotton
grommets at head and nut, under the washers. The top of the
ballast casting is difficult to calk, so it is a good plan to put a sheet
of wicking or canvas impregnated with paint between the keel
casting and the wooden fin, before boring for the ballast bolts.
All seams in the wooden fin, and between it and the keel, should
be well calked; it is a good plan to lute the pieces making up the

wooden fin before bolting it together. The wooden fin is most easily assembled by edge-bolting the pieces together in a unit with short drifts or spikes, taking care to keep clear of the places where the ballast bolts will be bored. The heads of the ballast bolts should be well countersunk in the ballast casting and plugged with cement or lead, or even wood.

In a well-designed fin-keel hull, the floor timbers are heavy in proportion to the size of the boat and are carried out to the sides as far as is practical. The keel forward and aft of the fin is usually faired off and the fin is streamlined. In some designs the top of the fin is shaped out of thick stuff so as to fair into the bottom athwartships. This shaping will have to be done with a large gouge and a hollow plane. A template should be made for each station in the way of such a molded timber, in order that the proper shape may be cut, and both sides of the fin be alike.

There are a number of designs having metal fins, such as the well-known Star Boat. The tops of these fins have a flange which should be let into the keel until it is flush. The use of a piece of saturated canvas between the metal and wood is also important here. The fin bolts pass through the fin and keel, sometimes through the floor timbers as well. Occasionally a design is seen in which the fin is made with a metal plate without a flange; avoid these, as it is quite impossible to properly fasten such a structure.

## Keel Types, Plank Keels

The plank keel is another special type used in sailing craft. This form of keel is practical when there are very hollow garboards, the latter standing almost vertical in the midsection. If the keel is to be wide enough to allow proper fastening, the plank keel is easy to build. It is really a laminated keel, as will be seen in the sketch. Keels of this form are sometimes seen in deep centerboard hulls. The best way to build a boat having this form of keel is upside down. The molds having been set up, the inner keel is first put in place. The floors are spaced off and secured to the keel. The hull is then ribbanded and framed, and a garboard is clamped in place, its bottom cut flush with the bottom of the inner keel. After both garboards have been fitted, they are nailed in place and then the outer keel is bent and secured over the inner keel and the raw edges of the garboards. This is a cheap, strong construction and

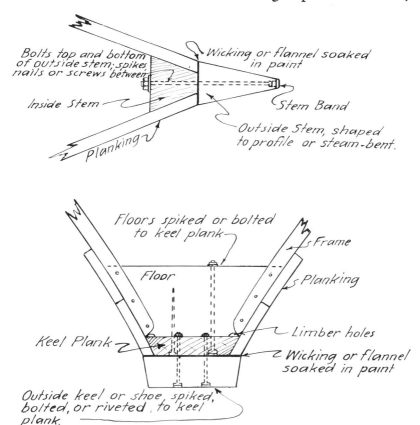

Bolts top and bottom
of outside stem; spikes
nails or screws between

Wicking or flannel soaked
in paint

Inside Stem

Stem Band

Planking

Outside Stem, shaped
to profile or steam-bent.

Floors spiked or bolted
to keel plank

Frame

Floor

Planking

Keel Plank

Limber holes

Wicking or flannel
soaked in paint

Outside keel or shoe, spiked,
bolted, or riveted, to keel
plank.

54. *Two-piece stem, and below plank keel construction used in
light hulls having "hollow garboards," either keel or centerboard, inside ballast.*

was used at one time in the old Tancook Whalers of Nova Scotia.
It is also used in some small fishing craft in the United States. Canvas or wicking saturated with paint should be placed between the
inner and outer keels. The plank keel is not suited to boats having
outside ballast.

### Laminated Stems

In some cases it is easiest to build up a stem, or a sharp stern, in
two pieces, to avoid the labor of rabbeting. The inner stem is set
up on the stocks and the hull planking allowed to run by it.

When the planks are secured, each plank is sawn off flush with the face of the inner stem. It is best to do this as each plank is fastened in place, not to wait until the boat is all planked. A piece of saturated wicking, flannel, or canvas is then put over the face of the inner stem and the raw ends of the planking. It may be held in place with a few copper tacks. The outer stem is placed on the inner stem and fastened with through-bolts, screws, and nails. This is the stem used in many flat-bottom hulls. It may also be used in round-stem hulls; the inner stem is cut to shape and the outer stem steam bent and put on cold. This is the practice followed in building the stems of the Jonesport Peapods, some Hampden boats, and many strip-planked hulls. If done with reasonable care, there is no serious objection to such construction.

## Keel Types, Heavy Timber Keels

Plate 21 on page 185 shows the keel structure of a heavy and large hull. It will be noticed that the horn-timber is built in the same manner as that of the smaller hull in Plate 24 on page 206. The rudder port or well is built up like a centerboard case. The round stern is shaped with a laminated frame or "grub beam," or may be made of short, heavy timbers as shown in the plan view. There are really two sternposts; the inner is carried up to deck and tenoned into a block let in between deck beams, or is notched into a single, heavy deck beam. The outer post that supports the rudder is called a "prick post" and is also carried to deck. It forms the forward ledge of the rudder post well. Both sternposts are either tenoned or dovetailed into the top of the keel. The frames are sawn, of course. The drawing shows the detail of a frame in the bow or stern fitted with a strongback in place of a floor timber; this construction is used in the so-called "cants" (that do not actually cant or set at an angle to the center line of the hull) in modern wooden hulls. The strongback passes over the deadwood and is only necessary where great strength is required. The plate shows a strongback at every cant, except those in way of the sternposts; this is unusual, as strongbacks are generally placed only on every second or third cant frame. The keelson is laminated; if it had to be sprung, this is the best way to build it. All heavy fore-and-aft members—for example, the shelf and clamp—in such a boat as this can be laminated also.

The keel and molds are now set up on the stocks and the rib-bands are in place. Before describing the framing and planking of a round-bottom hull that is the example of construction, the succeeding two chapters will be devoted to flat- and V-bottom construction. Before leaving the keel structure, however, a few remarks and suggestions are in order.

### Remarks and Suggestions, Timber

In ordering timber for the keel, in fact for the boat at all, insist on air-seasoned stock rather than kiln-dried stuff. If air-seasoned stock is not available, as it probably will not be, it is better to accept the partially unseasoned stock received directly from a saw-mill. Kiln-dried stock will swell and shrink very markedly and will therefore cause great difficulty in a boat after she is completed. If the boat is built under cover, kiln-dried decking can sometimes be used to advantage, however. If the home-built boat is small, the timbers will not be large and the partially seasoned timber from the mill will dry out quite fast. Another matter of importance in ordering timber for the keel is how it is sawn. This is not of great importance in very small boats or those having laminated or built-up keels, perhaps, but in a boat having a long keel in a single timber be careful to order that the "heart is to be boxed." A boxed heart timber has the heart of the tree inside the stick. A timber of this description will not take a "cast" or become permanently crooked when seasoning; neither will it "cup" or become bent across its greatest width. Nothing is more trouble-some than a keel which is not straight and it is very difficult to spring a crooked keel into the stocks.

### Marking

Another thing that is important: do not scribe the face of a timber (such as the face of the stem, or the top or bottom of the keel) along the grain with a timber scribe, scratch awl, or other sharp instrument. Such a scribed line will often start a severe check, particularly in green oak. It is safest to do all marking on the keel and other timbers of a boat with a carpenter's pencil.

## Breaking Auger

If an auger breaks when boring a deep hole do not become upset. A good many boats have an auger bit serving as a drift in their keels. Many a bit has been broken after it has pierced two timbers; drop a clench ring over the broken end, cut off the projecting shank, and rivet the head. If the bit breaks inside the hole, draw out the remaining portion of the auger and fill the hole with hot tar or tallow and put a wooden plug in it. Then drill a new hole.

## Drift Stuck in Hole

If a drift bends and cannot be drawn, cut it off, plug the bottom of the hole if it is for a through-fastening, and drill a new hole. These are accidents that happen in every yard or boatshop and are not the sole property of amateur builders. Through-fastenings can usually be driven out if the bolt fails, but even here it is possible to find that the fastening cannot be removed.

## Graving

If there is a bad knot in a large timber, yet it is not so large as to seriously weaken the stick, cut it out with a chisel and fit a square or rectangular block into the hole. Make sure the bottom of the block is in reasonably close contact with the bottom of the hole. Pay the hole with luting or with hot pitch and drive in the block, fastening it with a few nails. This is called "graving" and is a form of patching that should be done more often than it is. A bad knot or damaged spot will be a fine place for rot to start if not graved. In oak it is not uncommon to find that what appears to be a small soft knot on casual inspection is a serious amount of rot when opened up for graving. Therefore, cut for graving before going to the labor of shaping a stick. In selecting a stick look at the knots, probe them with an awl or bore a small hole, and look at the ends for checks or "shakes" that indicate damage to the timber. Pitch pockets in yellow pine are not objectionable unless they are very large and deep.

## Clear Stock

In choosing stock for the keel and heavy timbering do not expect to get all clear stock. This is a favorite specification with some designers, but, if followed, would result in a fortune being spent on timber; and then the boat would last no longer than one built of timber having a few knots, if reasonable precautions were taken. Perfection is easy to demand but very, very difficult to obtain. Long timber, clear of knots and perfectly sound, is something that exists largely in imagination, not in boatshops or yards.

## Paying and Preservatives

Be careful to pay all joints in the keel and to plug all unused holes made by temporary fastenings or accidental drilling. Due to the lack of well-seasoned timber, many builders paint the keel and deadwood inboard of the rabbet with creosote or other wood preservatives. Care should be taken not to get the creosote outside of the rabbet on the stem and stern above the water line as paint will not cover it well. If an accident should happen, wipe off the creosote at once and put a little aluminum paint over the spot after the creosote has dried. Creosote is rather dangerous to handle; do not get it in your eyes.

## Squaring Molds or Frames

In setting up molds and sawn frames, the method of squaring to the center line used by old-time builders is worth knowing. A nail is driven on the center line on top of the keel a few feet away from the mold or frame. A measurement is made from this to the sheer or a water-line mark on the mold or frame on one side, then checked against the mark on the opposite side. If the frame or mold is square to the center line the two measurements will be the same. Many builders do not cut the rabbet in the stem until the ribbands are being put in place; then each is notched into the stem at the proper bevel. These notches are then joined with a faired rabbet, cut with chisel and slick. There seems to be no particular advantage in this, compared to cutting the rabbet before setting up, if the loft work is done with reasonable care.

## Checking

If a boat is built slowly, it is probable that the keel timbers will check somewhat; painting with orange shellac will prevent serious damage. If the checks are large enough to warrant filling, use deck-seam compound or luting; do not use anything that sets up hard and so prevents the wood from swelling tight again. The practice of filling checks or rents with white lead or putty is occasionally the cause of rot. If creosote is used there is no need to fill the checks.

## Boxed Frames

If the heel of the frames are to be let into the keel, "boxed," that is, use a piece of framing stock as a gauge to ensure a reasonably close fit.

## Sternpost Tenons

In fitting a tenon for a sternpost, drill athwart the keel, through the mortise, before stepping the post; then mark the position of the hole on the tenon of the post with an awl or pencil. Remove post and bore hole in tenon about $\frac{1}{16}$ inch higher. This will cause the pin to pull the tenon into the mortise when the post is stepped and fastened. In a small boat $\frac{3}{8}$-inch oak pins, cut long and with a slightly tapered point, should be used.

## Fishtail and Gripe Plates

In large boats having a very heavy post, too heavy to handle easily, a dovetail is often used instead of tenon and mortise; it is backed up with two "fishtail plates," one on either side, and the two through-fastened. The top fastenings of these plates are in the post, the bottom fastenings in the keel. The plates should be let in flush. The forefoot of a large vessel is also tied together with a "gripe iron" in the same way. The "iron" takes different forms in each section: in some places the builders use "irons" shaped like wide horseshoes; in others they use circular rings or plates, or fishtails, or rectangular plates. These plates are either of galvanized wrought iron or of bronze, with the riveted fastenings of the same material as the plates.

## Centerboard Slot

The method of cutting the centerboard slot has been mentioned; in detail, it is to bore a few holes at one end of the slot and, with a chisel or slick, open up the holes enough to permit sawing. With a ripsaw, saw down the line of the slot on both sides, working alternately from top and bottom of the keel. The use of a corner chisel will give clean ends. The slick can be used to true up and finish the slot. Some builders bore out the slot with a large number of holes, then chisel and saw. This is a good plan with thin keels, such as plank or sprung keels.

## Close-Fitting Timber

If a really close fit is required between two timbers, chalk one face of the joint with blue carpenter's chalk and join; when separated, the chalk deposited on the piece not chalked will mark the high places that need to be planed off. Builders of boats are ingenious and it would pay the amateur builder to watch some professional builders at work, as there are countless tricks of the trade.

# CHAPTER FOUR

# FLAT-BOTTOM HULL CONSTRUCTION

## Building Methods

THERE are two ways to build flat-bottom hulls. One is to build "by guess and by God"—without plans. This is the method used by many skiff builders. A middle mold is made up with flare of sides to suit the builder's ideas; then a stem is made. Next two planks of sufficient width and length are cut to a suitable shape, for the sides. These are fastened to the stem, the middle mold inserted, and the two planks bent together at the stern with a rope made in a loop with a staff inserted and turned, as a Spanish windlass. The transom is cut and fastened, the ends of the planks of the sides sawn off, the bottom edges beveled, and then the bottom is cross-planked. A middle thwart or two is fitted and the center mold removed. With a dash of paint the hull is considered complete. Now this method turns out good boats—but only after a lot of experience. By trial and error, the builder learns how to cut the bottom of the side planks, either before they are fastened to the bowpiece and bent around the middle mold, or after. He also knows how to cut the sheer, but these rule-of-thumb dimensions only work when a fixed amount of flare is used for every boat the builder turns out. For this reason no variation in shape can be figured. There is no rule of proportion that will be practical to apply when flare is varied. It is obvious, then, that this method is not suited for amateur building, except in the roughest and most hurried construction. It should be added, however, that in some cases it is possible to build from a design by this method, if the shape of the sections permits the expansion of the side planks or if a half-model is made

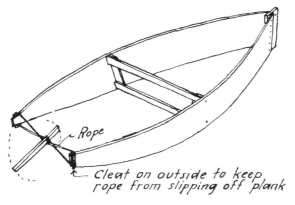

_Rope_

— Cleat on outside to keep
rope from slipping off plank

_55. Spanish Windlass_

by which the sides may be expanded to scale. In most yacht construction, however, the flat-bottom hull constructed from plans
must be built on molds and a set of stocks, like any other type.
This second method is the best from all points of view. It permits
the variation in model that makes building interesting.

## Importance of Good Design

The qualities of the flat-bottom type of hull have been discussed and so need not be dwelt upon again. For certain conditions and purposes there is no better type, in spite of the rather
widespread prejudice against it. As in all other types, the excellence of a flat-bottom hull depends wholly upon the excellence of its design, careful building being assumed. Much of the
criticism of flat-bottom hulls can be traced to an unfortunate experience with some poorly designed example.

## Lofting

Assuming that a design has been found that appeals to the
builder and fits the specifications of model mentioned in the
chapter on plans, the first step is to loft the plans. The principles
of lofting that were explained in the chapter on this subject will,
of course, apply. As there are only two fore-and-aft fairing lines,
the sheer and rabbet, and as the sections are usually straight sided,

there is little work involved in laying down the lines. Do not permit this to lead to slighting the job, however, and it is well worth while to work out the construction drawing on the loft plans. If the sides of the boat are to be curved in section, the design will show how they are to be faired (beware of one that doesn't). Usually this is done by striking diagonals through the topsides in the body plan and then fairing in the half-breadth; in rare cases water lines are introduced. No buttocks are required and in the smaller and more simple designs there is no keel; in large craft there must be some form of keel, which will be detailed in the design.

After the lines are laid down and the body plan faired, the thickness of the planking and deck is struck off, on each section.

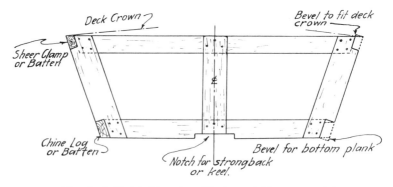

*56. Typical Mold, Showing Fitting of Clamps and Logs*

If the design calls for sheer clamps and chine logs these must be laid off on the sections so that the molds may be properly notched. These members are rectangular in section when roughed out, remember, and so will require a moment's thought. The top of the chine logs, and of the sheer clamps, will not parallel the bottom of the hull athwartships unless they are beveled, because of the flare. The outer and bottom corner of the chine log and the outer and upper corner of the sheer clamp must form the respective lines of chine and sheer at the inside of the planking. It is usual to cut the notch for the sheer clamp square to the sides, the depth of the clamp being taken at the inside of the side planking from the sheer. This brings its outer and upper corner to the sheer line at inside of planking and the top may be beveled off after the sides are in place. The chine cannot be fitted in this manner; the thickness of the chine log is first laid off parallel to the flaring sides, and where the line of thickness crosses the inside of plank line of the bottom as a beginning point the required depth of the chine log is set off. A line through this square to the side of the hull is the top of the chine log. The bottom of the chine, at the outer and lower corner, will project beyond the correct chine line at inside of plank and can be beveled off before the side planks are in place, or both side plank and chine logs can be beveled together before laying the bottom plank. If a fine finish is desired, the top of the chine logs is beveled so as to parallel the bottom; this is particularly desirable in an open boat as it prevents water lodging on top of the chine, in the angle formed by it and the inside of the side planking. If there is no chine log or sheer clamp it is a good plan to loft battens in their place and to notch the molds for them. These battens will help a good deal in shaping and beveling the top and bottom of the side planks.

## Picking Up, Molds, Bevels

The picking up of the stem, stern, and keel and the building of molds have been described in the chapter on lofting. The rabbeting of the stem should be lifted from the loft plan and the expansion of a raking transom should be developed there; there is no more reason for "try and fit" construction in a simple flat-bottom hull than in an ornate round-bottom cruiser. The number of molds required is governed by the shape of the boat. Experience is the only guide in deciding on a minimum number; it is safest to make a mold for every station shown in the loft body plan. The making of the molds for flat-bottom hull construction is too obvious to require explanation. Four or five pieces of timber will be used in each mold; be certain to get the molds strong enough. Where possible, a bulkhead should be utilized to take the place of a mold. This saves bother in fitting a bulkhead later and ensures a stronger boat. The bulkhead can be laid out in the loft plan and made to the proper fit and bevel without difficulty before setting up. The bevels of a flat-bottom boat can be lifted directly from the loft plan with an adjustable bevel, using the bottom or chine line in the profile, and the sheer and chine in the half-breadth plans.

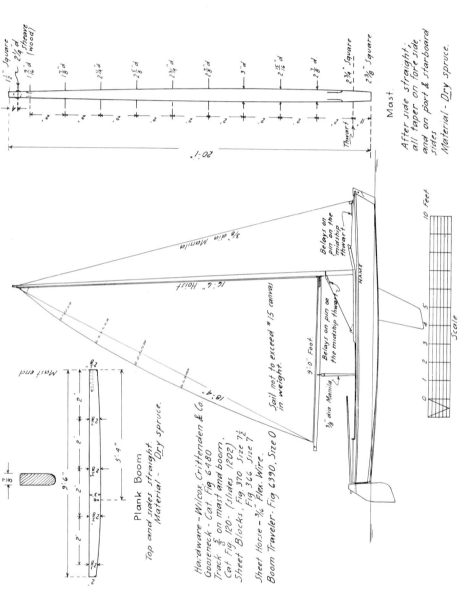

**Mast.**

After side straight, all taper on fore side, and on port & starboard sides
Material - <u>Dry spruce.</u>

20:1'

1½" Square
2¼" d
2¼" sheave (wood)
1½" d
1⅜" d
1¾" d
2¼" d
2⅝" d
2¾" d
2⅞" d
3" d
2½" d
2⅞" d
2¾" Square
2⅞" Square

Thwart
'll
2'   2'   2'   2'   2'   2'   2'   2'

**Plank Boom**

Top and sides straight.
Material - <u>Dry spruce.</u>

Mast end
7/8"
9'6"
5'-4"
2'   2'   2'

Hardware - Wilcox, Crittenden & Co.
Gooseneck - Cat. Fig. 6480
Track ⅝ on mast and boom.
Cat. Fig. 120 - (slides 1202)
Sheet Blocks, Fig. 370 Size 7½
Fig. 366 Size 7
Sheet Horse - ³⁄₁₆ Flex. Wire.
Boom Traveler: Fig. 6390, Size 0

3/8" dia Manila

16':6" Hoist

Sail not to exceed #15 canvas in weight.

9'-0" Foot

18'-4"

Belays on the pin on the midship thwart

Belays on pin on the midship thwart

3/8 dia Manila

NAME

Scale

0   1   2   3   4   5                    10 Feet

PLATE 25. *Sail Plan for a 16-Foot Hampton Flattie*

## *Stems*

Stem construction in flat-bottom hulls varies a good deal. The most common in yacht designs is the regular rabbeted stem. In some cases the laminated stem is used, shown in the cut on page 209. Another variation of the stem is the "New Haven style." This is made without an outside stempiece and is best suited for straight stems (without any curve in the profile). The inner stem is a piece of oak, triangular in section. The sides are cut with mitered

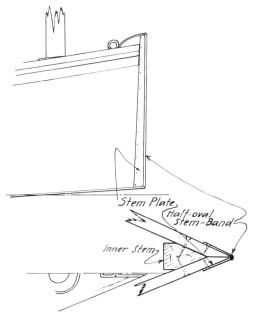

*57. New Haven Stem Construction*

ends and are fastened to the inner stempiece with screws or nails. The miter permits the ends of the plank to form the sharp edge of the cutwater. This is covered with a sheet of brass bent to form an acute angle and secured to the planking with brads or countersunk screws. By shaping the brass in two pieces and brazing these together it is possible to build a curved stem in the same manner. This form of brass cutwater was once popular in high-speed powerboats, though built with rabbeted stems. The brazed

plate is rather troublesome to build, however, if for a curved
stem. When the brass cutwater is used, its after edges do not
parallel the line of the face of the stem in profile; the top, at the
sheer, does not reach as far aft as does the bottom, at the chine.

## Sterns

The three common sterns in flat-bottom boats are the transom
(either plumb or raking), the sharp stern, and the round stern.
The transom stern has been discussed in the chapter on lofting.
The sharp stern is made like the bow. If the rabbet is straight, it
is little trouble to fit the side planking in one length into both the
bow and stern when these are set up on the stocks. If the rabbet
is curved in both stem and stern, there is usually some difficulty;
if only one is curved, fit that first and the end with the straight

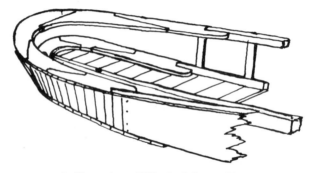

*58. Round or Elliptical Stern Frame*

rabbet can be easily fitted afterward. The round stern can be
made actually round, viewed from above, or in a flattened or
sharpened ellipse. The stern in profile is usually given a sharp
rake and makes a very handsome finish. The construction is not
difficult, if understood. In the loft plan the shape of two frames,
one horizontal at sheer level and the other at the slant of the
chine in profile at its level, are laid out. The frames at sheer and
the chine are expanded and beveled on the loft plan, following
the general principles given for expansion of transoms. The forward ends of these frames are laid out so that they may be
fastened to the chine logs or to the sheer clamps, as their position
requires. The side plank is run as far aft as the shape of the half-

breadth of the hull permits, without having to steam-bend the plank. Beyond this point, and around the stern, vertical staving is fastened, fanwise. To give finish, a piece or two of thin wool is bent around the stern at the sheer [after being cut to fit without having to be bent edgewise (called "edge-set")] and over this a piece of half-oval or half-round oak is bent to form a guard. The drawing shows the appearance of this. Both the strip and the guard must be steam-bent, usually in two pieces.

## Keels, Setting-Up

The keel construction will be shown in the plans and must be lofted. When built, it will form a backbone on which to set stem and transom, as well as molds, on the building stocks. Most flat-bottom boats are built upside down, as this is the easiest position in which to plank them. If there is a keel, the stem, transom, and molds may be mounted on it and the whole then secured upside down on the stocks. Any type of stocks suitable to building upside down may be used, and the one chosen should be worked out on the mold loft plan first so that the molds may be made to fit the setup with the minimum of labor. The remarks in the last chapter on placing the molds to allow for bevel should not be forgotten. When the molds are in place, the sheer clamps and the chine logs are fitted and fastened in place. Then planking of the sides can be started. If there is no keel, the molds, stem, and stern are set up on a bearer, or on the shop floor. In the latter case a temporary sprung keel of rough plank may be required. If there is a bulkhead it is set up exactly like a mold, except that it is beveled and so does not have to shift to face a station line. The sheer clamps and chine logs (or the battens in their places) are fitted and fastened, and then the planking of the sides is started.

## Building Right Side Up

If the boat is too large and heavy to turn over, she must be built right side up. Such craft will have a keel on which the molds may be mounted. The keel should be supported by posts which can be moved; there must be no fore-and-aft bearer as it would be in the way when cross-planking the bottom. Use as few supports to the keel as possible and utilize shores, under the molds, in their place. Fasten the latter so they can be shifted easily. If the hull is fore-and-aft planked on the bottom, the keel may be set up like that of a round-bottom hull with fore-and-aft bearer. The important consideration in planning stocks for building any flat-bottom boat right side up is to allow enough room under the hull to plank the bottom. There should be not less than 3½ feet between the bottom of the hull amidships and the shop floor. This will give sitting headroom in which to work.

## Chine Timbers, Bevels

The fitting of the chine logs has already been described in the remarks on lofting flat-bottom hulls in this chapter. Where possible, an attempt is usually made to obtain logs in one length. However, this is not always convenient, or possible, due to the shape of the boat, or its length. If the vertical curve is moderate, it is usually possible to edge-set the chine logs enough to give the proper curve. If this is not practical, then the logs must be sawn

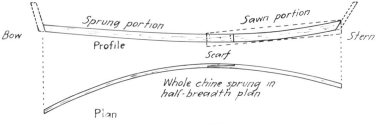

*59. Scarfed Chine*

to the required vertical curve, scarfed, and bent in the molds to the desired curve in half-breadth. The scarfing of sprung, or sawn, chine logs is generally done with the cut of the scarf vertical; its length is usually about eight to ten times the smallest dimension of the chine log. To obtain the shape of a sawn chine log, clamp or temporarily nail a thin plank on the molds when set up, as though planking was being started. This plank should be wide enough to permit a reasonable length of the chine log to be laid off on it, allowing for the vertical curve of the chine line in the molds. Tick off the lines of the sections represented in each mold and the height of the notches cut for the chine logs in the molds

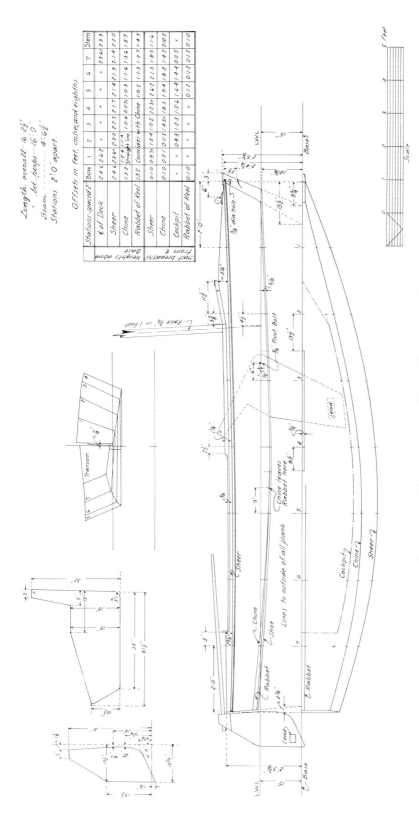

PLATE 26. Lines for a 16-Foot Hampton Flattie

Length overall--16'2½"
" Aft.perps--16'0"
Beam---- 4'6½"
Stations 2'0" apart.

Offsets in feet, inches, and eighths.

| Stations-spaced 2' | | Bow | 1 | 2 | 3 | 4 | 5 | 6 | 7 | Stern |
|---|---|---|---|---|---|---|---|---|---|---|
| Heights above Base | ℄ of Deck | 2·4·6 | 2·6·2 | x | x | x | x | x | x | 2·3·6+ | 2·3·3 |
| | Sheer | 2·4·6 | 2·3·6+ | 2·3·0 | 2·2·3 | 2·1·7 | 2·1·4 | 2·1·3 | 2·1·4 | 2·2·0 |
| | Chine | 1·3·2 | 1·3·2 | 1·2·4 / 1·1·4 Straight line | 1·0·4 | 0·11·7½ | 1·0·3 | 1·1·6 | 1·3·6 | 1·5·7 |
| | Rabbet of Keel | 1·3·2 | 1·3·2 | Coincides with Chine | | | 1·0·2 | 1·1·3 | 1·2·7 | 1·4·3 |
| Half-breadths from ℄ | Sheer | 0·1·0 | 0·9·7½ | 1·5·4 | 1·11·2 | 2·2·3+ | 2·6·2 | 2·1·3 | 1·8·5 | 1·1·6 |
| | Chine | 0·1·0 | 0·5·1 | 0·11·3 | 1·4·5+ | 1·8·3 | 1·9·4 | 1·8·2 | 1·4·2 | 0·10·2 |
| | Cockpit | | 0·8·5 | 1·2·3 | 1·5·6 | 1·6·4 | 1·4·4 | 0·11·5 | | |
| | Rabbet of Keel | 0·1·0 | 0·1·0 | x | x | x | x | 0·1·2 | 0·1·2 | 0·1·0 |

Scale
0  1  2  3  4  5 Feet

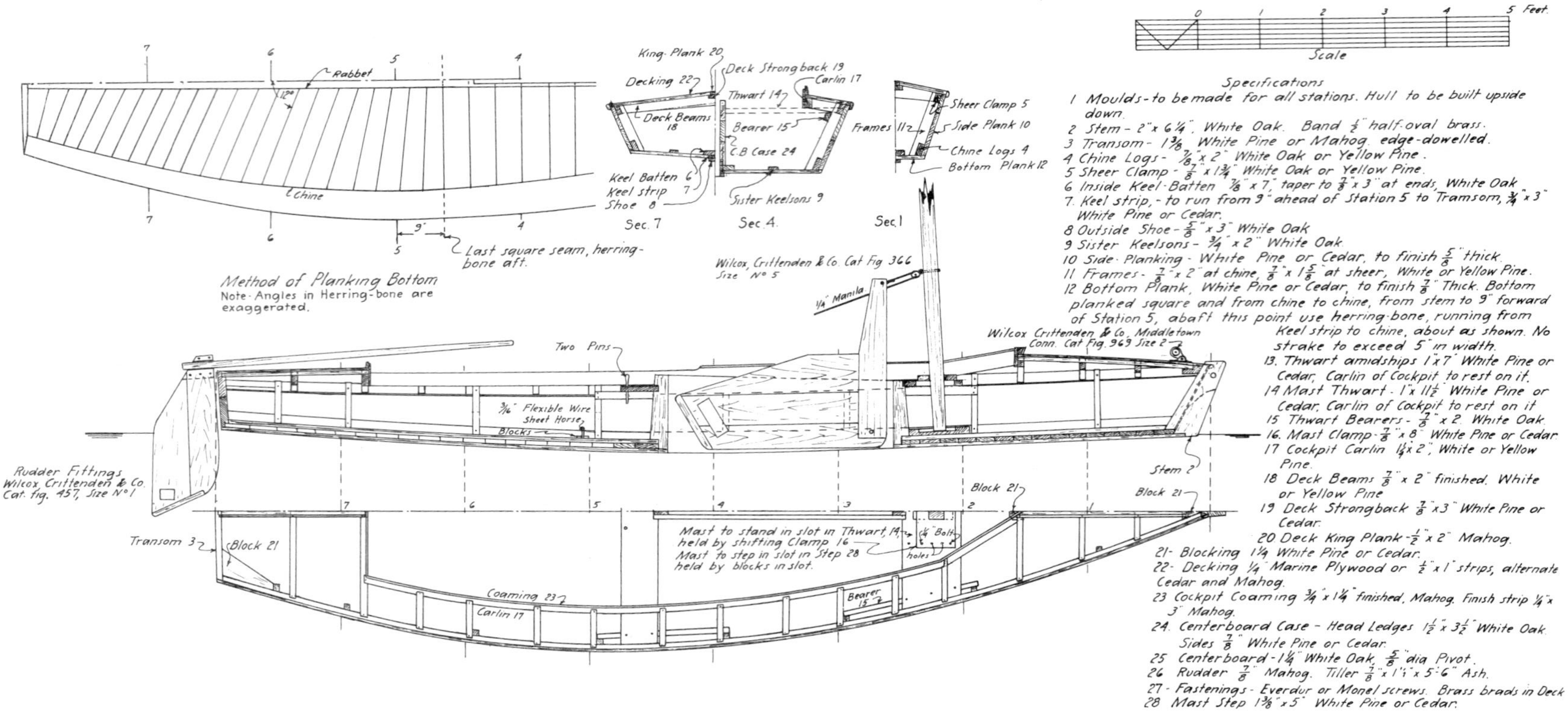
Scale
0 1 2 3 4 5 Feet
Specifications
1 Moulds - to be made for all stations. Hull to be built upside down.
2 Stem - 2" x 6 1/4", White Oak. Band 1/2" half-oval brass.
3 Transom - 1 3/8" White Pine or Mahog. edge-dowelled.
4 Chine Logs - 7/8" x 2" White Oak or Yellow Pine.
5 Sheer Clamp - 7/8" x 1 3/4" White Oak or Yellow Pine.
6 Inside Keel-Batten 7/8" x 7", taper to 7/8" x 3" at ends, White Oak
7. Keel strip, - to run from 9" ahead of Station 5 to Transom, 3/4" x 3" White Pine or Cedar.
8 Outside Shoe - 5/8" x 3" White Oak
9 Sister Keelsons - 3/4" x 2" White Oak
10 Side Planking - White Pine or Cedar, to finish 5/8" thick.
11 Frames - 7/8" x 2" at chine, 7/8" x 1 5/8" at sheer, White or Yellow Pine.
12 Bottom Plank, White Pine or Cedar, to finish 7/8" Thick. Bottom planked square and from chine to chine, from stem to 9" forward of Station 5, abaft this point use herring-bone, running from Keel strip to chine, about as shown. No strake to exceed 5" in width.
13. Thwart amidships 1" x 7" White Pine or Cedar, Carlin of Cockpit to rest on it.
14 Mast Thwart - 1" x 11 1/2" White Pine or Cedar, Carlin of Cockpit to rest on it
15 Thwart Bearers - 7/8" x 2. White Oak.
16. Mast Clamp - 7/8" x 8" White Pine or Cedar.
17 Cockpit Carlin 1 1/4" x 2", White or Yellow Pine.
18 Deck Beams 7/8" x 2" finished. White or Yellow Pine
19 Deck Strongback 7/8" x 3" White Pine or Cedar.
20 Deck King Plank - 1/2" x 2" Mahog.
21 - Blocking 1 1/4 White Pine or Cedar.
22 - Decking 1/4" Marine Plywood or 1/2" x 1" strips, alternate Cedar and Mahog.
23 Cockpit Coaming 3/4" x 1 1/4" finished, Mahog. Finish strip 1/4" x 3" Mahog.
24. Centerboard Case - Head Ledges 1 1/2" x 3 1/2" White Oak. Sides 7/8" White Pine or Cedar.
25 Centerboard - 1 1/4" White Oak, 5/8" dia. Pivot.
26 Rudder 7/8" Mahog. Tiller 7/8" x 1' 1" x 5' 6" Ash.
27 - Fastenings - Everdur or Monel screws. Brass brads in Deck
28 Mast Step 1 3/8" x 5" White Pine or Cedar.
Rabbet
12°
Chine
9"
Last square seam, herring-bone aft.
Method of Planking Bottom
Note - Angles in Herring-bone are exaggerated.
King Plank 20
Decking 22
Deck Strongback 19
Thwart 14
Carlin 17
Deck Beams 18
Bearer 15
C.B Case 24
Keel Batten 6
Keel strip 7
Shoe 8
Sister Keelsons 9
Sec. 7
Sec. 4.
Frames 11
Sheer Clamp 5
Side Plank 10
Chine Logs 4
Bottom Plank 12
Sec. 1
Wilcox, Crittenden & Co. Cat Fig 366 Size No 5
1/4" Manila
Wilcox Crittenden & Co. Middletown Conn. Cat Fig. 969 Size 2
Two Pins
3/16" Flexible Wire Sheet Horse
Blocks
Stem 2
Rudder Fittings Wilcox, Crittenden & Co. Cat. fig. 457, Size No 1
Block 21
Block 21
Transom 3
Block 21
Mast to stand in slot in Thwart, 14, held by shifting Clamp 16
Mast to step in slot in Step 28 held by blocks in slot.
1/4" Bolt
holes
Coaming 23
Carlin 17
Bearer 15

PLATE 27. *Construction Plan for a 16-Foot Hampton Flattie*

on the plank. Be sure to allow for the bevel of the top and bottom of the chine logs. When this plank is removed from the molds, the shape required for the sawn chine log can be obtained by connecting the notch tick-marks with lines swept by means of a batten. When the plank is cut to these lines, a template for the part of the chine logs to be sawn is obtained. If there is a twist, or roll, to the side it is easiest to cut the notches in the molds a little shallow and to bevel the outboard face of the chine logs after they are secured to the molds. If the notches are found to be too deep, shim out the logs when fitting.

In large hulls the whole chine log may have to be sawn, due to its size, but in small hulls the only part requiring to be sawn, as a rule, is the run, from abaft the midsection to the transom. The scarfs in the chine logs are sometimes staggered a little so as not to fall opposite and are well in the middle third of the length of the boat. However, most builders consider this an unnecessary refinement in construction and let the scarfs fall opposite and where the length of material dictates. Unless the boat is exceptionally light in scantling there is really no serious objection to this practice. Laminated chine logs are rarely necessary and should be used only when the flare of the sides is great enough to make avoidable the possibility of bottom, or side, fastenings being driven in the full depth of the seams between the laminations.

## Sheer Clamp

The sheer clamp, if one is required, can usually be bent into the notches in the mold without difficulty, as it is ordinarily a lighter timber than the chine log. As a rule, the sheer clamp in a flat-bottom hull is really a batten at the sheer and is between the side planking and the frames. Occasionally, however, the sheer clamp is inside the frames and so cannot be put in until the frames are in place. The setup on the stocks and the details of design must control the sequence of fitting the sheer clamp, in this case. If the sheer clamp is too heavy to bend it should be laminated. Keep the fastenings in the laminated sheer clamp well away from the top where the clamp is to be beveled, and also notched for the deck frames. Single timber sheer clamps should be scarfed in the same manner as chine logs, but laminated clamps need only have the laminations butted and staggered.

## *Fastenings, Stem and Stern*

Both chine logs and sheer clamps should be carefully fitted and secured to the stem and to the stern frame or transom. Screws or boat nails are commonly used in small boats, spikes and bolts in large craft. To secure the chine logs and sheer clamps to the molds, use the thinnest wire nail that will hold. Very often no fastenings are required to hold these members to most of the molds; the spring of their curves will suffice with the addition of a few cleats nailed to the top and bottom edges of the molds. Use as few fastenings as possible, as they will have to be cut when the molds are removed, later. The method used to fit the chine logs and sheer clamps to the stem depends so much upon the individual design that no hard and fast rule can be given. However, the ends of these members are usually beveled, or "snied off," to lay snug against the sides of the stem and may sometimes be through-fastened, with the bolthead and nut countersunk into the log and clamp and the countersink plugged with pitch or luting material. Through-fastenings are sometimes possible at the stern frame also. Care should be taken in placing such fastenings to avoid splitting the chine logs or clamps. Another common condition, at the ends of the chine logs and sheer clamps, is to find that they must butt against the inside of the stem and against a transom plank, without the use of a side frame or cleat. In such a circumstance, no direct fastening between the stem or transom and the chine logs and clamps is really effective; the strength of the joint is obtained by the side planking or by knees. For that reason the members may be held to stem and transom with temporary cleats. Notching the stem for the chine logs and sheer clamps is rarely possible and of doubtful value. The sheer clamps are sometimes secured to the stem by a horizontal knee, the "breast hook," and to the transom by "quarter knees."

## *Side Planking*

The planking of the sides of a flat-bottom hull is usually a simple matter. There are two considerations: the length and width of material available and the shape of the hull, which, with the first consideration, will govern the number of strakes required. As to length, this is rarely of great importance except as far as labor

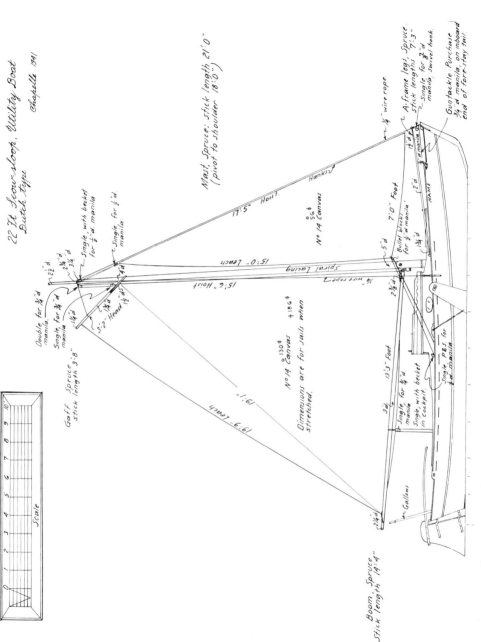

22 Ft Scow-sloop, Utility Boat
Dutch type
Chapelle 1941

Mast, Spruce: stick length 21'0"
(pivot to shoulder 18'0")

¼" wire rope

A-frame legs, Spruce
stick lengths 7'-3"
Single for 1" d
manila swivel hook

Guntackle Purchase
¾" d manila, on inboard
end of fore-stay rail.

17.5" Hoist.

Hanks.

7'-0" Foot

5'-6"
No 14 Canvas

1" d
manila

1½" d

2" d

NAME

15'-0" Leach

Single with becket
for ¼" d manila

Single for ⅛" d.
manila

Spiral Lacing

¼" wire rope

Bullet block
for ½" d manila

5" d

2¾" d

Double for ⅞" d.
manila

Single for ¾" d
manila

2½" d
2¾" d
¾" d.

3'-2" Head

1" d.
1¼" d

1½" d
2¾" d
¼" d

Gaff, Spruce 3'-8"
stick length 3'-8"

15'-6" Hoist.

No 14 Canvas 130⁰
+ 18⁰⁶

Dimensions are for sails when
stretched.

13'-3" Foot

3⁰ d

Single for ¾" d
manila
Single with becket
in cockpit.

Single, P&S for
⅝" d manila

19'-6" Leach

19'-1"

Gallows

Boom, Spruce
Stick length 14'-4"

2¾" d

Scale
0 1 2 3 4 5 6 7 8 9 10

PLATE 28. Sail Plan for a 22-Foot Scow Sloop, Utility Boat of the Dutch Type

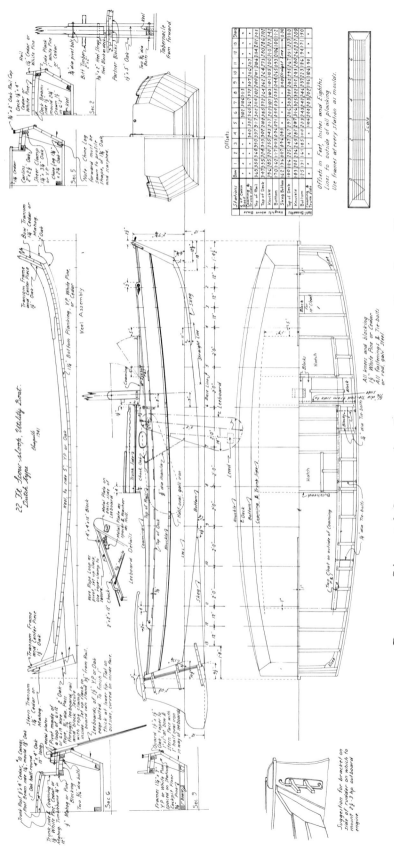

PLATE 29. *Lines and Construction Drawings for a 22-Foot Scow Sloop*

is concerned. Usually it is possible to get plank long enough to run from bow to stern in boats up to about 24 feet long, without great difficulty. If the hull is longer, the planks will have to be butted or scarfed. The width of the plank is more often a matter of difficulty and it is usually necessary to use two or more strakes to the side, or to piece up the sides at bow or stern to reach the height of sheer there. It is rare to find a design for a flat-bottom hull in which the side planking must be spiled. Boats having lap-strakes in the sides are an example. The rule that governs many builders of flat-bottom hulls is to use as few pieces of plank as possible in the sides, so as to save labor.

## Sheer Plank, Scribing Butts

Assuming the hull is not lap-straked in the sides, the first step is to select a plank for the sheer strake, if the whole side cannot be made of a single strake. This must usually be a rather wide plank, due to the combination of sheer and flare. If plank long enough to run the full length of the hull is available, well and good; if not, the length must be obtained by using two planks. The sheer strake is sprung on the molds and shifted up and down until it appears that its position permits the greatest depth possible at the point of the least freeboard, or at the bow or stern. The bottom of the plank should be smooth and straight. The plank may be held in place on the molds by a few clamps to molds, or sheer clamp, or by a couple of helpers. The forward end of the plank should be brought into the bow rabbet as much as possible; it obviously will not fit until it has been cut to the proper shape. The after end of the plank may be allowed to lie where it will for the moment. While it is in this position, the rabbet of the bow must be scribed on the plank so it can be shifted ahead into proper position in the next fitting. In some cases this may be done by use of the compass. This is the art of scribing, which must be mastered by every boatbuilder.

To achieve a well-fitted joint by scribing, the beginner might start by drawing parallel lines on the end of the plank, say, an inch apart and parallel to the lower edge of the plank. Now the compass is opened enough so that, with its point in the rabbet (on the inner or middle line), the pencil point will be able to mark the surface of the plank at the point that the end of the

plank is farthest from the rabbet. With the pivot point in the rabbet, and with the compass locked at the opening just described,
the curve or straight line of a rabbet may be transferred to the
plank by drawing the compass from top to bottom, taking care
that it is slanted to the rabbet so that an imaginary line from the
point to pencil always parallels the lines on the plank (parallel to
the latter's bottom). The most common mistake in both scribing
and spiling (the two are practically the same operation) is the

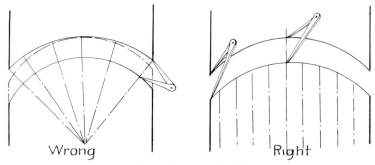

Wrong                                    Right

*60. Principle of Scribing*

tendency to keep the compass line (point to pencil) perpendicular to the *arc* of a curve, as it is drawn along such a curve. If the
arc of the curve of the rabbet were on a true radius, it will be
apparent that scribing with the compass line (point to pencil)
perpendicular to the arc would result in a scribed line, not of the
same radius, but of a smaller one which obviously cannot fit (see
cut).

When the end of the sheer plank or "strake" is scribed, its position is marked on the molds and the plank is removed; the end is
then cut to the scribed line. If the rabbet line is straight, the
scribing can be done by laying a 2-foot folding rule with one edge
in the rabbet, or along its outer line, and the other on the surface of the plank; draw a line along the edge of the rule on the
plank and this is the proper cutting line to fit the stem rabbet.
When the end of the plank is cut and smoothed, it may be
checked against the rabbet by holding the plank in its former
position. This will prove the cut and also verify the angle of the
rabbet. If any adjustment is needed it will be obvious now.

Now the plank is clamped into place, making certain that its end is snug in the rabbet of the stem, and that it is in its former position in regard to depth. A line run along the top of the sheer batten or clamp can now be drawn on the inside face of the plank; this will be the line used to cut the sheer line in the sheer strake. Now note this. The pencil line must be drawn so that it will stand above the actual sheer on the inside of the plank (which is the upper and outer corner of the sheer batten or clamp) to allow for the bevel that will have to be cut there, in order to lay a deck, or washboard, or rail. The amount of flare to the sides will govern the bevel, of course. If the sheer batten or clamp is the same thickness as the planking, then its upper and inboard corner can be used as the guide line and the marking pencil held in a level or horizontal position while marking. Otherwise it is best to scribe with a compass, with the amount allowed for bevel picked off the loft plan or obtained by careful measurement from the work. If the boat has a transom and the plank runs by it, it will be enough to reference the end of the sheer, leaving the extra length to be cut off at the proper angle and bevel after the plank is secured and fastened in place. The plank is now removed and cut to the marked sheer; one sheer strake is now ready to be fastened in place. Use this as a template to get out a duplicate. When both are ready they may be fastened in place. It is best, usually, to fasten the plank to the stem, along the "bearding" (between the inner or middle line and the bearding line of the rabbet). Care must be taken that the plank is snug in the rabbet and sprung enough, around the molds, to ensure that it is set in the proper place and that the cut sheer of the plank stands above the actual sheer line on the molds, at the inside of the plank, sufficiently to allow for the bevel to be cut later. The plank may now be fastened, working from forward aft, to the sheer clamp, and temporarily nailed to the molds. When the transom is reached the plank may be sprung in by hand or by a Spanish windlass until it bears; after it is fastened, the overrun of the length is then cut off at the proper rake and bevel, so that the end of the strake is flush with the face of the transom.

When one sheer strake is in place, its opposite is then fitted and secured. If the strakes must be in two lengths their butts must be fitted when both lengths are clamped, or secured, in position. After the forward one of the two is cut, duplicated, and secured, the after is likewise marked, cut, duplicated, and secured. The

butt or joint must fall between two molds and the butt must be
spliced by a piece of plank fitted and secured inside. The length
of the butt block should be about 12 times the thickness of the
side planking and its width should be sufficient to allow it to
overlap ½ inch, or thereabouts, onto the next course of strakes, or
plank. The butt block, in a sheer strake, will fit snug against the
bottom of the sheer clamp or batten, unless the latter is temporary; then the batten will have to be cut to fit the butt block.

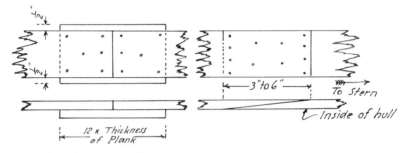

*61. Planking Butt Block and Plank Scarf Used in Lap-Strake*
*Construction*

In this case, cleat the butt temporarily until the whole plank is
secured except for the butt; then cut the batten and fit the butt
block. Use luting in the butt and on the faying surfaces of the butt
block (in other words, between the butt block and the plank).
The next pair of strakes need no fitting except at the stem, transom, and where they cross the chine at bow or stern. The marking of these strakes follows the same practice as the sheer strakes,
where they need to be cut to fit. The bevel must be allowed for,
along the chine, so the scribed line on the inside of these strakes
must stand outside of the true chine line enough to allow for
beveling. It is very easy to forget this and spoil a plank.

When the plank is fitted, it is well to lightly bevel its top, to
allow for a calking seam; in a small boat the seam should be open
a full 1/16 inch, or a little more, at the outboard face of the planking and closed at the inside face. When the plank is bent over
the molds and partially secured at the bow, it is a good plan to
nail blocks to the molds, below the bottom of the strake, on
which to drive wedges that will force the strake against the one

above, while it is being fastened. Take care not to mar the edges
of a plank with wedges or hammer blows.

### Shift of Butts

If there is a third band, or strake, of planking required, it must
be fitted in the same way. Butts should be shifted fore or aft of
the ones already in; three frame spaces is the rule, but this does
not help much in deciding the shift in a boat having no frames.
In this situation shift the butts about six to ten times the depth
of the strake, from the butt above or below it.

### Stealers

Very often there is a long, thin wedge of wood formed at each
seam in the run, by the strakes intersecting the bottom of the
chine logs at very acute angles. This wedge is apt to split or break.
The best way to avoid trouble is to cut off the wedge so that a

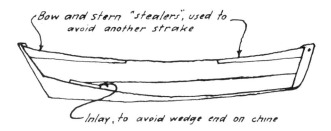

*62. Side-Planking Methods*

butt is formed an inch or so wide. Then chisel a little out of the
next strake, along the chine, so that a short, rectangular piece of
plank, an inch or so wide and about a foot long, can be fitted in.
This piece will cross the seam of two strakes at an angle, parallel
to the run of the chine, and will be backed and secured by the
chine log; it may be edge-fastened as well. If the stern is sharp and
the rabbet of the sternpost is straight, there will be no difficulty
in fitting the side planks, as the top and bottom of each strake

is ticked for the rabbet, where the plank being fitted runs by the sternpost. If the sternpost rabbet is curved, and the strake is made up of two lengths, lap the butt, scribe, and fit the end of the plank to the rabbet; remove and cut. Then replace with the end of the plank fitted to the sternpost rabbet and mark the line of the butt on the inside of the strake; remove, cut, and replace. Take care in fitting plank to have the molds marked so that you can replace the plank in the same position for each step in fitting.

Another problem in fitting side plank occurs when the sides are in a single plank. Very often it will be found that the plank is wide enough at amidships but lacks width to reach from chine to sheer at bow or stern, or both. In this case, fit it to the hull as far as it will cover, marking where its top, allowing for bevel, crosses the sheer line. After the plank is completely fitted, remove and, at the points where the sheer crossed the top of the plank, cut down an inch or two; then rip from the bottom of this cut, or cuts, to the end of the plank, parallel to the original top edge of the plank. Now replace the plank on the molds and secure. Pieces of sufficient width may now be fitted in the gaps left at bow or stern, or both, by the strip cut out. The notch formed at the inboard end of these fitted pieces is of sufficient depth to avoid the objectionable wedges that would occur if the cutting down were not performed. The narrow butts formed at the inboard ends of the fillers, or "stealers," can be backed by butt blocks if they are not on the sheer clamp; they may be edge-fastened also.

### Lap-Strake Sides

If the sides are to be planked lap-strake, the bottom strake of the sides must be fitted first and must be of sufficient width to bring the first lapped seam well above the chine. Because of this limitation, this form of planking (applied to flat-bottom hulls) is used only in small, light boats. The lines usually show the height of the laps and so can be established in the loft plan and transferred to the molds. The height of the laps should be marked at the edges of the molds, so that the marks can be seen when the plank is in place, being fitted. This done, the lower strake is fitted along the chine in the manner previously described. The top of the plank must be wide enough to extend above the marks

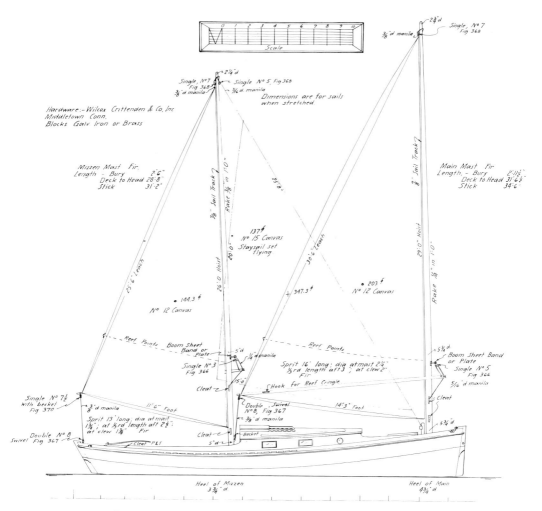

Scale

Single, Nº 7
Fig 368
3/8" d manila

Single Nº 5, Fig 368
3/16 d manila

2 1/4" d

Dimensions are for sails
when stretched

Hardware:- Wilcox Crittenden & Co. Inc
Middletown Conn.
Blocks Galv Iron or Brass

Single, Nº 7
Fig 368
3/8" d manila

2 3/4" d

3/8" d manila

Mizzen Mast Fir.
Length - Bury        2'-6"
Deck to Head 28'-8"
Stick                 31'-2"

Main Mast Fir
Length - Bury        2'-11 1/2"
Deck to Head 31'-6 1/2"
Stick                 34'-6"

137#
Nº 15 Canvas
Staysail set
flying

203#
Nº 12 Canvas

144.3#

347.3#

Nº 12 Canvas

Reel Points    Boom Sheet
Band or
Plate

Reef Points

Boom Sheet Band
or Plate
Single Nº 5
Fig 366
5/16 d manila

Single Nº 3
Fig 366

1/4" d manila

Sprit 16' long; dia at mast 2 1/4"
1/3 rd length aft 3"; at clew 2"
Fir

5'-0"

Hook for Reef Cringle

Cleat

Cleat

Single Nº 7 1/2
with becket
Fig 370

3/8" d manila

11'-6" Foot

Sprit 13' long; dia at mast
1 3/4"; at 1/3 rd length aft 2 1/4";
at clew 1 3/8"    Fir

Double Nº 8
Swivel Fig 367

Double ; Swivel
Nº 8, Fig 367
3/8" d manila

14'-3" Foot

Cleat

Cleat      5'-d

Becket

Cleat P&S

5'-d

Heel of Mizzen
3 3/4" d

Heel of Main
4 3/4" d

PLATE 30. *Sail Plan for a 30-Foot Sharpie Cruiser*

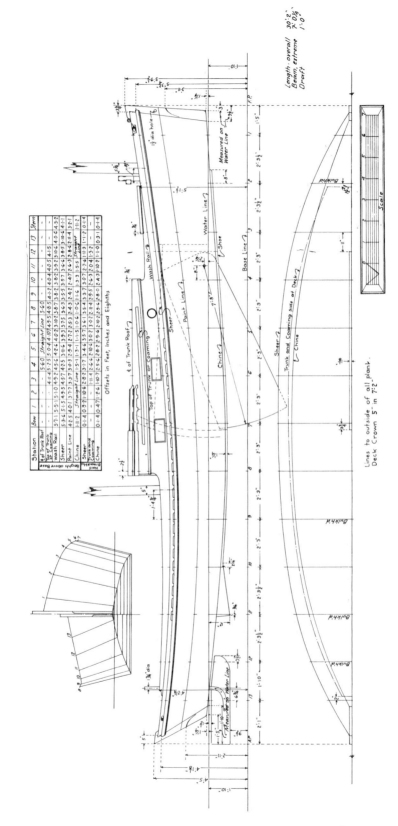

PLATE 31. Lines of a 30-Foot Sharpie Cruiser

the amount of the lap called for in the plans, at the least point. It is probable that the top of the bottom strake will not parallel the marks. When the bottom strake is otherwise fitted and clamped into place, the inside is ticked at the lap-line height from the molds. Then the plank is removed and, with the compass, new marks are made at the distance equal to the specified width of the

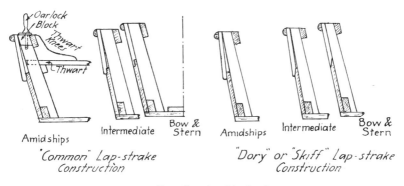

63. Lap-Strake Methods

lap from the first series of marks. A line swept through the new marks gives the top of the lower strake. The top being cut, the strake is rabbeted at bow and stern, beginning at the outside face of the plank a couple of feet inboard of bow and stern and running to half the thickness of the plank at the ends of the strake, at bow and stern. The width of this sloping rabbet is the width of the lap of the two strakes.

The bottom strake is now secured in place. When fastened, its top edge must be beveled a little along the outside face of the strake, so that the next strake above will bear the width of the lap. Usually the width of the lap is drawn on the plank with a pencil; then a short staff of straight plank is made, its length equal to the width of the strake above. If the sheer strake is the one above, then the staff is as long as the greatest width of the sheer plank, measured off the molds. This staff is laid on a mold with its lower end at the depth of the lap and its top at the seam above or with its inside edge on the sheer mark. This serves as a gauge to measure how much will have to be cut off the top outer face of the bottom plank to give the correct bevel for the lap of the two strakes. When this is done, the planks for the next strakes are selected

and one of them is sprung over the molds with its bottom at
the lowest point, a little above the top of the lower strake. The
bottom of the upper strake must now be scribed to fit the lower
line of the lap bevel below. This is spiling, and is done on the
same principle as scribing. The compass is set in the same way
and is held perpendicular to the straight edge of the upper strake,
not to the curve of the strake below. However, instead of sweeping in a continuous line, short arcs are marked on the upper
strake 4 to 6 inches apart. When the upper strake is removed,
the arcs are connected by a line swept in with the aid of a batten. This is the cutting line for the bottom of the upper strake.

The upper strake, when cut to shape, is placed back on the
molds and fitted to the line of the bottom of the lap marked on
the lower strake, to check. The end at the rabbet of the stem can
now be fitted, care being taken in shifting and scribing so that
the plank, when moved back into place, will fit the lap in the
lower strake. This will usually work out without undue difficulty.
At the stern, the upper strake should run past the transom in
the usual manner. When the upper plank is fitted, it is clamped
into its proper position and its upper edge is marked off from the
molds in the same manner as the lowest strake; if the upper is the
sheer strake then the sheer is scribed from the sheer batten or
clamp. The end of the strake may be held in the rabbet of the
bow by screwing a couple of cleats to the side of the stem, with
one end of each overlapping the rabbet enough to hold the plank
while fitting. When the top of the upper strake is marked and cut
it is ready to fasten, after a duplicate has been made. The first
step is to scribe the lap width on the inside of the strake. Then
a rabbet is cut in the ends of the lower edge in the same manner
as was done in the top of the lowest strake, but on the inside of
the upper plank, instead of on the outside as in the lower. When
the upper plank is set in place these rabbets will enter one another and so the projection of the lap disappears at bow and stern
and the planking becomes flush along the rabbet of the stem and
at the stern. If the upper is not the sheer strake then its top outer
edge must be beveled and rabbeted as was the lower strake. If
the upper is the sheer strake then the sheer must be marked and
cut as previously described. Lap-strakes need not be butted; they
should be scarfed in order to lap.

## *Fastenings, Nails*

Fastenings for the side planking will normally be the same as used for the bottom. It may as well be said that there is a good deal of ignorance in regard to fastenings among yachtsmen. Where the thickness of the timber permits, the best plank fastening is the boat nail—if it is properly made and has a good head. Where cost and strength are prime considerations, the hot-dipped, galvanized-iron boat nail is unsurpassed. The nail should be chosen

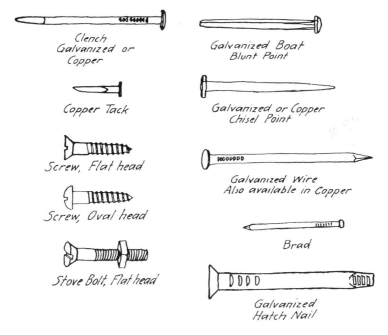

*64. Plank Fastenings*

with care—the head should be large and regular, oval or round. The edges of the shank (it is rectangular in section) should be sharp and there is no harm in roughness. The galvanizing should be thick and bright. Smooth, thinly coated or plated nails, with small irregular heads and long-tapered shanks, such as are seen in horseshoe nails and ordinary "cut nails," should be rejected. The length of the nail should be decided by the timbers through which it is driven; the rule is that the "penny" of the nail should be the number of eighths of an inch in the thickness of the plank through which it is driven. If the nail is to be driven in softwood, however, the "penny" should be two eighths greater than called for in the rule. The application of this rule to hull planking is subject to some practical qualifications. If the framing is too thin to permit the application of the rule, the length of the nail is equal to the thickness of the planking, plus the thickness of the frame, minus ⅜ inch. If the nail is to go through two timbers and be bent back into the wood after it has passed through ("clenched," in other words), its length is equal to the total thickness of planking and frame plus ¼ inch if the head is countersunk and plugged; plus ½ inch, if not. Good galvanized-iron nails can be clenched. In choosing a nail, use as long and thin a nail as can be driven. Boat nails are supplied with a choice of two points, chisel or blunt. The latter holds best and should be used except for clenched fastenings, when the chisel point is best.

"Penny" is the expression of length; the following are the standard penny lengths and inch equivalents. Twopenny equals 1 inch; 3 equals 1¼ inches; 4 equals 1½ inches; 5 equals 1¾ inches; 6 equals 2 inches; 7 equals 2¼ inches; 8 equals 2½ inches; 9 equals 2¾ inches; 10 equals 3 inches; 12 equals 3¼ inches; 16 equals 3½ inches; 20 equals 4 inches; 25 equals 4¼ inches; 30 equals 4½ inches; 40 equals 5 inches; 50 equals 5½ inches; 60 equals 6 inches. The thickness of a boat nail varies somewhat with the make, and each make with the length. The holding power of the boat nail has been thoroughly tested both in practice and in laboratory experiments. Its only weakness is the relatively small head, which may allow soft planking to be pulled over the head without withdrawing the nail. If the planking is of softwood or is under ⅝ inch in thickness, when finished, the round-shanked "wire nail" or the "hatch nail" are preferred by many builders. These nails have less holding power in the shank but greater power in the head. The "hatch nail" is sometimes sold as a "light boat nail." Clench nails are made of both galvanized iron and copper (or alloy); these are round-shanked nails having oval heads. The shank is straight and without taper, until within a short distance of the point. These nails are rarely clenched; they are commonly used as rivets in planking. Copper tacks are used for nailing the laps in lap-strake boats; the tack is a small-cut nail and it is clenched

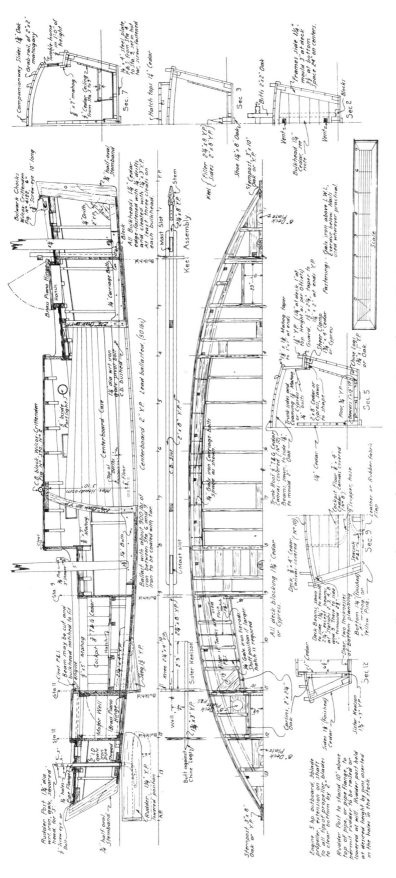

PLATE 32. *Construction Plans for a 30-Foot Sharpie Cruiser*

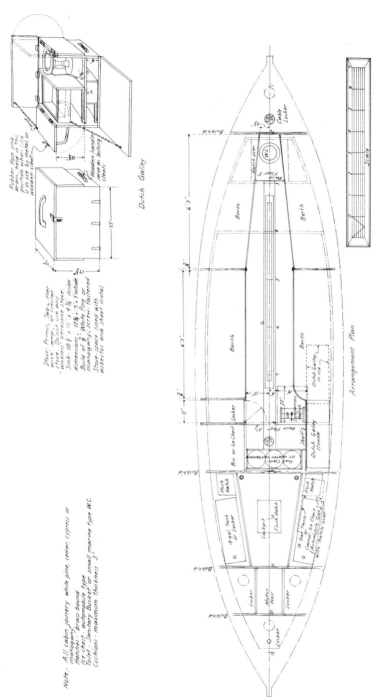

Dutch Galley

Rubber tube sink
drain held in this
position when not
in use by metal or
wooden cleat

Wooden handle
screw fastened to
wooden cleat

Stove: Primus, Imp or similar
wick lamp, or similar
stove. Do not use any
wickless kerosene stove.
Sink - 10¾ x 15 x 4¾ inside
dimension; 12¾ x 15 x 5 outside.
Build of ¾ White Pine or
mahogany; screw-fastened
Stove-space lined with
asbestos and sheet metal

Note:- All cabin joinery white pine, cedar, cypress or
mahogany; brass bound
Hatches - automobile type
Ice-chest - automobile type
Toilet - Sanitary Bucket or small marine type WC.
Cushions - maximum thickness 3"

Arrangement Plan

PWC

Cable Locker

Berth over

Knee Floor 3"

Berth

Berth

Berth

Bin or Ice Chest Locker

Knee Floor 3"

Dutch Galley
in use

Companion Hatch

Dutch Galley
Stowed

Fuel Tank
or water container

Flush Hatch

Flush Hatch

Cockpit

Flush Hatch

18 gal. Tank
or Locker

18 Gal Tank
or water
Containers
(Automobile)
Ice Chest
with hatch over

Locker

Motor
Well

Locker

Locker

Scale

PLATE 33. *Cabin Plan for a 30-Foot Sharpie Cruiser*

over, after being driven through the laps. Except for the hatch and clench nails, most boatbuilders do not use round-shanked or wire nails in boat construction.

Boat and hatch nails are now obtainable in various noncorroding alloys. Also special forms of barbed nails of such alloys are available; these have excellent heads and good holding power. Most of the alloy nails are very expensive compared to galvanized iron. Copper nails of any description have very little holding power unless their points are clenched or riveted. Riveted fastenings are usually made with copper or alloy clench (or "clinch") nails with a small "burr" (washer) dropped over the point after driving through. The point is then cut off in the clear and the remaining portion of it riveted over on the burr; this will be explained later. Nails in the planking should be bored for; boat and hatch nails with drills, or auger bits, smaller than the shank of the nail. Clench nails are drilled for with bits about the same size as the shank of the nail, when of copper.

### Fastenings, Spikes

Spikes, used only in heavy boat construction, run from 3 to 14 inches in length, and from ¼ to ⅝ of an inch square in the shank. All are chisel point, but may have conical, oval, or flat heads, as desired. They must be bored for in the same manner as nails. Spikes are usually of galvanized iron or steel, but may be obtained of noncorroding alloy.

### Fastenings, Screws

Screws are much favored by yachtsmen. The galvanized steel screws are strong, but the galvanizing process roughens the threads and makes them very difficult to drive. This fault in their threads also damages their holding power. Alloy and bronze screws are more satisfactory in this respect, but are more expensive. On the whole, they are not as strong as the steel screws and unless properly bored for will often wring off when being driven. This is particularly the case when a power screw driver is used and the screw driven through some soft planking material into an oak or elm frame. It is not exceptional to find, on survey, 10 per cent of the screw fastenings broken under these conditions. Brass screws are of little value in boat construction as they corrode and are weak in resistance to wringing off. The screws having flat countersunk heads are most commonly used for plank fastenings; they are bored for and the heads are countersunk and plugged, or "bunged." Their length is measured overall. Round-headed screws are used where the fastening is temporary or subject to occasional withdrawal. Their length is measured from the bottom of the slot to the point. The proper length of screw to use is three times the thickness of the timber through which it passes. Standard lengths of screws range from ½ to 6 inches and gauges from 2 to 24, depending upon length.

The gauge of a screw should vary with the hardness of the wood in which it is to be driven, for given lengths. To drive a screw, first bore a hole slightly less than the diameter of the shank and of a depth at least one half the length of shank from head to thread. In hardwood it is usually necessary to drill deeper than this and the best way to decide the proper depth is by experiment. In hardwood it may be well to bore through the first piece of timber with a drill of about shank diameter, and then bore a leading hole about half the length of the thread in depth. If the screw is smeared with soft soap, before driving, it will go home more easily and with less danger of wringing off. If the head is merely countersunk, the hole should be prepared with a countersink bit. Drills and countersinks combined in one bit can be used for drilling for screws that are to be bunged. The round-shank twist drills are best for boring for screws, using a push or automatic drill for small screws and a brace or breast drill for large. Screws are used where the timbers being fastened are not of sufficient thickness to hold nails. For that reason the ends of planking in the bow rabbet or the butts in planking are usually screw fastened. In light material the screw is considered the best fastening—say, in planking up to ⅝-inch thickness, finished. Often the impact of driving a nail is undesirable for some reason; here the screw is the answer to the problem. The rule is: "use nails where you can, screws where you must."

### Butts, Fastenings, Bolts

Planking butts in small boats can be screw fastened; in larger boats it is usually possible to employ nails. However, bolts can sometimes be used to great advantage. The bolts commonly used are a form of short stove bolt having a round or conical head, with a slot in it like that in a screw. These are usually supplied with square nuts. Carriage bolts are also used for the same purpose in very large wooden hulls. The bolt will serve better than a nail or screw to pull a butt fair, so that the planks bear completely on the butt block. The heads should be countersunk and plugged. The use of rivets and clench nails will be described in the chapter on lap-strake construction.

## Spacing of Fastenings

The spacing of fastenings in planking and elsewhere cannot be specifically laid down. In the stem and transom the fastenings can be spaced about 2 inches apart in the majority of hulls. Fastenings driven into end grain should be spaced around 1¾ inches apart. Planking is secured to frames, or to chine and sheer timbers, with fastenings spaced two or three to each plank, or 4 to 6 inches apart. Common sense is really the best guide, however.

## Bottom Plank, Chine Bevel

With the sides in place, the bottom can be laid. First the chine logs and the lowest plank of the bottom must be beveled. If the hull is building upside down this is a simple matter. A straight-edge long enough to reach across the hull from chine to chine is required, as are also a drawknife, plane, and broad hatchet. The straightedge will serve to check the bevel as it is cut. The outer and lower corner of the chine log is the correct line of chine. If there is a strongback down the center of the hull, made of a sprung plank, this must be secured in the notches in the molds and to stem and transom or stern. If there are two other strips parallel to this, or nearly so, on either side, these must be put in place. These are usually called "sister-keelsons" in flat-bottom and V-bottom hull construction. When the beveling has been completed, and the fore-and-aft members are in place, the plank for the bottom should be selected.

In a cross-planked bottom the board should be selected and prepared with a few points in mind. First, random widths can be used, but narrow stock is better than wide. Secondly, the board must be fitted to the hull with its end grain in the proper position, so that it will not "cup" and make the bottom like a washboard. Look at the end of a plank and note which way the annual rings of the wood turn in relation to the faces. The board must be laid on the chines so that these annual rings are curved *downward* against the chine. If they are allowed to be laid with the curve upward, they will cup. This rule should be followed when planking any flat or straight surface.

It is usual to begin planking a flat-bottom boat's bottom at the

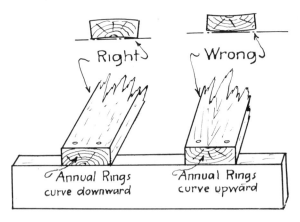

*65. How to Lay Plank*

stern, if she has a transom or is square sterned; start amidships, laying plank square to the center line and working alternately fore and aft if she has a sharp or round stern. As each plank is fastened in place, its overrunning ends are sawn off along the face of the lowest plank of the side, at the bevel fixed by the flare of the sides and, where necessary, sawn at the centerboard slot. It is easier to saw off each plank as it is laid, rather than to wait until the bottom is completely planked. It is an excellent plan to nail or, better, clamp blocks to the chine logs, so that the inside edge of each bottom plank may be wedged against its neighbor, while being fastened. Clamps will assure that each plank is bearing on the chine logs and strongback. The fastenings should be completed in each plank before going to the next one. The edges of the bottom plank will require some beveling to allow calking; the same width of seam on the outside of the planking as was used in the sides is required. Before starting to plank the bottom, lay strips of flannel, wicking, or calking cotton, soaked in paint, along the chines and centerboard case logs.

If the bottom is planked fore and aft, the boards should be so fastened that the curves of the annual rings shown in the ends of the plank curve against the frames. The construction of flat-bottom boats with bottoms planked fore and aft is sometimes quite different from that used in cross-planked hulls and will be described later. If the flat-bottom hull is built right side up and cross-planked on the bottom, the operations are no different from those already described, but beveling the chine logs becomes a rather tedious job. The roughing of the bevel is best done with an adz.

## Smoothing, Calking, Tools

When the bottom is planked, it and the sides should be planed smooth, sanded, and then calked and painted. For calking material use calking cotton used by boatbuilders, not the short strand stuff used by plumbers. Calking cotton comes in bundles and strands may be shredded out so as to make one to fit the size of the seam. Start by driving the strand into the seam of a bottom plank at one chine, with a little of the strand projecting outboard from the end of the seam, which can be driven into the exposed end of the seam. Use a calking iron and a mallet to drive the calking. The irons may be obtained from a marine supply house and can be purchased in various sizes and shapes. Ten irons make a set; these will be described later. Take a "creasing" or "making" iron and drive the calking along the seam, gathering it in small loops with the iron each time it is driven. The loops should vary in size as the width of the seam widens or narrows. The loops or folds should touch one another when in place. After the seam is lightly calked and driven, go back over it with the iron and drive it home so that there is room for puttying or filling the seam and drive in the end into the exposed end of the seam. Driving blows should be of equal force all along the seam. The iron should be held so that its slightly curved blade edge is level in the seam; if it is tipped along the direction of the seam, the edge will cut the strands of the calking. The calking can be driven too hard as well as too lightly. It must not be driven through the seam, but should be in a hard bunch, or rope, about halfway through the seam. If the latter is too narrow, it can be forced open with a "dumb" iron. It is a good plan to paint the seam before driving in the calking. This binds the calking; the wet paint will swell the cotton so that all voids are filled. This is less messy than dipping the cotton in wet paint before driving. The calking can be driven dry, but will not last as long as if driven in wet paint. If driven dry, the calking should be payed, or painted. This can be done, after driving, with a thin brush having stiff bristles. There is a regular "seam brush" made for the purpose which can be obtained at water-front hardware stores, as a rule. The seam may be filled with white lead putty, or seam composition, or hot marine glue, as circumstances warrant. Calking requires some practice, but the principles are soon grasped. In very light boats the seam may be calked with a strand of wicking, which is run in with a "calking wheel." In this case there are no loops. The seam may be practically closed when the wheel is used; it is opened with the wheel before running in the strand of wicking. In using a calking wheel, great care is necessary to avoid having the wheel jump out of the seam. Operate the wheel by a pulling, not a pushing, motion.

Calking irons are designed for every type or position of seam. For calking planking, the ordinary calking iron, called a "making," or "creasing" iron will serve. This iron may be had in varying sizes, with blades of varying thicknesses to fit almost any seam. The sizes are BB, Crease, $\frac{1}{32}$ inch thick; No. O, Crease, $\frac{1}{16}$ inch thick; No. 1, Crease, $\frac{1}{8}$ inch thick; No. 2, Crease, $\frac{3}{16}$ inch thick; No. 3, Crease, $\frac{1}{4}$ inch thick. The blades vary from $1\frac{3}{4}$ to $2\frac{1}{2}$ inches in width. For the garboard, along the keel, the "bent" iron is used; this has a blade bent sidewise so that it can be driven into an angle which could not be reached with the common iron. A deck or "dumb" iron is somewhat like the common, or crease, iron but has a thick blade and very little taper. It is used for widening narrow seams. A sharp, or "butt," iron has a long, sharp blade and is used for calking very short or narrow seams and corners. The "spike" iron is used for calking corners and fastenings or bungs; it has a very narrow blade. The "clearing" or "reefing" iron is a blade with a sloping edge; it is used to clear out old calking from a seam. The only irons an amateur builder really needs are a few creases, a dumb, and a bent. The calking wheel comes in only one size; it is a small metal wheel held in a wooden handle. Professional calkers use a calking mallet as it drives better and relieves some of the vibration to be found in an ordinary mallet or hammer. A "reaming iron" is a large iron

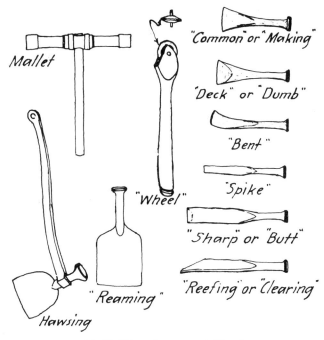

Mallet

"Common" or "Making"

"Deck" or "Dumb"

"Bent"

"Wheel"

"Spike"

"Sharp" or "Butt"

"Reaming"

"Reefing" or "Clearing"

Hawsing

66. Calking Irons and Tools

wedge with a wide, rather thin blade. It is driven into seams of large wooden vessels prior to calking, to open the seam and hold it open while the calking is being driven in. The "hawsing iron" is somewhat similar, but has a long handle attached; it is driven into seams after the calking has been set with a light iron, to drive it home or "hawse" it. The hawsing iron is used only in calking large, heavy boats.

### Remarks on Calking

Calking will stay in place better in softwood than in hard. The cotton should make an impression on the sides of a seam, to stand properly. This forms a tight seam, with the cotton making a continuous groove in the sides of the seam as the wood swells. Very light blows are required to accomplish this with cedar or white pine planking. Mahogany and yellow pine require blows somewhat harder; oak and many tropical hardwoods require very heavy blows and hawsing. If an impression is not made in the sides of the seam the swelling wood will close the wedge-shaped seam and spew out the calking. Do not try to calk with a screw driver, chisel, or putty knife; it is just asking for trouble. In large seams, oakum is used; this is rolled or "spun" in strands of sufficient thickness and driven like cotton, but not looped. Drive very lightly when only a few strands of oakum are used; heavy blows will break the fiber. Oakum will last longer than cotton calking but is more difficult to handle in small seams. A "strand" of cotton or oakum is about the size of the seam opening, before being driven.

## Finishing

A word about smoothing. This should be done before the calking and should be a finished job. Then, when the calking is completed and the seams puttied, a light sanding will make the bottom and sides ready for the first coat of paint. The bottom can receive two or more coats of antifouling bottom paint but the topsides may well be allowed to wait until just before launching, as they will become dirty and stained while the hull is being finished.

## Righting

If the boat is being built upside down, she must now be turned over to finish the top and deck. Much depends upon the size and weight of the boat as to how this is done. If the boat is small enough for a few men to lift, friends of the builder can be called in. It is a good plan to insert some notched spreaders inside the sheer clamp between the molds to give additional strength. It may be necessary to rest the hull on its side momentarily while turning her over, and these spreaders will prevent undue straining. If the boat must be turned over by mechanical means, she should be strengthened with heavy spreaders fixed to the sheer clamps and extending outboard a few feet. These spreaders can be notched so that they extend down a little inside the hull, or may be doubled with the shorter and lower piece a snug fit between the sheer clamps. Some builders nail these to the hull, or a lashing may be passed around the hull, outside the chines and bottom, to hold the spreaders in place. All the spreaders should be of the same length and their ends should be in line. Tackles or chain hoists are then rigged to the ends of spreaders, near each end of the hull, and to ridgepoles, or roof truss.

When all is ready the tackles are set up and the weight of the hull freed from the stocks. All shores, braces, and supports are removed and all tools and lumber cleared away. Sleepers are then laid on which the hull will rest when righted. The tackles are manned, the whole hull is lifted clear of the stocks, and then one side is lowered until the spreader ends are on the floor or ground. If the tackles are placed properly in regard to the hull, the upper side can now be lifted enough to bring the spreaders up and down. It should then be possible to force the hull over and to drop it right side up by lowering away slowly and carefully. If the boat is heavy the spreaders should extend a number of feet farther out from the hull on the side which will be lifted than on the side first lowered. The higher the boat can be lifted from the stocks before starting to turn her over, the easier the operation. Of course, a wide boat is much more troublesome to handle than one having a narrow beam. In most narrow boats one side can be lowered to the ground with jacks and the other side hoisted without first lifting the whole hull. When the hull is on the sleepers, it is blocked up level athwartships and a base line stretched inside from stem to stern at some water-line level. The blocking is adjusted to bring this base line level, using a string level. Now a base line is available by which superstructure, joinerwork, and construction can be measured and plumbed.

### Frames

If there are to be frames in the sides of the hull, these can now be fitted. These frames, in a cross-planked flat-bottom boat, are really nothing more than cleats laid on the flat and nailed to the planking between the sheer clamp or batten and the chine log. In some designs these frames are deep enough to be notched over the clamp and log, and fastenings driven there. Usually the frames

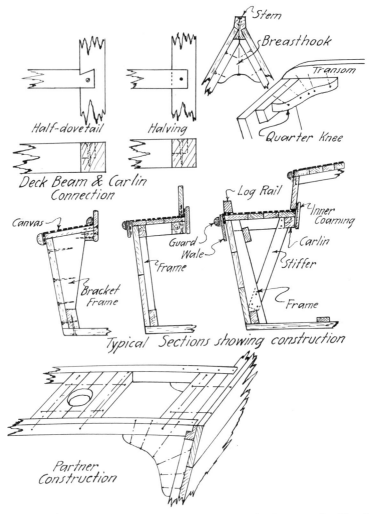

67. *Flat-Bottom Hull Construction, Details Commonly Used*

are not beveled, but allowed to stand square to the curve of the sides. If the boat has washboards, or narrow decks along the sides, the frames may be placed with their edges against the side planking and shaped deep enough to act as knees to support the deck, in lieu of beams or blocks. If these are beveled they may be laid off on the loft plan and their bevels lifted; or they may be measured directly from the boat. If some of the frames are to be located where the molds now are, lay them aside until the molds have been removed. This can be done as soon as a few deck beams are in place, or when thwarts are fitted.

### Fitting Deck Beams, Removing Molds, Etc.

The deck beams should be made up from the loft pattern and can be cut to the correct length prior to righting the hull, if desired. Their position being laid off, fitting may be started. It is usual to put in those nearest the middle of the boat first. If there are thwarts, these should go in before the deck. They should be made up from the loft drawing, as by that means the bevels of the thwarts can be predetermined. The thwarts may have to be notched for the frames and may be supported by bearers run fore and aft on the frames. Most small, flat-bottom sailing hulls require a thwart at the after end of the centerboard case and this should be well fitted and as snug as possible. Where the sheer clamp is against the side planking and at sheer height, its top is

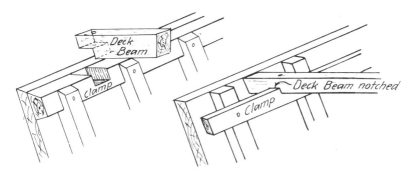

*68. Connection of Deck Beams to Sides*

notched to a depth of one half the depth of the deck beam. The latter's ends are also notched on the underside to the same depth. This permits the deck beam to drop down so that its top is flush with the outboard and upper corner of the sheer clamp, which is the proper sheer height, of course. The bottoms of the notches should approximate the proper bevel; they rarely do, however.

The ends of the deck beams are secured to the sheer clamps by nails or screws driven down through the deck beams and into the sheer clamps, at the notches. This gives a strong and simple construction. If the sheer clamp is inside the frames and under the deck beams, the molds will have to be removed before fitting the beams. If some of the beams can be fitted before removing the molds, they should be made up and secured. If not, or if no thwart or beams can be secured amidships, the hull must be stayed together with temporary crosspieces. Three or four are usually enough; if in doubt, fit crosspieces between each pair of molds. These crosspieces may be the spreaders used for turning over the hull. In any case they should fit snugly inside the side planking, at the sheer, to prevent the sides from falling in when the molds are removed. The ends of the spreaders inside the hull should be temporarily, but firmly, secured to the sides with cleats. When this has been done, the molds may be knocked out or removed by sawing them and breaking joints. Fastenings driven into the molds can be knocked out and plugged if they are in the side planking, but must be nipped off if they are in the chine logs or sheer battens, unless the latter were merely temporary. If the sheer battens are to be removed, they should be cut and pulled out, after the molds are all out. Take care not to disturb the spreaders. If the molds are screwed together, they may be knocked down and preserved. If this is the case, reassemble and bundle them up with the templates, and store them away safely.

### Deck Beams, Fitting and Fastening to Clamps

Once the molds are out of the way, the missing frames may be put in place and the sheer clamps made up. When these pass inside the frames they are usually pieces of plank nailed or screwed to each frame and secured to the stem and transom with cleats, knees, or blocks. The plans should show the designer's intent. Sometimes the deck beams are notched, so as to hook down over the top of the sheer clamps; this is usually done by fitting in the hull. If it is found that it is difficult to force a sheer clamp into the hull, it may be put in place in two lengths, scarfed or butted (butt block between clamp and side of hull), or made up in layers, laminated, of thin pieces. Once these members are in place the deck beams can be put in. Whichever the method employed, do not remove a temporary spreader until a deck beam or thwart is fitted and secured close to it. It is much better to

secure the deck beams to the sheer clamps than to attempt to
fasten them to the heads of frames. If the sheer clamps are properly fastened to the frames, and this is easy to do, the deck beams
fastened to the clamps are much stronger than those fastened to
the heads of frames. It is usually difficult to drive a fastening
through the side of a deck beam into the side of a frame, because
of the curve of the sides and the obstruction of frames or molds.

## Carlins, Fitting, Fastening, Tie Rods

Carlins are fore-and-aft members of the deck frame; they support the coamings of the cockpit, the cabin trunk sides, and the
hatch coamings. Usually they are the same depth as the deck
frames, but may or may not be as thick. The carlins supporting
the cockpit coamings and the cabin trunk sides are often sprung,
to allow these erections to follow the curve of the sides of the
hull and the crown of the deck fore and aft. The ends of the deck
beams are butted into the carlins, where the former are cut by
the latter. It is more or less a draftsman's convention to show a
half-dovetail to make this butt. The end of the deck beam runs
into the carlin half the depth of the former and half or the whole
width of the latter. The halving of the deck-beam end is shown
with a half-dovetail and the carlin notched accordingly. The
point of the half-dovetail is in the direction of bow or stern, working either way from amidships. The ends of the carlins are similarly shown, but with the points of the half-dovetail outboard,
where they are cut by deck beams. This is a fine finish, but it is
doubtful if there is any practical value to such a laborious butt
joint in small boats under 60 feet overall as there is so little timber
involved. The ends of the deck beams and carlins might as well
be halved without the half-dovetail. A good fastening driven
from the top of the deck beam, through the halving, into the
carlin will give sufficient strength for most hulls. A still easier
way is to butt the ends square and to hold in place with a lag
bolt driven through one member into the end of the other. This
is rather weak construction and tie rods between the carlin and
sheer clamp on each side are necessary. Sometimes the ends of
deck beams and carlins are not halved, but are half-dovetailed
their full depth; this is only possible when the members to which
they join are of greater depth. The method employed depends

upon the amount of time the builder wishes to spend on work-manship. The various dovetails are pretty, but halving is the quickest method; in any case the decking will cover the work-manship employed.

## Partners, Blocking

If there is a mast, the partners may be heavier in scantling than the rest of the deck beams. Also there will be blocking, or knees, worked in between the deck beam and partners, at mast and along the sheer. Blocks are also to be fitted for small deck open-ings and as foundations for deck fittings, such as windlass, winches, cleats, and fair-leads or deck blocks. All blocking should be snugly fitted between the members on which it bears. Fastenings are usually of less importance than fit in all knees and blocking. Around the mast, in a boat having a set of partners, the block-ing, or blocking and knees, is through-fastened fore and aft, from deck beam to deck beam. If this is called for, the partners should either be made up outside the boat or assembled and secured be-fore any other of the deck beams are set in place, to allow the fastenings to be driven. The most common through-fastening for deck blocking and knees is a rod, threaded at both ends, driven and set up with nuts and washers. On heavy boats the rod may be riveted instead. The depth of the blocking and knees is given on the plans as a rule. It should not be less than two thirds the depth of the deck beams where there is likely to be strain. Much of the blocking is not under strain and can be nailed or screwed to the beams, as the fastenings merely serve to hold the blocking in position until the decking is in place and the deck fitting se-cured.

## Washboards, Covering Boards

If the boat has washboards it is probable that they are sup-ported by the side frames, acting as brackets. The tops of these must be cut to the proper crown. Then the top of the sheer clamp and side planking must be beveled to fit this crown. The line of the sheer has been marked, either by the outer and upper corner of a sheer clamp, or by a pencil line traced along the top of the temporary sheer batten on the inside of the side planking. This is the control line by which the proper height of the top of the

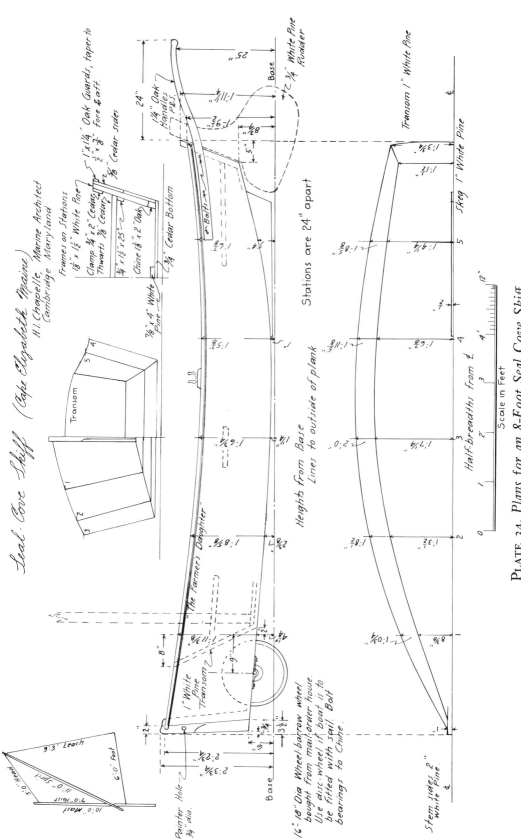

Plate 34. Plans for an 8-Foot Seal Cove Skiff

brackets, and deck beams, too, is fixed at the sides. The bevel can be cut with the same tools used for cutting the bevel in the chine logs, and a short straightedge, or adjustable bevel, will serve to check the cut against the deck beams, or tops of the side brackets. When the bevel has been cut, the fitting of the washboards is a relatively simple operation. Usually the washboards are one plank wide; it is obviously impossible to make the plank in a single length and to spring it in place, edgewise. The usual practice is to cut the washboards out of wide plank in short lengths. Sometimes the butts are scarfed and edge-fastened; this is a strong and workmanlike finish. In many boats the washboards are merely butted, with butt blocks below deck. No directions are necessary for shaping and fitting the washboards; if in one width, they must be wide enough to permit beveling along the sheer to meet the flare of the sides, and along the inside of the carlins to allow the coamings to stand according to the plans. When the washboards are fitted they are fastened to the deck beams or brackets and also along the carlins and sheer clamp or strake. It is a good plan to insert calking, wicking, or flannel, soaked in paint, along the top of the sheer strake before fastening the washboards. The washboard is usually fitted when there is a deck laid; then it is called the "plank-sheer" or "covering board." Only when the deck is canvas covered is the washboard, or covering board, omitted.

## Decking

The laying of the deck plank in a flat-bottom hull is usually made as easy and simple as possible. If the deck is canvas covered, the center plank is laid first, and then the planks on each side, alternating from side to side, until the deck is completely closed in. The long wedges formed by the deck planking along the sides of the deck are of no great importance as they will be covered with canvas; it is a good plan to edge-fasten them to the adjoining deck plank, however, with brads. The size of deck plank is given in the plans; when the deck is canvased there is no particular point in using very narrow stock. However, the deck plank should be laid with the annual rings curved against the deck beams or the deck will soon show seam ridges which will quickly cause wear in the canvas. If the deck is not canvased, it is usually wise to use plank not exceeding 4 inches in width. Where deck plank butt into the covering board they must be supported. A strip may be screwed along the inner edge of the covering boards to support the wedge-shaped butts of the decking in a small boat; blocking between the deck beams is necessary in a large hull. Tongue and groove stock is sometimes used for canvas-covered decking. It is hardly necessary to discuss a bright deck and the special methods of laying it, as it is rare that this class of deck is employed in a flat-bottom hull.

## Canvasing Decks, Fastening, Painting

After the deck is laid, the openings for hatches, cockpit, and cabin trunk should be trimmed ready for coamings and the whole deck planed and sanded. Then the canvas may be laid on the deck. Canvas for decks and cabin roof tops usually ranges from 7 to 11 ounces, 10- or 11-ounce canvas for decks that receive much usage. The canvas can usually be obtained in lengths equal to the deck length, but often must be made up of more than one width to cover the expanse of beam. It is very common to find decks in which the canvas is glued or cemented to the deck plank. This, contrary to popular belief, is not a good practice as wood will often swell enough to put such a severe strain on the canvas that it splits along the seams. On the other hand, a canvas deck laid in wet paint will be as smooth as a cemented deck; yet the bond will break before the canvas splits and replacement of canvas is a much easier task. Very successful decks result from laying the canvas on a dry deck without cement or paint. Experience and observation indicate that the life and appearance of the canvas deck is not improved by cementing it to the plank; the method used to paint and finish it is the important consideration. Whether the canvas deck is laid dry, or in wet paint, the canvas should be perfectly clean and dry. The canvas should first be stretched along the center line of the boat, tacking it at the ends of the boat and along the center line, when it is stretched as taut as possible. In a small boat, two men can stretch the canvas hard by rolling the ends around a staff to give a grip for the hands. If the boat is over 20 feet long it is a good plan to clamp the ends of the canvas between two staffs, after rolling it around one, then to clap on tackles to give a fore-and-aft pull. A bridle can be secured to the ends of the staffs to take the hook of the blocks of the tackles.

When the canvas has been stretched and secured along the center line, it is then pulled out to the sides of the hull and tacked along the side of the decking, or to the top of the sheer strake, if the guard is to be of sufficient depth to cover tacks so placed. The canvas should be secured with ½-inch copper tacks having good flat heads. Space the tacks about 3 inches apart, or a little less if the canvas is thin and light. If laying the canvas in wet paint, iron out all air bubbles and creases with a wooden block, before tacking. It is best to stretch the canvas over all deck openings and then tack, before cutting the canvas for them. Put tacks only along the seams and where required; do not scatter them promiscuously about the deck. At the cockpit coamings and cabin trunk sides, tack the canvas at the corners before cutting for the openings, then cut back enough to allow for a flap which will turn up or down, as shown in the plans. If it turns down inside the carlins the flap should be stretched and tacked as soon as cut; if not, it may be tacked along the opening on deck. When the canvas is stretched and smooth, it may be trimmed a little clear of the tack heads. If the canvas is laid in wet paint, it may be given a coat of priming; this should be thin and brushed into the canvas. If the canvas is laid "dry," most builders dampen it by sprinkling with a whisk broom dipped in water after it is in place. This shrinks the canvas, and painting is begun before the canvas dries out. After the priming coat is dry, two or three flat coats are put on, finishing with a good deck paint. It is well not to try to get a glossy deck, as the result will be a short-lived job of canvasing. If too much paint is laid on, the surface will crack, or "alligator," and in time the canvas itself will crack. Builders have many ideas about painting canvas; most of them seem to work well enough. Some dampen the canvas with water and paint while wet; others depend upon stretching well.

There are only a few "don'ts": do not use airplane dope, unless you expect to sell the boat before you have to recanvas the deck. Glue and cement should be avoided for the reason already mentioned; if you do use it, get rid of the boat before the deck requires recanvasing. These materials will cement the canvas to the deck so securely that it is easier to redeck the hull than to scrape or burn off the canvas, in most cases. Sometimes it is desirable to paint a canvas awning on the top, yet not paint it underneath. This can be done by wetting the canvas thoroughly and painting the top while still sopping wet. The water will prevent the paint from penetrating the canvas and will retard drying enough to form a film, which will settle and cement to the surface of the canvas as the water dries out from underneath the awning.

## Remarks—Seams, Spacing of Fastenings

The only important matters not yet mentioned in regard to canvas-covered decks are: be sure the deck is smooth and fair in crown, and thoroughly clean of dust and dirt, before laying the canvas. Rubbing in the prime coat of paint with a smooth wooden block (the paint being rather thick and the canvas dampened with water before the paint is laid on) will help to get a glossy deck, if you are willing to pay the price of such a bit of finish. If the canvas is to be made of two or more widths,

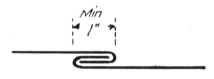

69. Deck Canvas Seam

the seam should not be formed by merely butting the canvas. The best way is to take the canvas to a sail or awning maker and have him sew the lengths together, with an inch overlap and a double seam. Another way, to be used when this is not convenient, is to double the edge of the piece first laid, with the edge upward; then lay the next piece with the edge doubled back, downward, to interlock with the first flap. The width of the flaps should be an inch or so. When the flaps are tacked together in wet paint, the result will be a tight seam. Tacks had better be spaced about 1 or 1½ inches apart, along such a joint.

## Hatches, Deck Erections

The erections on deck can be built when the deck is completed and the guards, half-rounds, or rub battens fastened along the sheer. The construction of deck erections is shown in the plans and few comments are necessary. Generally speaking, it is best to set the coamings of cockpit and hatches, and cabin trunk sides, on top of the deck and secure them with through-edge bolts, or with long screws from under the carlins. The inside face of the carlin and the raw edges of the deck and canvas can then be covered with a thin "inner coaming," or finish piece. In half-decked boats, where a tight deck is of no particular moment, the coaming of a cockpit is often nailed to the inside of the carlins and a piece of quarter round is then run along the seam on top of the deck, against the coaming. The construction of a cabin roof is the same as that of the deck, but will be discussed in a later chapter. Hatches may be required in a flat-bottom hull and their construction may be detailed on the designer's plans. However the hatch is formed, there is one important point to remember in building a tight hatch cover: the corners of the frame must be halved together. In laying out the frames, note which way the planking of the top will run. Make the framepieces that cross the hatch-top seams with the halving cut from the bottom of the

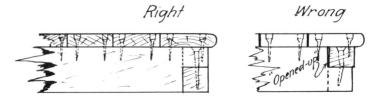

70. *Hatch Frame Construction*

pieces; the framepieces running with the planking with the halving are cut from the top of the pieces. When put together, the pieces across the run of the planking will reach from edge to edge of the frame, and, when the planking is fastened, will prevent opening up of the frame. If this plan is not followed, the frame will open as the swelling of the planking will cause the end fastenings of the outside planks to tip the frame at the top of the corners.

## Deck Fastenings

Fastenings in the deck and deck erections are usually nails and screws. The hold-down bolts in a cabin trunk can usually be made of rod threaded at one end, or both, as desired. The bolts should be so arranged that they can be taken up from below deck. Space hold-down bolts about 12 inches apart when possible; keep clear of the portholes or cabin openings.

## Centerboard Case

Centerboard cases should be made up and fitted to the hull, if not a part of the keel structure. When the case is completed, its bottom can be scribed to fit the bottom planking or the strong-back inside the planking. Fastenings are usually screws, or nails, driven from under the bottom. Take care that the board is placed exactly as shown in the plans; also that the mast partners and step are also exactly as shown there.

## Leeboards

Leeboards are rarely seen in this country, but are useful alternatives to a centerboard. In a small boat, the leeboards may be pivoted to the sheer strake with a machine bolt. This should be placed so that it passes through a frame and the sheer clamp if possible, or through blocking bearing on the frames. In a large boat the pivot bolts are subject to heavy strains and should be so fitted that the leeboards can become "broken winged" without tearing loose from the hull. This is caused by neglecting to lift the weatherboard, which is then forced away from the hull by the leeway of the boat, bringing a tremendous leverage on the pivot bolt and often tearing the board away from the hull. This can be avoided by using a bushing in the board and using two eye-bolts, eye within eye. One eyebolt goes through the hull, the other through the bushing in the board, loosely. The bushing may be omitted by employing two eyebolts connected by a link. The best way to secure these bolts is to have slots cut in the shanks and to drive in wrought-iron wedges over washers. Nuts will corrode on the threads and make removal difficult. If the pivot is above the deck line, the same result may be accomplished by using a few links of chain as the pivot. In a well-finished job, the pivot bolts should be cast of bronze and made in a gooseneck or universal joint form, or eye-in-eye, or two eyebolts connected with a link.

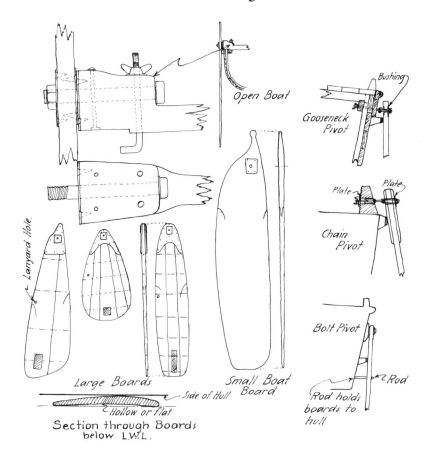

Open Boat

Gooseneck Pivot

Bushing

Plate

Plate

Chain Pivot

Bolt Pivot

Rod

Rod holds boards to hull

Lanyard Hole.

Large Boards

Small Boat Board

Side of Hull

Hollow or flat

Section through Boards below L.W.L.

71. Leeboards

Another plan is to confine the board to the hull with an iron bar, shaped to pass outside the board just above the chines, with its ends secured to the hull beyond the sweep of the board along the side. The leeboards should be made in a streamline form (cut lengthwise) in cross section or wing shaped. The flat side is faced outboard from the hull and the curved, shaped side against the hull. There should be a rub guard to take the chafing of the boards when down; this should parallel the water line or sheer. The boards should be ballasted so that they will sink. In rough water service the board is long and narrow; for smooth water service the boards are shorter and wider. The board can be proportioned roughly thus: one half the boards' length must be below the chine; their width should be about one half the length. The boards should be fixed so that they will tumble-home when both are down, that is, their lower ends should be farther from the center line of the hull than they are at the pivots. There are many ways of raising or lowering leeboards; heavy boards may be operated by a chain and a gypsy wheel, the latter mounted on the cabin roof and turned by a shaft and a crank in the cockpit. A trough over the cabin roof will prevent the chain from chafing. The gypsy may be locked by a catch on the crank. By this means one board is automatically lifted as the other is lowered. The boards should be also fitted for tackles, as emergency lifts.

## Power Installation

Power installation in a flat-bottom hull requires mention. The engine beds should be fitted with cross-bearers that reach to, and rest on, the tops of the chine logs. Usually there is a great deal of pitch to the shaft line in a flat-bottom hull and it may be wise to check the angle before selecting an engine, as some will not operate well at marked angles of pitch. Universal joints can be utilized, but are not satisfactory if over a slight variation, between the angle of the shaft and that of the engine, is required. If an outboard engine is to be mounted on the transom, the latter must be cut to fit the engine height (shaft length) and be well fastened and braced.

## European Setup—"Dory" Type

Flat-bottom hulls, with their bottoms planked lengthwise, are often set up in a manner entirely different from that described in this chapter. The bottom is expanded from the loft drawing and assembled with cross-cleats or frames. A setup is then made of posts, or cross-bearers, with their tops set to heights required to give the profile curve of the bottom. The latter is then set on these stocks and forced to the proper curve by stays or braces, wedged to the roof truss of the shop, or to a ridgepole and stem and stern setup. The sides are then put on with molds or frames to give the required flare. The sides extend down over the edges of the bottom and the chine logs are often omitted. When required, they are put in place just before the side planking is put on. This method is often used to build dories, but is more widely used abroad. The bottom is difficult to repair and the construction is not well suited to stand the strains set up in a sailing hull. The more common method of setting up a flat-bottom hull whose

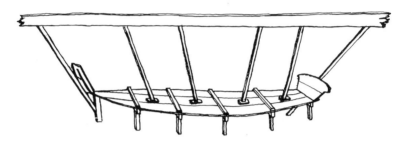

*72. Dory Setup, Used in Europe More Generally than in America*

bottom is planked lengthwise is to set up frames as molds and to fasten keel, chine logs, and sheer clamps to them; then put on the sides, and finally the bottom. This is the usual setup used for V-bottom hulls planked lengthwise on the bottom. The edges of the bottom planking are exposed along the sides when the hull is built in this manner.

### Bottom—Cross Planking vs. Fore-and-Aft Planking

The comparative advantages of cross-planking to lengthwise planking in the bottoms of flat-bottom hulls have been discussed in the first chapter. Many yachtsmen are under the impression that the seams of a cross-planked hull offer much greater resistance than when fore and aft. Observation of full-sized hulls does not bear this out and tank tests abroad are reported to have indicated some advantage in cross-planking at certain low speeds. At high speeds there appears to be some distinct advantages to cross-planking, but as yet the information is not sufficiently complete to draw definite conclusions. Ordinarily, the relative speed of the flat-bottom hull cross-planked with reasonable care is the same as that of a similar hull planked lengthwise on the bottom with equal care. The question, then, is not so much a matter of relative speed as of relative ease of building.

### Method of Expanding Side Planking

The expanding of the sides of a flat-bottom hull, so as to build without stocks from plans, in the "by guess and by God" method, is sometimes possible. It is doubtful that the results are as accurate as is desirable, but the possibilities vary with the design. To find whether this is practical, check the body plan in the loft drawing. If the sections there show that the sides are parallel to one another in *every* section, then the sides can be expanded. The process is somewhat like that used for expanding a transom. First a line is struck across the sides of the sections in the body plan; this is drawn like a diagonal and must be at right angles to every station it crosses. The two sides of the diagonal must correspond in the body plan; the diagonal must intersect on the center line and cross the base at equal distances from the center line. The first step will be to expand this line to find the true spacing of the stations. This may be done by fairing the line in half-breadth as a diagonal, marking the batten at each station in this elevation while it is on the floor. The batten is laid out on a straight line and the expanded spacing of the stations marked off. The stations are then drawn as perpendiculars to this line, extending a short distance above and below it. Next the distances from the diagonal, in the body plan, to the sheer and to the chine are laid off on a measuring staff for each station, measuring along the flare of the side. These measurements are transferred to the expansion and are set off on the corresponding stations there. So far there is little likelihood of trouble. The expansion of the ends of the sides is likely to be difficult, however. Perhaps the most accurate way is to draw another diagonal like the first and to expand its length, stern to rabbet of the bow, in exactly the same manner. If there is a reasonable difference in the height of the two diagonals in the body plan, the ends (when expanded) will be sufficiently decided to enable the proper rakes to be laid out. When the sides are being laid off, the two diagonals are parallel and the same distance apart in the expansion as they are in the body plan, measured along the flare of the sides, of course. When

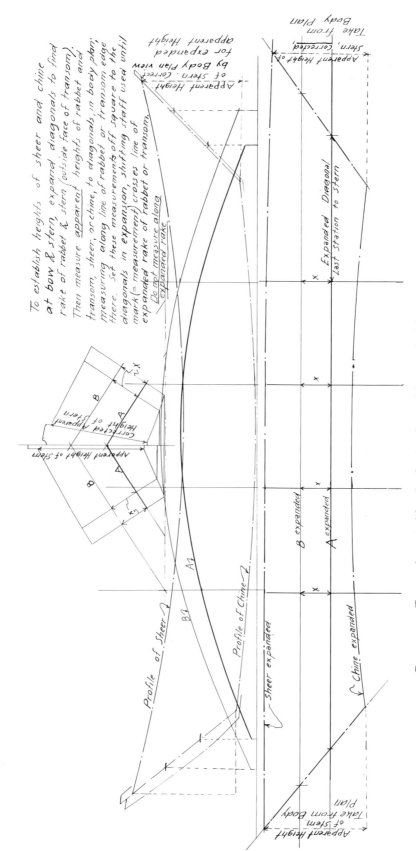

To establish heights of sheer and chine at bow & stern, expand diagonals to find rake of rabbet & stern (outside face of transom).

Then measure apparent heights of rabbet and transom, sheer, orchine, to diagonals, in body plan; measuring along line of rabbet or transom edge there. Set these measurements off square to the diagonals in expansion, shifting staff used until mark (= measurement) crosses line of expanded rake of rabbet or transom. Do not measure along expanded rake.

Apparent Height of Stern. Correct by Body Plan view for expanded apparent Height

Apparent Height of Stern, Corrected. Take from Body Plan

Take from Body Plan

Expanded Diagonal
Last Station to Stern

B expanded

A expanded

Chine expanded

Sheer expanded

Profile of Sheer

Profile of Chine

Corrected Apparent Height of Stern

Apparent Height of Stern

Apparent Height of Stem
Take from Body Plan

Plate 35. *Expansion of side plank of a dory. Lines to inside of plank (see text).*

the expansion is faired the true shape of the sides is outlined (see Plate 35). It is possible to correct for bevels from the loft plan, as only the top and bottom require correction. From this point on, the builder follows the method as outlined in the first part of this chapter, except that he makes his molds from the lines drawing. If the sections shown in the body plan are not parallel in the sides, then either the usual method of building over molds must be followed or a half-model can be accurately made by which the shape of the sides may be traced in the expanded form, to scale, in order to build "by guess and by God."

Flat-bottom boats have been built with strip sides, but there is no practical advantage. Occasionally a boat of this model is seen with the side planking spaced so the seams run as in a round-bottom boat. Here, again, there is no practical advantage, except appearance in a high-sided hull.

# V-BOTTOM HULL
# CONSTRUCTION

## Advantages of V-Bottom

THE construction of a V-bottom hull differs but little from that of the flat-bottom hull, in principle. On the whole, however, the V-bottom is the more difficult of the two models to build. This must be qualified by the remark that the difficulty in construction of the V-bottom is almost entirely a matter of hull design. The advantages of the V-bottom over the flat-bottom are greater displacement without an increase of driving power, less pounding when upright, better performance under power at medium and high speeds, and better sailing qualities in light airs. The flat-bottom hull has the advantage in lightness of draft, ease of building, and often in speed under sail in fresh breezes, because of greater stiffness and therefore greater sail-carrying power. It is evident that there is a greater range in possibilities of design in the V-bottom. It is possible to obtain designs of this model varying in form from the modified sharpie, having many of the good qualities of both the flat- and V-bottom combined; to the common V- or dead-rise model, having the advantages of the V-bottom model alone; or to the multi-chine hull, approaching the round-bottom in qualities and construction.

## Variations in Construction

The many borderline designs of V-bottom hulls, ranging from slightly modified sharpies to the multi-chine types, make it necessary to discuss as many of the variations of model as possible when describing the construction. Of the many variations, the most common may be classed as the modified sharpie, having very little dead rise (or V to the bottom); the model having an arc-bottom in cross section (as the Stars); the ordinary V-bottom planked crosswise or lengthwise; the power hull having curves in the sections, but still a V-bottom; and the multi-chine hull that is almost a round-bottom in some designs. The planking methods employed vary with the model, as a rule, and are ordinary carvel, lap-strake, and batten seam (ribband carvel). There are, of course, many combinations of construction methods used in some V-bottom designs, but the basic methods will apply to their building.

## Design

The importance of a good design is just as great in the V-bottom as in any other model. The requirements in design that make for easy construction have been described in Chapter One, and the qualities of the model were also discussed. There is little to add. The shape of the chine in profile is a matter that has been a subject for controversy among designers. Tank tests and observation show that the chine should be rather straight in the profile if speed under sail is the important requirement. On the other hand, speed is obtained at the cost of pounding. In order to do away with this the chine is often rockered (or curved in profile) a great deal. This overcomes pounding when upright, to a great extent, if the chine is quite high on the bow—but at cost of speed under sail. Even this greatly curved chine line will be of little value if the bow is full on deck, viewed from above. The builder must judge for himself which type of chine profile is most desirable for his purpose. If seaworthiness is of great importance, great beam and freeboard should be avoided; these have more effect on seakeeping ability than the chine line profile, perhaps. No wide, high-sided, light-draft hull is desirable for heavy weather work, whether she be V- or round-bottom, sail or power.

## Lofting

The design having been chosen, the loft plan must be drawn. The steps necessary to obtain a proper lofting job have been

described in Chapter Two. In most V-bottom hulls, the fairing
is done with the sheer, chine, rabbet, and sometimes the bottom
of the keel. If the hull is flat-sided and has no curves in section,
no buttocks or diagonals are required. If the bottom is an arc
athwartships, as in a modified sharpie model, these arcs are usually
on one radius, or a series of radii, as given in the lines, and so
buttocks and diagonals are not required. Occasionally, however,

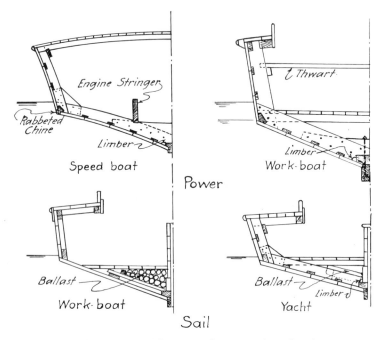

73. *Common V-Bottom Construction Sections*

the bottom of such a design requires fairing; this is done by
closely spaced buttock lines. In hulls having curves either in topsides, bottom, or both, the fairing should be carried out with
diagonals, water lines, and buttocks, as in a round-bottom hull.
The multi-chine hull can usually be faired by the various chine
lines. The designer's lines will usually be the best guide, and need
be added to only when there is an obvious lack of fairness. In case
this appears, the complete beginner had best discard the design, as
experience is necessary to refair a faulty set of lines.

Changes in the design, while lofting, are often very tempting. The urging of friends to "improve" a design by making the hull longer, wider, or higher-sided than shown in the plans should be emphatically rejected. If you had enough confidence in a designer to buy his plans you will do well to use them and not to take the advice of well-meaning friends, or self-appointed "experts" who happen along. Once the design is chosen, stick to it; don't attempt to change the bow, stern, freeboard, headroom in the cabin, or to lengthen the trunk or alter the position of the centerboard. If you do, you are asking for trouble of the most expensive and heartbreaking kind: a boat on which a lot of labor and material have been expended but which is not satisfactory under sail or power, or is not stiff enough, or is so ugly that the builder is ashamed of her. Don't change the size of timbers, either in the frame or deck structures. Don't raise the engine, or change its position, from the height and position shown in the plans. Don't add to the weights above the water line and then expect the boat to be as stiff as others of the same design without the additional weights. If the boat was designed for some individual make or size of engine, use the one the designer specified. If the plans call for an engine of a certain horsepower, do not plan to use an engine of greater or lesser power. Don't increase the tank sizes without consulting the designer—and follow his advice. It cannot be too strongly emphasized that one change in the plans of a boat will invariably lead to a whole string of changes, which is likely to end in disaster.

## Templates, Molds, and Frames

Patterns and templates should be made from the loft plans wherever necessary. As in the flat-bottom hull, the ease of fairing the lines should not lead to slighting this part of the construction. During the lofting of the plans the sequence of the various parts of construction can be planned and noted. The difficulties can be studied and often solved. Don't allow the natural urge "to get started" make you rush through the lofting in order to get to work with tools. The position of sawn frames must be carefully checked and the templates marked, so that they may be located on the stocks with their bevels fair, if the bevels are lifted from the loft plans. The construction of the molds is simple; most molds

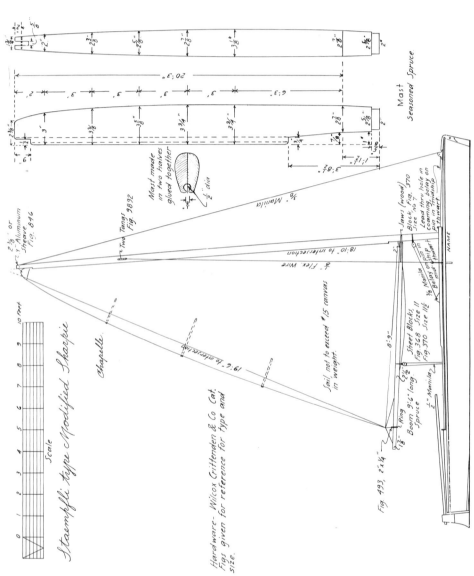

PLATE 36. *Sail Plan of a 16½-Foot Staempfli-Type Modified Sharpie*

may be made of five or six pieces of plank. Their construction is very similar to that used in flat-bottom hull molds and requires no description. If frames are used, instead of molds, it is usually easier to lift the bevels from the loft plan, using a bevel board, than to bevel the frames after they are set up; yet either practice can be followed, as will be explained. A well-finished V-bottom frame is beveled inside and out; this must be done by mold loft bevels, not when set up.

## Setting Up

Setting up is a very important step. Perhaps the most common fault, in most amateur setups, is lack of strength. This shows up when the sprung keel is used in some stocks; in others the whole setup goes out of line when one side plank is being sprung on. These weaknesses can only be overcome by using large enough timbers in the stocks and molds, and by proper bracing of both stocks and molds, when the setup is being built. These remarks apply to any form or type of setup, upside down or right side up. Most V-bottom hulls are built upside down; whether built this way or right side up, the suggestions on the setup of flat-bottom hulls in Chapter Four apply. In V-bottom boats having heavy keels sawn to shape, the weight of the keel may be so great that it is impractical to handle it when completely assembled. It is well to consider this in planning the setup; if the keel is to be put on the stocks in sections, these must be fastened together and this must be planned for, in designing the stocks. If it is possible to get help enough, or to rig hoisting gear, to handle the heavy timbers, this enters into the problem. If there is a sprung keel, there is no difficulty except, perhaps, the bending of the timber specified. If it is found that the timber required is too stiff to bend over the molds, steaming or soaking in hot water may help. If this does not make it limber enough, the keel will have to be laminated. If the keel is made up of a batten inside, with the keel attached to it, there should be no trouble in bending the batten, or in bending each separately, if the plans require it.

## Setting Up Frames, Beveling on the Stocks

Setting the molds properly has been described in Chapter Three and the instructions given there apply only to molds, not to sawn frames, when the latter are set up without being first beveled. If it is planned to bevel the frames after they are set up, the position of the frames should be indicated on the keel or stocks by the station, or frame, lines, as taken from the loft plan. The frames are then set so that those *forward* of the middle station, or of the point of greatest beam, have their *after* faces on the marks; those frames *abaft* the middle station have their *forward* faces on the marks. By this means, one edge of the frame, *from* which the bevel of the other edge is cut, is the true outline of the section shown in the loft body plan. Beveling is done by bending a thin batten over the frames, by which the amount of bevel required at each frame can be ascertained. Cutting can be done with a broad hatchet, draw-knife, and plane.

### General Notes on Frame Construction

The construction of the frames will be shown in the plans. In general, the frames are built like molds. The parts of the frames, at the chine, may be halved together and secured by a cleat or "gusset." In some designs the parts are butted and the heavy gussets are used. More rarely, the two parts are lapped and a knee is used, instead of a gusset. The knee stands on the bottom part of the frame, to which it is edge-fastened, with one side against the side part of the frame, to which it is side-fastened. In small craft, frame fastenings are either screws, nails, or rivets; in large hulls, bolts are used. The gussets should be laid out in the loft plan to obtain a uniform appearance and proper length for strength. While this is being done the fastenings of the chines to the frames must be considered and decided upon. The floor timbers should be as long as possible; they are sometimes made thicker than the rest of the frame to allow for edge-fastening to the keel. It is very important that the frames have their tops tied together with cross-spalls. Occasionally a design permits the cross-spalls to be replaced with deck beams, which can be cut to shape, fitted, and permanently fastened from measurements taken from the loft plan, before setting up the frames. In building the frames, the limbers should be cut before setting up. These are openings through the frames at the top or side of the keel, to allow bilge water to drain through the frame spaces to the pump intake. In light craft, plywood is sometimes used for the chine gussets; do not fasten the

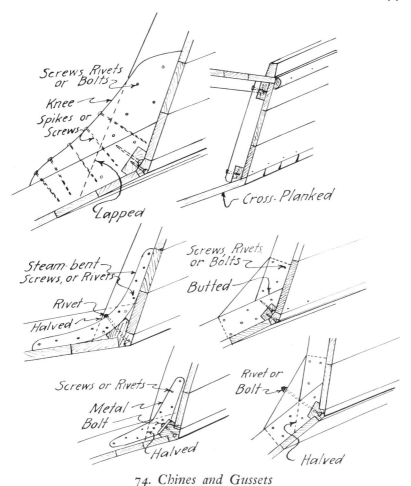

74. *Chines and Gussets*

chine logs to it, as edge-fastenings in plywood are not good. Metal gussets are sometimes used; set them in pitch or paint where they bear on the wood. Heavy boats have white-oak chine gussets, or knees. Fastenings in the gussets must be laid out to avoid splitting them, or the frames. In most V-bottom hulls the sheer clamp is on the inboard faces of the frames so no notch is cut for it. Notches must be cut for the keel and chine logs, however, and these should be laid out in the loft body plan—the chine logs particularly, as they will not center under the chine line at bow, or bow and stern, if there is much rocker in the chine fore and aft. The frames should be built with the gussets and cross-spalls on the side away from the station marks, when it is planned to set them up and bevel with battens.

### Notches for Batten Seams

Batten-seam construction will be described in detail later. The notches for the ribbands used in this construction should be cut as the planking is spaced, or "lined off." The fitting of the chines should be taken from the loft plan in this type of construction.

### Fitting Notches for Chines, Clamps, Etc.

If molds are used, and there is no bottom framing (bottom cross-planked) the treatment of the molds, chines, clamps, and fastenings follows that given flat-bottom hulls.

### Building Modified Sharpie Keel, Chines, Sides

The modified sharpie hull, having the chine lines meeting the keel rabbet at the bow, is the easiest V-bottom type to build, as a rule. Usually the bottom is cross-planked, though fore-and-aft planking is sometimes required. The keel is usually of the sprung type and is laminated, with keel and keel batten. The building procedure is the same as employed in ordinary flat-bottom hulls, except for the keel structure, and for the bottom planking. The chines are beveled to fit the rise of the bottom in the same manner as is used for flat-bottom hulls; the keel batten can also be beveled in the same way. The sides are planked as in a flat-bottom hull.

### Modified Sharpie, Cross-Planking Square on Bottom

If the bottom is to be cross-planked, its treatment depends upon the hull shape and the ideas of the designer. Some hulls can be planked "square," that is, the bottom planks lay at right angles to the center line of the hull fore and aft. Others must be planked herringbone fashion, with the bottom plank set at an angle to the center line, sloping aft from center line to chine. If there is more than an inch or two of dead rise amidships, it is always best to plank the bottom herringbone fashion, to avoid the twist in the bottom planks that will appear at the ends of the hull, if planked square across.

In square planking the bottom of a modified sharpie, the first bottom planks to be fitted are the two at the bottom of the transom. These can be fitted in about the same way that bottom plank is fitted to a flat-bottom hull, except that a little attention must be given to fitting the planks at the rabbet. If the keel is wider amidships than at the stern, the butts of the planks resting on the keel batten, or in the keel rabbet, will not be square to the edges of the planks, of course. The butts should therefore be scribed with the edge of a 2-foot rule or short straightedge. When the two sternmost planks are fitted and fastened, the other bottom planks are made up in turn, working port and starboard sides together. When the bow is reached, the last planks will be triangular in shape, due to the shape formed there by the meeting of chines with the keel rabbet. It will be found that these planks can best be cut with the grain running fore and aft, parallel to the keel. Some designs have a block forefoot, which is flush (on the outside) with the outside of the bottom planking. The after end of this block should be fitted with a cleat laid in luting and well fastened to the block; this will back up the seams along the block where the bottom planking joins it. Some care is required to fit the last bottom plank against the block, but as all lines are straight only careful handling of tools is necessary. The annual rings in all bottom plank should be curved against the chine logs and keel batten, of course. If the keel is not chamfered so that the butts of the bottom planking can be cut square to their surface, the beveling should be done so that the whole of the end of a bottom plank is snug against the keel and bears fairly on the chamfer cut in the keel batten. The latter is sometimes chamfered before the keel is set up, but in most cases is chamfered or beveled after the keel and molds are assembled on the stocks. In this case the keel batten is beveled in the same way as the chine logs, and at the same time.

## Double-Ender Bottom

If the hull is sharp-sterned, the same method of planking can be used, but the first pair of planks laid on the bottom are usually amidships, the rest of the bottom being laid by working alternately forward and abaft of the middle.

## Calking

Calking and smoothing the bottom and sides follow the methods specified for flat-bottom hulls.

## Modified Sharpie, Cross-Planking Herringbone on Bottom

If the modified sharpie has a square raking transom, the cross-planked bottom will be laid herringbone fashion. The first two planks of the bottom are usually parallel sided and are fitted along

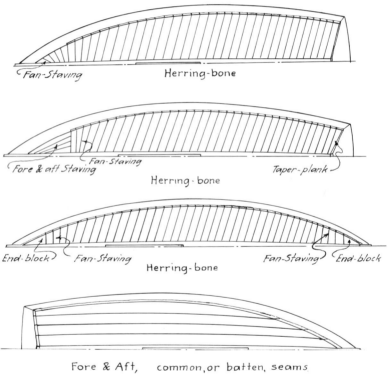

75. *Bottom-Planking Methods*

the bottom of the transom. Their butts against the keel must be cut at an angle to the rabbet and therefore must be scribed. Bevel may also be required, if the keel is not chamfered so that a square-cut butt can be used. The bottom is then planked up, using parallel-sided stock, until a point about one fifth or one sixth the length of the bottom, from the heel of the stem, is reached. Here the planks are tapered, usually, so that the last seam, before the triangular bow planks are reached, is square to the center line of the hull. These tapered planks will have to be spaced off by marking the position of the square seam, and then spacing back so as to find the dimensions of the butts and outboard ends of the tapered planks. It will be found that these tapered planks are narrowest at the rabbet. The only important consideration, in spacing the tapered planks, is to avoid getting them so narrow on the keel rabbet that insufficient room for fastenings results. It is a good plan, therefore, to space off the bottom plank from about amidships to the bow, previous to planking forward of the middle length of the bottom.

### Herringbone Bottom on Double-Enders and Square Stern Hulls

The application of the herringbone to sharp-stern hulls, or to the hull having a plumb square stern, is governed by the amount of dead rise amidships, as before mentioned. As a general rule, the herringbone bottom should be used. The angle at which the bottom is laid in these hulls is governed by arbitrary judgment—usually about 12 degrees to the hull center line. In a plumb, square-stern hull the aftermost planks of the bottom must be given a good deal of taper and must be narrowest at the chine ends. Some builders taper a number of the stern planks so that the extreme angle of rake to the bottom seams is finally reached a half-dozen strakes from the stern. As the bow is reached, the planks are again tapered, but with the narrowest ends at the keel in order to come square at the bow. In sharp stern hulls, the arbitrary rake of the bottom seams is established amidships and carried to the ends without change, when both ends finish in the modified sharpie style. The amount of rake aft in herringbone planking, from center line to chine, should not exceed 15 degrees to the hull's center line. Experience shows that giving greater rake than this results in a weak bottom unless a number of sister-keelsons, or fore-and-aft bottom battens, are used to reduce the unsupported length of each bottom plank.

## Bottom Herringbone with Block Ends

If the herringbone fashion is used in combination with a block at the forefoot in lieu of staving, the strakes must be tapered so that the seam at the block is square; do not attempt to carry the herringbone seams to the block, even though this can be done in double-ended modified sharpies without blocks in the ends.

## Modified Sharpie Planked Fore and Aft on Bottom

If the bottom is planked fore and aft, the frames must be beveled, either before being set up on the stocks, by use of loft bevels, or after being set up, by using a batten sprung fore and aft to measure the bevels required for each frame. The hardest plank to fit is the garboard, which is the first to be fitted and fastened in place. This must be spiled on; to do this, spring one plank over the bottom as close to the rabbet of the keel as possible. In a modified sharpie there will be little or no twist to the plank. The ends of the plank may run beyond the chine at the bow, or beyond the transom, or both if not in two lengths. Take a compass, open it so that, with the pivot point in the rabbet, the pencil or marking point will reach the plank at the place or places where it lays farthest from the keel. With the compass, scribe short arcs on the board, spaced about 6 inches apart. Remove the plank and, with a batten, strike a line passing tangent to the arcs. Take care that the line is truly tangent to every arc, as by this means the setback of the line is always parallel to the rabbet, as in scribing. Cut to this line and refit, to be sure that the garboard is snug in the rabbet before making the duplicate, or fastening. The other planks of the bottom do not need to be scribed and all will run out to a thin wedge along the chine forward. If possible, the widths should be planned so that no seam will intersect the chine aft in a square-stern boat. The planks may be secured before being cut along the chines; inlays may be employed to avoid the thin wedges at the seams if the width of chine logs permits.

## Side-Planking Lining Off

It has been assumed that the sides are planked in the same fashion as in flat-bottom hulls. Should it be desired to obtain a more

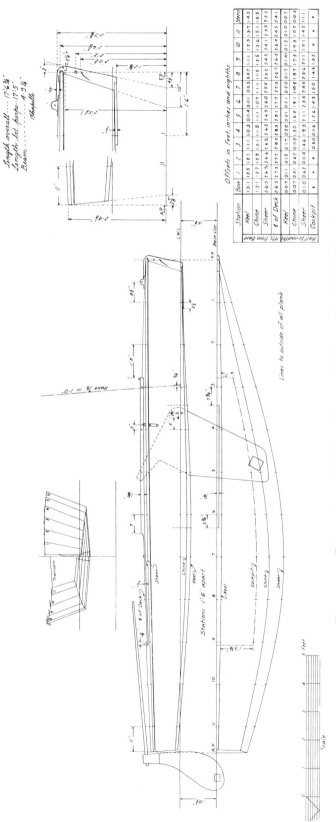

Offsets in Feet, inches and eighths

| Station | Bow | 1 | 2 | 3 | 4 | 5 | 6 | 7 | 8 | 9 | 10 | 11 | Stern |
|---|---|---|---|---|---|---|---|---|---|---|---|---|---|
| Keel | | 1-3-1 | 1-2-5 | 1-1-1 | 1-0-3 | 0-11-4 | 0-11-0 | 0-11-0 | 0-11-3 | 1-0-7 | 1-1-1 | 1-2-3 | 1-3-7 | 1-4-5 |
| Chine | | 1-3-1 | 1-2-7 | 1-2-5 | 1-2-1 | 1-1-5 | 1-1-1 | 1-0-7 | 1-1-1 | 1-1-5 | 1-2-5 | 1-3-6 | 1-5-1 | 1-5-5 |
| Sheer | | 2-6-5 | 2-6-5 | 2-6-6 | 2-6-5 | 2-6-5 | 2-6-2 | 2-6-0 | 2-5-5 | 2-5-2 | 2-4-5 | 2-4-1 | 2-3-5 | 2-3-2 |
| ₵ of Deck | | 2-6-5 | 2-7-3 | 2-7-7 | 2-8-2 | 2-8-3 | 2-8-1 | 2-7-7 | 2-7-3 | 2-6-7 | 2-6-2 | 2-5-4 | 2-4-5 | 2-4-1 |
| Keel | | 0-0-7 | 0-1-5 | 0-1-7 | 0-2-0 | 0-2-1 | 0-2-1 | 0-2-0 | 0-1-7 | 0-1-4 | 0-1-2 | 0-1-0 | 0-0-7 |
| Chine | | 0-0-7 | 0-3-1 | 0-6-7 | 0-11-0 | 1-3-0 | 1-6-5 | 1-9-1 | 1-10-2 | 1-9-7 | 1-7-5 | 1-4-3 | 1-0-5 | 0-10-3 |
| Sheer | | 0-1-0 | 0-6-2 | 0-11-4 | 1-4-6 | 1-9-3 | 2-1-1 | 2-3-5 | 2-4-5 | 2-3-6 | 2-1-1 | 1-9-1 | 1-4-2 | 1-1-1 |
| Cockpit | | " | " | 0-8-0 | 0-11-6 | 1-2-6 | 1-4-3 | 1-5-0 | 1-4-6 | 1-3-5 | " | " | " | " |

Half-breadth, Hts. from Base

PLATE 37. *Lines of a* 16½-*Foot Staempfli-Type Modified Sharpie*

Length overall ---- 17′6¾″
Length L.W.L. Above -- 17′5″
Beam ---- 4′9¾″
Chapelle

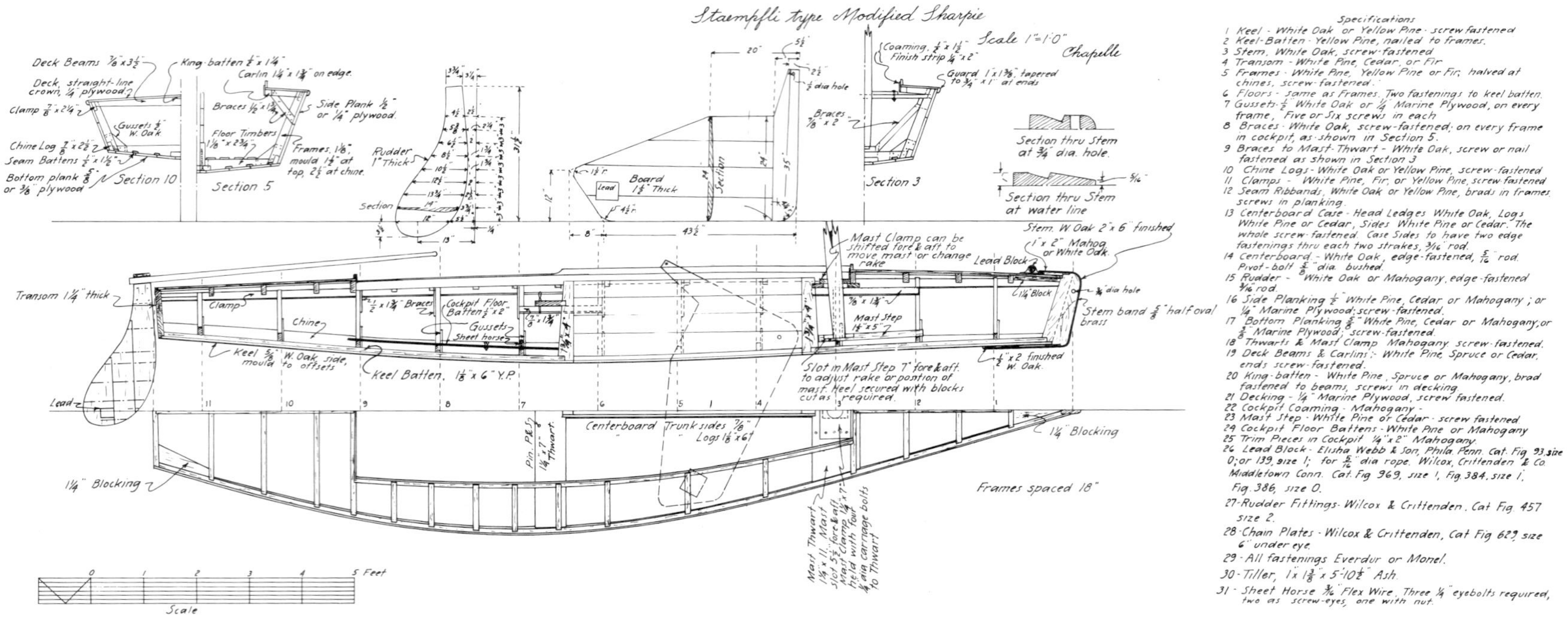
Staempfli type Modified Sharpie
Scale 1" = 1'0"
Chapelle
Deck Beams 7/8" x 3 1/2"
King-batten 1/2" x 1 1/4"
Carlin 1 1/4" x 1 3/4" on edge.
Deck, straight-line crown, 1/4" plywood
Clamp 7/8" x 2 1/4"
Braces 1/2" x 1 3/4"
Side Plank 1/2" or 1/4" plywood.
Gussets 1/2" W. Oak
Floor Timbers 1 1/8" x 2 3/4"
Frames, 1 1/8", mould 1 1/2" at top, 2 1/2" at chine.
Chine Log 7/8" x 2 1/2"
Seam Battens 1/2" x 1 1/2"
Bottom plank 5/8" or 3/8" plywood
Section 10
Section 5
Rudder 1" Thick
Section
Board 1 1/8" Thick
Lead
Section
Braces 7/8" x 2
1/2" dia hole
Coaming, 1/2" x 1 1/2"
Finish strip 1/4" x 2"
Guard 1" x 1 3/8", tapered to 3/4" x 1" at ends
Section 3
Section thru Stem at 3/4" dia. hole.
Section thru Stem at water line
Stem. W. Oak 2" x 6" finished
1" x 2" Mahog or White Oak
Lead Block
3/4" dia hole
1 1/4" Block
Stem band 5/8" half oval brass
Mast Clamp can be shifted fore & aft to move mast or change rake
Mast Step 1 1/4" x 5"
Transom 1 1/4" thick
Clamp
Chine
Braces
Cockpit Floor Batten 1/2" x 2"
Gussets
Sheet horse
Keel 5/8" mould W. Oak side, to offsets
Keel Batten, 1 1/8" x 6" Y.P.
1/2" x 2 finished W. Oak.
Slot in Mast Step 7" fore & aft to adjust rake or position of mast. Heel secured with blocks cut as required.
Lead
Centerboard
Trunk sides 7/8"
Logs 1 1/8" x 6 1/2"
Pin. P & S
1 1/4" x 7" Thwart
1 1/4" Blocking
1 1/4" Blocking
Frames spaced 18"
Mast Thwart 1 1/4" x 11. Mast slot 5 1/2" fore & aft Mast Clamp 1 1/4" x 7" held with four 1/4" dia carriage bolts to Thwart
Scale
5 Feet
Specifications
1 Keel - White Oak or Yellow Pine - screw fastened
2 Keel-Batten - Yellow Pine, nailed to frames.
3 Stem, White Oak, screw-fastened
4 Transom - White Pine, Cedar, or Fir
5 Frames - White Pine, Yellow Pine or Fir; halved at chines, screw-fastened.
6 Floors - same as Frames. Two fastenings to keel batten.
7 Gussets - 1/2" White Oak or 1/4" Marine Plywood, on every frame, Five or Six screws in each
8 Braces - White Oak, screw-fastened; on every frame in cockpit, as shown in Section 5.
9 Braces to Mast-Thwart - White Oak, screw or nail fastened as shown in Section 3
10 Chine Logs - White Oak or Yellow Pine, screw-fastened
11 Clamps - White Pine, Fir, or Yellow Pine, screw-fastened
12 Seam Ribbands, White Oak or Yellow Pine, brads in frames, screws in planking.
13 Centerboard Case - Head Ledges White Oak, Logs White Pine or Cedar, Sides White Pine or Cedar. The whole screw-fastened. Case Sides to have two edge fastenings thru each two strakes, 3/16" rod.
14 Centerboard - White Oak, edge-fastened, 5/16" rod. Pivot-bolt 5/8" dia. bushed.
15 Rudder - White Oak or Mahogany, edge-fastened 3/16" rod.
16 Side Planking 1/2" White Pine, Cedar or Mahogany; or 1/4" Marine Plywood; screw-fastened.
17 Bottom Planking 5/8" White Pine, Cedar or Mahogany; or 3/8" Marine Plywood; screw-fastened.
18 Thwarts & Mast Clamp Mahogany screw-fastened.
19 Deck Beams & Carlins:- White Pine, Spruce or Cedar, ends screw-fastened.
20 King-batten - White Pine, Spruce or Mahogany, brad fastened to beams, screws in decking.
21 Decking - 1/4" Marine Plywood, screw fastened.
22 Cockpit Coaming - Mahogany -
23 Mast Step - White Pine or Cedar - screw fastened
24 Cockpit Floor Battens - White Pine or Mahogany
25 Trim Pieces in Cockpit 1/4" x 2" Mahogany.
26 Lead Block - Elisha Webb & Son, Phila. Penn. Cat. Fig 93, size 0; or 139, size 1; for 5/16" dia rope. Wilcox, Crittenden & Co. Middletown Conn. Cat. Fig 969, size 1, Fig. 384, size 1, Fig. 386, size 0.
27 - Rudder Fittings - Wilcox & Crittenden. Cat Fig. 457 size 2.
28 - Chain Plates - Wilcox & Crittenden, Cat Fig 629, size 6" under eye.
29 - All fastenings Everdur or Monel.
30 - Tiller, 1" x 1 3/8" x 5'-10 1/2" Ash.
31 - Sheet Horse 3/16" Flex Wire. Three 1/4" eyebolts required, two as screw-eyes, one with nut.

PLATE 38. *Construction Plans for 16½-Foot Staempfli-Type Modified Sharpie*

highly finished topside job, the planks of the sides may be cut with taper so that all seams will run more or less with the sheer. Except for the labor of cutting the plank to the required shape, there is no great difficulty in doing this. The first step is to decide how many strakes will be employed. It is a pretty universal rule that no top-side strake above the water line should exceed 7 inches in width, when in place. In a small boat, under 30 feet in length, 3 to 5 inches is a reasonable maximum. The width of planking stock available will have much to do with fixing the number of strakes used. Due to the shapes required, it is practically impossible to give a rule that will show how much loss of width to expect. Most builders plan as they go, altering the widths if necessary, and perhaps adding a strake if it looks as if the planned number is going to cause difficulty.

Assuming a modified sharpie is to be planked in this fashion, the builder takes a straight batten, say, 2 inches wide and ¾ inch thick; this he bends around the side of the hull on the stocks, from bow to stern, with its bottom about 5 inches below the sheer at its lowest point, which will be on a mold or frame. In springing the batten he allows it to bend naturally, resting on every frame or mold; he does not spring its ends up or down, that is, he does not "edgeset" the batten. A few short brads or nails will serve to hold it sprung in position.

Now the bottom of the batten, being straight, is the line of the bottom of a straightedged plank, allowing 5 inches of width at the lowest point of the sheer. By measuring the width, bottom of batten to the sheer line (allowing for the necessary bevel at the sheer for deck) at bow and stern, the builder has the width of plank that will be required to get out the sheer strake 5 inches wide. If he has stock enough for the two planks, and of the required width, he can go ahead. If not, he will have to reduce the width at the lowest point of the sheer, or order stock of the required width. The batten is removed and the plank for the sheer strake on one side is clamped into place, its bottom at the mark on a mold or frame for 5 inches at the lowest point of the sheer. The sheer is then scribed on the plank. If the ends must stand some distance from the sheer marks on the molds, or from a sheer batten, due to the width of the stem, it is well to fit the bow end as is done to side-plank in flat-bottom hulls (as described in the last chapter), before scribing the sheer. Once more, don't forget to allow for the beveling of the sheer. The plank, being scribed for sheer and the bow end fitted to the rabbet, perhaps, is sawn to the marks. The builder knows that one of the indications of a good job of "lining off" is that the planks in the topsides, above the water line, look as if they were parallel when in place. However, he knows that if the seams are actually measured parallel in a profile drawing, and then constructed that way, the optical illusion caused by the sweep of the side will make the strake look actually wider at bow and stern than amidships. If the flare of the sides is not the same in all molds or frames, but the slope, or flare, of the sides increases at bow and stern, he will cut the bottom of the sheer strake parallel to the sheer just cut, because the roll-in of the plank will give an apparent taper when in place. On the other hand, if the plank must roll outward at the bottom at bow and stern, due to decreased flare there, he will cut the bottom of the sheer strake so that its ends are narrower than its middle. When the sheer strake has been fitted, and its mate made, they are fastened into place. If the hull shows great flare at a point slightly abaft the bow, as in many powerboats, the bottom of the sheer strake is established by bending a light batten over the frames in the desired position, and marking each frame before shaping the bottom of the strake.

Then the builder fixes the width of the chine strake in the same manner, using the batten. If the stern is deep enough he will attempt to bring the top of this strake to the transom, if width of material available will allow; if not, he will have to end it on the chine. While the batten is in place, with its top representing the top of the lowest strake of the side, call it the "chine strake," the builder measures from the top of the batten to the underside of the sheer strake at stern, bow, and point of lowest freeboard. By these measurements he will estimate the number of strakes he will have to use. It is obvious that the roll of the side will possibly cause some variation in width of strakes at some part of the hull, and so he may find that he will have to change his estimate in order to get the most out of his planking stock. However, that does not worry him now; he will wait until he has some more plank on before coming to a final decision.

The next step is to put on another pair of planks under the sheer strakes. In a well-lined-off planking job, these should be a little narrower than the sheer strake. He looks at bow and stern to see how far he has to run, up and down, in order to close the opening between the chine and sheer strakes. He decides that, according to his estimate, he should have four strakes between the chine and sheer strakes. One strake will have to be a little wider at the bow than elsewhere, and a little wider at the stern than amidships; this won't look well in the topsides. Therefore he plans to either alter the top of his chine plank by bowing it down amidships, or to get the odd-shaped "closer" or "shutter" below the water line.

## Closing Sides

Having come to a conclusion as to how the shutter will be handled, the builder marks the position of the top of the chine plank, as represented by the batten, on the frames or molds and removes it. He has decided that the two strakes below the sheer should be so cut that they appear to parallel the underside of the sheer strake and that they are to be 4 inches wide amidships. He marks the spacing of the two strakes on the midship mold, or point of lowest freeboard, then springs a plank over the molds or frames with its top overlapping the bottom of the sheer strake and its bottom well below the mark representing the bottom of this strake when finished. The ends must come low enough at bow and stern to allow for the width of end that will enable the bottom of the strake to appear parallel to the sheer strake; that fixes the width of plank he must use. Getting inside the boat, he runs a pencil along the underside of the sheer strake, making a line between frames or molds on the new plank, which represents the top of the new strake. He also transfers the mark of the bottom of the strake on the frame, or mold, amidships to the plank. Now he removes it, saws the top and draws the bottom parallel, or nearly so, to the top, using the principle that guided his decision in the sheer strake. He then puts the strake back in position and fits the ends. After making a mate, using the first as a template, he fastens both into place. If he finds that he has not width enough to overlap the sheer strake a little, in marking, he fits the plank to the frames, or molds, a little below the sheer strake, spiles the top, cuts and replaces to fit the ends, and marks the depth of the bottom from the mark on the side of the amidship mold, or frame, at its edge. The next strake is fitted in the same manner.

Now the builder has two more strakes and the chine strake to fit. He already has the top of the chine strake established, as he thinks it ought to stand; with his dividers, he spaces the widths of the two strakes above the chine strake on each frame, by dividing the space in two. If it appears that the roll of the sides is such that these two strakes would develop great widths at the ends and narrow widths in the middle, it is brought home to him that he will have to cut the top of the chine strake lower in the middle than at the ends. When he has decided this, he planks on down, using the same method as before but using the marks he finally establishes for the bottom of each strake when checking the spacing on each frame. He may even widen or narrow the strake immediately above the chine strake, if most of it is going to be below the water line, in order to maintain the greatest possible width in the chine strake.

The description of this operation of planking up is much more complicated than the actual construction, and the apparent uncertainty of the builder is not as great. If the sides do not change flare fore and aft of amidships there actually is no uncertainty necessary in spacing off the planks. It is often assumed that it is only necessary to divide each frame or mold, and the stem and stern, from chine to sheer, by the same number of spaces, to lay off the planking. This can only be done on a small boat; on a large hull it will be found that it will be impossible to get plank wide enough to cut the edge curves necessary in such a method of lining off.

## Remarks on Lining Off

When laid out flat, the sheer strake, and those parallel to it, will often show an S shape, and though appearing parallel edged in place, actually will not be; lining off such a plank will show why the width of the planking available is so great a consideration. The characteristics of a well-planked hull are: the sheer strake appears to be a little wider than the others in the topsides and to have its bottom edge almost parallel to the sheer, perhaps with a very little more curve fore and aft than the sheer, if the hull is rather straight on top; the rest of the strakes should appear to parallel the bottom of the sheer strake, or nearly so, in the manner the bottom of the sheer strake follows the sheer. When the water line is reached, the builder no longer regards appearance, but closes in to the chine in the best way he can with regard to stock available. However, even here a good workman will try to keep his seams fair,

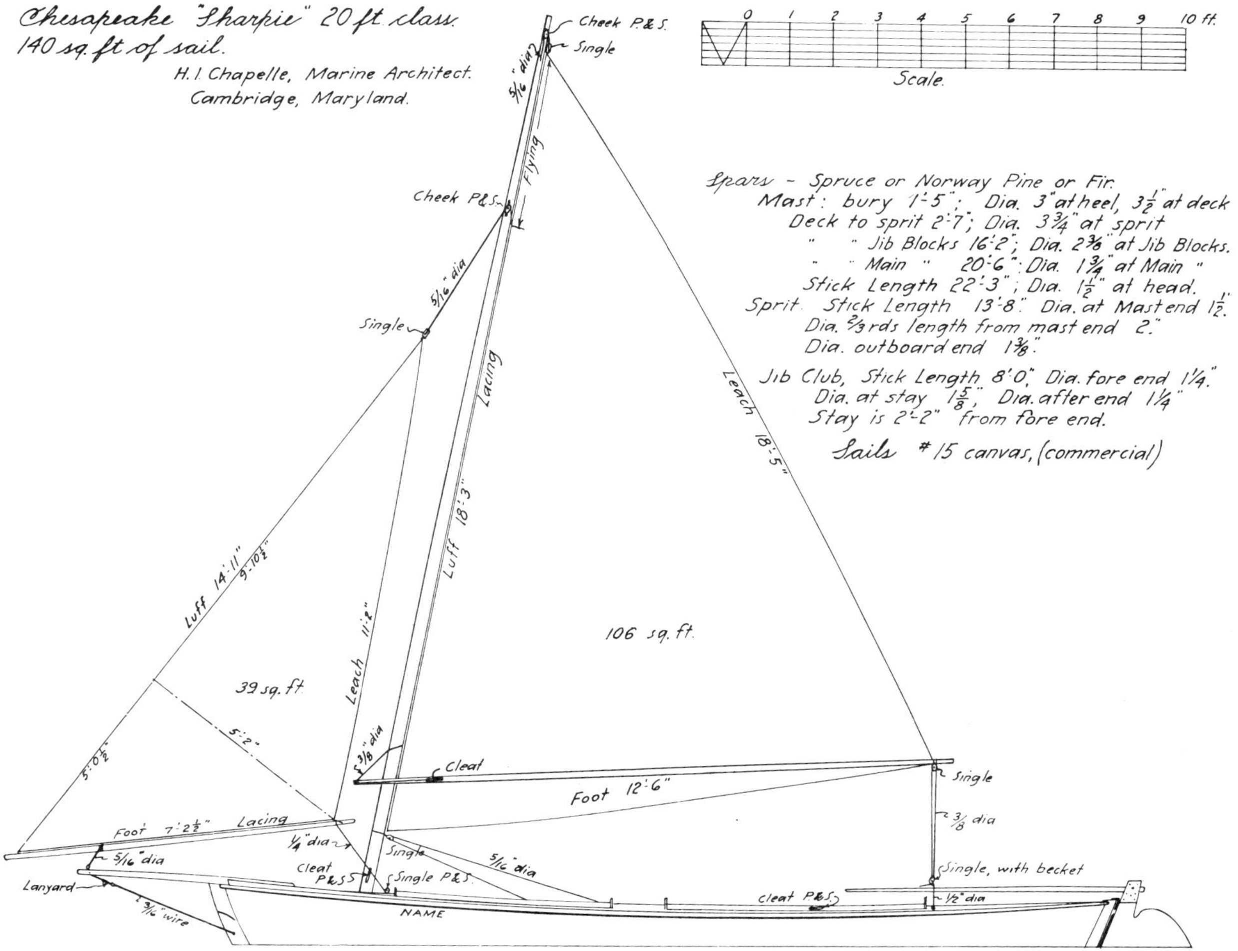

Chesapeake "Sharpie" 20 ft class.
140 sq. ft of sail.
H. I. Chapelle, Marine Architect.
Cambridge, Maryland.
Cheek P.&S.
Single
5/16" dia
Flying
Cheek P&S
5/16" dia
Single
Lacing
Luff 18'3"
Leach 18'5"
106 sq. ft.
Luff 14'11"
9'10½"
39 sq. ft
Leach 11'2"
5'2"
5'0½"
3/8" dia
Cleat
Foot 12'6"
Single
3/8 dia
Foot 7'2½"
Lacing
1/4" dia
5/16" dia
Single
5/16" dia
Cleat P&S
Single P&S
Single, with becket
Cleat P&S
1/2" dia
Lanyard
3/16" wire
NAME
0 1 2 3 4 5 6 7 8 9 10 ft.
Scale.
Spars - Spruce or Norway Pine or Fir.
Mast: bury 1'5"; Dia. 3" at heel, 3½" at deck
Deck to sprit 2'7"; Dia. 3¾" at sprit
" " Jib Blocks 16'2"; Dia. 2⅜" at Jib Blocks.
" " Main " 20'6"; Dia. 1¾" at Main "
Stick Length 22'3"; Dia. 1½" at head.
Sprit. Stick Length 13'8". Dia. at Mast end 1½".
Dia. ⅔rds length from mast end 2".
Dia. outboard end 1⅜".
Jib Club, Stick Length 8'0". Dia. fore end 1¼".
Dia. at stay 1⅝". Dia. after end 1¼"
Stay is 2'2" from fore end.
Sails #15 canvas, (commercial)


PLATE 39. *Sail Plan of Chesapeake Sharpie, 20-Foot Class*

and in the same general order as the topside seams. In order to prevent too much sweep-up on the stem at the top of the chine plank in some hulls, it may be necessary to hog the top of the strake instead of leaving it straight, or dropping it amidships as described. The strake above the chine is usually considered the shutter; this is the strake that may be of any width the combination of space and material requires. However, if it is exposed above the water line it is well to use the chine strake as the shutter. The important feature in lining off a shutter strake, or any strake in fact, is to retain enough width at the ends of the plank to allow for at least two well-driven fastenings there. Too often, planking jobs are seen in which the ends of the planking are so narrow, along the stem or transom, that they become mere strips with hardly enough room for a single fastening.

### Regular V-Bottom Hulls, Construction, Ribband Seams

The next type of V-bottom construction to be described is that in which the chine runs up on the stem and by this means increases the dead rise at the bow over that amidships. This is the most popular model of V-bottom built by amateurs. The construction of the hull, so far as framing and setting up are concerned, follows the plan generally used in flat-bottom hulls, except for the keel structure. This may be of the sprung type, or may be built up as in a round-bottom hull. If the hull is cross-planked, there are usually no frames in the bottom and the hull is built over molds, like a flat-bottom boat. If the bottom is planked lengthwise, there are sawn frames, and these are used instead of molds. The construction, in any case, has been covered by what has been said previously. The side planking may be that used in flat-bottom hulls, or may be the spiled type just described. In some yacht types the sides are batten-seam construction. This is made in the same way as the spiled planking but, as each plank is fitted, its seam is marked, the plank removed, and a notch cut in the frames to take a ribband. It is usual, in flat-sided V-bottom hulls, to use somewhat wider plank, in the side, with seam battens than would otherwise be employed. The ribbands should be fastened in the frame notches with brads or screws and then fastened to the planking on each side of the seam from the inside. Screws are the most satisfactory fastenings here. They should be bored

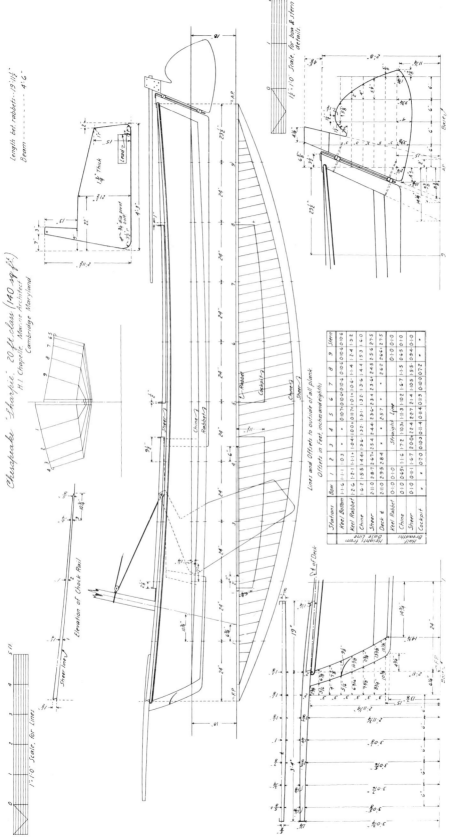

PLATE 40. Lines of a Chesapeake Sharpie, 20-Foot Class

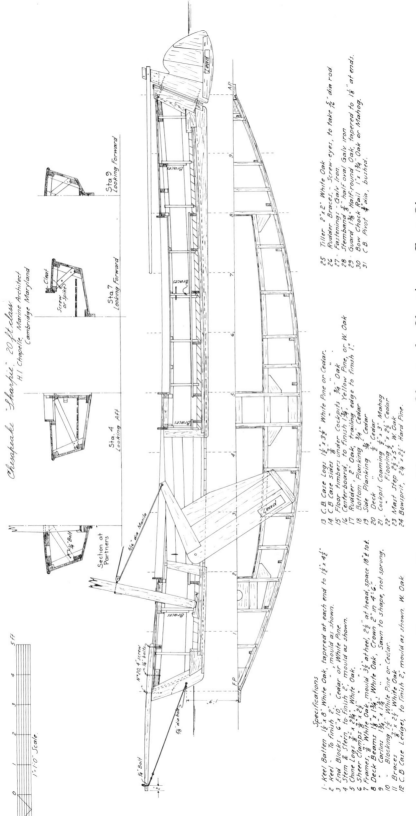

PLATE 41. *Construction Plans of a Chesapeake Sharpie, 20-Foot Class*

for with care, so as not to split the ribbands. If the ribbands and planking are very light, use copper tacks, clenched on the inside, instead. These can ordinarily be used by starting a small hole with an awl, but a very small drill in a pushdrill handle is safer. The art of clenching nails will be described when round-bottom lap-strake construction is discussed.

Many designs having the batten-seam type of construction call for the bottom seam battens to parallel the center line of the hull; it is best to place these as the bottom planks are fitted, as there will usually be a slight sweep in the ribband if the edges of the bottom plank are straight. The ends of all ribbands used in batten-seam construction must notch into the stem, transom, or chine, wherever they land. This is laborious, and professional builders question whether the saving in frames (the frames can be wider spaced with seam battens than without) is not counterbalanced by the notching, as far as time and labor are concerned. The ribbands must have their outer surfaces flush with the outside faces of the frames and must bear fairly on the strakes on each side of the seam. It is a good plan to lute the faces of the ribbands heavily before planking over them. If screws are required to hold the ribbands in the frame notches, mark their positions on the outside of the planks, as the latter are put in place, to enable the plank fastenings to be properly staggered in the frame. Ribband fastenings should be directly under the planking seam in all frames; no fastenings should be driven through plank, ribbands, and frame in most hulls.

### Regular V-Bottom, Cross-Planked on Bottom, Fashioning Ends

If the bottom is cross-planked, it should be done herringbone fashion in almost every design, unlike the modified sharpie. There is a practical reason for this: the difference in the curves of the rabbet and chine, as seen in the profile plan, would necessitate twist in planks laid square to the hull's center line. It is only in rare cases that the regular V-bottom hull can be planked square across on the bottom; this is when the rabbet of the keel and the chine are parallel in the profile plan. When the keel rabbet is a straight line and the chine a curve, as might be the case in the forward part of a V-bottom hull having a marked forefoot, the twist in square planking would be very great. The angle at which the bottom plank stands to the center line of the hull should be about 12 degrees, using fan-shaped staving at the ends to come up to the stem rabbet and transom bottom, or to the end blocks. In small double-enders the bottom can be laid herringbone with both ends filled in with fan-shaped staving; the forward portion has the widest ends of the fan-shaped staving at the chine, while aft the fan staving is reversed so that the wide ends are at the keel rabbet. Fore-and-aft staving in the ends is also used, a wide floor frame being

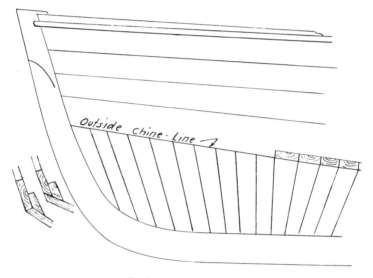

Outside chine·line

*76. Reduced Bevel at Chine*

worked into the hull at the place or places where the seam of the last cross-plank is to rest (being brought square by fan-shaped staving from the herringbone, at this point); and then the short fore-and-aft staving is worked in, using plank about one fourth thicker than the cross-planking.

The fastenings are deeply set, or countersunk, and the staving is then dubbed fair to the rest of the bottom with adz and plane. All staving, in the ends of a V-bottom, whether fan shaped or fore and aft, requires a little fitting at chines and rabbet so that each piece bears properly at these points. In some boats the fore-and-aft staving is a little harder to fit than the fan staving, but is considered superior in lasting qualities. The builder can usually decide the type of staving most suitable for the boat he is building by testing the bottom with short pieces of plank after the chines are in place on the molds. A full bow, at the chine line, will usually have to be staved with fan-shaped stuff; the very sharp bow having a marked forefoot can best be fore-and-aft staved. Very often a little study of the loft plan will enable a builder to see what must be done. If there is little dead rise and not much difference in height of chine and keel rabbet at the stem, or stem and stern in a double-ender, the use of end blocks is most satisfactory. These have already been discussed in previous chapters. The chines will have to be fitted to the top of the blocks. In small craft the top of the blocks runs flat across, from chine to chine, so the inside edge of the chine logs must be cut down from the bevel used elsewhere along the bottom. It is a good plan to back the seams formed by the inboard end of the block, or blocks, and the cross-planking of the bottom, with a cross-batten, or false floor timber. All herringbone bottom plank should be laid with their annual rings in the same position as in a flat-bottom boat. The bottom should be formed with calking seams; never attempt a "tight seam job" (planking with the seam closed tight at both the inside and outside faces of the planking) in any cross-planked hull, whether V-bottom or flat.

It is always well to use narrow planking in the bottom of a cross-planked hull, particularly when herringbone is used. If the dead rise is great and—even with the herringbone—there is some twist in the planking, it is a good plan to increase the thickness of the bottom strakes by one fourth so as to permit fitting at chine and keel rabbet, rather than to attempt to twist the strakes. An increase in the angle of the bottom planking to the keel rabbet may help the situation. In any V-bottom having great dead rise, the bevel of the bottom planking becomes excessive along the chine as the bow is approached. This may be overcome by suddenly stopping the bevel of the bottom of the chine strake at some arbitrarily chosen point on the chine; from there to the bow, fit the bottom planking against the square bevel of the chine strake. This requires the ends of the bottom strakes, in a cross-planked bottom, to be beveled a little to fit against the bottom of the chine strake. This effectively covers the raw ends of the bottom strakes and makes a better calking seam than excessively beveled ends. The same principle can be applied to fore-and-aft bottom planking, though it is less easily done.

## Regular V-Bottom Fore-and-Aft Bottom Planking

Boats of the regular V-bottom model, with the chine carried high on the stem, are often required to be planked fore and aft on the bottom, their shape requiring all, or most of, the bottom plank to end on the stem. Without doubt, this is one of the hardest hull forms to plank. Even when the stem is well rounded on the forefoot, as in most sailing hulls of this form, it is usually necessary to steam-bend the garboard strake, at least to get it to the stem rabbet without breaking or splitting. This is also the case with hulls whose fore-and-aft planking runs to the chine instead of to the stem, outside of the garboard. When the garboard is to end on the stem, the builder may as well prepare to steam this strake, before trying to fit it, as to "wait and see."

## Steaming and Boiling Plank

When plank must be steamed in order to be bent or twisted, the easiest way is to boil the ends requiring treatment after the plank has been fitted. Any large, square, metal tub will serve. Fill the tub about three quarters full of water and set over a fire. While waiting for the water to boil add a few handfuls of rock salt or soft soap. Obtain a few pieces of flannel, or sacking, with which to wrap the end of the plank. When the water is boiling, wrap the plank end in the cloth, as far as the twist is to extend, and place it in the tub. With a dipper, saturate the cloth with hot water. This must be continued for quite a long time, say, about an hour, wetting the cloth above the water line in the tub at five-minute intervals. At the end of the period remove the cloth and bring the plank to the hull, fit and secure it to the bow with a few cleats on the side of the stem, and a clamp or two, then gently but firmly bring it around the molds, forcing it into the keel rabbet and clamping at each frame. If the forward end of the plank is tapered to a thin wedge, due to the rounded rabbet of the stem, it is a good plan, prior to boiling, to screw a cleat across the outside of the plank near the stem, but clear of the rabbet and also clear of the keel, to keep the plank from splitting. It will help if boiling water is poured on the plank while it is being bent. If a large tank can be obtained, long and wide enough to take the whole plank for the length of the twist, the cloth is omitted and the whole end is inserted and well boiled. This is the easiest method, of course. An old hot-water boiler, with one end cut off, will serve. The steel farm tanks used for watering stock, which may be obtained from the mail-order houses at very low cost, are even better. For

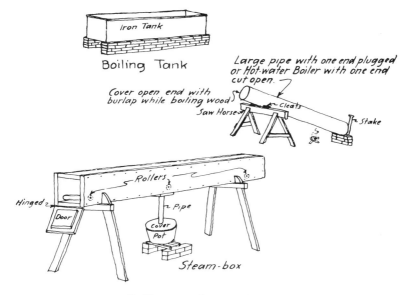

*77. Boiling Tanks and Steam Box*

plank, a tank 1 by 2 by 6 feet is a useful size. Boiling is more practical than steaming, as few amateur builders care to go to the trouble of building a wooden steam box and then attaching a boiler to it. Steaming is a slower operation than boiling. It is doubtful if boiling harms timber any more than steaming; at any rate, either will kill the dry-rot spores. The boiling tank may be set on loose brick or concrete blocks, and the fire fed with scrap lumber, or a couple of single-burner oil stoves may be used instead. Boiling water is required, not just hot. Incidentally, the plank will be so hot that gloves will be required when handling it. The subject of steam bending will be discussed again in a later chapter.

## Regular V-Bottom. Fitting Garboard, Spiling

The fitting of the garboard, prior to boiling, is not a difficult matter if a thin template is used to obtain the first fit. An experienced builder can spile off the plank accurately enough from a wide batten, but the beginner will usually waste less stock if he makes a template. This can be of ⅜ or ½ inch plank, wider than the proposed garboard, that can be twisted, to the roll of the bottom, cold. The spiling is done in the manner already described. First fit the plank to the rabbet roughly, by cutting the end to the approximate curve of the stem rabbet with a hatchet. The after end should run by the stern if the garboard is to be in one length. The template should be brought as close to the keel rabbet as it will come without edgeset. The roughly shaped fore end is in the bow rabbet, held by clamps, or cleats screwed to the side of the stem. The compasses are set with the opening equal to the greatest distance from any point on the rabbet to template edge. The arcs are now scribed; along the keel the spacing may be from 3 to 6 inches, but on the stem the spacing should be from 1 to 2 inches. The arcs should be about quarter circles. When this is done, remove the template and, with a batten, run a line *tangent* to the arcs. Cut to this and then fit to the hull. If carefully done, the template will fit very closely; a few shavings may have to be removed with the plane.

The top of the garboard can be struck off on the template if desired. To do this, the bottom planking should be lined off. As this must be done in any case before steaming the garboards, it will be described now. In most V-bottom hulls, the top of the garboard is straight before being sprung over the frames. This makes a sharp sweep-up to the top edge at the stem, which is unsightly and, if other bottom planks are to end on the stem, runs the strake up the rabbet too far. For that reason it is often well to spring a curve into the top of the garboard, making it wider in the middle than forward. This is "hogging" the seam. In some hulls the ending of the garboard forward is of great importance. This is true of V-bottom hulls in which all the bottom plank run to the rabbet of the stem, as in round-bottom hulls. There is no rule for finding the end; it is largely a matter of experience with a given hull form. However, when faced with this problem, it is usually safe to end the garboard on the stem, or on the keel at the stem, at a height found by projecting the top of the garboard amidships to the stem, parallel to the load water line. This is not always possible, but at least should be approached as nearly as the hull form permits.

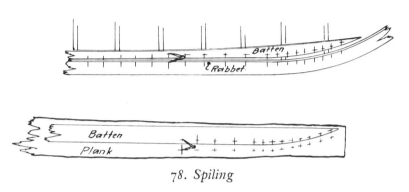

*78. Spiling*

The stern end of the garboard on this form of hull is usually a little narrower than at amidships. A batten can be sprung over the frames, to represent the top of the garboard and edgeset to give the proper hog. The frames can then be marked for the width of the garboard and the template marked to suit, while being checked. When this has been done, and the curve swept in with a batten on the template, after it has been removed from the hull, the top may be cut. Now the template will be the exact shape of the garboards and may be used as the pattern for the pair of them.

If a template is not made, a fairly wide spiling batten is used in the same way, but is not cut to fit the rabbet after being removed. It is handled in this manner: the spilings are marked on the batten as on the template, the batten then removed and the line swept in on the batten tangent to the arcs. As the batten may be used again, this can be done with chalk. The batten is then laid on one of the planks to be used for a garboard and, with the compasses set at the same radius as before, the arcs are swept on the plank, using the tangent points formed by the original arcs and the chalk line as radius points. The edge may then be outlined with a batten and a line drawn tangent to the new arcs on the plank; this is the edge of the garboard against the rabbet. The top is laid off as outlined for a template. When one garboard is fitted, the mate of it can be made, using as a pattern the template or the first garboard made. While the batten or template is being spiled, the rabbet can be checked and faired, if necessary, to give good bearing and a tight seam.

## Advantages in Use of Spiling Batten

This method may be used for obtaining the outline of any plank, from sheer strake to garboard. It is used by most builders instead of overlapping one strake over the other when striking the top or bottom of a new strake; it gives a better opportunity to see how the width of the plank can be utilized to the best advantage. When the spiling batten is removed from the hull it is laid on the plank close to the edge of the latter, and then shifted as required, to avoid getting a knot in the edge of the strake, or to avoid sapwood or other objectionable spots. The advantages of this are plain: the plank does not have to be unclamped and shifted as would be the case if the seam were laid off in the manner first described. However, the overlapping method has advantages in speed and accuracy in a small boat; it is probably well suited to the beginner, who must feel his way along in order to find the process most suited to his skill.

## Fitting Bottom Plank Outside of Garboard

When only the garboards, and perhaps part of another strake, run to the rabbet of the stem, the other bottom planks are fitted without taper, or spiling, as in the bottom of a modified sharpie planked fore and aft. The fitting of the planks at the chine becomes a source of some difficulty, however, as the bevel of the edges of these planks is usually excessive, which makes fastening very trying.

## Fitting Bottom Plank, Running to the Stem

If all the bottom planks are to come to the stem rabbet, in a V-bottom hull, it is probable that their ends (called "hood ends") must be quite narrow and that the chine strake on the bottom will have to be very wide and therefore an unusually wide plank in the rough is necessary. This will sometimes have to be pieced up with "stealers." Very often all the bottom plank will have to be steamed or boiled at the fore ends; the builder should not force the planks edgewise, or edgeset them, as this will very probably strain the hull out of line. The method of lining off the bottom of such a hull is similar to that used to plank a modified sharpie's sides, but very much more difficult. It may be permissible to tender a suggestion that no amateur attempt the building of a hull having this bottom planking until he has built some round-bottom hulls, in order that he have sufficient experience in lining off under varying conditions of hull form. This method of planking the V-bottom requires as much skill in lining off and fitting as any round-bottom hull.

## Improvisation to Suit Materials

Perhaps the builder has to improvise in planking the bottom of a V-bottom. To illustrate: the builder is planking the bottom of a V-bottom hull lengthwise and is putting on the garboard strake. He finds that the stock he has available will not bend to the required twist at the stem. After breaking a number of planks he decides that his stock will not stand the twist even with ample boiling. This should not cause him to give up: there are a number of things he can do, depending upon the locality where the building is being done and upon the type of boat he is building. First, he can obtain stock of some other timber than the designer specified; oak or elm will steam-bend much better than mahogany, white pine, white cedar, fir, or spruce. Therefore, he can try a garboard of oak or elm. It may be, however, that the additional weight of the oak, or elm, is a factor that forbids its use. Still the problem can be solved. He can fit his garboard as far forward as his stock will stand the twist of the bottom and put in a false frame on which the forward end will bear. Then he can fan-stave the bow, or put in the thick fore-and-aft staving, used in the herring-bone bottom. Of course, none of these alternatives is as desirable as carrying out the plans and specifications, but very often it is a practical matter of overcoming the problem, or giving up building the boat. The timber available has to be used without regard to the designer's desires, in many cases. Unfortunately, some plans specify timber for some portion of the hull which is entirely unsuited for the twist or bend required. Mahogany is often specified; it does not always respond to steaming or boiling. Sometimes better results are obtained by soaking the wood in cold water (that is, water not heated) for a long time, say, a month, prior to using it. Very dry wood is often unsuited to sharp bends or twists, even when steamed; green stock of the same timber is better for the purpose.

## Other Methods of Planking—Lap-Strake

Other forms of planking are sometimes required in the V-bottom hull. Lap-strake topsides are used in both power and sailing craft occasionally. The fitting of this kind of planking is like that used in round-bottom hulls and will be described when special construction is discussed. In general, the fitting of the plank is the same as in flat-bottom hulls having sides of this type, but the lining off is of greater importance. Likewise, plywood construction is often used in small craft and will be discussed in a later chapter.

## Arc Bottoms

Before leaving the planking of V-bottom hulls, it is desirable to speak briefly of the hull having the bottom athwartship in an arc—as in the Star Class hulls and some other small-class racers. This form of hull is commonly planked lengthwise, over sawn frames, and is built like a modified sharpie, planked in the same manner. If the arc of the bottom varies in radius, toward bow or stern or both, the bottom plank should be put on somewhat narrower than in the modified sharpie and some of the strakes can be tapered in width toward the ends. The taper should be slight, however, or a great deal of unnecessary work will result. Usually the strakes on either side of the center are tapered a little; the others are parallel sided but their edges are not straight: they curve toward the center when viewed from below. It is possible to cross-plank such a hull form, if the arc in section is not great. There must be a rather heavy inside keel, or strongback, down the center and sister-keelsons are required on either side. These are let into the molds before being secured at the chines, their number depending upon the beam and thickness of the bottom. The span between two

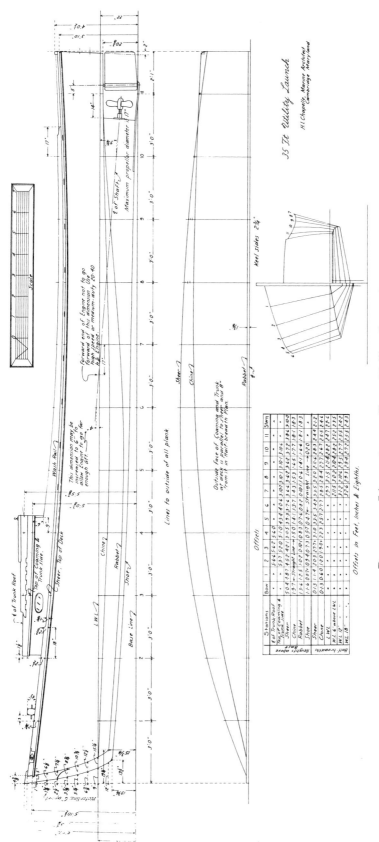

H.I Chapelle, Marine Architect
Cambridge, Maryland

Maximum propeller diameter 17"

Forward end of Engine not to go
forward of this dimension with
high speed or medium auxy 20-40
h.p Engines.

This dimension may be
increased to 6" to
allow Engine to go far
enough aft.

Outside face of Coaming and Trunk
at deck is parallel to sheer and 8"
from it in Half breadth in Plan.

Lines to outside of all plank

Keel sides 2½"

Offsets

| Stations | | Bow | 1 | 2 | 3 | 4 | 5 | 6 | 7 | 8 | 9 | 10 | 11 | Stern |
|---|---|---|---|---|---|---|---|---|---|---|---|---|---|---|
| Heights above Base Line | ℓ of Trunk Roof | | | 5.4.6 | 5.4.6 | 5.2.0 | 5.0 | | | | | | | | |
| | Top of Coaming & Trunk Side | | | 5.3.7 | 5.2.0 | 5.1.0 | 4.3.4 | 4.0.4 | 3.0.7 | 3.0.1 | 3.0.1 | 3.0.4 | | | |
| | Sheer | | 5.0.4 | 4.8.7 | 4.5.2 | 4.2.1 | 3.11.5 | 3.9.3 | 3.7.4 | 3.6.3 | 3.6.2 | 3.7.2 | 3.8.4 | 3.9.0 | |
| | Chine | | 1.9.7 | | | Straight line — 1.5.0 | 1.4.1 | 1.3.7 | 1.4.3 | 1.5.3 | 1.6.5 | 1.7.7 | 1.8.1 | 1.8.3 | |
| | Rabbet | | 1.3.6 | 1.2.5 | 1.0.2 | 1.0.4 | 0.8.3 | 0.7.6 | 0.8.2 | 0.9.0 | 1.0.4 | 1.1.4 | 1.4.1 | 1.8.1 | 1.8.3 |
| | Shoe | | 1.1.6 | 0.8.9 | 0.9.4 | 0.7.3 | 0.5.7 | 0.4.7 | — Straight Line — 0.2.0 | | | | | | |
| Half breadths | Sheer | | 0.3.1 | 1.1.4 | 2.0.3 | 2.7.7 | 3.1.0 | 3.3.5 | 3.4.3 | 3.3.5 | 3.2.0 | 2.9.4 | 2.8.3 | 2.4.4 | 2.1.2 |
| | Chine | | 0.1.3 | 0.6.0 | 1.2.0 | 1.9.0 | 2.2.3 | 2.5.7 | 2.7.7 | 2.8.5 | 2.8.4 | 2.7.7 | 2.6.7 | 2.5.5 | 2.4.4 |
| | L.W.L. | | | | | | | | 1.9.7 | 1.11.5 | 2.1.4 | 2.2.7 | 2.4.7 | 2.8.6 | |
| | W.L. 6 above LWL | | | | | | | | 2.0.3 | 2.0.2 | 2.0.4 | 2.3.2 | 2.5.2 | 2.8.6 | |
| | W.L 12″ | | | | | | | | | 3.1.2 | 2.0.4 | 2.3.5 | 2.7.7 | 2.5.5 | 2.4.2 |
| | W.L 18″ | | | | | | | | | 3.7.4 | 2.9.3 | 2.9.4 | 2.7.2 | 2.5.5 | 2.4.3 |

Offsets in Feet, Inches & Eighths.

## PLATE 42. *Lines of a 35-Foot Utility Launch*

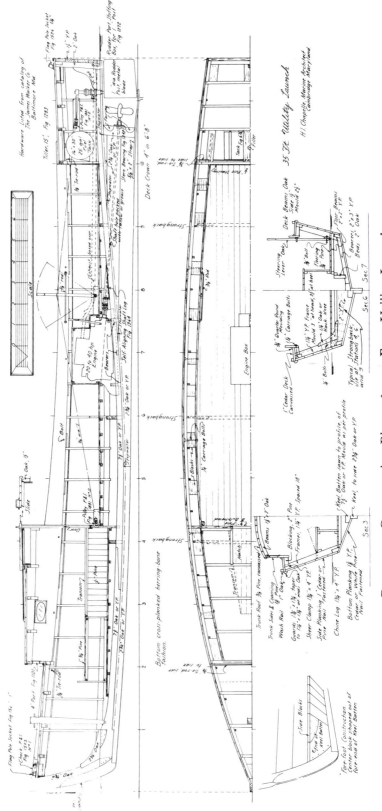

PLATE 43. Construction Plans of a 35-Foot Utility Launch

sister-keelsons, or between the strongback and the sister-keelsons, should not exceed 18 inches, edge to edge, in any boat built this way. The reason is that, unless there is ample support, the bottom will straighten out. To hold this form in shape there must be a few frames or bulkheads to give support to the fore-and-aft members. The use of cross-planking in such hulls is rare and it is doubtful if there is any advantage that warrants its use, in hulls of the size commonly employing the arc bottom.

### Multi-Chine Hulls

Multi-chine hulls are planked fore and aft on the bottom. In construction and planking they develop special problems for a builder. The frames are sawn and beveled—the side timber of a natural crook, if possible, and the bottom timber of straight-

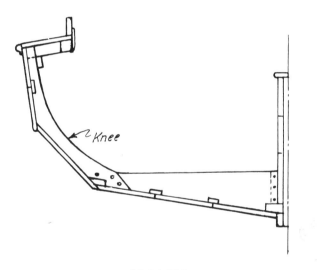

79. *Multi-Chine*

grained stock. The floors are made as in other V-bottom frames. By using natural crooks (timber that has grown in a curved or crooked fashion) it is possible to avoid the use of gussets at the lower chines, as the heel of the side timbers may be given enough spread to allow three good fastenings to the bottom frame timber. The lower chine is usually fitted with a chine batten; the frames are notched and the batten secured in place, then beveled to the outer face of the frames. The upper chine (or chines) is often made by a lap-seam, as in a lap-strake hull, or a chine batten is used. This is a very troublesome seam to make as a lap-strake at a chine line if there is much angle, as the bow and stern are approached. Do not attempt to make a rabbet in the lap at bow and stern; use the "dory lap" instead.

## Lining Off for Multi-Chine Hull

The lining off of multi-chine hulls is likely to be troublesome in some designs. Generally, the ideal is to make the planking between two chines of one width in the topsides. This is rarely possible, so often two or three strakes must be fitted. As all strakes must come to the stem rabbet, just as in a round-bottom hull, the strakes often show a good deal of edge-curvature when spiled off. In many designs there is a great deal of twist required in the bottom plank, so steaming is necessary. If the bottom is planked with some of its strakes landing on the chine, as in a modified sharpie, the lower chine logs must be fairly heavy—more so than when all the bottom plank have hood ends on the stem rabbet. The planks of a multi-chine hull are usually spiled by laying a batten on the frames, centrally between two chines, but allowing it to bend without edgesetting, and then spiling to both chine lines, in one operation. This can be done when two strakes are required by using one edge of the batten to represent the straight edge of each of the two strakes. Multi-chine hulls usually are not very easy to plank, in spite of their apparent simplicity.

## Fastenings, Bunging

Fastenings of the planking, in V-bottom hulls, are those used in flat-bottom hulls. These have already been discussed, but the method of finishing the fastenings outside the plank require mention and, as the V-bottom hull is usually better finished than a flat-bottom, this is an opportune time to look into the matter. It is usual to counterbore for plank fastenings. The depth of the counterboring, or countersinking, is fixed by the thickness of the planking, which in turn fixes the depth of the plug, or "bung," used. In thin planking it is quite plain that the countersink cannot be deep; yet if the depth of the plug is not about two thirds its diameter it will not stay in place well. One half is the absolute minimum. When this problem arises, the fastening should be countersunk and the hole puttied. The rule for counterboring is that the plug diameter be no larger than necessary to allow the head of the fastening to enter its hole. The countersink is bored first, then the leading hole for the fastening. When the fastening is driven home, plugs (which can be purchased of varying sizes and woods) are dipped in varnish, or thick paint, and then driven into the countersink. A good job requires that the grain in the plug be in line with that of the planking. Use a wooden mallet to drive the plug and take care not to crush it in driving, by too heavy a blow. When the plug is driven home, let the paint or varnish harden for a day or so, then cut off the plug outside of the planking with a *sharp* chisel. Don't be too hurried in doing this, or you may have plugs broken off below the surface of the plank, or may make rents in their grain which cannot be smoothed out. Plugging fastenings should be done before smoothing and calking the hull.

## Fastenings, Puttying

The most common objection to puttied fastenings is the liability of the putty to fall out after a period of service. This is caused by improper treatment in preparing the hole for the putty. Nevertheless, this has caused many yachtsmen to conclude that a good job of fastening is indicated by bunged heads. If puttied heads are to be used, the countersunk hole should be as rough as possible, inside. If screws are to be used, the countersinking can be done with a barefoot ship auger, instead of a Foerstner or Jennings bit, or a combination countersink and drill. This will give a rough-sided hole which will hold putty quite well. If nails are used, and the planking stock is of softwood, the nailheads can usually be set, with a "nail set," deep enough to take a little putty. The rough hole formed by the set head of a boat nail in white cedar or white pine will hold putty indefinitely. If the nailhead is too large and flat to be set, or the planking too hard, the head must be counterbored for, with a barefoot ship auger. The argument in favor of using boat nails in cedar and pine planking is that due to the softness of these woods countersunk fastenings weaken it seriously; the boat nail with its head set does not have to enter the wood as deeply as the countersunk head with plug; the puttied head will hold in these timbers better than bungs.

It may be concluded that softwood planking should be nail fastened, with heads set about ⅛ inch below the surface of the planking; hardwood planking should be nail or screw fastened and the heads bunged, if possible. When puttying the holes, it is a good plan to touch the sides of the holes with varnish, which should be allowed to become sticky, or "tacky," before the putty is applied. Marine glue is sometimes used on both bungs and putty to hold them in their holes, but it is more troublesome to use than varnish or paint. Seam compounds or glues are sold that may be used instead of putty in filling countersinks. Hatch or wire nails are often used without countersinking or setting the heads, but not in yachts. In lap-strake planking the heads of the copper tacks and clench nails are usually not countersunk, but are exposed in either a painted or varnished hull. When the planking is very thin and screws are used, it is possible to plug the head with plastic wood, using varnish as a binder. The plastic wood does not need to be very deep, say, 1/16 inch. When applying, let it stand above the surface of the plank until dry, as it shrinks while drying. It can then be planed flush with the planking.

## Righting, Removing Molds

The planking completed, the boat is ready for righting (if built upside down) and for the construction of the deck framing and the removal of the molds. As far as these are concerned, the information given in the last chapter applies. It cannot be too strongly emphasized that molds, if used, should not be removed until the hull is well braced athwartships with deck beams, or cross-spalls. When the frames are sawn, it is well to refrain from removing all the cross-spalls to get in the sheer clamps, if the clamps are inside the frames as is usual. At least the cross-spalls amidships should be left in place until some deck framing replaces those removed.

## Knees

The fitting of knees inside the hull should be done when the deck beams are being fitted. The vertical knees are the "hanging knees" and usually fasten to the underside of deck beams, and to the inboard face, or side, of hull frames with screws, rivets, or bolts, depending upon size. Knees resting horizontally between the deck beams are "lodging knees" and serve to stiffen the deck in lieu of blocking. There is no special skill required to fit these knees; the important thing is to so fit them that they bear fairly on the surfaces to which they are fastened. The fastening that passes through the apex of the angle formed by the faces of the knee is the "throat fastening"; on this comes the greatest strain. If rod is used for riveting, be careful to use good clench rings. Other knees are fitted like lodging knees, at the bow and quarters; these are respectively the "breasthook" and "quarter knees"; they are similar to those used in flat-bottom hulls. The faces of knees that bear on frames and beams should be luted before securing the knee in place.

## Decking

As a hull becomes more difficult to build, because of its model, it is usual to find better finish, or better deck joinery, required of the builder. This applies particularly to decks and deck erections. In most small V-bottom sailing and power hulls, the canvas decks described in the last chapter are employed. However, occasionally large V-bottom hulls are designed with bright decks. Also the plan view of the coamings is no longer angular; oval and round cockpits, and rounded corners to the cabin trunk, are not exceptional. If the coaming and trunk sides are to be varnished, the workmanship must be better than when painted.

## Deck Framing Tie Rods

If the cockpit or cabin trunk is rounded in plan, filler blocks cut to the proper curves are inserted at the corners formed by the junctions of carlins and deck beams, where required. These are shown in the deck-framing plan, which is part of the construction drawing furnished by the designer. In most V-bottom hulls, tie rods are required between the carlins of the trunk and cockpit and the hull sides. These rods hold the deck beams firmly home in the carlins and prevent the deck from opening up. Their diameter will be shown in the construction plan or specification, and their location can be scaled off the blueprint. The rods are commonly of galvanized steel or wrought iron, cut to length and threaded at both ends. Two nuts and two washers are required for each rod. The method of securing the tie rods at the hull side varies and the plans will show the designer's intention. Sometimes the rods are through both frame and sheer clamp; this is rather troublesome to accomplish as the frames are often so small as to make drilling difficult, and the fastenings of the clamp are often in the way. In small craft these are usually screws or nails, but in large hulls bolts or lags will be required to fasten the clamps. When this position of tie rod is required it is well to spot the position of the rod before fastening the clamp. In some designs it is necessary to insert the tie rods before planking the sides, but occasionally the tie rod is made with a head which is countersunk through the planking and the hole plugged. If the planking is under ⅞ inch when finished, the tie rods should be inserted before planking. In most designs the tie rods are only through the clamps, in the spaces, or "bays," between the frames. This will usually require some slope outboard to the tie rods, from the middle of the inboard face of the carlins downward to the middle of the outboard face of the clamps. This can usually be bored accurately enough by eye and no jig is required. The boring should be done with a long-shank ship auger, or with a bit in an extension fitting, in a common brace, if it will reach. If drilled in this manner there will be no bent tie rods resulting from holes drilled out of line. The rods can then be driven through both carlins and clamps from inside the hull; there is nearly always enough space, between the side planking and the clamps, to enable the washer and nut to be put in place. Sometimes it is necessary to revolve a rod, in its holes, to thread on the nut in a tight place; a pipe wrench is handy for this.

When the outboard washer and nut are in place, the inboard washer and nut may be attended to. Do not draw up the tie rod so much that the clamp or carlin is sprung out of line; no great tension is necessary—only enough to bring the washers snug against the timbers. If the pitch of the rod is great, it is a good plan to partly countersink the washer so that it bears on the carlin completely, not just on one side. When the tie rods are in place, the surplus rod projecting from the carlins should be sawn off.

There is one thing that the builder should observe in fitting carlin tie rods: the thickness of the inside coaming or finishing

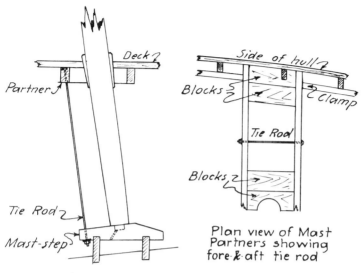

Deck

Partner

Side of hull

Blocks

Clamp

Tie Rod

Blocks

Tie Rod

Mast-step

Vertical Tie Rod

Plan view of Mast Partners showing fore-&-aft tie rod

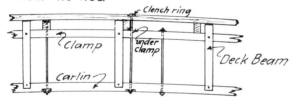

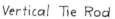

Clench ring

Clamp

under clamp

Deck Beam

Carlin

Carlin Tie Rods

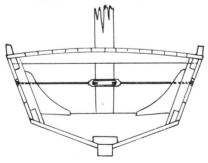

80. Tie Rods

strip compared to the depth the nuts and washers of the tie rods will stand out from the carlins when in place. If the countersink for these, in the finishing strip, must be so deep that there is danger of the drill breaking through the inboard face of the strip, then the nut and washer should be countersunk a little into the carlin. Occasionally it is necessary to fit tie rods fore and aft, to hold two partners or beams from spreading. These must be located as shown on the plans; it is usually a lot easier to complete the partners and insert the rods before putting any of the other deck beams in place. In large V-bottom hulls it is often highly desirable to tie the whole hull together athwartships in line with the end of a large deck opening, or at the partners of the mast of a sloop or cutter. Such a tie rod should be heavy and should be made of two galvanized-steel or wrought-iron rods, each headed at one end and threaded, one right and one left, at the other. The heads should be of the countersunk, flat-top type. The length of the rods should be a little less than the beam of the hull, from outside of plank (at the proper height) to the center line. These rods are inserted through the side planking and a frame, or frame and knee, and joined at the center line by a turnbuckle link. There should be countersunk clench rings or reamed washers under the heads—head and top of washer flush with the planking. Such rods as these are not required in small craft, but only in large, or those that must carry heavy loads.

The use of tie rods between the deck and mast step, or floor timber, in sailing craft is required to prevent the rigging or halyards from causing the deck to lift or hump at the mast. The rods used for this should be headed on one end and threaded on the other; the head in a deck beam on a washer, the whole countersunk. These rods are inserted before the deck is laid as a rule, though occasionally the design requires the head to be countersunk and plugged in the decking. The heels of the rods are usually set up with nut and washer under the mast step. Once in a while it is necessary to set up a rod to a floor timber, or frame, with the bottom planking in place. When this is required, drill the floor, or frame, for the rod, taking care to stop well short of the bottom plank. Then, with a chisel, cut a small rectangular hole from the side of the frame, close to the bottom plank, to intersect the drilled hole. The hole in the side of the frame must be large and deep enough to take the nut and washer, and the rod will have to be revolved to thread into the nut. The rod may be inserted in the hole in the deck beam and its length marked on the side of the floor or frame timber prior to cutting the hole for the nut and washer. As it is usually impractical to bore both the deck beam and floor timber, or mast step, with a long-shanked auger, the rod may be inserted in the hole in the deck beam and dropped to spot the position for the second hole. This avoids a lot of measuring.

## Bright Decks

Varnished or oiled decks are called "bright decks" and are perhaps one of the highest tests of workmanship a builder has to meet. They should not be attempted by a beginner who is not skillful in the use of tools. A tight deck of this type cannot be expected, as a rule, until the second season after it is built. Even teak decks take the first season to thoroughly "settle into place." At the end of the first season, or beginning of the second, the builder should expect to recalk and refill the seams in a bright deck; if he does not have to, it is usually good luck rather than good workmanship alone. In planning a bright deck that must be tight, as in a cruiser, it must be remembered that it is impractical to lay such a deck of less than 1¼ inches in thickness. If the boat is half-decked (partly open with short end decks and narrow side decks), a strictly tight deck is not so important and the decking may be a good deal thinner. In these boats the bright deck is sometimes built of alternating strips of white pine, or cedar, and mahogany. In large craft the deck is laid of white pine, white cedar, or teak. The seams are calked and filled, or "payed," with marine glue, or colored seam compound. Generally speaking, the bright deck is a good deal heavier than a canvas-covered deck, in hulls up to about 30 feet in length. The reason for this will be obvious when the construction of bright decks is explained.

In ordering material for bright decks, it is very important that the mill be given a full-sized drawing of the cross section of the deck plank wanted, that the timber be specified as "quarter-sawn," and that it be clear and without defects. It should be made plain to the mill that the planks must be planed fair, straight and smooth. The material for the covering boards and other trim will probably be of mahogany or teak, to get the contrast in colors that makes bright decks so handsome. If teak decking is used, the covering boards and trim are of the same material, sometimes painted to give contrast.

## Types of Bright Decks

Bright decks are of two types. In one the decking is laid sprung to the sides and the ends notched or "nibbed" into a center trim-piece called the "king plank." The covering boards are usually tapered fore and aft from amidships; very often the king plank is also tapered. The second type has the decking laid straight and

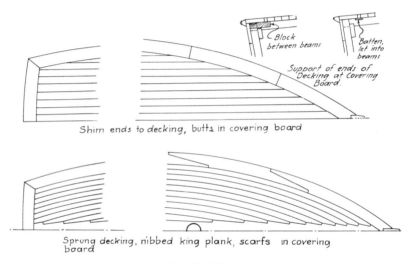

Shim ends to decking, butts in covering board

Sprung decking, nibbed king plank, scarfs in covering board

*81. Decking*

parallel to the center line of the hull; the ends are nibbed into the covering boards fore and aft, or finish in long, wedge-shaped ends ("shim ends") inside the covering boards. The latter is used in small boats having no rails of any kind. The choice of which type of deck to use is best decided by the plan view of the cabin trunk and cockpit. If the sides of these are curved and follow the sides of the hull more or less parallel, the curved decking is the most attractive and practical. If the sides of the cockpit and trunk are straight and parallel the center line, or have a very slight curve, or are straight lines, in plan view, that neither follow the center line nor run with the sides, the straight decking is used.

## Design, Shoring Beams

The first step in building a bright deck is to decide on the artistic design most suited to the boat. No rules can be given; the builder's ideas of beauty must govern. It is a good plan to work out a scale drawing of the deck plan, with decking and covering boards carefully drawn to scale. This will enable the builder to order the right amount of stock as well as to see how his ideas will appear when carried out. This done, the builder must prepare his deck beams. It is a good plan to put in some temporary shores or supports under the beams: the best way is to place a fore-and-aft girder under the beams along the center line and then to shore this up with posts on the floor timbers, using wedges to put a little strain on the beams. Do not slack off any vertical tie rods.

## Covering Board and King Plank. Laying Deck

If there is to be a nibbed covering board, or if the deck planks are to have shim ends, its width and taper are worked out in the scale plan. In a small boat the widths of the covering board on each deck beam are set off and notches cut to take a permanent ribband which will be edgeset into the notches, and center under the seam or nibbing. The top of this ribband will be flush with the top of the deck beams. In a large boat, requiring a tight deck, the ribband on each side is replaced by blocks set in between the deck beams. These should fit snugly on the beams and should have the ends against the beams well luted. If there is to be a king plank, a thin plank is sometimes let into the deck beams along the center line of the deck on which the king plank is secured. The thin plank is called a "deck strongback"; it should be an inch wider than the king plank, cut with a taper if required. Blocks should be used instead of the deck strongback in large hulls fastened in place after the nibbing is cut. At the mast partners, in a small boat, it is usual to make the king plank wide enough to pass around the mast hole, with a few inches to spare. In large hulls this is neither practical nor attractive, so additional pieces of trim are laid alongside the king plank to form a rectangle at the mast hole; this rectangle is called a "mast bed." Very often the mast bed is pieced up of thicker stock than the decking, in which case the king plank is also made thicker and its top chamfered to bring it to deck thickness along the points of the nibs.

The hatches may require nibbing pieces, or "margins," which will avoid feather, or shim, ends in the planking, when cut to form the hatch opening, in a deck laid with the side of the hull. Or, if the deck is laid straight, and there is a slight sweep to the

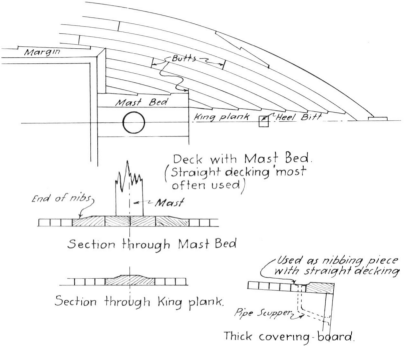

Margin

Butts

Mast Bed

King plank    Heel Bitt

Deck with Mast Bed.
(Straight decking 'most
often used)

End of nibs

Mast

Section through Mast Bed

Section through King plank.

Used as nibbing piece
with straight decking

Pipe Scupper

Thick covering-board.

82. Decking

sides of the cabin trunk and cockpit, it may be desirable to fit a wide plank on top of the carlins, fore and aft, and one edge running with a seam in the decking, to serve for the same purpose as a margin; the wide plank is of the timber used for decking. Across the stern, or top of the transom, a covering board must be fitted to take the after ends of the decking; this is sometimes nibbed. In any case the ends of the decking must be supported underneath by a deck beam or blocking. Margins may be placed at the fore end of the cabin trunk and at the after end of the cockpit, and on the fore-and-aft sides of hatches. If the fore end of the trunk is rounded the margin is usually omitted. The corners of all margins and covering boards are mitered. The butts in the covering boards may be scarfed, or butt blocks used. In the first case the fitting must be very accurate in order to be tight; in the second, an edge-driven stopwater is desirable. Covering boards and margins are usually screw-fastened, with the heads bunged. The deck planking, if sprung, should be almost square in section in a large boat; rectangular in section in a small. In the latter case the strips may be made so that they can be laid with the narrow edge to the beam; the long side of the rectangle is then equal to the required deck thickness. In a very strongly crowned deck, as in a small boat, there is no need of having the decking made to form the seams; the crown will give enough spread to the seams at the top of the decking when laid. In a large boat the deck planks should be formed narrower on top than on the bottom. The cross section can be drawn to indicate this. The whole side of the plank should not be drawn sloped; the depth of the seam would be too great. The depth of the seam should be about two thirds the depth of the plank in white pine and cedar; two thirds to three quarters in hardwood decking. The width of the seam should be planed to be about $3/16$ inch in a large hull, when marine glue or seam compound is to be used. One eighth of an inch is about the minimum width of seam used in bright decks, in medium and large-sized hulls.

In laying the deck, after the covering boards, king planks, mast beds, and margin pieces are in place, the sprung decking is started along the side covering boards. The straight decking is started at the center line, sometimes with a wide thick plank, a little thicker than the deck and about as wide as three strakes, laid on the center line. It is necessary to plank on each side of the center line alternately in order to have the nibbing of each pair of planks at an equal distance from the stem and center line. It is very important that the seams be of equal width throughout the deck, in order that the nibbing work out correctly and the deck look well when the seams are filled. The ends of the planks that are nibbed are usually squared; then the side of the plank toward the nib is snyed off to a width of one half, or even less, the width of the plank, and for a length equal to that required by the angle at which the deck plank intersects the covering board, or king plank. The sketches show this better than can be explained in the text. The method of fitting the end of a plank to be nibbed is to spring it into its proper position on the deck, with its butt against the covering board or king plank. It is a simple matter to draw the nib to be cut in both planks by using a straightedge to project the

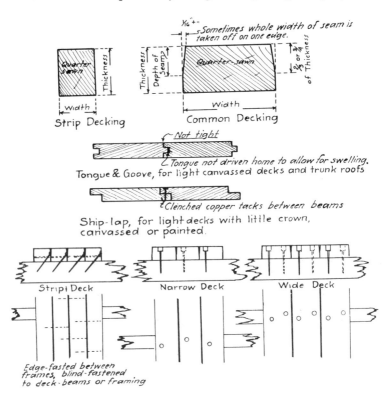

*83. Decking and Deck Fastenings*

butt into the covering board at the required angle. The nibbing in the covering board, king plank, or margin piece is cut with a sharp chisel, and this requires a good deal of skill with the tool. If blocking is used under the nibbing, not fastened, the nibs are easily sawn out. In a sprung deck it is possible to omit the king plank and to interlock the butts at the center line, as shown in the sketches. This is called "herringbone finish." Butts in the deck planking are usually fitted with butt blocks; the butts in adjoining planks should be at least three deck-beam spaces apart. On large vessels butts are brought on a deck beam. If the deck is over ¾ inch thick, stopwaters may be fitted. Butts should be

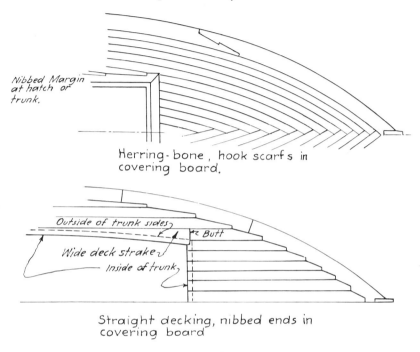

Nibbed Margin at hatch or trunk.

Herring-bone , hook scarfs in covering board.

Outside of trunk sides

Butt

Wide deck strake

Inside of trunk

Straight decking, nibbed ends in covering board

*84. Decking*

coated with varnish on the end grain of the planks before being brought together. Nibbing ends should also be varnished. The after ends of deck planking are often nibbed into the stern or transom covering board.

## Scarfing, Covering Boards, Splined Decks

In fitting the margins and covering boards it is usually best to mark their outer edges first, then lay off the inside line. In large boats the covering boards are hook-scarfed, instead of butted. In shaping deck plank by hand, square up the deck stuff and then plane the edges to the required bevel for about two thirds or three quarters the thickness from the top. This should be done very carefully to be sure that the resulting seam is of the correct width. Splines are sometimes used in place of a filled seam. These are strips of some dark wood, mahogany or teak as a rule, wedge shaped in cross section. After the deck seam has been calked

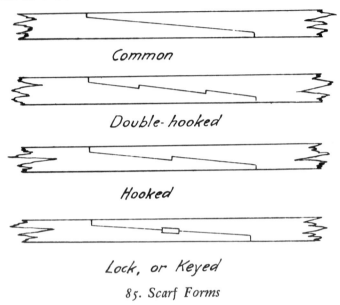

*Common*

*Double-hooked*

*Hooked*

*Lock, or Keyed*

*85. Scarf Forms*

these strips are fitted into the seam and then glued into place. Usually a few small copper brads are added to back up the glue. A splined deck is very handsome, but extremely difficult to construct. Both planking and splines must be well seasoned.

### Fastening Decks

Decks are usually fastened with galvanized boat nails; the heads are countersunk and bunged. If the decking is very narrow, and over ⅞ inch thick, blind-nailing is sometimes used: the nails are driven through the edge, in a sloping direction, as in laying the floors of houses ashore. Galvanized brads or wire nails are used. In narrow decks each plank is given one fastening into each deck beam, taking care to stagger the fastenings in the same beam as each strake is laid. In wide stock, two fastenings can be used, but must also be staggered on the deck beam, of course. In strip-planked decks, in which the strakes are too narrow to be fastened with boat nails countersunk, bronze or brass brads are used; their heads are sometimes lightly set and the holes filled with putty, colored to match the wood. Seams in strip-planked decks are usually filled with varnish, no glue or seam compound being used. Canvas-covered decks are fastened with flat head galvanized wire nails or screws, countersunk and puttied.

## Calking, Glue, Seam Compounds

Calking a bright deck requires caution. No marks should be made in the planks and the calking should be set well down into the seam. If the seam is to be filled with glue, obtain a good grade of marine glue for the purpose. This requires heating to apply. Instructions are attached to the package and should be followed carefully. Some glues can be melted by merely putting the glue in an iron ladle and applying direct heat; others must be heated with steam, usually by placing the container in a pot of boiling water. When the glue has become sufficiently fluid to use, it is poured in the seam with a lipped ladle, or funnel-shaped container known as a "paying shell." The lip of the ladle, or the spout of the paying shell, should not be permitted to rest on the edges of the seam; the lip or spout should be held 2 or 3 inches from the deck, to prevent air bubbles from forming. It is best to fill a seam in two operations, filling half the depth each time. Any glue that spills, or piles up on the seam, should be removed with a scraper operated diagonally across the seam when the glue has cooled and set. Most glues shrink very little and so the seam should be filled about level full. Colored seams are obtained by using deck-seam compounds. These do not harden completely and are not very expensive. The container is heated by placing it in boiling water until the compound becomes soft. Then it may be applied to the seam with a puttyknife, like putty. It is a good plan to apply two coats of varnish to a bright deck before using seam compound as it will stain the wood unless this is done, and accidental smears are almost impossible to avoid. When the deck has been varnished, these smears are easily removed without leaving marks on the deck. With glue, no varnish should be used. The deck is planed, sanded, and then the seam filled with glue. When the seams are hard they are smoothed off and the deck varnished. With the seam compounds it is necessary to smooth and sand, then varnish, before applying the compound. The compounds will not stand scraping when cold. The seams should not be filled with compound above the top of the seam, or the seams smoothed while the compound is warm.

## Painted Decks

Painted decks are usually laid in the same manner as bright decks, but the decking is not clear stock, since knots and minor faults can be covered with paint. Even marks caused by faulty workmanship can be masked, so the deck is quite easy to construct. The same rules as to thickness required for calking and for seam depth and width apply. Usually painted decks are not nibbed, though this is sometimes done, and the deck strakes run to a shim end at the covering boards, or king plank. The seams are sometimes filled with putty, but glue is much better. Compounds are sometimes used, but care should be taken to obtain a compound that can be covered with paint; some will stain through.

## Oiled Decks

Instead of varnishing or painting a deck, it may be oiled. This is not a suitable plan for a yacht's deck, but is satisfactory in commercial and fishing craft. The deck, when calked, payed, and smoothed, is given a few coats of oil. The common floor oil used in factories and offices ashore is employed; finishing oils used in furniture and cabinet work are not suitable. Hot pitch is used to pay seams in most oiled decks. The calking is oakum instead of cotton.

## Deck Joinery

The construction of cabin trunk sides, cockpit and hatch coamings, and other deck erections is usually detailed on the plans. Occasionally, however, some detail is omitted and so the amateur builder must know the common methods of construction used in deck joinery. A good deal of care is required to make hatches, trunks, and skylights tight. It is important to remember that flimsy, ill-built deck joinery will spoil the appearance of an otherwise well-built boat. Strength in the deck joinery is as necessary as in the hull structure, but excessive weight and awk-ward construction are to be avoided.

## *Bitts Bowsprit*

If there is a bowsprit heel bitt, or "samson post," or if the windlass is mounted on a bitt, the fitting of the bitt, or samson post, is important. In most hulls the timber is carried to the top of the keel, or stem knee, forward and steps in a tenon (which should be drained). If there are two bitts, side by side, they are usually brought down on each side of the deadwood, or stem knee, and through-bolted athwartships. They should never step on a floor timber or frame. At the deck the bitts should be se-cured to a deck beam and should pass through the deck strong-back, or blocking, and be wedged with cedar or white-pine wedges. If there is a bowsprit, the heel of this is tenoned into the single samson post, or is passed between the double bitts and through-bolted athwartships. In small boats, in which there are no bitts, or samson post, the heel of the bowsprit is often bolted through a deck beam. Except in very small craft, the bowsprit should be kept a little off the deck by properly placing the tenon and permitting the stemhead to stand a little above deck level, or by shimming up at the stem and at the heel bolts. It is a good plan to cap the bitts and samson post with sheet copper or brass, or a wooden cap, to cover the end grain. Bitts should have the corners rounded off where the hawser or line will be bent.

## *Hatches*

If there is a hatch forward, it should be through-bolted, through its coaming and carlins, or deck beams. This hatch is apt to be a source of annoyance if it is not tight. The hatch top should be built as suggested in the last chapter, page 264, unless it is to be fitted to slide, in which case it will be built like the companion-way to be described later.

## *Cabin Trunk*

The cabin trunk sides must be cut to the fore-and-aft sheer of the deck; they are made up of a single width of planking in small boats, two or more planks doweled together in larger craft. The corners are built with a rabbeted corner post, the outer corner of which is rounded off. The corner posts are usually notched at the heel so that part of the post will overlap and stand on the deck, and part will extend down inside the corner formed by the intersection of the carlin and deck beam. This permits a good fastening through the corner post into the deck beam, or carlin. Sometimes the rabbet is omitted in the corner posts and the trunk sides and ends are either lapped or mitered. In this case the corner posts are triangular, or square, in section and are wholly inside the carlin and deck beam. While strong, this type of corner post is out of place in a well-finished hull. Laminated corner posts can be used to avoid cutting a rabbet in the rounded type; they are built up with an inner and outer piece. The latter is rounded on the outer corner and serves to cover the end grain of the trunk ends and sides. Unless built with care this type of corner post will leak. The trunk sides should stand on top of the decking and be through-bolted, edgewise, to the carlin, through all. For setting up trunk see page 347.

In placing the through-bolts, take care to keep clear of the portholes and of the cabin-roof beam ends. In small craft, where the trunk sides and other coamings are too light to edge-fasten with through-bolts, long screws are used; these are driven up through the carlins, beams, and deck from below. In large, or very heavy, hulls the cabin trunk sides are often made of narrow stock, the ends of each course of which are halved together vertically at the corners, somewhat as in a log cabin. Through the halving a through-bolt is drifted into the deck and beams when the sides are completed. Each course, or layer, of narrow stock is edge-fastened as laid, and then the whole edge through-fastened when the top is laid. The ends of the cabin-roof beams notch into the inside faces of the trunk sides their whole depth; the notch is usually half the thickness of the trunk sides in depth. The top of the beam, when in the notch, is flush with the *inside* edge of the top of the trunk sides; the outer edge must be cut down to the bevel required by the crown of the cabin roof. If the trunk sides are too thin to allow notching for the beams, a strip is run fore and aft along the top inside edge of the trunk sides, into which the roof beams are notched. The ends of cabin-roof beams should be nailed to the trunk sides with boat nails. If a bearer strip is used, however, screws should be used to fasten it to the trunk sides and also to fasten the beam ends.

In order to get the trunk sides properly laid out, it is always best to work out the full-sized sections and expansion on the loft plan. As there is a bevel at the deck, to suit the crown, in addi-

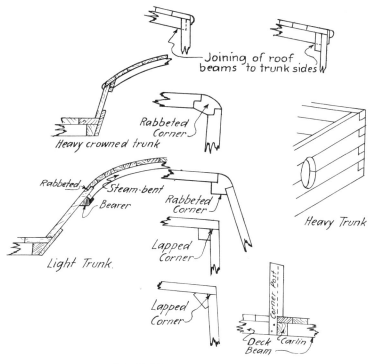

*86. Cabin Trunk Details*

tion to the one at the cabin roof, it is practically impossible to get the trunk sides correct as to height by any other method.

If there are fittings on the cabin roof, blocking must be inserted between the beams for foundations. If a mast goes through the cabin roof, a well-braced partner is required, which should have hanging knees at the trunk sides with their lower arms reaching to the level of the bottom of the carlins of the deck. The position of the cabin-roof beams must be accurately laid off. Use the loft plan to check this. Cabin-roof carlins are fitted in the same manner as deck carlins. The half-dovetail is sometimes used in the ends of both cabin-roof beams and carlins. The ends of the trunk are usually constructed in the same manner as the sides; if the after end is in the cockpit, it should stand on the flooring or deck, preferably on a rabbeted timber laid athwartships over the cockpit floor or beam and through-fastened to the floor beam. The after end of a trunk in a cockpit is usually planked vertically or paneled; thus the rabbeted timber, or "waterway," is laid with the rabbet facing aft and the paneling, or planking, of the bulkhead is fastened from the outside of the trunk. If the trunk end stands on deck, the end is usually of one or two planks, laid with the grain running athwartships. If two or more planks are required in the ends, they should be doweled together with iron pins, or battened on the inside; the companionway door frame will serve as battens in the after end. The cabin trunk roof is usually canvas covered.

## *Tumble-Home in Trunk Sides, Rake of Ends*

In setting up the cabin trunk sides, the "tumble-home" should be fixed. The plans usually specify the amount; if not, ¼ inch to each foot of height in the trunk side is a good allowance. Tumble-home means that the top of the sides of the trunk at the roof is nearer the center line of the hull than the bottom at deck. The ends of the trunk should be perpendicular to the base, unless high. In the latter case the forward end of the trunk should show a slight rake aft; the top at center line can be abaft the bottom, at a rake of about ⅛ inch per foot of height. This will prevent the optical illusion that makes the trunk appear to fall forward.

## *Ports, Deck Lights*

Ports cut in the sides and ends of the cabin trunk must be tight. If the port is fixed, that is, does not open, the glass is usually set in the trunk without a metal frame—in all but highly finished yachts. These ports may be round or oval. They should be marked from a single pattern, to be certain that all are alike, if so required, and should be located accurately from the plans. Don't shift them to suit your eye or you may find that one will come on a bulkhead, when you come to put in the joinerwork in the cabin. The hole, when marked, can be cut by boring a series of holes and cutting between them with a keyhole saw, finishing off with a chisel, rasp, file, and sandpaper. To fit the glass to the shape of the opening is an unnecessary task. It is much better to let in a square of glass on the inside of the trunk, by a shallow rabbet around the port; then secure the glass with a light frame of wood or metal. A broken glass can thus be easily replaced. The porthole should be cut so that it will drain outboard; it is a very common fault to cut portholes so that a little water stands against the glass at the bottom of the port. When laid up for the winter, this water may freeze and cause the glass to crack. Ports that open are available in many different shapes and sizes.

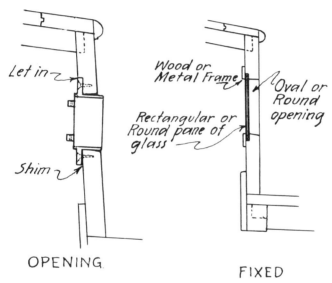

OPENING                          FIXED

*87. Fitting Trunk Ports*

Galvanized ports are preferable to bronze, as the latter are easily strained if clamped tight, when closed, by the attached "dogs." The strained port frame will always crack the glass. In ordering portlights, specify diameter of opening, thickness of the trunk sides, and, if bronze, how finished (plain or bright). It is no longer customary to use the outside finishing ring, or outside frame, so order the portlights without these. The use of any outside ring, or frame, makes the ports too prominent, by increasing their apparent size. The omission of the outside finishing ring requires that the port frames fit very closely the holes cut for them, leaving room for a strand of calking all around. The edge of the port frame should project through the trunk side and show as a narrow bead around the port on the outside. This may necessitate the inside finishing ring of the port (a part of the frame casting and not a separate piece like the outside ring) being let into the inside of the trunk sides. Some builders set the port frames so that they will drain by this means; the result is that the frame of the port will project from the outside of the trunk a little more at the top than at the bottom, to which there is no objection. An opening port that will not drain is a great nuisance, as every time it is opened a teaspoonful of water is spilled into the cabin, usually right on a sleeper in a berth.

Ports can be purchased with screens that fit into the frames from the inside; windscoops for the ports are also obtainable. All ports that open are fitted with a rubber gasket, which prevents leakage when closed. Ports always open inboard. Lightweight ports are available and are used where weight must be kept to a minimum. Where there are both fixed and opening ports in a trunk, and uniformity of appearance is desired, the fixed ports may be obtained with inside ring and frame. All port frames, and the glass in fixed ports without frames, should be set in white lead or seam filler. It is often desirable to light some locker, or other portion of the hull, where portlights cannot be used. Deck lights are useful for this purpose. These may be obtained in various shapes and sizes, with or without frames. The type having a corrugated bottom to the glass is generally used when the decking is thick enough; there is often no frame, as the glass can be held in place by a series of large iron staples driven over the glass. These also form an excellent guard against breakage. Bronze frames are often used with this and other forms of deck lights. The older form of deck light was in the form of a prism or eight-sided pyramid; it gave good light but was dangerous where headroom was scant. All deck lights should be lightly calked with cotton and set in seam compound or glue.

## Skylights

Skylights are very difficult to build so that they will open, yet be watertight when closed. Various plans are used to ensure watertight joints where the top meets the coaming. In spite of the many years in which this form of hatch has been in use, it must be admitted that there has been very little success in finding a wooden skylight that will stay tight after a few years of service. The sketches show some of the more common designs of skylight, but practically all are subject to leakage when warping and shrinking take place in service. The most satisfactory skylight that the writer has been able to design was made with a fixed top, in which the rectangular "marine cabin windows" were fitted. These are merely rectangular opening ports, with metal frames. The window was fitted to open outward; this was a hindrance, but was

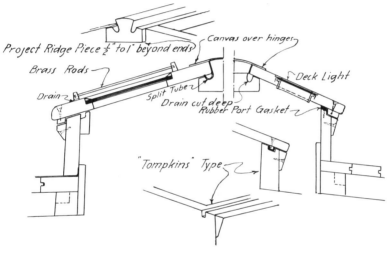

88. Skylights

counterbalanced by the fact that the skylight was tight. In place of a framed glass in the top of a wooden skylight, fixed ports can be used in a plank cover. Most skylights, having an opening cover, soon require a canvas skirt fastened along the edges of the covers and also a canvas hinge cover. These are not very sightly but are preferable to cold water down the back of one's neck from a leaking skylight. The coamings of skylights should be halved together like the coamings of hatches. Dovetailed corners are sometimes seen but are unsuitable. The coamings should be edge-fastened through the cabin roof into the carlins or beams.

As in all hatches, the raw edges of the roofing and canvas covering should be hidden with an inside finish strip, or inner coaming. Small skylights often have the long "piano hinge," but the strap hinge is preferable. There are many locking and raising devices for skylights, and the builder can usually find the type most suited to the particular requirements of the job in a marine hardware dealer's catalogue.

## Companionways, Doors

Companionways, like the skylights, are inclined to develop leaks after leaving the builder's hands. There are a great many ways of building the slides and the best way to understand the most common methods of construction is to study the accompanying sketches. Fixed lights are often put in the cover, fitted in the same manner as deck lights. The slides are screw- or through-fastened to the carlins and cabin-roof beams. The bottom of the slides should be drained; continuous scuppers are better than just two at the hatch. Doors should be of the drop type, if watertightness and strength are very important. Hinged doors, while more convenient, are practically impossible to make tight, or very strong, in a small cruiser. If possible, the bottom of any door should stand well above the deck or cockpit floor.

## Cockpit

The cockpit coaming in a small cruiser is fitted in the same way as the trunk sides. The floor is supported by athwartship beams, the ends of which rest on a fore-and-aft piece nailed to the inside of the frames; or the ends may be hung from the deck beams and carlins above with long bolts made up and fitted like tie rods. The latter method is often used when the space alongside the cockpit is utilized for tanks. In a seagoing cruiser the cockpit floor should be laid fore and aft of plank as thick as the decking; in a small boat the floor should be canvas covered and light flooring can then be used. If the cockpit is to be "self-bailing" it must be reasonably watertight. The cockpit sides and ends should be vertically planked, or paneled, with waterways fitted in the same manner as at the after end of the trunk. If the cockpit floor is canvas covered, the edges of the canvas should turn up on the sides

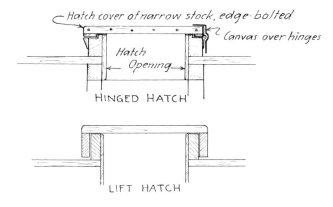

*89. Hatches*

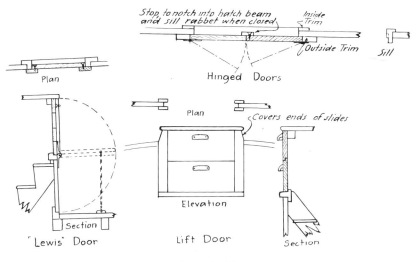

*90. Trunk Doors*

and ends, and should be covered with a finishing strip like a "mop board" in the rooms of a house ashore. The cockpit sides and ends, at the deck, are covered with a thin finish strip on top of the deck; or, if the cockpit is built before the deck is laid, by the decking, which in turn has its raw ends covered by an inside

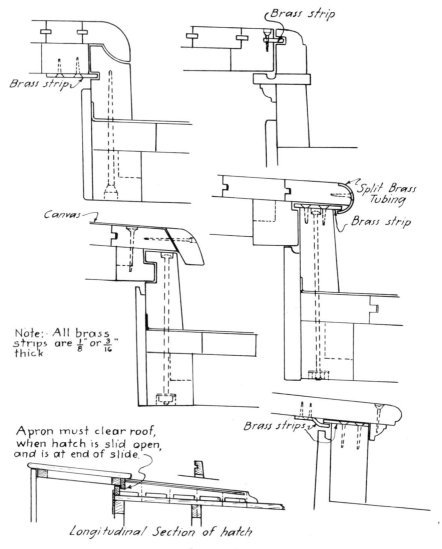

Brass strip

Brass strip

Split Brass Tubing

Brass strip

Canvas

Note:- All brass strips are $\frac{1}{8}$" or $\frac{3}{16}$" thick

Brass strips

Apron must clear roof, when hatch is slid open, and is at end of slide.

Longitudinal Section of hatch

*91. Companionways*

coaming around the cockpit. The cockpit scuppers should be installed before the cockpit floor is laid; they will be discussed in a later chapter.

If the cockpit, or trunk, or both, have round ends, the coamings

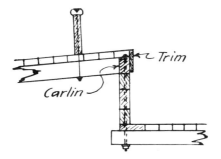

*92. Cockpit Construction*

will have to be steam-bent. If the curves are too sharp or the timber too dry to stand bending, then vertical staving must be used. The staving is usually tongue-and-groove stock, without the beaded edges seen in shore structures. The staving can be

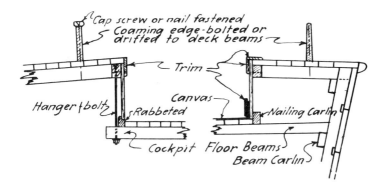

*93. Cockpit Construction*

stepped in a rabbeted waterway laid on deck, but it is usual to place the staving inside the carlins and deck beams, or blocking, allowing the deck to come home against it. While neater, this method is not as tight as when the waterway is used.

### Streamlined Cabin Trunks

The so-called "streamlined" cabin has come into quite general use in recent times. This is marked by large sectional curves at the intersection of cabin roof and sides and by large, rounded corners. These must often be carved out of a solid timber or made up "bread-and-butter" fashion in laminations. Practically speaking, this class of deckhouse is most unsatisfactory, for the corners will open up, or check, if the timber used is not perfectly dry and well protected with varnish or paint. There is no marked saving in weight by this construction and there is no advantage, other than appearance, in boats whose speed is under 35 knots.

## *Windows*

There are a great many possibilities in the fitting of cabin trunks that give opportunity for the builder to show ingenuity. The use of sliding, hinged, or drop windows instead of ports is an example. These are often quite satisfactory if properly built. Their design depends upon their location and surroundings; obviously no instructions can be given as to their construction. Like

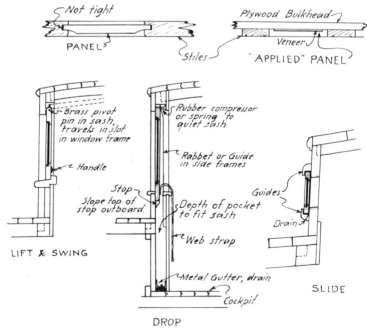

*94. Cabin Windows*

any sliding, or folding, fitting on a boat, the sliding windows must have plenty of clearance in the slides to prevent their sticking when swelling of the wood takes place. Drop windows are used in the deckhouses and trunks of powerboats; though they serve their purpose, they often rattle. In fitting such windows it is desirable to fit rubber stops to hold the frame firmly and thus prevent vibration. The sketches show the details of construction most often used in cabin windows.

### Finish of Details, Rails, Guards, Moldings, Paint

Finishing the exterior of the hull is a very important part of boatbuilding. There are certain things in this that mark a well-built boat and show whether or not the builder appreciates his opportunities of exhibiting knowledge and workmanship. None of these things are particularly hard to do. First, the rails (or the strips running aft from the bow in many small boats, called the "bow chocks") offer an opportunity for "finish." These rails, made of strips of wood called "log rails," should not be mere rectangular-section pieces bent along the edge of the deck. The log rail should be shaped both in section and longitudinally. In profile, the rail should usually be a little higher at the bow than elsewhere; from the bow the rail height should taper very gradually to the stern. In plan view the rail should be thicker at the stem and gradually taper aft, so as to be parallel sided at some point about one fourth the length of the boat from the bow. Another variation of this is to make the fore end of the rail thicker than the rest, but, instead of tapering the sides, they run aft parallel for a short distance, then drop to the required thickness of the rail in a short, hollow curve *on the inside of the rail*. The parallel part of the rail serves to support the metal "chock," or fair-lead, through which the anchor or mooring line is passed.

In section, the rail is narrower on top than at the deck, the taper being on the *inside* of the rail. The bow-chock rail is similarly fashioned. If the rail is capped, the top of the rail may have a tongue cut in it, which enters a groove in the underside of the cap, in a well-finished hull. Otherwise, the cap is merely set on top of the rail and fastened. In such a job the fastenings must be closely spaced, to prevent the cap from buckling away from the rail and showing open spaces between the fastenings. The cap is not centered over the top of the rail; it should overhang the top of the rail more on the inside than on the out. The after end of the cap should have some kind of a finish piece where it joins the transom; usually these are of knee shape. Similarly, a false knee is often used at the fore end of the rail caps, to join them at the stemhead or over the bowsprit.

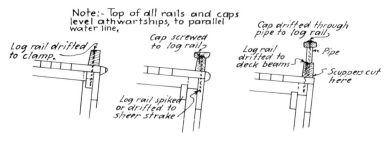

*95. Rails and Fastenings*

The log rail should not be set on the deck with its outside face flush with the edge of the deck; it should be set back ⅛ inch, more or less according to the size of the boat, to emphasize the sheer. The cap or top of the rail, athwartships, should be level. The guards or half-rounds, or half-ovals, run along the sheer fore and aft to protect the sides and the deck edge, or to cover the edges of the canvas on deck, should be tapered fore and aft from the point of least freeboard. Not only should there be a slight taper in the profile, but also in the plan view. The fore end of the guards should never be carried ahead of the face of the stem; this is the mark of the lubber. The guards should always stop abaft the face of the stem in profile, where they are snyed off to fit the sides of the stem, as they approach it at an angle. If the sides of the stem are so beveled that the guard will not die out against it, cut the guard off a little ahead of the rabbet and round the outer edges in a "streamline" nose. At the stern the end of the guards may stop short, flush with the after face of the transom, and finish off with a narrow metal half-oval bent over the guard ends fore and aft, running around on to the transom. This will need to be heat-treated in order to put a twist in it that will enable the parts on the transom face to parallel the water line or deck when viewed from astern.

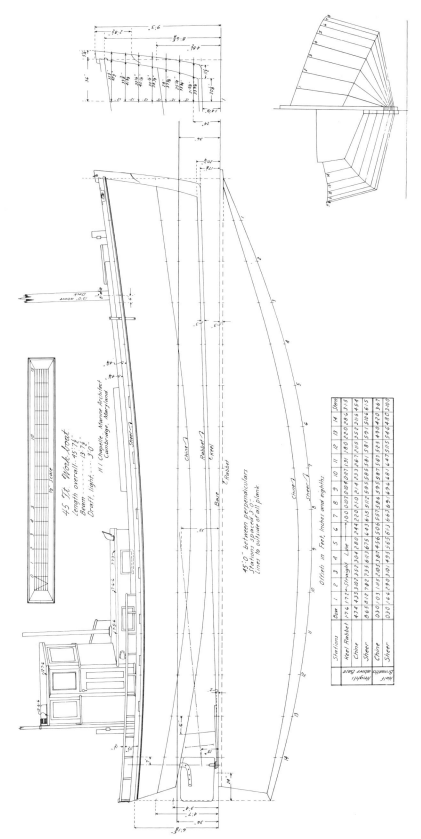

PLATE 44. Lines of a 45-Foot Workboat

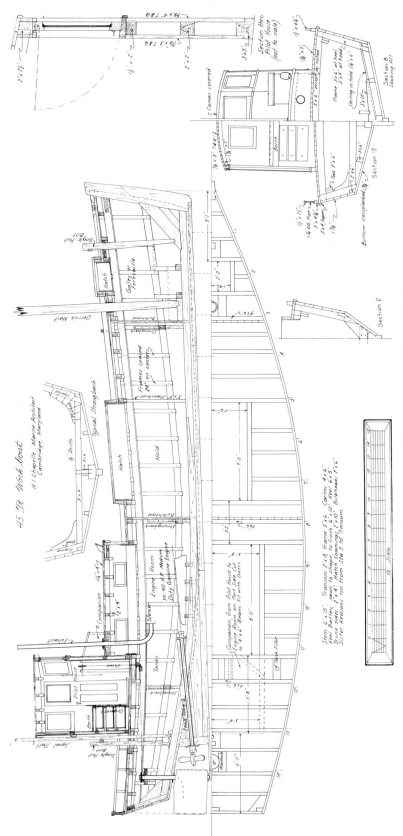

PLATE 45. *Construction Plans of a 45-Foot Workboat*

In finely finished hulls the guard ends, aft, are sometimes capped with bronze castings, which fair into the finished strip of bronze run around the transom edges. The half-round used to cover the seam formed by the intersection of the cabin trunk roof with the trunk sides should be similarly tapered fore and aft, the greatest width and depth being over the point of lowest freeboard in the hull. The apparent height of the trunk may be reduced by the use of a narrow strip fitted under the half-round along the sides of the trunk. This should also be tapered toward the ends; it will give an additional line, which creates an optical illusion of a lower side to the trunk. The rule for these additional lines is that those above the sheer of the hull tend to be straighter than the sheer, becoming straighter as they become more distant from the sheer; those below the sheer become more curved, so that the boot top would have more curve in its top than the sheer. The use of arrows and other fancy moldings or hollowed-out lines, "cove lines," in the hull has happily been decreasing in recent years. If a cove line is necessary, make it narrow and let it die out short of the bow and stern, without any arrowheads or feathers. If the bow needs ornament, use a vine scroll or other conventional foliage. This should be carefully proportioned; it is much better to have it too small than too large. In choosing the painting scheme remember that a varnished transom creates the illusion of a shorter boat than actually exists, so don't employ it if the freeboard is high.

The finish of the top of the stem is important; as has been mentioned in an earlier chapter, don't saw off a stem at deck level unless there is a bowsprit. If there are dents, or hammer marks, in the hull, fill them with a mixture made by adding white lead to the paint you are using. Add white lead until the paint is very thick and lay on as smoothly as possible with a broad putty knife. If it is desired to have this dry very quickly, use spar varnish as the base, instead of paint. This dries very quickly and great care is needed to get it smooth since, when dry, it will not sand down as easily as the surrounding paint. Painting will be discussed later; here it can be said that if you are using a semigloss topside paint, use it for all coats; do not use flat. If a full gloss is used, it is better to use flat coats to build up the color. The important thing is to put the first, or prime, coat on very thin; use plenty of turps and do not try to get the paint to cover the wood well. It is a good rule to put on a number of thin coats in preference to a few thick coats of paint.

## Special Details of Construction

There are many details of construction used in V-bottom hulls that have not been mentioned; these are special methods rarely used. In cross-planked hulls, the stern is sometimes planked fore and aft for a short distance forward of the transom, as was described for the bow. This is done in order to give a good deal of shape to the transom, the bottom of which may be made in a hollow V, as in the old New York pilotboats and the yachts of the eighties. This idea is often carried to its extreme by inserting blocks at the after end of the side planking at the sheer. These blocks are shaped so that the transom can be tumbled-home, as in the well-known Friendship Sloop.

## Rabbeted Chine Logs

The rabbeted chine has not been described; though unsuited for amateur builders, it must sometimes be employed. It should be first laid off in the loft plans and the sections drawn in on the body plan for every frame. In lofting these sections, it must be remembered that the rabbeted chine log is really being partially expanded. To do this, there must be a base from which to establish the sections. This is obtained by making the inside of the notches for the chine logs, in the frames, all of the same angle to the body-plan center line. The back, or inside of the logs, is made "normal" in this way, that is, it requires little or no twist. When the sections are laid out as described it is possible to ascertain the size of stick required in the rough. Then a batten is bent into the frames, when set up, to find the expanded spacing of the chine sections shown in the body plan. By the use of templates made from the body-plan sections of the logs, and the spacing batten, the shape of the rabbeted log may be laid off and the timber cut. The forward ends of the logs are merely roughed out, as there is often some twist in the logs that requires the rabbets to be cut after the chine logs are in place. A small rabbeted chine is much easier to make than a heavy one, as the light log may be forced a little without straining the hull. Some craft, having fairly angular chines, can have their chine logs rabbeted by merely placing the rough stick in the frames and finding the bevels and angles directly from the hull. In this case, the chine logs are usually rectangular in section, in the rough state, and can be notched so that one corner stands in the frame, the inner face of the log standing vertical, or nearly so, and more or less parallel to the side of the hull, as a flat-bottom boat!

## Engine Stringers

In high-speed power hulls of the V-bottom type, the engine stringers are important strength members. These hulls, being lightly built, require careful fitting. The engine stringers stand outboard of and against the engine beds; in some cases the engine beds and stringers are one. In either case, the stringers are carried as far fore and aft as the hull form will permit. The plans should show this and detail the construction required in these members. Usually the stringers are notched over every floor timber they cross, and are bolted. These notches must always bear; if they do not, shims should be placed in the notches to make a bearing for the stringer. If this is not done the hull will vibrate and work at high speed. Laminated, or built-up, stringers are often used.

## Open Rails

Open rails are used in V-bottom hulls in some sections of the country. These are made of a log rail and cap, the two separated by pipe stanchions. The log rail is first fitted and secured and then the spacing of the stanchions is laid off and leading holes drilled. Galvanized iron pipe is cut to the required lengths. The cap is then cut to shape, or sprung, securing it to the bow first, and along the sides, with temporary braces or cross-spalls. The forward stanchions are set first; when the cap is brought to the proper position in reference to the log rail, the cap is bored and a driftbolt started. The pipe stanchion is placed under the cap and the drift driven into it; then the heel of the stanchion is brought to the leading hole in the log rail and the drift driven home. It will be seen that the driftbolt passes through the pipe. It is a little difficult to set the stanchions at the proper rake unless the cap is blocked or braced into its proper position before marking and boring for the drifts. The cap can be laid out in the loft plan, and the sheer expanded, before making the pattern. This is rarely done, but is undoubtedly the easiest and most accurate way to do the job. In marking and setting stanchions, profile patterns can be made for each pair so that the top of the log rail will serve as a base for fitting the patterns to find the rake.

## Watertight and Fireproof Bulkheads

If watertight bulkheads are required, it is best to make them of two courses of planking laid diagonally, one course at right angles to the other. Canvas is often used between the two courses. The bulkheads are secured to frames, on canvas, or wicking, in thick paint, white lead, or marine glue. The frame must be calked and made watertight, along the planking; the best time to do this is while the planking is being fitted. Then a strip of wicking may be run along the edge of the frame, between it and the planking. The frames on which the watertight bulkheads are fastened should be completed, with the bulkhead in place, prior to setting up. Watertight bulkheads are usually located on the forward side of a frame in the forebody; in the afterbody they are on the after side. If the bulkhead is to be fireproofed, this is usually done by placing sheet asbestos on one face of a watertight bulkhead and covering it with sheet metal. These bulkheads are actually neither watertight nor fireproof in the strict sense of the words, but serve to delay sinking or burning an appreciable length of time. The diagonal-planked bulkhead should be screw- or rivet-fastened, and bolted to the frames. If there is no deck beam at the top of the bulkhead, a false beam should be worked in.

The use of plywood and strip-planking in V-bottom construction will be dealt with in a later chapter.

## Importance of Strength in Deck

Like the flat-bottom hull, the V-bottom depends largely upon its deck framing for strength, if the hull is over 25 feet long. It is well to remember this when framing, particularly if the builder has been tempted to lengthen the cabin trunk, or change the deck arrangement, from that shown in the plans.

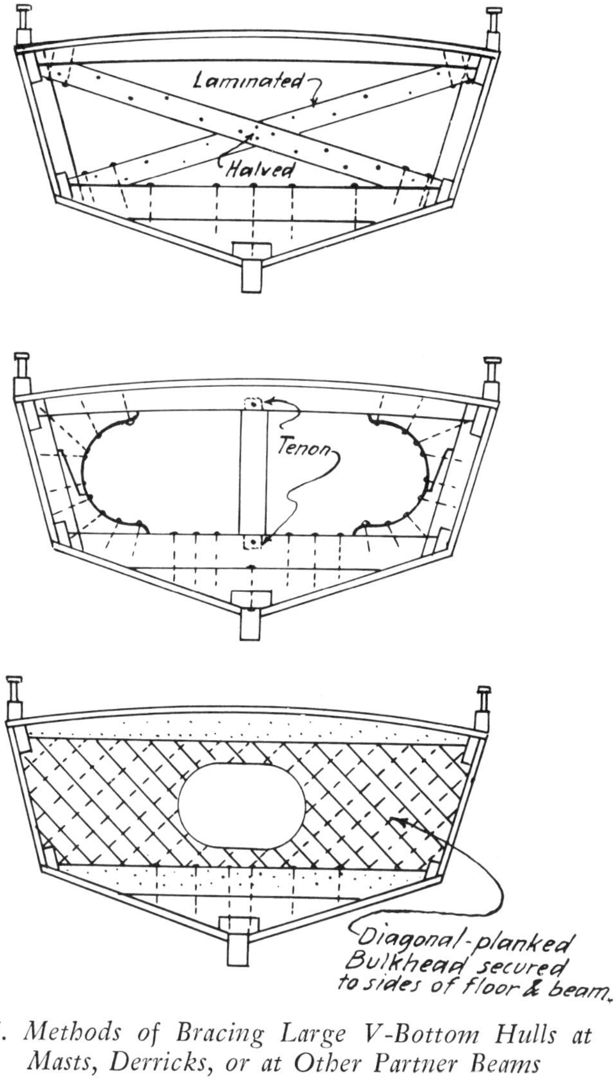
Laminated
Halved
Tenon
Diagonal-planked
Bulkhead secured
to sides of floor & beam.

*96. Methods of Bracing Large V-Bottom Hulls at Masts, Derricks, or at Other Partner Beams*

## Ballast

Most V-bottom sailing hulls, and some powerboats, need inside ballast. This is usually scrap iron, such as salvaged window weights or short lengths of car rails. Ballast of this type should be dipped in hot pitch before being put in the hull. Very often the designer does not give an accurate estimate of the amount of ballast required, due to variation between the theoretical weight and the actual weight of materials used in construction. The plans usually show the water line as she will set in the water with rig, engine, and ballast in, tanks full, but not with personal gear and cruising equipment aboard. Therefore, the amount of ballast that is required is that which will bring her to her proper trim, as shown in the plans. If there is much dead rise, or if the boat is launched with spars in place and ballast is called for by the designer, be sure to put in at least a quarter of the estimated amount before launching. Ballast in power hulls usually is stowed in either end of the hull, to bring the fore-and-aft trim to that shown in the plans. In sailing craft the ballast usually is required about amidships, or a little abaft of it. The ballast should be stowed under the cockpit, or cabin floor, which will serve to hold it in place.

The ballast material should be carefully placed so that it cannot move, and so that the weight on each side of the keel is the same. If it is necessary to stow it fore and aft of amidships, in order to get in the required amount, it is a good plan to limit the fore-and-aft spread to the middle half of the length of the boat in most designs. The spread athwartships should not exceed one half the beam at the chines. Most V-bottom hulls require the bulk of their ballast abaft the middle length. In a boat planked athwartships on the bottom, the ballast should rest on battens, laid athwartships between the keel and the sister keelsons, and resting on them. If this is not possible, due to the lack of sister-keelsons or to the shape of the ballast, fore-and-aft battens should be used: first, to spread the weight over as much of the bottom as possible; second, to keep the ballast clear of the bottom plank for drainage and ventilation. Boats planked fore and aft on the bottom should have battens laid athwartships for the same reasons. If the ballast can be so arranged that it rests on frames instead of the bottom planking, this should be done.

Along the outside of the ballast, when in place, stops should be secured, to prevent the ballast shifting into the bilge. These can be battens nailed to the bottom frames or the cockpit floor beams, running fore and aft. If much ballast is required, ballast boxes can sometimes be used. These are long, narrow, wooden boxes built into the hull along each side of the keel, or center-board case, in which the ballast is stowed. The top of the ballast boxes should be below the load water line, if possible, in most V-bottom hulls. If on trial it is found that a small, open V-bottom hull tends to trim by the head, the corrective ballast may be cast into the skeg to advantage. Otherwise, a small ballast box con-taining lead should be secured to the inside face of the keel bat-ten at the place, found by trial, that gives the required trim. Many V-bottom hulls require a good deal of experimenting to bring them to proper trim and to give the necessary stability; this is particularly the case with cruisers having much dead rise.

## Side Planking Edge-Fastened

In V-bottom hulls requiring great strength it is rather common to edge-fasten the strakes in the side planking between the frames. This not only stiffens the sides between the frames but also adds to the longitudinal strength of the hull. The fastenings are usually driftbolts spaced about 6 or 8 inches apart, well stag-gered. When this type of fastening is used, it is necessary to start planking at the chine, of course, and rather narrow strakes are used above the chine strake. The well-known Chesapeake Bay dead-rise hulls often have edge-fastenings in the sides.

## Setting Up Trunk Sides and Coamings

Molds set up on deck are usually required to bend cabin trunks and cockpit coamings to the proper flare or tumble-home. These molds, two to four in number, are like those for a flat-bottom skiff and are set up across the deck from carlin to carlin at their proper stations. Template stock can be used to scribe the deck edge and to line off the top edges. The bevels may be lifted from the deck and crown of roof. Molds should be notched to fit be-tween the carlins and should remain in place until sides or coam-ings are in place.

# CHAPTER SIX

# ROUND-BOTTOM HULL CONSTRUCTION

## Possibilities of Construction

ROUND-BOTTOM hull construction is not beyond the capabilities of the amateur boatbuilder. Even a beginner at the art, having reasonable ability in the handling of common carpenter's tools, can construct some of the round-bottom models. The choice of design for a round-bottom hull covers a wide range of possibilities; these have been discussed to a great extent in Chapter One. Most powerboat models and sailing craft having the dinghy form of hull are, in general, the most suitable models for the home builder. Not only is the hull shape an important consideration in the choice of a design; the specifications must also be carefully studied. Unless the amateur builder has professional help, he should not attempt to build the very lightly constructed and highly specialized racer, nor should he undertake a hull whose design calls for a great deal of outside ballast. Of course, the facilities available to the builder are factors that play a part in the selection of a design. These matters have been discussed previously, in Chapter One, and, beyond emphasizing the need for a realistic approach to the selection of a design, there is nothing that need be added here. The qualities of the round-bottom models have been described; from this information the amateur builder can form an opinion of what is most suitable for his requirements and skill.

## Amateur Designs

Those who wish to design and build a boat should heed a word of warning. It takes years of study and experimenting to design highly developed racers and class boats, and a great deal of skill to build them. If you feel capable of designing a boat, choose a small, simple hull for your first attempt. All designers, amateur and professional, are benefited by the experience of building from their own plans. It is so easy to draw something that is so very difficult to build.

## *Lofting, Contracted Length, Sheer Expansion*

The design having been chosen, the lofting described in Chapter Two must be carried out. The directions given there are sufficient for lofting most designs; however, a few additional matters require attention. These apply to hulls in which there are certain problems in lofting and building. In some cases, where there is insufficient length of space to loft a hull to its correct length, it is possible to draw the lines contracted in length. By this means, the body plan is correctly shown and the fairing fore and aft is tested. To loft a set of lines in the contracted form, all frame or station spacings and all fore-and-aft dimensions must be divided by the same factor, usually 2. This results in the stations being spaced half their proper distance and the overhang, or rake, of bow and stern being one half the correct amount. While the body plan can be lifted directly from the loft plan to make molds, the stem, stern, and keel have to be redrawn to make templates, or laid off from the offsets (as checked in the loft drawing) directly on the timber to be used. Bevels can be lifted by use of the bevel board and corrected spacing measurements, but the labor is increased somewhat. The disadvantages of the contracted method are obvious when it is necessary to plot the shape of deadwood (or keel timbers that must be pieced up), or when a transom has to be expanded. For this reason the contracted method of lofting is used only in small craft having straight keels for most of their length, such as canoes, rowing craft (shells, barges, and wherries), and small-power and sailing craft having sprung keels, vertical transoms, or sharp sterns, open or half-decked. Small V-bottoms are sometimes lofted by the contracted method.

Powerboats that have great flare in their forward sections, combined with a moderate amount of sheer, require special lofting treatment in one respect. In most cases, a boat of this form built exactly to the sheer shown in the profile, in the lines, will

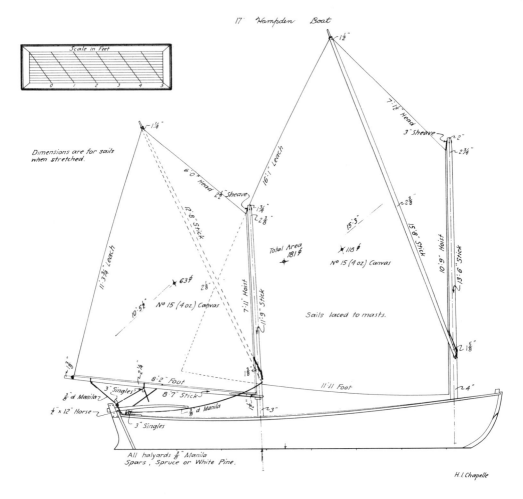

17' Hampden Boat

Scale in Feet
0 1 2 3 4 5

Dimensions are for sails
when stretched.

1½"

7'1¼" Head
3" Sheave
2"
2¾"

6'0" Head
2½" Sheave
1¾"
2⅞"

16'1" Leach
15'3"

12'8" Stick

11'3¾" Leach

15'8" Stick

Total Area
181 ♯
× 118 ♯
No. 15 (4 oz.) Canvas

10'9" Hoist
13'6" Stick

× 63 ♯
2⅞"

10'5½"  No. 15 (4 oz.) Canvas

7'11" Hoist
11'9" Stick

Sails laced to masts.

2⅝"

2⅝"
2¼"
3" Singles
8'2" Foot
8'7" Stick
⅜" d Manila

¾" d Manila

11'11" Foot

2'4"

¾" d Manila
¾" x 12" Horse
3" Singles

1¾"
2'3"

All halyards ⅝" Manila
Spars, Spruce or White Pine.

H. I. Chapelle

PLATE 46. *Sail plan of a 17-foot Hampden Boat. See also*
*Plates 10 through 20.*

appear to be humped at the point of greatest flare, when viewed at certain angles. This is an optical illusion which should be foreseen and corrected. The manner in which this is done is as follows: The lines are first completely faired in the loft plan. Then a batten is sprung along the sheer line in the half-breadth plan and the position of each station in the forward part of hull is ticked on the batten, at the intersections of station and sheer lines. The intersection of the sheer with the stem rabbet line is also ticked on the batten. It should be observed that the stations chosen to be ticked on the batten may be limited to those in which there is flare, say, in the forward fourth, or fifth, of the hull length. The batten is then moved to the loft profile and, with the aftermost tick on the corresponding station there, the batten is sprung along the sheer, carrying the ticked portion of the batten forward of the stem in a fair curve. When this has been done the curve is tested by removing some of the nails or awls holding the batten abaft the stem rabbet, on the profile of the sheer line. If the curve has been properly projected forward of the stem, the batten will remain in place along the sheer line.

Now mark the ticked stations, and intersection of sheer and stem rabbet, from batten to loft paper, or floor, and identify. Remove the batten. It will be seen that the marks thus transferred are all forward of their proper position. They must be measured in height from the base line and transferred aft to their proper position on the sheer elevation. This is done with a measuring staff. Through the points so obtained, a new and corrected sheer line is drawn in the profile. The half-breadth sheer remains the same but the body plan will require correction or sheer height and flare in the sections will be affected. The effect of expansion is to give the hull a "canoe sheer" and raise the height of the stem. This method of expansion will usually prevent the illusion of a hump in the sheer line. The amount of correction, it will be seen, is fixed by the expanded length of the sheer line in half-breadth and therefore is governed by the amount of fullness in the deck line, or sheer, in this view. Some designers mark their lines as already expanded; if this has been done the correction described is omitted, of course. In powerboats having the hogged, or humped, sheer in profile, no sheer expansion is required. Sheer lines that are perfectly straight in profile are rarely seen in round-bottom hull designs, fortunately. This sheer line is impossible to expand and when built is subject to such illusions that it often appears to have waves in it.

In open boats a form of sheer called the "powder-horn" has been used. In this form there is a deliberate hump upward in the sheer about one fourth, or one fifth, the over-all length of the hull abaft the stem. This is to give freeboard at the critical point in a sailing hull, the "shoulder" where she is most likely to ship water. The powder-horn sheer is not hard to build and in clench-built hulls is often the normal lining of the lap of the sheer strake. In lofting a round-bottom hull it is important that all fairing be accurate and all intersections of water lines with buttocks should be correctly placed in each view. Even professional builders are prone to look upon lofting as a necessary evil, to be made as short an operation as possible. This point of view often leads to loss in labor and material, when construction is actually under way. The builder should not let the common urge to "get started" cause him to do the loft work in a slipshod, hasty manner.

## Setting Up, Ribbanding

The setting up of the stocks, backbone, molds, and ribbanding have been described in Chapter Two; the operations explained apply to nearly all types of round-bottom hulls and there is little that need be added. In ribbanding off small hulls, the ribbands are sometimes secured to the molds, and stem and stern, with "staging nails." These are wire nails formed with two heads, one a short distance below the usual head. The lower head acts as a stop that prevents the nail from going home its full depth, yet gives a bearing that will prevent the ribband from springing out from the molds or timbers. The projecting outer head is used to withdraw the nail when the ribbands are being stripped from the hull.

## Bent Frames, Preparation of Keel

It is assumed that the hull is set up and ribbanded, that she is right side up and that she has bent frames. The first step is to secure the frame stock; this should be young white oak or rock elm, sound and clear of knots and blemishes. White oak is most commonly used, but elm is equally good. The builder should carefully select the frame stock for length, then stack it so that the short pieces can be reached when they will be used. The stock must be cut to the required size before being boiled or steamed. The spacing of the frames is next laid off on the keel sides. If the heels of the frames are to be notched, or "boxed," into the keel, these can then be cut. Use a short length of frame material as a gauge. The bottom of the boxing is at the bearding line as a rule, though it is sometimes desirable to cut deeper. The angle at which the frame meets the keel sides can be determined by use of the short piece of frame stock, using the lowest ribband, or two, as a guide. The boxing should be cut to fit the heel of the frame closely, and should be deep enough to permit one fastening to be driven through the frame into the keel within the boxing. Boxing the heels of the frames has become a draftsman's convention, like half-dovetailing deck framing. Boxing is rarely absolutely necessary. It is of assistance in stepping frames that are bent hot, particularly in the ends of the hull, where the frames stand at an acute angle to the keel side. The boxing is rarely tight around the heel of the frame and, unless creosoted or otherwise treated, is an excellent starting place for rot. The heel fastening of the frame to the keel is of little importance structurally and only serves to hold the frame in place during construction. The use of boxing, therefore, is largely a matter of personal preference. In this country the boxing is usually cut to fit a square heel; abroad, the heel of the frame is slightly beveled off on the inside and the boxing cut to fit the reduced heel. The keel and deadwood being ready, the next step is to mark the frame positions on the sheer batten or upper ribband. This will ensure the frames standing plumb. It is necessary to measure from mold to mold parallel to the center line and then square out the position of each frame; the frame spacing does not measure the same around the sheer ribband as it measures along the center line, obviously. A thin batten can be used to mark the other ribbands, so the frames will stand parallel.

## *Floors*

The next step depends upon the builder's preference. If the floor timbers have been lofted and their bevels lifted, the floors can be made up and secured in position, taking care to stagger the fastenings to avoid any chance of splitting either floors or keel. If the floors have not been lofted, the framing goes into place first and then floors are fitted.

## Types of Bent Frames

Framing can be done in two ways; the most common method in small craft is to bend the frames, while they are hot, directly in the boat. This is practical when the frames are light and bent "on the flat," that is, bent so that the widest faces of their cross sections are against the ribbands and planking. If the frames are large in section, say, over 4 square inches of area in cross section, it is best to bend the frames over special molds and to fit them to the hull after they are cold and set to shape. This is particularly the case if it is desired to bend the frames on edge, or to bevel them. In finely built hulls, the frames are often tapered so that they are largest at the heel, smallest at the sheer. If this is to be done, fit some chocks, made of plank, to the top of the work-

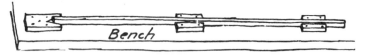

*97. Chocks for Planing Frames*

bench; these chocks should be in pairs just far enough apart to hold the frame. The end to be reduced in size may be held with an end stop made of another block. The frame is usually tapered on its inside face only, by planing.

## Canting Frames

The question of canting some of the frames should be considered, when the bow is full on deck or the stern sharp. This is done by reducing the frame spacing on the keel somewhat, so that the frame spacing around the sheer will be about that used in the middle portion of the hull. The plans will indicate that the frames should be parallel their full length, but in practice this is impossible unless the frames are beveled. As a result, the frames usually are permitted to take a natural cant in the ends of the hull. It is well to take advantage of this natural tendency to splay out, to respace the frames at the heel so that the frame spacing at the sheer clamp is approximately the same throughout the length of the boat.

## Cold Frames

If the frames are to be bent on molds and fitted after they are set, the molds should be made. A steam-bent frame may be sprung open from a curve a good deal when cold; so it is necessary to have only one or two molds, or "forms," by which the frames are shaped. To find the shape of the mold, take the section in the loft plan showing the sharpest curve, pick this up and make a

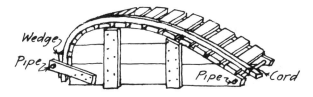

*98. Bending Form*

rough template. Make a form as shown in the sketch; but, in shaping the mold, give it a good deal more curve than the template, holding to the general character of the curve of the template, however. The amount of extra curvature required may be approximated by laying out the form curve so that the two ends of the frame may spring away from the form four times the frame thickness and still be within the curve shown in the template. The form may be made of two rough planks, or of more battened together, cut to the proper curve on one edge. These shapes are set up, with the curved edges on top, and a couple of feet apart. They are then joined with narrow planks or battens with open seams. At one end an iron pipe is inserted; at the other two cleats are nailed and another piece of pipe inserted. The accompanying sketch shows how the form looks when set up. The frame is inserted under the pipe held in the two cleats at one end and then is bent slowly and steadily over the form.

When completely bent, the free end is secured to the iron pipe, in the form sides, by tying with twine or rope. The frame is left on the form overnight. Then it is removed, and stayed by tack-

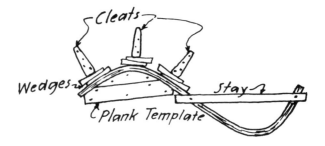

*99. Bending Frames on Floor*

ing a batten across the curve, which serves to hold it in shape. The form should be wide enough to hold a number of frames at a time, not less than ten. If the frames are large they may develop "runs," or show splinters, on their upper faces when bent over the form. This may be prevented by obtaining a piece of strap

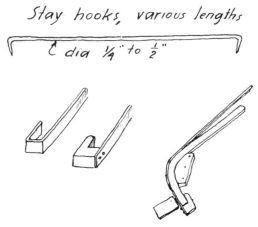

*100. Bending Straps*

iron as long as the frames and of the same width. The thickness should be from ⅛ to ³⁄₁₆ inch, depending upon the length and size of the frames. One end of the strap should be shaped into a square-angled hook which will slip over one end of the frame to be bent. The frame and strap are inserted under the pipe in the cleats and both are then bent over the molds, the strap on top, of

*101. Ripped Frame*

course. If the frames show a tendency to break in spite of every precaution, they must be ripped from the end nearest the curve. After being bent, the two parts formed by ripping may be fastened together by copper rivets if desired.

Reverse curves are formed in two operations. First, the large curve is formed over the molds or form; when cold, it is removed from the form and stayed together with a batten. Then the end to have the reverse is steamed, or boiled, and bent over a form made by nailing a template to the floor of the shop or to the top of a workbench. Very often the reverse formed in the second

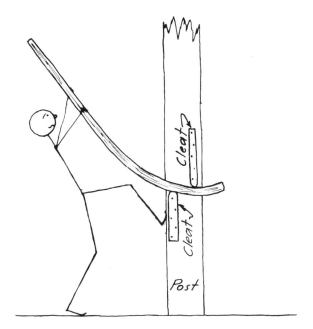

*102. Straightening "Cold" Bent Frames to Fit Ribbands*

operation is the sharpest curve of the two in the frame; the latter may have to be ripped to allow the reverse to be formed. Blocks inserted between the form and frame while bending will serve to give increased curvature. Securing the end of a frame while it is partially bent over the form will give decreased curvature. Shifting the frame while placing it in the form will permit a wide variance in shape of section that will enable most of the middle part of the hull length to be framed without much springing of the frame stock, bent over a single form. A frame bent over a form, and put in the boat cold, may be straightened, but remember that the amount of curvature cannot be increased. A frame may be straightened by inserting one end between two blocks nailed to a post (the direction of the curve of the frame upright) and then pulling down on the free end. Do this a little at a time, testing the frame against the ribbands on the hull after each trial.

## End Grain

In bending frames, the grain in the end should be noted. The frames should always be bent so that the annual rings run more

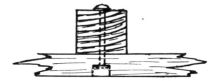

*103. End-Grain Position in Bent Frames*

or less parallel to the ribbands or planking. The annual rings should never approach at right angles to the ribbands, or planking, as the frame is then easily split in fastening.

## Hot Frames, Beveling

If the frames are to be bent, while still hot, directly in the boat, make a handle about 2 feet long with a square hole in it. This will be inserted over the head of the frame, to bevel it by twisting, after the frame is set in place but before it is wholly clamped.

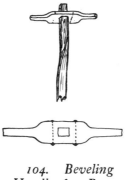

*104. Beveling Handle for Beveling Bent Frames*

## Cold vs. Hot Frames

Bending the frames on a form, and fitting them in place while cold, is probably the best method when building a boat single-handed. Once all the frames are bent over the form and stayed, the builder can frame up the hull as his time permits. He may spend as much time as he desires in beveling the faces of the frames and in fitting the heels. When the frames are taken directly to the hull from the steam box or boiler, however, the bending, fitting, and beveling of the frame must be done quickly, while the frame is still hot and flexible. As one man must bend the frames from the inside of the hull if she is upright, or from the outside if she is upside down, it is often difficult to secure the clamps unless another man can work from the opposite side. In a boat over 20 feet in length, three men are required to frame properly: one to take the frames from the boiler and pass them into the hull; another to step and bend them; and a third to nail the heels and clamp them to the ribbands. If the operations are not carried out speedily many frames will be broken.

## Bending Frames, Material Treatments

The preparation of the frames for bending has been described up to the point of steaming, or boiling. The remarks on these two methods, as applied to planking in the last chapter (page 298), are pertinent to framing or other bending. The choice of equipment can be governed by the suggestions given there. There are a number of matters that deserve attention, however. First, the woods that respond to steaming and boiling; these are generally hardwoods. Where the curvature is to be very great, rock elm, ash, and hickory (true and pecan) are the best, as they withstand great deformation. Less extreme bends can be made with white oak, beech, birch, maple, and red gum. Douglas fir and yellow pine can only be steamed or boiled to very slight curves. Mahogany is of a similar nature. Teak is not easily made pliable unless it is but partially seasoned. Most of the tropical hardwoods cannot be steamed, or boiled, so that they will stand the effects of a sharp bend. The sharper the bend, the greater the weakening of the timber caused by deformation of the fibers. For that reason, a hull requiring very sharp bends in the frames (as in a Friendship Sloop) is not strengthened by the use of large bent frames, or by frames bent on edge. The so-called "canoe frames"—thin, wide frames bent on the flat—are the strongest frames for this type of hull; stiffness must be obtained by the use of longitudinal clamps, stringers, and shelves, and by the use of long floor timbers carried well out and up the sides of the hull. It is a good plan to place all framing stock in water prior to steaming or boiling; this prevents the wood from drying out and becoming brittle. It is a common mistake to place frames in the boiler, or steam box, before the water in the boiler is sufficiently hot to boil or steam. This results in "cooked" frames in extreme cases; these are dead, brittle frames caused by application of dry heat, or too slow boiling.

The water in a boiling tank should be made as hot as possible; the use of soft soap or salt is most common as a means of raising the boiling temperature. It is also claimed that the use of soft soap helps to hold the heat in the wood longer, after removing it from the boiler or steam box. If a steam box is used, the efficiency is greatly increased if pressure can be obtained in the box. The exact length of time required to make a timber pliable depends upon so many factors that general rules are unsafe. Perhaps the most common rule is to leave the timber in the boiler or steam box one hour for every square inch of cross section. However, this is only a rough approximation and should not be accepted as an accurate guide. The safest way is to place some samples in the boiler or steam box and then withdraw pieces occasionally for testing, keeping close record of the time. There should be no difficulty in steaming or boiling timber if the proper woods are available. It should be remembered that the wood must be as pliable as possible before starting the operation of bending. One characteristic of steam-bent wood is that it will tend to increase its curvative, after cooling and being held to shape, when the wood becomes drier; when the wood becomes wetter the curvature tends to decrease. Obviously the latter condition is to be expected in boats.

## *Framing Up, Cold Frames*

In order to simplify the description of the operation of framing, the method used when the frames are placed cold will first be described. Framing should start amidships. The first frame may be placed inside the ribbands (or outside, if the setup requires) and shifted up and down until the position in which it fits best is decided. Then the heel is cut to the proper length and bevel. If necessary, open the curve of the frame a little. Set the frame in place, put in a permanent heel fastening, and then put in some temporary fastenings at some of the ribbands. These can be wire nails driven through one corner of the ribbands into the frame, with the heads protruding enough to permit easy withdrawal. The opposite frame is then prepared the same way and secured. Sometimes a frame will be found that has insufficient curvature for the position for which it is tried; lay it aside, as it may be of use forward in the hull. Step the frames alternately forward and abaft the midsection, taking care that they are square to the keel. When the bow is approached, or a sharp or very narrow stern, the frames may be canted or beveled. The amount of bevel required can be measured by eye or lifted by a compass measurement from the ribbands; the frame is then removed to a workbench and the bevel cut with a drawknife and plane.

It is too much to expect that the bevels will be perfectly correct, but they can be checked later when the planking is being put on; additional cutting can be done then, or shims inserted between frames and planking where required. If the ribbands are inside the frames, as may be the case when the hull is built upside down, it

is well to bevel after the frame is secured in place. Again, do not
attempt to force more bend into a frame than it originally had.
If the frames do not have sufficient curvature, steam or boil some
more, and pad the curve on the bending form so that a sharper
curve can be obtained. If frames are canted forward, or forward
and aft, the heels should be properly beveled against the sides of

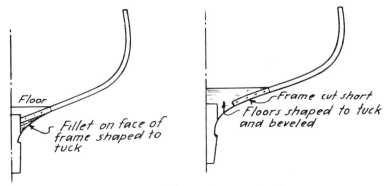

*105. Forming Sharp Reverse in Frames*

the deadwood or keel. If there is a very sharp reverse curve, close
to the keel near the stern, to which it is found impractical to bend
the frames, do not give up or botch the job. There are two courses
open: one is to rip the frames as suggested before; the other is
to let the heels of the frames run into the keel where they will
and then fill below the frames with a shim, shaped to the required
curve. Another variation of this is to form the sharp reverse
curve in the floor timbers and cut the heels of the frames off, a
little short of the sides of the keel. Sometimes it is desirable to pad
out the sides of the deadwood, where the heels of the frames butt
against it, to give something to fasten the heels to; this pad is
made of a batten nailed to each side of the deadwood and notched
along its bottom edge for each frame. If the frame is forced to
a sharp reverse curve it will be unfair, due to deformation, and
will have to be faired up with a spokeshave. As a rule, the extremely sharp reverse curves along the keel should be formed in
the floors, and the frames cut short of the keel. Such floor timbers
should be lofted, as that is the only way the builder can be certain of having the two sides alike.

## *Framing Up, Hot Frames*

If the frames are to be placed hot and bent in shape over the ribbands, the builder should spend a little time making sure his helpers understand what is to be done and the need for speed. The helper, who passes the frames to the man who bends the frames (usually the "boss" of the job), should understand that he is to keep the frames in the boiler or steam box hot and that, as he passes each frame to the "boss," he is to pass it in such a manner that the receiver knows how the bending face stands in relation to the annual rings. The receiver, or builder, steps the frame in its boxing, or against the keel on its marks, and then the man who is to handle the clamps cuts the heel with a saw, so that the heel stands against the side of the keel. In bending, the feet, knees, and hands should be used, first "walking up" the frame and then pulling the frame in with the hands so that it bends more than necessary, then letting it spring out against the ribbands. The frame should be worked in this manner very quickly, taking care that it is on the position marks. The beveling handle should be dropped over the head of the frame and, as required, the bevel twisted in, while the bending is being done.

While the builder is doing this, the other helper is clamping the frames to the ribbands. Use only a few clamps; they should not be set up tightly until the frame is entirely bent to the ribbands. After setting up the top clamp, tap the head of the frame with a mallet so that the frame will be forced down against the ribbands; then tighten all clamps. If the hull is built upside down, tapping is not necessary. In this case, the bending can best be done by standing on the ribbands or, in a very small boat, on the floor or bench. In small boats the bender can also handle the clamps, so only two men are required for the job. Frames that extend from sheer to sheer across the keel, in one piece, should be bent and secured in one operation; this requires two men, each working on a side, with a third operating the steam box or boiler and passing frames. As before, framing is started amidships, working alternately forward and aft. The tops of the frames are allowed to stand above the sheer; they can be cut off after the planking is in place. If a frame breaks or runs, throw it aside and try another: don't hope to patch it satisfactorily later, for it can't be done. If the timber won't stand the bend, rip it and then steam, or boil, and bend in place. If the reverse is so sharp along the keel, aft, that it is difficult to form the curves in the frames, don't hesitate to shim; curse the designer if you wish.

If the frames cannot be twisted to give the bevel, set them to more than the proper curve by inserting blocks between the ribbands and the frame, and then clamp. When they are cold and set to shape they may be removed and beveled, as was done with frames put in place cold. Always step the frame at the keel and bend from this point outward, making sure the frame is bearing on each ribband. As each frame is clamped in place watch for places where the frame is not bearing on a ribband; tap the end of the frame and use a clamp to work it into place. Wire nails may be used in the ribbands and frames where there is no great strain, so that the clamps can be shifted to the next frame. Always twist the frame more than actually required for a bevel; as it is slacked off it will come back some. The same principle is used in bending; bend more than needed and allow it to spring back. Watch out for flat spots and buckles; a clamp rightly placed may save a frame.

It is a good plan, on a heavily framed boat, to add some cross-spalls between the molds, securing them to the top ribbands. After framing, some of these can be transferred to the projecting frameheads. Brace some of these spalls to the overhead beam or to the bearer. Transfer the sheer marks on the molds to the nearest frame. If the molds are in the way of a frame, then these may be removed and the frame bent in place. Before removing any mold, however, make sure that the surrounding frames are well braced so that the hull will not change shape. This means that not only must the cross-spalls be in place on the frames, or upper ribband, but that these must be prevented from moving vertically. Hence the cross-spalls must be braced or stayed to the overhead beam, or to the bearer of the setup.

As a general rule, designers try to place the mold stations clear of all frames, so the molds can stay in place until the hull is planked. When this is not the case, careful builders often re-space the stations in the loft plan, after fairing, so that the molds will not have to be removed for any frames. When there is much tumble-home in the topsides it is a good plan to tie the projecting heads of each pair of frames athwartships to make certain that no flat spots develop in section through the heads of the frames "casting out." Like tying the ribband ends, this is often neglected, with the result that unfair places show up in the planking of the topsides when the boat is completed.

## Extra Frames, Strapping

In a sailing hull it is a good plan to check the plans to see where the chainplates come; it may be necessary to add a frame, or part of a frame, in the way of the chainplate fastenings. Occasionally the frames are doubled, side by side in the wake of the partners, that is, where the partners' ends meet the hull sides. If there is diagonal strapping of bronze or steel in the hull sides, some builders insert them before bending the frames; others work them in between frames and ribbands after framing. If the frames or strapping are at all stiff, the strapping should go in before the frames. These straps must be cut into the frames so that they are flush and are usually fastened to each frame. The notching of the frames and fastening of the straps can be done as the ribbands are removed, one by one, for planking. Care must be taken that the straps are located and the ends fastened as shown in the plans.

## Suggestions

Most of the trouble that beginners have in bending frames is caused by not boiling, or steaming, the frame timber long enough, or by not obtaining the proper timber for the purpose. The use of test pieces will overcome the first difficulty; the proper selection of timber, the second. Of course, it is often impossible, or impractical, to obtain perfectly clear oak or elm, but the portion of clear stock should be sufficient for those frames requiring the greatest curvature. The less perfect stock can be used where the curvature of the frames is slight. It is best to bend the stock toward the knotty side, whenever possible. The substitution of elm for oak is often the solution of a problem. The other woods suitable for severe deformation can be used, even though they are less satisfactory from the standpoint of durability. The most important aim in framing is to avoid broken or fractured frames; the use of shims, or floor timbers, in reverse curves, and ripping to form lamination, will overcome all difficulties. In extreme cases the frame may be wholly laminated; this should be done over a

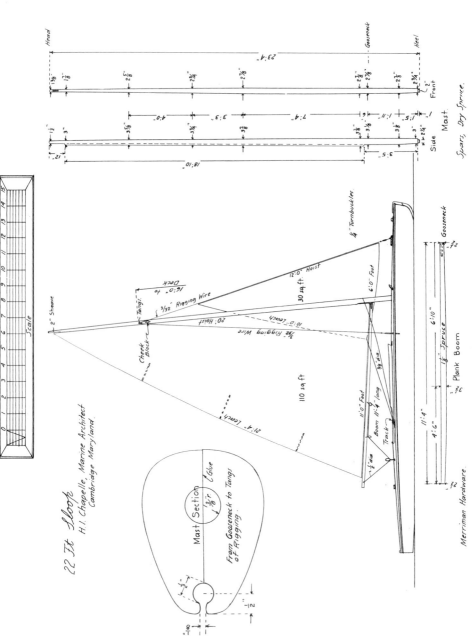

PLATE 47. Sail Plan for a 22-Foot Racing Sloop

form, if possible, and the two laminations secured together before being permanently fastened in the hull. In all laminated construction the use of wood preservatives is advisable. If it is not practical to laminate over a form, this may be done directly in the hull, taking care that the two layers make a reasonably tight joint. This can only be done by bending the inner layer on top of the outer, beginning from the keel, using a large number of clamps. Both layers should not be bent hot in one operation together. In rare cases it is necessary to bend frames without application of steam or boiling; this can be done by using frames made of a number of thin laminations, each bent separately, cold. As each lamination is bent, and added to the frame, it is glued with marine glue. When the frame is completed, the whole series of laminations may be through-riveted at suitable intervals. Such a frame is very strong but, unless well painted and protected, will not last a great length of time.

## Floors, Fitting

If the floor timbers have not been lofted and already secured in place, they may be fitted when the frames are all stepped. The siding and depth of the floors should be shown on the plans. Usually the siding (thickness) is about one-quarter greater than the fore-and-aft width of the frames, unless the latter are very wide. The depth of the floors is greatest over the keel (this portion of the floor is the "throat") and least at the outboard ends; here the depth is usually equal the depth of the frame. If the floor timbers are very shallow in the throat, it is best to make them up of crooked timber ("natural crooks"); usually it is both necessary and possible to make them of straight-grained stock, oak or yellow pine. Under the mast step and engine it is common to use either heavier floor timbers than elsewhere, or to place a floor on every frame if this is not required in the rest of the hull. Floor timbers are most often required to be fitted to every other frame. Metal floors are sometimes needed, particularly under tanks in the bottom of the hull; templates must be made for these and they then can be made of welded strap iron galvanized, or cast of bronze.

To obtain the template of a floor, either wood or metal, from the hull, take two pieces of thin plank and scribe one side on each piece, then lap them endwise to get the shape of the full floor. The laps may be held with brads or tacks, after the fitting has been checked; small clamps are very useful in holding the two pieces while checking the fit. Only that part of the floor timber that bears on the planking and keel need be templated; the top may be struck off when laying out the timber. A template should be made for each floor timber required. The position of each floor timber can be decided by consulting the plans; usually the floor timbers are on the sides of the frames, those in the forebody on forward sides of the frames and those in the afterbody on the after sides of the frames. The reason why the floors are usually placed in this way is that an edge of the frame may be used as the outline to be scribed on the template; the edges of the floor timbers are to be beveled from this line or edge. In rare cases the floor timbers are fitted on top of the frames. In this case the templates are scribed from the sides of the frames nearest the midship frame, and the bevels cut from the resulting line. By these means the exact amount of wood needed in each floor timber is outlined and no extra allowance for the bevels is required. As each floor is templated it may be cut out of the lumber on hand for that purpose and secured in place. If the keel is narrow, the floors are secured to it with a single fastening, staggered in relation to the center line of the keel. Usually, however, it is possible to place two fastenings; in this case they should be staggered in relation to the athwartship center line of the floor timber.

If there is room, the floor fastenings are often drilled with a flare from the vertical, so that they are farther apart on top of the floor than they are at the top of the keel. In large craft, the fastenings may often be offset in the wide floors so that they may actually cross, clear of one another, in the keel. Take care that the floor timbers are square to the keel and against the frames. It may be necessary to tap the heel of a frame fore or aft, to bring it snug against the sides of the floor. Do not try to force a frame to come flat against a floor; the necessary bevel in the frames caused by the sweep of the ribbands will prevent this, unless the frame is forced out of bevel. In other words, it is more important that the frame bear on its full width on the planking than to have it bear its full depth on the floor timber. Some builders go to the trouble of trimming the sides of the frames or floors so that the

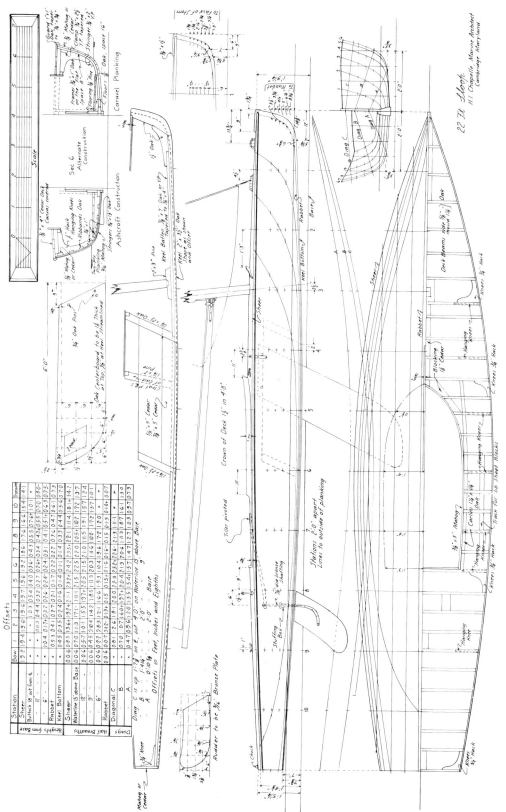

PLATE 48. *Lines and Construction Plans for a 22-Foot Racing Sloop*

depth of the frame may bear fully upon the floor timber; this is thought to "look neater," but has no practical advantage.

At least three fastenings are required to secure the heel of each frame to its floor timber. In small craft, under 40 feet, these fastenings should be boat nails. In larger craft, two carriage bolts will probably be required, though spikes can be used. If the floors are on top of the frames, very few fastenings are required, as the planking fastenings can be made long enough to pass through planking and frames into the floors where necessary. There is no particular advantage to placing the floors on top of the frame except where the frame depth is too slight to take edge-fastenings of sufficient diameter.

## Floors, Bevels

When each floor is fitted and fastened, it should be beveled. The easiest way to do this is to start fitting and securing the floors from amidships, working alternately forward and aft, and beveling as each floor is secured. This can be done by using a short straightedge, which, laid fore and aft on the outside of the frames in way of the floors, will indicate the amount of wood to be trimmed off the floor on the side to be beveled. The cutting can best be done with a sharp adz, but a broad hatchet and spokeshave will serve; a compass saw, or keyhole saw, can be used where the bevel is great. If the floors are on top of the frames, the bevels will have to be scribed from the top edges, using the edge nearest amidships for the controlling shape and the edge nearest the bow and stern for the bevel side. In this case the beveling must be done before the floors are secured in place, of course.

## Fitting of the Heels of Frames

The type of floor timber and keel will govern the fitting and beveling. In many small craft, where there is no back rabbet, the ends of the frames land on top of the keel. The heels of the frames are usually tapered so that the face on the keel top bears as much as possible. In dinghies and other small, flat-floored hulls the frames are often lapped over the keel and no floor timber is used. In this case there should be an inside batten or keelson on top of the frames over the keel. The frames are placed in the hull so that each pair is sufficiently offset from one another to permit the lap without fore-and-aft twists or bends.

## Limbers

The limbers in the floor timbers should not be overlooked. In some cases the floor timbers are not notched the depth of the back rabbet and the resulting openings, on each side of the keel, over the frames, serve as limber holes. In all other types of floors, holes should be cut either on top of the keel or on top of the frame. The bay between the floor timbers should be filled with some material, such as paraffin or pitch, to the level of the bottom of the limber holes, when the boat is planked, to ensure the proper draining of the bays. If the frame heels do not come to the keel, the limbers can be cut in the floors at the corner formed along the keel sides by the bottom planking.

## Equipment for Bending Frames

There are variations in bending equipment from that already described. Large timbers are often bent on a floor instead of a form. A strongly built floor is drilled with a series of ¾-inch diameter holes, the flooring being about 1½ to 3 inches thick. The shape of the frame is chalked on this floor and the frame bent between locust or iron pins inserted in the holes. This is similar to the iron "bending slab" used in steel shipbuilding to shape the frames. Blocks nailed to a floor are sometimes used instead of forms. To stay the frames after they are bent, iron staples, like those described in Chapter Three, page 184, are made up in assorted lengths; these are driven into the sides of a frame after it is cold and has been removed from the bending form. The iron strap used to prevent frames from developing runs or splinters may have a wooden hook instead of having its end shaped by a blacksmith, to take the end of a frame. The wooden hook should be riveted to the strap with through-rivets and should be of oak or locust. A block and tackle may have to be used to bend large frames, using either forms or floor.

## Longitudinal Members

The fore-and-aft members, such as keelson, stringers, clamps, and shelves, cannot be installed until the molds are removed in most setups. The exceptions are when sawn frames are used, or when these members are notched into the molds in an upside-down setup.

### Sawn Frames, Modern Construction

The procedure for setting up sawn frames was described in Chapter Three, page 184. The common practice is to build a shifting platform on each side of the keel, and level with its top, when on the stocks. The end of the platform nearest the stern is at the aftermost "square frame." After the pieces of the frames are

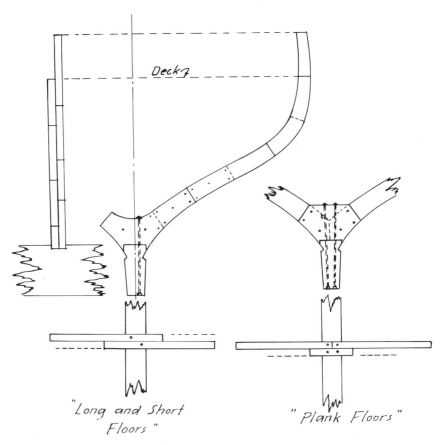

"Long and Short Floors"

"Plank Floors"

*106. Sawn Frames "Double"*

shaped from the molds, the latter are assembled to form a complete half of each frame. The pieces are brought to the platform in order and assembled, using the assembled mold as a constant check for each frame. When the whole frame is assembled it is raised and stepped on top of the keel, the platform being shifted as progress warrants. It is important that the work be done with great accuracy and that all marks on the molds be transferred to the frames and checked. The construction of a sawn frame of straight-grained timber is such that it has little strength by itself; it is of great strength when the planking and ceiling are in place, however. The use of straight-grained timber is almost a necessity in recent times, natural crooks being almost impossible to obtain in the sizes usually required. For this reason the floor timbers are best placed straight across the keel, "plank floors," as in a bent frame. Each frame has one floor timber; floors are usually arbitrarily placed on the part of the frames nearest the ends of the ship. The matter can best be decided when lofting the construction.

When natural crooks are available, the floors are formed by what is known as "long and short floors," in which there are actually two floor timbers to each frame. As each frame is made up of two layers there is no clumsiness in this. Single sawn frames are used in small craft, when wood for bent frames is unobtainable. These frames are lofted in a single layer, so to speak, and are usually set up like V-bottom frames, with those forward of amidships having their after faces on the station lines, and those aft of amidships with their forward faces on the station lines. The cleats that are used to join the pieces ("futtocks") of the frames are on the opposite sides from the station mark. The floors are fitted as in bent frames. The beveling is done on the frames when they are in place, as in V-bottom frames, though, of course, it can be done on the loft plan if desired. Instead of using cleats to join the futtocks, the butts may be edge-scarfed to make a neater and lighter job. The butts of all sawn frames should be well secured; bolts are used in large craft while screws or clench nails are used in small. The futtocks of double frames should be fastened together with wooden pins or treenails if possible; iron spikes, drifts, or nails otherwise. The wooden fastenings in the futtocks are most desirable, as they will not foul the plank fastenings, or the drill used for them. If treenails are used they should go through the frame fore and aft and be wedged on each end. Sawn frames are a good deal heavier than bent frames but, once in place, are stiffer. If made of natural crooks, both single and double frames are very strong. Single frames are widely used in southern waters, where they are made of heart yellow pine, live oak, or some of

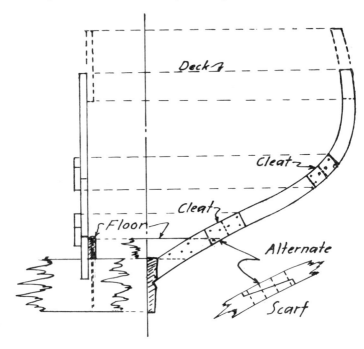

*107. Sawn Frame "Single"*

the tropical hardwoods such as madeira or black mangrove. Single sawn frames should not be less than 1-inch siding, even in a very small boat.

## Planking Difficulties

The planking is the next job after framing, in most cases. The common carvel planking is most popular. This is "lined off" in the same general way as explained in the chapters on flat- and V-bottom construction. The art of lining off is not one that is easily described; a very fine job is usually the result of some experience in a given model of hull. It may be said that the most common difficulty in planking arises when the projection of a straight line around the sections, in its natural, or normal, curve, is too widely departed from. This results in the need for excessively wide planks, in order to get the edge curves necessary in some of the strakes. Another common difficulty is traced to carrying the garboard too far forward on the keel rabbet; this results in the hood ends becoming too narrow along the stem rabbet and an unpleasant upsweep to the planking seams forward. The use of a few general principles will overcome these difficulties to a great extent.

## Lining-Off and Planking

As was mentioned in the last chapter, the top of the garboard should approximate a line parallel to the load water line when the garboard is in place. This does not mean that its top must be a straight line, viewed from the broadside, but that the heights of the tops of the ends should be within the limits of such a line. The fear of the shim end in the forward end of the garboard is the cause of many builders' carrying the strake too far forward. It should be remembered that the shim end will be backed up by the back rabbet, or keel batten, in most boats. Where this is not the case, it is possible to saw off the shim at some convenient point and form a hook in the next strake above that will fill the space formed by the cutoff end of the garboard.

The planning of the topside strakes is the same as described in V-bottom construction in the last chapter. The mode of planking usually followed is first to put on the garboards, then the sheer strakes, using an arbitrary width for each as described in V-bottom construction. Many builders continue planking down from the sheer strake a couple of strakes, at least, before beginning to plan the intermediate strakes. This is usually possible without developing difficulties farther along in the job. The builder decides this by observing the amount of curvature required in each strake; if it appears to be increasing rapidly in each successive strake he stops and lines off. This is done by bending a straight-edged batten around the hull, letting it take a natural bend. The batten is usually first placed so that the after end and top edge run from the intersection of the transom, or stern overhang, with the sternpost rabbet (the "tuck" in builder's parlance) along the turn of the bilge, or as close to it as the batten will normally run. The batten should be from 3 to 6 inches wide; too narrow a batten will take an unnatural curve and mislead the builder. It is intended that the top edge of the batten represents the normal position of a straight-edged strake on every frame. By spacing either way, above or below the straight edge of the batten, the spacing, or widths, of strakes may be found. As a result, the builder can plank down to the batten, from where he stopped on the topsides, and be assured that the edge curves in the strakes are coming back to a straight line.

Having done this, in most hulls, it is possible to plank on, by

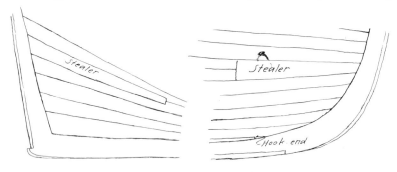

*108. Planking Stealers*

working up from the garboard, to a closing strake or shutter just under the turn of the bilge. This is often the strake whose top is represented by the straight edge of the batten. It can be seen that— if after planking a little above the garboard it is found that the edge curve is becoming too great—it is possible to employ the straight-edged batten twice, if the planking is not carried too far. The placing of the second batten line will be obvious to the builder, in this case, although a general rule cannot be given that will apply to even a majority of hulls. If the run of the planking is such that it is impossible to close up at the sternpost as fast as elsewhere, without the use of abnormal widths of planking there, the use of a triangular-shaped stealer may be necessary. This need not run to a shim end forward; the strakes above and below the stealer, or either one alone, may be notched, or "anchored," to permit the forward end of the stealer to be a narrow, square butt, backed up by a butt block between the frames where the butt falls. It is a good plan to try to carry the stealer to as near amidships as possible; it is usually just below the tuck, say, two or three strakes. In some cases it is used as the shutter as well. Stealers forward are sometimes required; these are of different form and serve to carry two strakes to the stem in one. When it is found that the hood ends of two strakes are too narrow, they are cut off somewhere abaft the stem and carried forward with a single stealer. This stealer is widest at the butt where it meets the ends of the cutoff strakes and narrowest at the stem.

The use of the normal line, the straight-edge batten applied to the hull in a natural position, is the secret of economical planking and good lining off. With the batten in place, the builder can foresee how to use the timber at hand to the best advantage and can even edge-spring the batten forward or aft to widen the hood ends in the topsides. The spacing off of the plank widths is best worked out roughly by laying off on the midship frame and those nearest the bow and stern. After the spacing is roughed out and corrected where necessary, the final marks can be placed on every frame. This is not necessary when the builder is experienced, but is usually a good plan for a beginner. In selecting stock for planking, it is usual to use the wide stuff below the bilge and in the sheer and garboard strakes. The topsides to the water line should be apparently parallel edged and rather narrow. At the turn of the bilge the strakes should be made as narrow as the builder deems necessary. The harder and quicker the turn of the bilge, the narrower the strakes will have to be. This often permits a more rapid closing in at the stern than would be otherwise possible; in some cases this is highly desirable. No strake should be so narrow that two fastenings into the frames or stem and sternposts are impossible. Sometimes it is necessary for a rather wide strake to run into the curve of the bilge. Any attempt to bend the strake crosswise will split it. It is necessary to hollow the inside of the plank, in this case, to make it rest fairly on the frames. As the outside must be rounded in smoothing off, such a strake should be a little thicker than the rest of the planking to allow for the reduction in thickness that results from "hollowing and rounding." Years ago good builders took pains to hollow and round all planking, wherever necessary, but this is rarely done now except in the most expensive craft.

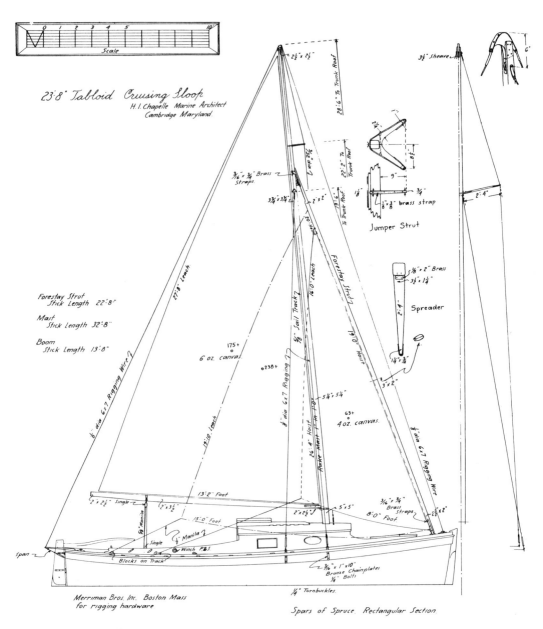

**PLATE 49.** *Sail Plan for a 23-Foot Tabloid Cruising Sloop*

The sequence of planking is by no means ironclad. The first strakes put on may be either the sheer or garboard strakes; but these two strakes are put on before any others in any case. With these two in place, the builder may put on the topside strakes or work alternately up from the garboard and down from the sheer, closing with the shutter. It is only in large craft, requiring staging to plank, that the sequence has any importance; here the topsides are planked to the turn of the bilge as soon as possible, so that the staging may be removed.

## Widths of Strakes

The widths used in lining off planking vary with the size and type of boat; however, the following finished widths taken amidships are about average. The garboard is usually from 7 to 12 inches wide, the sheer strakes from 4 to 7 inches, the topside strakes from 3½ to 6 inches, the broad strakes above the garboard from 5 to 9 inches, and those at the turn of the bilge from 3 to 5 inches. The ends will be narrower, of course.

## Planking Methods

The methods used in planking have been described in Chapter Four, page 228, and in Chapter Five, page 284, but as there is bound to be some difference between planking a flat- or V-bottom hull and planking a round-bottom hull, instructions will be given for this operation. Assuming the garboard is to go on first, the lumber stock is inspected and it is found that the two widest planks available are both a little over 13 inches wide, so far as usable lumber is concerned. Allowing for trimming, it appears safest to plan on garboards about 10 inches wide. This dimension is laid off on the frame having the greatest girth, measuring from the rabbet of the keel after removing the ribband, or ribbands, that would interfere. The point of greatest girth may be ascertained by bending a thin batten over the ribbands, or on the frames, and checking the length from rabbet to sheer. In most hulls the top of the garboard should not be a straight-edged plank; some hog is usually required. If it appears feasible to make the top of the garboard straight, the use of a straight-edged batten tacked to the frames, with the straight edge passing through the mark just made and the batten sprung to a normal curve around the frames, will serve to check the idea. If it appears that the garboard is run too far ahead or too high on the stem by this means, the straight-edged batten should be removed and a stiff, square-sectioned one substituted. With the latter batten an arbitrary curve may be laid off on the frames to represent the top of the garboard strake. The amount of curve in the top of the strake should be sufficient to keep any part of it to below a line parallel to the load water line, passing through the point of greatest width in the strake. The end forward will be fixed by the amount of curve in the top of the strake and by the angle at which the keel rabbet stands to the load water line.

When the batten is placed to the satisfaction of the builder, the top of the garboard is marked on each frame and the batten removed. The spiling batten may be next applied; the use of this was described in Chapter Five, page 300, and no further instructions should be necessary to obtain the shape of the garboards. When one is completed and fitted, it is used as a pattern for its mate; both are then fastened in place. If the rabbet needs truing up, it will be apparent while spiling, or fitting, the garboards. Some of the frames may need additional smoothing up to obtain a good bearing on the planks.

### Removing Ribbands

As each strake is prepared or lined off, the ribbands in way of it should be removed. All of the ribbands should never be removed prior to planking; this would cause the hull to change shape and become unfair. The interference of the ribbands may be troublesome in lining off, but extreme accuracy in the latter operation is not necessary, as corrections can be made as each strake is laid out after the ribbands that interfere are removed.

### Garboard

In fitting the garboard it will be found that the straighter the rabbet of the keel and sternpost, the easier it is to fit this strake. Perhaps the most troublesome garboard to fit is one in which the rabbet edge is a complete curve, from top forward to top aft. This is required when the intersection of the rabbet on the sternpost with that on the keel is a fair and sweeping curve. When faced with this design, the builder should cross-batten the garboards on the outside, before forcing them into place; otherwise a split strake may result. Steaming or boiling this end of the garboard is often a desirable practice. If there is much fullness in the sections forward, near the keel, the garboard may have so much twist that steaming or boiling is required. In planking a full-ended hull with cedar or mahogany, it may be found that the planking will not stand the twist required; rather than be content with a fractured plank, it is better to substitute oak or elm garboards. If this is done, be certain that the stock is well seasoned. The garboards are the most troublesome planks to fit in most hulls: that is why most builders like to get them out of the way as soon as possible.

### Sheer Strake

Next the sheer strake is fitted. Again an arbitrary width is taken. This may be checked against the stock on hand by bending a wide, straight-edged batten through the mark representing the width of the sheer strake to check the actual width of plank required, as described in Chapter Five, page 287. Usually the greatest width of plank is required where the flare of the sides is greatest, as in the forward sections of many powerboats. For the beginner, it is a good plan to transfer the sheer marks on the molds to the frames. This can be done with a stiff, square-sectioned batten, sprung along the sheer marks on stem, stern, and molds if a ribband was not fitted in its place, or is not accurate. This batten, when in place according to the marks on the molds, should be carefully "sighted"; this may be done by standing off from the hull a considerable distance, if possible, and inspecting the curve formed by the batten from various angles. This sighting of the sheer will enable the builder to see and correct any unfairness, either at the molds or between them.

When the sheer has been sighted on both sides of the hull, the frames between the molds may have the sheer marks struck on their outside faces and referenced by tick-marks on either their forward or after sides. This done, the use of the straight-edged batten to ascertain the width of the sheer strakes is made more accurate. Once the width of the sheer strake is decided, its bottom is established with a square-sectioned batten, running it through the width mark on the frame of greatest girth and to the bow and stern as required to appear parallel with the sheer when viewed broadside on. If this is done while the sheer batten is still in place, the appearance of the sheer strake is more easily visualized. When satisfied with the batten's position, the marks representing the bottom of the strake can be struck off on every frame. Now the strake can be spiled off. The spiling batten can be a wide, straight piece of thin plank if the sheer is fairly straight, but often must be made up of two pieces, lapped in the middle at a slight angle (when lapped and the batten stood on edge, on the floor, the middle should be clear of the floor 6 to 8 inches). The batten should be $\frac{1}{8}$ to $\frac{3}{16}$ inch thick and from 3 to 6 inches wide, planed smooth on both sides. This is clamped to the frames with its upper edge a little below the sheer batten or marks, allowing it to take a normal curve. Take a compass, open enough to reach from sheer marks to well onto the batten at the widest opening between them, and scribe at every frame. Take care to make good, full arcs. Reference the marks on the batten with chalk; the batten will be used a number of times and the chalk can be rubbed out after each spiling.

Mark the stem rabbet on the batten and the butt, if there is one. This may now be removed and the spilings set off on the plank to be used for one sheer strake, reversing the operation of the compass, from batten to plank. The method of spiling has been thoroughly described, so need not be repeated here. In cutting the top of the sheer strake, make the necessary allowance for the bevel formed along it by the decking; this can be estimated from the loft drawings. Once the top is cut, the bottom may be picked off by transferring the distance, sheer to bottom of strake, as marked off on the frames, to the strake being shaped. When the sheer strake has been fitted for sheer, its end may be cut to fit the bow rabbet. Usually two marks at top and bottom of the spiling batten are enough, if the rabbet is fairly straight at the end of the strake, but in hulls where the strakes at the bow are wide, and where the curvature of the rabbet is marked, end spilings may be required. When the first strake has been completed it is used as a pattern for its opposite, and both are then fastened in place. In full-ended or sharp-sterned hulls the sheer strakes often need steaming or boiling; even a substitution of timber is necessary in

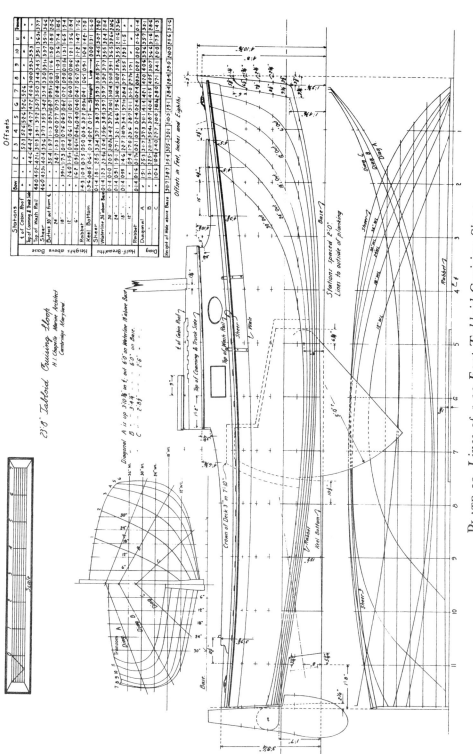

23'-0" Tabloid Cruising Sloop

H. I. Chapelle Naval Architect
Cambridge Maryland

PLATE 50. Lines of a 23-Foot Tabloid Cruising Sloop

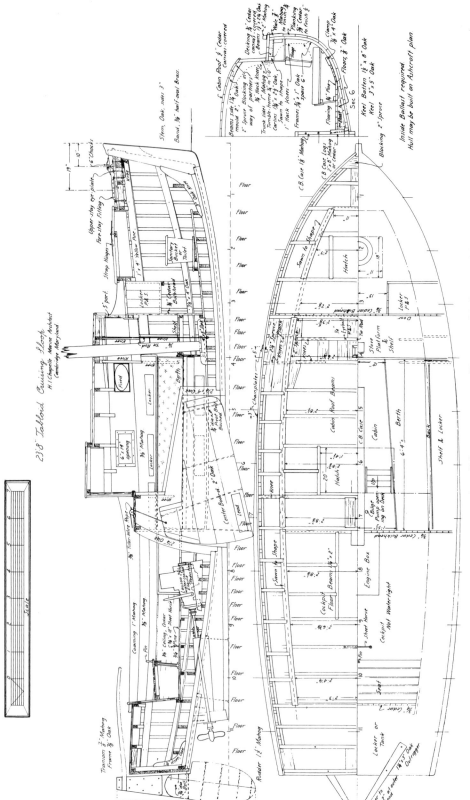

PLATE 51. *Construction Plans for a 23-Foot Tabloid Cruising Sloop*

extreme cases, as in the garboards. Incidentally, in a hull planked with softwood a hardwood sheer strake is desirable. After the sheer strakes are ready to be put in place, see how the sheer clamp must be fastened, as it may be desirable to fasten these strakes only temporarily so that the fastenings of the sheer clamps may be driven from the outside of the frames later. The bevels at the top of the sheer strakes are best cut when the deck beams are in place and decking is being laid.

## Butts

The butting of strakes, when they must be in two lengths, should be done with butt blocks fitted between the frames. These should be of oak or hardwood, and wide enough to overlap ½ inch onto the adjoining strakes; they should also be of the same thickness as the strakes. The tops of all butt blocks should be well rounded on the inside edge, to drain properly; otherwise a damp pocket will be formed to harbor rot. It is a good plan to leave a small space at each end of the butt blocks, between them and adjoining frames, to aid in draining. The butts should be nailed, screwed, or bolted, three to five fastenings in each plank, according to size. A weak butt block is the result of poor workmanship, or quality of fastenings.

## Long Strakes

Some yachtsmen have made a fetish of single-length strakes, running in one piece from bow to stern; some have gone to the extreme of actually paying a large premium to have a hull built with no butts in the planking. A little common sense should indicate how illogical this is: a hull must be built with joints in its structure, the planking butts being the least important, structurally. The strongest type of end-to-end fastening of plank is the lap; the butt block is really the same thing as a lap. Nevertheless, in craft over 50 feet in length the butts in the topsides can be too numerous; this often results in the hull "working," or changing shape, due to the accumulated movement possible in the many fastenings of the butts. However, two or three butts in the sheer strake of a large vessel will cause no weakness. It is not particularly difficult to build the topsides of a hull having a transom with single-length strakes, providing they are available; but to fit these to a double-ender or to a transom hull in the way of the sternpost is far from easy. Certainly the advantages of the single-length strakes are not important enough to warrant the cost of obtaining the necessary plank, in any but hulls under 20 feet long. In butting planking, however, the builder should never resort to the lubberly practice of butting on a frame, without a butt block. This is a highly dangerous practice in all but the largest of wooden hulls, where there is ample backing for three or more well-staggered fastenings. Butts in planking should be staggered; those in adjoining strakes should not be nearer than three frame spaces and the longer portions of strakes in the topsides should be shifted alternately forward and aft. Butts in the same space between frames should be separated by three or four strakes.

## *Topsides*

With the sheer strakes in place, a few topside strakes can be spiled and fitted. The bottom of each should be struck off on the frames with the square-sectioned batten, and the top edge spiled. When the spiling has been transferred to a plank, the bottom edge is laid off from measurements lifted from the frames and the ends cut. Always fit the fore end first, or the forward portion of a strake in two lengths. When the strake is ready and has been fitted, its duplicate is made. These are then fastened in place. When preparing to put a strake in place, have the clamps ready and also prepare wedges, blocks, and shores. After a plank has been clamped to the frames, nail or clamp some blocks to the frames, above or below the strake as the position permits, and then force the strake edgewise against its neighbor by driving wedges between these blocks and the edge of the strake opposite the edge to be set tight. This should not edgeset the strake; it must be cut to fit, but will ensure a tight seam. If there is a great deal of flare forward or aft, do not forget to bevel the edges of the planking so that the calking seam will be open on the outside and closed on the inside, not the reverse. Sometimes, due to hull shape, a finished plank cannot be fitted without great difficulty; in this case a thin template can be made and fitted correctly before strake is cut. Though somewhat wasteful of material, it often saves a great deal of labor.

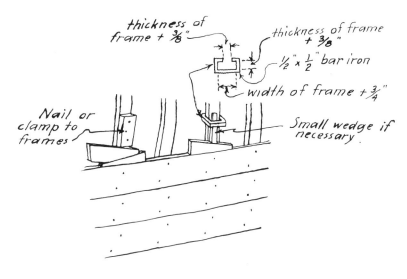

*109. Wedging a Strake*

## Lower Strakes and Shutters

When the strake below the sheer strake is in place, the builder may put in the one below, or drop down to the strake immediately above the garboard. This is laid off and spiled in the manner employed in other strakes. When this strake is completed, the builder may feel it desirable to work out the dividing line, that is, the straight seam formed by a straight-edged batten run from the tuck forward. This should be just under the turn of the bilge amidships, in most hulls. In some jobs it is really not necessary to use this batten at all, but the beginner should employ it nevertheless, since, due to lack of experience, he has not the necessary judgment to decide the question. When the batten is being located, care may be needed to obtain the best results. In a full-bowed hull some shifting will be required to prevent the fore end of the batten from being too high on the stem; if possible, it should be at, or just below, the load water line at the stem. In rare cases it may be desirable to do a little "faking" and edgeset the batten downward at the bow.

When the batten has been finally placed, all the other strakes may be laid off. This is done by first dividing the frame of greatest girth by the number of strakes required from batten to the last strakes put on, above and below it. If there are four above and six below, for example, the same number must be spaced off on the frames closest to the bow and stern on either side of the batten edge. If it is found that the six below the batten are only 3 inches wide at the bow and that at the sternpost all must be 12 inches wide, it is plain that a stealer is required. This will permit the closing, or shutter, strake to be of odd size and the six original strakes can be made arbitrarily 10 inches on the sternpost, leaving a 12-inch shutter there which will run out abaft amidships, at a point that may be arbitrarily chosen after all but the shutter is in place. This done, the builder planks up, alternating above and below the shutter. When this is reached, he may choose the point where the last two strakes part edges to cut the hook for the fore end of the shutter stealer, or may go forward of that. He can cut the square butt for the stealer with keyhole saw, ripsaw, and chisel if the strakes are fastened, or he can use temporary fastenings and remove the strakes to form the hook. Temporary fastenings can be formed by nailing the planks to the frames, after drilling, with nails passed through small blocks of wood or by using staging nails having upper and lower heads to facilitate withdrawal. Shores will probably be necessary also. Forward stealers are fitted in the same manner.

## Marking for Planking

Earlier discussion of lining off the planking should be sufficient to enable the builder to decide on the proper widths for each strake, not only with regard to the material in hand, but also to obtain a workmanlike appearance. It is not necessary to work out the spacing for the strakes above and below the straight-edged batten on every frame: every fourth frame is ample. A batten run through the marks for each strake will enable more marks to be made. An experienced builder marks very few frames and may not even batten off, but this is not for the beginner.

## Shutter Position

The shutter strake should be one that can be put on without great twist and that requires no boiling or steaming. As it will be impossible to use clamps, the other strakes being in the way, cleats may have to be nailed through adjoining strakes into frames (boring for the nails), or shores and wedges used liberally.

## Hollow and Round

Hollow such strakes as require it; these are usually at the turn of the bilge amidships, or at the same position in the counter, or near the transom. The inside faces of some strakes in a reverse curve formed near the keel may require rounding. This can be done with a plane—a round-edged iron in a scrub plane for the hollowing and an ordinary jack plane for the rounding. The amount of hollow or rounding can be measured by placing a straight stick across the frame where the strake is to fit and measuring the round or hollow. The fitting need not be perfectly smooth.

## Fastenings Required

Fastenings should be three to a frame in the wide strakes, two fastenings to each frame in the narrow strakes. Take care in drilling to stagger them in the frame. The garboard, and the strake above it, should be fastened to both frame and floor timber, two in the frame and one in the floor, in one strake, and the reverse in the other. Fastenings are usually placed in the garboard, to pass into the back rabbet if there is one, or into the keel batten. It is a mistake to place these fastenings too close together, or to let a fastening pass through the edge of the strake, in the rabbet, where it will interfere with calking. Two fastenings in every frame bay are usually sufficient. When there is neither back rabbet nor keel batten, no fastenings can be used.

## Tight-Seam Planking

By careful workmanship it is possible to build a hull in which all planking seams are so tight that calking is not required. This calls for accurate spiling and beveling of the seams. The planks, before being set in place, have their edges slightly crushed with a specially shaped pair of metal wheels set in handles, something like a calking wheel. One wheel has a hollow edge, formed in a shallow V and a little wider than the edge of the plank; the other has the V reversed, so that its apex is in the center of the rim of the wheel.

Both are fitted with guides to enable the user to apply pressure to the wheel without having it run off the edge of the plank. As each plank is shaped, one edge is crushed with one wheel and the opposite edge with the other. This, when applied to the planks in proper order, forms a very slight tongue-and-groove effect, made by the crushed fibers of the wood at the edges, or center, of the plank edge. When the strakes are forced into position, the seam is made tight. When completely planked and planed off, the hull is washed with boiling water, which swells the crushed fibers and closes the seams so tightly that they can hardly be seen. This "tight-seam" construction is suitable for small craft having thin planking, but should not be used otherwise. Tight-seam planking puts an enormous strain on plank fastenings, so these must be of the very best quality—never brass.

## Refinements

There are countless refinements in planking that are used by the best of the professional builders; many of these can be used to

*110. Shiplap Seams*

advantage in amateur boatbuilding, where cost of labor is not a matter of importance. For example, the outboard faces of butt blocks are rounded fore and aft to make the planking butts fair; the sheer strake is made thicker than the others and then shaped on the outside face to form a molding, or a wale; the butts in the planking are edge-scarfed instead of straight-butted; the sheer strake is edge-fastened to the one below it; seams made shiplap; and, of course, there are also other forms of planking than carvel.

## Double-Skin Carvel

Lap-strake, strip, and diagonal planking require certain details in construction and will be dealt with later. This is true with the forms of double-planking in which one layer, or skin, of planking is laid diagonally to the keel center line. However, a common form of double-planking is constructed with both layers running fore and aft, the seams in one layer being at about the center of the strakes in the other layer. This form of planking is not easy: the inner layer, or course, of planking must be perfectly fair and the seams close. The strength of a lightly framed hull is greatly increased by double-planking, but, unless there is some preservative or watertight material between the two courses, double-planking is not long lived. In certain designs, however, double-planking is highly desirable and a builder should know how to proceed.

Usually the inner skin is thinner than the outer. The stock should be ordered so that there is some allowance for smoothing and fairing, to permit the two skins together to finish to the required thickness. In the topsides and bottom very little allowance need be made, but in those strakes at the turn of the bilge and in the sharp reverse sectional curves there must be ample to allow for hollowing and rounding, plus fairing and smoothing. Between the two skins there is often silk or muslin, laid on the inner skin with marine glue, paint, varnish, or (rarely) airplane dope. The outer face of the inner skin and the inner face of the outer are often treated with some of the patented wood preservatives that will not resist paint (creosote cannot be used). To obtain the best results, there should not be more than one butt in any strake. The sheer and garboard strakes are one in course; the lower edge of the sheer strake and the upper edge of the garboard strake are rabbeted to form a shiplap; the depth of the rabbets on the outside of the strakes is equal to the thickness of the outer skin. The vertical depth of these rabbets must be sufficient to permit fastenings to be placed in the rabbets, and staggered slightly. Therefore, the shiplap rabbet so formed is at least ¾ inch wide.

There are various ways of putting on a double skin. Usually the inner skin is first completed with light fastenings into the frames, then the fabric put on and coated, and finally the outer skin put in place. The obvious difficulty is in attaching the spiling batten and the planking while fitting the outer skin. This is ordinarily done by using staging nails, or nails driven through small wooden blocks before using as a temporary fastening, care being taken to drive these through the inner skin into frames. The holes made are carefully filled with the glue, paint, or varnish used on the fabric, before placing the outer strakes in position and fastening permanently. In some yards the inner skin and outer skin are put on together, inner and outer in pairs. The fabric is put on in strips a little wider than the strakes. This allows clamps to be used on most of the strakes. Perhaps the greatest disadvantage is that the use of strips makes a messy operation, as the glue, or whatever adhesive is used on the fabric, gets spread over everything, unless the greatest care is taken. The fastenings in double-planking are usually through all: two or three fastenings through each outer strake in each frame, five or six through both skins between the frames. These last are usually screws driven from inside the hull, though clenched copper tacks driven from outside are sometimes used when the skins are very thin.

The fastenings in frames are either rivets or screws. At least two fastenings should be placed in the rabbets of the sheer and garboard strakes, between frames. Unless the double-planking job is a good one, the results will be disappointing; poor fitting or lining off is emphasized by double-planking. As the inner skin acts as butt blocks for the butts in the outer, and as the inner skin is thinnest, care must be taken not to spring the inner skin at the butts of the outer skin. Wide frame spacing is undesirable in double-planking for this reason. Except in power craft subject to rapid vibration, double-planking is an unnecessary refinement as a rule. Double-planking, with the inner skin diagonal, is preferable when the hull is subject to wrenching strains, as in lifeboats or other rowing craft that must be beached. Double-diagonal is even better for this class of hull.

### Breaking Strakes, Bending Plank

In fitting strakes into place it is not uncommon to break a plank; in some designs this is very likely to happen. When a plank must be bent sharply, it is a good plan to bend it into place, using clamps to hold it, before doing any fastening. If a plank is bent hard, and fastened as it comes to bear on each frame, it will often break at a fastening, or while being drilled for a fastening. Saw cuts, across the inside face of a plank, can be resorted to in extreme cases; these should not be over one third the thickness of the plank in depth, and closely spaced.

### Edgeset

As a general rule, edgeset should be avoided in planking. In large hulls, however, it is often necessary to edgeset a good deal

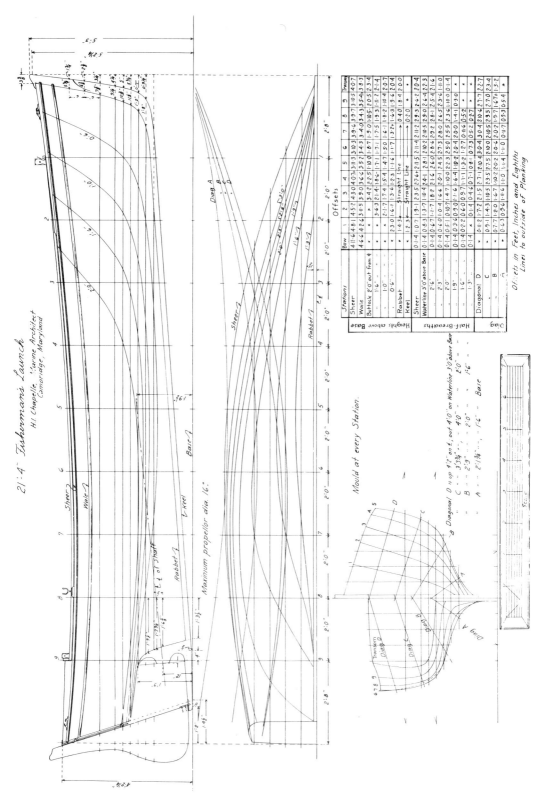

PLATE 52. *Lines of a 21-Foot Fisherman's Launch*

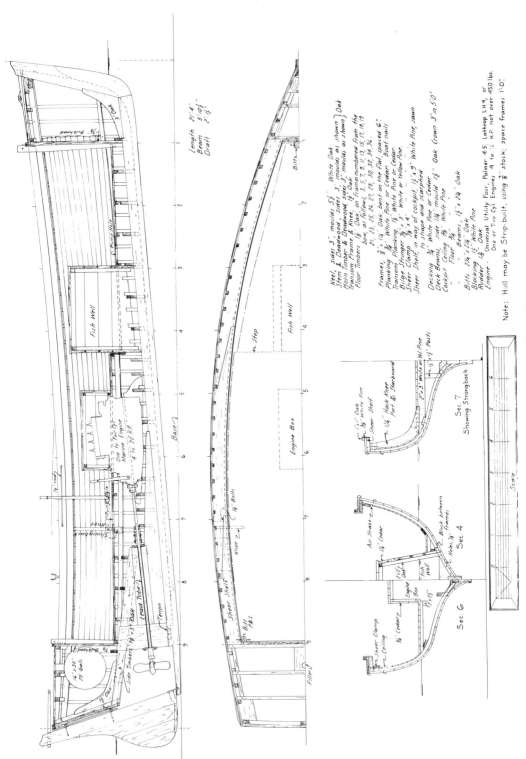

PLATE 53. *Construction Plans for a 21-Foot Fisherman's Launch*

of the planking in some hull forms. The amount of edgeset in any strake should be very slight, however. In any lightly framed hull edgeset is ruinous and should never be resorted to, except in strip planking.

## Notes on Fastenings, Rules for Size

The fastenings in planking have been discussed earlier and there is only a little to be added. The use of alloy nails, such as Monel, has become popular. It has been found that nails of this type should be driven home and set in one operation; if they are driven and the setting put off, they appear to "freeze" and either will not go home or will be extremely hard to set up. Care should be taken, while boring for plank fastenings, to keep clear of all frame or floor-timber fastenings. Look before starting to drill. The use of tree-nails for securing planking is now limited to large hulls. The diameter of the treenails used in the planking is $\frac{1}{4}$ inch larger than the iron bolts used in the butts. Two-inch planking requires $\frac{1}{2}$-inch diameter butt bolts, $\frac{5}{16}$-inch diameter spikes, and $\frac{3}{4}$-inch diameter treenails. Two-and-a-half to 3-inch planking requires $\frac{5}{8}$ to $\frac{3}{8}$ to $\frac{7}{8}$ inch. Three-and-a-half to 4-inch planking requires $\frac{3}{4}$ to $\frac{7}{16}$ to 1-inch bolts, spikes, and treenails—in that order.

The old rule for the thickness of the bottom planking in inches was length, plus beam, plus depth, in feet, divided by 50. Bilge strakes were $\frac{L + B + D}{40}$-inches of thickness. Bilge to planksheer was to be $\frac{L + B + D}{55}$. In large vessels, treenail fastened, great care must be taken that the treenails are well-seasoned locust, or white oak. The frames and planking should also be well seasoned. Due to the lack of such timber, spiked planking is in greater favor. Treenails should be wedged; those that do not act as through-fastenings may be "fox-tailed" or "blind-wedged"; this is done by splitting the point of the treenail slightly and setting an oak wedge in it before entering it in its hole. When driven home, the wedge is forced into the treenail by the bottom of the hole. The driving end is then sawn off flush with the outside of the planking and wedged; the outside wedge is usually required to be driven at right angles to the grain of the planking, so as not to cause "fastening rents" or checks. Through-treenails are wedged on the inside of the ceiling or frames, in the same manner as employed outside the planking.

## Removing Molds

The planking completed, in the small-bent frame hull, the molds are removed and the longitudinal members placed. The molds should be taken out carefully, so as not to disturb the cross-spalls or frame ties. In boats over 25 feet long it is usually easiest to dismount the molds and remove them in pieces.

## Keelson

If there is a keelson, this should be put in first. Sometimes it is possible to make this member in one length, but usually it must be scarfed. In sawn-frame hulls the heavy keelson should go in before the foremost frames, or cants, are stepped. Scarfs in this timber should not come nearer than three frame spaces to scarfs in the keel. If there is much curve in the keelson, this must be cut into it, or the member laminated. Springing a large keelson to a profile curve should not be attempted. The fastenings are usually drifts carefully located so that they do not foul the floor-timber bolts. When the keelson is used, the floor-timber bolt is single and on alternating sides of the center line of the keel; the keelson bolts are also single, through each floor timber, and staggered to alternate with the floor bolts. The keelson bolts are long enough to pass through the floor timbers into the keel. The ends of the keelson must be well secured to the deadwood at each end of the hull; otherwise the member is of little value structurally. Usually the ends rest in notches cut in the top of each deadwood and are drift-bolted. When heavy loads are to be carried, the keelson should be notched on the bottom to lock into every floor timber. In small craft, having keelsons, such as bent-frame dinghies, the keelsons are in single lengths and are easily sprung into place; the fastenings are screws or nails driven through the frames into the keel, or keel batten. The ends are fastened to the bow and stern deadwood knees.

## Sheer Clamps

The sheer clamp is next placed. The position of this, in regard to the sheer, is of particular importance: it must be at the proper

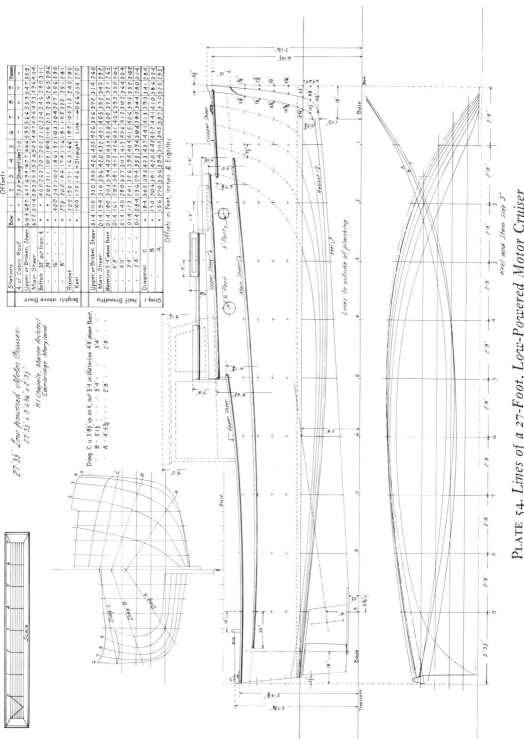

27'3½" Low-powered Motor Cruiser
27'3½" x 8'6¾" x 2'3½"

H.I. Chapelle, Marine Architect
Cambridge, Maryland

Offsets in Feet, Inches & Eighths

Lines to outside of planking

Keel and Stem Side 3"

PLATE 54. Lines of a 27-Foot, Low-Powered Motor Cruiser

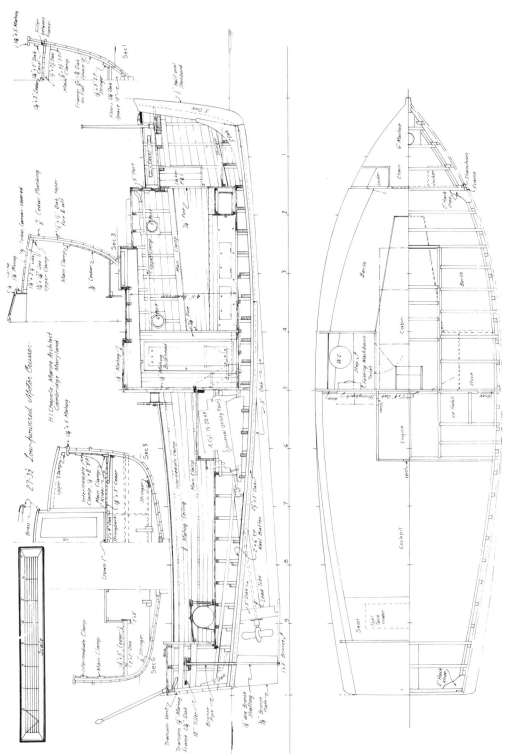

PLATE 55. *Construction Plans for a 27-Foot Motor Cruiser*

height to allow the top of the deck beams, which rest on the clamp, or are notched into it, to come flush with the sheer line, or top of sheer strake. It is a good plan to check this position by the loft plan as the ends of the deck beams are rarely square. If lofting cannot be readily done, the deck beams can be made up and a few temporarily placed to serve as a guide in fixing the proper clamp position. In practically all round-bottom hulls the sheer clamp is under the deck beams, on the inside face of the frames, sometimes beveled on top for the underside of the beams. In all but small craft this member is scarfed. The length of the scarfs in all the longitudinal members is usually about two frame spaces long and the scarfs are so placed that no two, in keelson, keel, keel batten, bilge stringers, or shelves, are in the same bay between the frames; the stagger is from two to three frame spaces. The scarfs are edgewise, running from top to bottom, and are edge-fastened with long screws, or carriage bolts, in most designs.

In working craft the sheer clamp is sometimes butted and a long lap piece is run on the inside face of the clamps, through-fastened, to act as a butt block. Usually the clamps are tapered fore and aft, which is a great help in bending them into place. Clamps are often troublesome to force into place, due to the edgeset needed. In some designs it may be necessary to spile the sheer clamps in order to avoid excessive edgeset that would cause them to break, or make it impossible to force them to the proper position. In edgesetting the clamps, ripping the ends will often help to obtain the required sheer and twist. The forward ends of the clamps usually butt on the after face of the stem, or its apron, and are held to it by a knee, the breasthook, placed on top of the clamps and fastened to both the stem and clamps. The after ends of the clamps usually butt against the transom frame and are secured to it with quarter-knees, placed either on top, or against the inside face, of the clamps.

If the specifications call for the clamps to be bolted to every frame, and to the end knees, it may be desirable to place the sheer clamp before finally fastening the sheer strakes, if the bent frames are inside the ribbands as usual in hulls built right side up. It may also be desirable to steam or boil the ends of the clamps before forcing them into place. The clamps are usually secured to the frames with screws or nails in small craft, lags or bolts in large. Rivets are perhaps the best fastenings in small- and medium-sized hulls; these can be driven from the outside, through sheer strake, frames, and clamps, the heads bunged. One fastening to every frame is usually required, unless the clamps are very wide. It will be found necessary to have help in putting the longitudinal members into place. Have plenty of clamps, shores, cross-spalls, and wedges on hand before starting the job.

## Shelves

The shelves, if required, are the next to go into place. These are secured to the inside faces of the clamps, with their tops flush with the top edges of the clamps, as a rule. Usually rectangular in section, beveled on their outboard faces, and tapered toward the ends, the shelves are generally easily forced into place, edgewise, particularly if scarfed. Sometimes it is necessary to build up the shelves of laminated strips. The outboard faces must be beveled where the flare or tumble-home is great. The shelves are usually fastened to the clamps between the frames, if bolted. If screwed or nailed, the fastenings may be staggered from the clamp fastenings, in the frames, to avoid splitting the latter. The ends of the shelves may stop short of the ends of the hull, or may run under the breasthook and quarter-knees, and be fastened to them. When the latter is the case, the breasthook and the quarter-knees are not put in until the shelves are in place. The sequence of placing the upper longitudinal members should be studied before planking, so that fastening is not a troublesome problem. In fitting the shelves, care must be taken that the deck beams will bear on them when in place. The best mode of accomplishing this is to use a few deck beams, set temporarily in place, to check the bevels of the shelves. If the shelves are of very heavy timbers, in the plans, the shelves must be templated and sawn to shape, scarfing short lengths together. The purpose of the shelves is to stiffen the sides of the boat and to give additional strength to the deck. Very often the deck beams can be bolted to the shelves instead of to the clamps; this is the case when the shelves are bolted to the clamps in turn.

## Bilge Stringers, Pointers, Offside Shafts

The bilge stringers should be placed with care in a cabin boat. From the plans the approximate position can be measured off;

then a light batten, sprung inside the boat in the position thus found, will serve to mark the frames and to check for edgeset and normal bend. It is necessary to consult the plans to see if the position thus marked will interfere with the joinerwork on either side of the cabin. When both sides are marked, the stringers can be put in place; they are exceedingly troublesome to handle as there is usually nothing to clamp them to. Cleats nailed to the frames, shores, and braces, and temporary fastenings have to do. The ends of the bilge stringers sometimes stop short of the stem and stern; in other cases they run to the after side of the stem and to the transom frame, where they are secured with blocks or knees, acting as breasthooks and quarter-knees. The stringers are usually spiked, nailed, or screwed to the frames, from the inside. In large sawn-frame hulls the bilge stringers are usually made up of two or more thick strakes. These have some through-fastenings, driven from outside the hull planking and bunged there; most of the fastenings are spikes or drifts, driven from the inside of the hull.

In most sawn-frame sailing and power hulls, pointers are used also. These are laminated plank, placed inside the frames, running from the forefoot to the sheer clamps at an angle of about 45 degrees to the keel, raking aft. These serve to tie the cants securely together at the inside of the frames. First, fillers are placed so that bearing will be given the through-course over the bilge strakes or stringers. Then the through-course of the pointer is sprung into place on each side, fastened with drifts or spikes to every frame, through the filler pieces and stringers. The upper ends are through-fastened to the sheer clamp, with the pointer's upper ends snug against the underside of the shelves. The heel is secured with a breasthook, or pointer knee, to the deadwood at the heel of the stempost. In building a craft having this member, it is usual to work on both the longitudinal members and planking at the same time, with two gangs, so that fastenings are rarely a problem. When pointers are used, the ceiling, or inside the frame planking, is cut at the pointers; the latter should not be put on over the ceiling.

In many auxiliaries, the shaft is not in the deadwood but is placed to one side, or "offside." When this is required, the position of the shaft line must be taken from the drawings and transferred to the hull so as to find where the shaft log must be placed, both as to fore-and-aft and athwartship location. The foundation for the

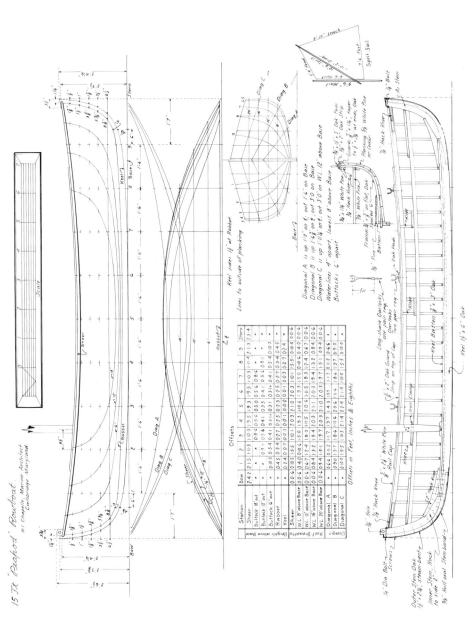

PLATE 56. Plans for a 15-Foot Peapod Rowboat

shaft log fitting must then be secured in place. This is usually a piece of hardwood plank. Its length is usually about twice the length of the shaft log fitting, or a little more, as required by the shaft angle. Its width is about one and one half the total width of the shaft log fitting. Its thickness is enough to permit notching over frames. If the shaft will pass through a frame when in place, the frame is cut out for the width of the foundation piece. The latter is snug against the inside of the hull planking when fixed in place; it should be set in wet paint or white lead, liberally applied. Fasten the foundation piece with nails or screws driven through the planking from the outside, taking care to stay clear of the shaft hole that must be bored later. Fasten to the frames from the inside with nails, screws, or lags. Through-bolts are only required in large hulls. Line up the shaft and bore the shaft hole through planking and foundation piece. It is best to line the hole with a lead sleeve, made of lead tubing, reaching from outside the planking to inside the foundation piece, flanged as required at each end. The stuffing box is part of the shaft log fitting; the adjustable type is recommended and may be fastened with lags or hanger bolts to the foundation. If the inside stuffing box is used, the foundation piece must be shaped on top, thicker at the forward end, to serve as the log and to support the stuffing box. The lead tubing must be fitted in this type also. The shaft log fitting is strongest.

## Ceiling

If the boat is small and a ceiling is required, this can be put in now, or later. In a large sawn-frame hull it usually is placed before the deck beams are all in. Ceiling, in a small bent-frame hull, serves to make a neater cabin; it is made of thin tongue-and-groove pine, cedar, or mahogany in some designs, in others of strips with an open space in lieu of a tight seam. In either, the first piece is put on just below the sheer clamp, allowing a narrow opening between the top of the first ceiling piece and the bottom of the sheer clamp; this is the "air-strake." It is usually possible to edgeset the first piece of ceiling enough to force it into position, but if the stock is too wide its top should be spiled. The other strakes are then placed, no taper or shaping being given them until they run into the bilge stringers. Here they are fitted snug to the top of the stringers, allowing shim ends to form where necessary. Below the stringers, the ceiling is carried to the top of the cabin floor, or in very small craft it may stop above the bilge stringers at the top of the bunks, or seats, along the sides. The ceiling is nailed to the frames with finish nails, or is screwed in rare cases. If strip-ceiled, a small wooden block is used as a gauge to space the strips. In sawn-frame hulls the ceiling is often used to strengthen the hull. Here the ceiling is made up of planks as thick as, or thicker than, the outside skin. In a very fine job the ceiling may be lined off and spiled like the outside planking, but usually only those planks in which shape is absolutely necessary are spiled.

*111. Ceiling Clamp*

The ceiling is clamped in position with a special ceiling clamp; this is like an ordinary steel C-clamp except that the lower portion of the C is not formed—in fact, the shape is like half a T (Γ), or an L upside down. The lower stem is coarsely threaded and is tapered. A hole is drilled into the frame on which the clamp will be used, then the stem is screwed into the hole. When deep enough to hold, the clamp is set up like the ordinary C-clamp, with a screw in the top arm of the clamp. As pressure grows on the clamp the stem binds in its hole in the frame. When the clamp is removed, the hole in the frame is plugged. The ceiling is spiked to the frames with occasional through-fastenings in the thick strakes, as before mentioned. After the ceiling is in place, in a large vessel, it is calked; large seams are wedged with white cedar strips, or wedges. This serves to prevent the ceiling from working and so stiffens the vessel longitudinally. As the ceiling is put on, the inside of the planking, the frames, and the outboard faces of the ceiling planks are treated with some wood preservative, but should never be painted. When the ceiling is in place, in a large vessel, "strong-backs" are run athwartships over the after frames, say, on every other after cant on top of the ceiling, and through-drifted to the frames. These serve as floor timbers in, or near, the counter.

Large double-ended hulls may have pointers aft, instead of strong-backs.

## Engine Stringers, Beds

Engine stringers or beds should now be placed. In order to set the beds at the correct angle, a wire or chalk line is run through the shaft hole to represent the center line of the shaft. Care should be taken to line this up in the center of the shafthole and to make it straight. From the engine catalogues, or installation plans, the position of the top of the beds in relation to the shaft line can be found, and the spacing athwartships of the beds also. Careful measuring, and leveling with a carpenter's level, will ensure sufficient accuracy. It is best to set the top of the beds a little lower, say, $1/16$ or $1/8$ inch, than called for in the installation dimensions; this will permit the use of thin metal shims in aligning the engine. The beds may rest on top of the floor timbers, in which case they should be notched over each floor, or may be secured to the sides of fore-and-aft stringers, which are notched at the floors instead. The beds, or stringers, are bolted (or drifted) to the floor timbers, after making certain the beds are parallel and lined up correctly. In small sailing hulls having auxiliary engines, the beds often run out aft against the planking and careful fitting is necessary there. All engine beds should be of hardwood, or can be capped with structural-steel angle bars.

## Sister-Keelsons

Sister-keelsons are rarely used in round-bottom hulls; in large craft they are often placed alongside the center keelson and through-drifted to it and to the frames. In small, wide, flat-floored craft they are sprung into place like bilge stringers, usually stopping short of the ends of the hull. They either pass over the floor timbers or along the frames just outside the ends of the floors and are fastened to the frames like stringers. If heavy timber is required, they should be sawn to shape and bevel.

## Breasthooks, Quarter-Knees

Breasthooks and quarter-knees are usually of hackmatack or oak; they should be fitted with care. Rivets, drifts, through-bolts, and screws are used for fastenings, according to the size of the knees. They can be fitted by making a thin wooden template to fit the place in which they are to stand; it is rarely worth while to loft them. Their bearing faces should be treated with a wood preservative, or should be well luted.

## Mast Steps

If there are mast steps, these can be placed now. Usually these are blocks of oak, or other hardwood, in which a tenon is cut to take the mast step. In sailing craft it is a good plan to make the tenon longer than needed so that the rake of the mast can be adjusted without disturbing the mast wedges at the partners. A small hole, or series of holes, should be drilled so as to drain the tenon or slot. When the slot is used, blocks are set in it on either side of the mast heel, fore and aft, to lock it in position; the blocks should be a drive fit and may be held with a wire nail in addition. To vary the rake, the blocks can be altered. The step is usually placed on top of the floor timbers, and runs fore and aft. It is drifted, bolted, spiked, or nailed to the floors. In very small craft, such as dinghies, it is screwed to the frame tops or to the top of the keel or keel batten. In heavily sparred or canvased vessels the steps should have two through-bolts or rivets, athwartships, to prevent splitting. In some craft, particularly ketches, there is often reason for stepping a mast on a "bridge," or thwart. This must be done with the mizzen of small ketches, very often, to clear the engine reverse gear, or the propeller shaft. The bridge, or thwart, should be placed according to the plans, making certain that it is at the correct height above the shaft line. The ends should run to the sides of the hull, at the inside of the frames. To support the bridge, or thwart, a fore-and-aft member is fastened to the insides of the frames, on both sides of the boat; this is the bearer, or carlin. Its length should be at least two frame spaces. The carlins should be of sufficiently heavy material to prevent bending under strain and should be well fastened to the frames, using bolts, rivets, nails, or screws, as size permits. These will have to be driven from outside the planking, in large craft; nails, screws, and spikes can be driven from the inside. The thwart rests on these carlins and is bolted to them. The mast steps in a tenon, or hole, in this thwart; a slot can be used to advantage here, too. Do not fasten the thwart permanently until the engine and propeller shaft are installed, as it would be in the way.

## Tank Beds, Etc.

If there are tank foundations or beds, or large tanks, to be installed, it is well to get these out of the way before placing the deck beams. Many builders put the engine on its bed at this point, but do not line it up or fasten it in place. If this is done, the engine

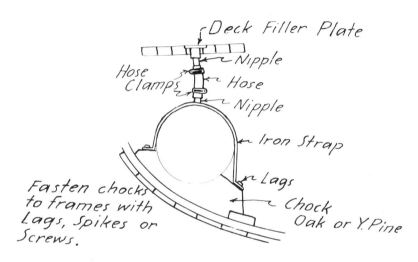

*112. Tank Chocks and Filler Assembly*

should be covered with a tarpaulin, or boxed over, to protect it from damage and dirt. Also it is a good time to look over the plumbing, exhaust piping, wiring, and cabin or toilet fittings, to see what can be installed now while there is plenty of room to work.

## Deck Beams and Framing

When ready to lay the deck beams, the loft plan can be used to make them up to lengths required. The fitting of these has been described in previous chapters. Now it is only necessary to discuss the less common methods of fitting beams and the problems that arise occasionally. In sailing craft the deck is an important part of the structure, as far as strength is concerned. It is important, then, that the fitting be accurate and that the whole of the deck framing be well secured. At least a few beams, running clear across the hull, are desirable in any but the small open craft, and even these require thwarts for the same reason—strength. In making any changes from the designer's plans, as far as deck arrangement is concerned, do not cut any deck beams. The beams that run from side to side are to be carefully located according to the plans, as they often are placed by the designer to support deck structures or joinerwork. Care must be taken to get the beams square to the center line of the hull; the easiest way to do this is with a steel tape, one end made fast to a nail in the top of the stem at the hull center line. If the beam is square, its ends must be equidistant from the nail on the stemhead. The fastenings of the beam ends are important; as has already been pointed out, the fastenings should be in the clamp or shelf, not in the frames. The carlins should be fitted as described on page 257 and tie rods fitted, if required (see pages 257 and 311 to 315).

There are other ways of fitting carlins than have been described. One way is to place the carlins under the deck beams; this can be done only when headroom below deck is not important, as along the cockpit, for example. Another method sometimes used is to butt the beams against the carlins, and then to secure them; a wide

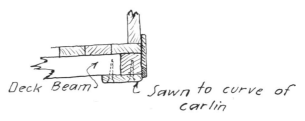

*113. Carlin and Plank*

plank is fastened on the underside of the carlins, overlapping the underside of the beams enough for their fastenings. This gives a stiff carlin, which is desirable, and easy construction, but adds weight and is liable to rot if there are deck leaks. Along the sheer, in place of the usual clamp and shelf, the builders of Friendship Sloops fastened a shelf only; this was made up of short lengths of wide planking scarfed together and sawn to shape, both in plan and elevation. The heads of the frames were notched into this and nailed, or spiked, to it. The deck beams halved into the inside edge of this shelf and the ends were also nailed and spiked. The scarfs formed in this type of shelf were edgewise, and edge-fastened. It is probable that the surprisingly long life of this type of hull can be traced to this deck construction, as well as to good selection of timber. Certainly the framing was usually so poor that there was little strength there.

It has been said that in most boats the deck beams are cut from a single pattern. This is true, with two exceptions. One, of course, is when the center line of the deck is arbitrarily established to give a certain profile, as in small powerboats, runabouts, or sailing racers. Here each beam must be lifted from the loft plan and a crown pattern laid off. It may even be necessary to fair up such a deck with buttocks, in the loft. Another exception will be found when laying the deck of a full-bowed hull, with beams cut to one template. When the beams are in place and a batten laid along the center line on top of them it will be found that a dip will appear a little abaft the stem; this can be cured only by shimming the beam, or cutting a new one, or two, with a little more crown. In wide hulls, over 40 feet in length, it is a good plan to add a little to the specified deck crown, when lofting, as the deck of a wide hull has a tendency to flatten out a little unless well supported. In sailing craft requiring deck strapping, the size and position of the straps will be given in the plans and they must be placed in the hull as shown. They are let into the deck beams so that they lie flush with the top of the beam. Straps that cross will have to be cut a little deeper into the beams near the point of crossing. The straps are fastened to every beam and to each other where they cross; the ends are likewise fastened, either to a plate fastened to the deck beams, or beams. In small craft, and powerboats having wide cockpits, there are often no beams along the cockpit sides: blocks resting on the shelves, or clamps, answer the purpose. These blocks are usually nailed to the tops of the clamps, then the carlins nailed to them. The grain in the blocks should run fore and aft. Tie rods have already been thoroughly discussed in Chapter Five, page 311. Blocking and decking have likewise had attention in that chapter.

## *Bulwarks*

Before laying the deck it may be necessary to set up stanchions for the bulwarks in some hulls. These are required only in large hulls, where log rails are inadequate. In hulls having bent frames, the stanchions are very rarely the heads of the frames, carried to the proper height, but, more commonly, are pieces inserted between the planking and the clamps, between the frames. The latter is preferable in all boats. If a stanchion needs repair it may be removed without having to disturb the planking or decking, whereas if it is a frame head the damaged part must be cut off below deck and spliced, or cleated, which usually requires some planking to be removed. There is only one difficulty in stepping the stanchions: to get them to stand fair and to carry out the shape of the topsides. This can only be done by first lofting the stanchions. It is sufficient to use merely a line to represent each one in the loft plan—as they will cant and so need little or no bevel—to get the sectional curves in their outer faces. This can be done by first spacing them off on the half-breadth plan, roughly indicating the cant of them there, from deck to rail cap. The half-breadth of each can be transferred to the rail and deck in the loft body plan, where it is then possible to sketch the sectional view of the stanchions. It is unnecessary to fair them up; the body plan sections will be so close together that the stanchion lines can be drawn by eye, using the sections as a guide. Low bulwarks rarely require so much trouble, however, and can be set and shaped largely by eye.

It is a good plan to loft the rail cap, for a pattern at least, by which the stanchion heads can be faired to the lines shown in the design. If the hull has much curvature in the topsides, the curved faces of the stanchions must be carried below deck to a depth equal to half the height of the bulwark above deck. When the stanchions are larger, in section, than the frames, the insides of the stanchions are notched at the top of the clamps, and are reduced in thickness from there down. This enables the stanchions to be easily set for height. The stanchions should be set in place and tacked temporarily to hold them in the correct position. The rail-cap templates can be partly assembled and used to correct the heads of the stanchions to obtain the correct flare. Expanding the rail cap in the loft is not difficult: first a batten is fitted to the profile sheer line and the stations and ends of the rail cap are ticked off. Removing the batten to a convenient straight line will enable the expanded distances between stations, and stations and ends of the sheer line, to be laid off. Squaring station lines out from the straight line, at the expanded spacings, and then setting off the corresponding half-breadths of the sheer at these stations will give a line that is the correct, or expanded, outline of the sheer line—

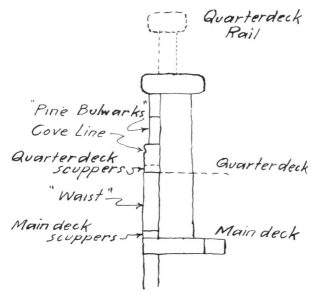

*114. Schooner Bulwarks*

that is, the outside (or inside if the lines are so drawn) of the sheer strake at the underside of the rail cap.

The plank-sheer is now fitted. This is not an easy job for a beginner, and it is best to use a thin template for the job. The plank-sheer will be sawn to the plan of the sheer and sprung to the elevation. The outside of the template can be spiled from the outer corner of the top of the sheer strake, after the latter is beveled to the crown of the deck, using the beams as a guide. When the outside edge is spiled and cut the template can be placed against the inside of the stanchions and the notches required for each stanchion marked, for width and depth. As the edge of the template, when the notches are cut, will have to go to the outside edge of the sheer strake, the notches are cut the depth of the stanchions, inboard to out, plus the thickness of the planking on its beveled top edge. After the notches have been marked and cut, and the template fitted, the ends are marked for scarf, or butt, as desired; then the inside edge of the plank-sheer is laid off and the template cut. Now a pattern for one piece of the plank-sheer is ready. This is laid on the timber to be used and the marking done. First the outline is cut without regard to the notches. When this is finished, instead of cutting the notches the markings are used to cut a series of square holes, one for each stanchion. If the templating was done accurately, allowing for the spring of the sheer by springing the template while marking, the finished piece of plank-sheer should be so accurate that it might be tapped down over the standing stanchions along the mid-length of the hull, if desired. It is easier, however, to remove the stanchions in way of the piece, fit and secure the piece, and then to replace the stanchions.

When all the plank-sheer is in place, and all stanchions replaced, then the latter may be permanently fastened, after being checked with the rail-cap template. Two fastenings are sufficient for each stanchion, one fastening near the sheer and one at the heel of the stanchions. This method of fitting gives a tighter plank-sheer. If the timberheads are the stanchions, however, the plank-sheer will have to be notched the depth of the stanchions plus the thickness of the beveled top of the sheer strake; then the space between the outboard faces of the stanchions and the outside face of the sheer strake will have to be filled with blocks. Another method is to fit the plank-sheer to the inside of the sheer strake and then put in a strip along the top of the sheer strake, the thickness of the deck, along the outside faces of the stanchions. Neither of these two alternatives is really desirable, but will be necessary if the frames form the stanchions. This is because the natural canting of bent frames makes it impossible to drop the plank-sheer over the timberheads in most jobs. After the stanchions are faired and secured, the seams at the plank-sheer should be wedged with white cedar wedges, each in width equal to the full length of the seam (on face or sides of a stanchion). The wedges should be driven in luting or wet paint, no calking used.

After the stanchions are wedged, the rail cap is secured (it should be fitted before the plank-sheer) and the bulwarks planked up. If the bulwarks are open all along the deck to form the scuppers, calking can be used around the stanchions if desired, though this is not the best practice even here. All stanchion fastenings, where the stanchions are not part of the frame timber, should be driven through the planking from the outside (heads bunged or puttied) or from the inside, through sheer clamp and ceiling. Inside fastenings can be screws, to advantage. Repairs or replacements of stanchions are then made very easy.

## Bulwarks, Sawn-Frame Construction

In sawn-frame construction, double or single, the stanchions are usually a part of the frame, forming the uppermost futtock. The advantage of this, in a hull having high bulwarks, is that the fairing of the stanchions is easier and more accurate, since the whole frame, from floor to stanchion top, can be picked up from the loft plan and checked when assembled. The disadvantages are that the beveling of the inside of the stanchions makes extra work, and damage in service will be hard to repair. If the stanchions are part

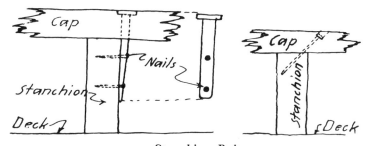

*115. Stanchion Bolts*

of the frame, they should be carried no lower than necessary to place one fastening opposite the air strake. This fastening should be a carriage bolt that can be reached through the air strake if the joinerwork permits. Additional fastenings in the stanchions serve no useful purpose and only make repairs more difficult. The heads of all stanchions should be treated with preservative or luting; the best construction is to tenon the heads into the underside of the rail caps. The fastenings of the cap to the stanchions should never be driven vertically into the stanchionheads; the holding power of such fastenings is slight, due to the fastenings standing in the end grain of the stanchions. By driving the fastenings at an angle to the stanchion, say, about 60 degrees to the top of the rail, a stronger hold is obtained. Each stanchion requires one cap fastening; this should be driven alternately from the right and left, along the line of stanchionheads. The fastenings should have their heads luted and bunged; leakage along the bolts or fastenings will cause rot in the stanchionheads. "Side bolts" are sometimes used for this reason; these are round spikes, or bolts, having a flattened shank near the driving point; in this are two or three holes, large enough for boat nails. The side bolt is driven vertically in the cap, located so that the flattened shank will run down one side of the stanchion, against its side face. When the bolt is driven, it is secured to the stanchion by nails driven through the holes in the shank of the bolt, into the side of the stanchion. The rail cap should be scarfed and edge-fastened, the scarfs placed between pairs of stanchions in every case.

## Scuppers

Scuppers cut in the bulwarks should be completed before placing the lowest plank of the bulwarks permanently in place. The most common type of scupper is a slot, cut on each side of the stanchions, in the bottom of the lowest plank of the bulwarks. The slots are from 3 to 5 inches long, and from $\frac{1}{2}$ to 1 inch wide; they are usually cut for about one half the deck length of the hull, equally on each side of the point of lowest freeboard. If there are no stanchions, the scuppers need not be so numerous: a 35-foot hull needs only six to eight on a side. Too many scuppers spoil the appearance of the topsides. The most common shape of the slot scupper is a flattened U, upside down; a cupid's bow shape is sometimes seen, however. Pipe scuppers are common in the larger yachts; these are of lead pipe, running from the deck, just inside the plank-sheer or waterway, to the side of the hull just above the load water line and below the copper paint line. The scupper pipe usually passes down between the skin and ceiling, though in a yacht it is usually better to locate the pipe just inside the ceiling, if the molding of the frames is small. The lower opening of the scupper pipes, in the side of the hull, should be covered with oiled leather flaps, nailed or tacked to the forward side of the opening; these act as automatic valves and prevent the scuppers from spouting on deck when the vessel is moving in a seaway. The inside

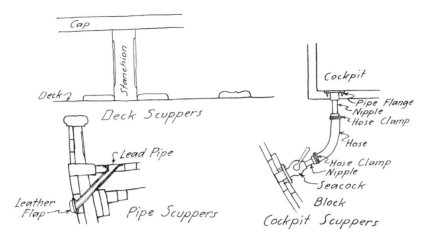

*116. Scuppers*

diameter of the scupper pipes should not be less than 1 inch; only three or four to a side are usually required. Pipe scuppers are more expensive than slot scuppers, but have the advantage of not staining the topsides.

## Ports

If there are ports to be cut in the sides of the hull, these can be marked and cut, in the same manner as trunk ports. In way of all ports, the planking should be blocked on the inside, the blocks fitted like butt blocks, and large enough to take all port-rim fastenings. As in trunk ports, the outside rings or frames are best omitted. If the ports are too large, too near together, or too numerous, they will spoil the appearance of a boat. Usually they must be as high as possible, just low enough to clear the underside of the sheer clamps; note the way they are to swing open. If the hull is ceiled, the space between planking and ceiling must be fully blocked in the way of each port; the inside rim is fastened through the ceiling into the blocking. The blocking must drain and wood preservative should be used on and around it, between planking and ceiling. In ceiled hulls the inside rings of the ports are sometimes boxed through the ceiling so that the frame is on the inside of the planking.

## *Hawseholes*

Hawseholes and pipes can be located and cut before laying the deck, though this is by no means necessary when hawseholes are above the deck far enough, so that the deck is not cut for the hawsehole castings. When pipes are desired, however, they should be put in place before the deck is laid, as only then can sufficient room be had to do the job properly. In order to discourage the unnecessary use of hawsepipes, it should be said now that there is no excuse for them in hulls having less than 12 feet freeboard at the bows. Obviously, this limits their use to large craft. One reason this is true is that the anchor most commonly used is the "stockless" Navy Anchor, which is not brought to deck but is stowed by drawing its shank into the hawsepipes. With heavy anchors, this is a definite advantage; unfortunately, however, the stockless anchor is very inefficient for its size and weight. This is particularly marked in small anchors of this type. Therefore wise seamen avoid its use in all but the largest of hulls, such as steamers. In a sailing yacht it is a useless and lubberly affectation. If the anchor is to be stowed on deck, the hawsepipe serves no purpose, unless the freeboard is so great that the line from windlass to anchor, when the vessel is at anchor, is broken at the hawse to an excessive degree, and then only when the hull is so large that it is possible that the strain at the hawse is so great that the anchor cable may "cut down the bows." This has happened in some large wooden five- and six-masted commercial schooners, but it is doubtful if the average boatowner need worry about this possibility in his vessel. Hawsepipes, then, may be omitted. Only the professional builder needs to know how to fit them. They must be set at such an angle to the load water line that the anchor will come home in the pipes; the best way to assure this is to cut the lower and outer holes first, then fit a rough, square, wooden pipe to represent the hawsepipe. This can be tested by hoisting the anchor, or a wooden model, into the pipe, to verify the angle. The angle the hawsepipe takes to the water line will be found to be over 45 degrees.

Hawseholes, however, are practical in almost any boat having bulwarks or knightheads, or both. They can be cut, in small boats, with any auger bit, assisted by a chisel. First, their position should be found. The height, in relation to the deck, can usually be taken from the plans. The position in reference to the hull center line can be fixed by attaching one end of a chalk line in the position the anchor cable will be in when belayed at the windlass, or bitts, or at the chain wildcat of the windlass, and stretching it forward so that it stands at a slight angle outward to the center line of the hull, say, 2 or 3 degrees. Mark the position of the string on the rail and plumb it down to the required height outside. With a small auger or drill, drill a leading hole for the hawse on each side, taking care that it is in the same position, relative to height and center line, on each side; also, that it comes through inside in the same relative position. Usually the hawseholes stand at a slight angle to the water line in a fore-and-aft direction, the in-board end higher than the outer.

Now, if the hawsehole is small enough, it may be bored; other-wise, it will have to be cut out with a chisel and gouge. In the latter case its outside outline must be established. The best way to do this is to take a light steel rod, the same diameter as the

117. Hawse Scriber

leading hole already drilled, to a blacksmith and have him bend one end in a hook that measures, from the center of the rod to the center of the hook end, the radius of the hole required. When the hook end is sharpened to a point, the tool is ready for use. The long shank is inserted in the leading hole, the inboard end may be supported to form a jog if necessary, and then the outline of the hole can be scribed on the outside of the planking by revolving the hook, allowing the shank to slide in and out in the leading hole so that the point bears on the planking constantly. By reversing the shank in the leading hole the inside can be scribed. Cut the holes from both sides, meeting in the middle of the bulwarks or knightheads, to be certain of a neat job. If a casting is to be fitted to the hole, make a rod of wood, the diameter of the hole, insert it and cut off on inside and out, so that the cuts are flush with the inside and outside of the bulwarks, or knightheads. Make a right and left. If these plugs are sent to an experienced foundry, a molder can shape the castings from patterns on hand; or the foundryman can have patterns made. If this is not practical, the plugs can be sent to one of the established marine hardware dealers, who will have the castings made. If chain is used, the castings are of galvanized iron; otherwise bronze castings are used.

In a cheap boat where a manila anchor rode will be used, and chain never employed, the builder can line the hawseholes with heavy lead tubing, flanged and tacked (with copper tacks) on the inside and out. Of course, nicely cast bronze flanges and hawse are handsomer. Another scheme is to cut the hawse out of iron or brass pipe, the flanges out of iron or brass plate, then weld or braze the outer flange to the cut pipe. The sharp corners must be carefully built up, and then rounded by filing. The inner flange is screwed or nailed to the bulwarks or knightheads; the outer flange is fastened in the same manner to the outside planking. In large craft the outside flange should be through-bolted to the knightheads; therefore the holes for fastenings in the inner flange must not be opposite those in the outer. A holding fastening is often driven through the bottom of the casting from inside the bulwarks, in the pipe portion, down into the knightheads, when the strain on the pipe is to be great. It is one of the curses of professional boatbuilders that they rarely succeed in placing the edge-fastenings of the knightheads and hawse timbers, or the log-rail fastenings, so that they are not met when cutting the hawseholes. If the amateur has the same misfortune he must resort to cold chisel, hack saw, and profanity, like the professional.

## Decking

The laying of the deck has been discussed in previous chapters and so requires no attention now. Therefore the space available may be given to a few random comments on deck framing details and deck joinerwork that have not received attention.

### Remarks, Laminated Construction

Partner-beam construction in sailing craft is an important part of the structural strength of a hull. In boats in which the mast or masts pass through the cabin roof, great care is needed in fitting partners to ensure the necessary strength and watertightness. This is really a matter for the designer to decide upon, as far as he is able: the builder is responsible for carrying out the plans accurately and making good joints. Laminated deck- or cabin-roof beams may be required; in small craft, when the mast passes through the trunk roof, the partners there may be formed of one or two wide plank, laid athwartships and sprung to the crown, underneath the roofing. The outer ends of these are let into the top edges of the trunk and fastened there. Knees may be omitted if the rig is not heavy. Steam-bent knees can be used in the trunk,

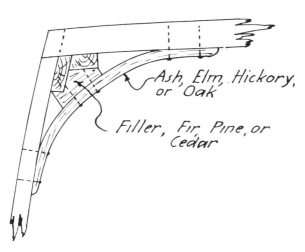

*118. Bent Knee*

if desired; these are made by bending square stock over a mold and fitting cold. They are very strong and light. It is desirable that a throat block be fitted in the throat of the knee so formed; this serves as a strut and should be through-fastened as in the throat-fastening in the solid knee. Laminated bent knees may be made if it is impossible to bend the size of stock required in one piece. All laminated structures are best made up out of the hull, by bending each layer and assembling cold. Between each lamination use marine or waterproof glue, then fasten with a few through-fastenings, such as copper rivets. Finally smooth up, fit, and then carefully paint before securing in place. The life of laminated beams, knees, partners, or other members of a structure, is governed by the protection given them against the accumulation of moisture in and between the laminations.

## Gluing

The use of marine and waterproof glues has increased in recent years among boatbuilders and designers. It is to be feared that the enthusiasm for this material has led to faulty ideas and conclusions. In the first place, a properly glued joint is extremely strong. Another advantage is in the light weight of such joints. A joint that is properly glued will last a very long time under the proper conditions. Against these advantages stand some very serious disadvantages: a glued joint requires skill and knowledge to make properly; all timber is not suitable for gluing; all so-called waterproof glues are not strictly waterproof under any or all conditions of usage; and the life of glued joints in a boat is in proportion to the amount of protection it receives during its life. The builder who uses any of the standard marine or waterproof glues may be certain of the excellence of the material; the glues used hot are probably more waterproof unprotected than those used cold. Failure of a glued joint, using these materials, is due to improper use, workmanship, timber, or design. Wood surfaces that are to be glued must be true and very smooth. There must be a continuous film of glue between the surfaces, no dirt or air bubbles. The consistency of the glue must have some relation to the pressure used in clamping the pieces together while the glue is drying and setting; use light pressure when the glue is thin, heavy when the glue is thick. There is no rule by which the pressure required can be arbitrarily stated; experience with given materials is the only guide. Glues applied cold should be under pressure longer than those applied hot.

In practice, straight plain joints are generally to be preferred to dovetailed or machined joints. End-butt joints are no good whatever. Scarfs should be used instead; the slope of the scarfs should be 1 in 10, in mahogany, 1 in 15 in hardwoods, such as white oak. End-to-side-grain joints are usually unsatisfactory unless dowels or tenons are used. The finishing of a glued joint should not be attempted before the glue has dried. Most glues will dull cutting tools when dry, so sharpen often. The life of glued joints

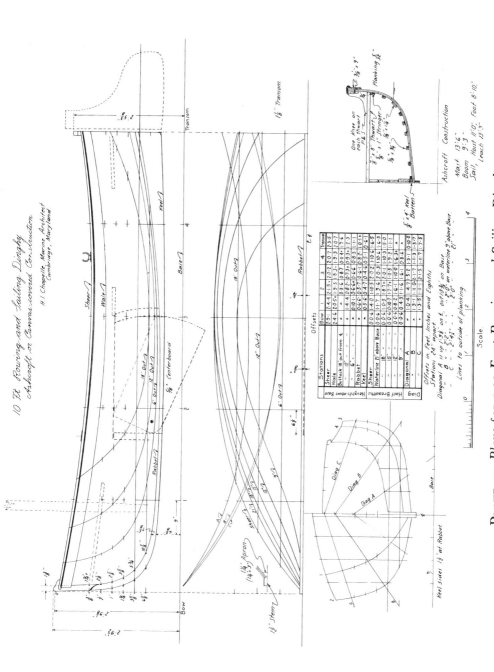

PLATE 57. Plans for a 10-Foot Rowing and Sailing Dingby

is improved by impregnation of the wood with waterproofing materials; the glue manufacturer should be consulted as to the proper treatment. The ideal gluing condition is reached when the moisture content of the wood is that which it is subject to in service after being glued; the difficulty of obtaining this in marine work is obvious. For these reasons, marine lamination, using glue, is commonly given the additional support of a few metal fastenings, when the structure is to be so placed that it cannot receive periodical inspection and protection (painting or varnishing) in all parts.

## Deckhouses

In large craft having deckhouses, foundations—"sills"—should be laid on deck. These are usually of heavy timbers, bolted through the decking to the beams or carlins; the studding, or framing, of the deckhouse is tenoned into the tops of these sills. The bottom of these timbers, like trunk sides, should be cut to the deck sheer. The corners of the sills are usually halved together with the lap of the halving parallel to the deck. These joints, and the seams along the deck, must be calked. The planking, or sheathing, of the deckhouse should rabbet into the top of the sills; shiplap seams in the sheathing are preferable to all others. If there is no ceiling in the deckhouse, the sheathing must be thick. Edge-fastening of the sheathing should be done, if possible, in preference to heavy studding. If the house is ceiled inside, or paneled, the studding must be placed close enough together to support it. If the deckhouse is lightly sheathed and ceiled, the sheathing seams can be splined or shiplapped. The roofs of all deckhouses are best canvased, particularly if there is to be a stove in the house. Bright deckhouse roofs will invariably be neglected and will eventually leak. A stop should run around the edges of deckhouse roofs to prevent water draining down the sides of the house and leaving stains and marks. Pipe scuppers are fitted inside the sheathing, draining out through the sides of the sills, on deck.

## Cockpits

Cockpits in seagoing boats should be strongly built and, if self-bailing, should have scupper pipes of sufficient size to drain the cockpit quickly. Copper or lead tubing is often used for cockpit scupper pipes in large boats, steam hose being employed in small craft. In laying out the scupper pipes for the cockpit, and elsewhere, care must be taken that there are as few bends as possible, so that the pipes can be cleaned out with a wooden stick (wire will punch holes in lead pipe scuppers); no pockets that will not drain outboard should be permitted. Cockpit scuppers should lead to just above the load water line, inside the copper paint, or to at least a foot below the water line. If the scupper outlet is at the water line, or less than a foot below, the outlet may freeze and fracture when the boat is laid up afloat in the winter time. All pipe outlets in the hull, scupper, or plumbing that are very close to, or below, the water line should be fitted with seacocks or valves. Where these are secured to the inside of the planking, there should be foundation blocks, through which the outlet and seacock fastenings are passed. The block should be secured to the planking. Cockpit scupper pipes are sometimes crossed, so the port scupper empties to starboard, and vice versa; this prevents the leeside flooding.

## Copper, Bronze, and Brass

Copper and bronze should be used for all piping, fastenings, or fittings on which strains will be put. Brass fastenings, piping, and fittings will corrode and become brittle. Bronze should be specifically ordered as "Navy bronze," not just "bronze," if strength is important.

## Deck Joinery

Deck joinerwork requires little discussion: its construction is largely a matter of skill in the use of tools. The few matters that have to deal with watertightness and strength have been discussed in the earlier chapters. The effect of the deck arrangement on handiness of working the boat when she is complete should not be forgotten in the enthusiasm for deck joinery or fittings. Offside openings should be avoided in sailing craft. To some extent, ventilation is affected by the deck arrangement, in cabin craft. If the arrangement makes it necessary to fit ventilators, some provision is required to make them watertight. The most

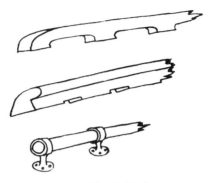

*119. Grab Rails*

common method is to build a box without a bottom, step the cowl ventilator in the top, near one end, with its bottom just clear of the deck; the box is then fitted over a stub ventilator pipe in the deck (which stands a few inches above the deck and is either fore or aft of the bottom of the ventilator). The box has a few scuppers along its edge on deck. The stub pipe is fitted with a screen. This

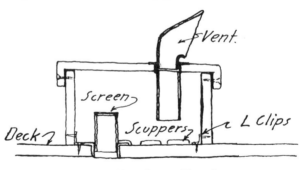

*120. Ventilator Trunk*

type of ventilator takes up some deck space, but is quite simple and practical. There are also numerous watertight ventilators on the market. In thinking about cabin ventilation, it is well to consider the fact that hatches and skylights that can be opened either forward or aft (hinged athwartships) are better than those hinged to open on each side of the center line of the hull. Deck plates, for ventilators or other purposes, are often required. The brass, screw-cover type of plate is useless: the threads are soft and

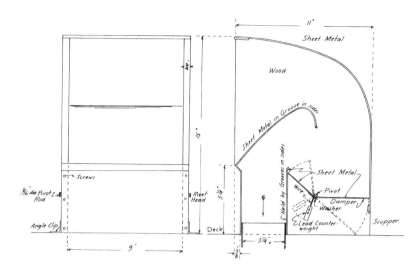

*121. Improved Box Ventilator*

fine, so are easily crossed, or corrode enough to make opening the plate doubtful. Deck plates of other metals, or fitted with bolts, or bolts and bars, are to be preferred. All screens should be of fine copper mesh, with wooden frames to rest in a rabbet, or on strips, on the inside of the hatch coamings.

## Locks

In the matter of hatches, skylights, and companionways, locking can be done from the inside of the boat, using hooks and eyes or sliding bolts. When screens are used there may be some difficulty in locking the covers, so it is usual to have locks on the inside of the screens also. If the boat is left for a short time the locked screens are sufficient, but if the boat is left for a long period the screens can be removed and the covers locked. Hatches that are not used often, as entrance hatches or for ventilation, should be locked from the inside by a bar across the beams, or carlins. The bar can be connected to the cover by hooks and eyes, the hooks being fitted to the bar so that they can be taken up with wing nuts. If the hatch is small, a single eye bolt secured to the center of the hatch cover with a riveted staple, and to the bar

with a wing nut, is sufficient. These connections to the cover
prevent the use of screens, however. Slide hatches should be
locked by padlocks. Mortise and rim locks are not suited for the
purpose unless the hatch is so arranged that locking hinged doors
will lock the hatch cover. The most common way of fixing a lock
to a slide hatch, fitted with lifting doors, is to place a long staple
in the hatch frame that will reach through a slot in the door, when
the hatch is closed, far enough for a padlock to be inserted. A
bronze plate around the slot gives an excellent finish. A hasp

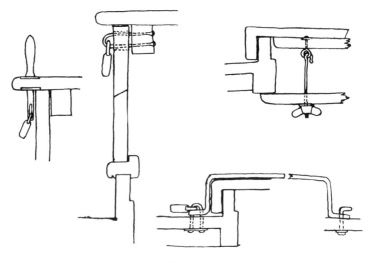

*122. Hatch Locks*

fixed to the side of one of the slides, with a staple plate on the
hatch-cover side, can be used in some cases. Never put a hasp on
the underside of the hatch; it will hang down when the hatch
is open and is then a source of danger to passing heads.

Only bronze padlock cases should be used. Lift-off hatches,
that must be locked from the outside, can be fitted with a metal
bar across the top, padlocked to staples in the tops or sides of the
coaming or on deck. The bar should be fore and aft. If a hasp is
used in such a way that it does not cover its fastenings, these
must be through-bolts set up on the underside of the hatch cover,
or rivets. Sliding bolts that can be locked are sometimes found
in hatches; these are usually on the doors, through-fastened; the

bolt enters a pocket in the underside of the hatch cover. If hinged doors are used, a bolt at the top of one of the doors, inside, will enable the locking of one door to lock both doors and hatch. Inside door locks, or hook and eyes, are also desirable. Mortise locks can be used on doors that are thick enough; otherwise rim locks must be employed, or hasp and padlock. The objection to rim and mortise locks on small craft is that they are usually so situated that their parts are subject to rapid corrosion.

## Hinges

Strap hinges are stronger than butt hinges and are therefore preferable for outside doors and hinged hatches. The straps should be secured with through-fastenings so as to prevent their removal from the outside. In small doors and hinged hatch covers the brass piano hinge can be used to advantage as it is somewhat stronger than the common butt hinge. Offset hinges are often required, so that a door may swing clear of its casing.

## Chain Locks

Locks on small commercial craft can be made of a chain and riveted staple, or a metal belaying pin dropped through a hole in the hatch cover outside the doors and locked by a padlock passed through a hole in the point of the pin. Chain can also be used for cargo hatches.

## Mast Tabernacles

Tabernacles, by which it is possible to lower masts, are strangely missing in American boats. Apparently, if you live above the bridge, you don't have a sailboat, or keep it miles away. By stepping masts in tabernacles, they can be raised and lowered without having to call on a rigger or a boatyard. There are numerous tabernacle designs. The more common ones are made of two heavy planks, stepped on each side of the keel, or keel batten, and through-fastened athwartships. At the partners there is a mast stub inserted between the planks; this either stands on deck or on the deck blocking. It extends up a few inches above the deck, with its top cut at an angle, fore and aft, so that the after edge of the top of the stub is higher than the forward. Two through-fastenings are driven through the planks and stub athwartships. Above the deck, the planks pass on each side of the mast; in way of the planks, the mast is square. The butt is cut to fit the angle of the mast-stub top. The pivot bolt is near the top of the planks; the height of

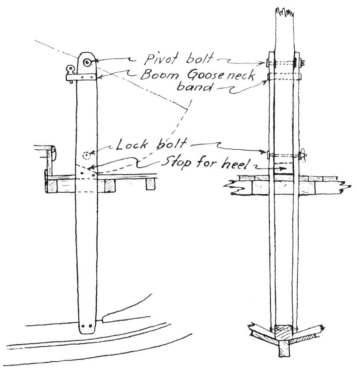

*123. Tabernacle (After Tiller)*

the pivot is fixed so that the mast will lie parallel to the load water line when lowered, and be clear of the cabin trunk hatches or skylights. The pivot bolt is usually bushed in the mast.

To hold the top of the tabernacle firmly together a U-shaped gooseneck band is bolted to the two planks, passing around abaft the mast; the boom is on this gooseneck. At the heel there is either a removable bolt fitted with a wing nut or a pin with a cotter in it. To lower the mast, the heel pin is removed and the running forestay slacked off, allowing the mast to fall aft into a boom crotch or other support. To raise, a spar or boathook is placed under the forestay to make a proper hauling angle, and the mast raised until its heel comes home against the sloping top of the mast stub, when the heel pin may be passed through. The

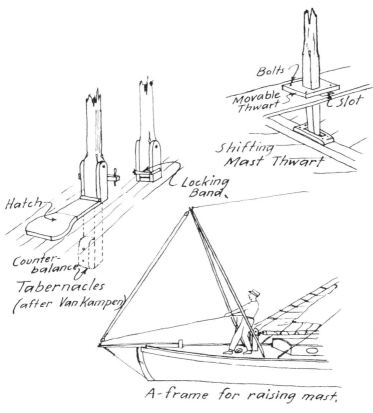

A-frame for raising mast.

*124. Mast Tabernacles*

boom gooseneck should be on the tabernacle U-strap, not on the mast. In other designs there is no mast stub; a heel strap around the after side of the tabernacle just above the deck serves the purpose. Sometimes, in Holland, the heel of the mast reaches below deck and is counterweighted to make hoisting easier. In this case there is a long narrow hatch at the fore side of the tabernacle through which the heel passes when raising or lowering the mast. As there can be no fore partner, ahead of the mast, the after one must take all the strain, so should be heavier than usual. The pin rail is usually a straight piece of wood across the after side of the tabernacle. The boom is always on the tabernacle, not on the mast. To aid in hoisting the mast, the Dutch use an A-frame, either permanently fixed or to unship, the heels of which step at the foremost chain plate on each side, or opposite the center line of the mast, with the head reaching to the forestay just above the block on the bowsprit, or stemhead, through which it reeves. When the mast is lowered, this A-frame lifts up at the forward end with the stay (or its block if a purchase is used on its end instead). This acts as a shears to raise the mast. If the bridge is very low, the A-frame may have to be unshipped.

## Stepping Masts on Deck

Masts stepped on deck have come into favor not only in power-boats, but also in sailing craft. Such a mast is wholly supported by its shrouds and stays; its advantage exists only when a very long, light spar is required, usually hollow, which must be stayed not only to stand but also to remain straight. Such spars are only used in highly developed sailing racers. The other use of the mast stepped on deck is in powerboats, where the mast is nothing more than a flagstaff. Because of the appearance of such masts in noted racers, some yachtsmen seem to think the mast stepped on deck should be used on cruisers, on the grounds that the heel of the mast interferes with a pet arrangement scheme. This is not quite the case, as the mast that is stepped on deck puts a tremendous thrust on the partners, so these must be supported under the deck with one or more stanchions, a bulkhead, or the partners bridged and trussed in such a way that headroom is effected. If the shrouds and stays are not kept properly set up, the mast on deck may go out of line, or even over the side; so it will be seen that such a rig is hardly desirable for the average week-end and vacation sailor, or the shorthanded ocean cruiser. The stepping of such a mast must be carefully designed; it is a job for a naval architect, not for the builder. Not only must the partners be constructed exactly as shown in the plans but, also, the chain plates must be placed exactly as shown.

## Fitting Hardware

The fitting of the hull ironwork, or hardware, is actually done when rigging, yet provision must be made while building, even before planking. Chain plates, for example: these are sometimes placed between the frames and planking, passing through the covering board or plank-sheer. The outside of the frame, or frames, on which the chain plates are fastened must be cut down the thickness of the chain plates, to fair in with the planking. Care must be taken that the frames, on which chain plates are secured, bear on the sheer clamp, inside; if not, shims must be inserted. If the chain plates are outside they are let into the planking about half their depth in a well-finished hull, the outside of the chain plate having beveled corners this deep. All staples, or chain plates, for backstays, bowsprit shrouds, or topmast stays must be through-fastened to frames, or to the sheer clamp through a block inserted between clamp and planking. Eye bolts for foot-ropes of the bowsprit must pass through frames. On any but very small boats, all these supplementary chain plates or staples should be through-fastened with bolts or rivets, not fastened with screws or lags.

## Calking and Smoothing

Smoothing up and calking the round-bottom hull is little different from the methods used in other types. Planing the hull is the first step, which can be done roughly when all the planking is completed. First go over the hull to make sure all fastenings are in place, set, or bunged. Plane down the seams, then all the planking. This can best be done, as a rule, with a short wooden or wood-soled plane. The wooden plane is less likely to leave marks or bruises than the iron plane and cuts easier. A good scraper is the best tool for smoothing a hull planked with hardwood. Professionals hold the blade in their hands but the amateur will require a handle; an adjustable handle is handy. If the hull is planked with white pine, cedar, or mahogany, however, the amateur should not attempt to use a scraper on it; scraping softwood requires great care and practice. When smoothing a hull, run the hand up and down over the planking; curiously enough, you can feel unfairness that you can't see. Take long cuts with the plane wherever possible. When the hull is smoothed it may be sanded, or this may be allowed to wait until the calking is done.

Cotton calking is used in planking up 1½ inches in thickness; oakum, in thicker planking. If the planking is under ⅝ inch in thickness, calk with the wheel. In calking, first clean out the seam. Start the calking material into the seam, holding a making iron between the thumb and second finger of the left hand; the first finger holds the cotton or oakum in position. The iron lies across the palm, steadied by the remaining fingers. This gives the best control of the iron and calking, and lessens the danger of severe injury to the left hand when driving. In making the cotton into the seam, it is not stretched along the seam but is driven into it in small loops. Each time the calking is made into the seam a little is looped back and forced into the seam with a light blow. The loops should be from 1 to 3 inches long, depending upon the width and condition of the seam. When the seam is wide the loops are shorter and more calking is tucked in than when the seam is narrow and tight.

After a couple of feet of seam have had calking tucked in, go back to the starting place and drive the calking home with even, heavy blows of the mallet. Do not permit the iron to tip in the direction the seam runs, as the corners of the blade will break the calking if this happens. If the seam is not tight on the inside it shows a poor job of planking. While excusable in a first boat, it is not in any other. If the calking is not driven through, the "open seam" may be tight, but it is a good plan to set the calking in marine glue. This is a messy job, but it is the only way to make sure the open seams are watertight; in the case of a really bad seam it may be necessary to insert muslin soaked in glue into the seam, before calking, or even to trim the seam on the outside and drive in a batten wedge. Of course, it is much better to remove the offending strakes and replace them with new ones; this is a matter between the builder and his conscience. Oakum, if used instead of cotton in a narrow seam, should not be driven hard as the few strands possible are easily broken.

## Bent Floors

There are many variations of construction details in round-bottom hull construction; mention of them will serve as a reminder to the builder of some possibilities when orthodox methods will not serve. In the case of floor timbers, it may be found that a tank, engine, or other fitting is so low in the hull that the usual sawn floor timber will not do. Metal floors may be unavailable. In this case, bent floors can be used to advantage. These should

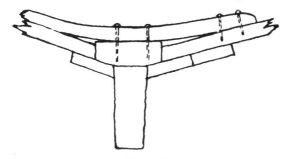

*125. Bent Floors*

be of heavier stock than the frames, and should be bent over a mold and placed in the hull when cold. To be really strong, the bent floor timbers must be so shaped that they not only rest on top of or alongside the frames, but also must touch the top of the keel or keel batten at the hull center line, where a fastening is required. If the curve required to do this is excessive, insert a block between keel and floor and fasten through it.

## Double-Bent Framing

Double-framing, of a sort, can be accomplished in bent frames by bending an inside frame, inside the bilge stringer and sheer clamp, and fastening it to the outside frame with fastenings driven through spacers (blocks) inserted between the inner and outer frame. This type of construction is useful when a stiff hull is required with bent frames; usually only a few frames need to be so doubled. When this construction is desirable it is best to put in the inner frames before fastening all the strakes permanently. However, this depends upon the type of fastening required; the inner frame should be bent over a mold and inserted cold, of course. This type of frame is rarely used, except in light hulls.

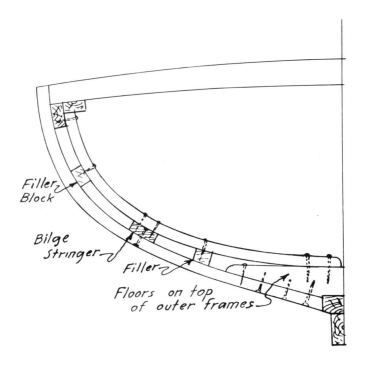

*Filler Block*

*Bilge Stringer*

*Filler*

*Floors on top of outer frames*

*126. Double-Framing*

## Intermediate Shaft Bearing, Alignment

When the propeller shaft must be long, it has to be supported. A bearing is required for this, so some foundation must be allotted it. Measure from the coupling of the engine to the position of the inside stuffing box, or inside shaft log, and locate a place two fifths the length from the stuffing box, or log (or three fifths the length from the engine coupling), for the bearing. If this comes on a floor timber it is well; if not, it may be desirable to fashion a false timber or to place a block on top of the keel.

This bearing should be well fastened. If the bearing is not correctly placed, vibration and noise will result. Another thing that must be planned in a long shaft is flexibility. Any wooden hull will change shape enough, as the timbers become moist and swell, to bind a long propeller shaft by throwing it out of line; this happens even in the very short shafts used in auxiliary yachts. If the shaft is long, and must be made up of short lengths (so it can be removed without tearing the hull to pieces), there should be a flexible coupling at the ends of each section, and the sections supported by one or two bearings spaced about 40 times the shaft diameter. In short shafts the use of a flexible coupling at the engine is good practice. In ordering bearings and stuffing boxes, be sure they are a little oversize for the shaft, in a wooden hull, so that the shaft will not bind when the engine goes slightly out of line. The tolerance usually permitted is about .025 to .03 inch in the diameter, in all shafts. In lining up the engine before launching, do not make permanent bolting; after the boat has been afloat a few days she will have changed shape slightly and the engine should be realigned then. The engine usually has to be lowered one shim, though occasionally the reverse is the case. In placing a propeller, be sure there is not less than $1\frac{1}{2}$ inches between the blade tips and the bottom; or one tenth the propeller diameter, or greater.

## Large Centerboard Cases

Commercial schooners or sloops having centerboards require a well-built centerboard case. In large vessels the keel stops at each end of the slot and sidepieces (pocket pieces) are lapped to the keel, to form the sides of the slot; usually the ends of the pocket pieces are actually scarfed to the sides of the keel forward and abaft the head ledges. The frames are half-dovetailed into the outboard faces of the pocket pieces and wedged on the flat side. The thickness of the centerboard is $\frac{1}{4}$ inch for every foot of length. Yellow locust or white hickory is superior to white oak for heavy centerboards. Burr oak is used in some parts of the country instead of white oak. The diameter of the pivot bolt is one half the thickness of the board, through-bushed in the board. The length of the centerboard is a matter of design. Roughly it may be found by adding the draft to the water-line length; the sum is multiplied by four; the square root of the product is the proportionate length of the board in a large vessel. The head ledges are 1 inch thicker than the centerboard. Their width is at least one and a half times the thickness. The case sides should be

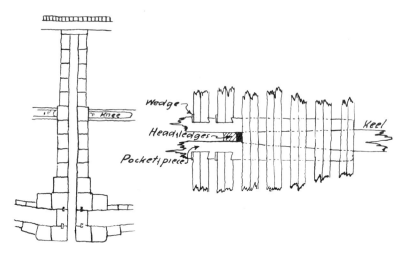

*127. Centerboard Case for a Large Commercial Schooner*

of narrow stock, the lower part as thick as the head ledges, the upper part 1 inch less. The fastenings are edge bolts, strake by strake—four bolts athwartships in each strake at the head ledges. The cap of the case is at the underside of the main deck beams; it is half as thick as the upper strakes of the case. Offside cases have already been described (Chapter Three).

## Shifting Centerboards

In small craft a shifting centerboard is a good feature. The case must be longer than the board, of course, and some mode for shifting the pivot in the case or board is necessary. The most common method is to hang the pivot to a bronze strap on each side of the board, the tops of the straps being held together by a wooden spacer above the board, at level of top of case. The straps are held to the case by a wing-nut bolt passed through the case sides and spacer; another is required a little below. By having a number of holes in the top of the case, their position found by experimenting, the board may be shifted to suit the weather or the trim. Another method is to pivot the board unusually high in the case, or at the upper forward corner of the board, and to shift the pivot pin.

### Shifting Mast

In small open or half-decked sailing craft the mast is usually stepped in a thwart. These boats are very sensitive to weight and trim, so the ability to shift the mast and sail slightly is often an advantage in racing. To accomplish this, the heel of the mast must be in a slot in the step, secured by blocks in the slot or other means. One alternative is to have a slot in the heel of the mast; the step is a plank on edge, the heel being secured by a pin passed through athwartships. This is suitable for few craft, however. Mechanical devices have been developed for the same purpose, but they are usually rather expensive. Marine hardware dealers can furnish information on available fittings of this type. To shift the mast in the thwart, the most simple method is to cut a slot, fore and aft, in the thwart in which the mast will travel. To hold it in position, a short thwart fitting snugly to the mast is secured to the top of the first thwart. The short thwart is nothing more than a short piece or square of plank the same thickness as the thwart, bolted to the latter. The bolts can have wing nuts to make them easy to remove. They should be loose in the holes. A series of holes for these bolts enables the whole rig to be shifted fore and aft an appreciable amount. A sliding iron clamp can be worked out to accomplish the same result and an ingenious builder can develop many gadgets of this type.

### Cleats

In making fittings, wooden cleats are preferable to metal ones; they can be made of oak or locust. If there is going to be a strain on them, as in the case of cleats used for halyards or sheets, through-bolt or rivet them. Don't depend upon screws: spike or lag if through-fastening is impractical. A cleat should not be fixed so that it is in line with the strain coming to it; it should be turned 15 or 20 degrees to the line of strain. Make the wooden cleats large enough for the ropes belayed on it, and high enough to be of

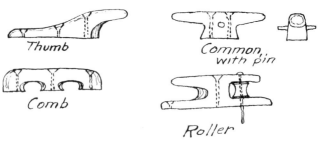

*Thumb*

*Common,*
*with pin*

*Comb*

*Roller*

W ooden  Cleats

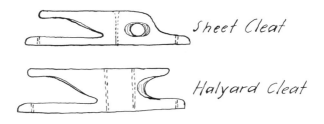

*Sheet Cleat*

*Halyard Cleat*

*Lewis Cleats*

*128. Cleats*

some use, when belaying in a hurry. Low, small cleats look neat, perhaps, but are useless if too short to hold the turns, or so low that two hands are required to force the rope under them. There must be two fastenings in every cleat. All cleats should be off the deck when possible; put them on the sides of the trunk or cockpit coaming, on the inside of the rail, or on top of the house in preference to the deck.

### Preservation of Timber

Preservation of the structure of a hull depends upon proper ventilation in all parts. This is not always possible, unfortunately, in many yacht arrangements. As a result, other protection must be used, even though less effective than ventilation. One method is creosoting, or the application of commercial wood preservatives. Creosote is the cheapest; the odor is objectionable to some, however. Odorless creosotes are marketed, though possibly less effective than the commercial creosotes. These are applied with a brush in most hulls; impregnation is better from the standpoint of preserving, but is impractical if done before the timber is shaped. The parts of the hull to be treated are the frames, floors, deadwoods, inside of keel structure, stem and stern inside the hull, and knightheads below deck. The inside of the planking, below the water line, may also be treated. It is impossible to paint well over creosote; if painted surfaces are to be treated, some of the other commercial preservatives are preferable.

In addition to this treatment, salting has advantages. This is done by placing rock salt between the frames, outside the clamps and inside the sheer strake. This is accomplished by inserting thin battens between the frames while building. These have their ends notched into the frames, or are held with copper nails. The battens should be bored with a small drill, to drain, the holes well spread over the batten. The battens form stops which prevent the salt from falling into the bottom. The stops should not be a very tight fit, between clamp and planking. Another idea is to put the salt in bags, held behind the clamps with spring clips. Salt most suitable for this work is the commercial rock salt used in making ice cream, which is in coarse grains. The prime advantage of salt is in the prevention of mildew inside a boat. The ends of a boat, inside, should be creosoted, or painted with wood preservative every three years. Raw linseed oil is useless as a wood preservative; boiled oil is somewhat more effective. Boiled linseed oil is used under painted or varnished surfaces occasionally. Its value is in resistance to penetration of moisture in the wood.

As a general rule, it is undesirable to paint or varnish the inside of the planking of a boat. In open boats, however, this is not particularly harmful as the direct rays of the sun reach all parts of the interior. If there are decks or cabins, however, painting the inside of the planking, either in the bottom or topsides, will lead to rot. If not creosoted, the inside of the planking can be given a couple of coats of kerosene oil, while the hull is building, and left unprotected afterward.

## Guards

Heavy guards are often required on motorboats, particularly those used for commercial work. These should be tapered fore and aft, both in depth and thickness. The inside should be slightly hollowed, to fit the round of the sides. The bevel formed by the flare of the hull sides should be allowed for, either on the inside or outside face, so that the guard will not slope downward from the side of the vessel. Scarfs should be used instead of butts. It is useless to place a heavy guard at deck level and attempt to fasten

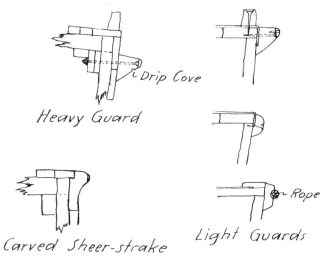

129. *Guards*

it to the hull with screws or lags. The guards must be low enough so that through-fastenings can be used; these should pass through guard, planking, frames, and clamp. If the frames are not wide enough for these fastenings, the latter should pass alongside the frames, very close to them, in passing through planking and clamp. If there is any tendency for the clamps to spring outward, this may be remedied by placing a small piece of framing behind the clamps, close to any guard fastening. Carriage bolts, set up on washers, are the only fastenings suitable for the heavy guards of commercial hulls and motor sailers. It is a good plan to run a cove along the underside of a heavy guard; this should be out near the outboard face. The cove serves to prevent hull streaks caused by water dripping from the guard at the cove.

# CHAPTER SEVEN

# LAP-STRAKE, AND OTHER CONSTRUCTION METHODS

*Lap-Strake Construction—Advantages and Disadvantages*

PLANKING a boat carvel fashion, as described in the last chapter, is but one of many possible methods. However, boats planked other than carvel fashion usually have to be designed to suit the method by which they are to be planked. It is true that it would be possible to plank a boat designed to be carvel-built in some other manner, but as a rule this should not be attempted except in strip building. Lap-strake construction is the favorite method of planking boats that must be very light and strong, or that must carry heavy loads in shallow, very rough water. A hull planked lap-strake, or "clench-built," is very flexible and no calking is required except in large craft.

Although it has many advantages, the use of lap-strake planking has been circumscribed by certain important limitations. The lap-strake planking method requires wide stock, particularly as the size of the hull increases. This method of planking can best be carried out with hardwoods, such as oak or elm, except in very small craft (such as canoes and dinghies), where cedar or mahogany is often used. Furthermore, lap-strake planking is much easier to use in some hull forms than in others; those having fairly straight keels are the most satisfactory. Lap-strake is not used in hulls having a large amount of ballast outside. A good deal of skill is required to line off a lap-strake hull; no stealers can be used, so an error in lining off is really serious. Repairs to the planking of a lap-strake hull are difficult. Relatively thin planking must be used;

while this is an advantage in some hulls it is a disadvantage in others.

### Uses of Lap-Strake Construction

The scope of lap-strake construction, in the United States, has always been rather limited; only small craft such as dinghies and canoes are built in this fashion, in most parts of the country. Except for the Jersey Sea-Skiff type of hull, running to 50 feet in length, no large craft have been built lap-strake in recent times. Years ago there were a number of sailing boats, lap-strake, ranging from 15 feet to 50 feet in length (such as the Block Islander), mostly double-enders. In Europe the lap-strake construction has been applied to hulls of far greater size: cutters, schooners, and brigs; in medieval times, ships. The famous English Cutter of the American Revolutionary War period, and later, was clench-built. Boats used on open beaches in England were almost invariably lap-strake.

### Timber and Model

The effect of available timber on hull design cannot be better illustrated than by clench-built hulls: where oak and elm were available, clench-built hulls were often full-ended; where only softwoods were to be had, clench-built hulls were sharp-ended, as in Scandinavia. Hardwood-built hulls had narrow and numerous strakes; softwood hulls had wide and few strakes. The effect of timber on the shape of the midsection was to permit hardwood hulls to have flat floors, great beam, and hard bilges, while the softwood hull usually had rising floors, slack bilges, and little, or moderate, beam.

### Frames

Frames of lap-strake hulls can be either sawn or bent. The latter are used in small boats, or those in which light weight is important. Sawn frames were used in the Block Island boats and in most of the large European clench-built hulls.

### Fastenings

Fastenings for lap-strake hulls may be either copper or galvanized-iron nails, riveted or clenched. Screws may also be used,

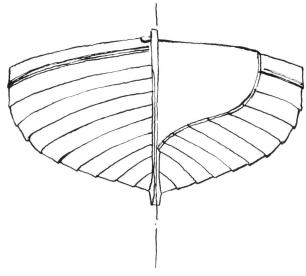

*130. Lap-Strake*

either for fastening the planking to the frames, or at the laps, or at the plank ends. Galvanized-iron nails are often used in clench building. The point is driven through the timber and turned back in the direction from which it is driven, then forced into the inside of the frames or planking, as will soon be described. As a result, the iron nail must be of soft wrought iron, well galvanized, to stand such handling without fracture or loss of galvanizing. Because of the difficulty in obtaining such nails, copper or alloy nails are now used.

## Planking and Construction Timber

The woods used for lap-strake planking are white oak, rock elm, yellow, white, or red pine, larch, cedar, and mahogany. Frames are made of white oak, rock elm, ash, if bent; oak, apple, or tropical hardwood, if sawn. Floor timbers are of oak, elm, apple, or ash. Keels are of oak, yellow pine, larch, or mahogany.

## Design

The choice of a design for a lap-strake boat is governed by the factors outlined in Chapter One, with certain additions. If the wood available is not capable of being steamed, sawn frames and a sharp-ended hull must be planned on; the midsection should have rising, or hollow, floors and there should be slack bilges and little, or no, spring to the keel rabbet. If hardwood is available that can be steamed, the hull may be sharp, or full-ended; it may be flat, rising, or hollow-floored. Bilges may be hard or slack, beam narrow or wide, and the frames bent or sawn.

## Lines, Lofting, Setup, Stocks

Lines drawn for a lap-strake hull are always to the inside of the planking, as the laps would make drawing the lines to the outside of the planking unnecessarily difficult. If it is desired to use lines designed for carvel planking, the thickness of planking deducted

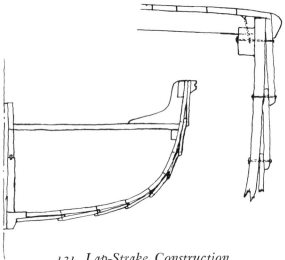

*131. Lap-Strake Construction*

may be less in lap-strake construction than would be required in the carvel-planked design. There is no set rule, but it is safe to assume that a lap-strake hull will require one half the thickness required for carvel planking, if built of hardwood; two thirds, if built of softwood. Lofting of the design should be carried out as in any round-bottom hull, and templates and molds made in the usual way. The keel and deadwood are also built as in any round-bottom hull. These are commonly set up on bearers, or strongbacks, set on posts or horses; the hull is built right side up. The sawn frames, usually single but sometimes double, are set up as in any sawn-frame hull. If bent frames are used, molds are set up in the usual way. These are stayed in position and tested with fairing ribbands; the latter are not fastened to the molds by most builders. Lap-strake hulls having bent frames require few molds; the planking is used to shape the boat by experts. An experienced builder can turn out a creditable job with only the midship mold, but the beginner should not attempt this.

### Lining-Off

With the molds in place, and faired up, planking is started; the bent frames are put in place after the planking is completed. First, the number of strakes must be decided upon. Narrow strakes are best for the beginner: they are easier to shape and fit, give a stronger boat, and do not require as wide stock as wide strakes. The only disadvantages are that the boat is made heavier with

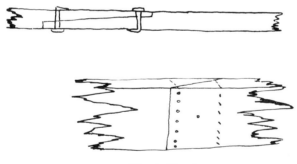

132. Plank Scarfs

narrow strakes and that the greater number of laps increases the number of fastenings to be driven. The lining-off may be done with a flat, straight-edged batten at the normal line along the bilge, then spacing off on either side, batten to sheer, and batten to rabbet. It must be kept in mind that no stealer is possible, so all strakes must run the length of the hull. The ends of the strakes must be wide enough for two fastenings. It may take a number of attempts to work out the lining-off so that the strakes can be cut of narrow stock, look well, and not make the hood ends too narrow.

The number of strakes used in a lap-strake hull should vary with its shape, size, and the stock available. If the boat has a transom that is stepped high up on a sternpost, without a counter, remember that one seam, or lap, must run to the tuck—where the transom meets the sternpost rabbet. It is by no means necessary that all strakes be of the same width, however, so the builder has some leeway in lining off. As in carvel planking, the widths of the garboard and sheer strake may be established arbitrarily; the other planks are shaped to vary in width and sweep for the sake of appearance and as required by the hull form.

## Garboards

The garboard is put on first, in a lap-strake hull. This is often in two lengths, scarfed at the butt. The latter is always a little forward of amidships. To get out the garboard, make a spiling—as usual in a round-bottom hull—of the rabbet. Strike off the top of the garboard with a batten. Lay off the garboard from the spilings and measurements at the molds for width. The planking of

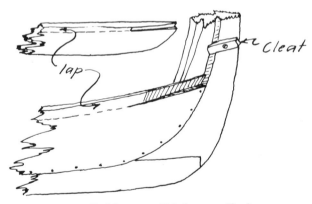

*133. Rabbets or Shiplaps at Ends*

a lap-strake hull must be well-seasoned stock, particularly if oak or elm is used. In lining off, the top of the garboard must be arbitrarily established, as in carvel planking. However, a little more sweep-up, to the laps forward, is permissible than is the case in carvel plank seams. The garboard will probably need steaming, or boiling, to work it into place. In a hull that requires great twist in the garboard, it may be well to template the strake for a "cold fitting." When the garboard has been templated and fitted, the garboard may then be made and set in place without having to remove it from the hull for fittings; this is a good plan with any

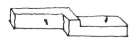

*134. Lap Gauge*

plank that must be steamed or boiled. Once the template is made, both garboards can be shaped; otherwise the first fitted is used for a pattern of the second. If templating is not done, and the garboard is steamed or boiled, it is necessary to spile very carefully. Then if the garboard does not fit it must be left in place until cold before being removed for fitting. In this case it may need a second steaming or boiling if the twist is great. To hold lap-strakes to the stem and sternposts, wooden blocks or cleats are temporarily fastened to the posts, by screws. Once a strake is in place, the cleats are removed and the screw holes plugged or puttied; then the cleats are shifted for the next strake.

If the garboard is in two lengths, it is best scarfed. To do this, the butt is cut off in a miter box so that the scarf is across the thickness of the plank; the length of the scarf is to be from 3½ to 8 inches long, as the thickness of the plank permits without showing excessive feather edge. The scarf should stand so that the end of the scarf, outside, is aft of that inside. The miter box should be made up of two wide pieces of plank, separated by a spacer at the bottom a little thicker than the thickness of the hull planking; a saw kerf at the proper angle will guide a backed miter saw, used for such work; if the strakes are too wide for the backed saw to be used, a stiff cross-cut saw can be used. A fine-toothed saw should be used for this work.

In American lap-strake construction, butt blocks are often used, particularly in powerboats. The butt block is fitted in the same manner as in carvel planking, except it does not reach the full width of the strake, and does not overlap the adjoining strakes. The butt block used reaches from the top of the strake below to the top of the strake being butted; in other words, the butt block width is equal to the width of the strake minus one lap. In American practice, also, the rabbets in the laps at bow and stern, to be described, are not used. Instead the American builder uses the dory lap and often backs the seam so formed by a batten which runs one or two frames beyond the bevel of the dory lap, in line with the lap seam. The batten and dory lap are screw-fastened, as there is rarely room enough to rivet at the bow. The frames are notched for the seam battens, as a rule. The advantage claimed for this, over the usual rabbet in the lap, is greater strength; for this reason many builders of power lap-strake hulls use battens at the seams in the bow. At the stern most American builders do not rabbet the laps, unless the stern is sharp. Here they notch the transom edge for each strake so that the full thickness of the lap is carried right to the stern.

Before nailing the garboard into place, gauge the amount of lap to be given the next strake at the garboard top. This should be from ¾ to 1¼ inches, depending upon the size and shape of the boat. The line of fastenings is sometimes gauged; this is at half the lap width. Except at the turn of the bilge in hard-bilged hulls, the width of the laps in all strakes is the same; therefore, a lap gauge is useful. This is a 1 by 1 by 5-inch piece of wood, cut with a jog in the middle on two sides, and with nails driven through on each side of the jogs to scribe the width of the lap on one side, and the fastening line on the other side, if desired. By reversing the gauge, with the jog on top or bottom of a strake, the nails will scribe the width of the lap with one arm, the fastening line with the other.

## Fastening Garboard

The lap set off, the garboard is fastened to the stem, sternpost, and keel. This should be done with boat nails or screws, using as long a fastening as the scantling of the keel and posts permit— usually about four times the thickness of the plank. Holes must be drilled for these fastenings; they should be nearly at right angles to the face of the back rabbets. The fastenings should be not more than 3 inches or less than 1 inch apart. If the molds are known to stand fair, yet the strake will not come home against it due to the shape of the hull lines, pull the strake to the mold by a temporary fastening just below the lap line scribed on it. No fastenings of this kind are placed above the scribed line for the lap.

## Luting and Fastenings

Planking scarfs should have thin brown paper, set in marine glue (muslin may be used instead of paper), placed between the faces of the scarfs before fastening. Luting is sometimes used but is not as good as wet glue and paper, or muslin. The best fastenings for scarfs of this kind are copper tacks, about ¼ of an inch longer than the thickness of the planking. These should be driven through the scarfs, close to the featheredges; the heads of the tacks on the featheredge side should be at each end of the scarf. After the tacks are driven through, the points are neatly turned down with a light hammer. The tacks should be ⅜ or ½ of an inch apart. If the planking is thick enough, a couple of clench nails, rivets, or screws may be driven at the middle of the scarf. The scarfs in any strake in a lap-strake hull should not be fastened until the strake is nailed at the ends, rabbets, and laps. Hence the strakes must be clamped together at the scarfs to fasten. Scarfs may also be made with jogged ends, in the usual fashion of scarfs —a good plan with softwood.

## Supporting the Garboards

In fitting the garboards, it may be found that they bulge between the molds, due to their thinness. A block or batten screwed to the top of the keel, reaching a little more than two thirds the distance from the side of the keel to the top of the strake, will overcome this; clamps or nippers applied to block and strake will hold the latter in place. The floor timbers may be fitted as soon as two or three strakes are fastened in place, to replace these blocks.

## Beveling and Rabbeting Laps

When the garboards are in place, the lap established by the scribed line must be beveled. This is done with a sharp plane, using a short block of wood, a little longer than the width of any strake, as a gauge. This is placed with its top edge at the line on the mold struck off to represent the top of the strake above and its lower end overlapping the garboard. The amount of bevel required will be enough to allow the inside face of the gauge to rest on the outboard face of the garboard the full depth of the

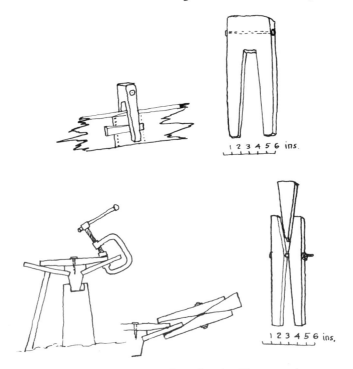

*135 Clamps Used in Lap-Strake Construction*

lap. At bow and stern, the lap must die out and the planking come flush on the outside at the rabbet of the stem, sternpost, and along the after face of the transom. To accomplish this, the bevel, as it reaches within a short distance of these points, dies out and changes to a rabbet, as wide as the lap and half the thickness of the planking at the rabbets, or transom face. This rabbet will begin at nothing, then, and gradually increase to half the thickness of the planking at the hood ends. This must be cut with a very sharp chisel, and perhaps a bullnosed rabbet plane. The rabbet need not be long: 5 or 6 inches is long enough in a 16-foot dinghy.

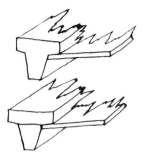

*136. Keels Used in
Lap-Strake Hulls*

One rule for the length of these rabbets is 12 times the thickness of the planking. They really form a shiplap.

## Planking Up

When these rabbets are cut, the next strake is spiled off. The bottom of this strake must reach to the lap line scribed, or gauged, on the top of the garboard. The top will be decided by the batten line struck on the molds in lining off. The strake is fitted in the same manner as a carvel strake, but overlapping the garboard, of course. When fitted and temporarily secured, the lap is scribed at the top of the strake and the fastening line is scribed at the bottom. Then the strake is removed and the lap of the bottom is scribed on the inside of the bottom; the short rabbets are then

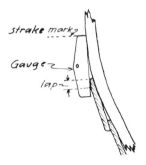

*137. Checking Lap Bevel*

cut at each end, so that the strake will fit into the rabbets, or shiplaps, on the outside top edge of the garboards. This done, and its mate made, the strake is then replaced, with its mate, and permanent fastenings are driven. It will be noticed that no bevel is required on the inside, bottom edge of the strake. The top is then beveled and rabbeted at the lap, as was done in the garboard. All the rest of the strakes are spiled, fitted, beveled, and rabbeted in the same way, until the sheer strake is reached. The top of this requires no lap bevel, of course, but allowance must be made for the bevel of the gunwale, or deck, along the sheer.

## Planking Notes

The bilge strakes may sometimes develop a good deal of curvature when laid out flat. This may be so great, in some hulls and with some methods of lining-off, that it will be necessary to scarf the planks so that the grains of the two parts are at a slight angle to one another; this scarf should be aft of amidships. The bevel, at the lap, may be the full thickness of some strakes. It should be noted that the harder the bilge, the less is the amount of lap possible there.

Due to the fastenings along the lap, a little edgeset to some of these strakes in the bilge will do no harm. To set the spiling batten for an edgeset strake, the batten must be edgeset also. This may be gauged by setting the batten in place, clamping it at the bottom near the middle length and fore end. Then springing down the after end edgewise will turn the upper edge at the middle inward against the mold; when the upper edge comes home against the mold, the amount of edgeset is fixed. The after end is then clamped and spilings made. When the batten is removed for spiling the plank the edgeset is lost; this must be obtained in the strake by clamping it in the same manner and springing it while fitting.

In setting strakes make sure both sides are alike as to height and position of laps, and that the lap edges showing outside the hull are fair and smooth. The lower and outer edges of every strake, exposed at the lap, should be slightly rounded to prevent splinters developing. The sheer strake is usually a little thicker than the other strakes, to serve as a wale. The after ends of strakes on the transom should not be cut off until the strake is permanently fastened in place. The old builders often worked a cove line along the bottom edge of the sheer strake. It is plain that the beauty of the lap-strake hull depends upon the lining-off of the strakes, and laps. In some ways, lap-strake planking is the severest test of the builder's craftsmanship and sense of proportion. Tightness of a lap-strake hull depends upon the accuracy of the beveling of the top edge of each strake as it is placed, and upon skillful fastening.

## Riveting and Clenching

To do a lap-strake job, the builder must know how to rivet and clench, preferably the former, using copper nails. To rivet, use copper nails. With these, obtain burrs (small washers) to fit. First drill a hole through the lap of the two planks, or a plank and frame. In softwood the hole should be a little smaller than the nail diameter; in hardwood it should be the same size. Tap the nail through with the head driven home, then force the burr, or "rove," over the point. A hollow-pointed punch, called a "rove-iron" or "rove punch," is used to do this. After the burr is driven against the wood, the point of the nail is cut off with nippers, leaving enough to form a "head" over the burr. The amount of nail left projecting from the burr, after nipping off the point, should be about one and a half times the diameter of the nail. A helper then holds an iron against the head, a "holding iron," or the top of a heavy ball-pein hammer, or even a flatiron will do. A piece of steel shafting, with the end ground slightly rounding, is a good holding iron. The cutoff end may now be headed with light blows of a small ball-pein hammer, using the rounded ball end of the hammer head. In softwood use very light blows, working the shape of the head gradually.

Clenching a nail is somewhat harder and requires practice. The hole is bored as for a riveted nail and the nail is then started. As the nail is driven through, its point is turned over in a hook by holding the face of a hammer against the side of the point, then following the point around to form the hook. When the hook is formed, the point of the nail is ready to re-enter the wood, before the head is quite home outside. The head is then driven home, the holder-on inside the hull using a heavy hammer face to force the point deeply into the wood. He finally finishes the clenching by tapping the crown of the hook down while the man outside holds his hammer against the head. There is a trick in doing this that can only be learned by experience. A somewhat easier method is to first drive the nail nearly home, then form the hook with a pair of roundnose pliers, after which the head is driven home and the hook forced into the wood, then tapped down smooth. The point of the nail hooked over must not re-enter in the same

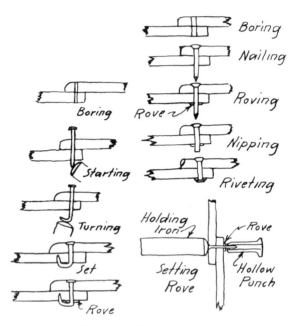

*138. Clench Nailing and Riveting*

line of grain; it must cross the grain at nearly right angles or splitting will result. Sometimes a burr is placed over the point of the nail before forming the hook. Making a re-entering hole with an awl will help in clenching a nail. Most builders prefer to rivet rather than to clench; riveting will pull two pieces of wood together better than clenching, as a rule. Clenching is perhaps preferable when softwood planking is used, but riveting is best in hardwood. Care must be taken that the holes are of the right diameter in riveting; otherwise the nail will bend outside the planking in driving, or, if too large, the nail will bend in the hole while riveting. The beginner will find riveting most suitable for work in clench-built hulls. The heads of fastenings are not countersunk, as a rule, in lap-strake hulls.

## Floor Timbers

The planking completed, the floors are usually set in place next; these are scribed from templates. It is necessary to suggest that in a hull in which the molds are widely spaced the floors should be placed before the planking is completed. If the floors are placed when the garboard and two strakes above it are in place, in such

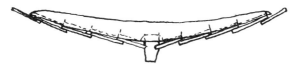

*139. Scribing Floors*

a hull, the strains on the garboard fastenings, during construction, are lessened considerably. If molds are numerous this is not usually necessary, however, unless the planking is very thin. The floors are often jogged for the laps and the planking is through-fastened to the floors with rivets, or clenched nails.

## Lap Fastenings

Fastening the planking at the laps is best done with rivets. These should be bored for along the line scribed in the laps for fastenings. It is well to mark the position of the frames on each strake after it is in place, before fastening the laps, so that the latter fastenings will not be foul of those in the frames. Usually two fastenings are placed in each frame bay.

## Frames

With the laps fastened, and the floors in place, the frames may be stepped. It is generally considered easiest to bend the frames over a mold and place them in the hull cold, unless they run from gunwale to gunwale in one piece. In this case they should be placed hot. Cold frames are often beveled and jogged around the laps; this cannot be done with frames placed hot. In bending hot, a series of holes are bored along the frame lines for the fastenings; these serve to guide the bending of the frames. If the man inside the hull, who bends the frames, wears soft-soled shoes, he can use

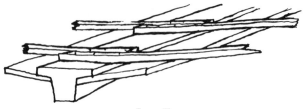

*140. Lap-Frames*

his feet effectively in bending frames hot, by "walking them in." The frame should not be pushed to bear on the keel, or bilge, by merely shoving it into a hard bend there, but should be worked into the bilge from the keel outward; or, if the frame is continuous from gunwale to gunwale, two men inside should work the frame down, keeping it nearly straight across, above the keel, as long as possible, so that it bends in a fairly continuous curve. When worked down, it may be fitted into the sharp turn of the bilges by first pulling the heads of the frame inboard and forcing the curve with the pressure of one foot, then releasing the frame head, allowing it to snap out against the planking. This should be done a number of times before a frame is worked into a sharp turn of the bilge.

Riveting of the frame should be done while it is still warm, so that it can be pulled home against the planking. It must be held while a few rivets or clench nails are driven. Some of these will be driven through the planking clear of the laps; drive those in the laps first, then those clear of the laps. Usually only one fastening is driven clear of the laps, in each strake; this is usually above the middle of the distance between laps, outside, so that it is driven where the frame touches the strake on the inside. If the frames are jogged over the laps, the fastenings clear of the laps, into the frames, are often two in number in each strake and frame. Frames running from gunwale to gunwale are only useful in flat-floored hulls; those having rise to the floors should have the frames crossed or lapped on top of the keel, or brought down alongside the floor timbers. In boats that require great strength, the short frames run down the sides of the floor timbers, with intermediate frames crossing on top of the keel between the floors. The floors are not fastened to the short frames; both are fastened to the planking instead.

## Jogged Frames

Jogged frames are often fitted hot and temporarily secured; when set and cold the inside laps are scribed on the frames. The latter are then removed and shaped, then refitted and fastened.

*141. Jogged Frame*

The extra work of making these frames is warranted only when the boat is used for landing on rough beaches. The extra support given the planking, between laps, by jogged frames is desirable under such conditions. Jogged frames are often used in large lap-strake hulls.

## Gunwale

In open boats, built lap-strake, the gunwale (sheer) must be finished in some manner. The most common way in small boats is to saw off the frames at the sheer line and run a sheer clamp, or stringer, along the inside of the frames level with the gunwale. Outside the planking, a guard is placed, also level with the gunwale. The clamp is usually riveted at the frames through all; the guard screw, or nail, is fastened to the frames, through the sheer strake. This plan is popular as the boat may be easily drained and cleaned inside by turning it upside down. In boats in which this is impractical, because of size, the sheer clamp is put in, in the same manner as just described. Then the sheer is capped: this is done by nailing a thin strip of wood along the sheer, wide enough to reach from the outside of the sheer strake to the inside of the sheer clamp. If a guard is desired, it may or may not be placed at the sheer so that its top lies flush with the top of the cap strip. The reason for the cap strip is to protect the heads of the frames from moisture and rot. Oarlock sockets are stepped in blocks between the frames, with or without the cap.

### Thwarts

Thwarts are secured to the hull by carlins, or stringers, which run fore and aft along the inside of the frames at the desired height; these are screw, or nail, fastened to the frames, as a rule, but may be riveted through all. The thwarts rest on top of these and are nailed, or screwed, to them. In large, open boats thwart knees are required; these stand on top of the thwarts, with one arm along the top of the thwart and the other upright against a frame,

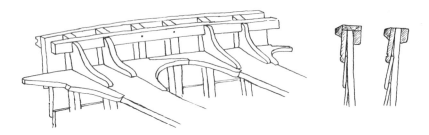

*142. Gunwale and Thwarts*

the top of the arm reaching to the gunwale and notched over the sheer clamp. At the outboard ends of each thwart in the middle third of the boat there are usually two of these knees; sometimes only one is used, however. The seat in the stern, or "sternsheets," which is a low platform used in the stern of a working boat instead of the seat, is supported by the thwart carlins or by beams athwartships. Quarter-knees and breasthook should be fitted. The mast thwart should have thwart knees and should have its ends notched for frames.

## Floor Boards

Floor boards should be fitted to the top of the frames, to protect the bottom. Unless lightness is very important, the floor boards are best made with tight seams; batten floor boards allow dirt to accumulate in the bottom between the frames.

## Frame Scantlings

No suggestions have been made as to the proper size of bent frames for use in a lap-strake hull; this is a matter of design. Most builders make them square in section if bent hot; the thickness and width of the frames are about twice the thickness of the planking. Frame spacing is about 12 times the plank thickness. Wide, thin frames, bent on the flat, are used in some boats. The thickness is about one and one half the thickness of the planking; the width is about twice the thickness. Notched frames are about two and one half the plank thickness, in depth; in width, twice the plank thickness.

## Stiffening, Sea-Skiffs' Keels

Lap-strake hulls are very flexible; if it is necessary to carry a heavy load in the boat and to sail her, or to come alongside other craft a great deal, the hull should be stiffened along the gunwale by using a heavy sheer clamp. The more popular method, however, is to insert lodging knees at each side of the thwarts; these rest on top of the thwart carlins and are fastened to them, with the other arm secured to the fore, or after, edges of the thwart. The long arms of these knees are against the inside of the frames. In some designs the long arms are so long that they meet one another in a scarf halfway between each pair of thwarts. The knees should not be notched around the frames on which they bear. The short arms fit into a shallow notch on each side of the thwarts, and may be through-fastened, edgewise, through the thwarts. The Jersey Sea-Skiffs have a flat bottom, made of thick plank with splines in the seams, in lieu of a keel. Three or four planks make up the bottom, and the lap-strakes begin at the edges of the bottom, which is carvel, of course. These craft are much like round-sided dories in model.

### Diagonal Construction—Ashcroft System

Diagonal planking has become very popular in some parts of the world, particularly New Zealand. There are a great many methods of planking a boat in this manner, but the one most suited to amateur builders is the Ashcroft system. This was introduced in England some years ago and has become a popular method for planking dinghies. The planking is very thin, laid on the hull in two skins, both at an angle to the keel and both raking in the same way. A very satisfactory job of planking can be done with a little care.

### Types of Hull for Ashcroft System

The Ashcroft system of planking is not suited to all hull forms. It works best in the dinghy form of hull, though it may be used in almost any hull having no hollow in the after sections. The keel should be straight or slightly rockered and there should not be hollow garboards anywhere in the body plan. If outside ballast is required, it should be on a fin or skeg. This system of construction can be used in hulls up to about 30 feet in length, but it is most suitable for smaller boats. Batten keels should be used in all sizes.

### Setup Framing, Sheer Strakes

The hull is lofted in the usual manner. Molds and templates must be made. The setup is to be upside down; the molds should be carried to a base line above the sheer, in lofting. In making the molds, extend them to this line and fasten a cross-spall across each with its ends extending about 3 inches outside the sheer marks on the molds. When the molds are upside down, the tops of these cross-spalls should be at the sheer marks. Get out the backbone in the usual way, setting it up on the stocks upside down. The molds are set up as in any round-bottom hull. The Ashcroft system requires no transverse framing, longitudinal framing being used instead. The longitudinal frames consist of a number of stringers, or ribbands, running from bow to stern and spaced about 5 inches apart amidships. Except at the turn of the bilge, these stringers should be small in section: ¾ of an inch by 1 inch will be large enough for an 18-foot hull. The bilge stringers should be a little heavier, say, ¾ of an inch by 1½ inches. The molds, stem, and stern must be notched to receive these. The notches in the molds should be a little wider than each batten so that the molds can be easily removed. The stringers can be held in the notches by tying them in pairs across the boat. At the turn of the bilge, round the outside faces of the stringers there, so that the planking can bear on the full width of the stringer faces.

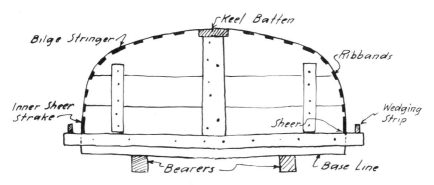

*143. Mold for Ashcroft Hull, Set Up for Planking*

The ribbands must be firmly in place against the molds to give solid bearing. The ends of the ribbands are screw-fastened in the notches at bow and stern. There is no ribband at the sheer, as the sheer strake will be in two thicknesses; the inner is notched into the molds to serve in place of a sheer batten, and the outer is put on as a wale, over the diagonal planking. Before notching for the sheer strake, the latter must be spiled off. This is done as in carvel planking, the width of the sheer strake being arbitrarily fixed by the builder to suit his ideas and stock. The inner sheer strake, after being cut and fitted, is used as a pattern to make three more duplicates, giving two inside and two outside strakes. The inner strakes are then set in place on the molds, using them as gauges to cut the notch in each mold. The keel batten must be correctly beveled for the planking before the latter is placed.

### Stiffening

Because of the thinness of the inside sheer strake, it must usually be supported by a temporary outside stringer or "wedging strip";

this is bent around the gunwale on top of the projecting ends of the mold-cross-spalls and fastened to each. These extra stringers should stand off from the molds about 1¼ inches. In a boat over 18 feet long, it may be well to add some ties between the molds; these may run between (and under) the extra stringers and are nailed to them. Some hardwood wedges should be made. It is a good plan to check now and see that all fore-and-aft members are in place: carlins for the thwarts, sheer clamps if there is to be a deck (these can go inside the inner sheer strake, or a thick inner sheer strake can be used instead, thus making the extra stringers outside at the sheer unnecessary). The keel batten should be well secured, but it is best not to place the outside keel until the planking is completed.

## Scantling

The planking is to be in two equal thicknesses: ⅛ of an inch by 3 inches in an 8- to 10-foot boat; ⁵⁄₃₂ of an inch by 3 inches in an 11- to 14-foot boat; ³⁄₁₆ of an inch by 3 inches in a 15- to 18-foot boat; ¼ of an inch by 3 inches in a 19- to 28-foot boat; ⁵⁄₁₆ of an inch by 3 inches in 28- to 30-foot boats. White pine, larch, cedar, mahogany, or duali are good timbers for planking. The scantlings used for the sheer strakes should be mentioned: ⅜ of an inch in an 8- to 10-footer; ½ of an inch in an 11- to 14-footer; ⅝ of an inch in a 15- to 18-footer; ¾ of an inch to 1⅛ inches in a 19- to 28-footer; and ⅞ of an inch to 1¼ inches in a 28- to 30-footer. There should be five stringers to a side in an 8- to 10-footer; six in an 11- to 14-footer; seven in a 15- to 18-footer. Larger boats should have theirs spaced 5 inches at the midsection. Eight- to 10-footers have stringers ⅝ of an inch by ¾ of an inch; 11- to 14-footers, ⅝ of an inch by ⅞ of an inch; 15- to 18-footers, ¾ of an inch by 1 inch; larger boats: for each 3 feet in length above 18 feet, add ⅛ of an inch to both width and thickness of the stringers. Bilge stringers should be from ⅜ of an inch to ½ of an inch wider than the rest; if great strength is required, increase the thickness ¼ of an inch over the other stringers. All planking and stringers should be clear stock.

## *Fastenings*

Plank fastenings are brads, ¾ of an inch to 1 inch. A small push drill is the best tool for boring the necessary holes. Small C-clamps, or homemade wooden wedge clamps like those used in clench building, are necessary. Between the two skins there should be some form of luting. This can be the luting already mentioned, or can be whiting mixed in linseed oil to the consistency of pancake batter. This is liberally applied to the strakes of the first skin before any strake of the outer skin is laid in place. Other materials than luting can be used, such as strips of thin muslin set in marine glue or airplane dope.

## *Planking Schedule*

As has been said, the Ashcroft system of planking requires the two skins to run diagonally to the keel, or center line of the hull. The strakes of the outer skin are over the seams of the inner skin. Each strake laid after the first two or three of the inner skin are in place will be alternately outer and inner. This enables strakes of both skins to be clamped to the stringers. Boiling or steaming the strakes will be required; the planking is so thin that sponging with boiling water will be sufficient in the smallest hulls.

## *Planking*

If the keel is not in place on the keel batten (and this is best), mark the center line of the keel on top of the keel batten. With a small, straight batten, strike a line across the keel, on each side of the center line across the first few stringers, at an angle of about 45 degrees to the keel center line, raking aft. This can be done on both sides, at a point a little forward of the point of greatest beam. This is the rake of the strakes. Take one of the pieces of planking, planed straight on both edges, and clamp it at the gunwale, either to the inner sheer strake or to a block or wedge, against the outer stringer so that it bears on the inner sheer strake; bend it fairly at the marked angle. Take care that the edges bear on the stringers; clamp the strake at each edge as it comes to bear on each stringer, and finally clamp it to the keel batten. This temporary strake will show whether or not there is any adjustment necessary in the angle the strake stands to the keel. There must be no bulging at the edges of the strake. It is a good plan, if bulges appear, to slack off the clamps from the turn of the bilge to the sheer and reclamp, working from bilge to sheer. This may indicate that the position of the strake at the sheer may have to be changed. Occasionally it will be desirable to increase the angle at which the strake stands to the keel; very rarely it may be necessary to decrease it. In either case, the amount of change will be very slight; the variation is due to some feature in the lines.

After the first strake has been checked, it may be fastened. These fastenings are not under great strain as the real plank fasten-

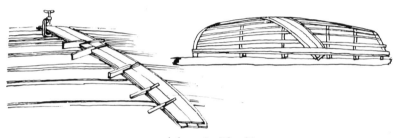

*144. Ashcroft Planking*

ings will be driven when the outer skin strakes are set in place. Therefore the inner skin fastenings may be short brads or tacks, driven into each stringer and into the gunwale and keel batten. Use just enough to hold the strake in place—the fewer the better. Saw off the end of the strake along the center line of the keel batten so that a miter is formed there when the opposite side receives the equivalent strake. Saw off the end at the gunwale a little clear of the sheer line, or, if not too long—it should not reach more than one inch beyond the sheer—let this wait. It is most important that this strake, and the ones laid on either side of it, lie flat and fair, without bulges. It is worth while experimenting until this can be accomplished, before fastening a strake.

When one strake is secured, fit its mate on the other side, taking care to duplicate the angle and lay. The second strake may be fitted forward or abaft the first. Secure it at the gunwale so that one edge touches the edge of the first strake; bend it over the stringers so that it touches the edge of the first strake again at the keel batten. It will be found that it is impossible to make it touch the first strake, all along its edge. The opening formed, between the two strakes, will be greatest near the turn of the bilge, and the width of the opening will vary with the form of the boat. As the ends of the boat are approached, the width of the opening will decrease. Take a compass and open it a little wider than the widest part of the opening between the two strakes and scribe the new strake so that a line is drawn on it parallel to the edge of the first strake, against which the second strake rests. It should be kept in mind that the second strake must be clamped so that its edges bear on the stringers reasonably well, before scribing.

Remove the strake and cut to the scribed line; fair and smooth the cut edge with a plane. Replace on the hull and fit. It is not necessary that the seam formed between the first and second strakes be absolutely tight. Clamping will have to be done along the edge away from the first strake, but the use of a batten under the screw of the clamp, reaching to the side against the first strake, and the judicious use of a few wedges under the batten here, will bring the edges of the second strake to bear on the stringers. Fasten the second strake as the first and trim the ends in the same way. Put on its mate on the opposite side of the hull.

## Outer Skin

Now the first outer strake may be laid. Like the first inner strake, the edges are parallel. It must cover the seam formed between the first and second inner strakes, so it must lie as nearly as possible at the same angle as the seam. Fit it roughly first and mark the inner skin so that it can be replaced in the same position as tried. Remove it and lute the marked position; then replace the strake and fasten, working from the gunwale to the keel batten. The fastenings pass through the inner skin strakes, into the keel batten, stringers, and gunwale. Those in the stringers and sheer strakes should be long enough to pass through all and be riveted or clenched on the inside. Three or four nails are required at the end on the keel batten; in each stringer there should be three nails, two within ⅜ of an inch of the edges and one in the center of the strake. Two rivets should be placed at the sheer strake, about ¾ of an inch from the top of the inner sheer strake and close to the edges of the outer diagonal strake. Two more rivets

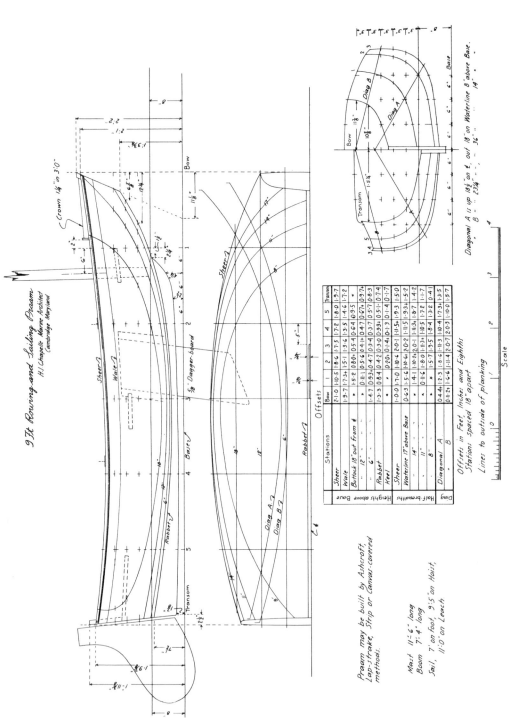

9 Ft Rowing and Sailing Praam
H.I Chapelle Marine Architect
Cambridge Maryland

Crown ¼" in 3'0"

Praam may be built by Ashcroft,
Lap-strake, Strip or Canvas-covered
methods.

Mast 11'-6" long
Boom 7'-4" long
Sail, 7' on foot, 9'-5" on Hoist,
11'-0 on Leach

Offsets

| | Stations | Bow | 1 | 2 | 3 | 4 | 5 | Transom |
|---|---|---|---|---|---|---|---|---|
| Heights above Base | Sheer | 2-1-0 | 1-10-5 | 1-8-6 | 1-7-5 | 1-7-2 | 1-8-0 | 1-9-7 |
| | Wale | 1-9-7 | 1-7-3+ | 1-5-1 | 1-3-6 | 1-3-5 | 1-4-6 | 1-7-2 |
| | Buttock 18" out from ℄ | * | 1-5-2 | 0-8-0 | 0-5-4 | 0-6-4 | 0-9-5 | * |
| | 12" " " | * | 0-11-1 | 0-5-6 | 0-4-1+ | 0-4-7 | 0-6-7+ | 0-9-7+ |
| | 6" " " | 1-4-7 | 0-9-3 | 0-4-7 | 0-3-4 | 0-3-7 | 0-5-7 | 0-8-3 |
| | Rabbet | 1-3-3 | 0-8-4 | 0-4-2 | 0-3-0 | 0-3-9 | 0-5-1 | 0-7-4 |
| | Keel | * | 0-2-0 | 0-1-4 | 0-1-3 | 0-1-4 | 0-1-4 | 0-1-7 |
| Half-breadths | Sheer | 0-0-0 | 1-7-0 | 1-10-4 | 2-0-1 | 1-11-5+ | 1-9-3 | 1-5-0 |
| | Waterline 17" above Base | 0-6-3 | 1-5-6 | 1-10-6+ | 2-0-2 | 1-11-5 | 1-9-3+ | 1-5-2 |
| | 14" " " | * | 1-4-1 | 1-10-2+ | 2-0-1 | 1-11-3+ | 1-8-7 | 1-4-2 |
| | 11" " " | * | 0-11-6 | 1-8-0 | 1-11-3+ | 1-10-5 | 1-7-2 | 1-1-7 |
| | 8" " " | * | 0-5-7 | 1-3-5 | 1-9-5 | 1-8-4 | 1-3-2 | 0-4-1 |
| Diag | Diagonal A | 0-4-4+ | 1-2-3 | 1-8-6 | 1-11-3 | 1-10-4 | 1-7-3+ | 1-3-5 |
| | B | 0-5-6 | 1-6-6+ | 1-11-4 | 2-0-7 | 2-0-3 | 1-10-0 | 1-5-7 |

Offsets in Feet, Inches and Eighths
Stations spaced 18" apart
Lines to outside of planking

Diagonal A is up 18½" on ℄, out 18" on Waterline 8"above Base.
B " " 23¼" " " 36" " " " 14" " "

Scale

PLATE 58. Plans for a 9-Foot Rowing and Sailing Praam

are then driven at the bottom of the inner sheer strake in the same manner. If appearance is important, rivets in the sheer strake are preferable to clenched nails. Copper fastenings in stringers and sheer strakes are recommended; iron, or bronze (or alloy), nails can be used in the keel batten.

All fastenings must be drilled for. A helper is a great aid in fastening; he can watch the inside to be sure the diagonal inner strakes are in position and that the drilling is being done properly for the through-fastenings. The keel-batten fastenings are not clenched or riveted, and are not through-fastenings. Later, fastenings will be required between the two skins, placed between the stringers. The skin fastenings should wait until the planking is finished. In a hard-bilged hull there is a tendency for the skins to bulge slightly between the stringers; do not be alarmed at this as the skin fastenings will overcome it to a great extent. When one outside strake is in place, fit its mate on the other side of the hull.

*Inner Skin*

The third inside strake is now fitted; this is done in the same manner as the second. It will be noticed that each strake is scribed along one edge only and that the amount of shaping will decrease as the ends of the hull are approached. Fewer fastenings will be required in the inner strakes also. When this strake is fitted and in place, make and place its mate. Now the second outer strake is put on, over the seam of the second and third inner strakes; this is scribed and fitted as the second inner strake. It is worth while to take a little more care in fitting the outer strakes, in order to get reasonably tight seams. Use plenty of luting between the two skins. If the inner strakes do not bulge, the outer strakes will lie smooth. The two skins can be clamped together, using C-clamps and battens, in fitting the outer strakes, so that their edges are home on the inner skin. As the ends of the hull are approached, the shaping of the edges of the strakes will decrease, as has been said. In some hulls, however, the shaping may take an entirely different form: the edges of some strakes may become convex instead of concave. The strakes that end on the transom edge and stem rabbet will require careful fastening. It is a good plan to put a little calking cotton, say, three or four strands, between the inner skin strakes and the transom edges and also in the stem rabbets.

## Trouble

If, in planking, it is found that some strakes bulge and cannot be brought fair along the edges, it is a sign that the strake is too wide. In most hulls there will be no serious trouble, but short, wide hulls having sharp ends may show bulging in some strakes unless the width of these strakes is reduced. If the lines show marked changes of form in the ends it will be found much easier to plank the boat with somewhat narrower strakes than specified earlier in this description. As in all round-bottom hulls, it is important that the fairness of the longitudinal curves of the side be maintained at the stern; there is often a tendency in the stringers to come inboard under pressure. This cannot be overcome by tying the ribbands abaft the stern, as they stop short at the transom frame.

The best way to avoid this difficulty is to have a mold close to the transom; if this has not been done it is usually possible to tack cross-spalls across the hull at each pair of stringers. Care must be taken, in fitting these, that the stringers are not forced outboard enough to be unfair. It would be best to place these cross-spalls before the planking crosses the mold forward of the transom, but unfortunately the stringers do not go out of fair until under the strain of planking, so the precaution of cross-spalls should be taken if the molds are widely spaced. The fastenings in the stem and stern cannot be riveted or clenched, of course. A full bow will require the boiling of some strakes. It is hardly necessary to explain why all outer strakes should be fitted before luting the inner skin.

## Narrow Strakes, Goring

In some hulls, the Ashcroft system may be rather difficult to apply. Narrow strakes will usually answer, but in some cases it may be easier to "gore" a strake or two. This consists of cutting a long narrow V down the center of a strake, starting from one end, usually that at the sheer. The width of the V can be found by first ripping the strake along the center for a foot or two and then fitting, allowing the two parts formed by the saw cut to overlap. By marking the overlap on one part, the width of the V is found. If there is a tendency to bulge at the bottom of the V, make it deeper.

### Keel, Skeg, Skin Fastenings

After the hull is planked, put on the keel or skeg. If there is a centerboard, saw out the slot in the planking, where the ends of the latter overlap the slot in the keel batten. At the fore end of the hull, the planking may form a ridge along the keel-batten center line; this may be planed off to the width of the keel or mitered along a filler strip under the outer keel. If in planking it is found that the ends of the strakes in this part of the hull will not lie on the keel batten, it is evidence that the bevels of the sides of the keel batten are faulty. In sharp-bowed hulls the ends of the strakes may stop short of the center line of the keel batten the half-breadth of the outside keel or skeg. A filler may be cut,

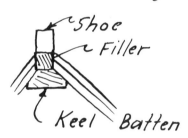

*145. Filler Strip for Shoe,
Forward*

the thickness of the two skins and the width of the outside keel. This is placed on the keel batten to fill the space between the ends of the strakes, running fore and aft, before placing the outside keel. The builder will find such dodges as this are the natural ways of overcoming an individual difficulty.

If there are spaces in the ends of the hull, inside, which are "slack" due to poor fitting, fill them with hot marine glue or paraffin. This can be done after turning the hull right side up. After righting the hull, the molds may be removed, leaving cross-spalls at the sheer to prevent the hull from changing shape. The skin fastenings that hold the two skins together between the stringers can be driven, partly before the molds are removed and partly afterward. In a small boat these are usually clenched copper tacks or nails; in a large, they may be screws driven from the inside of the hull. In driving these skin fastenings, any slight bulges in the edges of outside strakes should be pulled up smooth. Such bulges may be pulled up, before drilling for the fastening, by screwing a cleat to the outside skin over the bulge, forcing the bulge out temporarily. Then fastenings may be driven on either side of the cleat to hold the gain; when the cleat is removed another fastening may be required in its place. The screw holes can be puttied or filled with plastic wood, or a rivet can be driven in the holes. When these matters have been taken care of, the outside sheer strake can be fastened, riveting it through the two skins and the inner sheer strake, and screwing the ends through all, into the stem and transom edges. Finishing the hull from this point on is like that of any other round-bottom hull.

## Watertightness

The watertightness of the Ashcroft planking depends upon the material placed between the skins. As the area covered on each side of an inner skin seam by an outer strake is so large, there is little difficulty in obtaining a tight hull. Repairs to the planking of the hull planked in the Ashcroft manner are difficult. In large hulls the life of the planking is not likely to be as long as that of carvel or lap-strake. This is the case with all double-skin planking, however.

## Double-Diagonal

In large hulls the double-diagonal planking can be used to advantage. This is done by first laying the whole inner skin in the Ashcroft manner, but raking forward. Fasten this to the stringers with staging nails. When this skin is complete, start the fitting of the first outer skin strake in the Ashcroft manner but raking it aft so that it crosses the inner skin seams at about a right angle. The staging nails in the inner skin will have to be removed in way of this strake, for fitting. When the strake has been fitted, varnish or glue the inner skin and lay thin muslin while this is still wet. The muslin should be torn in strips about 2 or 3 inches wider than the outer strakes. Lute over the muslin and fasten on the outer strake. At the edges of this strake, drive the fastenings through small cleats that will overlap the edges; these serve to hold the next strake while fitting. The second outside strake is put on in the same manner, taking care that the muslin under it is overlapping the edges of the first piece put on. Only the outer edge of this and the rest of the strakes need be fastened with cleated nails. As the planking progresses, these may be removed and replaced with regular fastenings. The skin fastenings are driven as in the Ashcroft system. The use of a temporary outside batten keel is required to hold the keel end of the outside strakes.[1]

## Double-Skin, Inner Diagonal

Double-skin planking, with the inner skin diagonal and the outer skin carvel, is not extremely difficult. The inner skin is laid diagonally, raking aft as in the Ashcroft system. The whole of the inner skin is laid as in double-diagonal planking just described. The muslin or silk is employed in the same manner as in the latter method. The inner skin is usually fastened with staging nails, or nails in cleats, though in a large boat it may be well to use permanent fastenings instead. The outer skin is then lined off carvel fashion, and the first strake fitted, then secured, with the edge against which the second strake will rest held with cleated nails. The cleats will help to hold a spiling batten and the second strake while fitting. When this strake is fitted and placed, the cleats are split and the nails driven home, in the first strake. It is very important that the inner skin be smooth and fair. As in regular double-skin carvel, good lining off of the outer skin is required; and, like it, the diagonal and carvel should not be attempted by the beginner building his first boat.

## Strip-Planking Limitations

Strip planking is a form of carvel in which narrow strips are used instead of the usual strakes. It is a popular form of plank-

---

[1] The complete handbook of the Ashcroft system of planking has been lately republished in a fifth edition, revised and rewritten by Edwin Austin, published by Captain O. M. Watts, London, England.

ing in some parts of the United States, but is not favored by professional builders because of the large number of fastenings required. However, since it is relatively easy to fit, strip planking is suited for amateur construction. It can be used on any hull form designed for carvel, though a long, narrow hull is easiest to plank with this method, as it is with other systems. As in clench-built hulls, the frames are bent in after the hull is planked, but the strip-planked hull requires very few frames. The disadvantages of strip planking are: the weight compared to clench-built hulls, the amount of labor in fastening, the desirability of having machine tools available, and the difficulty in repairing the planking in the finished hull. The strips used instead of strakes are narrow enough to be edge-fastened with galvanized wire finishing nails, as a rule. In most hulls the strips are 1½ inches wide, but in large hulls 2- or 3-inch strips are used and the edge-fastenings are increased in size. In large craft of 50 or 60 feet length, the strips are edge-fastened with long spikes. The appearance of strip planking depends upon the seams; to obtain a satisfactory appearance, it is necessary to bevel the edges of the strips, so that the seams are reasonably tight. One scheme to overcome the labor of this is to use a power shaper (or "sticker") to hollow the bottom edge and round the top edge of each strip. By this means, the upper strip sets down over the lower strip and can be swung out of line of the faces without opening a seam. The best practice in strip planking is to combine straight, parallel-edged strips with some that are tapered each way from the middle. This requires the use of a bandsaw, if the labor of getting out the strips is to be lessened.

### Lofting and Setup

The strip-planked hull is lofted and set up in the usual way. It is easiest to build a hull, planked with strips, right side up. The molds should be close together, particularly in the ends of the hull. The whole structure should be well braced, as in setting up for other types of planking. Ribbands need not be fastened to the molds and are required only at the sheer, to stiffen the molds and to check the fairing.

## Lining Off

It is a good plan to line off a strip-planked hull in this manner: take a pair of dividers and set them at the width of strip the builder intends to use. Space off the mold of greatest girth, from rabbet to sheer, to see how many strips will be required to plank up each side. Then take a thin, rather narrow batten and line off the molds, beginning at the sheer. The strips should be parallel-

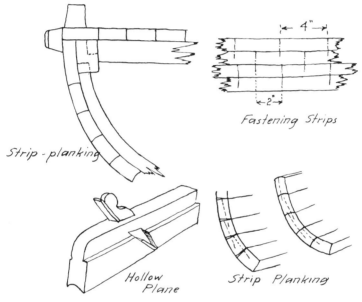

Strip-planking

4"

Fastening Strips

2"

Hollow Plane

Strip Planking

*146. Strip Planking*

sided from the sheer down to a little above the turn of the bilge. Line these off, marking the edges of the strips on the molds and bow and stern so that the position of each strip can be found later. Now line off from the keel up, beginning with the gar-board. This is usually a tapered strip, the taper arbitrarily fixed so that the ends of the strips are not less than 1 inch wide. With this lined off, the spaces between the top of the garboard marks and the marks for the lowest parallel-edged strip can be checked on the mold of greatest girth, then set off on the bow and stern, or on molds very close to them. This will show how much taper

would normally be required in strips filling these spaces. Since
there must be one fastening, into the bow or stern, at each end
of the strips, it is apparent that they should be not less than
seven twelfths the greatest width of the strips. If the spacing
indicates that the ends of the strips must be narrower than this,
a forward or after stealer will have to be used, to reduce two
strips to one, before the stem or stern is reached. Usually the
arbitrary taper of seven twelfths the width of the strip is required
only at the forward ends of the strips; the after ends are wider.
If necessary, a stealer aft can be added, as in carvel, to gain on
the stern. While lining off, the appearance of the seams should
be considered. It may be desirable to use some tapered strips in
the topsides, if the sheer is flat. If there is great flare in the hull
forward it may be well to plan on a spiled sheer strake or spiled
strips, to prevent an apparent wave in the seams in the flare. In
lining off the bottom, it may also be wise to start with a spiled
plank garboard, with the top shaped to overcome the effects of
great drag to the keel rabbet. Or, if the hull is wide and flat, a
plank garboard running from a shim end forward to a shim end
aft, close to the stern, may be useful. It is worth while to spend a
little time in lining off the strips, as planning may save trouble
when planking up. If care is used, the strip-planked hull will
show as good a job of lining off as a regular carvel job.

## Making Strips

It is a good idea to get out templates of the two types of strips
used; the straight, parallel-edged ones, and the tapered ones. One
template of each type will usually serve. The tapered template
can have one edge straight as the strips will be edgeset anyway,
when in place. The templates can be taken to a woodworking
shop, where they can be used to get out the strips. In sawing the
strips, allow a little extra width for beveling and smoothing. If
the strips must be scarfed to obtain sufficient length, get out the
two pieces that make up one strip with lots of overlap so that
the scarfs can shift when planking up; they must not come close
together in neighboring strakes. If it is intended to use hollow and
round edges, mark the strips that are tapered so that the fore end
can be quickly identified; then take the strips to the shaper and
hollow the bottom edge and round the top of each, except the

bottom of the garboard strip and the top of the sheer strip. Both of these should be about one fourth wider than the other strips so that any loss in fitting will not make the strakes run short of width in these two parts of the hull planking. A few extra strips should be run off to allow for spoilage; 10 per cent is the usual allowance.

### Planking Schedule, Fastenings, Garboard

The planking schedule is to work from the keel rabbet upward to the sheer. The garboard goes on first. Fit this by spiling if necessary, edgesetting if strips are used here. If a plank garboard is employed, put in some floor timbers to which it can be fastened. If a strip garboard is used, it is edge-fastened to the keel, using galvanized finishing nails, or larger fastenings if required; these are closely spaced. Small craft fastened with nails have

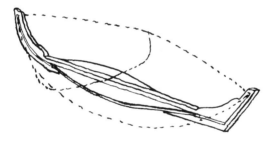

*147. Plank Garboard for Strip Planking*

4-inch spacing; spikes should be spaced 6 to 8 inches, according to size. The edge-fastenings should all be drilled for and well set when driven. Mark the position of each fastening on the outside of the strip so that new fastenings in the next strip will not foul them. The end fastenings are usually single and are driven as in carvel construction. When one garboard is in place, fit and fasten the mate.

### Planking-Up

The next strip is a tapered one; it is set in place and the ends fitted. It may be held to the molds with clamps or staging nails. After fitting, remove and lute the top edge of the garboard. Then set the strip in place and secure. Then edge-fasten to the garboard, as was done with the latter strip, and finally fasten at bow and stern. If the edges require bevel (the hollow and round edges not being used), this must be done before luting the top of the garboard. Only one edge of each strip need be beveled. After a little experience this can be done largely by eye. The beginner will need to scribe the inside edge of the strip between the molds before removing the strip for trimming. The strips are put in place, one by one, working on each side of the hull alternately and edge-fastening from the middle toward either end. If the strips must be scarfed, the forward strip is fitted first, as in carvel. The scarfs need not be long: sufficient length to drive two fastenings is ample. No individual scarf fastenings are necessary; the usual edge-fastenings of the strake will serve not only to secure the strake but also the scarf.

When planking up, it may be found that the strips are not coming to the lining-off marks, due to loss in width in beveling, or hollow-and-rounding. Do not attempt to correct this until the sheer is reached. The wider strip, used here, will correct the loss; if not, use a still wider strip. Allow for the bevel of the top of the sheer, to take the deck or gunwale cap. As each strip goes into place, do not hesitate to twist it and edgeset it so that it fits tightly against the molds and the strip below. The method of fastening prevents an accumulation of stress in the hull that could cause it to change shape. The use of waterproof glue between the strips is a good plan if the wood is well seasoned and the seams smooth and tight.

When the hull is planked, it is smoothed off in the usual manner, the frames having been bent in as in clench building. A thin batten bent inside the boat, to represent the position of the frame, should be used to line off the frames. The fastenings of the frames should be bored from the inside of the hull, prior to bending the frames. Heavily planked, strip-built hulls often have only two or three frames; these are placed where the strains are greatest—-at the mast partners or thwarts and at the ends of the cockpit and under the engine beds. A sheer clamp is often fitted against the inside of the sheer strake, into which the deck beams are notched and fastened, as in sharpies and other boats without frames. If there are enough frames, however, the sheer clamp is inside the frames as usual.

## Strip Scantlings

It is impossible to give minute dimensions for the thickness of strip planking. In very small boats it is between ⅜ and ½ of an inch. Fifteen- to 20-foot hulls have strip planking between ½ and ⅝ of an inch. Twenty- to 30-foot hulls have between ¾ of an inch and 1⅛ inches; 30- to 50-foot hulls, 1⅛ to 1¾ inches. Larger hulls often have strips nearly square in section amidships, from 2 to 3 inches thick.

## Edge-Boring

In boring for any plank edge-fastening, when either the diameter of the fastening or the depth of the boring is great, a helper is useful. If he puts his hands flat on the side of the plank being edge-bored he can feel the drill if it comes near to either surface of the plank, before it breaks through. As the drill sinks he should try to keep his hands opposite the point. By this means, the boring can be corrected before actually breaking the surface by off-boring.

## Notes

Steaming or boiling strips may be required in some hulls. Strip planking, well fastened, makes a hull very stiff longitudinally and has all the advantages of laminated construction. It is excellent for motorboat hulls subject to vibration. The life of the planking depends upon the watertightness of the seams: so lute well. If the strips are made up by hand, wooden molding planes to make the hollow and round can be used instead of beveling. Making strips by hand is a rather tedious job. Sometimes it is desirable to use a narrower strip than planned, at some place in the hull, such as at the turn of a hard bilge; hand cutting is then necessary. The beginner should understand that strip planking is a slow job; time saved elsewhere in construction by use of strip planking is the best excuse for its use in preference to ordinary carvel.

## Plywood Construction

The development of waterproof plywood in recent years has led to a new method of planking, using panels of this material.

So recent has been the development of this material that the technique of building hulls with it has not been fully explored. At present the material is limited to chine-model hulls; the round-bottom plywood hull (built of veneer somewhat on the Ashcroft system) requires special equipment out of reach of the individual builder and is only economically possible in stock-built

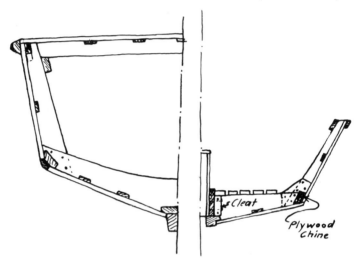

*148. Plywood Construction*

models. The hull of a plywood-planked boat should be designed so that the sheets, or panels, of the material can be applied. To some extent, the panels limit the hull design, as large compound curves are not possible. The limitations of the panels in this respect are best illustrated in a sheet of paper.

## *Advantages*

The advantages of plywood are such that it is particularly suited for amateur builders. The use of large panels, which may be obtained in varying sizes and thicknesses, enables a hull to be planked easily and rapidly, with very few seams. Not only is the material very strong, but it is also very light when compared to other forms of hull planking. The lasting qualities of the material are generally excellent, assuming reasonable care in building and upkeep. It should be emphatically pointed out that plywood must be painted or otherwise protected against dampness, which will cause reaction in the wood making up the panels, even though it will not affect the adhesive. The panels are flexible and stiffeners, or frames, are required in the hull planked with plywood. At the time of writing, large plywood hulls are more expensive than hulls of the same size planked carvel. It is doubtful if there is any particular advantage in large plywood sailing hulls, the light weight of which would be of no value. Large power hulls, of plywood, might show to better advantage, however. It is very important that the edges and ends of the plywood panels used in planking or constructing a hull be sealed or covered; the raw edges of a panel must never be exposed.

## Scantlings

Because of its great strength, plywood planking could be much thinner than any other form of planking. However, the panels are so flexible that it is recommended that planking panels be not less than 60 per cent, in thickness, of carvel planking. When weight is important, the thickness of panel must be carefully considered. If too thick the weight of planking will be unnecessarily great; if too thin the hull will be too flexible or the framing will have to be so increased that weight is added there, to an excessive degree. As the stock panel thicknesses do not always work out at 60 per cent of carvel, 75 per cent is commonly used instead.

## Limitations

To some extent framing can be made of plywood. The sole difficulty is that the edge-fastenings of plywood are of the same character as end-grain fastenings in timber. It is necessary, therefore, to use fastenings 50 per cent longer than would be used elsewhere. The use of cleats, secured to the sides of a plywood frame, to which the planking is fastened, is common, but adds to the weight of the frames. Plywood chines, sheer clamps, or stringers are practical; use chines, however, only when the flare and dead rise of the hull are great enough so that planking fastenings in the chine cross the laminations at slight angles and do not follow the seams between the plys. Plywood stiffeners in the hull must be carefully fitted and well fastened to be effective; the material is not sufficiently rigid to form large stiffeners subject to compression without the addition of timber to the stiffener. Plywood bulkheads subject to compression should be framed and stiffeners of timber added to prevent "blowing." Tension structures of plywood need no additional bracing. Except in very small craft, plywood should not be used for knees under the mast partners.

### Sealing and Cutting, Fastening

In planking with plywood there will be little difficulty if the hull has been correctly designed for such construction. As each piece is fitted, the edges should be sealed with clear resin sealers made for this purpose, or marine glue, aluminum paint, or good spar varnish. If any framing is of plywood, sealing should be done after fitting but before finally placing the member in the hull. The amateur builder, to whom time is not usually a matter of prime importance, can apply a number of coats of sealing material. Make sure the sealer covers the raw edges completely. Use a fine-toothed saw on plywood; a panel saw is also very useful. At the chine, use a batten between the bottom and sides, to form the outside chine angle; this protects the raw edges of panels above and below the chine. Muslin, set in hot marine glue, may be used instead, in very small boats. Fastenings are not countersunk. Screws are generally used to fasten plywood and are driven home so that the countersunk head compresses the surface fibers and the countersink is thus formed by pressure. A screwdriver bit in a brace is best for driving these fastenings by hand; be sure the driver bit is properly ground to fit the slots of the screws used. Use a good quality of screws—never brass, which will not stand hard driving.

Never attempt to countersink and bung, even in thick panels. Use butt blocks luted with glue, or some of the mastics made for this purpose. Scarfs can be used, 12 times the thickness of the panel in length, but are very hard to make by hand. Panels can be scarfed together by the makers so as to obtain long lengths, but, of course, this is rather expensive, and is therefore not ordered very often. Plywood seams should be calked in the same manner as thin carvel planking. Fastenings along the seams may be as close together as the timber underneath the panels will permit.

While there is no danger of splitting a panel, the frame, or timber under a seam, may be split by improper fastening. In the best grade of plywood construction, the panels stand in batten-formed rabbets at the chine, keel, stem, transom, or stern, and at the rail. Plywood can be used to advantage in the chine gussets of small V-bottom or flat-bottom hulls.

## Finishing

Finishing plywood planking requires certain precautions, particularly if the surfaces are fir. This timber will surface check, and the grain will rise when exposed. To reduce this to a minimum, paint with a clear resin sealer as a prime coat. It is a good plan to paint the inside of all panels after they are fitted but before finally fastening them in place. The outside can be primed afterward. The sealer keeps dampness out of the panels and acts as a preservative to some extent. Panels can be had in birch and mahogany surfaces; these, too, should be sealed with a clear resin sealer, or varnished with spar varnish before painting. The maker should be consulted before applying commercial wood preservatives in order to avoid using an unsuitable chemical. Waterproofing the surfaces by other means than the sealers listed is another matter on which it is best to consult the maker. It will be found that the manufacturers of marine plywoods will co-operate and give useful advice on the latest practices in plywood construction and finishing.

## Bending

The bending of plywood deserves special attention. Steaming or boiling may be resorted to, if necessary. Because of the structure of plywood, there is a more limited range to bending by this means than with a simple timber. Too much bending will put great tension on the outer ply and great compression on the inner ply. These may eventually fail, even though they do not at the time they are bent. Extreme bends may be made by cutting shallow saw kerfs across the compression face before bending. The saw kerfs should be close together and not more than one third the thickness of the panel in depth. The kerfs can be filled with marine glue before fastening the panel in place.

## Decks

Plywood is coming into wide use for decks. The sole difficulty is in the compound curves required in some decks; cutting gores and taping the seam formed are sometimes resorted to. Plywood planks, cut in wide strakes, can be utilized; the seams should be backed with battens. It is possible even to plank a hull not designed for plywood construction by this means, using a batten-seam construction, but, of course, there is little practical advantage in this, compared to the use of timber.

## Plywood Frames

The possibility of using plywood frames in round-bottom hulls would be an interesting study. If it were possible to find a manufacturer who would stock a line of frames bent in manufacture to a relatively few curves, extremely strong framing would be available; these could be steamed or boiled to slightly modify the curves and to set the bevels in the ribbands. Heavy plywood stringers and clamps would have definite advantages in some hulls. The application of plywood to joinerwork, both on deck and below, has obvious possibilities and is much used in stock boats. The swelling and shrinking of plywood are so slight that it may be canvas covered by gluing or cementing canvas to the whole face of the panel; this will form a very hard, water-resisting surface, either on decks or sides and bottoms of hulls. It is a good plan to paint a plywood hull inside and out, and to take pains to keep her well painted after launching.

## Panel Sizes

Stock fir panels vary somewhat as to structure as their thickness increases; the thinnest panel is $\frac{1}{8}$ of an inch and the thicknesses increase by eighths to $\frac{7}{8}$ of an inch. The panels measure from 4 by 6 feet to 4 by 16 feet, but the largest size is not available in all thicknesses; 4 by 10 feet or 4 by 12 feet are the largest in some cases. The number of plies used varies with the thickness and also with the surface material; fir panels are usually 3-ply to $\frac{3}{8}$-inch thickness and 5-ply above. Birch, mahogany, and teak-surfaced panels are available in thicknesses from $\frac{1}{16}$ to $\frac{7}{8}$ of an inch; panels thicker than ³⁄₁₆ of an inch are usually 5-ply. It is sometimes very difficult to get panels other than those made of fir in local supply houses; if teak or mahogany panels are required, order them well ahead of time.

## Fiber Panels

The use of waterproof pressed-fiber boards in place of plywood is possible. The structure required is the same as in plywood construction. The pressed-fiber boards have about the same advantages as plywood, but do not withstand sharp blows as well and must be treated like canvas on battens; a stout floor is necessary in the cockpit to prevent damage in stepping into the hull.

## Canvas-Covered Hulls

Canvas-covered hulls are built only in the very small sizes, dinghies and canoes. The structure of these is basically a carvel-planked hull covered with canvas. The planking is very thin and is supported by wide, thin, closely spaced frames. No attempt is made to get watertight seams in the planking. The planking, usually ¼ or ⁵⁄₁₆ of an inch thick, is tacked to the frames and to the stem and stern. No rabbet is required at the stem; the inner stem is merely beveled off to take the planking. After the hull is canvased, the steam-bent outer stem and an outside keel are added. The inner keel is sometimes a batten, but generally one strake of the bottom planking forms the keel, the shoe outside being the real keel member.

The molds are set up and ribbanded off as in a carvel-planked hull, usually upside down. The frames are then bent over the ribbands and the planking is laid on. No attempt is made to line off to get a good appearance to the seams, since they will be masked by the canvas. The gunwale stringer is inside the frames, in the form of a sheer clamp, and is put on with the ribbands. If there is a heavy keel, it is on top of the frames, or is notched on the underside to fit over them, as a keelson, and is also put on the molds with the ribbands. Thwarts or spreaders are often put in with the ribbands or with the gunwale stringer. The planking is given a coat of paint and the canvas is stretched over it and tacked.

The canvas is usually stretched by clamping the ends between two timbers and hauling out with a small tackle. The canvas is tacked to the hull at keel and gunwale, or at the ends of the hull and gunwale if no keel is used, beginning at the middle of the hull and worked both ways toward the ends. The process is much like that used in laying a canvas-covered deck. The ends are tacked last and then the canvas is trimmed off wherever necessary. The canvas is then painted with a number of coats until a smooth surface is built up. This method of building is simple and easy, and the resulting hull is tight and strong. The only disadvantage is that the canvas is easily damaged by landing on beaches or grounding on rubbish. As a rule, the last members to go on a canvas hull are the guards. Copper tacks are used for fastenings wherever possible. If it is desired to build up a glossy surface on canvas, dampen it lightly with water and then paint with very thick paint. When this has been done, and while the paint is still wet, rub it into the canvas with wooden blocks. This will form a hard prime surface when dry and can be worked perfectly smooth. The other coats can then go on. Putty, dissolved in benzine, and applied in numerous coats to build up a surface, is used for a canvas filler by some.

## Canvas-Batten Construction

Some canvas-covered hulls are not planked; the canvas is laid over ribbands. This construction is used only in very light canoes or kyacks. Though very simple, this method does not produce a very strong covering and should be used only in hulls that must be carried about a good deal. No description of building is necessary as the plans from which the canoe is built will be self-explanatory. A form of iron pliers, used by upholsterers for stretching fabric, may be used for stretching canvas.

## Rowboats

Rowboats are worthy of discussion; they are among the most common types built by amateurs. A good rowboat is one that rows easily, is a good carrier, a good seaboat for her size, and is sufficiently stiff for safety. If the boat is used as a tender to another and larger boat, she must be light enough to be lifted on deck, either by hand or by davits or other gear, and she must tow well. In most cases it is also necessary that the boat have a fixed limitation on length, so that she can be stowed on the deck of a cruiser. As a result, most tenders on small yachts are too small to row well, carry well, or to be good seaboats. If there is a great distance

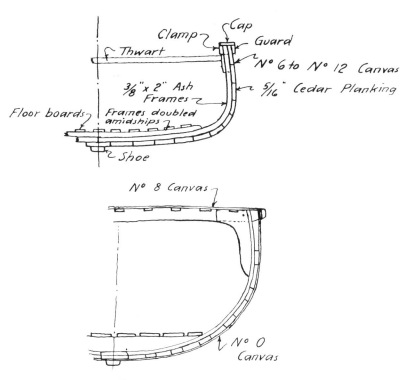

*149. Canvas and Batten, 15-Foot Canoe*

to be rowed, the short yacht dinghy is very tiring. It is unfortunately true that it is quite impossible to get a really fine rowboat in lengths under 14 feet. A boat shorter than this will stop between each stroke of the oars, with a headwind, and will not "run." The lighter the short boat, the more objectionable she is in this respect. Probably the least desirable rowboat, from the standpoint of handling under oars, is the praam, without a long skeg, either flat- or round-bottom. Such a boat will not run straight, will not maintain way between strokes, and is often unsafe in even a moderate amount of rough water. In spite of this, the type is often necessary to the yachtsman with a small cruiser.

Flat-bottom rowing craft have a bad name generally; the fault which led to this is excessive rocker to the bottom. The well-designed flat-bottom skiff has her chine profile perfectly straight from the heel of the stem, aft and slightly downward, to about one third the over-all length. From here the chine starts to curve through the middle third; the after third is the run, formed by bringing the chine up in a sweeping curve, slightly flattened near the stern, to a little above the water line. The hull should have the heel of the stem nearly touching the water when empty. The transom should not be so shoal that there is a sharp upturn to the chine aft. The run should not be so short that it comes up from the bottom in a short, quick arc.

Flat-bottom hulls do not row well when short and wide. Prams are best designed with V- or round-bottoms. Though almost never seen, there should be both a bow and a stern skeg on a pram if she is to row well. The bow skeg can be much like the one at the stern, but shoaler and rounded off in profile forward. The pram usually tows well and the bow skeg will not destroy this advantage if the towing ring or grommet is low in the skeg at the bow.

V-bottom rowing hulls are not very common for some reason; they are excellent pulling boats if properly designed. Here, again, good rowing qualities depend upon length, but a short boat may be designed so that she is a practical tender. A short V-bottom hull should have a strong sheer if used in rough water. A properly designed V-bottom tender will tow very well. She should have a long, straight skeg; the forefoot should be shoal or well rockered. The dead rise should be slight and the beam moderate. Such hulls are sometimes to be found among the plywood tenders.

The round-bottom tender should be high-sided, wide, rather flat-floored, and should have a great deal of sheer, if she is under 14 feet in length. The lack of sheer is one of the most common faults. The stern should be wide in a short boat. Double-ended round-bottom tenders are often splendid rowboats for their length. If the stern is full at the gunwale, the boat will carry better than if she is alike at bow and stern. Nevertheless, the boat shaped like a New Bedford Whaleboat, or the smaller Jonesport Peapod seen to the eastward on the Maine coast, is one of the finest rowing types for use in rough water, or where a long pull is common. For rough water, weight is somewhat desirable, as long as it is not excessive. These double-enders usually tow fairly well. If they are rather flat-floored they are very stiff and carry well. Fairly hard bilges are desirable in a boat that must carry heavy loads; slack bilges are best in a boat for long pulls. The run of a transom-sterned dinghy should not be full and short, but should be long and as flat as the depth permits.

### Bilge Boards

Bilge boards are not very common, except in racing craft designed for very high speed under sail—the Inland Lake Scows for example. The bilge boards are of various forms, some pivoted in the usual way and some of the dagger form. The cases are small and are placed opposite to one another, one in each bilge. They are fitted so that they stand at an angle to the water line athwartships, tumbling home. This causes the boards to splay outward at the bottom when down. Though the boards are small, the cases should be quite strong and well braced. Usually the slots for the bilge boards come through the deck and so the deck beams are cut in the way of them. If this is done, carlins (running along each side of the cases at the slots) should be fitted and well secured to the through-beams at each end of the slots; the cut beams should be well fastened to the carlins. Often these carlins are of plank, laid on the flat. The headledges of the cases should stand on a bed fitted to the inside of the bilge planking and fastened to it, and the headledges should pass through this bed with their ends on the inside of the planking. The frames that are cut for the slot should notch into the beds and be fastened there. The case sides usually stand on the beds or are rabbeted into them. The headledges tenon into the deck beams at each end of the slot.

As weight is important, the size of the beds and carlins must be only enough for strength. Usually the designer will give complete details of these cases in his plans. The angle the bilge boards stand to the water line, when down, viewed end-on, is usually about 72 to 75 degrees. Roughly, they may be figured to be perpendicular when the hull is heeled 15 or 17 degrees from the vertical. Bilge boards might be used to advantage in multi-chine hulls, or even in V-bottoms.

## Remarks

The various substitutions in construction and planking for orthodox methods that have been described should be looked upon only as possibilities when they are suited to the hull design, the use to which the boat is to be put, and the materials available. It may be well to keep in mind the fact that no method of building is strictly "easy"; any method requires work—careful work—and time.

# CHAPTER EIGHT

# JOINERWORK, PLUMB-
# ING, INSTALLATION,
# SPARMAKING, AND
# FINISHING

## Proportion Completed

*W*HEN the hull is completed, the amateur builder may feel that the boat is nearly done; but this is true only when the craft is a small, open boat. If there is a cabin, the building is by no means "nearly done" at this stage of construction; the amount of work required to complete the boat is in direct proportion to the amount of accommodation. Much time will be consumed in making cabin fittings, doing the plumbing and wiring, installing and fitting the engine and its controls, making spars, fitting rigging and its hardware, and painting. The greater the number of gadgets in the cabin and on deck, the more time required to build and properly install them; also time will be required to make the necessary changes in design of these gadgets, which always seem to be necessary to make them work. It is well to keep the fact in mind that professional builders look upon a cruiser as only about one third complete when the hull is planked and the deck laid. This will explain why the construction seems to make such slow progress in the "finishing-up" stage.

## Checking Hardware, Schedule of Work

When the hull is completed and the deck laid, it is a good plan to sit down and carefully study the plans and specifications.

Check over the list of fittings and hardware to make sure all are on hand. Inspect the hardware and see how each piece is to be fastened, and then make sure the proper fastenings are on hand. Don't overlook such details as bronze or brass lags, bolts, eyes, flat or oval head screws, pipe fittings, wiring fittings and fixtures, door hardware, and the many other small things a boat requires if she has a cabin. The few hours spent in this checking may save days when actually working on the boat. Next, think about the best way to schedule the work: should the engine be completely installed before the joinerwork? If the latter is put in first will there be great difficulty in connecting the plumbing, or in wiring? Suppose the joinerwork is put in first—will some of it have to be pulled out to connect the exhaust pipe or to put in ballast? In answering such questions as these, it will be apparent that careful planning of the work is required. In many cases it will be impossible, or impractical, to complete all the plumbing before doing some of the joinerwork, or vice versa. If you wish to avoid discouragement and annoyance, make sure you have the necessary materials and tools on hand before starting to work. If, on the other hand, you wish to experience a proper "headache," just sail right into the work, planning to get what you need when you need it, and to work with such materials as happen to be at hand. After completing a boat in this fashion you will be fitted to understudy an acrobat, or the carnival "rubber man," if you remain reasonably sane, but it is an excellent bet that the boat will neither be satisfactory nor like the plans.

## Installation Schedule

If there is a motor, it is usually best to install it and the tanks before doing the cabin joinerwork; often it is desirable to do at least part of the engine installation before the deck joinerwork is completed. The propeller shaft and its bearings, or stuffing boxes, should usually be put in place, the engine temporarily aligned, the tanks and their foundations placed, the engine exhaust pipe partially completed, and the engine piping started before much of the joinerwork in the cabin is built. If there is cabin plumbing, some of this should also be done—the outboard connections particularly. In some boats the cabin plumbing can be completed gradually, with the joinerwork; in others it will be better to complete the plumbing first. Except in rare instances, wiring is less likely to be troublesome and may be done when the cabin joinery is completed, but not painted.

## Instructions for Installation

The engine and tanks should be installed and fitted as shown in the plans and specifications. The engine manufacturer usually gives complete general instructions, in the instruction book or pamphlet accompanying the engine, for piping and wiring the engine and for installation. It is well worth the builder's time to read and follow these instructions.

## Engine Beds, Drip Pan

The engine beds, or stringers and beds, must first be prepared. These are shaped according to the plans, as explained earlier. They must be well secured to the floor timbers, or bearers; care must be taken so that they are in contact with each floor timber, or bearer. Chocks, or braces, placed against the sides of the beds may be required, if the beds must be high, to prevent lateral motion. The drip pan, if one is required underneath the engine, should first be placed. This is a shallow metal pan with a drain cock at one end and is used to catch any leakage of oil, or overflow of fuel, near the engine. The pan may be of copper or galvanized iron. The drain cock should usually be off-center and must be at the low end of the pan. The width of the pan should be that required to fit it between the engine beds. The length of the pan should be sufficient to permit it to reach from a little forward of the engine flywheel to a little forward, or a little abaft, the coupling. The depth of the pan is obviously decided by the height of the engine beds above the floor timbers and by the shape of the engine base. If possible, the depth of the pan is sufficient to clear the engine base by 5 or 6 inches. As there is a possibility that the pan may rattle or drum, most builders insert felt weather stripping between the floor timbers and the bottom of the pan, and also between the sides and the engine beds.

To make the pan of practical use, there must be room under the drain to insert a suitable receptacle—a small pan or pail. If this cannot be done, the pan will have to be pumped out, or the pan might be omitted. In auxiliary vessels it is often impossible to make the pan deep enough to prevent its spilling when the hull is heeled, in which case the pan is of no practical value. In these craft it is a better plan to make the floor timbers at each end of the engine space water and oil tight; then use a separate bilge pump for the space. As a general rule, the drip pan is practical only in powerboats.

## Location of Engine

With the pan in place, the position of the engine should be accurately marked. This may be done by scaling the plans, if no dimensions are given by the designer. Usually the most convenient dimensions are along the shaft line, either from the deadwood at the flange of the inner stuffing box, the outside end of the skeg, or the intersection of the shaft line as projected to the center line of the rudderpost, to the face of the engine half of the coupling at the engine. When the scaled dimension is found, it may be laid off by stretching a chalk line or wire through the shaft hole for the shaft center line and measuring. A steel square can be used to transfer the measured points from the shaft line to the beds. The catalogue or installation drawings will give the dimensions from the coupling face to the after lugs, which are the only ones that need to be marked on the beds. It is important that the marking be accurate.

## Hoisting in Engine

The engine may now be hoisted into the hull. This may require help; if the engine is heavy it is often desirable to call in professionals, house or furniture movers, who have the required gear, rather than to attempt to handle the engine with makeshift equipment. The engine manufacturer usually gives instructions for making fast the slings required to hoist an engine; these should be followed to prevent damage to some part of the engine.

## Placing Engine and Checking

When the engine is lowered into the hull, the after lugs should be brought to the marks on the beds, but the beds should not be bored for the lug fastenings until the shaft is aligned. When the engine is in place, insert the propeller shaft and check it for length and alignment. If the shafthole is not in alignment it must be corrected. Handle the shaft and couplings with care; any damage will prevent proper alignment.

## Lining Up, Fitting Shaft

Lining up the engine and shaft is no easy task; it requires both care and patience. It is done by shifting the engine until the faces of the coupling at the engine are in contact all around their circumference. The shaft must first be placed into the after half of the engine coupling. The shaft must fit the coupling very accurately, and a key between shaft and coupling is necessary. If the shaft cannot be inserted into the coupling without driving, do not hammer the coupling. Heat it in a pail of boiling water until it expands enough to permit the shaft to be pushed into place.

## Shaft Length, Ordering Shaft

A good deal of trouble can be avoided if the shaft has been ordered correctly. Its length can be scaled from the plans; it is a useful precaution to check this on the loft plan. The diameter of the shaft is found in the engine manufacturer's catalogue; it is governed by the engine coupling. In the event that a shaft of the required diameter is not obtainable, use a shaft larger than the required diameter rather than smaller. The larger shaft can be machined to fit the coupling; do not machine the coupling unless it was obtained without being bored. The shaft may be ordered from a marine hardware dealer and should be specified to be "machined." This includes truing up the shaft so that the face of the coupling is square to the center line of the shaft, and cutting the keyway at the engine coupling, as well as tapering and cutting threads and keyway for the propeller. It is a time-saving plan to order shaft and propeller as a unit so that they may be both correctly machined before being received by the builder.

## Engine Beds, Plates and Shims

So far as the engine beds are concerned, it is assumed that they were built and lined up according to the plans, and to fit the engine. The method of lining them has already been described.

If the engine is very heavy, or if the engine beds are of softwood, recent practice is to top the beds with structural steel angles, or to use channels instead of beds inside the engine stringers. The tops of these, or of the beds, should be from $\frac{1}{16}$ to $\frac{1}{2}$ inch below the bottom of the engine lugs, depending on the size of the engines, to allow for shims. These shims may be of thin sheet metal, or may be a patented article purchased from a marine hardware dealer under the name of "adjustable engine bed shims." Jacks, a chain lift, or tackle, and a crowbar will be required to shift most engines in lining up. Softwood beds are sometimes topped with hardwood strips, 2 or 3 inches deep and fastened clear of the engine lugs.

## Shaft Bearings, Etc.

If the shaft is long, intermediate bearings may be required. The placing of an intermediate bearing has already been mentioned. Supports for a shaft should be spaced about 40 x diameter of shaft. In ordering bearings and stuffing boxes it will be found that there is a selection possible that will fit almost any condition or use. Take the inside stuffing box; this is obtainable in many shapes and sizes. Usually the "self-aligning" type is preferable. If a sprung keel is to be fitted, the adjustable, or "self-aligning," shaft log is used. Marine hardware dealers' catalogues illustrate the standard designs. The outside stuffing box, or stern bearing, is available in many shapes. Some are watertight stuffing boxes, while others are merely bearings to be used when there is a tight, inside stuffing box. If there is a skeg or deadwood, it is usual to use a watertight bearing outside and a stuffing box inside, connected with a lead tube, or a bronze pipe or tube. If bronze pipe or tube is used, the stuffing box and outside bearing are purchased in a unit, designed and threaded to take the pipe or tube. Struts are sometimes used instead of the skeg, or sternpost, bearing; the adjustable single-arm strut is preferable in small craft. The bearings, used in struts, stuffing boxes, intermediate bearings, and outside bearings, are made of various materials, to suit many requirements. Babbitted bearings are very common; they are easily aligned, usually being poured with the shaft in place. They wear out quickly, however, and are best suited for inboard bearings that can be oil lubricated.

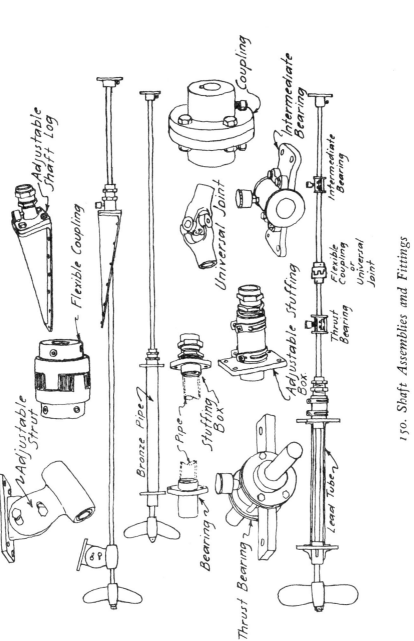

150. *Shaft Assemblies and Fittings*

Adjustable Shaft Log

Coupling

Intermediate Bearing

Flexible Coupling

Adjustable Strut

Universal Joint

Intermediate Bearing

Flexible Coupling or Universal Joint

Thrust Bearing

Bronze Pipe

Pipe

Stuffing Box

Adjustable Stuffing Box

Bearing

Thrust Bearing

Lead Tube

Rubber bearings are excellent for all outside stuffing boxes, bearings, or struts. They are lubricated with water; the housing of the bearing is designed to scoop water through the bearing for this purpose. In fitting, the opening of the scoop must be clear of any obstruction. The bearing must be rather long, however, and careful alignment is necessary. Flax-packed bearings are used in large vessels where the shaft speed is low. The housing is large and is packed with braided flax, impregnated with lubricant, cut into rings to fit the shaft. The joints in the rings are staggered, when the rings are in place. As a rule, the designer will specify the make and type of bearing, or stuffing box, required. Rubber bearings are used where the water is shallow, and grit and sand are in suspension.

Wood bearings, of lignum vitae, are used in large craft; water lubrication is required. The lignum vitae is furnished in a long sleeve which is slipped into the housing to replace a worn bearing. It is used only on shafts of large diameter, moving at low speeds. Thrust bearings are required when the shaft is made up of a number of short lengths coupled together, or when two lengths are coupled with a flexible coupling. The thrust bearing must be placed on the length of shaft to which the propeller is attached and is therefore just inboard of the inboard stuffing box, or shaft log. Thrust bearings are sometimes used for intermediate bearings in heavy hulls.

## Couplings

Couplings are required if the shaft is in two or more lengths. The engine coupling comes with the motor; all others must be ordered as separate units. The regular shaft coupling is like that of the motor; it is fixed and is not flexible. Though often used, it is not as desirable as flexible couplings in a wooden hull. Flexible couplings are of two forms, one using fabric held between two "spiders" to give flexibility, the other the well-known "Universal Joint." The fabric coupling is preferable in heavy boats; the "Universal Joint" can be used in small craft. These flexible couplings prevent the shaft's binding when it is slightly out of line. "Universal Joints" are often required when a boat is powered with an automobile engine which cannot be set at the required shaft angle. However, the break in the line of the shaft cannot be very great and a thrust bearing between propeller and "Universal Joint" is necessary. When the shaft installation is unusual it is necessary to consult a designer, or the engine manufacturer, as to the proper fittings. If the shaft is to have flexible couplings, or "Universal Joints" without a break in the line of the shaft, aligning will be made easier if regular fixed couplings are used to line up the shaft. The fixed couplings are removed and replaced by flexible ones when the final alignment is made.

## First Shaft Alignment

The shaft and its fittings on hand, the first alignment can be made. This is temporary, and is to fit bearings, shims, and lug bolts. The final alignments are made after the boat is launched, one alignment before the trial run and the final one two or three weeks from the trial date. To make the alignment on the stocks, insert the shaft in its hole, lining it up to the position shown in the plans. The stern bearing, inside stuffing box or log, or the strut and log, should be in place; these can be lined up prior to inserting the shaft by using a wire or chalk line through the shaft hole as a base, or center line, for the fittings. It is usually easier to line up the fittings with the wire or chalk line than with the shaft, as the wire or line can be more easily measured for position. When the shaft has been inserted, the after half of the engine coupling is keyed onto the shaft. Then the faces of the two halves of the coupling are brought together. If the faces do not bear along the circumference of the coupling, the shaft and engine are not in line. A feeler gauge can be used to check the opening between the coupling faces. The spacing between the faces of the coupling should be within .002 inch all around the circumference. Strips of paper inserted between the faces of the coupling will serve instead of a feeler gauge; when the coupling is properly aligned it will take an equal amount of force to pull out each of the strips from between the closed faces. Shift the engine vertically and laterally, using shims (or adjustable shims) under the lugs, until the coupling is correctly aligned. Test by revolving the shaft, with the engine half of the coupling stationary; the faces should be closed throughout a complete turn.

When proper alignment is found, drill the lug fastening

holes; the fastenings are usually lags or hanger bolts. Bolt down the engine so that it cannot move, but remember that this is not the final bolting. If the shaft is made up of short lengths, or is so long that an intermediate bearing is required, support the shaft at midlength, between stuffing box and engine coupling, in lining up. When this is done, the intermediate bearings can be properly placed and aligned. Multilengths should be coupled with fixed couplings for alignment, the flexible couplings being put in their place after the alignment is made. The alignment of the shaft and engine is usually made easier if the shaft is first brought to line by two bearings, say, strut and shaft log.

## Mounting Propeller

When the first alignment of engine and shaft is complete, the propeller may be mounted on the shaft. The propeller hub is bored to fit the shaft when ordered and the keyways in both hub and shaft are cut. It is usually necessary to force the wheel onto the shaft; do not hammer the hub without placing a block of wood over the hub to receive the hammer blows. When the propeller is in place, the nuts may be threaded on the shaft and locked with a cotter pin. Sometimes the nuts are covered with a fairing piece screwed on, overall.

## Alterations from Plans

The location of the propeller has been discussed. In case an error has been made in ordering the shaft, certain changes are usually permissible. It is best to have the wheel a little nearer the rudder than the deadwood, if a change in wheel position is necessary. Except in high-speed motorboats, the engine can usually be shifted a few inches forward, or aft, of its designed position without harm, but the effect of any change must be carefully studied. In high-speed power craft, however, it is distinctly unwise to shift the motor from its designed position. If the propeller must be shifted aft a little from its designed position, the possibility of padding the stern bearing to bring it nearer the hub of the propeller can be considered. With reasonable care taken in measuring for the shaft there should be no occasion to shift the propeller or engine, however.

## Suggestions

The inboard stuffing box, or log, should not be so close to a coupling, or thrust bearing, that it is impossible to repack the stuffing box. Bearings should be strongly secured to their foundations. Live-rubber pads can be inserted under inboard stuffing boxes to increase flexibility. Lubrication of all inboard bearings and stuffing box, by means of grease cups, or grease gun fittings, is desirable. In fastening inboard stuffing boxes, use long lags or hanger bolts, so that there is no danger of splitting the deadwood. Use plenty of white lead under the pads of all stuffing boxes or shaft logs.

## Tanks

The tanks can next be put in place. Their foundations naturally depend upon the shape and size of the tanks. Round tanks are easiest to install and are much cheaper than tanks of other shapes. Round tanks should rest in chocks firmly bolted or spiked to the frames, or floor timbers. The chocks should be rounded out to fit the tanks, and should bear on the tank at least one fourth its circumference, if possible. The tank may be held in the chocks by iron straps over the tank; the ends may be bolted, lagged, or screwed to the chocks, or hull timbers and chocks, as position permits. Chain or wire, set up with turnbuckles, can be used if desired. In some cases it is possible to secure the tanks by upper and lower chocks held together with tie bolts. Rectangular and oval tanks, or tanks shaped to fit the hull, are sometimes specified. Both square and oval tanks are easily chocked. Tanks molded to fit the hull are often difficult to secure, particularly those that fit against the side of the hull. These are often tall and narrow in section. The builder will have to make templates of each end of the tank, the shape of which is taken to the inside of the frames. If the tanks are in the way of a bilge stringer the tank should not be notched, but rather the tank is shaped so that it is inboard of the stringer and also inboard of the frames the depth of the stringer. The top of the tanks should not be carried to the underside of the deck beams but should be at the level of the underside of the sheer clamps. This will give room for the necessary deck connections and for inspection of the connections. The bottom of the shaped tanks should not be a sharp edge; a flat bottom should be formed so that a suitable foundation can be built.

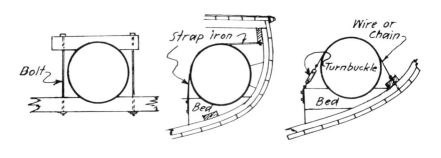

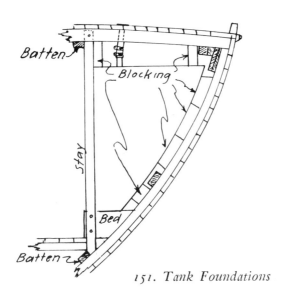

151. *Tank Foundations*

When the builder is planning such a tank it is always necessary to make a scale drawing, showing the shape and dimensions of the tank. On this can be located the inlet and outlet, the vent and the drain, also any baffles and inspection or cleaning manholes, or plates, that are required. In locating these, be sure that their position is not only in accordance with the layout of the space available but also clear of any framing or timbering in the hull. It is necessary to locate the various deck plates first, then plan the connections to the tank, to see if the positions of these connections will work out properly. Room to make pipe connections, or to fit hose, is necessary. Too many yachts are so planned that there is no room for these necessary jobs. The shaped tanks must be set on solid chocks and the tanks held in place with straps or timbers. Large tanks should always be ordered with baffles so that the contents will not swash about and make an unpleasant noise. In fitting shaped tanks, remember to support the side nearest the hull framing, if the tank does not rest on the frames. If not too high, the top of a shaped tank can often be utilized as a shelf.

Copper tanks must be carefully supported as they are relatively weak. Wooden supports should be spaced not more than 18 inches apart as a rule, both on the back and front of shaped tanks, as well as on the bottom and ends. Round or oval tanks should be closely chocked, and square or rectangular tanks are best supported by a floor or by battens. Tanks of various forms are often placed under the cabin floor or alongside the cockpit; the structure surrounding them will suggest the best method of constructing the foundations and securing them in place. In any case, the tanks must be held firmly in place and must not be able to move in any direction. In sailing craft the tanks should be as low as possible, if they are large in proportion to the size of the hull.

## Tank Details

In ordering tanks, or in planning them, specify the filler to be at least 1½ inches in diameter. The vent opening should be about one third the diameter of the filler opening, never under one fourth. These are on top of the tank. The outlet may be in the bottom or at one of the ends. If the tank is made to order, the outlet should be of the same diameter as the feed pipe on the motor, never smaller. A drain plug, or cock, in the bottom of a tank is a desirable feature; it should be at least ¾ inch in diameter and there should be room for a receptacle under the drain outlet. In large tanks there should be manholes, or removable plates, for entering the tanks to clean them. Fuel oil tanks usually require "clean-out" manholes, even in small sizes. Diesel

engine tanks may require to be tapped at the top for a return
line; this is often run to a pipe fitting in the filler pipe line,
however. Copper water tanks should be tinned inside. Filler
pipes in both water and fuel tanks should be as far outboard as
the tank position allows. In planning shaped Diesel oil tanks it
is common to find the outlet required at the top of the tank;
a pipe from this to within an inch or two of the bottom of the
tank must be fitted by the tank builder, and directions should
be given him. Many designs require tanks to be of excessive
capacity in proportion to the size of the boat, and this leads to
tanks so large that they are difficult to fit, as well as to other
faults.

### Exhaust Piping

With the tanks secured, it is usually possible to begin piping
up. The exhaust line may be put in first. There are a great many
ways of piping and fitting an exhaust line. In sailing craft, having a gasoline auxiliary engine, the exhaust line is often difficult
to install properly, due to crowding. It is often wise, therefore,
to install much of this piping before the deck is fully laid. The
engine catalogue or instruction book should be consulted as to

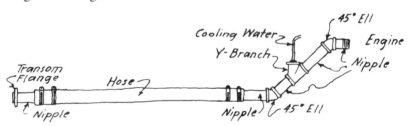

*152. "Wet" Exhaust Line without Muffler*

the diameter of the exhaust pipe. The piping may be of slightly
greater diameter than the exhaust outlet on the engine but
should never be smaller. The two most common methods of
installing the exhaust line are to eject the cooling water through
the exhaust line or to use a dry exhaust pipe. With the first
method, a loop is formed in the exhaust pipe as soon as it leaves
the engine and the cooling water injected on the downward

side of the loop, toward the exhaust opening of the hull. Between this point and the hull outlet is a silencer or muffler; the water is passed through this and is ejected out of the hull outlet. This is a cheap way of obtaining a cool and reasonably quiet exhaust. The dry exhaust is used on commercial craft; the exhaust leaves the engine and runs aft a short ways, then

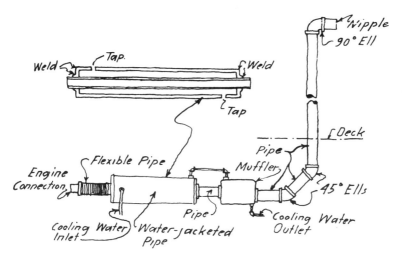

*153. "Dry" Exhaust Line*

runs up to a stack or outlet on deck. The "dry" muffler is usually on end, on deck. The exhaust outlet is usually carried well above deck and is capped with a pipe ell and nipple, to keep rain water from entering. Both types of exhaust require condensation traps just abaft the engine.

Exhaust piping for either method is made of cast-iron pipe or welded tubing. Cast-iron pipe is preferred as it can be easily broken up to remove, while steel tubing or malleable iron pipe must be cut up with a torch. Threaded pipe will corrode together so that it cannot be broken with a wrench. A third type of exhaust is used in expensive craft; this is a dry exhaust in which the exhaust pipe is cooled by a water jacket. This requires a pattern which must be made before the water-jacketed exhaust can be built; the pattern must show the shape the line

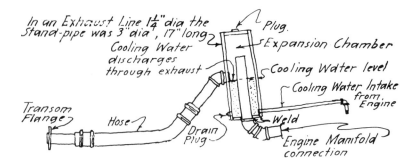

In an Exhaust Line 1¼" dia the Stand-pipe was 3" dia', 17" long

Cooling Water discharges through exhaust

Plug.

Expansion Chamber

Cooling Water level

Cooling Water Intake from Engine

Transom Flange

Hose

Drain Plug

Weld

Engine Manifold connection

*154. Use of Standpipe in Place of Loop in a "Wet" Exhaust Line in an Auxiliary Cruiser*

will take as far as it is cooled. The water-jacketed exhaust line is very expensive. Flexible pipe couplings, made of corrugated steel, are used with this type of exhaust, placed at the engine manifold.

## *Remarks*

Common black cast-iron pipe and pipe fittings are usually required for the exhaust pipe. Forty-five degree elbows are used instead of 90-degree ells. Y-fittings, or tapped elbows, are used to inject the cooling water; it is better to inject the whole flow of the cooling water instead of using only part of it. A tee can be used for a condensation trap at the engine manifold. In some cases it is easiest to use steam hose for the greater part of the exhaust line abaft the muffler, but usually the line can be made up of lengths of iron pipe joined with short sections of steam hose, secured with clamps. Use two hose clamps to secure a piece of hose to one piece of pipe, spacing them about one half the pipe diameter apart. If one inch is left between the ends of the iron pipe, inside the hose, there is enough flexibility to permit the exhaust line to follow the side of the hull.

In nearly all exhaust lines, the muffler is best placed a little abaft the midlength of the line, measured from manifold to outlet. In sailing craft it is often easiest to use the "North Sea Exhaust"; in this the exhaust line is brought aft to a tee, from which there is an outlet on either side of the hull. The outlets

are masked with a clamshell vent fitting, opened aft. The muffler is usually just inboard of the tee, in a loop formed there to
prevent water backing up the exhaust line. If the line is water-
cooled without a jacket, the loop must be at the engine. Dry
exhaust lines, not water-cooled with a water jacket, should be
insulated where they pass through decks or deckhouses. Water-
cooled exhaust pipes, with injected water, require insulation

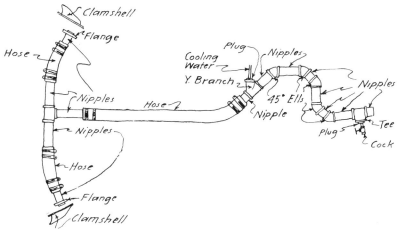

*155. Assembly Sketch of a "North Sea" Exhaust Line for a Small
Auxiliary*

only to the point where the cooling water enters the line. This
is usually done with ground asbestos mixed with a little plaster
of Paris (a teaspoonful to a pound). This insulation is usually
reinforced with chicken wire wrapped around the pipe, or with
a sheet metal jacket. Very often there is no silencer, the cooling
water acting as a muffler. Exhaust lines should be supported every
four feet from the hull side, or from below; never from the deck,
as this would cause drumming and vibration. The muffler should
have support and should not depend wholly on the piping to
keep it in place.

The outlet of any exhaust, having its outlet in the hull side or
stern, should be close to and above the water line when the boat
is at rest. Underwater exhausts are not usually successful. From
the outlet, the exhaust should rise to a point as high in the hull
as possible before looping down to the engine. Rubber or leather

flaps over the outlets are useful in slow-speed hulls, acting as valves to prevent water entering the exhaust pipe. They also have a muffling effect. A cheap muffler can be made by placing a section of automobile tire inner tube over the exhaust outlet in such a way that the exhaust gas passes through it. On any exhaust line

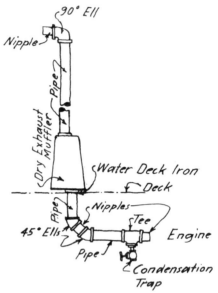

*156. Typical "Dry" Exhaust Line of
a Workboat*

there should be a flexible connection between hull and engine manifold. A water-jacketed line should have a corrugated flexible union, or coupling, at the manifold; if the line is long there should be another at the hull outlet. A dry stack exhaust should have a metal flexible connection at the manifold. Two engines should never exhaust into the same exhaust line. The stand-pipe exhaust, shown in the cut, is best when the engine is below the water line.

## Outboard Connections

Outboard connections for engine and plumbing are best marked and bored, and the fittings bolted or screwed into place, before the cabin floor is laid. The engine cooling-water intake should be well below the water line when the boat is in motion;

usually the best place for it is in or near the garboard. If the boat is flat on the bottom, it may be well to place the intake in the run, where it will not choke with mud or sand if the boat runs aground. If the intake is aft in the run, be sure that it is in a position where it is not affected by propeller or rudder eddies. A scoop may be necessary; in any case the intake opening must have a screen. The toilet connections should be placed as close to the toilet as space permits; the inlet to the pump must be forward and below the discharge outlet. A leather or rubber-fabric flap is placed over the outlet of the discharge line if the toilet is forward. There should be a screen over the inlet. Seacocks should be installed on all underwater hull connections; with these the line is closed when the handle is at right angles to the line. The galley sink outlet should

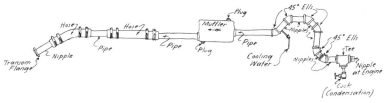

*157. Typical "Wet" Exhaust Line*

have a leather or rubber-fabric flap; this will usually prevent spouting. The bilge pump hull connection should always be above the water line when the hull is at rest; the best place for it is just below the painted water line, or boot top, where the bilge water will not cause a noticeable stain. Fuel tank drains sometimes have hull connections, if the tanks are above the water line, to enable the tanks to be drained overboard. Draining is illegal if done when the boat is afloat in coastal waters; it is well to have a pipe plug in the outlet of such a line so that draining can only be done when the boat is hauled out.

Cooling boat engines with fresh water has obvious advantages; this can be done by means of a tank, and a cooling coil attached to the outside of the hull. There are various systems of this type on the market, some of which require but one through-hull connection. Fresh-water cooling is particularly desirable with converted automobile engines. Directions for the installation of such systems are obtained from the maker. No special hull construction is required.

## Fuel, Piping, and Plumbing

Fuel piping is usually done with copper tubing, the connections of which are "pressure fittings." A "flaring tool" and a tube
cutter, or hack saw, are necessary for this type of piping. Only
tees and valves are required (except for couplings), but elbows,
crosses, reducers of various forms, and check valves are obtainable. Pipe-and-tube connecters, elbows, tees, and check valves
may also be obtained. Tube unions and pipe-to-tube plugs or
"bushings" are also standard fittings. As the copper tubing is easily
bent in gentle curves it is not difficult to install without many
fittings. In bending, fill tubing with fine sand to prevent flatten-
ing. In making pipe-to-tube connections remember that tube sizes
are given in outside diameters while standard pipe sizes are to
inside diameter. Fuel piping and salt-water piping are made of
standard brass pipe. Litharge is used in brass pipe and copper tube
joints instead of red lead, as a rule. Vent pipes or tubes, for tanks,
should have no 90-degree ells; if possible they should be formed
of bent tubing. The vent outlets for fuel tanks should be outside
the cockpit and cabin trunk in sailing craft, outside the hull under the guard in powerboats. If the vents lead upward they should
be protected from rain water by bending the outlet downward
to form a "gooseneck." The tubing is secured with brass or copper clips, fastened with copper tacks, to beams or bulkheads.
Where the fuel lines connect to the engine there must be either
flexible tubing (made of braided or woven copper), or a loop
made in a complete circle to prevent vibration or engine movement from fracturing the lines. If there are two water, or fuel,
tanks it is best that they both empty into a single pipe line with
individual tank cutoff valves (each tank being emptied separately) with check valves between cutoff and tank. If the tanks
are connected without check valves the lee tank will fill as the
boat rolls, while the mate empties if the cutoff valves are not
operated. In fuel tanks this will result in uneven engine performance, when the tanks are low. In sailing craft such a connection
might have dangerous effects on stability. Filler pipes are connected to the deck plates with pipe nipples, to which are connected short hose unions, secured with hose clamps. This type of
connection will not only prevent pipe fracture caused by vibra-

tion, or tank movement, but will also permit the correct adjustment of the piping, from the perpendicular nipple in the tank to the off-perpendicular nipple in the deck fitting, without special pipe fittings. Obviously, the deck plate and nipple will be off-perpendicular due to the crown of the deck.

## Hose, Etc.

Wherever possible, small boat piping is best done with rubber hose. This is far cheaper than tubing or piping, since it is easier to follow the run of the side, or to make twists and turns, or loops, with hose than with pipe or tubing. The advantages of rubber hose, in addition to the two mentioned, include the low cost of replacements, or repairs, and ease of removal in case of stoppage. There are various types of hose: steam or radiator hose, gasoline hose, noncollapsing suction hose, and metallic oil hose. The diameter of hose is usually taken inside, running from $\frac{3}{8}$ inch to 4 inches. Suction hose is useful on water intake lines for the engine, or in pump suction lines. Toilet pumps and most small bilge pumps require only ordinary rubber water hose, as they lack sufficient power to collapse this hose. Water piping, under the cabin floor, should be placed so that it can be reached when the boat is completed, without tearing out the joinerwork, and so that it is protected from ballast or stores. In spite of appearance, exposed piping in a boat is a seamanlike feature. Cockpit scupper pipes have been discussed; hose is preferable to lead piping. All boat piping should drain so that there will be no pockets in the piping that will hold water and permit bursting through freezing. Hose should be used where draining is impractical. The piping of fixtures will be discussed when the joinerwork has been described. In ordering pipe and fittings, it is a good plan to diagram the line, to record the position of each fitting ordered.

## Joinerwork

The first step in cabin joinerwork is to lay the cabin floor beams. These are placed according to the plans, of course, taking care that one is placed under each bulkhead in the cabin. A temporary floor is then laid over the beams. The reason the permanent floor is not laid immediately is to allow the bulkheads to stand on the beams rather than permanent floor. If this is not done, it is impossible to open up the bilges, as the whole cabin floor cannot be removed without tearing up the joinerwork. The main bulkheads are built first, their location being taken from the plans and carefully checked. Any error in placing these will usually lead to serious trouble; a berth may be too short, or there may not be room enough for the stove, or some other cabin fitting. Bulkhead construction varies with the type and size of boat and is a matter that should be decided by the plans and specifications. Should this not be the case, the following is general practice. Small craft often have plywood bulkheads, using waterproof plywood panels. In these the whole panel may sometimes be utilized; the shape of the bulkhead is first lifted from the mold loft drawings, or templated from the partly finished hull. The bulkhead is laid out, its shape and any required openings cut, and it is then placed in the hull in a single unit. In planning this, make certain that the panel can be passed through the hatches or deck openings. If not, it will be necessary to cut the panel into smaller sections, or to place the bulkheads before the decking is completed.

Plywood bulkheads require stiffeners; these are either rabbeted pieces placed at the corners or are part of the door trim. If the bulkhead falls between deck or trunk-roof beams, it is secured to the underside of decking or roofing with suitable moldings. The bottom of the panels rests on the cabin floor beams and may merely be toenailed; the panels will be locked in place when the cabin floor is laid on either side. Joints in the panels are covered with strips, or are backed up with a stiffener. If the hull is ceiled, it will be necessary to cover up the joint between the bulkhead and the ceiling with molding; this will also serve to secure the bulkhead to the sides of the hull. The advantages of plywood bulkheads are lightness, strength, and quietness—they do not squeak and groan when the craft is under way. They are not cheap, however, and it is doubtful if their use saves much labor, as securing them is often a laborious problem and the work of trimming doors, corners, and openings is greatly increased over plank bulkheads.

In heavy or large craft, plank bulkheads are required. These are usually framed and the plank is laid vertically. When the hull is ceiled it is necessary to step the plank against a molding, or on

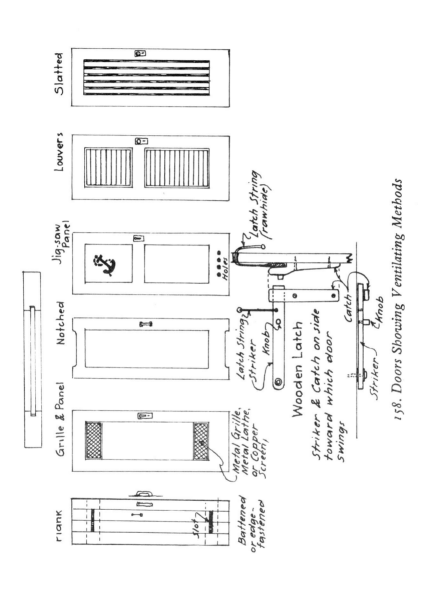

Plank

Battened or edge-fastened

Slot

Grille & Panel

Metal Grille, Metal Lathe, or Copper Screen,

Notched

Jig-saw Panel

Holes

Louvers

Slatted

Latch String
Striker
Knob

Latch String (rawhide)

Catch

Wooden Latch

Striker & Catch on side toward which door swings

Striker
Knob

Catch

158. Doors Showing Ventilating Methods

a rabbeted sill, bent to the side of the hull. The top of the bulk-head may be against a beam, or may be secured with moldings between the beams. Light plank bulkheads may be made of tongue-and-groove ceiling; heavy bulkheads are sometimes tongue-and-groove also. Tongue-and-groove ceiling should be ordered without beading, square-edged. The beaded stuff is diffi-cult to keep clean and to refinish. Double plank bulkheads, made of two layers of planking separated by framing, are used only in large craft. Paneled bulkheads are becoming rare; modern cheap panel work is done by building the bulkhead of plywood and then applying the stiles and rails. Attractive paneling can be obtained only by careful planning; the bulkhead must be drawn to scale and the height of the rails and width of the panels studied with relation to the surrounding cabin furniture and structure. The modern trend toward extreme plainness of finish is the reason why paneling is no longer common. Built-up panels are superior to ap-plied panelwork, but machinery is necessary. The placing of elec-tric light fixtures should be planned while laying out bulkheads; single plank, plywood, and single-thickness paneled bulkheads will expose wiring, unless the wiring can be covered with mold-ing or the stiles of the panels. Improperly placed moldings will spoil the appearance of any bulkhead. Double bulkheads are less of a problem in this respect, but should be wired as built.

## Berths, Cushions, Etc.

The berth fronts and other fore-and-aft partitions can next be built. Berths are of many types and any special requirement in their construction will be covered in the details attached to the plans and specifications. For this reason only the standard types of berth construction will be described, as these are not usually detailed. The common fixed berth needs little explanation. The front is built first, with the frame of the top. The front may have doors, lift-out panels, or drawers. It is usually built of plank or plywood but is sometimes paneled. The bottom is nailed or screwed to a frame piece, laid fore and aft on the cabin floor, or hull ceiling. The top of the front is secured to the front frame of the top. It is usual to lay the top planking of the berth so as to come flush with the outside face of the front, overlapping the planking of the front. Then a rail is secured to the front, standing

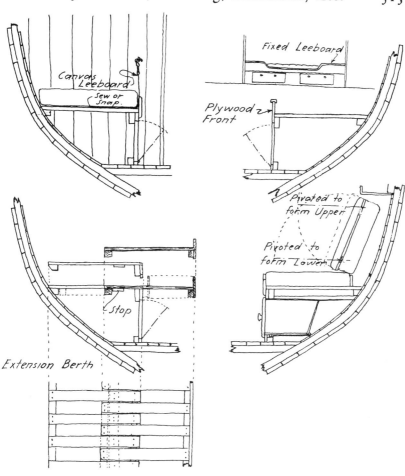

*159. Berths*

above the top sufficiently to hold the mattress or cushion in place. The top planking is often laid with open seams, for the sake of ventilation. The top of any berth should be built with the cushion in mind. Innerspring mattresses and cushions require a solid berth top; air and sponge rubber mattresses may be used with canvas berth tops; hair and kapok cushions may be used with plank or rope berth tops. Backs are usually built of plank; the back cushion is made with a loop at the top, through which a cord or rod is passed, to hold it to the back.

## Extension Berths

Extension berths are very common; the top pulls out to form a wide berth. The additional cushion width required to form the wide berth is obtained by employing the back cushion, which slides down as the bottom cushion is pulled out. The front of the berth is made in the usual way, but it is heavily framed. The top is made of strong battens laid athwartships, spaced wide apart. The sliding portion is made on a separate frame and its top battens slide between the battens of the fixed portion. The outboard portion of the sliding frame is below the battens and rides on the undersides of the fixed battens. The inboard, or front, frame is outside of the front of the berth and to this the rail is attached. When the berth is extended the frame should usually be supported by movable legs to the cabin floor, or by a track or rail on adjoining bulkheads. The sketches show the common construction of this class of berth.

## Folding Berths

Folding canvas berths are often employed. The canvas is usually battened to the hull side or ceiling and is extended by a rod attached to its front. This rod is secured at the ends by chocks attached to adjoining bulkheads. By having a number of notches in the chocks it is possible to vary the amount of slack in the berth and its width. When folded, the front rod is shifted to a chock close to the back batten, or otherwise stowed. Pipe berths require no explanation. Canvas berths of either type should not be stretched tight; the canvas should be permitted to sag. The front rail of a berth is often made high at the ends to prevent the occupant from rolling out when the boat is rolling. This destroys the comfort of the berth as a seat. Removable rails, or "leeboards," are sometimes fitted, but stowing them is usually a problem, so they remain shipped.

If a berth must be used as a seat a suitable leeboard may be made of canvas; a strip is attached to the underside of the cushion with snaps, so that most of it can be drawn up in front of the cushion. The top of this portion is roped. The ends of the rope can be secured with hooks or snaps to eyes in the adjoining bulkhead, thus forming a canvas leeboard for the berth that can be stowed under the cushion when not in use. The standard length of a berth is 6 feet 2 inches, but longer berths are usually desirable. Berths measuring 6 feet 4 inches are now becoming common. The least width, measured at the widest part of the top, should not be under 21 inches; the least headroom between

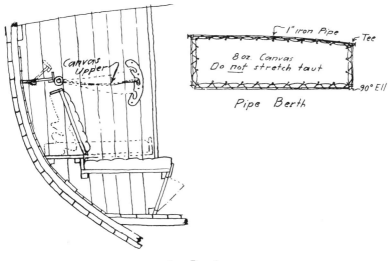

*160. Berths*

an upper and lower berth should be at least 21 inches also. All seats and transoms should be at least 16 inches wide and the top of the cushion should be not less than 12 inches and not more than 16 inches. The lower the seat, the wider it should be. Headroom over all seats and transoms should be 3 feet to 3 feet 6 inches.

## Strength of Joinerwork and Doors

There is no need to give minute instructions for building cabin furniture, such as tables, workbenches, lockers, hampers, shelves, and bookcases. These are shown on the plans and the construction is simple. It is important, however, to make all cabin joinery strong and securely fastened to the hull. This can be done only by adequate framing and fastening. Locker and other small doors should be made amply strong; it is best to make both the doors and the openings with square corners, rather than off-square, as hanging is simplified. Large doors may have to be off-square occasionally, but this should be avoided whenever possible. Deckhouse doors often have to be off-square for the sake of appearance.

## Gadgets

There are possibilities for ingenuity in fitting the cabin, but it is well to proceed with caution in the development of folding, sliding, and disappearing "gadgets." Many of these are very taking on paper, or in the boat while she is new, but a year or two of hard service often shows up weaknesses that lead to the discarding of these ideas. The effect of shrinking and swelling or corrosion of materials exposed to dampness is the prime cause of the downfall of many a handsome gadget. It is usually the inexperienced owner, or builder, who goes in heavily for "new" fittings. This is not to say that all gadgets should be passed over; rather it is to suggest that too much emphasis can be placed on fittings of this type.

## Iceboxes

Iceboxes require some attention. Every owner has ideas on the subject; perhaps no part of a boat is more revealing of the owner's and designer's sea experience. Except in houseboats, the icebox fitted with doors is out of place; yet it is safe to say that the majority of seagoing and coastwise yachts have this type. The disadvantage of the common icebox would not be so obvious if the box were placed athwartships with its doors opening forward or aft. However, this is rarely done and the box is placed so that the doors open toward the center line of the hull, with the result that the contents are often spilled. To overcome this, the boxes are fitted with racks, drawers, bars, and other gadgets; but try to take out something from the back of the icebox when it is blowing weather! The icechest, therefore, is the only practical seagoing refrigerator. This is merely an insulated box with a lift, or hinged, top. The ice is held by a grating at one end; the rest of the box is given up to food. Usually the ice compartment is a little higher than the food compartment, but the former has a lip, or dam, separating it from the latter. The ice compartment must have a drain and the lip, or dam, prevents water from entering the food compartment. The drain always raises the important question of how to dispose of the water from the melting ice. Some iceboxes and chests are high enough above the water line so that the waste may be piped overboard, but this is not usually possible. Sometimes the box, or chest, is fitted with a waste tank

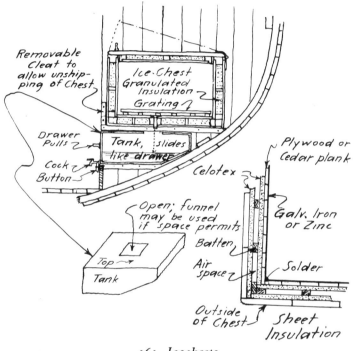

*161. Icechests*

which can be emptied from time to time through a drain cock. Still another plan is to allow the waste to drain into the bilge, an insanitary and rot-producing practice. Due to the animal and vegetable matter in the ice, the waste water is likely to cause an odor and attract vermin. The ideal icechest would be one in which the waste tank could be removed and taken out of the cabin for scalding and cleaning. In small craft the whole icechest should be capable of being removed for this purpose. In craft up to 40 feet in length the icechest is rarely of such great capacity that this is impractical.

The built-in icechest, or box, has a disadvantage not shared by the removable chest: it is common to find dry rot in the neighborhood of the built-in chest, particularly in back of it. This is due to condensation and lack of ventilation, both of which are difficult to avoid in the built-in chest. Unfortunately it is difficult

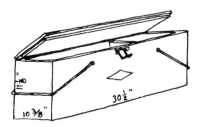

*162. Camp or Automobile Icechest Obtainable in Various Sizes*

to obtain a stock icechest, except in very small portable types suitable for only the smallest cruiser.

The construction of an icechest is not extremely difficult; a suitable box can be made which is lined with celotex or other insulation board. The best method is to place a lining against the sides and bottom of the box, then fit a thin frame of battens before putting in a second lining. This forms an air space between the two linings. Inside of the second lining of insulation a sheet metal lining, galvanized iron, is fitted; this must be watertight, which can only be accomplished by soldering the joints in the sheet metal. The cover is made in the same way. In a box having a capacity of over 25 pounds of ice, a wood lining between the insulation and the sheet metal, say, of plywood, is useful. The sketch shows typical icechest construction. If the chest is mounted on a platform it is usually possible to place a waste tank under the chest and make both removable. Many owners require icechests much too large for their boats.

## Fuel Locker

The stove platform is usually fitted for a pan locker or fuel bin. If the latter, it should be lined with sheet metal for coal, painted with creosote for wood.

## Drawers

Drawers are often required in cruisers, in both cabin and galley. Only one type of drawer is really suited, in which the drawer front overlaps the face of the furniture. This is done to permit

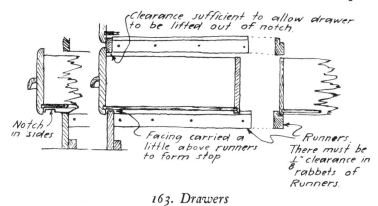

*163. Drawers*

notching the bottom so that it will be self-locking, as shown in the sketch. All drawers and locker doors should be made with ample clearance, so that they will not stick when swelling takes place.

## Bins

Bins are often preferable to lockers with doors, or to drawers. The bin door should hinge at the bottom and sides may be formed by wooden, metal, or canvas ends that will prevent the contents of the bin from spilling out on each side of the door when it is opened. Bin doors usually open to an angle of 45 degrees to the perpendicular; the sides are fitted so as to prevent the door opening farther.

## Workbenches and Table Tops

Workbenches and sink tops in the galley are best made of hardwood. The pieces should be battened and glued together before fitting and sanding. Polished metal tops, on workbenches and tables, are as practical aboard a boat as glass calking tools, however attractive they may be in the kitchen of a city apartment. Dishes will slide around enough aboard a boat without the aid of polished metal launching ways. All tables, shelves, and tops of bureaus and buffets should be fitted with leeboards; these may be made of thin battens set on edge and secured with brass dowels

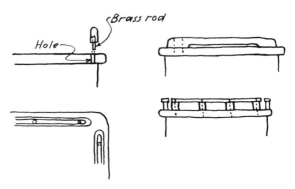

*164. Table-Top Leeboards*

to the tops of these pieces of cabin furniture. By gluing the dowels in the strip but having a loose fit in the furniture top, the leeboards can be easily unshipped for cleaning, or if they are in the way on a table. Fixed leeboards are made by fastening a strip or molding to the edges of the top of a piece of cabin furniture. The ends or corners should be left open so that cleaning scuppers are formed.

## Tables

Tables, unsupported by a centerboard case or bulkhead, are often difficult to secure properly. The cabin floor is usually too thin to give adequate support and it is very common to find that the table legs cannot be placed on the floor beams, due to the dimensions of the table. If this is the case, it is better to support the table from the cabin roof beams, using pipe or tubing, or even wood, if the cabin arrangement permits. If this is not possible, heavy blocking between the cabin floor beams must be resorted to, in order to obtain a secure fastening for a table.

## Cabin Arrangement

It is not the purpose of this book to suggest details of design, except where practical matters intervene; there are many books that discuss the questions of cabin arrangement to a minute degree and describe a variety of cabin furniture. To these the builder can turn if he must work out a cabin arrangement of his own.

## Cabin Floor

As the cabin furniture is built, the permanent cabin floor can be laid. It is usually desirable to have this made of planking thicker than ½ inch in all but very small craft, as there is bound to be some fixture that must be fastened to the floor clear of a floor beam. Tongue-and-groove stuff makes the best flooring, as the closed seams make the accumulation of dirt in the bilges much slower than would be the case with ordinary planking. Grating floors are sometimes used, but have obvious disadvantages. The flooring in the cabin should be made in short, narrow sections that can be easily handled and removed through the hatches. Lifting rings, that will lie flush in the floor when not in use, are very desirable. If any part of the floor must be fastened, use screws. For convenience, the floor and its supports should not be of hardwood if fastening is required; oak floors and floor beams make fastened flooring practically impossible to remove, as the fastenings "freeze."

## Ventilation

Ventilation of all parts of the cabin joinerwork is very important. The use of gratings, latticework, venetian-blind panels, cane or metal grills, or holes bored in solid panels should be considered. Jigsaw cuttings in panels are now popular, using the silhouettes of birds, anchors, ships, or other decorative motives. Whatever is used, it is not sufficient to place openings in the upper panel of a locker door; openings in the bottom are also required. Openings are required in all inside doors and under seats and transoms; in fact, all closed cabin joinerwork should be ventilated. Holes are usually bored in a series, often diamond shaped, or in lines. Small gratings may be used in the cabin floor.

## Trim

The use of facing, or molding, strips, to cover raw ends of timbering or joinerwork, requires careful planning. Such matters as facing the underside of deck or cabin roof beams, carlins, or trimming around hatches and skylights are often worth considering. The material used should be narrow and should be finished to contrast with the predominating finish of the whole cabin. It is possible to overdo this and some restraint is necessary. As in hull construction, the first principle of cabin joinery is not to expose the end grain of any plank or timber; the use of miter-joints, rabbeted pieces, or corner posts, strips, and facings usually solves any difficulty.

## Fastenings

Joinerwork fastenings vary a good deal. Any panels, or parts subject to occasional removal, should be fastened with oval-headed screws with small copper washers under the heads. Countersunk heads can be used if "cupped washers" are available. All brightwork, i. e., varnished joinery, should be brass or bronze fastened. Finishing nails should be used wherever possible; usually these are of galvanized iron, but brass or bronze-alloy nails are available. Oval-headed brass nails, called escutcheon pins, are often used in light work. Usually all nail- and screw-heads are countersunk and plugged or puttied, but in brightwork it is permissible to allow brass fastenings, nails, or screws to show. Screws are very valuable joinerwork fastenings, since the structure in which joiner fastenings are driven is often so light that nailing is difficult. In selecting fastenings for joinerwork, be sure they are adequate for the use.

## Hardware

Hinges and locks or latches in the cabin should be bronze or brass; iron is used only as a last resort. Brass-plated steel hinges and door hardware will not last; galvanized iron will last longer. If brass hinges are unavailable, light inside doors can be hung on heavy sole leather and the latches may sometimes be made of wood. Hinges are made in many forms; a marine hardware dealer's catalogue will show the more common marine types. Butt hinges are used in most cabin doors; they are the type used in doors at home. If a door is subject to great strains, or is large, strap hinges are used. Often a door must swing out from its opening, to clear a molding or frame; offset butt hinges are made for this purpose. Icebox hinges are straps, of special form, fitted so that an offset-front of a door (offset outward from the surrounding door frame) can be handled. Continuous, or piano, hinge is used either as a butt or strap hinge for small openings, or windows, occa-

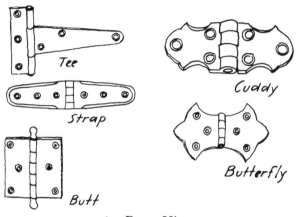

*165. Door Hinges*

sionally on hatches, tables, and bins. Spring hinges, giving self-closing doors, are used on small lockers and particularly on doors of bins. Small, fancy hinges, called "butterfly hinges," are used only on lockers; they are of the strap variety, being wholly exposed on the casing. Marine butt hinges are usually "loose-pin" so that a door can be removed without removing the hinges on either door or casing. In deciding whether to use a loose or fast pin, the way the door is to swing and lock, in regard to the pin, should decide the point—in outside doors at least. Outside doors, swinging outward, require fast pins.

    Latches, door handles, locks, and catches are available in many types and sizes. Cupboard turns and catches are used for locker doors of small size, or doors in a small boat that are latched from one side only. Toilet doors are latched from both sides. Small, thin doors of this type require "rim locks" which are applied to one face of the door. Thick doors, over 1 inch in thickness, usually have mortise locks, mortised into the door. Hanging a door with butt hinges and fitting a mortise lock is a slow job for even a skilled man. One of the most desirable qualities, and one not often found, in any marine door lock, latch, or catch is quietness; most fittings rattle in a highly annoying manner. Door hardware should be fitted, but not secured, until after painting is completed. In general, cabin hardware requires careful selection and consideration.

In planning the cabin joinerwork, it is well worth while to study many marine hardware catalogues. The possibilities of using certain pieces of hardware, if observed ahead of construction, will often save hours of work and often a good deal of trouble as well. The swing of each door must be decided and the type of hinge and latch selected with regard to the door and casing. Incidentally, if a paneled door has narrow stiles and the rails are tenoned as usual, the mortise lock should be of the tubular type as it is very trying to cut a square mortise in the end grain of the middle rail, where it stands in the tenon.

## Wheelboxes

Wheelboxes, in both power and sailing craft, should always be very strongly made and secured, particularly when engine controls are mounted on the side of a box. The wheelbox framing should be of oak and the side on which the engine controls are mounted should be well cleated to prevent splitting. The whole structure should be bolted to the deck, or bulkhead, and screw-fastened throughout, so as to be dismountable. In planning, be sure there is enough room for both steering gear and controls; the latter take up a surprising amount of room inside a box.

## Ladders

Steps and ladders must be built to fit the place in which they stand. The sides, or stringers, should be fitted first, so as to establish the position of the foot of the steps or ladder in relation to the hatch. Headroom in a hatchway is often spoiled by improper placing of the first step. A person usually leans forward as he steps up, but it is a good plan to place the lowest step so that its front edge is within the hatch opening when viewed from directly above. In stairbuilding ashore, the height of each step, or "rise," is approximately 7 inches and the depth of each step, or "tread," is approximately 10 inches. Using this as a trial, the builder tries to come as near to it as conditions allow, following the rule "twice the rise per step, plus the tread, equals 24 inches." In marine work, however, this rule is rarely applicable. In the first place, there is usually insufficient "run" (length horizontally from front of lowest step to back of highest step) for the "rise" (perpendicular height from cabin floor to deck). In the second place, the seaman usually likes stairs that can be mounted very quickly. For these reasons, the stairs used on boats are usually made like stepladders, open between steps, but with wider treads. The width of the steps or treads is usually from 5 to 8 inches; the rise per step is from 10 to 14 inches. The width between the sides, "stringers," is from 16 to 30 inches; in small boats 20 inches is a good average.

The back of the steps should never be closed in, either with solid risers or with sheathing laid vertically against the back of the steps and slanting with the underside of the stringers, until the tread is about 8 inches wide. The treads can be fastened to the stringers in a number of ways, rabbeted and cleated. It is usually best to rabbet the end of each tread into the stringers. Handholds should be cut near the top of each stringer, between steps, if the rise of the ladder exceeds 5 feet. In most boats the layout of the cabin requires the ladders to be unshipped to enter some compartment or locker; for this reason the ladders should be built of soft, light wood, not oak. Usually the stringers can be made of plank from 1 to 1½ inches in thickness, the steps or treads of ¾- to 1-inch plank. If weight is very important, the steps can be of ¾-inch plank, with stringers each built up of two hardwood strips, with softwood cleats acting as spacers and brackets combined with rod braces, as on some stepladders. The ladders must be secured so that they will not fall; usually this is done by using hooks and eyes at the top of each stringer, to secure them to the bulkhead. It is better to step the bottom of the stringers in cleats or wooden sockets, nailed or screwed to the cabin floor, in addition, to depending upon hooks and eyes alone. If preferred, metal fittings can be obtained from marine hardware dealers that will answer for hooks and eyes.

## Floor Coverings

The coverings for floors and steps are not matters offering any great difficulties. Whatever is used should be proof against mildew. It is of very great importance to use something that is not slippery, either dry or wet. Any openings in the floor that are used as hatchways should have a section of floor covering cut to fit with the edges of the opening covered by brass strips attached to the hatch cover. This binding is screw-fastened and should be from 1 to 1½ inches wide, weighing 2¾ to 3½ ounces per foot. A T-shaped hatch molding, which is screwed to the sides of the hatch cover, with one flange forming a binding on top, is also available.

## Height of Tables, Etc.

The height of tables, bureaus, workbenches, and stove tops depends upon the headroom of the cabin, or on the piece of furniture in question. If the headroom is sufficient for standing, say, 6 feet 1 inch, and the owner of average height, the height of these should be 34 to 40 inches above the floor, except tables, which should be 12 inches above the cushions of seats or transoms. Swinging tables, which compensate for the roll of the hull, are practical in large yachts but do not seem to be very satisfactory in small craft, due to the quick motion of the latter and the great weight of ballast required in such tables. Desks and dressing tables are usually about 30 or 33 inches high.

## Stove Platform

The stove platform must be figured to fit the stove purchased, as to height and other dimensions. The top of the platform should be strong enough to enable the stove to be adequately fastened down. This is done in various ways, depending upon the size and type of stove. Heavy, cast-iron stoves are secured to the platform top by screws through the feet, in addition to which turnbuckles, or wire lashings through the lashing rings on the ends of the stove, are necessary. A long eyebolt, shackled to the lashing ring and passed through the platform top, set up with a nut and washer under the platform, will do very well. If the stove is close to the deck, or to a bulkhead, protection from scorching is necessary. The best protection is obtained by use of sheet asbestos. This should not be tacked directly to a bulkhead, or to any flat surface; thin batten spacers should be placed to form an air space between the asbestos and the surface in question. The asbestos must have some protection: zinc or some other suitable sheet metal, or nonscorching tile, should cover it. Asbestos should also be employed under the stove, combined with sheet metal or tile if desired. The top of adjoining worktables, or locker tops, should be similarly protected, where the cook will be likely to lay a hot stove lid or pan.

Small stoves, burning oil or alcohol, should stand in a shallow metal pan which will catch drippings and oil. If the stove is under the deck, be sure its top is about 18 inches below the carlins or beams; the drying effect of heat from the stove will otherwise cause trouble in all but canvased decks. Oil tanks, for stoves, should be separated from the stove by sheet metal, or a bulkhead of wood sheathed with asbestos and sheet metal. A little planning to allow for laying down hot plates, pans, stove lids, or for cleaning spilled food or fuel from around the stove, will add to the value of the stove platform.

### Plumbing Fixtures and Plumbing

Plumbing, so far as fixtures are concerned, needs little attention. It is assumed that the plans specify the type and size, or make, of each fixture required. As in joinerwork, it is very important that all plumbing fixtures be securely fastened to the hull or cabin floor. If a hand basin is to be fixed to a light bulkhead, a backing block must be screwed or bolted to the bulkhead to give support. Bolts should be used wherever possible. Toilets should be lagged or bolted to blocks, if it is impractical to bolt them directly to cabin floor beams. Fastening to the cabin floor alone is insufficient. In placing toilets, be sure that there is enough room between the cabin floor and skin of the hull, under or near the toilet, to make the necessary connections. Hose connections for toilet and hand basins are usually preferred to pipe, as has been suggested earlier. If either is below the water line, it will be necessary to pump out the waste, and there should be a loop to above the water line in the waste pipe. Usually, however, the hand basin waste is run into the toilet and discharged by pumping that fixture. As the toilet is commonly below the water line, and must be flushed, pump toilets are standard marine equipment. The waste of this should be looped to from 12 to 20 inches, depending where the toilet is placed in regard to the hull center line, above the water line when the boat is at rest. In motorboats without sails of any kind 8 inches is sufficient. The length of the waste line, from the highest point of the loop to the hull outlet, must always be 1 foot longer than the distance from the highest point in the loop to the toilet connection on the fixture, to prevent siphoning. Hose is suitable for the loop and piping; lead piping can be used also, but is both expensive and troublesome. In fitting hose to the waste or intake of a toilet, avoid turns that tend to flatten the hose.

### Above-Water Toilets

While it is common to see the ordinary marine toilet used in installations above the water line, toilets specially designed for this position are preferable. These have the advantages of being cheap, having no valves to cause trouble and requiring very little piping. One type requires no pump, being operated by an intake scoop and a siphon shoe outside the hull. Another type requires a navy-type bilge pump for use when the boat is at rest. The latter is marketed under the name of "Strathru Marine Toilet," the former "Chesapeake Marine Toilet." The James Walker Company, of Baltimore, Maryland, lists these useful fixtures.

### Basins and Sinks

Where the waste from a hand basin is injected into a toilet, it is usually necessary to use flattened tubing under the toilet seat, if the bowl is not fitted with a special connection for the purpose. This tubing will have to be long enough to be secured with clips to the adjoining bulkhead or locker face, if hose is used for the rest of the waste line. If tubing is used instead of hose connections, be careful to order the hand basin with tube fittings. If the hand basin is well above the water line, the waste can be run to a hull connection fitted with a flap; it is well to put a valve in the waste line, in this case, that can be easily reached. Sinks are often a difficult problem, so far as the waste pipe is concerned. Often the galley is so arranged that the sink is well outboard and so is subject to spouting, or flooding, when the the boat is well heeled. The only cure for this is a valve in the waste line that can be easily reached from in front of the sink, and a flap on the hull connection. The valves used in waste lines should be "gate valves," not "globe valves." Flooding of a galley sink could be overcome if the makers could be induced to fit the waste plugs with a "breech-block screw" instead of using the ordinary metal and rubber stopper. Waste pumps are rarely used on galley sinks but would be practical when the sink must be close to the water line in elevation. A loop in the waste line would be necessary, fitted as in toilets. Water pumps, to serve basins and sinks, are obtainable in many forms; in placing them the most important thing is to be sure that there is room to use them without striking the user's elbow on some near-by structure.

## Bilge Pumps

Bilge pumps for small boats are available in many types but are usually of the so-called "navy type," having a brass barrel. This type of pump should have hose connections and should be firmly fastened to a bulkhead or to a mast. The intake must be in the lowest part of the bottom and should be fitted with one of the standard strainers, to be purchased with the rest of the hardware. The well may be screened to advantage, using galvanized metal screening having ¼- to ½-inch mesh; this can be formed in a square box to fit between the floors and around the strainer. The outlet in the hull should be extended inside the ceiling, or frames, so that it can be reached, if it is necessary to break the hose connection there. This can be achieved by placing a pipe nipple, threaded at one end, in the hull connection. Most yachts have inadequate bilge pumps, should a serious leak develop.

## Engine Controls

Engine controls are perhaps one of the most trying parts of an engine installation job. It is rare to find the controls planned in advance so that, when this job is reached, it is necessary to work out a complicated system to avoid obstructions already in place. Most professional builders call in a mechanic experienced in this work, in preference to attempting it themselves, and the amateur builder would do well to follow suit. Usually the engine manufacturer, or his agent, can suggest a skilled man. If it must be attempted by the builder, the engine manufacturer's instruction book should be consulted and the amount of movement in the clutch and reverse gear, and the spark, choke, and throttle, measured. The connections between these and the hand controls must be rigid; brass pipe is generally used when the engine is

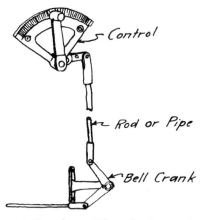

166. *Spark or Throttle Control*
*Fittings*

large. Flexible controls, using wire, can be used on spark, choke, and throttle when the distance from the controls on the engine to those on the wheelbox does not exceed 6 feet; if longer than this, it will be necessary to experiment to see if operation is possible. Bowden wire and casing for this purpose can be obtained to the required lengths from marine hardware dealers.

As in all boatbuilding and joinerwork, control installation can be best worked out by making full-sized drawings. By this means the measured movement of each control can be laid off and the arc of travel of each bell crank or hand control plotted. By lengthening or shortening the arm of a bell crank or hand-control crank, the "throw" of the engine control can be adjusted to fit the movement desired in the hand levers. When the control is once planned, the necessary fittings can be ordered in a unit from the marine hardware dealer. Rods will serve to connect the controls in small engines, but usually it is safest to use pipe instead.

## Steering Gear

It is impractical to attempt to give directions for the installation of all possible fittings, such as automatic bilge pumps, hydraulic or electric engine controls, certain mechanically operated wind-lasses, and similar gear. Each of these requires special knowledge which is commonly obtained from the instructions accompanying the fitting. Steering by the common methods, however, can be explained; the installation of most methods of steering is not very difficult. Steering by a tiller on the head of the rudder requires little attention here; it is only necessary to call attention to the necessity of ample strength in that part of the tiller fitting over, or into, the rudderhead. Open powerboats are often steered from amidships, or forward, by a lever, operating the rudder with wire or light rope attached to a yoke or quadrant on the rudderhead. The rope or tiller line is continuous, running around the gunwale or cockpit and held in small metal or wooden fair-leads. Commercial small-boat operators often have a good deal of slack in this line and merely wrap the slack around the lever, which is pivoted low in the boat, either to the floor or side of the hull. This enables the tiller line to be cast off and the steering done by merely holding the tiller lines, from any part of the boat, even on deck at the extreme bow.

Steering wheels are of many types; sailing craft usually employ a wheel attached to a gear which operates the rudder. This gear is mounted either directly over the rudderhead or just forward of it. There are many types of these gears made, to suit almost any requirement of mounting. Usually the catalogue illustration shows the gear correctly mounted; in most gears foundations are required only at the ends of the gear. Lags are often used to secure the gear to the foundations, but through-bolting should be resorted to whenever possible. In selecting a gear, it is important that the rudderhead fitting be the same diameter inside as the rudderhead (except when the rudderhead is outside the transom). Usually the designer specifies the type of gear necessary.

Powerboats, having wheels, steer in various ways. In very small craft, a wheel and drum are mounted on a bulkhead or on an instrument panel board; the steering is then done by a quadrant, tiller, or yoke, on the rudder, connected to the drum with tiller lines made of bronze wire, covered with braided waterproof linen. The tiller lines are in one piece, running from quadrant arm to quadrant arm, around the drum. The tiller lines must be secured to the drum. Often the fitting required is furnished with the steerer. If not, a U-bolt or staple must be used. The number of turns, on each side of the staple, must contain the length of line required to put the tiller, or yoke, hard over from the central

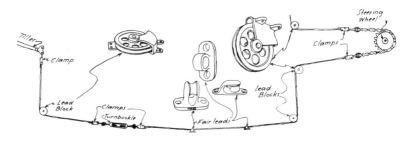

*167. Sketch of Steering Cable of a Powerboat*

position. Both windings must be in the same direction, so that as one winding is unwound the other winds.

Chain and flexible wire may be used in the same manner, if the size of the boat requires. If wire is used, it should be standard "wire tiller rope," with which wire rope clamps are used, and both chain and wire require turnbuckles. The latter should be so placed that they do not foul any lead blocks required to carry the tiller line along the sides of the hull. Of course, these turn-buckles must also be placed so that they can be easily reached for adjustment. Tiller lines should be set up so there is a slight amount of slack, never set up so the lines are taut. If chain is used, a wild-cat is used instead of a drum on the steerer; in this case the chain makes contact for only half the circumference of the wildcat. Grip is obtained by the shape of the scores in the wildcat. The chain must lead downward on either side, however, and so lead blocks under the steerer are necessary.

Another common type of gear employs a short chain on a sprocket at the wheel, to which are attached wire tiller lines. The chain used is of the roller type. Here, again, the lead blocks under the steerer should be employed; the height from the center of the lead blocks to the center of the wheel sprocket must be a little greater than the amount of chain required to move the quadrant from the center position to hard over, on either side. The length of the chain is the length of the arc, through which the yoke, tiller, or quadrant swings, from hard over to hard over, plus half the circumference of the sprocket, plus four chain links. Some method of stopping the swing of the rudder should also be used, so that the rudder cannot swing so far that the steerer jams. If the usual tiller or quadrant is used, blocks or vertical pieces of timber secured to the rudderpost thwart, or to deck beams, or both, against which the fitting will strike when the rudder is hard over, will serve. Outboard rudders are often fitted with chains, one on each side, secured to a staple at each side of the transom and to the after edge of the rudder, just above the water line.

In some craft—particularly those with sharp sterns—blocks, properly beveled, are secured to each side of the sternpost to act as stops. If the rudder and post weigh less than 60 pounds, stops are rarely necessary. When wire or rope is used, lead blocks are required at all angles made in the tiller lines, unless they are only 2 or 3 degrees, when tiller line fair-leads will serve. These can be obtained from marine hardware dealers, as can all types of tiller lines, lead blocks, and quadrants or yokes. In lining off steering lines and lead blocks, use a piece of cord to make sure the leads are practical before securing the blocks or fair-leads. In mounting all steerers it is very important that the wheel and drum, sprocket, or wildcat, be rigid; through-bolting to strong timbers is necessary. The less common steering gears include rack-and-pinion, worm gear (such as is used in automobiles), and various mechanical or electrical devices. These require very careful installation, and the beginner should call in a practical mechanic to aid him in most cases.

## Stoves and Chimney Stacks

The stove requires little skill to install. The oil and alcohol stoves for marine work, now on the market, are safe and easily secured in place. No chimney is required. Stoves can be obtained that are mounted on gimbals, but it should be noted that these require a good deal of room in which to swing. In a small boat gimbal stoves are rarely used. Gas stoves can be obtained and, if properly installed, are reasonably safe. The gas tanks must be located outside the cabin, on deck, and the pipe connection must be tight. Piping is done with copper tubing, using as few fittings as possible in order to reduce the number of joints to a minimum. The gas tanks must be so installed that they can easily be removed when empty and replaced; the tanks should be in a deck box and covered, but not tightly. Oil and gasoline stoves should have their tanks well away from the stove, preferably on deck also.

Coal and wood stoves require chimneys, of course. These are easily installed; there are a few things, however, that should not be overlooked in placing the chimney for a coal and wood stove. If it is necessary to use elbows, the horizontal run of the pipe should pitch up from the elbow nearest the stove. The chimney should be placed so that there are not more than two elbows. The diameter of the chimney should not be less than that called for by the stove manufacturer. Perhaps the most common trouble in stove installations is lack of draft, or the downdraft in sailing craft when under sail. These faults are due to improper location of the stack on deck. A stack placed in the lee of a deck structure or mast will often cause trouble, as will also one under the main boom of a sailing boat. Unfortunately, the stack position is often forced upon the builder by the cabin arrangement, so it cannot be changed. In this circumstance the fitting at the top of the stack is often of very great importance. If the stack must be in close proximity to a deck structure, the top of the stack must be carried above the structure; if this is not advisable then a cross-pipe must be carried athwartships so that the ends of the cross-pipe extend a little outboard of each side of the deck structure. There is usually little trouble in powerboats if this is followed. In sailing craft the problem is often very troublesome and cannot be met by merely extending the stack. Here the fitting at the top of the stack is of prime importance. Cross-pipes are often used in commercial vessels but are usually too cumbersome for small craft. If the stack comes up through a cabin trunk, a practical cross-pipe can be made by using a sheet metal hood, U-shaped, set directly on the top of the trunk.

The chimney or stack should be carried about half the height of the hood above the cabin roof. The length of the hood should be not less than six times the stove pipe diameter and the width across the base one and a half times the pipe diameter. The height of the hood should be two times the pipe diameter. The hood is set athwartships and so can exhaust on either side. Elbows at the top of the galley stack are of little value as they require constant adjustment. The standard "Liverpool Head," which is fitted to the top of the stack, is very popular in power yachts but is most unsatisfactory in sailing craft. A better fitting for these is the head used at Gloucester, Massachusetts, called the "Seattle

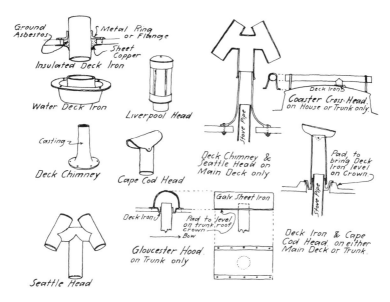

*168. Galley Stack Fittings*

Head." This is a T-shaped head that cannot produce a down-draft and is cheap. In addition to these two heads, there are a great number of others available: the "Cape Cod" or tipping hood, revolving or spinning heads, and a number of patented ones. The latter are usually rather expensive; their advantage over the Seattle Head is usually in their smaller size and lesser liability to be fouled by running rigging.

The stack on deck or cabin roof should be stepped on a "water deck iron"; the chimney is brought into it. Thus the stack is usually a little greater in diameter than the chimney. This is to prevent water running down the sides of the chimney. In spite of this precaution, however, it is almost impossible to avoid ugly stains on the chimney below deck if galvanized-iron stove pipe is used. Copper is preferable for this reason. A damper should always be placed in the stove pipe, close to the stove, to adjust the draft.

The method of securing the stove has already been mentioned in the description of stove platforms (page 526). There are many types of oil stoves available: both wick and pressure kerosene as well as pressure gasoline and alcohol models. The wickless kerosene stoves are useless in a boat as they must be level to operate properly. If marine oil stoves are not available, the old "wick lamp" type will serve in a small cruiser quite well. The "Primus" is perhaps the best small marine oil stove.

## *Mechanical Ventilation*

In all decked hulls having engines, ventilation of the engine space is required, except when the engine is under a box in the cockpit. In the latter case, louvers in the box, or other openings, are all that is usually necessary. The system of ventilation should always be so arranged that air is drawn in through one ventilator and expelled through another. If there are only two ventilators they should be placed so that they are at diagonally opposite corners of the engine room or space. The intake pipe of the forward ventilator should merely enter the engine room or space, but the exhaust ventilator should be piped to the bilge, or to below the level of the bottom of the engine. Ventilating piping is usually required to accomplish this. The piping should be galvanized-iron stove piping or ventilator pipe whenever possible. The exhaust system should often be equipped with a blower; these can be obtained from any marine hardware dealer and are equipped with suitable electric motors. The blower should be secured to a bulkhead, or to the underside of the deck; there is a flange at the exhaust end of the blower for this purpose. The blower requires at least one elbow, as the intake is usually on the side of the blower. Wooden ventilating trunks can also be used and these are most easily made of plywood. The ventilator on deck, cabin trunk, or deckhouse roof must stand on a pad so as to be vertical; the choice of fitting is great. In selecting ventilators, the size of the blower should be considered: the ventilator should be of the same diameter as the blower exhaust, not smaller.

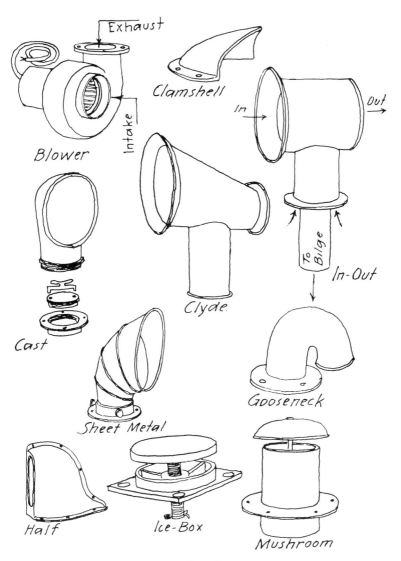

Exhaust

Clamshell

In → Out →

Blower

Intake

Cast

Clyde.

In-Out

To Bilge

Gooseneck

Sheet Metal

Half

Ice-Box

Mushroom

169. *Ventilators*

The height of the ventilator may be important; see that there is room for the ventilator chosen, under a boom or other obstruction.

## Fire Extinguishers

Fire extinguishers are also necessary in power craft and auxiliaries. In small craft these may be of the small hand types, the stations for which should be chosen with care so that they are available in case of fire or explosion. In large craft, regular piped systems are generally used; the installation of these is explained by instructions accompanying the equipment.

## Wiring

Wiring is rarely done by the builder, an electrician usually being called in to do the work. This is preferable to an attempt to wire by an inexperienced person. Most boats require a number of circuits: one for the cabin lamps, one for the running and navigation lights, one for the radio, and one for the engine. Splicing is to be avoided as far as possible. The cable should be marine quality and must be waterproof; all fixtures and fittings should be designed for marine use. Great care should be taken, in wiring, that no fastening is driven into the cable for any reason whatever. All connections should be taped. Switchboard and fuse box are usually required. All wiring should be placed so that it can be inspected, yet the appearance of the cabin should not be spoiled by random placing of wiring. All cables should be secured to bulkheads or roof with brass clips fastened with tacks or screws. Junction boxes should be used in large craft, so that additional connections can be made after the boat leaves the builder's hands. If the builder must install the wiring himself, he should obtain one of the many electrical handbooks before beginning work. Fixtures are usually mounted on pads; they may be selected from a marine hardware catalogue to suit use.

## Lamps

Kerosene lamps and running lights are commonly used on small craft. These are obtainable to suit all sizes of craft. No recommendations need be made here; the builder can consult marine hardware catalogues and select lamps and lights to fit any boat. It might be observed, however, that the method of mounting cabin lamps on gimbals now used in most cabin lamps could be greatly improved upon. As now mounted, the lamps must be removed from the gimbals to fill or clean by unscrewing small nuts; for some unfathomable reason these are invariably ball shaped. When these are laid down they usually roll out of sight. If the lamps were mounted in a fixed gimbal ring by a "bayonet catch," a half-turn of the lamp in the ring would release it from the gimbal for filling and cleaning. The number of lamps required is difficult to estimate; the more irregular the cabin layout, that is, the more corners and offsets formed in it, the greater the number of lamps required. Small kerosene lamps are of little candle power, so many are often required. In many cases an estimate of two lamps for every person accommodated in the cabin will serve.

## Cushions

Cushions should be made to fit the berths and transoms or seats. Cost usually is the basis for the selection of cushion construction. Perhaps the best is the cushion, or mattress, made of sponge rubber covered with fabric or imitation leather. At least this is true as far as length of life of the cushion is concerned; however, some people object to the odor of a rubber cushion. These cushions are quite expensive. Another suitable cushion, or mattress, is one made of rubberized hair; this, too, is water- and mildewproof, but rather expensive. Common hair- or cotton-filled cushions, with or without innersprings, are often used, but kapok filling is preferable to either common hair or cotton.

If fabric is used to cover the mattress or cushion, there should be a removable cover instead of a fixed one. Kapok or sponge rubber should be used for cockpit cushions; the covers should be of waterproof material. The cushion maker must be given a paper pattern of each cushion or mattress, cut to the exact shape of the cushion, or mattress, without allowance for seams and taking up. Patterns should be marked as to top, front, and position in boat; any reduction in thickness for changes in height of plank top of berth or seat should also be marked. Strong wrapping paper can be used for these patterns. Mark with wax crayon.

Cushion backs should be patterned in the same manner as seat cushions; specify how the backs are to be fastened to the seat: snap buttons, or rod, or cord loop. All buttons in a cushion or mattress should be nonrusting; leather is often used. Mattress pads, without innersprings, are usually 5 inches thick; cushion pads are 3 or 3½ inches thick. These are sometimes used with separate springs. The plans should show the required thickness of cushions and mattresses. If there is a bevel at the back of a mattress, or cushion, it is more expensive than when the back edge is made plumb. Bevel-edged mattresses and cushions are therefore avoided.

## Deck Fittings, Windlass

The placing of fittings on deck should now be started. The windlass can be placed first. The numerous types of windlass available make exact directions impossible. First, the windlass must be rigidly mounted and should be secured with through-bolts if mounted on deck. If mounted on the bowsprit heel bitt, or other bitts, the bearings can be lagged to the after side of the bitt posts. The type of windlass required will be specified by the designer. In mounting a windlass on deck, be sure it stands high enough to make operation easy; most windlasses are mounted too low. Crank-operated windlasses, in particular, should be mounted high. Often there is no reason that the windlass could not be mounted on the after side of a mast to advantage, particularly on small cruisers. The lead of the cable or chain, through the hawse, or from the rolling chocks on a bowsprit, should be considered; the lead of chain from these fittings to the wildcat theoretically should be square to the axle of the wildcat, but in practice an angle of 3 or 4 degrees is possible. It will be found that the farther aft the hawseholes are from the stem rabbet, the wider the windlass should be.

If roller chocks are used on the bowsprit, or on sides of the stem, English fashion, a narrow windlass is preferable. Small capstans are not very practical. They have one advantage, however: they can be mounted off center, on either side of the hull center line. In ordering windlasses for chain, consult the designer's specification for size of chain; this is usually BBB or Crane

Chain. Most builders buy large, heavy chain first and send a short section of it to the windlass maker, or marine hardware dealer, to make certain the windlass ordered will take it. This is

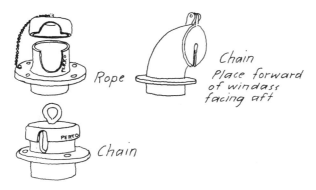

*170. Chain Deck Plates or Navel Irons for Anchor*
*Chain Lockers*

not usually necessary with small chain and windlasses, however, but it would be safest to order chain and windlass from the same firm, asking that the windlass be checked against the chain.

## Chain Plates

If the chain plates are outside the planking, they may now be placed. They will show to the best advantage if they are made to stand in line with the shrouds. This can be easily accomplished by taking the angle of each off the blueprint, using the sheer line, or edge of deck, as the base line. If the chain plates are made as usual, of bar or strap metal, the tops must be bent inboard to stand with the shrouds when viewed from forward, if turn-buckles are used in the shrouds. This should be done while fitting the chain plates, not after they are secured. The top of the chain plates may have to be drilled for a link or for the jaws of the turnbuckles; in either case it is a mistake to drill a hole that just fits the bolt of the turnbuckle jaws, or the link; a little tolerance is desirable. An oval-shaped hole is most desirable, as this gives enough clearance to prevent binding.

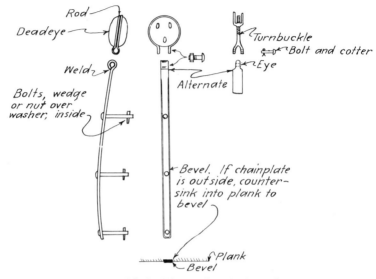

*171. Chain Plates, Large Vessels*

Fastening the chain plates should be done carefully. Do not use too many fastenings: a single bolt of large diameter through planking, frame, and sheer clamp is worth three small fastenings in planking and frame. All chain-plate bolts should be through-all, set up on the inside. Before setting up these bolts, place a grommet of calking under the chain plate, around the bolts. Clench rings, instead of flat washers, should be used inside. Bob-stay plates and bowsprit shroud plates should be secured with

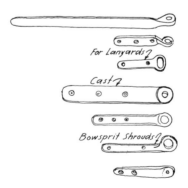

*172. Small-Boat Chain Plates*

through-fastenings and should line up with the wire. All outside strapping, such as chain plates, should be let into the planking slightly. This makes the strapping less liable to damage and much more sightly, as there are no openings visible between straps and

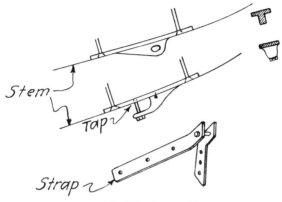

*173. Typical Bobstay Fittings*

hull. Chain plates should never be made of half-oval straps; these will appear heavy and awkward when in place. Boltheads may or may not be countersunk, but countersinking gives the best appearance.

## Chocks

Chocks can also be placed. It is rarely possible to fasten these with anything but screws or hatch nails. Screws are usually the most practical fastenings. Set the chocks in wet paint, or varnish, and make certain they bear on the full length of their flanges. Chocks let into the log rail should be fitted to lock into place, with very little strain brought on the fastenings. The placing of the chocks should be shown in the plans. Powerboats and small sailing craft often use chocks in place of hawse fittings; these chocks should be strongly secured.

## Powerboat Deck Hardware

Deck hardware on power craft—consisting of cleats, metal bitts, davits, and flag sockets—can be placed from the blueprints, but it is a good plan not to place all hardware in sailing craft but to wait until the boat is being rigged and to place hardware to fit the lead of the rigging. Very often the plans are not correct in this respect; it is often impractical for the designer to fix the leads of gear on the plans, as so much depends upon the fit and cut of the sails.

## Davits

Davits on power craft should be stepped very securely. They may be obtained, with the necessary fittings, from marine hardware dealers. If the davits cannot be supported by a substantial bulwark, they must have their heels below deck. The heel fitting can be placed on a block secured to the hull frames with lags, or through-bolts, but in fitting this look out for the exhaust piping and steering cable. The deck fitting should be in a wide covering board; if in a canvased deck, use a false covering board laid on top of the canvas, along the sheer of the boat.

## Lifting Eyes

Small power and light sailing craft should be fitted with lifting eyes; these should be carefully selected to withstand the load put on them in hoisting the boat out. There are many types on the market, to fit all sizes and weights of hulls. The most common type of lifting eye is made of two fittings, one on deck and the other on the keel, connected by a rod threaded into each fitting. The fittings should be through-bolted, of course, in all but the lightest of hulls. Heavy hulls require the eye and rod to be in one unit, set up as a through-bolt, from deck to underside of keel. If a lifting eye, or eyes, must be fitted, the designer should be asked to design and place them; these are not matters for haphazard guessing. Even when it is not intended to hoist a power-boat out of water, bodily, with hoisting gear and eyes, one well aft will often be very useful for making minor repairs to propeller, rudder, strut, or stern bearing.

## Cost of Hardware

In fitting hardware it is desirable to keep in mind the cost. Too often a plainly finished hull is fitted with the most expensive bronze or plated hardware, with incongruous results. The finish of the hardware, and its cost, should certainly have some relation to the finish and basic cost of the hull. A great deal of money can be spent foolishly if the builder's enthusiasm for "fine hardware" runs away with his judgment. "Use only what is needed" is a fine rule, but one admittedly hard to follow.

## Requirements for Painting and Varnishing

Painting and varnishing are important matters to the boatbuilder. In the first place, there is a common misunderstanding: the finish of a boat is not a matter for a last-minute decision, as many seem to think. If the boat, or any part of it, is to be finished "bright," either with varnish or oil, the wood and workmanship must be fitted to the finish. Nothing is more unsatisfactory to both owner and builder than an attempt to varnish a surface originally planned to be painted. Upkeep of brightwork is another matter that must be considered; to retain a good appearance all brightwork must receive constant attention, while the boat is in active service. Any neglect will require extensive repairs to the finish. It is not practical to attempt bright finish when the lumber used is not of the best grade. Paint finish is therefore the most suitable for the average boat, where attention to upkeep is subject to limitation and where low-cost lumber is used in construction.

## Advice

Most of the advice to be given in painting is elementary. The surface to be painted must be smooth, dry, and clean of dust, grease, or dirt. On this must be built up the finish, using a series of coats; one or two thick coats are useless. Each coat of paint should serve a purpose and only marine paint should be used. Only good-quality paints will stand up in marine work; cheap paint will not last. It is well to leave experimenting to others and to buy paint from recognized marine paint manufacturers. As each coat is applied, time must be allowed for it to thoroughly dry before the next coat is started. Sanding down each coat, except the last, is necessary if a really smooth surface is desired. This is very tiresome but cannot be avoided if a good finish is expected.

## *Painting*

The first coat laid on is the "prime coat." This is sometimes
flat paint thinned down with turps; sometimes the painter mixes
his own primer, or uses one of the prepared primers. In any case,
the prime coat is put on as thin as possible, no attempt being made
to cover well. Some put on a coat of boiled linseed oil and allow
this to thoroughly soak in before putting on the prime coat. This
is claimed to give a smoother finish than would be possible by
applying the prime coat to the bare wood. Another plan is to first
shellac the bare wood, using thin white shellac. This serves to fill
the grain of the wood, but probably at the cost of adhesion in the
prime coat. Aluminum paint is also used by some builders, particularly when the wood is stained. This will give excellent
coverage, it is true, and will hide severe stains, but at the cost of
adhesion in the finish coats. In these days of chemical paintmaking
it is a good plan to paint as the manufacturer directs, taking care
that all coats are of the same brand of paint. Mixture of brands
might result in a chemical action that would damage the surface
and life of the paint. Pure lead paint is still accepted as standard
by most professional painters; if this is used there is little danger
of trouble, as long as all the brands used are lead paints.

Mixed primer can be made by dissolving pure white lead with
turps, stirred until smooth. The mixture should be fairly thick.
Add a little red lead, enough to make the mixture a light pink.
When ready to use, add linseed oil in the same quantity as the
turps used. Test on a piece of wood. If you cannot see the grain
through the first coat laid on, the primer is too thick and should
be thinned by the addition of equal parts of turps and oil. If prepared paint is used, it should be thinned as directed by the manufacturer; if prepared primer is used, the instructions on the can
should be followed exactly. Lay on the prime coat and allow to
dry thoroughly, then sand lightly and dust before starting the
next coat. Sanding should be done with medium weight of sandpaper; do not be alarmed if it appears that most of the prime coat
is rubbed off—there is enough in the pores of the wood for a
foundation. Be certain the surface is clean before starting the
new coat.

The second coat should be primer slightly thicker than the

first coat. Care must be taken that the paint has no lumps or dirt in it; strain the paint through cheesecloth if there is any doubt as to its cleanliness or smoothness. The second coat, when dry, should be rubbed down with very fine sandpaper, then thoroughly dusted.

The third painting should be done with a flat coat of the color chosen for the finish, if a full enamel is to be used in the final coat. If, however, the final coat is to be a "semigloss," then it is usually necessary to mix the flat coat with semigloss, half and half. If semigloss is applied over a flat coat, flat spots will usually appear in the final coat. Usually it is a good plan to thin the third coat slightly, but this is not a matter that can be ruled upon arbitrarily as each brand of paint requires individual treatment that can only be learned by experience with it. If in doubt, it is usually safe to thin slightly with turps only.

When the third coat is dry, sand very lightly with very fine sandpaper and dust. The final coat should then be laid on. Before doing this, however, clean up around the work so that there will be no dust; wet the ground or floor around the boat if necessary. If painting can be done indoors, close the shop tightly, even though it is stuffy. If the work must be done in the open, pick a dry, still day, but not a cold one. The final coat will be either a semigloss or an enamel. Open a new can and stir thoroughly right down to the bottom of the can. Most enamels and semigloss marine paints are quite thick but should rarely be thinned. Thinning of the final coat, if necessary, should be done as directed by the manufacturer, usually by adding a little linseed oil—rarely turps. Apply the finish coat with a large, soft brush, brushing in more than one direction. Do not start a surface unless you can finish it in the same day. After completing the final coat, leave the shop closed and allow plenty of time for drying. Even when the paint is dry it will be soft for some time, as long as ten days if the humidity is high at the time.

## Suggestions

The method described will give a fine surface if patience is used. However, this care is only necessary when the finish of the woodwork warrants an equally fine paint finish. In many cases the use of three coats, primer well sanded, flat coat lightly sanded, and then the finish coat, will be all that is necessary. Mixing colors, to get a shade not standard, is inviting trouble later, when it may be necessary to touch up some surface. Lining off two colors requires care and patience. First, the line should be struck off in pencil after the prime coat is on. The color above the line is first completed, then the one below, taking care to avoid over-running the line. When the first color is dry, the second is started. Lining off by use of scotch tape is sometimes possible; a small sheet of tin held in one hand and placed on the line while painting to it will answer in most jobs. In working two colors on a flat surface the tape is satisfactory.

## *Varnishing*

Varnishing is much like painting, except that no undercoats are required. Success depends upon having a well-finished surface before varnishing. Bright finish shows up every scratch and mar, so exceptional care is necessary if a fine finish is desired. The wood must be dry and all dust must be removed. After sanding the wood, it must not be allowed to get wet; many woods will mark if this happens. It is sometimes necessary to apply stain, to artificially color the wood. Stains can be obtained ready mixed and these are preferable to mixing one's own stain. Most hardwood, and the mahoganies, require a penetrating stain; pure aniline dye is sometimes used. After a stain is applied, it is allowed to stand about half an hour and is then rubbed off with clean, coarse sacking, or old, clean canvas. Evening up the tones in mahogany or oak can be done with bleaches; for mahogany, use graded mixtures of chloride of lime and water. Dark spots in oak and mahogany can be bleached out by using a mixture of oxalic acid and water, a teaspoon of the former to a pint of the latter. Prepared bleaches can be purchased in most large paint stores.

All bleaches should be applied in diluted coats to accomplish their purpose: a strong bleach might do more harm than good. If desired, a good filler can be had by painting the wood with one or two coats of linseed oil, allowing these to soak in before the first coat of varnish is applied. Varnish should not be thinned; brushing out the varnish while applying is important. Four coats of varnish are considered necessary in a good job; when each coat (except the last) is dry, it is lightly sanded and well dusted before the next coat is laid on. Dirt, dust, and marks on the wood are usually the cause of poor appearance in varnish work, if the woodwork is suitable. Only marine varnish should be used in a boat, inside or out.

## *Brushes*

Brushes are an important factor in good painting and varnishing. Only good brushes are to be used, and a good brush is pretty expensive. Rubber-set bristles are the most popular. Before using a new brush, soak it in water for a day and there is less likelihood of its losing bristles. Most professional painters trim the flat brushes by tapering them from the top of the bristles (where they are held to the handle by a metal band) to the tip. The width

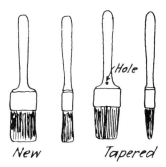

*174. Preparing a Paintbrush*

of the tip is usually about half the width of the brush at the band, viewed edgewise. The broadside view also shows a slight taper at the sides. The tapering can be done with a small pair of shears.

There are brushes for all purposes. For priming and flat coats a brush 2 to 3 inches wide is commonly used. For finish coats a narrower brush is preferred, say, $1\frac{1}{4}$ to $1\frac{3}{4}$ inches. Brushes for lining off are often very narrow, $\frac{1}{4}$ or $\frac{1}{2}$ inches. For bottom paint a 4-inch brush is popular. Bevel point brushes are used for lining off also; these are sold as "sash brushes." Varnish brushes are often round or oval; flat varnish brushes are often bought with long bristles. Generally speaking, the bristles of a varnish brush should be softer than one used for paint; brushes used for enamel should be softer than those used for flat coats. For lettering and striping, the narrow camel's-hair artist's brush is useful; standard lettering brushes are more common, however. The bevel point sash brushes are most useful of all for lining off against projections—under the rail caps, for example.

The builder should have a brush for every color and purpose. This costs money and so the care of brushes is important. To keep a brush in working order, drill a hole through the handle, just above the band holding the bristles. This should be large enough to allow the brush to be threaded on a heavy wire. Next, obtain a deep pan, or can, deep enough so that the bristles of any brush will not touch the bottom when the brush is threaded on a wire laid across the top of the pan, or can. It is a good plan to have a number of these pans, so that brushes can be separated for purpose and color. When through with a brush, wash out the bristles in turpentine, flicking the turps out. Then place it on the wire so that it stands upright in the pan. The pan may be filled with water or turpentine. If the brush is not to be used for a long time, it may first be thoroughly cleaned in turps and flicked dry, then carefully washed out in warm water with a little soap powder in it. The brush should then be flicked dry and hung up in a warm, dry spot.

## Schedule, Remarks

Before using a new brush on the work, try it out by painting a piece of scrap lumber; this will work out any loose bristles and dirt. Keep one wide, soft brush for dusting. A rubber drip cup, to fit around the handle of a brush, is very useful for overhead work. The tendency of a beginner to overload the brush with paint must be avoided: do not try to cover too much surface with one brushful. Painting cannot be hurried if a good job is desired. The usual schedule of painting a new boat is as follows—prime coat outside, prime coat inside, bottom paint, inside flat coat and finish, outside flat coat and finish, and final coat of bottom paint. The bottom paint requires no primer. Some put on a coat of red lead, or a primer, before using nonfouling paint; this gives a smooth surface perhaps, but shortens the life of the bottom paint very markedly and damages the antifouling qualities. In choosing bottom paint, it is a good idea to make inquiries among local boatmen concerning the types and brands of paint in favor along the water front. It is usually found that some type or brand is generally preferred, due to the powers of a given paint to withstand local conditions. In waters where worms are exceptionally troublesome it is not uncommon for painters to add creosote to bottom paint, or to use a prime coat of creosote, thinned with turps, or heated. The addition of creosote, or its use as a primer, will often give a mottled effect to the bottom, but this is less objectionable than a worm-eaten strake.

At least two coats of bottom paint are required; one is put on after priming topsides and interior, the second just before launching. When the boat is launched, the last coat should be tacky. Though two coats of bottom paint will usually serve, three are better in a new hull. Racing bottoms are usually painted with a gloss paint, made for the purpose, having slight antifouling qualities. This paint is commonly built up of three coats, using one as a primer by thinning the paint with turps. Sanding between each coat is resorted to, but this cannot be done with regular antifouling bottom paints as they are too soft. In applying all standard brands of paint, be sure to consult the dealer and read the instructions on the can. Often a brand will develop certain oddities: for example, a standard yacht black can be laid on and then must be rebrushed sometime later before it will dry in a reasonable period. This quality was found in only one brand, however, and might not exist in paint made at a later date. Experimenting with a brand of paint, before using it on the new hull, is therefore necessary.

There is a question as to the desirability of using expensive paint on a new boat. This is raised because of the unseasoned planking commonly used and because some planking will not hold paint as well as others. If a boat is built of unseasoned timber, or even partially seasoned stock, there is no question as to the economic desirability of using cheap paint, for no paint will retain a good surface or give proper protection when applied to poorly seasoned stock. It is a matter of common sense, therefore, to use a cheap brand the first year and then to burn this off and apply a standard brand at the beginning of the second year. This is not to say that a hull built of green or partially seasoned stock is desirable, but it is foolish to assume that all boats are built of perfect materials. Some timber does not take paint well: cypress and yellow pine, as well as some tropical hardwoods, have this quality. If these are used for planking, it may take a year or two before a really satisfactory surface can be obtained.

## Straight Boot Top

Striking the boot top, or bottom paint line, is not difficult if the line is straight. First, level the hull athwartships and then mark the height of the line on bow and stern. The height of these points on the hull may be laid off from dimensions obtained by scaling the drawings. Then erect gallows, or horses, at bow and stern; the height of the top of these should be level with the marks at

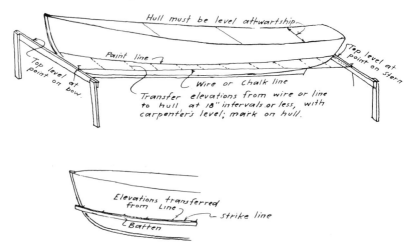

*175. Common Method of Striking Water Line or Boot Top*

each end of the hull, and should be also level across. Next, a chalk line, or wire, is stretched over the gallows, or horses, and set up taut. With a carpenter's level, it is possible to level from the line to the hull, at short intervals. Marks obtained on the hull in this manner may then be lined off by tacking a light square batten on the hull so as to have a marking edge. The line may be marked with pencil or "raced" in (cut in) with a race knife.

## Sheered Boot Top

Boot tops that are sheered are more difficult. They are usually lined off by measurements taken from the sheer of the hull, which are found by scaling the plans at convenient stations. These measurements are, of course, plumb, and must be leveled into the hull. A new cloth tape is often used as a plumb line, a suitable weight being attached. When marks are obtained on the hull, they are faired in with a batten, as with straight boot tops. It is always necessary to sight in the paint line and to check both sides, before cutting the lines into the planking. Attach the lining-off batten to the hull with as few brads as possible, so as not to force it into an unfair position by bringing the inside face to bear fully on the hull planking.

## Painting Scheme, Deck Paint

The color which a boat is painted is a matter of personal taste. The only important question relating to this is in regard to deck paint. In hot climates, offwhite, light gray, or yellow, or very light green, is preferable to dark colors. In cold climates dark colors will serve, but warm tones are undoubtedly best. This also applies to cabin floors. Dark colors, or dark woods finished bright, are hardly suitable for cabins, unless used in moderation to form a contrast to light colors or woods. Painted and varnished decks are very slippery when wet, unless treated in some manner to prevent this. Perhaps the most common method of overcoming this objection to painted and varnished decks is to sprinkle them, while the paint or varnish is still wet, with fine sand; this can be done satisfactorily by using a large salt shaker and very fine, sharp, clean sand. Another way is to use pumice stone, ground fine. This powder is mixed with the paint, using about a teaspoonful to the quart. There are also some "nonskid" paints on the market which are quite satisfactory. The only fault of these is that they are dull and give the effect of a flat coat rather than a gloss deck. Practically this is preferable, but some owners object to it. The painting of canvas decks and trunk roofs has been discussed in an earlier chapter; slipperiness is overcome in the same way as on wooden decks.

## Spars, Rigging, and Sails

Spars, rigging, and sails are matters about which a builder must have knowledge—spars, particularly, since the builder usually makes them. Rigging is best done by a professional rigger if a great deal is required; the builder must know the principles, however, so that he can properly place the rigging fittings and supervise the work. The sails should be made by a professional sailmaker, but the builder must know how to bend them and to lead the running rigging that works them. In general, modern small sailing craft are usually overrigged; this has been brought about by the necessity of trusses to hold the excessively light masts, often used, in place. There is a question, at least, as to the desirability of these masts in small boats, particularly in those boats denominated as "cruisers." Not only do light masts and the involved rigging they require add greatly to the cost, but also the rigging must cause resistance, due to windage, when the boat is on the wind. The increased emphasis on truss rigging, in recent years, is very curious when viewed in the light of the emphasis on "streamlining" of masts, fittings, and even hull topsides, seen in racing craft. In very small craft the great popularity of truss rigging is undoubtedly due, partly at least, to fashion rather than to practical necessity. It would seem that the interest in aerodynamic design of sails would extend to rigging, eventually, so that future rig design will parallel airplane wing design, where exposed truss rigging has been entirely eliminated.

## Sparmaking

Although sparmaking requires knowledge, solid spars are not particularly difficult to build, as a rule. Some hollow spars are not very difficult either, but others not only require great skill and experience but also a good deal of equipment. Solid spars, or those pieced up of two halves, can be built by a beginner; the box-shaped hollow spars are but little more difficult. Round or streamlined hollow spars, built up of a number of small ribbands glued together, or spars built of veneer, are not for amateur construction: only well-equipped and experienced professional builders would attempt to make them. Even these would usually call on the services of experienced sparmakers or shops. Solid spars are also difficult when built up of small timbers glued, or banded, together. The strength and lasting qualities of any glued spar depend to a great extent upon the joining of the various parts;

this must be done with the greatest accuracy, so machine tools are almost a necessity.

## Dimensions

The dimensions of any mast, or spar, must be taken from the sail plan furnished by the designer. There should be no deviation from these under any circumstances. If a hull is designed for hollow masts, or spars, she must be so fitted; if designed for solid sticks, do not use hollow ones. At least, don't make a change without consulting the designer and obtaining from him new drawings showing the changes necessary in spar diameter and rigging arrangement.

## Timber, Solid Masts, and Spars

Spar timber for solid masts should be as clear of knots as possible. The smaller the diameter of the spar, the clearer the stock must be. For the average small sailing boat, the best spar timbers are Sitka spruce, white or Norway pine, and Douglas fir. The Northeastern spruce is usually full of small knots and is therefore not suitable for small spars. It may be used, however, for large sticks, if the diameter is reasonably large and the knots are sound—not larger than the diameter of a pencil. In southern waters spars are made of hard pine, longleaf, loblolly, rosemary, or Caribbean; these are very heavy and the hull fitted with them must have a good deal of stability in order to carry them to advantage. If a hull is designed for spars of a given material, or given materials, change to other timbers is not permissible. Solid masts and spars are best made of saplings, or tree trunks, rather than from sawn timbers. The latter are often cut so that the stick is cross-grained, or with the heart exposed only on one side of the stick. In selecting a spar stick it should be box-heart, if sawn. Northeastern spruce and Sitka spruce are very flexible when green, but stiffen markedly when fully seasoned. If green wood is used, do not be surprised if the mast bends excessively while the boat is new; the second season should show an improvement in the stiffness as the timber becomes seasoned. White and Norway pine sticks have the same quality but to a much less marked degree. All-heartwood sticks are preferred when these pines are used. Fir is less desirable than either spruce or the soft pines, being heavier and often weak, due to long slivers of grain not bonded. These often appear close to the heart, where they do the most harm. Small knots are permissible in soft pine and fir, if they are solid and not larger than those specified in spruce spar timber. It may be well to point out that large, heavy spars, such as used in workboats and some cruising yachts, need not be so clear of knots, and may have knots large as a quarter if they are not loose.

Spar timber, theoretically, should be well seasoned; this is best done by first removing all bark and then placing the sticks afloat, in water deep enough to permit floating at all times. If, however, this is not practical, and seasoned timber is not available, green wood can be used, but it will check very quickly. These seasoning checks are unsightly, but do not weaken the spar; if you value the life of a spar, do not fill the checks with putty, white lead, glue, plastic wood, or seam compound. The use of any filler will develop rot in the checks. If any protection is used at all, linseed oil, or wood preservative, squirted into the checks with an oil can, can be resorted to. Seasoning checks will open and close with the change in humidity of the air that occurs with each change in the weather.

### Timber, Hollow Masts and Spars

Timber for hollow, or pieced-up, spars must be thoroughly seasoned and must be free from knots and blemishes. Spruce and Douglas fir are the most suitable timbers for hollow spars, Sitka spruce preferably. If possible, the stock should run the length of the spar in one piece, but this is not an absolute necessity. Built-up solid spars and all hollow spars must be glued, so dampness in the wood must be avoided; the timber must be carefully stored in a dry place. These spars must be made under cover, of course.

### Length of Solid Spar Stick, Dimensions Commonly Used

A stick for a solid spar must be somewhat longer than the required finished length, so that end checks and shakes can be trimmed off. The "stick length" of a spar is its total length from end to end. In masts the length dimensions usually given are: the depth of the tenon, or depth of the socket in the step; the "bury" or depth from top of deck at mast hole to bottom of step socket; "hounded length" or length from top of deck at mast hole to the shoulder for the shrouds; "deck to pin" or length from top of deck to pin of the sheave for halyards of mainsail; "head" or length from shoulder, or sheave pin, to the top of the mast. Sometimes the mast dimension "heel to truck" is given; this is the over-all length ("stick length") of the mast. Boom and gaff lengths are usually taken from the after face of the mast to the end of the stick; from this length is deducted the space required by jaws, gooseneck, or track fitting. Do not mistake the dimension of the foot of the sail for the boom length; the boom must be longer than the foot of the sail. Bowsprit lengths are taken from the face of the stem, as a rule. Practice in dimensioning spars varies a little among designers; make sure you are right before cutting a spar for length.

## Diameters

The diameters of masts and spars are usually given at various places along the stick. Mast diameters are usually given at the heel, above the tenon, and at the deck or partners, again about halfway from deck to shrouds, at the shrouds and at the head. Booms and gaffs have three diameters given, one at each end and one at the middle or at the point of strain, as at the sheet or halyard bands.

## Taper

Masts and spars of fore-and-aft rigged craft are not tapered on all sides. The side of the mast nearest the sail and the bottom of the gaff and the top of booms and jib clubs are straight lines; the taper of these spars is on the sides, and on the face away from the sail. An exception to this rule is when the sails are loose-footed, that is, the foot of the sail is not secured to the boom except at the extreme ends. In this case the spars are tapered on all sides. Spars to which any sail is secured along its edge—by lacing, track and slides, hoops, or by the bolt rope inserted in a groove in the spar—should always be straight on the side toward the sail. The practice in bowsprits varies with the type of hull: in many all the taper is on the top and sides, the bottom being straight; in others the taper is on the sides and bottom or on all four sides. If the bowsprit is to appear bent, or "hogged" down, the taper is always on top and the bottom is either straight or is shaped to curve downward at the outer end. Spinnaker poles and yards are tapered on all sides; so are sprit booms. Box, plank, and T-booms are straight on top; the designer usually gives details for the construction of these spars when they are specified.

## Timber Sticks

The length of the stick required for a given spar should be from 3 to 5 feet longer than the finished spar; the diameter at the small end should be large enough, when squared, to contain the diameter of the small end of the spar. There is usually no difficulty in this, except in long masts where the diameter at the shrouds, or "hounds," is often so great that it is difficult to find a stick large enough at the small end. Fir sticks of great size may be obtained from lumber dealers specializing in spar timber, or may be obtained from the West coast; these are eight-sided when shipped. Squared timber is also used in some sections; large, heavy spars are often obtained sawn square, to save time in shaping. Small spars are also purchased square, in some sections. Except for the objection to sawn sticks mentioned earlier, this saves time in shaping. If a solid spar must be made to carry a large spread of sail for a given diameter, it is undoubtedly best to hew out the spar from a tree or sapling by hand.

## Hewing

The process of hewing spars is laborious and requires practice, but the results are worth the trouble, in large spars at least. The timber is brought from the water and is blocked up off the ground or shop floor so that the top of the timber is a little more than knee-high. The spar timber may be supported on leveled blocks or horses, so that it can be rolled over when required. The supports should be close enough together to prevent sagging at any time. Hewing is done with a broadax, or broad hatchet if the spar is small. The handling of these tools is very important, as carelessness will result in serious injury to the user. The advice of a highly skilled user is worth quoting: "keep the handle low, so that the end of the handle is lower than the blade when it strikes; then if the blade misses it will go into the ground, or chips, rather than into the foot, or leg, of the user." The use of this tool will be fully explained later. The stick must be as straight as possible. If it is curved, the spar must be cut to curve with the heartwood; this is often done in masts so that the curve of the finished spar is fore and aft, but never athwartships. Then the stays can be used to pull it straight, or nearly so. A curved boom or gaff is undesirable.

In shaping the spar keep in mind that the center of the heartwood of the stick should be the center of the spar, as nearly as possible. The sapwood should be hewn away as much as is practical. Hewing starts by picking the foreside of the mast, or the top of a boom, or underside of a gaff, and turning the stick so that this side is toward the worker. Hew a plumb spot at each block or horse; to do this the supports must stand level and a plumb bob is used to check the hewing. With cant hooks, or by rolling, turn the stick so that the opposite side is toward the worker; hew plumb spots at the supports. Roll timber foreside up and find center line at each end. Strike center line on stick with chalk line and chalk. Lay off the given diameters (the method of laying off spar tapers to a few given dimensions will be described later) at the predetermined stations on this line, using it as the center line for the given diameters, of course. The stations should not be over 6 feet apart. At each station notch and cut a plumb spot to the mark. Now the stick can be hewn from station to station, taking care to plumb the face hewn. It may help to strike off a line from station to station, on the rough surface of the top, to guide the hewing. It is not correct to hew one side at a time; either hew both sides together, or hew 6 feet on one side, then on the other, until both sides are complete. When two sides are hewn, turn the stick and repeat the lining off and hewing. The stick is now squared to the rough taper of the spar. It must now be eight sided.

To mark the stick for this, various gauges are used: the most common is a short piece of board with two nails, one at each end and with width apart equal to the widest part of the squared timber; then two pencils, or nails, spaced so as to divide the space between the end nails into the proper spacing to scribe the lines required to eight-side the stick. The gauge is operated on a tapered stick by always keeping the guiding nails in contact with both sides, turning the gauge sidewise (toward the direction it is moving) while drawing it along the stick. The old-time sparmakers used a folding (one-joint) two-foot rule. This was opened, and, with both ends tangent to the outside edges of the timber, and the rule along the station line, dots were made at the 7- and 17-inch divisions. This, repeated around the stick, divided the section there into an octagon.

The eight-siding of a square may be laid out as follows. Draw intersecting diagonals, from corner to corner, across the figure. Take a compass and, with one point at a corner of the square and the other at the intersection of the diagonals at the middle of the square, sweep an arc to the sides of the square. Repeat this with the pivot leg at each corner of the square, and strike in the necessary points to form an octagon; this laid off to the square of the butt of a stick will enable a gauge to be made. The stick is now worked to the lines, to make it eight-sided, using adz or drawknife. The spar can then be rounded with a drawknife. This should be done by drawing the tool at an angle, rather than directly toward the operator, so that spiral shavings are made. Large outside calipers are used to test the stick for roundness. The final step is to plane the spar with a jointer plane, taking out any unfairness. Scraping and sanding may be done just before putting the rigging over, prior to stepping the stick. Sanding is done with a spiral motion.

## Small Spars

Small solid spars may be made with less hard work; the cutting from eight-side to round can be done with a smooth plane, using a jack plane to jointer off. The broad hatchet will be found useful in hewing small masts and spars. If these are made from sawn timbers, the hatchet will speed up eight-siding. Hewing to a line should be mastered, using both ax and hatchet.

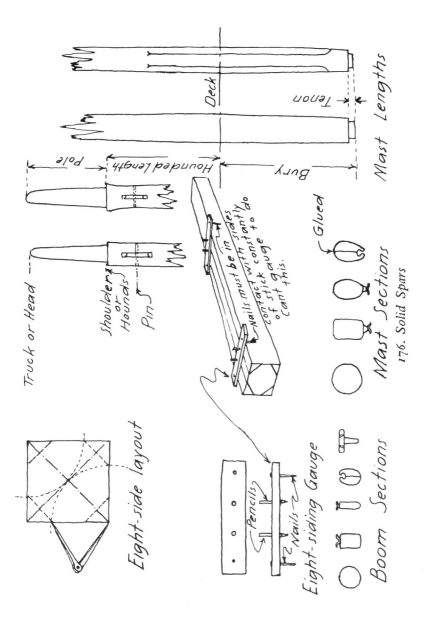

Mast Lengths

Deck

Tenon

Bury

Pole   Hounded Length

Truck or Head

Shoulders or Hounds

Pin

Nails must be in sides contact with constantly of stick gauge to can't this. do

Glued

Mast Sections

176. Solid Spars

Eight-side layout

Pencils

Nails

Eight-siding Gauge

Boom Sections

## Design of Taper

The design of a solid spar is often left to the builder. Perhaps only a few diameters are given in the plans, so the taper must be laid off in order to obtain intermediate diameters. There are many ways of laying off taper, but the following is perhaps the most common. Suppose a mast is to be laid off; diameters given are 5 inches at heel, 8 inches at partners, 6 inches at hounds, and 3 inches at truck. The taper is laid off from given dimension to given dimension. Measure the distance between each given di-

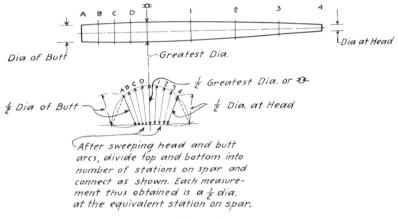

*After sweeping head and butt arcs, divide top and bottom into number of stations on spar and connect as shown. Each measurement thus obtained is a ½ dia. at the equivalent station on spar.*

*177. Spar Tapers*

ameter. If the distance from heel to partner is 5 feet, the distance from deck to hounds 30 feet, and from hounds to truck is 5 feet, it will be desirable to find a diameter at 2 feet 6 inches below the partners—at, say, 3-foot intervals above the partners to the hounds and at 2 feet 6 inches above the hounds. In other words, the number of stations at which diameters are wanted is decided.

This done, proceed as follows: lay off a straight line, on a piece of paper or plywood, the length of which is a few inches greater than the largest given diameter, and at the middle of the line erect a perpendicular somewhat higher than half of the greatest spar diameter. With a compass lay off the arc of half the largest given spar diameter with the intersection of the two lines just drawn as the pivot point of the arc. The arc should reach from horizontal line to horizontal line, passing through the perpendicular.

The greatest given diameter of the mast is 8 inches; the radius of the arc is therefore 4 inches. This is the height of the perpendicular from horizontal line to arc. Now, below the partners we want one intermediate station and above we want nine intermediate stations, or ten equal divisions of the length. Take the heel diameter first; this is 5 inches. Set the compass at half of this—2½ inches. With one leg at the intersection of the right-hand intersection of the arc and the horizontal line, sweep an arc on the first arc drawn. Then transfer the pivot point of the compass to the intersection of the two arcs and, with the same radius, sweep an arc from the intersection of the first arc and horizontal line below and up to the horizontal line again. This gives another intersection on the horizontal line inside the ends of the first arc drawn.

Now draw a straight line from this intersection to the radius or pivot point of the arc last drawn, which is above the horizontal line on the arc first drawn; the length of this line is half of the heel diameter. Now divide the arc with dividers or compass from the perpendicular to the intersection of the line last drawn with the first arc into two parts; the horizontal line from the perpendicular to the intersection of it and the line last drawn (half of heel diameter) into two equal parts; then connect the points thus obtained. The line so drawn is half of the diameter at 2 feet 6 inches below the partners. Then on the left-hand side of the perpendicular proceed the same way, using half the hound diameter for the arcs at the end of the first arc drawn and then dividing the arc and horizontal line, from the half-hound diameter to the perpendicular, into ten equal spaces, to give nine additional half diameters. Proceed as before and lay these off in exactly the same way as the first half diameter found for 2 feet 6 inches below the partners. Each half diameter found can be tabulated so that it is easily found when laying off the taper on the rough stick. The wanted diameter at 2 feet 6 inches above the hounds is found in the same manner, using half the hound diameter for the initial arc and the truck or head diameter for the second arc. The application of this method to any spar follows the directions just given.

## Mast Shaping

In shaping masts, consult the plans; sometimes the mast is swelled from a little below the hounds, to give a wider shoulder for the support of the shrouds, or the spreaders. At the partners the mast may be round, square, or eight-sided. Eight-siding is sometimes carried up to a little below the boom. If there is a reduction in the diameter of the mast, from a little above the hounds to the top, or truck, this must be noted and carried out. The details of spreaders or other fittings at the hounds will be shown in the sail plan; these should be sufficient to carry out the construction without instructions here. The mast should not be cut off at the proper length until it is fully shaped; be careful to get the right over-all length, to allow for heel tenon, and then make certain that the tenon is cut so any curve in the stick will be fore and aft, when the mast is stepped. It is a good plan to lay off the positions of all mast fittings and mark them with crayon, pencil, or chalk, so that the hardware may be fitted immediately. Very often a little reduction in the mast diameter, or spar diameter, at some point, will be necessary to fit the hardware. Under no circumstances should grooves be cut in a spar, or mast, to fit any hardware; the whole stick should be reduced if the hardware is too small, or new hardware should be obtained of the proper size. While a slight reduction in spar diameter, to fit hardware, is usually permissible, it is always better to correct the hardware rather than the stick. On the other hand, it may be found that the hardware is a little too large; in this circumstance the hardware on hand may often be fitted by inserting one or two thicknesses of canvas or leather. This should be seated in wet paint or varnish. Special care is necessary in fitting hardware to a green stick; if possible it is better to use some wood preservative under all hardware, in this case. This is particularly true under any sheet metal applied to a mast, or spar, to prevent chafe—as at the place where boom or gaff jaws ride, for example.

## Hollow Spars

Hollow spars are designed by the designer; he furnishes a sketch of the taper, or shape, required with the sail plan. This should be laid out full size, but fore-shortened as to length.

Usually the taper may be laid out using a length scale of 1½ or 3 inches to the foot, and the diameters full size. It will often be found that the after face may be used for a base line in the profile, but a center line will have to be established for the athwart-ship view. The selection of material has been mentioned. The size of material will be specified, or drawn, by the designer; the latter is usually accomplished in one or more cross sections. It is not the purpose of this discussion to describe all types of hollow spars; only those most suitable for the beginner, or for a shop with little equipment, will be given attention. It must be emphasized that the builder must make no changes in length, diameter, thickness of material, or placing of hardware when building a hollow spar, as these matters are strictly within the designer's field. The number of glued longitudinal seams in a hollow spar seems to have some relation to its stiffness; for this reason do not make up a spar of fewer parts than shown in the plans. For the beginner, the hollow square or box section mast is the most suitable. This may be built of four planks, usually tapered in thickness as well as in width. The longitudinal joints may be made square, using four planks of the same thickness, but it is better to make the fore-and-aft faces of thicker material than the sides, rabbeting them so that they cover the raw edges of the side planks.

The process of building is easy. The planks are carefully cut to shape and smoothed. The edges and rabbets should be sanded so that as perfect a joint as possible is made. Use casein glue and mix according to the instructions on the container. Do not do this, however, until you are ready to glue; clamp the spar as soon as possible after the gluing is completed. Speed in spreading the glue and assembling the spar is very important. The spar must be made solid in places: from heel to a little above deck, or at heel and at the partners, at the boom gooseneck, at the shrouds and stays, and at the head. If spreaders are used, the mast must be made solid in their wake. This is done by making softwood cores to fit inside the spar aand inserting these as the spar is assembled; it can't be done afterward. These cores are glued in place. The minimum length of a core, in any mast, should be 12 inches.

It is obvious that such a spar must be planned and laid out correctly, before assembly. The position of every piece of hard-

ware and the location of every fitting (spreaders, sheaves, goosenecks, and tangs, or bands) must be scaled off the plans and
marked on the planks for the mast, or spar, before assembly, so
that cores may be correctly placed. It is very important that the
cores fit accurately; they must be of the correct section and taper.
This job cannot be done quickly or hurriedly. The cap, or head

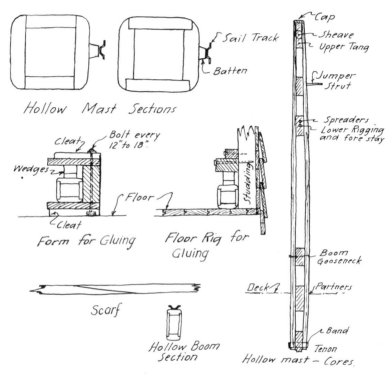

Hollow Mast Sections

Form for Gluing     Floor Rig for Gluing

Scarf

Hollow Boom Section

Hollow mast – Cores

*178. Hollow Spar Details*

core, must be made very carefully in one or two parts, so that
moisture cannot work down inside the mast. If possible, the cap
should be a separate piece from the head core, fitted to cover the
end grain of the fore-and-aft faces and sides. The heel should
be banded above the tenon. Sheet metal can be used in small
masts to make such bands; large masts require a regular cast, or
wrought, band. There is no use making a hollow spar if weight
cannot be saved over a solid spar; keep this in mind while build-

ing and do not let enthusiasm for strength lead you to make too long, or too many, cores, or lead you to too heavy hardware, bands, or spreaders.

When the spar is shaped, the clamps must be prepared. If C-clamps are to be used, prepare four hardwood battens the length of the spar, or a number great enough to equal this. These battens should be about ¾ inch thick and wide enough to prevent the clamp jaws from marring the parts of the spar. Enough clamps should be available to make a double row the length of the spar, spacing the clamps no more than 14 inches apart; 12 inches is preferable. Prepare a place to assemble the spar; this should be a bench long enough to support the whole spar, which can be fashioned of a wide plank fastened to a wall and supported by enough braces to prevent sagging. If this is not practical, use a straight, smooth floor. A few light brads will be useful in holding parts together before clamping; screws are not necessary. Only use enough to do the work; remember, too many add unnecessary weight. If enough clamps are not available, a gluing form can be built. If no suitable floor is available, build a U-shaped trough of heavy timbers, the sides cleated and through-bolted through the bottom. Assemble the spar in this trough, laid on its side, and wedge every 12 inches, against the top side of the trough. If a floor is available, a heavy piece of timber, or two, spiked to the floor, with a cap overhanging on one side spiked to the timber, will serve. Another variation of this is to spike two timbers to the studding of the shop sides and to wedge the spar under this. If the floor is used, it must be perfectly straight, or the mast will be given a permanent bend. It is sometimes necessary to shim up a mast for a slight irregularity in the floor. As the floor or form is straight, the spar must be set up with its straight side against the bottom side of the form or on the floor, the wedges against the opposite curved face. Masts are therefore assembled with their after faces down, on the floor or against the form.

In order to glue up in the least possible time, call in enough help so that each of the workers has only about 6 feet of surface to cover. All parts of the spar must be laid out and each worker must be instructed on the portion of the assembly he is to glue. The edges of the after face, away from the worker, are first covered with glue, laid on smoothly with a brush. Then the side away from the worker is erected and the cores set in glue, as required. Next the front edge of the first part of the mast placed in the form, or on the floor, is glued, the side of the cores toward the worker covered, and then the other side is set up. The top faces of the cores and the top edges of the last-erected sides are covered, then the forward face of the mast is set in place. Due to the curved taper of the sides and forward face of the spar, a few blocks may have to be secured to the form, or floor, to hold these in place, or it may be necessary for some brads to be driven. The last piece fitted, the forward face of the mast, can be wedged as fitted. Wedge loosely at first, to be sure all is in proper alignment; finally set up the wedges very hard, so as to squeeze glue out of every joint, working either way from the middle length. The wedges should be placed from 12 to 18 inches apart.

When the wedges are set up, leave the mast as it is for at least 36 hours, longer if possible. When as much time as can be spared has passed, the mast is removed from the gluing position by knocking out the wedges and is then placed on a bench, or on other supports, so that it lies straight; then it may be shaped, the corners rounded and smoothed up. Give it a coat of spar varnish, or a prime coat of paint, immediately after smoothing up. The life of a glued stick depends upon the care it receives; the glue must be protected at all times from excess moisture. Early morning, in the summertime, is often the best time to glue a mast, or spar; in the wintertime any warm day will do, but usually the shop must be heated, so that gluing should be done early in the day, before the air gets too dry. Quite a lot of humidity is desirable since the mast will be exposed to some dampness in use, even though protected by paint or varnish. In assembling a mast, it is best to cut all mortises for sheaves before starting to glue.

### Fitting Hardware

The fitting of hardware to masts and spars is a very important matter. So far as fit is concerned, theoretically the mast should be cut to fit the hardware, the latter being made to the proper dimensions. As has been suggested in regard to solid spars, this is not always the actual case. Perhaps all the hardware is not on hand when the spars are made or an error is made in ordering. It is not possible to get stock hardware to exact fit, even when the true diameter of a spar is found for the position in which the fitting is placed; stock hardware is not made to minute variations in diameter. Hence a certain amount of cutting and shimming is actually necessary, unless the hardware can be made to order after the spars are completed—a very costly and unnecessary proceeding in ordinary craft. A great deal of the stock rigging hardware usually used on small craft is unnecessarily heavy for the work it has to do. It would be impossible to discuss the various types of rigging hardware in use in the space available; in any case the designer usually specifies that required for a given job. The sail plan shows the position of each piece on the mast and spars. The fastenings of each piece are obvious and common sense is the best guide.

## Spreaders

Spreaders, or struts, are part of the sparmaker's job. These must be made to fit the rig. Their length and position will be shown in the plans. Note the angle they stand to the mast; this is approximately fixed by the shrouds they support. The spreaders should stand so that they bisect the angle formed at their outer ends by the shroud. Spreaders on round masts are usually fixed; those on square masts are usually hinged so that they can rise vertically. Swinging spreaders that can move fore and aft at the outer ends are useless; they are sometimes seen on old yachts, but were due to ignorance on the part of the rigger or designer. In fact, the spreader must always be fixed; hinges are useful merely for convenience in fastening. Once the spreader is properly set it must be locked in position by seizings placed on the shrouds above and below the spreader, or by rod lifts. The latter are angle braces from the top of the spreader to the side of the mast; one is placed on each side of the mast. Wire lifts for the spreaders are not good supports in the modern rigs. Jack stay spreaders, on the foreside of a mast, are commonly double and stand at an angle of about 75 degrees to one another, when viewed from the deck. They should also bisect the angle formed by their shrouds; usually this brings the jack stay spreaders perpendicular to the mast. If single, jack stay spreaders must not swing athwartships. Fixed spreaders are secured to the mast by light strap metal; screws in both mast and spreader are the usual fastenings.

The spreaders should be light and formed so that they do not look heavy; taper on all four sides is desirable for the sake of appearance. Angle clips of metal may be used, instead of hinges, on square masts for jack stay spreaders. Metal spreaders are usually of brass pipe, set in a clevis at the mast, so that the spreader hinges up and down or is set in pipe sockets. The outer end is first threaded and a nut, or two, threaded on; then a slot is cut into which the shroud is placed. Wire seizings on the shroud secure the spreader at the proper angle. Wooden spreaders are slotted at the outer end for the shrouds; a through-rivet or bolt, passed fore and aft through the spreader just inboard of the spreader ends, prevents splitting of the spreader by the shrouds. The shrouds should be secured in the slots by a band around the ends of the spreader, outside the shrouds, or by seizings to the spreader. If the spreader is used as a lookout seat or station, the fastenings and lifts need to be stronger than usual. Shroud spreaders usually have a length, from end to end, at least two thirds the beam of the hull at the mast, often the full beam at mast position. Jack stay spreaders commonly stand out from the mast about one ninth the length of the stay from spreader to mast head.

## Scarfing Masts

It is not desirable to scarf solid masts, but it can be done if no alternative exists. The type of scarf used is often the one seen in lancewood fishing rods. The ordinary hook, or plain scarf, can be used with metal bands at each end of the scarf, and in the middle. The location of the scarf has much to do with the type used; with all but the fishing-rod type the best location is at the partners or just below. Marine or casein glue should be used in the scarf. The fit of the parts of a spar scarf must be very accurate. Hollow spars may be made up of pieces shorter than the spar without difficulty as long as the scarfs are well shifted. The type of scarf in the planks should be that used in clench-boat planking, but the scarf should be glued instead of tacked.

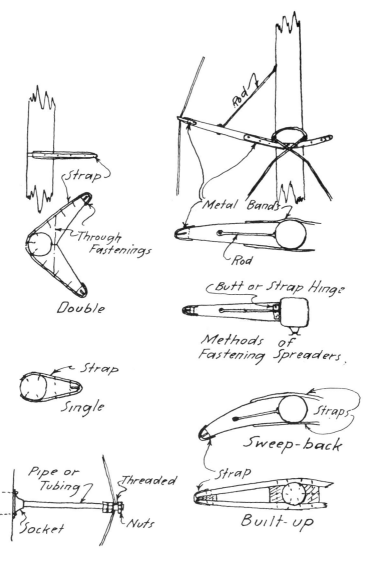

Strap

Through
Fastenings

Double

Rod

Metal Bands

Rod

Butt or Strap Hinge

Methods of
Fastening Spreaders.

Strap

Single

Straps

Sweep-back

Pipe or
Tubing

Threaded

Socket

Nuts

Strap

Built-up

179. Jumper Struts and Spreaders

## Streamlined and Round Hollow Spars

In discussing hollow spars, streamlined or round spars have been mentioned. As has been said, these are not suitable for amateur construction because of the number of parts required to make up a spar and the difficulty in clamping. The latter may be overcome, only at the expense of extra work, in this manner. Before starting to glue, blocks must be made to fit the spar on top and bottom when it is in the form, at each wedging or clamping station, so that the pressure is exerted on the whole surface of the spar. The difficulties of this are obvious when it is remembered that both gluing and clamping must be done very rapidly. Chain clamps are usually used for this work.

## Built-up Solid Spars

Built-up solid spars are best glued together before shaping the outside, as clamping is more easily done while the outside of the spar is in a rough state. These spars, and solid ones, having no shrouds, should have their greatest diameter at or a little above the mainsail boom.

## Rigging

The details of rigging—such as splicing wire and rope, and the power of tackles—have been covered in many books; it is too specialized a matter to be discussed here. The builder who wishes to attempt rigging himself must consult some of the books available on the subject. The use of sockets and clamps in place of splices in wire rigging has come into some popularity in recent years; directions for the use of these fittings are furnished by the manufacturer. It is important, however, that a builder know how to measure and cut rigging, and how to place deck blocks, fairleads, and how to reeve off running rigging. While the sail plan shows the tackles required, and the approximate position of their deck blocks, these must be checked before finally put in place.

First, the wire rigging must be measured and cut. This should be done before the mast is stepped. The best procedure is to carefully check the lengths of the spars and the position of the fittings, using a steel tape, against the dimensioned and scaled

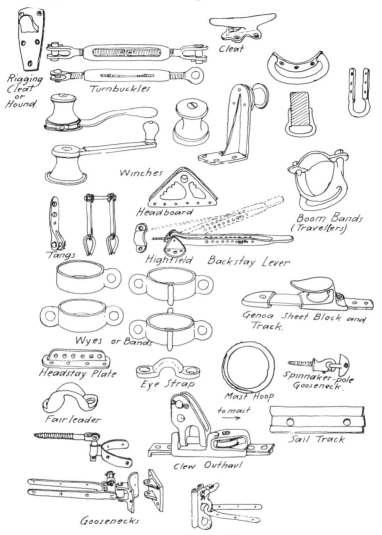

Rigging
Cleat
or
Hound.

Turnbuckles

Cleat

Winches

Headboard

Boom Bands
(Travellers)

Tangs

Highfield   Backstay Lever

Wyes  or Bands

Genoa  Sheet Block and
Track.

Headstay Plate

Eye Strap

Mast Hoop

Spinnaker-pole
Gooseneck.

Fairleader

to mast.

Sail Track

Clew Outhaul

Goosenecks

*180. Typical Rigging Hardware*

positions and lengths in the sail plan, noting any difference. Next, the hull should be carefully measured for the position of the stays. Then the mast positions should be carefully checked. Finally, measure from the center of the mast athwartships at various angles to the center line of the hull, to the eye of the chain plates, and then obtain the neight of these eyes in relation to the height of mast hole. This done, the rigging draught can be drawn.

From the offsets lay off the sheer of the boat on a piece of paper to a large scale, say, 1 inch to the foot. Draw in bow and stern and locate masts. From the sail plan transfer the required rake of masts and lay off the position of mast hole in relation to sheer as to height. Locate stay positions at each end of hull and then set off all required mast-heights. Draw in stays. The length of these can then be scaled, allowing for length of turnbuckles, which is a deduction, but adding allowances for splicing, or use of clamps, and for thimbles or other fittings specified by the designer, as well as for the circumference of the mast. Roughly, this is three times the diameter of the mast at the position a stay goes around it, but it is better to actually measure the stick at the required place, pulling the tape at the angle the stay stands to the mast when in place. Usually the eye of stays going around a mast is somewhat greater than three times the diameter. The allowance for splices varies among professional riggers; two to three feet is perhaps a common allowance. The whole of this may not be actually used but the rigger should have some length to spare. Mark the length scaled off the rigging draught and the itemized allowances and deductions along the stay. Also mark an identification letter on each stay. All fore- and mast-head stays, and springs, or backstays, can thus be laid off and dimensioned.

The shrouds must be laid off now. Each must be plotted so that it is viewed in a plane parallel to which it stands in relation to the hull center line. Lay off a base line representing the height of sheer at the mast and then set off the height of the mast hole in relation to it. This point is the top of deck at the center line of the hull, at the mast position, or the top of the trunk roof at center line and at mast position. Now, erect a perpendicular to represent the mast, setting off all necessary heights for shrouds, spreaders, and fittings. Then lay off the measurements of each chain-plate eye from the mast, as measured from the hull, on the base line; erect or drop perpendiculars and set off the height of each eye in relation to the mast hole. Each shroud may now be drawn, from its individual chain-plate eye to its position at mast head. The shrouds may now be scaled off and allowances noted as in the stays. It may be added that, in laying out the rigging draught, the half-breadth of the mast at stay and shroud positions should be drawn and allowed for. If spreaders are used, the half-breadth of these can be laid off at the proper height and angle, and the shrouds over them drawn in and measured. Jack stays can be laid off on the rigging profile plan in the same way. Accurate scaling and measurement are necessary in making a rigging draught.

Having marked the length, itemized allowances, and identification letter of each shroud and stay, the next step is to mark on the specified size and material of wire used. The designer will specify this in the sail plan, or specification. If not, the advice of a marine hardware dealer may serve, or the designer can be consulted. For the beginner, the best thing to do is to make a tracing of the rigging draught and send it to a firm that deals in rigging gear with instructions to cut wire and make splices, or fit sockets. The itemized allowances will enable them to correct any obvious error. The original drawing will enable identification to be made when rigging, and will serve to lay out some of the running rigging lengths if desired.

## Rigging Materials

Standing rigging wire may be of various materials: iron, mild or plow steel, galvanized, or stainless steel. The latter two are used most often in yachts. The wire is made in various ways; the number of strands and wires per strand vary with the work for which the wire is intended. One by 19, or 19 strand, is strongest and has the least stretch but is difficult to splice. Six by 7 is the most popular wire for standing rigging; it is readily spliced but is the least strong. Seven by 7 is a little stronger than 6 by 7 and will stretch less, but is stiffer. Wire seizing should be used for these; 1 by 7 of best charcoal iron, galvanized, from $\frac{9}{64}$ to $\frac{3}{32}$-inch diameter, or from $\frac{1}{16}$ to $\frac{1}{8}$ inch, can be obtained. Single wire is used for very small rigging wire, ranging from .021 inch for $\frac{3}{32}$-inch rigging wire to .041 inch for $\frac{3}{16}$-inch rigging. In handling a coil of rigging wire, do not pull it off the coil but roll the coil to prevent kinking. If rigging wire is cut, seize the wire on both sides the cut before making it, to prevent unlaying. Single-wire standing rigging is used in very small boats; this cannot be spliced, but can be twisted up and served, to form an eye. A better way is to seize with fine wire and paint. A rigging clamp is a necessity in making close splices for eyes, or thimbles, in all types of wire rope, except single wire.

## Notes

There is no space to discuss serving, seizing, worming, and cross-pointing; these matters will be fully discussed in books on rigging or knots and splices. Only general notes on standing rigging can be given, as well as a few practical suggestions. These follow. Rigging wire should be as small as possible to give sufficient strength, in racing craft. Stainless, or plow, steel should be used for this class of rigging. Cruising yachts and workboats should have heavier rigging, of iron, mild or plow steel, galvanized. Since the rigging of these craft receives less attention than in racing craft, a margin of safety to allow for corrosion and chafing is desirable. Stays on which jib, or staysail, hanks travel should be of steel in all craft. The bobstay can be of wire, chain, or rod; chain for the outer bobstay is best. Wire is most commonly used for bowsprit shrouds, but the outer may be of small chain in large craft.

As far as possible, turnbuckles aloft should be avoided. Bowsprit-rigging turnbuckles should be at the outboard end of the spar, not at the hull. The forestay of many small sailing craft will not remain taut when the jib is hoisted; this might be accomplished by bringing the forestay through a sheave at the stem or bowsprit and setting it up inboard. The tack of the sail could be hooked into a thimble spliced into this part so that, when the jib is hoisted and the halyards set up, the tack would pull the stay through the sheave, and so tighten the stay. The method of securing the stay could vary; a wire clamp to act as a stop at the sheave would serve. Another method would be to secure the end of the stay on deck with a turnbuckle inboard of the sheave; a short tail eye-spliced onto the stay just inboard of the sheave would serve for the tack.

Shrouds for small craft can be set up on themselves without use of turnbuckles or lanyards; rollers are used in the chain plates, and the shrouds brought through them on the inboard side. Thimbles are then turned into the ends. The shrouds can be set up with the main halyard, after which three seizings can be passed to secure each shroud. If turnbuckles are not available, long U-bolts made of small steel rod fitted with a plate and four nuts can be made to serve. Two shrouds on a side can be set up by one turnbuckle by using rollers in the chain plates and placing the turnbuckle fore and aft between them; this should be done only when a pair of shrouds are secured to the mast at the same height. If the mast is square, it is usual to secure the upper end of shrouds to the mast with tangs; these should be through-bolted to the mast with bolts not less than $\frac{3}{16}$ inch in diameter.

The means used to secure the shrouds to the mast usually decide how the track for the sail is to be attached to the mast. If tangs are used, the track is often screwed directly to the mast; if the shrouds are eye-spliced around the mast, the track must be set on a batten. Track battens should be wider than the track at the mast but narrower at the underside of the track. The track batten should be fastened to the mast with screws, or nails, before the track is attached; screws are used for the latter. The end of the track must be measured from the blueprint, allowing space above the boom gooseneck for threading on the slides and for a latch. The latter may be a piece of hardwood, or a short piece of track flattened at the lower end, and pivoted at the lower end by a screw; the latch prevents the slides from unshipping when the sail is down, yet allows the sail to be removed when it is desired to do so.

## Rigging Gadgets

Every book on yachting dealing with upkeep, cruising technic, and handling seems to contain useful rigging gadgets. Every experienced boat sailor has a collection of these and uses them at every opportunity. Some are more trouble than they are worth, but many exhibit ingenuity of a high order. The amateur builder should carefully observe all craft possible and note any useful gadget. This can be overdone, of course; common sense should prevent the adoption of a gadget that serves no necessary and practical purpose, or that leads to unnecessary expense. As in cabin gadgets, rigging gadgets must always work; mechanical or complicated ones are taboo with the experienced seaman.

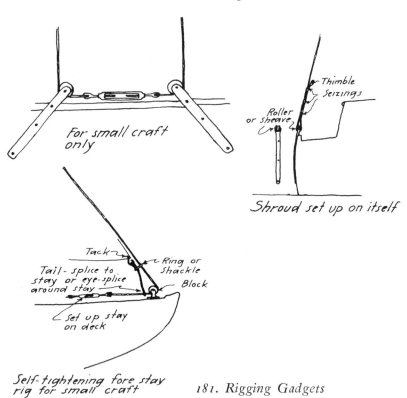

For small craft only

Thimble
Seizings
Roller or sheave

Shroud set up on itself

Tack
Ring or Shackle
Tail-splice to stay or eye-splice around stay
Block
Set up stay on deck

Self-tightening fore stay rig for small craft

181. Rigging Gadgets

## Running Rigging, Blocks

Running rigging should offer no great problem. The blocks required will be listed by the designer on the plans or specifications. Observe the blocks shown in this plan carefully; some have a becket by which the bitter end of the standing part of the tackle rope is secured. Blocks having this must be so ordered. Then consider how the block is to be attached to the spars, rigging, or deck. This is done with a hook, shackle, bolt, plate, swivel plate, eye, swivel eye, slide (to fit mast track), snap shackle, Coleman Hook, ring, swivel-eye shackle, lashing eye, bolt and spectacle, stiff jaw, swivel jaw, and bridle fitting. Each of these is designed to meet some requirement in fitting blocks. Marine hardware catalogues should be consulted, as each block is selected, in order that the order for the block may specify the correct fitting. Keep a separate copy of the block list, with notes as to identification and placing of each block ordered, so that no error in placing will result.

The way the block stands to its fastening is a matter that must also be taken into consideration. This is particularly true of blocks secured by shackles, hooks, eyes, bridle fittings, and Coleman Hooks. If the shackle stands so that its edge is in line with the sheave opening, it is called a "front" shackle fitting; if it stands so that the edges of the shackle are athwart the sheave opening, it is a "side" shackle fitting. This applies to the other fittings mentioned: if the side of the fitting is in line with the sheave, it is a "front" fitting; if the side or narrow edge of the fitting is at right angles to the sheave, it is a "side" fitting. Shackle fittings may be "upset" as well as either "front" or "side." An "upset" shackle is one in which the shackle is passed through the block while it is being assembled, so that the bolt or pin can be removed without the shackle coming free of the block. Regular shackle fittings have the shackle secured to the block by the pin, so that if this is removed the fitting is freed from the block. In short, an "upset" shackle is one standing in the block upside down, or pin up.

Special blocks, such as cheek blocks, snatch blocks, fiddle blocks, bullet (for jib sheets) and wire-rope blocks are also standard and may be obtained without trouble. If there is flexible wire running rigging, the blocks used for it must be designed for wire rope and should be so specified in ordering. The number of sheaves must also be noted in ordering any block; single, double, and treble sheaves are the most commonly specified numbers. Block sizes are usually in inches, measured on the length of the shell, not sheave diameter. Usually the catalogue will not only give this dimension but also the size of rope for which the block size is fitted. If there is any doubt as to the diameter of rope for which a block is suited, it is better to have the block large than small. The size and material of the blocks should suit the ship: small bronze yacht blocks look inadequate when placed on a plain-finished heavy cruiser, or workboat; on the other hand, a smart, well-finished racer would seem overblocked if she were fitted with regular fisherman-quality commercial blocks. Not only must the blocks fit the ropes running through them, but their size should have a natural relation to the size of the spars and hull. Blocks having wooden shells are preferable for rope, those having metal shells for wire. Bronze blocks, for rope, are popular, however, because of their small, neat appearance. It should be kept in mind, in choosing blocks, that very small, neat blocks often make tackles work heavily, while large blocks give easy working. Perhaps the most common fault in yacht rigging today is blocks too small for the work they are supposed to do; very often this is emphasized by sheets and halyards too small to handle comfortably under load.

## *Rope*

Rope used for running rigging is usually three-strand stuff; four-strand is preferred only when block sheaves are very small. It can be had in various sizes and qualities. The better the quality, the stronger it is for a given diameter and the softer it is to handle. The sizes of Manila rope are given in both diameter and circumference, except when the diameter is under $7/16$ inch, when diameter and "thread" are used; $1/4$ inch is 6 thread, $5/16$ inch is 9 thread, and $3/8$ inch is 12 thread. Diameter is now most commonly given, at least in this country. Treated ropes are often specified; these are treated with preservative that prevents rot, and, in some cases at least, reduces or practically eliminates rapid stretching. These treated ropes are often greasy, or stiff and unpleasant to handle, so are not very popular for running rigging. Some treated rope makes excellent lanyards, however, and is a cheap and satisfactory substitute for tarred hemp; "American All-Weather Rope" is an example. Rope sizes should be specified by the designer. It may be observed, however, that the diameter of the mainsheet is not so much a matter of required strength as ease in handling; if the sail to which the sheet is attached is 400 or 450 square feet in area, $1/2$-inch diameter sheets are strong enough but $3/4$ inch to $1/8$ inch diameter sheets are much easier to handle. Four-strand rope should be used for lanyards, as in deadeyes for example, as it will stand the hard turns necessary better than three strand.

## Stepping Spars

The rigging on hand, the shrouds, and stays should be bent to the mast and hoops put on, and the main, or peak, halyard rove off, before stepping masts. This operation can be done afloat in all boats or may be done before launching. Small masts require merely strength to walk them into place; heavy masts must be hoisted in with a derrick, or sheer legs. A single hoisting, or "gin," pole will sometimes serve. If this can be stepped on a wharf, or bridge, the mast may often be stepped very easily. Sometimes it is possible to use the gaff, or boom, of a larger boat to act as a derrick boom. Secure the hoisting line a little above the center of gravity of the mast with a topsail halyard bend. The mast must be hoisted high enough to clear all obstructions and its heel must be guided into the mast hole and step; to step, it may be necessary to use crowbars, or "prys," to work the heel into place. The way the mast is to face must be considered in fixing the gear. If the mast has much rake the hoisting line should be secured to the foreside of the mast; indeed this is usually the best plan with all masts, unless there is some obstruction that makes this impractical.

## Wedges

After the mast has been stepped, wedges should be made if required. These are best made of softwood, such as cedar, white pine, or mahogany. There are various ways of wedging masts. The most common way is to make narrow wedges with bevel edges and to drive them all around the mast so that they fit tightly against one another as well as wedging between mast and sides of mast hole. The top of the wedges usually stand 2 or 3 inches above the deck when driven home; the points will reach below the blocking of the partners. After driving, the points of the wedges projecting below the partner blocking are usually sawn off. Another plan is to use a square mast hole, much larger than the mast, and to fit a wooden collar around the mast, in two parts, and to wedge the collar. Square masts are usually wedged by four wide wedges, one on each side. Wedges should not be driven until the rigging is set up and the masts brought to the required rake and stand.

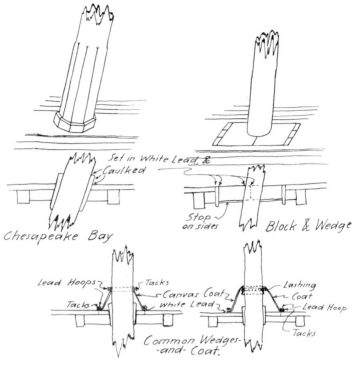

*182. Mast Wedges and Coats*

### Rake of Masts, Setting Up, Rigging

The rigging should be set up as soon as the masts are stepped. It is unnecessary to dwell on this operation at length; the utmost pains should be taken to bring the mast to the required rake by careful measurements and by plumbing. In large vessels a measurement is often taken from the hounds to the gammon iron, or other convenient point on the hull, to assure accurate rake. The masts should also be pulled plumb athwartships, taking care that the boat has no heel while this is being done. Setting up shrouds and stays should be done gradually; as the wire stretches the rigging can be set up to the desired tension. Many professional riggers deliberately cut some rigging wire a little short and insert chain links at the turnbuckles. As the rigging stretches out, the links can be removed. This is not necessary with the best grades of rigging, however.

In setting up the rigging of a modern boat, using the now fashionable hollow mast and attendant rigging, the aim is to set up taut enough to hold the mast straight and to allow no bends to appear anywhere along its length—not to set up so hard that "Home Sweet Home" can be played on the shrouds by some wandering harpist. The modern hollow mast is a compression member and is designed to stand a load with a fixed factor of safety. If the shrouds and stays are set up too hard the compression load is increased, and when the additional load of sailing is added the factor of safety is rapidly reduced. Solid masts should be set up so that there is a little flexibility; unlike hollow masts, bending to a moderate degree will not harm them.

## Mast Coat

Once the rigging is set up, the wedges can be driven. A mast coat is usually required; this is furnished by a sailmaker and is a piece of canvas cut to shape, so that it will fit around the mast and cover the wedges. It is usually secured to the mast and deck, or trunk roof, by copper tacks. A better plan is to place a narrow lead strip around the mast and another on the deck, through which the tacks are driven (through the mast coat into the deck or trunk roof). White lead or varnish should be used under the mast coat to ensure watertightness. Some owners prefer to first invert the mast coat around the mast and lash it, then turn down and tack to the deck.

If a block is fitted as a collar for the mast, and the collar wedged, no mast coat is required; the wedges are cut off flush with the deck and the whole is calked and painted. If the mast is square or eight sided at the partners, wedges may be so driven that they are watertight when calked and painted. This requires accurate fitting, however. Mast coats must be sewn to close them; this should be done after the mast coat is around the mast but before it is fastened, and the seam should be on the after side of the mast, on the hull center line. Care should be taken in tacking a mast coat to the deck to get it smooth and even. The coat should be painted in the same way as any canvas deck.

## Shipping Spars, Lacing Sails

After the rigging is in place, and the masts wedged, the spars should be shipped. This done, the sails should be bent. If the sails are to be laced to the spars, use a marlin hitch on the booms and gaffs, in preference to the more common spiral lacing. The sails should be·hauled out hand-taut along the booms for this operation. If the sails are laced to the mast, as they sometimes are in very small craft, use a spiral lacing. Usually the sailmaker fits the slides to a sail when a track is used; the builder furnishes the slides. The same is true of snap jib hanks. If hoops are used, and the jib is secured to the forestay by ring hanks, these must be in place before rigging starts. Hoops and ring jib hanks are lashed to grommets in the sails, using marlin.

## Placing Blocks and Leads

The placing of lead blocks and sheet horses can best be done after the sails are bent. First the halyards are rove off and the sails hoisted. This should be done on a quiet day, so that sheet leads can be fixed without the sails flapping. The horses for the sheets can often be placed from the plans, though movable horses for the jib or fore staysail sheets are best placed with the sails hoisted. It should be kept in mind that the sails will stretch. First the main sheet can be placed; its horse and blocks on boom and deck require little checking. It is a good plan to first secure the horse and traveler, then fit the boom band and ship the blocks, reeve off the sheet and fix the lead blocks, if any, by trying them in various positions so that the lead is fair; push the boom around to see that the sheet is leading properly under all conditions.

Gaff and jib-headed sails can usually be sheeted without trouble as long as they have booms. Boomless sails require experimenting with, however. A boomless gaff sail should be sheeted so that the deck block, when the sail is hauled flat, stands a little aft on deck of a line perpendicular to a diagonal drawn from the peak to the tack. A boomless jib-headed sail will usually sheet when the line of the sheet can be drawn through the clew so that it bisects the angle formed by the foot and leach. In a new sail the blocks on deck should usually be aft of the places found by the projection of the bisecting line, say, about 2 to 3 inches. Boomless sails should have the deck blocks mounted on tracks so the lead can be altered. Jib-sheet deck block positions can be found by laying off a line perpendicular to the stay, through the clew fitting, to the deck; the blocks should be set a little abaft the points so found if the sail is heavy, a little forward if light, say, 2½ inches. If the jib is fitted with a boom it requires no experimenting to place the horse or the deck blocks; but if a short club is used, the horse should be a movable one, or it will be necessary to experiment to find the right position.

The deck blocks for light sails—the genoa, staysails, spinnaker or parachute, and ballooner—should not be permanently fixed until the boat has been sailed with these set. The genoa sheet will pass outside the rigging, usually, and will lead about in line with the miter of the sail to the top of the rail or the edge of the deck, well aft. The deck blocks will have to be mounted on suitable tracks and the position of the blocks must be adjustable. These same blocks can then be used for the guy and sheet of the parachute.

Perhaps the hardest fitting to place is a deck, or coaming, winch, to handle the sheet of a genoa, or the sheet and guy of a parachute. If the winches are placed before trying out with sails hoisted, it is not unusual to find the leads from the sheet block wrong, or the winch in such a position that the user cannot brace

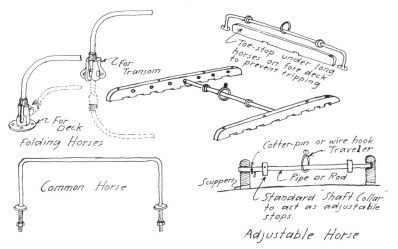

*183. Small-Boat Sheet Horses or "Travelers"*

himself to get maximum power on the winch and work the sail in a short space of time. In a racing boat, placing many fittings should be made a part of the tuning-up process, unless the deck arrangement is such that an obvious position for the winches exists. In placing deck fittings of this class it is important that the lead not be foul, that power can be exerted quickly, and that the fitting not be in the way of the crew. Winches are often used in small boats when they are really unnecessary, but in most boats fitted with the genoa jib they are an absolute necessity. The user of a winch should have a place where he can brace his feet yet have his arms clear, and there must be room abaft the winches for a member of the crew to tail the sheet, in all but the smallest craft fitted with this sail. The genoa is often a very difficult sail to set properly on a small cruiser.

### Staysails

Deciding the lead of sheets of staysails is best done by trial and error; some sheet to the deck, others to the end of the main, or mizzen, boom. It is unreasonable to expect to be able to do this without trying a number of positions, since not only the outline, or shape, of the sail has to be considered, but also the cut or draft. Flexibility in the position of deck blocks and leaders is always a good feature as it allows for shifting to meet changes in the fullness of a sail caused by stretching. This is true of all headsail sheets, as well as of all staysail sheets.

### Belays

The lead and belay of halyards is largely a matter of personal opinion. While the sheets may all be led within reach of the helmsman on even a fairly large boat, this cannot be done with halyards, except in small boats having light sails and spars. The reason this is true is that the lead is usually such that friction is too great and the full weight of the crew cannot be employed in hoisting. The clutter of rigging along the deck is another reason this is often objectionable. In a cruiser it is usually better to belay halyards in the rigging at the rail rather than at the foot of the mast. In racers this is not always practical, in which case a deck block is used at the foot of the mast with halyards below deck, or a hoisting winch is placed on the mast, from which the fall may lead to a cleat or pin on a band on the mast. If wire halyards are used, the mast winch takes the end of the fall, so no belaying pin or cleat will be required. When working out belaying positions, every effort must be made to prevent bunching of coils, which will result from many belays close together. Also the coils of a belay should be high enough off the deck to be out of the way and not to wash off the belaying pin, or cleat, easily. In small craft, where the halyard is led below deck and aft to the cockpit, the belay or winch must be easily reached yet not in the way. This is easy to say, but often hard to do.

## Suggestions

It is obvious that the subject of spars, rigging, sail bending, and placing of fittings has been only roughly outlined in this chapter. The subject is too involved to treat here, and constant change makes it impractical to attempt to give rules for these matters. Experience and the use of common sense are the best guides that can be suggested. A builder will do well to consult experienced racing and cruising men, so that he will be able to keep abreast of the latest developments in each field. The more boats you build, the more you will have to question and discover, since every boat will raise new problems. It is only the inexperienced who are dogmatic and "know all."

## Study

After a boat is built the builder should run or sail her, studying every part of the boat and the behavior of not only the boat, but also of the gear. By observing carefully, changes will suggest themselves that will result in improvement in the qualities and working of a hull. Also, the builder will see the desirability of some improvement in structure, or fitting, in the next boat he builds. Every builder should know how to tune up a boat reasonably well and only by sailing, or operating, a boat can this skill be obtained. In fitting out a sailing boat, the knowledge of how her gear is used is necessary before it can be fitted to the best advantage. That is why it is so important that a builder learn how to handle the boats he builds.

# CHAPTER NINE

# TOOLS AND CARE, PRO-FESSIONAL BUILDING

*M*ANY beginners find boatbuilding very difficult because of their inability to use the necessary tools, or
to keep them sharp. This is particularly true of those
tools that are not commonly used by hobbyists.

### Broadax

The broadax is a roughing tool; in the hands of a skilled user,
however, an amazing amount of work can be done and the timbers hewn will be very smooth. This ax can be obtained in various weights and patterns. The one best suited for heavy work

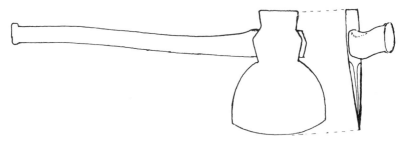

*184. Broadax*

has a deep bit and a cutting edge about 6 inches long. A short-
bit ax having a 7- to 8-inch cutting edge is best suited to light
work. The handles are offset to clear the hand which is nearest
the bit when cutting through timber. The bit should be hung
slightly out, or square with the handle, but never hung in. The

offset of the handle is either to the right or left, when holding the ax, according to the hand suited to the user. The amount of offset is about 4½ inches in 2 feet 6 inches of handle. The cutting edge should be ground to an arc having a radius of about 7 inches from the center of the eye of the bit. The grinding of the edge is greatest on the side toward which the handle is offset, or bent; some users do not like this, however, and grind both sides more or less alike. As it is quite impossible to buy a good handle, it will have to be made by the user. The stock should be hickory, or ash, and steam-bent at a sharp angle to give the required offset. This must be done when the stock is rough; after bending, the handle is worked to shape.

### Use

In using a broadax, stand with both feet close together. Before making a heavy cut, strike a line on the rough timber with a chalk line. With the broadax—or better, an ordinary ax—cut

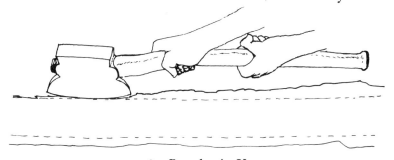

*185. Broadax in Use*

notches, or scores, every 8 or 10 inches; then split off between notches, taking care to stay clear of the chalk line in both operations. Next, hew down at one end of the timber with the broadax in a plumb line; this may be checked by holding a plumb bob and line against the timber from time to time. Take pains to have the ax fall plumb; do not hurry the cutting. Be sure to hold the ax so that the end of the handle toward the user is always below the cutting edge. Never cut sweeping blows along the timber. *Keep both feet together and the handle below the head of the ax or injury may result. Take your time and cut slowly and carefully.*

## *Adz*

The adz used by ship carpenters is a finishing tool. There are many patterns; the style used by those who fair or "line" sawn frames is hollow bladed, like a gouge. With this, a series of grooves are cut across frames to get fair spots, before dubbing between the grooves. The adz used by a dubber is from 5 to 5½ inches on the cutting edge and has lips turned up at the sides to give

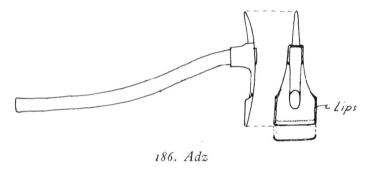

186. *Adz*

clean cutting. The adz used to square timbers is also lipped; its cutting edge is 6 inches. All of these are used to cut athwart the grain of a timber, not with it. Only the scarfing, or "strap," adz is used to cut at a slight angle to the grain. This is usually a narrow-bladed tool having a cutting edge of 2 to 4 inches and no lips; it is used to cut up to a shoulder in a scarf—hence its name.

## *Handles*

Adz handles, like those of broadaxes, are usually made by the user. Hornbeam, white ash, wild cherry, applewood, or hickory are used (these are also used for broadax handles). The adz is hung by holding a 2-foot rule along the handle with one end flush with the outer face of the bit. The other end is held at the center of the handle. Next the rule is swung to the cutting edge, pivoting at the handle. When swung, the end of the rule should project from the cutting edge from ⅝ to ¾ inch, according to choice of the user. By wedging the handle, the hanging may be changed. An ax or adz is "hung" to tip the blade to or away from the user, in line with the handle; "offset" is to tip the blade sidewise.

## Use

The beginner should begin to adz a flat surface. First strike slowly on the flat of the bit, without cutting. After the "feel" of the tool is had, try to take off the thinnest chip possible. When every cut gives chips of equal size and thinness, confidence in the tool will result. *Do not strike quick blows, or sweeping ones.* A good adzman, or axman, strikes easily, slowly, and accurately. The tools are too heavy to use with the rapid, sweeping strokes of the chopping ax; control is impossible if this is attempted. One more thing—the end of the adz handle in the eye of the bit must be flush with the outside face of the head.

## Broad Hatchet

The broad hatchet is but a miniature broadax and should be used in the same general manner. Its bit is usually ground almost entirely on the side away from that against the timber being cut; the handle is usually without offset as deep cuts are not taken. The hatchet is used to hew the edges of narrow timber, or plank, rather than for the face of wide stock. The cutting edge is usually about 4 or 4½ inches long.

## Remarks

The position in which the user of ax or adz stands is always important. Take care to have firm footing. When the adz is used on a timber lying on the ground or floor, stand on it, or close to it, with feet widespread and cut between them. If possible, stand a little to one side when cutting against an upright or high timber with this tool. When using a broadax, stand close to the timber being cut, feet close together, and swing the ax between you and the timber.

## Planes

Planes used by ship carpenters and boatbuilders are commonly those used by house carpenters and hobbyists. However, the older shipwrights trained to fine work will only use planes having a wooden sole, or planes whose whole body is wood. There is a good reason why the wooden plane, or wooden sole plane, is preferred; these will cut smoothly in all wood, either seasoned or dry, whereas an iron sole will cause a plane to stick, or "chatter," in green or wet hardwood. Iron plane soles will also mark work more readily than wooden-soled planes. Most of the wooden-bodied planes are made by the user, of beech, lignum vitae, live oak, or tropical hardwoods. The boat and ship carpenters seem to prefer narrow planes rather than wide ones. The planes commonly used are as follows: smoothing planes with bodies 8½ to 10 inches long, bits 1½ to 1¾ inches wide; jack planes 15 to 18 inches long, bits 1¾ inches wide; jointers 22 to 26 inches long, bits 1¾ to 2 inches wide. Spar planes are usually made with a hollow bit and sole, on various radii; they are usually about 10 inches long. All planes should have cap, or "double," irons.

## Use

The use of a plane requires little explanation. The correct way to hold the tool is with both hands; the hand toward the front of the plane should have its thumb against the back of the nob (on the cutter or bit side), not on the side away from the user. As the plane reaches the end of the stick do not allow it to tip. On the return stroke lift the rear of the sole off the work. In cutting across the grain, use a block plane; lift the front of the plane before the cutter runs off the edge. When using an all-wood plane, the thumb of the leading hand is toward the user. The fingers of this hand can be used to guide the plane on narrow work. Take reasonably long strokes in planing, but do not try to take such long ones that the position of the hands must be changed. The bit should be at right angles to the stroke; some hold the plane so that the cutting edge is at a slight angle to the direction of the stroke, but this is not correct. The amount of set, or exposure, of the cutting edge of the bit below the bottom of the *iron* and *cap* should vary with the type of plane and the hardness of the wood to be worked; the recommended amount of exposure of bit is—for jack planes—½ inch; for jointer, $\frac{1}{16}$ inch and, for smooth plane, $\frac{1}{32}$ inch. These are for use with softwoods. For hardwood, or cross-grained stock, reduce the set by about one half.

## Types of Planes

There are almost countless types of planes; the very numerous molding planes and the special planes used by coopers, joiners, and other tradesmen account for the number. Block planes, used for planing end grain, and the bullnose and rabbet planes are usually seen in boatshops.

## Use of Drawknife Spokeshave

The drawknife and the spokeshave are very useful tools; the former is used for heavy cutting and the latter for light. These tools are used extensively by sparmakers. Plankers and joiners use both tools also; planking may often be roughed out, if light, with a drawknife. The spokeshave is very useful for smoothing hollow surfaces on the outline of a rudder or similar conditions in joinery, as it will work when planing is impossible.

## Screw Drivers

Screw drivers should be ground so that there is a short parallel side above the point. Tapered points will jump out of the slot in the head of a screw. Screw drivers to fit all sizes of screws should be available.

## Bits and Augers

Bits and augers have been discussed in an earlier chapter; the professional boatbuilder has drills and bits up to ⅝ inch, when "hiring out"; the shop furnishes those larger.

## Use Of Saws

Saws have also been discussed; the set of the teeth of a saw is very important when making deep, heavy cuts in hardwood. For this work, the teeth are usually quite coarse and have much set, so that the kerf is wide enough to prevent binding. In using a hand saw keep right shoulder (if right handed) directly in front of cutting edge, grasp lightly, and do not press saw into cut to hurry it. *Use a long stroke, not a short, jabbing movement.* The saw may be twisted slightly in cutting, to direct the cutting edge along a line, or bent slightly to plumb a cut; use a try square against the blade now and then to get a square, or plumb, kerf. In heavy cutting the saw can be oiled or greased to make the work easier.

## Hammers

Hammers, sledges, and mauls require careful selection. Only good steel bits are of any use, as poor steel will chip or pit. Hammers should be chosen for the work they must do: light hammers for tacks and brads; heavy for nails and small spikes; mauls for large spikes; and sledges for drifts. When driving a fastening, the line of the handle of the hammer should always be at right angles to the center line of the fastening being driven; the handle must go down with the head.

## Measuring Tools

Tapes should be steel, not linen or cotton fabric. The short, flexible spring tape is very useful. Only good quality 2- or 3-foot rules should be bought. The 6-foot folding rules, while useful, are too easily broken to be used as an alternative for the usual folding 2- or 3-foot rule. Rules made to measure inside casements and doors are often very useful in joinery.

## Squares

Try squares and steel squares are a necessity and should be used only for the purposes intended. The try square, particularly, is often abused; do not use it to drive tacks!

## Wrenches

Wrenches should include two or three sizes of monkey wrench, as well as a pipe, or stillson, and perhaps some socket wrenches. These last are expensive if bought in large sets. The monkey wrench is the most useful for carpenters, but the stillson and socket wrench, as well as wrench pliers and mechanics' flat wrenches, are often useful in fitting out a boat.

## Scrapers

Scrapers are tools used to finish fine cabinet work, the outside of hulls, the decks, and the spars. Scrapers having a variety of handles and bits can be purchased. Most boatbuilders do not use a handle at all, preferring to hold the blade with bare hands. The best scraper blades for this purpose are pieces of large band saws. With a scraper made of this, a very fine shaving can be removed from a plank, leaving a smooth surface in its wake. Because of the smoothness of work scraped, this tool is widely used on hull topsides, after planing. It is easier to scrape hardwood than some softwoods, particularly those softwoods in which there is variation in the hardness of the grain. However, experience with the tool will enable the user to finish nearly all woods.

## Chisels and Gouges

Chisels and gouges are, of course, necessary. These have already been discussed in an earlier chapter; generally speaking, few tang-handled chisels are used by boatbuilders, socket handles now being preferred. In cutting with a chisel held in the hand, the tool is used for paring and is laid flat against the work. When using a mallet, the chisel, if small, is held near the point with one hand; heavier chisels are held by the handle. A chisel should not be driven so deep into the work that great effort is required to free the chips; light chisels should not be used for heavy work. Of course, chisels are not to be used as tack pullers, wrecking bars, or screw drivers.

## Sharpening Tools

All cutting tools need to be sharpened regularly when in use. A good grindstone and an oilstone are necessary. The high-speed hand, or power, grinder is a poor tool for sharpening; it is very easy to spoil the temper of a good tool with an emery wheel. The hand grinders should be turned slowly; high speed is not desirable. The slow-turning grindstone is safest. Select one with a fine-grained stone that runs true, without wobbling, and has a smooth, straight surface across its grinding face. A grindstone turned by foot pedals is most convenient for a small shop. The oilstone may be a natural stone, or one of the many artificial abrasive stones. The combination stones, having one surface fine- and the other coarse-grained, are preferred. For small tools that must be carefully honed, the Arkansas (soft) stone is best.

In using a grinder, or grindstone, the wheel must be kept wet when the tool is applied. Oilstones should be soaked in thin oil for several days when new, after which they should be kept clean and moist. On all fine and medium natural stones, and on all artificial stones, oil should be used, not water. Do not use lubricating oil, or grease. Any but very light, clear oil will glaze the stone. After an oilstone is used, wipe it off with a clean, soft rag so that neither dust, oil, nor particles of steel remain on the stone. If a stone becomes glazed, clean with ammonia or gasoline. If more treatment is required, scour with fine sandpaper mounted on a smooth block of wood. When not in use, keep a cover over a stone. In recent times the small hand grinder is often seen in boatbuilders' shops; this is because it is cheap and portable rather than because it is really preferred. The one advantage of this tool, however, is that attachments may be obtained for some types that permit correct beveling of tool edges.

## How to Sharpen Tools

Cutting tools are ground by sharpening against the edge. Thus the grinder and grindstone are revolved so that the wheel turns against the edge of the tool being sharpened. When honing on an oilstone, the stone is usually fixed and the tool is moved back and forth on its surface. The grinder or grindstone is used to grind the proper bevel, or to grind out irregularities in the edge. The oilstone is used to get a keen, lasting cutting edge.

## Bevels

Bevels are very important. Chisels require the following bevels: framing 25 degrees, paring 15 degrees, firmer 20 degrees. Plane bits are beveled at 25 degrees. Scraper blades are ground with both square edge and bevel; the latter is about 45 degrees. Chisels are now often ground hollow on the bevel. In grinding, use plenty of water and do not let the tool get hot, along the edge. Hold the tool steady so that the bevel is the same all the way across the cutting edge. It is well worth while to give attention to the accuracy of the bevel while grinding. When the tool is ground sharp it must then be whetted on an oilstone.

## Use of Oilstone

The oilstone should rest level and solid. Put on a few drops of oil and grasp tool or bit with both hands, if it is big enough. Place the tool on the stone at the proper bevel and rub back and forth, with the edge at an oblique angle across the top of the stone. It is possible to exert a good deal of pressure by bearing down on both hands. Hold the tool close to the edge being sharpened, whenever possible, so that the bevel will be accurate. Do not give the hands a scooping, or dipping, motion while whetting. Use the entire face of the stone as far as possible; reverse the stone once in a while, turning it end for end. Use the coarse side first, then the fine side. Drawknives are sharpened by holding the tool in a fixed position and moving the stone. Place the blade bevel up, with one handle flat on the workbench and the other projecting over the edge so it can be held with one hand. With the other, run the stone back and forth from one end to the other of the blade, being sure to hold the stone to follow the bevel. Gouges are whetted by placing them on the stone at the proper bevel and then moving sidewise with a rolling or swinging motion. In whetting or grinding the gouge, the tool is held at right angles to the stone or wheel, and then rocked to hold the bevel. Small stones, of various shapes, called "slips" are used to whet the inside of a hollow-edged bit and also to hone an auger bit. The cutting lip is honed from the lower side, to hold the bevel or angle; a file is often used to touch up the leading point and thread or the scoring nib at the outside edges of the cutting lip.

## Scraper Sharpening

Scrapers must not only be ground and whetted but also the cutting edge must be turned. The bevel-edged scraper, used for working on green wood, is first ground or filed to a 45-degree bevel. Filing can be done with an 8- or 10-inch mill file. Then hone with a fine oilstone. When a very sharp edge is obtained, lay the scraper blade on the bench with bevel down and toward you. Then, with a burnisher, or "steel," burnish cutting edge bright and shiny. Then, with burnisher, turn the edge so it is at right angles. This is done by successive strokes of the burnisher, varying the angle of the line of the burnisher from 5 to 10 and then to 15 degrees from the face of the bevel, finally bringing the edge to a right angle to the face opposite the beveled one. To do this, run the burnisher the full width of the blade. Finally, run the burnisher over and then its point under the turned edge rapidly, the last time under. The strokes of the burnisher under the edge must be with the point of the burnisher, of course. The square-edged scraper is draw-filed at right angles to the faces of the blade, then honed with the blade held perpendicular to the surface of the stone. Burnish flat, then turn one edge, or all four on both sides, using the burnisher as with the bevel-edged scraper. The burnisher should be of very hard, fine steel. A good one may be made by grinding a three-cornered saw file smooth and honing it on an oilstone. Grind the file on a grindstone with plenty of water so as not to draw the temper—do not grind on an emery wheel.

## Care of Tools

Keep tools clean and oiled; if rust appears, as it will, clean and polish the tool before using it. Sharpen if necessary. Have a suitable place for edge tools when using them so that the cutting edges will not be dulled and so that no one will be injured. Do not lay a chisel, ax, adz, or slick on the staging or hull where it is apt to roll off onto someone passing by or under. Saws should be sent to a professional for sharpening, as this is no job for an amateur.

## Turning Professional

The amateur builder often decides to turn professional. With experience, there is no great difficulty in this. However, all trades have some individual difficulties and these are the kind that the amateur rarely meets before becoming a professional. It is because of these difficulties in the boatbuilding trade that few boatbuilders ever become even comfortably well off financially. Some of these difficulties are in shop management, in the field of economics; others are in the practices that have grown up in the business.

## Preliminary

When the amateur builder decides to become a professional, he must expect to find some difficulty in getting work, in setting up his shop, and in obtaining skilled and reliable help. The general effect of this, usually, is to make necessary financial resources to at least a moderate amount. Occasionally an amateur will obtain a job before he actually turns professional; he does this usually by turning out a superior hull which has won the approval of a friend, or acquaintance. This may, or may not, be of assistance in setting up his business, *depending on whether his price was high enough to give a reasonable profit.*

## Yard

First, the shop must be considered. If the builder is wise, he will not depend upon building alone; rather he will depend upon repairs and storage, with building as a side issue. For this reason the shop must be suitably located for these varied requirements. Taxes must be investigated to see if stored craft are taxed and, if so, how much. The effect of high taxation on stored boats is disastrous as the owners can easily store their boats where there are no taxes on them, in most localities. In order to make repairs, a railway must be built, or purchased. These are not cheap if built by contract; if the builder makes his own railway a great deal of labor and time will be required. Storage sheds are not wholly necessary, perhaps, but are desirable in the long run. The building shed must be separate from storage sheds and should be used for building only. The reason that building alone is insufficient to support a yard is that it is a seasonal business to a great extent. Storage pays well, considering the investment necessary, and produces income before the building season really starts. Repairing is at its height during the boating season and thus pays while both building and storage are dull. There are exceptions to this, but there can be no question as to the superiority of the yard equipped to repair, store, and build over the yard that can do only one of these.

## Equipment in Relation to Work Done

Equipment of the yard is important where repairing and building are to be carried on. Machine tools are necessary; on the other hand there can be too much capital invested in machinery. If this is the case, the investment is so large that the interest on it becomes a serious burden. The problem is a difficult one and perhaps the best approach is from the type and quality of the work to be done, that is, whether the builder expects to cater to yachts or to commercial craft. If yachts are expected to furnish business, what quality of boats will be in demand? To a great extent, the quality of the work to be done in a yard depends upon its locality, its nearness to wealthy summer colonies or yachting centers. In some communities only cheap yachts, or commercial craft, will be in demand. Obviously, the shrewdness of the builder in choosing a location is very important to the success of his venture.

## Tools and Stores

This matter having been explored, the builder must equip his yard. This is an expensive job for the newcomer. The best rule to follow is to buy as little machinery as possible, at first. The exception to this rule is in high-grade yacht work and stock boat building, but it is safe to say that neither of these fields is suited for an inexperienced builder. He should usually start by building either small, cheap boats or commercial craft. A yard for either type of work can get along with a good band saw, planer, shaper, and jointer. The planer and shaper should be heavy-duty tools; the band saw should be a 36-inch tilting-frame saw. The tilting-table saw is not satisfactory for boat work. Rebuilt tools are far cheaper than new ones and will give good service.

Small tools, such as power drills and screw drivers, pipe and bolt threading kits, soldering and brazing tools, blow torches, and the multitude of small items required in a boatshop, are items of expense that must be considered when buying the machine tools. A list of these, picked out of the storeroom of a commercial yard, will be of interest: heavy- and light-duty power drills, drills and augers, power screw driver and bits, power hack saw, hand hack saw and blades, large blocks and miscellaneous rope, crowbars, cant hooks, wrecking bars, power grinder and grindstone, soldering kit, blow torch, two cross-cut saws, four large jacks and two small ones, sledge and two mauls, bolt cutter, pipe cutter, pipe threading kit, bolt threading kit, chain fall, files, set of socket wrenches, set of machinist's wrenches, large monkey wrench, reamers, paint brushes, scrapers, extra blades for band saw, putty knives, calking tools and mallet, seam paying can, oil cans, glue pot, bolt and rod cutter, anvil, pipe vise, machine vise, tube flaring tool, cold chisels, sanding machine, post maul, two large pipe wrenches and one small one, four rigging clamps, fifty C-clamps, two ceiling clamps, six large ship clamps, portable winch, breast drill, oil stove, and a brazing kit.

Stores consisted of such items as nails, spikes, tacks, brads, bolts, screws, rods, piping, hose, hose clamps, clench rings, washers, nuts, and tubing of various sizes, paint, sandpaper, putty, white lead, red lead, varnish, paint remover, oil and turps, pipe and tube fittings and valves, canvas, rope, calking cotton and oakum, sheet metal, strap metal, some half-oval brass and iron, a number of sizes of wooden plugs, glue, dowels, rags and waste, gasoline, lubricating oil, creosote, rigging wire, a few turnbuckles, wire clamps, sheaves, a few blocks, some chain, marlin, tar, litharge, alcohol, seam compound, shellac, lantern, two flashlights, seizing wire, chalk, crayons, pencils, tape, and rubber cement. Some of this was purchased in quantity, the rest accumulated from leftovers of various contracts and jobs.

## Fine Yacht Building and Stock Boats

The unsuitability of certain fields of business, for a builder newly started, has been mentioned. The high-grade yacht-building yards require a lot of experience to operate. It is questionable if the demand for such yachts warrants new yards being started. At any rate, the amount of capital required to start such a yard is very great and it is probable that few newcomers in the trade would consider the outlay. In explanation of the outlay required for high-grade yacht building, fine work, particularly finishing, can only be done with the best of machine tools, and the boatbuilding shop must be separated from both joiner and paint shop. Labor is also a great problem and the training of hands is one of the tasks of a builder in this field.

The stock-boat business has been highly touted as the best field of operations for the future. Without going into a lengthy discussion of the truth of this, it may be suggested that there are very marked difficulties in a stock-boat business. The often-made comparison of stock boats to automobiles is quite ridiculous; the comparison would be more apt if it were made between stock boats and houses. For every man who wants a stock house there are probably ten who would not consider one under any circumstance. The reputed saving in stock boats, to an owner, does not bear inspection since low cost is not only a matter of production; it is also a matter of building location. That is why it is possible to purchase a custom-built yacht, or to have one built in some yards and localities, at a lower cost than is possible in the better stock-boat yards. As a result, the stock-boat builder suffers constantly from competition outside his real field. However, the problem of the stock-boat builder is not in the production of a cheap, but attractive, boat; given enough capital it is possible to build fine boats in number at a surprisingly low cost. Rather the problems are, first, in finding a design that will sell in large numbers for a length of time; secondly, in organizing and maintaining a sales organization. Sales and advertising require a large capital outlay—often greater than the cost of a plant required for fine yacht building.

## Small Boat and Commercial Craft Building

Perhaps the two best fields for the newcomer are small-boat building, and commercial-boat building—both custom work. In either case the outlay for yard and equipment can be limited. It must be admitted that the profit in cheap boats is very small, and that commercial boats rarely cost enough to ensure large profits either, but an inexperienced builder is far less likely to get into financial difficulties in a low-cost boat than in a high-cost one. It is sad, but true, that though fine workmanship is admired, few will pay for it. To a builder, it often seems as if some owners were trying to drive him into bankruptcy by their insistence on better work than they are paying for. This is so often met with in all yacht building that builders agree that pleasure-boat building is more troublesome than commercial-boat construction. In the latter, the owner is not interested in fine workmanship; he wants the cheapest boat possible for his purpose, allowing for strength and long life.

## Bidding

This brings us to the subject of bidding. Before bidding can be started, the yard operator must know how long it takes to do a given job, such as to loft a boat of a given size, to set up the keel and to frame, to plank and to lay the deck. He must know how long it takes to build a berth, a wheelbox, a table, and other items of joinerwork. If he can break down each job that he has done himself, so that he knows the man-hours required to repeat it, obviously he can give a very accurate estimate of the time required to build a boat like any he has built before. The cost of labor is the biggest item in small-boat building, often reaching twice or three times the material cost. In large boats the cost of labor compared with materials varies with the finish; in working craft it may be as low as 75 per cent of the material cost. Percentages, however, should not be used in estimating; actual material costs and cost per man-hour are the only basis on which to work. Overhead, such as taxes, depreciation of machinery, tools and building, nonproductive labor, management and insurance, must be allowed for.

## Contracts and Clauses

Certain objectionable practices have grown up in boatbuilding which often lead to the downfall of the inexperienced builder. The first of these is signing contracts on the basis of preliminary plans and specifications. If asked to bid on a contract, do not give a "firm" bid on sketches of boats, or on outline specifications or on "preliminary specifications." Before signing a contract, be sure that the plans and specifications are final and complete. It is not what the owner or designer says about a "cheap boat" or "plain commercial finish" that counts; it is what the plans, specifications, and contract say. Too often, the builder listens to pleasant words about the cheapness of the boat he is asked to bid on, rather than reads the contract and specifications. The contract must receive *careful* reading; do not sign one in which the designer reserves the right to add plans to or to change those already on hand, after the signing of the contract, nor one in which work must be done to the "owner's (or designer's) satisfaction."

Other objectionable features in contracts are those relating to the furnishing of equipment, or fittings. Too often the designer plans to furnish all the expensive items of hardware and fittings, thus adding to his fee at the expense of the builder. If the owner reserves this right it is equally objectionable. However, it is practice for the owner to furnish his own equipment, such as pots, pans, linen, dishes, navigating equipment, bedding, and sometimes the cushions and dinghy. This is certainly not objectionable from the builder's point of view; but when necessary hardware is supplied by the owner, the question of time of delivery, and fastenings the hardware requires, always causes trouble. Very often the hardware and fittings furnished by the owner, or designer, do not fit the boat well and cause expensive improvision, for which neither designer nor owner will make the builder an allowance. It is important, therefore, to have an understanding in writing as to the financial responsibility for delay and extra work caused by lack of fastenings, or improper fit, of hardware and fittings furnished by others than the builder. If, for example, the owner, or designer, is to furnish the engine, some understanding must be reached as to exhaust, silencer, propeller shaft and propeller, controls, bearings and strut. If asked to bid on such a plan, it may be better to exclude engine installation and require the owner to pay for this on a material and labor basis. The installation of many of the larger engines will cost up to one third the list price of the engine, when tanks, controls, exhaust, propeller and shaft, struts, bearings and couplings, piping and wiring are all furnished by the builder. Do not use such a proportion for bidding, however; figure material and labor on each item.

Prices for work done by subcontractors, outside the yard, should be obtained in writing, before signing a contract, if the work is costly—as in the case of special tanks, or castings, for example. Make certain that the owner understands he cannot work on the boat while it is in the yard, under construction, and cannot give orders to workmen directly. Inspect the contract for penalties for noncompletion, or for the inability of the boat to make a required speed. Contracts containing these clauses are often unfair to a builder, as he cannot control these matters in all circumstances.

Another matter of great importance in a contract is changes. Most contracts call for authorization of changes in writing. Many builders neglect to carry this out, by not insisting on authorization, with the result that bills for such changes are not honored by the owner. In most states the time clause of a contract is broken when the owner authorizes changes, unless the authorization requires the clause to be maintained. In this case the builder can refuse to make the change, if he feels he cannot do the work without more time. It is a good plan to establish the practice of written authorization for changes; usually changing begins with some minor alteration of no particular importance and gradually works up to expensive matters, and resulting trouble, if written authorization is not required in every case. The builder does not have to make a change, if his work is to specification, but it is wise to make all authorized changes, if practical, and to collect for them in the form of "extras."

## Relationship between Builder, Owner, and Designer

The relationship of the owner and builder should be thoroughly fixed before signing the contract, if possible. That is, the exact amount of work the builder agrees to do for a given price must be thoroughly understood by both parties. The builder must remember that the architect is the agent of the owner, not of the builder (unless the latter pays the architect's fees). It is to a builder's advantage to avoid taking sides in any disagreement between owner and architect. It is very easy to find fault with either owner, or architect, but this does not help a builder. The builder's responsibility is only to carry out the plans and specifications, not to design, or operate, the boat. If you decide the architect is incompetent, finish the contract and then avoid bidding on any more work designed by him. If you take a dislike to an owner, finish your contract with him, and then avoid doing any more work for him. The best way to retain the respect of both the architect and the owner is to be businesslike in running your yard. Casual agreements and concessions only lead to ill feeling.

The professional builder could add a lot to the advice just offered, the bulk of which could be outlined in one sentence— "Don't forget you are dealing with human beings; don't expect to deal with angels." Professional boatbuilding is not an easy or get-rich-quick craft, but it is possible to operate a yard so as to make a reasonable profit and to retain customers and friends. The amateur builder, who has built one or more boats for himself, will not need a list of advantages to be found in boatbuilding, as his experience will have shown him what they are.

## Legal Equipment

The Motorboat Act of 1940 revised the Act of 1910 and the following are the important requirements as to equipment now in force.

CLASS A, up to 16 feet long:
Combination light in fore part of boat showing red to port and green to starboard from right ahead to two points abaft the beam—lights visible at least one mile.
Stern light, one bright, white light showing all around the horizon and visible at least two miles.
Lifesaving equipment, one life preserver, ring buoy, or buoyant cushion for each person on board.
Flame arresters, on each carburetor on all gasoline engines except outboards.
Ventilation, at least two cowl or equivalent ventilators capable of removing fumes and gases from the bilges in the engine compartment and from the vicinity of fuel tanks in all decked boats using gasoline or fuel oil of a flashpoint less than 110 Fahrenheit.
Fire extinguishers—one 1-quart carbon tetrachloride or one 4-pound $CO_2$ or one 1¼-gallon foam extinguisher.

CLASS 1, from 16 to 26 feet long:
Combination light as in Class A
Stern light as in Class A
Whistle, hand-, mouth-, or power-operated whistle audible at least ½ mile.
Lifesaving equipment as in Class A
Flame arresters as in Class A
Ventilation as in Class A
Fire extinguishers as in Class A

CLASS 2, 26 to 40 feet long:
   Side lights, properly screened to show red to port and green to starboard from right ahead to two points abaft the beam on both sides; visible at least 1 mile. Combination lights not permitted.
   Stern light as in Class A
   Bow light, one bright white light in fore part of bow showing from right ahead to two points abaft the beam on each side; visible at least 2 miles.
   Whistle, one hand- or power-operated whistle, audible at least 1 mile.
   Bell, one suitable bell
   Lifesaving equipment as in Class A
   Flame arresters as in Class A
   Ventilation as in Class A
   Fire extinguishers, two of any type specified in Class A

CLASS 3, 40 to 65 feet long:
   Side lights as in Class 2
   Stern light as in Class A
   Bow light as in Class 2
   Whistle, power operated, audible 1 mile
   Bell as in Class 2
   Lifesaving equipment, one life belt or buoy for each person on board.
   Flame arresters as in Class A
   Ventilation as in Class A
   Fire extinguishers, three of any specified in Class A

Equipment should be of the required size for each class; thus, Class 2 side lights should be used on Class 2 hulls only.
White lights, and combination lights on Classes A and 1, are not required on craft under both sail and power, but such boats must carry a white light or flash ready for immediate use as a warning light to approaching vessels.
Only *approved* equipment as listed should be on board.
The foregoing lists of required equipment apply only to vessels not engaged in commercial service.

# INDEX